SCOTLAND
1689 to the Present

THE EDINBURGH HISTORY OF SCOTLAND

General Editor
GORDON DONALDSON, D.Litt.

SCOTLAND

1689 to the Present

William Ferguson

The Edinburgh History of Scotland
Volume 4

MERCAT PRESS
1994

MERCAT PRESS
James Thin Ltd.
53–59 South Bridge
Edinburgh EH1 1YS

Hardback edition first published, 1968
Reprinted 1975
First published in paperback, 1978
Reprinted in paperback 1987, 1990, 1994

ISBN 0 901824 86 0 *paperback*

Printed and bound in Great Britain
by The Cromwell Press, Melksham, Wiltshire

PREFACE

In accordance with the aim of this series, I have tried to cover most aspects of modern Scottish history in a factual narrative that should at the same time provide some interpretation and, I hope, illumination. That the treatment is unequal is owing to many causes. Some topics are badly under-researched (this is particularly true of the last century or so) and others do not readily lend themselves to the highly condensed treatment that had to be their lot. But as far as space and the evidence available have permitted, I have tried to sketch the conditions of life and thought of the masses as well as the upper classes at various periods. Fundamentally, I see this book as being primarily concerned with a living, changing society and the forces that helped to shape it. I have not, however, resorted to apocalyptic ' models ' or sweeping sociological generalisations; instead, I have worked in the older historical tradition, not out of conservatism but simply because I believe it to be the best way of studying the past. Whether the result is good or bad, it is for others to judge.

It is a commonplace that books of this type are built on the labours of others and this one is no exception to the rule. My footnote references give some indication of the extent of my debt to scholars past and present. I should also like to express my gratitude for unfailing help to the staffs of the National Library of Scotland and of the Scottish Record Office in Register House. My experience with them is by no means unique, but that does not minimise my debt to them or the warmth of my appreciation. On a more personal plane, my colleagues John Simpson of the Scottish History Department in the University of Edinburgh and Donald J. Withrington of the History Department in the University of Aberdeen read the entire typescript and made many valuable suggestions. Together with a vigilant general editor, they rescued me from many dubious situations but did not always succeed, I fear, in rescuing me from myself. I need hardly add

that the poor things that remain are my own. That their number
is not greater is in large part owing to Mr. Douglas Grant and
his team at Oliver & Boyd who took such extraordinary pains
with the production of this book, much improving it in the
process. Finally, my deepest thanks go to my wife, who bore
patiently with the many inconveniences caused by this project.

W. F.

Publisher's Note

The opportunity created by the paperback edition has been taken to add a
postscript to chapter 13 bringing the coverage of this book up to date.
Similarly, the bibliography has been extended to take account of
important recent publications.

October 1977

CONTENTS

LIST OF ABBREVIATIONS

Particulars of the volumes referred to will be
found in the Bibliography

A.P.S.	=	*Acts of the Parliaments of Scotland.*
Cal.S.P.(Dom.)	=	*Calendar of State Papers (Domestic).*
D.N.B.	=	*Dictionary of National Biography.*
E.H.R.	=	*English Historical Review.*
Econ.H.R.	=	*Economic History Review.*
H.M.C.	=	Historical Manuscripts Commission.
O.S.A.	=	*Old Statistical Account of Scotland.*
N.S.A.	=	*New Statistical Account of Scotland.*
R.P.C.	=	*Register of the Privy Council of Scotland.*
Reg. Ho.	=	General Register House.
S.H.R.	=	*Scottish Historical Review.*
S.H.S.	=	Scottish History Society.
T.R.H.S.	=	Transactions of the Royal Historical Society

1

THE REVOLUTION SETTLEMENT

The Revolution of 1688-9 in Scotland, the origins of which have been discussed in the preceding volume,[1] was not a single event or even a logical series of co-ordinated events. Many Scots were bewildered by the sudden collapse of King James's authority, especially some of the episcopalians who ' were extremely overjoyed at the noise of the Prince of Orange's coming over, being so weak as to imagine he would make so dangerous an attempt only to secure their laws, and relieve them from their fears '.[2] James's folly, his flight to France, and the English convention-parliament's interpretation of this as abdication could not be foreseen. It is little wonder that Burnet described his downfall as ' one of the strangest catastrophes that is in any history '.[3] In Scotland the privy council was divided and soon bereft of any real authority, its position usurped by a *camarilla* made up of the remnar.t of the old presbyterian interest headed by the Earls of Glencairn and Crawford and Sir James Montgomerie of Skelmorlie. But the term ' presbyterian party ', then so freely bandied about, can hardly be taken at its face value, for by this time it was a political rather than an ecclesiastical interest. Only Crawford showed single-minded adherence to the old resolutioner policies; Montgomerie was more typical of the age, for, though supposedly a ' phanatick ', he was in reality a *politique* steeped in Whiggish notions of government and driven by lust for power. Office could not be found

---

[1] Gordon Donaldson, *Scotland: James V to James VII*, pp. 383-4.
[2] Earl of Balcarres, *Memoirs touching the Revolution in Scotland 1688-90*, p. 5.
[3] G. Burnet, *History of My Own Times* (1838), II. 397.

for so many saviours of the nation, and by the time a convention of estates met in March 1689 significant rifts had already appeared in the ranks of the ' revolutioners '. The ' court ' and ' country ' conceptions of politics already existed, and these differences were accentuated by the work of the estates.

Although influence was certainly brought to bear on the elections, the convention was not packed. It was as representative as conditions would allow: the Test Act of 1681 was waived, poll elections were held in the royal burghs, and some of those who had been forfeited under the old regime were allowed to sit in the convention. Only by such breaches of existing law could the convention reflect, in however rough a fashion, opinion in the country. But William's supporters did not succeed in determining the composition of the estates or the outcome of their deliberations, and so the course followed by the convention turned on the actions of prominent individuals both inside and outside that body. Many members were perplexed, most were awaiting directions either from local magnates or from the rival courts, and indeed when so much was uncertain there was little for it but to wait on events. This was particularly true of the numerous episcopalians present, for the nine bishops who appeared, believing that episcopacy stood or fell with King James, did nothing to clarify matters. Archbishop Paterson had already explained to the Archbishop of Canterbury the dilemma of the Scottish episcopalians: they felt themselves to be dependent on the crown and could not oppose it as their brethren of England had lately done; for ' here if the Court chance to frowne on us, it is far otherwise . . . so that our Bishops here ly open to farr greater tentations to yeeld to the importunities of Court than yours do.'[4]

From the opening day of the convention, 14 March 1689, it was clear that neither Williamites or Jacobites had the ascendancy and that much would depend on the large number of waverers. The Duke of Hamilton, who throughout the crisis of William's invasion had maintained the irresolute traditions of his house, was, to the consternation of all, chosen by the Prince of Orange to serve him in the convention. Hamilton never enjoyed William's trust and never deserved it; but at this important point he might, if overlooked, have caused trouble in opposition.

[4] W. R. Foster, *Bishop and Presbytery: The Church of Scotland 1661–1688*, p. 23.

One of similar stamp to Hamilton who felt abused by this arrangement was the Marquis of Atholl. Atholl had as little claim on King James for services rendered as he had on William; none the less, his frustrated ambitions now led him to make his peace with the Jacobites. He was accepted by them as their leader in the convention, although he was a mere pawn in such a complicated game. His power in the central Highlands and his entirely imaginary popularity with the presbyterians were Atholl's main recommendations. The first round in the struggle in the convention, therefore, was a contest between these two shifty opportunists for the presidency. This was an important matter since the president possessed not only certain tactical advantages but also a magnetic attraction for place-seekers and dependents, of whom the convention had rather more than its due share. By a narrow majority Hamilton carried it. Two days later, on 16 March, the reading of letters from the rivals for the crown shattered the declining cause of King James. That of William was moderate and conciliatory, couched in safe generalities, and quite incapable of producing either elation or despair in its audience. King James's letter was a very different proposition. The Jacobites, little dreaming of the nature of its contents, actually voted that it should be read to the convention though without casting any reflection on the legality of that body. To their dismay it turned out to be little more than a threat against all who forsook their natural allegiance. This alarmed the waverers among the episcopalians who feared that in the event of James's restoration their natural allegiance would be made to cover not just the king's majesty but also the spiritual claims of the pope. Rightly, this episode has been regarded as the main determinant of the course followed by the convention.[5] The reason is not far to seek. William had dexterously said nothing of church government, but had wisely confined himself to the safeguarding of the protestant faith. No such explicit guarantee could be had from James, and this everyone could see except the benighted bishops. At a stroke, his stupid letter reduced James's active sympathisers in the estates to a relatively small body of committed Jacobites of whom the chief was Viscount Dundee. Its effect on the waverers was soon shown by the vacillations of Atholl and other opportunists.

[5] Earl of Balcarres, *Memoirs*, 27-8.

Disgusted at the feeble leadership displayed by Atholl, Dundee concluded that nothing more could be done for James in the convention, and on the plea that his life was endangered by some vengeful western Whigs then lurking in Edinburgh he withdrew from the estates.   On 18 March he held a brief conference with the Roman catholic Duke of Gordon, whom he persuaded to continue holding Edinburgh Castle for James.   Deserted by Atholl, the Earl of Balcarres, and other prominent Jacobites who had agreed to quit Edinburgh and form a rival convention at Stirling, Dundee then rode out of the capital with a few attendants.   He carried on to his house of Dudhope in Angus, where he assured the convention, somewhat ambiguously, that he would live peaceably unless forced to do otherwise.   His idea of living peaceably was to organise a rising, but in this he met many difficulties.   In the crucial stage of the convention, therefore, the Williamites had matters all their own way.   Dundee was too precipitate, for he might have risked his life for James to more purpose by remaining in Edinburgh.   In the convention James's cause was now leaderless, since Atholl took no real part in its further proceedings; and he later, on the plea of ill-health, withdrew to Bath.   On 27 March a committee of the estates, composed of safe Williamites, was appointed to serve as an interim executive and to prepare and expedite the work of the convention.[6]   By the crucial month of April there was no one to speak for King James in the convention, except a few of the bishops, who attended irregularly and proved but ' dumb dogs '.   Dundee, who was declared rebel by the convention on 30 March and thus forced into premature revolt, found the bishops equally useless, referring to them scornfully at one point as ' the kirk invisible '.[7]

The first great question facing the committee of the estates concerned the throne.   In his instructions to Hamilton William recommended that the English precedent should be followed, but this merely revealed his ignorance of the situation in Scotland. In England it was possible to replace James by William and Mary with little or no amendment of the constitution,[8] but in

---

[6] *A.P.S.*, IX. 22.

[7] Dundee to Melfort, 27 June 1689, quoted in Mark Napier, *Memorials of Claverhouse*, III. 601.

[8] For the settlement in England see D. Ogg, *England in the Reigns of James II and William III*, ch. viii.

Scotland this could not be done. There it was not just James who had incurred criticism but the nature of the monarchy itself. Few politically minded Scots were happy with existing arrangements, and after the Revolution constitutional change proved unavoidable. On this matter there was a large measure of general agreement; the real problem concerned the nature and scope of reform. Aware that the demand for reform might cause trouble, William recommended that a union of the two kingdoms should be negotiated.[9] At this point Andrew Fletcher of Saltoun, famous later for his resistance to the Union of 1707, concurred on the grounds that 'we can never come to any trew setelment but by uniting with England in parliaments'.[10] The Scots showed some interest in the union project; but the English failed to respond, the matter dropped, and the estates set about putting their own house in order.

Thus on 4 April 1689 the convention with only five dissentients resolved that James VII had forfeited the crown, a resolution which strongly implied a contractual monarchy.[11] This idea was elaborated in the Claim of Right, which was accepted by the convention on 11 April and was by some at least thereafter regarded as the basis of the constitution.[12] In this important document the various shortcomings of James, a papist who had not even taken the coronation oath, were listed. Not only had he allegedly attempted to overthrow the protestant faith but he had invaded ' the fundamental constitution of this Kingdom, and altered it from a legal limited monarchy, to an arbitrary despotic power'.[13] The Claim of Right then laid down certain fundamental constitutional principles. No papist could be sovereign or bear office in the kingdom; the royal prerogative could not override law; the consent of parliament was necessary for the raising of supply, and parliament should meet frequently and debate freely; torture was not to be applied as hitherto without evidence or in ordinary crimes; and, somewhat anomalously, prelacy was condemned as ' a great and insupportable grievance and trouble to this Nation '. This last could scarcely be regarded as a fundamental constitutional principle and might more logically

[9] *Leven and Melville Papers*, pp. 2-3.
[10] Reg. Ho., Papers belonging to Andrew Russell, merchant in Rotterdam (N.P. 260/1), Fletcher to Russell, 8 January 1689. I am grateful to Dr T. C. Smout for drawing my attention to this source.
[11] *A.P.S.*, ix. 33-4.   [12] *Ibid.*, ix. 37-40.   [13] *Ibid.*, ix. 33, 38.

have been considered in the Articles of Grievances which were passed by the estates on 13 April.[14] These dealt mainly with the relations between legislature and executive; and in particular the committee of the articles was condemned, a development already foreshadowed in that section of the Claim of Right which demanded freedom of speech in parliament. On 11 April William and Mary had been proclaimed, and shortly thereafter a delegation consisting of the Earl of Argyll for the lords, Sir James Montgomerie of Skelmorlie for the barons, and Sir John Dalrymple for the burgesses carried to London the convention's proposals and the offer of the crown. On 11 May William and Mary accepted the crown of Scotland, arguably, though not certainly, on the terms of the Claim of Right and the Grievances. Whether the commissioners followed their instructions and required William and Mary to accept these documents before tendering the coronation oath was later the subject of keen debate in the parliament. The only untoward event on 11 May was when William objected to a clause in the oath which required the rooting out of heretics. He declared that he would not be a persecutor, and this difficulty was overcome only by an assurance that the phrase to which he objected was a mere form.

Thus far Scotland had caused William little trouble; but from this point to the end of his life that country must have seemed to him troublesome out of all proportion to its worth. One principal source of friction lay in the fact that many in the estates regarded the Claim of Right and the Articles of Grievances as the terms of a basic contract between crown and parliament and confidently expected them to be implemented in practice. In June 1689 Hamilton informed William of a widespread discontent ' lest the Government return to the old channels so often complained of '.[15] Already this unease was being exploited by disappointed place-hunters, chief of whom was Sir James Montgomerie. Argyll and Montgomerie had expected high offices from William; but Hamilton failed to support them, and a combination of the Dalrymples and Lord Melville instead gained the ascendancy with the king. This probably reflected the strong court influence of William Carstares, a Scottish presbyterian minister who was one of the royal chaplains. Carstares feared that Montgomerie was deeply implicated with the presbyterian

---

[14] *A.P.S.*, IX. 45.　　[15] *H.M.C., 11th Report* (1887), Pt. VI, p. 177.

extremists and might thus prejudice the chances of a moderate church settlement. Montgomerie, too, was known as a pronounced Whig in civil matters, whereas the Dalrymples, with their brilliant but pliable minds, were high for the prerogative. Sir James Dalrymple and his son Sir John further realised that only the retention of the royal prerogative could keep them in office, tarnished as they were by their association with what was then generally reprobated in the old regime. Thus the elder Dalrymple wrote to Melville as early as 9 April 1689, fulminating against a scheme to resurrect the act of 1641 whereby parliament would nominate to offices of state, council, and judicatures. 'That,' wrote Sir James, 'was to leave nothing to the King but an empty name.'[16] The appointments made by William after his coronation intensified the gathering strife and bitterness. The convention was turned into a parliament and an administration had to be formed. Hamilton became king's commissioner, the Earl of Melville secretary, the Earl of Crawford was made president of the parliament, and the Dalrymples received high legal offices. Sir James was, on the reconstitution of the court of session, to become its lord president, while his son, Sir John, became lord advocate, an office in which he had already zealously served King James. The Dalrymples were able but unscrupulous trimmers, and something in their conduct and bearing gave offence in an age which at bottom set little store by consistency. Indeed, a bill in the first session of William's parliament which sought to exclude from office any who had served in James's administration was aimed principally at the Dalrymples.

Those who were disappointed in the scramble for high offices readily found awkward matters on which to dilate in parliament. Chagrin gave leadership and direction to the dissidents who had existed even in the convention. Montgomerie was ambitious for power rather than the spoils of office, and this distinguished him from his contemporaries, most of whom could be liferented if not bought and sold. The average Scottish politician of the Revolution period anticipated the spoils system of the following century. One of the shrewdest of the younger politicians, prominent later in the reign as Duke of Queensberry, correctly diagnosed the country's ills: 'The country is mightily divided, not so much for or against your interest and government, as about

[16] *Leven and Melville Papers*, p. 10.

the methods of serving you and the persons employed '.[17]   Skelmorlie had hoped to be secretary and would settle for nothing less. Argyll, too, was affronted at being passed over and made common cause with Montgomerie.   More honest but less acute and influential pillars of ' the club ', as the opposition came to be called from its habit of concerting measures in Penston's tavern in the High Street, were Sir Patrick Hume of Polwarth, Fletcher of Saltoun, and Forbes of Culloden.   Many of the military officers were also smitten by politics of the factious, opportunist type, since, again anticipating the eighteenth century system, ' they beleiv thats the way to secur ther places or to ryse '.[18]   In addition some Jacobites like James Ogilvie acted with the club, partly to protect themselves from attack and partly to keep matters unresolved as long as possible in the well-founded belief that this might be of service to King James.

The disgruntled leaders of the club could exploit and inflame two widely diffused but ill-defined sentiments.[19]   There was a desire for some kind of presbyterian settlement and, secondly and not necessarily related to it, for the supremacy of parliament in the constitution.   More than presbyterian zealots looked back longingly to the halcyon days of 1641, when not only the bishops but the prerogative too had been vanquished.   If there were to be such a golden age again, the first object of attack had to be the committee of the articles.   Throughout the first session of parliament Hamilton, who was at odds with Crawford and poorly instructed from London,[20] found himself in a quandary.   His directions about church government were vague in the extreme. In July 1689 prelacy was abolished,[21] but what to put in its place could be gleaned neither from William's instructions nor yet from the tumultuous parliament.   The club would treat of nothing but the committee of the articles, conscious that until this matter was settled little of moment could be transacted—and so it proved.   Indeed, only three acts passed by the parliament

[17] Cal. S.P. (Dom.), 1689–90, p. 530, Lord Drumlanrig to King William, 29 March 1690.

[18] Leven and Melville Papers, p. 245, Sir John Dalrymple to Lord Melville, 8 August 1689.

[19] J. Halliday, ' The Club and the Revolution in Scotland 1689–90 ', in S.H.R., XLV., 143-59.

[20] For his instructions see Cal. S.P. (Dom.), 1689–90, pp. 126-8.

[21] A.P.S., IX. 104.

were accepted by the executive, and none of them contributed much to a solution of the country's ills. Numerous other acts passed the house but failed to receive the royal assent. Thus the law courts remained closed, since parliament refused to accept the king's right to nominate to judicial offices; the church was unsettled; and no supply was granted for the upkeep of the forces. Neither side was willing to compromise over the committee of the articles, and on 2 August 1689 Hamilton prorogued the parliament. He complained bitterly and justly of lack of direction from the king and of being by-passed in important matters by the lord advocate. Crawford, too, was contributing to the commissioner's troubles by pressing for presbyterian church government. Hamilton's position had been undermined and his efforts to soothe the club had been misrepresented to Melville, and doubtless to the king, as treacherous. On all these grounds he was glad to prorogue, and thus be free to travel to London in an effort to secure clear instructions and to defend himself against insidious attacks. The leaders of the club, Montgomerie and Lord Ross, also took advantage of the prorogation to go to London to set their grievances before the king. William swept them aside unheard, and the rebuff seems to have unbalanced Montgomerie, who then embarked on some desperate intrigues.

Hamilton was the readier to prorogue parliament in that Dundee was no longer a menace. Dundee is usually regarded as the paladin of these days. Much of his loyalty, however, sprang from political unawareness. James VII terrified his best friends, not in his personality, which was pleasing enough, but in his policies; yet to the end Dundee, like a good soldier, accepted and to the best of his abilities carried out orders, though there was no stauncher protestant in the British Isles. Besides, he would have found it difficult to fit into the new regime. Making his peace with William, his old commander, would have been easy, but to live down his past would have been difficult. Thus from the moment that he left the convention he was irretrievably committed to the cause of King James. At first he could do little and did not seem to pose a very serious threat to the government. Early in April he raised the standard of King James on Dundee Law, only to find in the northeast Lowlands many professions of sympathy but few recruits. He could, therefore, do little until he secured the help of the Highland clans. Major-General Hugh

Mackay, who was sent north to put down Dundee before the rebellion assumed dangerous proportions, was almost as badly off for troops and supplies, and for weeks they warily paced each other through the eastern and central Highlands, neither side really desirous of an engagement. Twice the Jacobite commander made a swift descent into the low country with the intention of joining his old regiment of dragoons which Mackay had placed in garrison at Dundee; on each occasion the rebels were thwarted and forced to retreat. So much noise and so little fighting led the government to regard the rebellion as a chimera. As one of the newsletters of the time put it: ' The Viscount of Dundee, with his troop, is in Lochaber, skipping from one Hill to another, like Wildfire, which, at last, will vanish of itself for want of fuel '.[22] The blaze, however, was more substantial than this, for already some of the chiefs had responded to Dundee's eager promptings. Their motives were mixed. Some, like Keppoch, would have embraced any cause that held out prospects of plunder; others, like Lochiel, feared the reinstatement of the Argyll family. By 25 May Dundee had about 2,000 men of the western clans gathered together, and it is a measure of his genius that he soon fathomed the strength and the weakness of such a force. The Highlanders were splendid guerrillas, excellent for a war of rapid movement in the hills but of little use in prolonged campaigning in the low country. Dundee made a brave show with this meagre force in the hope that he might convince James, who was then in Ireland, that the cause in Scotland flourished and deserved full support; and in the hope too that he might persuade the many hesitant Lowland lords that the real path of safety lay in serving King James. In neither task did he succeed to any appreciable extent. Only 300 raw Irish recruits under Colonel Cannon were sent to join the Scots, essential supplies of arms and money failed to appear, and the gentry of the northeast Lowlands, episcopalian and at heart Jacobite though they were, still held aloof.

But James's general could not keep to the hills indefinitely, the more so as Mackay, exhausted by his summer exertions, was now at King William's bidding proposing to contain the Highlands by fortifying key points just as Cromwell had done. Moreover, if the clans were to be held together some prospect of fighting and

---

[22] *Proceedings of the Estates in Scotland, 1689–90*, ed. E. W. M. Balfour-Melville (S.H.S.), I. 105 (25 May 1689).

of the spoils of war was necessary. Besides, Lord Tarbat had suggested to William the possibility of buying if not the loyalty then at least the neutrality of the chiefs, and already he had sounded Lochiel. The offer had been spurned, but prolonged inaction might render it attractive. For all these reasons Dundee had to make a move. The seizure of the castle of Blair in Perthshire for James by Atholl's defaulting factor, Stewart of Ballechin, and Mackay's anxiety to retake this vital position led to the battle of Killiecrankie on 27 July 1689. The terrain favoured the Highlanders, and their wild charge downhill broke Mackay's inexperienced troops. The result was a panic-stricken rout, and only with difficulty did Mackay manage to bring off part of his force. Fortunately for William, in the onset Dundee was killed and whatever advantages his victory opened up were lost. Cannon took over the command but failed to establish anything like Dundee's ascendancy over his motley force. On 21 August Cannon's lack of ability was revealed when the Highlanders were repulsed at Dunkeld by the stalwart defence put up by the recently formed and outnumbered Cameronian regiment under its young Colonel Cleland who, like Dundee, fell in his hour of victory. Thereafter the rebellion faltered, paralysed mainly by lack of leadership. The only other skirmish of any importance occurred on 1 May 1690, when at Cromdale in Strathspey Sir Thomas Livingstone surprised and routed General Buchan, who had superseded Cannon. Notwithstanding these reverses the rebels, safe in their remote fastnesses, refused to submit.

The real importance of Dundee's little war was political rather than military. After Killiecrankie the government was as fearful of further troubles as hitherto it had been negligent, and as a consequence it devoted more thought to the problem of the Highlands than was perhaps strictly necessary. The issue in the years 1690–1, however, was clouded by the recurrent dread of an invasion by an Irish papist army. This never materialised, but until Ireland was pacified by the Treaty of Limerick in October 1691 fear of such a move was one of the powerful factors in Scottish politics. In particular it forced the king and his ministers to court the parliament, if only to obtain supply to keep the small army in Scotland in being. Thus, in preparation for the next session, the management of parliament received close consideration from the executive. Sir John Dalrymple was foremost in this work, and on 4 February 1690 he sent the result of his scrutiny to Secretary Melville. Dalrymple concluded that ' the plurality of the Parliament is right for the King ' but that the presence of William was necessary to keep them steady.[23] The sharing out of offices by setting them in commission had sweetened some influential members; and the club was alienating many by its desperate shifts. The first Duke of Queensberry, one of the principal Jacobites, had become notably intimate with Montgomerie, to the satisfaction of the Dalrymples and others in the administration but to the consternation of such Whig zealots as Hume of Polwarth and Forbes of Culloden. They at last began to pierce the designs of Montgomerie, who was now actively engaging in intrigue with the Jacobites, and so they veered towards the court party. Argyll, too, was quick to take the alarm and draw away from his old associates, while Hamilton was in one of his celebrated ' humours ' and regarded as untrustworthy.

In a broader prospect, William's affairs were in the balance. He was preparing for his campaign in Ireland and could spare no time for the confused politics of Scotland. It was impossible for him to preside over the parliament in person and so the choice of the king's commissioner became more important than ever. Since Hamilton was such a dubious quantity a warrant for Melville to act as commissioner was secretly prepared. In large part the intention behind Melville's appointment was to placate the presbyterians, the more so as Hamilton was said to be attempting to join the Cameronians to the Jacobite interest. William not unnaturally felt that Melville, a moderate presbyterian, was the best answer to such a situation. The latter had throughout been in correspondence with the presbyterians, who wrote to him in the following strain—' wee, the Presbiterian pairtie expects ye will take us by the hand '.[24] Melville, in fact, was determined to replace Hamilton; but in order to do this he bound himself to the presbyterians, with results pleasing to them but adverse to himself.

With the ground thoroughly prepared the important session of 1690 went well for the administration. Montgomerie tried hard to rally the turbulent opposition of 1689, but the bulk of the

[23] *Leven and Melville Papers*, p. 392.

[24] *Leven and Melville Papers*, p. 270, Mr Thomas Dunbar of Grange to Lord Melville, 4 September 1689.

presbyterians put their trust in the new commissioner, and, besides, Montgomerie's intrigue with the Jacobites was leaking out. The poor showing of the opposition almost from the first day of the session, 15 April 1690, caused the Jacobite Balcarres to describe their activities in the most mournful terms: ' never men made a more miserable figure in any meeting '.[25] Melville made the most of his instructions, which included giving satisfaction over the question of the committee of the articles, the settlement of moderate presbyterianism, and the securing of men by gifts and promises. As an earnest of good will the bills refused by the last commissioner were touched with the sceptre, and in this way the Act of Supremacy of 1669 was abolished, and those of the ministers ejected in 1662 who survived were restored.[26] The lords of the articles were then abolished,[27] no compromise proving acceptable on this issue, and, deprived of this important committee, control of parliament became more difficult. On 7 June 1690 an act restored presbyterian government to the church on the model of 1592.[28] The Westminster standards were approved, though the covenants were tacitly dropped; but the only presbyterians who refused this Erastian settlement were the extreme Cameronians. So far Melville was faithfully carrying out the king's instructions; but an act to secure the transfer of patronages from private individuals to heritors and kirk sessions gave umbrage to William who had emphasised that it was only to be passed as a last resort. Most of the presbyterians, however, felt that such an attack upon private property was imperative since so many of the patrons were either hostile or lukewarm to their system. Carstares took the opposite view. He believed that after thirty years in the wilderness the presbyterian ministers were too dependent on the dogmatic humours of their congregations, and that to vest the right of presentation in the latter would turn the church into a bedlam. There was sense in both arguments, but Melville caved in to popular pressure. By the Act concerning Patronages of 19 July 1690, on payment by the heritors of a composition of 600 merks to the patron, the right to present ministers to vacant charges was to devolve upon the heritors and elders of the parish under the oversight of the presbytery.[29] The nobles and gentry were considerably annoyed by this act,

[25] Balcarres, *Memoirs*, p. 59. [26] *A.P.S.*, IX. 110-11.
[27] *Ibid.*, IX. 113. [28] *Ibid.*, IX. 133-4. [29] *Ibid.*, IX. 196-7.

and Melville's rivals seized the opportunity to undermine his position at court. Hamilton, out of pique, and the Dalrymples, out of envy, were the most dangerous of those who engineered the fall of Melville. Melville himself had no great abilities and, a serious fault in a secretary, he was a poor correspondent. But like all of William's servants he might have pleaded that his heaviest burden was the king's indifference to affairs in Scotland. It was unsatisfactory for the king's ministers in Scotland to seek directions from court favourites like the Dutchman Hans Willem Bentinck, Earl of Portland, and Carstares. The result was to stimulate the faction and intrigue in which the nation was already adept.

The final blow to Melville's prestige at court derived from the general assembly of the church of November 1690. It was the first to meet since 1653, although in 1689 the episcopalians had called for one in the hope of using their majority to make a compromise settlement without recourse to parliament. This the presbyterians had resisted—a prime historical jest that deserves to be remembered. In 1690 the basic problem was still how the presbyterians, a minority of the existing ministers, were to control a general assembly. True, in the south-west the ' curates ' had been rabbled by the Society People or Cameronians in the winter of 1688–9, although their lot was not the martyrdom hallowed by episcopalian tradition. Numerous other ministers had been ejected by the privy council in 1689 for failing to pray for William and Mary. Nonetheless, by November 1690, many who had been episcopally collated remained within the church, some of them doubtless Vicars of Bray but most still sincere believers in episcopacy. The assembly of 1690, therefore, was not as general as usual. Few ventured to Edinburgh from the episcopalian strongholds of the north-east, and the core of the assembly was made up of the sixty ' antediluvians ' who survived from those ejected at the Restoration. By the act of parliament restoring presbyterianism they alone were to exercise the governing power until the unreliable elements within the church were removed. In this work the statesmen, from the king downwards, counselled the assembly to be moderate, fearful lest harsh conduct should raise resentment not only in Scotland but also, which was more important, in England where the establishment was hostile to presbyterianism. Under the nervous direction of the high commissioner, nothing was done to offend. The three remaining Cameronian ministers—Lining, Shields, and Boyd—accepted the settlement even though they were not allowed to register protests at its uncovenanted, Erastian defects. The setting up of two commissions (one to operate north of Tay and the other south of it) to purge the church of unyielding episcopalians seemed at the time to be a reasonable step, but in it danger lurked. The high commissioner professed himself satisfied with the work of the assembly; yet within a few months the king was incensed by the unscrupulous way in which its commissions had exceeded their mandate. Ministers were not supposed to be judged by their past compliance with episcopacy, but all sorts of pretexts were used to extrude those who were found too sympathetic to the old order. Doubtless many refused to pray for William and Mary; but many of the episcopalian ministers were thrust out of their livings in a manner not dissimilar from the ' rabblings ' in the south-west. In the north-east attempts to extrude episcopalian ministers were resisted, and William was incensed by the reports he received of the northern commission's activities. The universities were also purged, though not certainly for the advancement of learning. The king did his best to moderate the work of the commissions, but his letters on this subject were disregarded. These unlooked-for events gave Melville's rivals an opportunity of which they were quick to avail themselves; they also contributed to William's unpopularity.

The handling of another pressing problem, the need for some kind of pacification of the Highlands, also discredited the king and his administration. Lawlessness was endemic in that area, owing in part, as has been ably argued, to the clash between clan loyalties and feudal superiorities, which tended to promote unrest.[30] To end this James VII had toyed with the idea of the crown buying up and reallocating superiorities so as to eliminate friction. To some of the clans, and especially the Camerons and MacLeans who had in the past suffered from the claims of the house of Argyll, this was an attractive policy. The restoration of Argyll implicit in the Revolution was therefore displeasing to many of the clans. But this cannot be made to account for all the troubles in the Highlands. The fact remains that many Highlanders thrived on disorder, as was evidenced by frequent

[30] A. Cunningham, *The Loyal Clans*, ch. IX.

raids or levying of ' blackmail ', activities that were as marked
before the Revolution as after it. In 1679, for example, the
disorders in the Highlands were only slightly less alarming to
government than the armed conventicles in the Lowlands.[31]
The main offenders were MacLeans, Camerons, MacDonalds and
MacLachlans. In August 1688 James dispatched forces to put
down rebels in Lochaber;[32] and indeed, one of the king's chief
worries on receipt of the news of William's expedition in November 1688 had been for the peace of the Highlands. It is, therefore,
hard to resist the conclusion that in its origins Highland Jacobitism
drew less of its strength from divine right theories of monarchy
than from ancient predatory traditions. Poverty was perhaps
the most powerful motive inducing loyalty to the exiled king, with,
as a close second, fear of the restored powers of the Earl of Argyll.

There were those in Scotland with intelligence enough to
discern this; but the mass of Lowlanders viewed the Highlanders
with fear and hatred, and not least those who lived exposed to
their depredations along the borders of the Highlands. The
western covenanters hated them as the children of Israel hated
the Philistines. Equally strong, if less pious, was the aversion of
the Jacobite episcopalians of the shires of Stirling, Perth, Angus,
Aberdeen, and the northeast plain. The difficulty of achieving a
durable pacification of the Highlands was, therefore, increased by
this mass of prejudice and, in some cases, justified fears. Thus the
government from 1689 onwards oscillated between two contrary
policies. The most consistent policy, although it was feebly
pursued, was that of curbing the rebels by force and devising a
system of policing to hold them in check. The building of a fort
at Inverlochy, which was named Fort William and placed under
the command of Colonel Hill, who had served in the same post
in Cromwell's time, was the keystone of this policy. But it led to
no mass capitulation of the rebels, mainly because the army in
Scotland was too weak to permit really effective measures to be
taken. In part this was due to the strain of William's wars elsewhere: for example, a fair proportion of the army in Ireland was
Scottish. But in addition the Scottish treasury was in a low
condition in the years of turmoil following the Revolution, when

[31] For revealing illustrations of this see *H.M.C. 6th Report* (1877), pt. 1, Argyll
MSS., pp. 616 ff.; and *R.P.C.* (3rd ser.), VI. 203 ff.

[32] *R.P.C.* (3rd ser.), XIII. 299-300.

the trade of the country declined and it proved impossible in many areas to uplift the cess or land tax. Therefore, the other policy, of trying to buy off the rebels, had its attractions, even if it were only to secure temporary gains. First in the field here with advice and offers of service was Viscount Tarbat, who, himself a Mackenzie, understood the Highlanders and knew to a nicety what would answer the purpose. He advocated not only an indemnity and money payment to the chiefs but also a realloca-tion of the troublesome superiorities.[33] William was impressed by the good sense of these arguments and, in the summer of 1689, at the height of Dundee's campaign, Tarbat was credited with £5000 sterling with which he tried hard to make a deal with the rebel chiefs. He was hampered by the ill will of the main office-holders in Scotland who did not like to be bypassed in this fashion; he did not carry sufficient weight and so failed to make any real headway. The opposition of the privy council proved to be the main impediment to such a policy, since it was feared that whoever made peace in the Highlands would win the favour of William and be preferred to high office. Argyll and Atholl were each covetous of such a triumph, but were inhibited by fear of losing their superiorities. These two Highland magnates, therefore, sabotaged the various attempts made by Tarbat and Hill, and went out of their way to counteract the really determined efforts made by Breadalbane in 1691.

John Campbell, first Earl of Breadalbane, resembled Tarbat in his intelligence and wary carriage, but he had a much more forceful personality. Like Tarbat, he saw that the real Highland problem was an economic one and that the prerequisite of im-provement was a durable pacification. Breadalbane bears a bad character in history, though his evil reputation is not wholly deserved. Self-seeking and ambitious he certainly was, but in these respects he did not differ from most of his contemporaries. He played little or no part in the Revolution, although he was suspected as a crypto-Jacobite: the truth seems to be that like many others he tried to keep a politic foot in both camps, deter-mined that whoever should win he would not lose. Thus, again

---

[33] *Cal. S.P.* (*Dom.*), *1689–90*, p. 131. King William to Lord Leven, 1 June 1689. Tarbat's negotiations are reported in several items in State Papers; see P.R.O., SP8/vol. 11, *e.g.* no. 5 which clearly brings out the opposition of Argyll and the army officers.

like many others, after Killiecrankie he inclined towards the established order, and by August 1689 Sir John Dalrymple considered him the ideal agent to break the Highland confederacy by negotiation. Tarbat and the Dalrymples could never agree, and it was the Master of Stair who brought Breadalbane forward as a counterpoise to the suave, insinuating Mackenzie. Breadalbane, though, would do nothing for nothing, and so he took his time about accepting the task. He wanted office and he wanted it quickly. Not until March 1690 did he venture to Edinburgh, where, in the old Scots manner, a pile of debt hung over his head. Melville thought that his price would be too high; but the king was prepared to meet it. Tarbat made one last effort in the Highlands in this same year, and it too came to nothing. The way was then cleared for Breadalbane, whose dreams of high office had been stimulated.

But for various reasons nothing could be done until the summer of 1691. For one thing, Breadalbane had been named by Lord Annandale, who had taken part in Montgomerie's plot, as being deep in that design. In the winter of 1689 Montgomerie had concocted a fantastic scheme whereby presbyterians and Jacobites were to work together for the restoration of James VII, who was supposedly to countenance a system of presbyterian church government. In fact Montgomerie was still engaged in his endless quest for power, and the presbyterians were to be used as mere cats'-paws. Melville's work as commissioner destroyed any basis for such a strange alliance, the plot was detected, and the main men involved tumbled over themselves to make abject, but disingenuous, confessions. The fullest relation was made by Annandale in London in the summer of 1690;[34] that of Lord Ross was less trustworthy, while Montgomerie, who had also gone to London in an attempt to win favourable terms, lost his nerve and went into hiding. Until his death in September 1694 Montgomerie was a fugitive, either lurking in London or plotting at St Germain. In the meantime it was confidently expected that the torturing of Neville Paine at Edinburgh on the direct orders of the king in December 1690[35] would amplify Annandale's account. Paine, an Englishman, was reckoned to be a mean creature, but he

---

[34] *Cal. S.P.* (*Dom.*), *1690–91*, 12 August 1690, pp. 92-4: but the main lines of the plot were known in June 1690.

[35] MS. R.P.C. (Acta), King William to the Council, 10 December 1690.

showed remarkable endurance and courage, and no additional information could be got out of him. Forgery and false testimony were rampant in those chaotic times; but although Breadalbane's complicity in the plot was far from being proved those who held office in Scotland were, or affected to be, convinced of it.

Thus when Breadalbane began to negotiate with the rebels in the summer of 1691 he could rely only upon the support of Sir John Dalrymple, who by this time shared the office of secretary with Melville. Melville was doubtful of the whole project, especially as it was now being pushed by his rival, the Master of Stair. Colonel Hill did his best to impede it, since he had hoped to bring off that coup himself and so justify decent provision for his old age. Neither Argyll nor Atholl could brook the thought of Breadalbane or any one else breaking the confederacy. In 1691 the only two men who actively and zealously promoted the policy of indemnity and purchase were the Master of Stair and the Earl of Breadalbane. The privy council and the army commander, Sir Thomas Livingstone, went out of their way to be obstructive. Also, unexpected difficulties arose among the Highlanders themselves. The news of the taking of Mons by the French revived their hopes of help from France. The chiefs also vied among themselves for the honour of holding out longest, and they haggled over the amount of money they were to receive. King William was preoccupied with other and more pressing affairs, principally the war in the Low Countries, and despite constant pleas from the Master of Stair and Breadalbane he could not be made to stir in the matter.[36] The upshot was a dangerous drift in which the good faith and temper of the parties concerned were sorely tried, and none more so than those of the precise, ambitious Dalrymple.

At a meeting with the leading chiefs at Achallader in Argyll in June 1691 Breadalbane, with the help of his kinsman Lochiel, had laid the basis of a settlement, whereby the chiefs were to receive sums of money in proportion to their status. The angry words that were later alleged to have passed between Breadalbane and MacIan, chief of the Glencoe MacDonalds, may indeed have an existence in fact; but only the most forced interpretation can link

[36] *H.M.C.*, *Finch Papers*, III. 131 ff. especially, pp. 154-5, Sir John Dalrymple to Lord Nottingham, 13 July 1691, urging the king ' not to delay the conclusion of this Hyland business nor to suffer the settlement of our nation to ly long over '.

them with the tragedy that ensued. None had suffered more in two years of anarchy than Breadalbane's tenants and none had plundered them more thoroughly than MacIan's men. In the light of this, hot words were understandable. MacIan, however, was too minor a figure to wreck Breadalbane's scheme. That was done more effectively by another MacDonald, Glengarry, who was the most obstinate of the rebels. It was Glengarry, prompted by Atholl, who upset prospects of a good outcome. He alleged that Breadalbane had signed certain secret articles at Achallader, the main tenor of which was to bind him to the service of King James. Hill and others in the government service were supplied by Glengarry with copies of this alleged secret treaty, and the accusation was gratefully received.[37] The original of this peculiar compact has not been discovered, then or since. William never took the allegations seriously, and Lochiel, who was well aware of the intrigues of Glengarry and Atholl, also regarded them with scepticism. It is hard to believe that such a ' politique blade ',[38] as Breadalbane appeared to a contemporary, would have delivered himself into the hands of his enemies, Jacobite and Williamite, in this careless fashion. What Breadalbane did undoubtedly concede was that the rebels, to save face, should be given time to secure James VII's consent to a capitulation; but this can only appear odd to those not versed in the niceties of seventeenth century warfare. Unfortunately, the privy council, which for sound reasons had not been consulted in this matter, disliked it and bade fair to wreck the entire negotiations by unwanted and inopportune military activity in the Highlands. Only with difficulty was the council restrained. In the months that followed, William failed to follow up Breadalbane's initial advantage, and confidence ebbed on both sides. The Master of Stair, as these vital six months passed, found himself labouring under an increasing load of criticism and his touchy nature began to react violently. All his difficulties he attributed to the bad faith of the Highland rebels. They had been offered fair terms and they had duped those who, in the face of strong opposition, had made these terms possible. That they had been promised certain benefits and that none of those benefits had materialised did not weigh with Dalrymple. As he saw it, the issue had now become very simple.

---

[37] *H.M.C. 15th Report*, pt. IX., Hope Johnstone (1897), pp. 173-4.
[38] *H.M.C. 11th Report*, pt. VI, p. 169.

If the rebels failed to take the oath of allegiance by 1 January 1692, the prescribed date, then they should be crushed by a relentless display of force. By the end of 1691 the Master of Stair looked forward to making some bloody examples, and in this attitude he was far from being singular. All this has a sinister appearance, especially when the papers dealing with it are brought together in one volume centring upon the Massacre of Glencoe.[39] But, in fact, it was a different situation that obtained in December and the first week of January. The conclusion was reasonable: if rebels refused to submit then they must be put down. Breadalbane, who still hoped for some success, shared this view, albeit reluctantly. The real danger lay in the late arrival of permission from King James for the rebels to come to terms. In so far as most of the chiefs took the oath by the required date Breadalbane's optimism seemed justified; and indeed the Master of Stair was disappointed at this unwelcome result. He found little comfort in the fact that Glengarry, young Clanranald, and Sir John MacLean of Duart had not come in. Glengarry's house of Invergarry was strongly fortified and not the best of targets for a punitive expedition operating on the cheap. Clanranald was a mere child and could be disregarded. For some reason, Sir John MacLean was always favoured by Dalrymple. The news received on 11 January that MacIan of Glencoe had failed to take the oath by 1 January was more to the Master's liking.

The story of the aged chief's strenuous but belated efforts to provide for the safety of his small clan needs no repeating in detail. With time rapidly running out, MacIan had presented himself at Fort William on 31 December 1691 in the belief that Colonel Hill might tender the oath: but this was not in the competence of a military officer, and in vile weather the old man toiled towards Inveraray, losing 24 hours by a delay forced upon him at Barcaldine Castle. He did not reach Inveraray until 3 January, only to find that the sheriff-depute, Campbell of Ardkinglass, was absent, recovering apparently from a hogmanay revel. Not until 6 January did Ardkinglass, touched by MacIan's entreaties, tender the oath. The technical irregularity was venial, but there

---

[39] As in *Papers Illustrative of the Highlands of Scotland*; *e.g.* Master of Stair to Breadalbane, 2 December 1691, p. 49: '. . . shortly we will conclude a resolution for the winter campaign. I do not fail to take notice of the frankness of your offer to assist. I think the clan Donell must be rooted out, and Lochiel . . .'.

were those in Edinburgh and London who were more than willing to clutch at straws. By some mysterious but evil work in Edinburgh, Ardkinglass' certificate was cancelled, and the matter never referred to the privy council as a whole. This was, perhaps, strictly legal procedure; but it is hard to see why the secretary in London was not informed of the full situation. All that reached the Master of Stair to begin with was information from the Earl of Argyll that MacIan had not, as earlier reported, taken the oath on time.

Why did the Master of Stair accept this news with such relish; why did he single out the MacDonalds of Glencoe for punishment; and why did that punishment take such an extreme form? The main reasons are frequently illustrated in the Master's correspondence at this time. The Glencoe MacDonalds were in his opinion, which was not ill founded, 'a sect of thieves', though Dalrymple's verdict on them was too sweeping and vehement. They were, the Master believed, Roman catholic, and in his correspondence he showed a marked preference for the protestant clans, notably the no less delinquent MacLeans. It has to be remembered, too, that the old unreasoning fear of popery had recently been revived in Scotland, not merely by the policies of King James but even more by the reported, and exaggerated, catholic atrocities in the recent disturbances in Ireland. And Dalrymple had served James VII until the Revolution; his enemies now spread rumours that he was still serving James. The Master could only dispel such insinuations by taking strict measures against the catholics. Thus, on 3 December 1691 he wrote to Lieutenant-Colonel Hamilton at Fort William: 'the MacDonalds . . . thats the only popish clan in the kingdom and it will be popular to take severe course with them'.[40] The Master was probably mistaken. Many of the MacDonalds, notably those of Clanranald and Glengarry, were indeed papists; but the Glencoe people were probably episcopalian. The widespread belief that the MacDonalds of Glencoe were Roman catholic rests mainly on the Master of Stair's misapprehension and is not supported by contemporary evidence of weight.[40a] None the less, the Master felt that an example was needed and that on every count MacIan's clan would best answer the purpose.

[40] *Papers Illustrative of the Highlands of Scotland*, p. 53.
[40a] W. Ferguson, ' Religion and the Massacre of Glencoe ', in *S.H.R.*, XLVI. 82-7.

The actual planning that resulted in the massacre remains obscure. Clearly, the treatment to be meted out to MacIan's wild brood was decided in London. That its chief architect was Dalrymple admits of no doubt; but the complicity of Breadalbane is debatable. The popular belief that the massacre was merely the result of a feud between the Campbells and the MacDonalds is untenable, despite the existence of bad blood between these clans. There is no evidence linking Breadalbane with the tragedy at all. Such evidence as is usually adduced rests on complete misinterpretation of the correspondence between Dalrymple and Breadalbane in the preceding December. At that time Breadalbane certainly accepted the need for force, all else failing, though not just on the MacDonalds of Glencoe but on all the contumacious rebels in the Highlands. In this wider context ' to maul ' them was feasible, but to put all to the sword certainly was not. In fact, on receipt of the first news of the massacre Breadalbane saw at once that, in his own words, ' that precipitat action in Glencoa . . . will produce [events] which ar contrarie to what I hav venturd My lyf and fortoun to have compleated in the Highlands, and that is peace '.[41] His whole correspondence at this time shows that he had been still zealously trying to promote his negotiation and that the massacre was the final blow to his hopes. The scheme was concocted in London by the Master, and, interestingly, it was condemned in the English privy council by the Marquis of Carmarthen as brutal and barbarous. This makes it difficult to believe that William was kept in utter ignorance of its details. Certainly, full knowledge of Dalrymple's plan would not have been as inconsistent with the king's character as Macaulay and others have maintained. William's essential ruthlessness was only held in check by his selfish good sense. He regarded the Highlanders as savages, and his patience, like the Master's, was exhausted. But whatever doubts there may be as to William's complicity that of Sir Thomas Livingstone is clear. Livingstone, who passed on the Master of Stair's instructions to the officers in the Highlands, knew what was intended. His original orders from the Master on 7 January 1692 were to march upon those rebels who failed to take the oath, smite them ruthlessly and not trouble about prisoners. These earlier instructions may be

[41] Reg. Ho., Breadalbane Papers, Letters, Box 4, 1690–99, Earl of Breadalbane to Colin Campbell, 15 March 1692.

C

regarded as equivalent to 'Letters of Fire and Sword', which were frequently invoked in seventeenth-century Scotland but rarely literally enforced. They may have been what Dalrymple had in mind, but, precisian that he was, by him they were literally interpreted. To these general instructions, however, the Master of Stair on 11 January added more precise directions as to the fate of the MacDonalds of Glencoe; and matters were further clarified by additional orders sent on 16 January, signed and countersigned by King William. Hill was similarly instructed. Neither Livingstone nor Hill, who passed these orders down the chain of command, can have failed to understand their import. No semantic discussion of such key-words as 'to extirpate' (whether it meant massacre or simply to scatter and disperse) can conceal the deadly purpose of these orders. The treacherous means to be used were also hinted at in Dalrymple's letter to Hill on 30 January: 'let it be secret and suddain, otherwayes the men will shift you'.[42]

The plan was set in motion late in January when Campbell of Glenlyon, with 120 men of Argyll's regiment, which was the only one available, was despatched to Glencoe. Whether Glenlyon understood at this point the exact purpose of his visit is not clear. He was a very small cog in a complicated machine, and, confirmed drunkard that he was, he could scarcely have been trusted with the full details. For almost a fortnight he and his men were hospitably entertained in the glen. On 12 February Glenlyon received from his immediate superior, Major Duncanson, instructions that could admit of no misunderstanding. All were to be put to the sword who were under seventy; but the soldiers engaged in such work were hardly likely to ask for non-existent birth certificates. Early on the morning of the 13th Glenlyon, to the best of his fuddled abilities, complied. Two of MacIan's sons, however, took alarm and with most of the clan escaped into the hills, where, in the hard winter conditions, many of them perished. Old MacIan and about 37 besides were butchered in the glen. Lieutenant-Colonel Hamilton who was supposed to co-operate in the massacre failed to come up in time, detained either by bad weather or gnawing conscience, and it was with anger that the Master of Stair heard of the partial failure of his plans.

[42] *Papers Illustrative of the Highlands*, p. 71.

Whatever the unfathomable secret history of this affair, it was an appalling blunder, and not to be assessed by the relatively small number killed. Nor can it be softened by comparison with other, and possibly even more brutal, Highland atrocities. What one lawless band will mete out to just such another is not the yardstick by which governments can hope to be measured; and no one in seventeenth-century Europe, despite the brutality of that age, could be deluded into imagining that it was. The treacherous means employed at Glencoe were not only shocking to the Highland tradition of hospitality but were also at variance with the elaborate code of military honour which still flourished. Thus, as the news leaked out, William and his government came under very damaging criticism. The French were the first to publicise the massacre, and were soon followed by the Scottish and English Jacobites. In Scotland, the indignation ran deepest of all, and not just for hypocritical reasons. Certainly it was accepted as a heaven-sent opportunity by the Jacobites, certainly it was eagerly taken up by those politicians by whom the Dalrymples were detested; but these groups could not command popular feeling. Indeed the reception given to the massacre in Scotland, Highland and Lowland, was symptomatic of a new and more humane climate of opinion. Besides, how could reasonable men condemn the ' Highland Host ' of 1678 and condone the Massacre of Glencoe ? And reason, after a century of religious fanaticism, was again beginning to assert itself. As to its results, the massacre did more than any other single event to promote Jacobitism in the Highlands. William and his government were thereafter discredited and distrusted, all the more since, despite a prolonged outcry, the affair was never satisfactorily investigated.

In the session of parliament of 1693, over which Hamilton once more presided, a noisy but poorly organised opposition threatened to withhold supply unless grievances were redressed. One of these grievances was the affair of Glencoe. The Master of Stair prudently absented himself from this session and the parliament was adroitly managed by the co-secretary Johnstone. In an effort to placate the opposition an enquiry into Glencoe was set up, which in the event did nothing. Again in the session of 1695, partly to allay opposition and partly too to bring down Dalrymple, a fuller enquiry was made, but the commission appointed was drawn mainly from the officers of state and government nominees. Its findings, therefore, were of the most guarded kind. The main charge was laid against the Master of Stair, to the satisfaction not only of the leader of the current 'club', Sir James Ogilvie, but also the king's commissioner, the Marquis of Tweeddale, and the co-secretary Johnstone. It proved impossible to act on the commission's findings, mainly because the king not only refused to allow trials to be held but actually promoted some of the suspects. Breadalbane could not be incriminated, but was for a few months imprisoned on the old charge that in 1691 he had betrayed King William's trust. William ordered him to keep silent, and by the king's authority Breadalbane was released. Johnstone and Tweeddale had secured their point, public clamours lingered still but in diminishing volume, and the Master of Stair, utterly discredited, was deprived of office and forced to keep resentfully in the background for the duration of William's reign.

It was partly in an effort to divert attention from Glencoe that William in his instructions to the commissioner Tweeddale in 1695 sanctioned the project for establishing an overseas trading company in Scotland. But these instructions were vague and the extent of the king's commitment was not very clear. Such a project had long been discussed, and was, in fact, merely one aspect of the quickening economic life of Scotland under the paternalist Restoration monarchy. The larger role played by parliament after the Revolution reflected, and possibly even exaggerated, these economic trends. The merchant interest could then exert pressure to initiate legislation, as in 1693 when the committee of trade of the estates recommended that legal sanction should be given to those who wished to establish overseas plantations.[43] From this to the act of 1695 setting up the Company of Scotland was a logical step, and one that was aided by the promptings of interested parties in England. There the jealously guarded monopoly of the great chartered companies caused resentment, and many London merchants were willing to invest in a concern as privileged as the 'Company of Scotland Trading to Africa and the Indies'.[44] Not only was the company to enjoy a monopoly of trade between Scotland and America,

<hr />

[43] *A.P.S.*, IX. 314-15. The terms were very favourable and anticipated those of the more famous act of 1695.

[44] *Ibid.*, IX. 377-81.

Africa and Asia, not only did it receive exemptions from customs and other duties for 21 years, but also any damage it incurred was to be met from public funds. Indeed so attractive was the company's charter that in its first two or three months of life the Scots had to struggle to keep control of the venture, so keen were London financiers to participate. It should be emphasised at this point that the original purpose of the company was indicated in its title. The ' Darien Scheme ', by which name the entire venture is often erroneously known, was a last desperate gamble, accepted partly because of the persuasive arguments of its originator, William Paterson, but mainly because of ultimate failure to secure English or continental backing.

The total capital of the company was not defined in the act, but half of it was to be subscribed by English interests. The directors of the company originally fixed its capital at £360,000 sterling but under pressure from the English projectors this was increased to £600,000, and within a fortnight of the company's books being opened in London in November 1695 half of this sum was subscribed or promised. Indeed, by increasing the amount of capital the London merchants rather put the Scots directors in a difficulty, and had matters continued on this footing there can be little doubt that real control of the company would have passed to London. Such a development would probably have been beneficial all round, for the experienced southerners would scarcely have allowed Paterson's grand vision to cloud their judgment; but the English and Anglo-Scottish merchants were forced to withdraw by the agitation raised in the English parliament by their outraged rivals. Thwarted here, the Scots determined to make an extraordinary effort and carry on by themselves. The strain proved heavy, and so they turned to Holland and the Hanse towns, not only for the building of suitable ships but also for financial backing. Probably as early as July 1696 Paterson's scheme for a great free port on the Isthmus of Darien, which would garner the wealth of both hemispheres, was attracting the directors of the company,[45] but knowledge of this possibility was not available to William's representatives in the financial centres of northern Europe when in 1696–7 they ruthlessly sabotaged the efforts of the Scots to secure backing. Sir Paul Rycaut, the English resident at Hamburg, openly warned

[45] F. R. Hart, *The Disaster of Darien*, p. 48.

the senate of that city, and the authorities in the other Hanse towns, that any who countenanced the Scots in this way would be regarded by William with hostility. Against such downright statements the Scots in vain produced their act of parliament of 1695, which William had already disavowed by thrusting the blame upon his Scots ministers. He had, he declared, been ill served over that matter, and Tweeddale and Johnstone, the latter of whom had given him timely warning of the dangers in the proposed act, were dismissed. So far, throughout the years 1696 and 1697, there was no diplomatic question involved. The affairs of the Company of Scotland did not upset any intricate web of diplomacy; the king disavowed and hampered the project solely to placate the clamours of vested interests in England. Throughout the prolonged crises in the company's affairs William was conscious of this, and more than once he recorded his disquiet at the thankless role forced upon him by the unsatisfactory bond between the two kingdoms.

Denied financial backing from abroad, denied the experience and control that would have accompanied it, the Scots decided to embark upon the Darien venture ill equipped in nearly every respect except optimism. They had no real experience as colonisers and very little in trade of the dimensions conjured up by Paterson's glowing vision. Their material resources in capital and shipping were slender and unlikely to survive reverses. But though Paterson was a commercial visionary neither he nor his scheme was quite mad. As a project the Darien venture was more soundly based than the great commercial gambles of the next generation, the South Sea Bubble in England and in France the Scotsman John Law's Mississippi Scheme. When Paterson wrote of the Isthmus of Darien as ' this door of the seas, and the key of the universe ',[46] he was not dreaming. By means of an overland route across the Isthmus the wealth of east and west was to be diverted from the Cape of Good Hope, and Scotland was to rival Holland as a great central emporium. What was really lacking was knowledge of the geography of the Isthmus and the extreme difficulty of transport between the Pacific and the Caribbean. In the spring of 1698 information on these matters was sought from Lionel Wafer, a ship's surgeon who had been on the

---

[46] ' A proposal to Plant a Colony in Darien ' (1701), MSS. cited in G. P. Insh, *The Company of Scotland*, p. 73.

Isthmus with the buccaneers and who had ready for publication a book on the area. Wafer's knowledge indicated that the intention of planting a colony on Darien was not as fantastic as is often supposed. The infringement of the sovereign rights of Spain, usually regarded as the wildest feature of the scheme, was, in fact, among the least of the difficulties involved. Certain parties in England were then thinking along similar lines, and the recommendation that England should plant a colony on the Isthmus was made in September 1697 by the commissioners of trade and plantations. Indeed, when the first Scots expedition arrived at Darien it found there an English ship bent, among other things, on seeking out a favourable spot for such an attempt. In a wider context, the whole history of the Caribbean in the seventeenth century had demonstrated how feeble was the Spanish hold on that area. This was evident not only in the English conquest of Jamaica, but also in the exploits of Morgan and other brethren of the coast against Panama in the decade 1670–80. As to claims of sovereignty, the matter is not as simple as it is usually made out. The Scots act of 1695 empowered the company to erect a plantation on any territory not ' possessed ' by any sovereign power. That the Spaniards claimed sovereignty over the Isthmus is certain; that they possessed the territory is not so clear.[47] If England had seriously undertaken such a venture she might well have succeeded. In brief, the failure of the Scots is to be attributed largely to their lack of resources and their inexperience; but that is a very different thing from saying that the enterprise itself was utopian.

Another factor which told heavily against the Scots appeared after the first expedition had sailed for Darien in the autumn of 1698, there to establish the colony of Caledonia. This was the threatened blow to William's complicated diplomacy concerning the Spanish succession. Charles II of Spain was in poor health and had no heir of his body to succeed him. How were the claims of the Bourbons, the Emperor, and the Elector of Bavaria to the vast Spanish empire to be settled? Following the Treaty of Ryswick, which ended the War of the League of Augsburg in

---

[47] On this whole subject see L. E. Elliott Joyce, ed., L. Wafer's *A New Voyage and Description of the Isthmus of America* (Hakluyt Society, 1934). In her introduction the editor points out that the Spaniards never controlled the area and that not until 1776 did they have a treaty with the Indians.

September 1697, this was the problem which mainly engaged William's attention. By the First Partition Treaty a compromise was reached which pleased all except the ambitious Louis XIV. But the Spanish crown and nation were ill content with the position of the cadaver on the dissecting table. The descent of the Scots upon Darien added to William's difficulties, and so in an effort to preserve his work he went out of his way to hamper the Scottish settlers, even to the extent of forbidding the English colonies in North America and the West Indies to have any dealings with Caledonia.

These instructions did not, as many Scots at the time alleged, ruin the first attempt at settlement; but they were remembered when the true reasons for failure, which were not flattering to Scots conceit, were conveniently overlooked. The first attempt ended disastrously because the directors of the company neglected to arrange for the adequate provisioning of the colonists. Not the hypothetical might of Spain but starvation and fever led to the withdrawal of the first settlers. The second main expedition which, ignorant of the fate of the first, arrived in 1699 failed for substantially the same reason—inadequate support. The Spaniards were easily routed at Tubuganti on 15 February 1700 by a mixed force of Scots and Indians, under Captain Campbell of Fonab. But the colonists were too few in numbers and too ill-supplied to hold out indefinitely, and in March 1700 they were obliged to capitulate on honourable terms. In the case of both expeditions, more lives were lost by disasters at sea after clearing from Caledonia than in the colony itself. The Company of Scotland survived this shattering blow, but in an enfeebled condition which restricted its activities. There was slight trafficking in Africa and the Far East, but the eastern voyages were also more eventful than profitable. The disaster of Darien undoubtedly left Scotland, which was at this time further burdened by a succession of bad harvests, in a desperate economic plight. This found expression in a mood of political intransigence.

As the affairs of the Company of Scotland lurched from crisis to crisis, only the most energetic management enabled William's ministers to contain a growing opposition in parliament. In this William was best served by the pliable James Ogilvie, former Jacobite and club-man, who on the fall of Johnstone in 1696 became co-secretary with the Earl of Tullibardine (Atholl's eldest son). In 1698 Ogilvie, created Viscount Seafield in that same year, proved to be one of William's mainstays in a noisy session of the parliament. Resentment at Rycaut's conduct at Hamburg was keen, and the directors of the company wished not only to protest to the king about it but also to have the support of the privy council. With difficulty they were dissuaded; but William did nothing to placate feeling in Scotland. Again and again he evaded the issue. The tactics of the opposition, therefore, were to put forward popular bills which were not acceptable to the executive and then to threaten to withhold supply if these were not touched by the sceptre. It was in this way, for example, that a bill for the equivalent of the English *habeas corpus* procedure was first agitated. In the end the Earl of Marchmont (another former club-man, Sir Patrick Hume of Polwarth), the commissioner, and Seafield, the president, managed to bribe and cajole a majority into letting the affairs of the company drop and even into providing two years' supply. To ensure compliance, the parliament was told to its face ' that the King was resolved that no man that opposed him should enjoy either place or pension of him '.[48] In face of this threat the ambitious place-hunters refused to press popular clamours to extremes, and thus deadlock in the session of 1698 was avoided.

But time did not run for the king. News of the failure of the first expedition to Darien, which reached Scotland in October 1699, increased William's unpopularity. It was then openly demanded that the company should have the use of the three Scottish frigates which ' were lying useless at Burntisland '. Under the act of 1695 a case of sorts could be made for this, but since such a move would merely have wrecked what little good faith Spain still reposed in William, the request was curtly refused. The king, though, was more worried by the affairs of Scotland than he cared to admit. The need for supply was imperative and he was rightly apprehensive of the outcome of the next session of parliament. His detailed instructions to the new commissioner, the second Duke of Queensberry, showed William's dread of what might ensue when parliament assembled in May 1700. Matters were to be handled with the utmost delicacy; a cess of at least six months was to be obtained, even at the cost of giving

[48] *Carstares State Papers*, ed. J. McCormick, pp. 400-2, Duke of Queensberry to Mr Carstares, 24 July 1698.

satisfaction over the demand for the frigates; but on no account was an act declaratory of the Scots' right to Caledonia in Darien to be accepted. The session went badly for the administration, and indeed after two stormy meetings the refractory estates had to be adjourned. William's regret for the failure of the first expedition was perfunctory and, to the members, unconvincing. The better to harass the administration, religious grievances were also dragged in. William's brusque treatment of the general assembly in 1692 and again in 1694, his act granting toleration to conformist episcopalians in 1695, and other slights, real and imagined, had roused the resentment of the presbyterians. The bulk of the parliament cared nothing for presbyterian crotchets, but they knew a useful tactical aid when they saw one; and so they did their best to enlist the aid of the disgruntled churchmen. The estates took up the business of Caledonia and refused to let it drop. On 27 May a resolution was introduced, declaring that the settlement of Caledonia was legal under the terms of the act of 1695, and that the parliament should support and aid the same.[49]

At this point Queensberry developed a diplomatic cold and the parliament was adjourned, not to meet again until October 1700. But it was in these months that the full tragedy of Darien became known. Already the house of lords, sensing the hopelessness of the *impasse*, was trying to interest the commons in a project for closer union between the two kingdoms. William eagerly accepted this as offering the one chance of a good outcome; but the house of commons proved to be as susceptible to chauvinist hysteria as the estates of Scotland, albeit with less excuse on this occasion. A bitter war of pamphlets arose in which angry and scurrilous tracts inflamed tempers in both countries. In one such, *The People of Scotland's Groans and Lamentable Complaints*, there was an ominous attack upon the injuries allegedly heaped upon Scotland as a consequence of the Union of the Crowns in 1603. As a result of this, it was stated, ' our Sovereignty and Freedom is violated, and Laws trampled upon, our Trade interrupted '.[50] These were dangerous statements and led to the confinement of the author and printer in the tolbooth of Edinburgh. Again, in June 1700, before the final stunning news from Darien was known, William was petitioned by a strong section of Scottish society which

[49] *A.P.S.*, x. 195.   [50] Quoted Insh, *op. cit.*, p. 218.

complained bitterly of the adjournment of parliament and the administration's failure to deal with the parliament's grievances. Even the Scottish ministers of state, Queensberry and Seafield in particular, echoed this appeal, only to receive the usual fobbing off. William, indeed, at this point committed his true thoughts on the Scottish problem to the Dutch Pensionary Heinsius: ' I am sorry to be obliged to tell you that affairs go on very badly in the Scotch Parliament. . . . What vexes me in particular is that this affair retards my departure for Holland, for which I long more than ever '.[51]

Scots hopes soared momentarily in June on the receipt of the news of victory at Tubuganti; but the enthusiastic bumpers with which this was toasted ended in an ugly riot, with the mob in possession of Edinburgh, smashing the windows of those who were reckoned to be ministerial in sympathy and releasing from the tolbooth such martyrs for the national cause as the author and printer of *The Groans and Lamentable Complaints*. Throughout, Queensberry slumbered peacefully at Holyrood, or at any rate did not venture from his bed. The ringleaders were never caught, which indicates that the rioters had the sympathy if not the active help of the bulk of the citizens. These high spirits were soon effectively damped by the black news of the surrender in Darien. Even William had to bow before the sullen resentment that swept through all classes in Scotland. Prompted by Seafield, he successfully interceded with Spain for the lives and liberty of several members of the first expedition who had been captured off Carthagena, carried to Spain, and condemned to death at Seville. But this could not dispel the ugly mood that gripped the Scots. The Jacobites, naturally, made the most of all this, and one of them, Dr Archibald Pitcairn, physician and accomplished Latinist, lampooned William in a witty rendering of Æsop's fable of the frogs who begged Jupiter for a king only to be given a stork. A fiercer expression of this mood was an inflammatory address which circulated widely and hinted darkly at the overthrow of the king's authority: a convention of estates was to meet in Perth, where the Highlanders, adopting for them an unusual role, were to provide a makeshift national guard. The administration could not afford to treat all this as idle bombast, whatever the glare of hindsight might enable modern commentators to

[51] *Letters of William III and Louis XIV, 1697-1700*, ed. Paul Grimblot, II. 415.

make of it. A real crisis was in the making. As one of Carstares's correspondents pointed out: ' God help us, we are ripening for destruction. It looks very like Forty-One.'[52] But the near unity which had strengthened the Scots in 1641 was lacking in the clash of interests in 1700. The wild temper was there, but held in check by divergent purposes. It was this, rather than the efforts of the administration, which prevented civil war. Queensberry weakly hoped that the presence of the king would make all well; but William by this time was safe in his beloved Holland and had no intention of exchanging it for the cold penury of Holyrood and an angry session in the Parliament House. In so far as the administration worked its own salvation, the credit must go to Seafield. He alone acted with spirit and effect. Bending every effort to the essential task of securing a ministerial majority in the estates, he personally canvassed the northern constituencies while Argyll took the western in a frantic quest for the way to members' hearts. Every inducement, every wile was employed to influence members of the estates, ranging from sums of money to the pettiest marks of favour. Money, indeed, was short, and only grudgingly was £1,000 sterling provided from London— with the fatuous instruction that it was not to be squandered.

The ninth session of parliament which opened on 24 October 1700 was tumultuous; but the ministerial phalanx, so hurriedly cemented together, held. Now that Caledonia was safely out of existence, William could take stock of it by expressing his sorrow for the losses incurred and his willingness to help the Scots to recoup themselves in any reasonable way. At last it was possible for the king to be sincere in this matter, but too late to soothe the ruffled feelings of his Scottish subjects. The critical question was whether the estates would pass an act asserting the company's right to Caledonia, in which case William would have lost whatever confidence Spain had in him and the second Partition Treaty of March 1700. Seafield's work, plus the fundamental hostility between Jacobites and presbyterians, enabled the administration to muddle through. On 14 January 1701 it was narrowly decided to present the king with yet one more address on the legality of the Darien venture and not to embody this claim in an act of parliament. On 1 February 1701 the last real session of William's parliament ended.

[52] *Carstares State Papers*, p. 527.

Within thirteen months the Jacobites were toasting ' the little gentleman in black velvet ', the mole whose burrowings caused William's horse to stumble and so to hurry on the king's death, which occurred at London on 8 March 1702. Latterly William's thoughts had been concerned mainly with the danger to the second Partition Treaty, which had been ignored by the will of Charles II of Spain who had died on 1 November 1700. France now had the prospect of the entire Spanish inheritance; but Louis XIV could not content himself with this and his aggressiveness in the Spanish Netherlands, by threatening Holland, made war unavoidable. Then in September 1701 James VII and II died at St Germain; and Louis, by chivalrously recognising James VIII and III, unconsciously helped William by providing not only a *casus foederis* of the Peace of Ryswick of 1697 but also justification in British eyes for William's war-like preparations. England and the Empire were bound to ally against France, and the coming hostilities in Europe occupied William's last days. His one contribution to the settlement of the Scottish problem was to recommend a closer union between England and Scotland.[53] For, dimly though he understood Scotland, William knew that the victory secured in the last session of parliament was fleeting and illusory. The essential problems remained and were to plague the early years of his successor, Queen Anne.

[53] Cobbett's *Parliamentary History of England*, v. 1341.

2

THE REIGN OF ANNE AND THE UNION OF THE PARLIAMENTS

In the background to the first half of Queen Anne's reign two matters stand out as being of primary importance: one was the dynastic problem and the other was the War of the Spanish Succession. The death of Princess Anne's last surviving child in July 1700 opened up the problem of the succession. The English parliament sought to solve it by the Act of Settlement of 1701 which recognised the claim of the Electress of Hanover and her issue; but in Scotland this act was resented as arrogant and one-sided. The Scots believed that in a matter of such fundamental common interest there should have been prior consultation, and the Scottish parliament studiously refrained from passing a similar measure. There was also a body of opinion in Scotland which held that the question of the succession could be used to make possible some redefinition of the connection between the two countries by purely constitutional means. There was widespread agreement in Scotland that the existing bond between the two kingdoms was unsatisfactory and that it was slowly strangling the weaker nation. The unionists believed this no less than the anti-unionists: but they disagreed as to remedies. The exigencies of the great European War were such that English statesmen were driven, albeit reluctantly, to pay serious heed to developments in Scotland, if only because France supported the exiled Stewarts.

William's death did nothing to solve outstanding political problems in Scotland, and indeed, by materially altering the system of government, did much to intensify them. William had made discreet use of his Dutch favourite, the Earl of Portland, to oversee Scottish affairs; but Anne, though by no means a nonentity, could not maintain this system and the task of supervising Scottish policy devolved upon her English ministers and particularly upon Godolphin, the lord treasurer. His initial policy was simply to keep Scotland quiet and subservient, and the less troublesome the means the better.[1] The first problem that faced Anne's ministers was whether or not to summon the Scottish parliament in terms of an act of 1696 whereby the parliament was to meet within twenty days of the sovereign's demise solely to secure the succession.[2] The express terms of the act were broken. The parliament met ninety and not twenty days after William's death, most likely to permit the privy council on 30 May to declare war on France,[3] an unpopular measure which would have had a stormy reception in parliament. The leader of the opposition, the Duke of Hamilton, seized on these irregularities to declare the parliament summoned for 9 June illegal. Failing to carry his point, Hamilton and 73 of his supporters ceremoniously withdrew from what was, indeed, a superannuated convention parliament. Their departure played into the hands of the commissioner, Queensberry, who seized the opportunity to pass a few acts, one ratifying the queen's succession, another securing the established church, and—most important of all—an act nominating commissioners to treat for union.[4] Queensberry knew that he was unpopular and feared that Godolphin might give way to demands for a general election; he therefore pinned his hopes on a satisfactory and speedy conclusion to the negotiations for union.

The scheme failed. To the discomfiture of the Court party in Scotland the cause of union foundered at this time. As a result of elections held in July 1702 the Tories secured a clear majority in the house of commons and they showed little interest in a complete union with Scotland. In the meetings held at the Cockpit in Whitehall the English negotiators, Whig no less than Tory, proved half-hearted in their approach, sometimes not even troubling to constitute a quorum. Finally, the outline of an

---

[1] *H.M.C. 14th Report*, pt. III, Seafield MSS., p. 198, Godolphin to Seafield, 13 March 1703.

[2] *A.P.S.*, x. 59-60, entitled, significantly, ' Act for the Security of the Kingdom '.

[3] Sir David Hume of Crossrigg, *Diary of the Proceedings in the Parliament and Privy Council of Scotland, 1700-1707*, pp. 82-3.

[4] *A.P.S.*, xi. 19, 25-7.

agreement for an incorporating union with full communication of trade was reached, but the whole project foundered upon the demands of the Scots commissioners for recognition of the rights of the Company of Scotland.[5]   On 3 February 1703 the negotiations were adjourned.   The English parliament displayed no interest in the proposed terms, and in fact these commissioners never met again.   But even if the English parliament had been favourable it is extremely doubtful if the proposed treaty would have been acceptable to that of Scotland.   Queensberry's rump parliament was no more; for, in spite of warnings that a new parliament would likely be beyond ministerial control, Godolphin and Nottingham overrode Queensberry and decreed that a general election should be held.   Seafield again was the main manager for the Court party, and he worked hard wheedling and ' influencing ' electors and elected.   Hamilton and his friends, however, worked to even better purpose, offering all things to all men.   Thus they strove, with remarkable success, to overcome ' the hopes of reward and the fear of punishment ' which the Court employed.[6]   A preliminary estimate reckoned that the Country party—the opposition—could count on 60 commissioners for the shires and 35 burgess representatives; this proved near the mark, for in the new parliament the Country party and its allies had a decided, if somewhat fluctuating, majority. Attempts were made in December 1702 to disrupt the Countrymen by inveigling one of their leaders, the Marquis of Tweeddale, into office but he refused to be drawn.[7]   The failure of the union negotiations was thus a stroke of luck for the ministry, since a treaty would hardly have passed such a hostile parliament.

In preparation for a difficult session slight but significant changes were made in the ministry.   This was done at the behest of the English ministers and was not at all to Queensberry's liking.[8]   Godolphin and Nottingham wished to have a ' broadbottom ' administration in Scotland, thus depriving the opposition of leadership.   Queensberry remained as commissioner, but Seafield, the indispensable trimmer, replaced Marchmont as

[5] Journals of these negotiations are in *A.P.S.*, xi. App., 145-61; and in P.R.O., State Papers (Scotland), ser. ii. S.P.54/2.

[6] P.R.O., S.P.54/1, No. 10, ? to Mr Keith, 7 August 1702.

[7] *Correspondence of George Baillie of Jerviswood, 1702–1708*, p. 9.

[8] P. W. J. Riley, ' The Formation of the Scottish Ministry of 1703 ', in *S.H.R.*, xliv. 114 ff.

chancellor, while Tarbat (created Earl of Cromartie on 3 January 1703), a Tory, became secretary. Tullibardine (who on 6 May succeeded his father as Marquis of Atholl) became lord privy seal. Cromartie and Atholl were supposed to be influential with the Cavaliers or Jacobites, who had done surprisingly well in the recent elections. The object was to prevent collusion in parliament between the Countrymen and the Cavaliers; but this uneasy alliance between the Court party and the supporters of King James soon broke down. The Cavaliers were episcopalian and demanded concessions for that communion, including the restoration of private patronage. At that point such a price could not be considered practicable politics, and in the event Cavaliers and Countrymen joined in mounting an assault on the ministry. For the ministry the session of 1703, which opened on 6 May, was an unmitigated disaster. The crucial issues (succession and/or union) were thrust upon the house by a numerous if somewhat disjointed opposition which refused to allow the ministry to broach these matters at its convenience. The ministers first moved supply,[9] which was desperately needed, only to be met with a massive onslaught on the constitutional *status quo*, comparable in intensity to the work of Montgomerie's club in its brief but hectic heyday in 1689. Tweeddale, one of the leaders of the Country party, countered the motion for supply by an overture for consideration of the succession and the terms on which a successor should be accepted.[10] Others of his party, notably Andrew Fletcher of Saltoun, regarded this as a mere base on which to erect more drastic measures. As Fletcher had already trenchantly put it: ' 'Tis not the Prerogative of a King of Scotland I would diminish, but the Prerogative of English Ministers over this Nation '.[11] He was ably seconded by Lord Belhaven, who alleged that the Scots had badly erred in 1603 ' by not making such Conditions of Government, and Rectifications of their Constitution, as might have preserved the Soveraignity and Independency of their Nation '.[12]

Nor was the ministry well served by some of its own members.

[9] *A.P.S.*, XI. 41, 19 May 1703. This was moved by the leader of the Cavaliers, the Earl of Home, before his party became disenchanted with the ministry.

[10] *Ibid.*

[11] A. Fletcher, *Speeches by a Member of the Parliament which began at Edinburgh the 6th of May 1703* (1703), p. 26.

[12] *A Speech in Parliament by the Lord Belhaven* (1703), p. 7.

It was the lord privy seal, Atholl, who introduced the first claim for an Act of Security, for what reason is not clear.[13] Atholl, an intermediary for the Cavaliers, may have been reflecting their disillusionment with Queensberry, but it seems more likely that, with the agreement of the other ministers, he was trying to prevent the opposition from introducing a more stringent measure.[14] If the latter was the intention, then it failed lamentably. The result after prolonged wrangling was the Act of Security, which carefully left the succession open, possibly as a bargaining counter but more likely to enable constitutional reform within Scotland to be carried. It stipulated that the successor should be nominated by the parliament, and should be of the royal line of Scotland and of the protestant faith; but unless the sovereignty of the kingdom were secured and guaranteed that successor would not be the person already designated to succeed to the crown of England. The purpose of the Act of Security, then, was to define the constitutional position on the death of Anne; to vest authority in the estates rather than in the existing ministry and its tool, the privy council; and to give teeth to these measures all the protestant fencible men were to be trained. It really foreshadowed a resurrection of the full programme that had been thrust upon Charles I in 1641. In vain the ministry sought to placate or divert the opposition by bringing in popular measures such as the Wine Act which, in spite of the state of war, permitted trade with France, thus bringing much needed funds into the treasury. Nothing would satisfy but the Act of Security which, in spite of the ingenious prevarications of the ministers, passed the house by a majority of 59 on 13 August 1703.[15] Queensberry was nonplussed by this unprecedented situation. Desperate for supply, he sought permission from the English ministers to accept the Act of Security but this was denied. His allies were already deserting him, with Atholl, Seafield and Cromartie openly veering towards the Cavaliers. The opposition was still on the rampage, passing an Act anent Peace and War which reserved decisions on these important matters for the estates, rumbling about a triennial act and debating Fletcher's scheme for limitations which, if implemented, would have vested full sovereignty in the parliament. Fearful lest worse should befall, the commissioner touched the acts of the session

---

[13] *A.P.S.*, xi. 45; Hume, *Diary*, pp. 101-2.
[14] *H.M.C.*, *Laing*, ii. 16-19.   [15] *A.P.S.*, xi. 74.

with the sceptre, excluding only the Act of Security, and adjourned on 16 September.[16]

The session of 1703 was a costly set-back for the Court. The question of the succession remained provocatively open; the union project, which Godolphin now warmly recommended to Seafield,[17] seemed to have foundered; much-needed supply was withheld; and, most disquieting of all, there was constitutional deadlock over the Act of Security. At last the abolition of the committee of the articles had produced a head-on clash between executive and legislature. The ' patriots ' claimed that there was no royal veto on decisions of the parliament, denounced such an alien importation, and asserted that parliament was a sovereign body. By the end of the session Queensberry had ceased to look for a deliverance by constitutional means and turned, naturally, to intrigue.

Already in late August 1703 the commissioner had some faint hope of a turn of fortune's wheel which would, from his point of view, put all to rights. The exiled court had eagerly followed this troubled session of the Scottish parliament and, after its usual fashion, concluded that hostility to the ministry must imply support, or at least the possibility of support, for the Chevalier. The Pretender's advisers were divided into two factions, one headed by the Earl of Perth and the other by Middleton. The Perth or Scottish faction, as it was sometimes called, felt that this favourable situation in Scotland should be boldly exploited ; but Middleton's party was much more cautious in its appraisal. The French showed some interest in a plan for invading Scotland, but Louis XIV's forces were heavily committed and troops could not be dispatched on the basis of mere guesswork. An emissary from St Germain was sent to Britain to sound out prospects and report back to Paris. The Jacobite ministers blundered badly in choosing for such a delicate role one of the shiftiest of the numerous rogues who professed to serve King James. This was Simon Fraser of Beaufort, self-styled Lord Lovat, head of clan Fraser, and a notorious outlaw. Fraser, hoping to ingratiate himself with Anne's government, betrayed the plot to Queensberry, lavishly gilding the details. If Fraser were to be believed, Queensberry would have the satisfaction of ruining not only Hamilton and Home but also his own colleagues, Atholl, Seafield and Cromartie, with Tweeddale and other leaders of the Countrymen thrown in

[16] *Ibid.*, XI. 112.　　　[17] *Stair Annals*, ed. J. M. Graham, I. 380-1.

for good measure. All would be stigmatised as Jacobite plotters, and indeed the only man of the first rank in politics entirely free from such a stain would be Queensberry himself. Atholl, however, got wind of the danger through Robert Ferguson the Plotter; he took prompt action to counterwork Queensberry and in the event ' Queensberry's plot ' brought about the downfall of its projector.

Queensberry, in fact, had discovered too much and yet too little. The English Whigs believed that Godolphin and Marlborough were also in correspondence with the exiled court; it was also believed that, in order to protect themselves, the ministers took advantage of a clash between the two houses of parliament to refuse to carry out a thorough investigation of Fraser's allegations.[18] The charges against Tweeddale and his friends were clumsy fabrications,[19] no sooner raised than exposed. Queensberry's stock at court slumped, helped by some adroit undermining by Atholl, Seafield and Cromartie. A delegation from the opposition (consisting of Roxburghe, Rothes, and Baillie of Jerviswood) went to London for the same purpose. Godolphin, aware that Queensberry was now a liability, set to work on this delegation, hoping to form from it a new Scottish ministry which could command a majority in the parliament. By May 1704 an agreement had been reached whereby Tweeddale and his friends —soon to be known as the New Party—were to form a ministry.[20] The main object was to carry the Hanoverian succession, and in order to popularise this policy the Act of Security was to be accepted in a diluted form.[21]

Two awkward circumstances wrecked the scheme. Tweeddale was unable to carry the bulk of his party with him, and, of course, the Cavaliers could not be brought to support such a policy. The new commissioner could never reckon on more than about 30 votes. An equally serious failure must be attributed to Godolphin, who denied Tweeddale the patronage that might have helped to win support.[22] Thus Tweeddale had to face a hostile

[18] G. Hilton Jones, *Mainstream of Jacobitism*, pp. 68-9.
[19] N.L.S., MS. 7104, No. 31, Atholl to Tweeddale, 11 December 1703.
[20] N.L.S., MS. 7104, No. 32, Marlborough to Tweeddale, 4 April 1704; and MS. 7121, Tweeddale to Godolphin, 18 May 1704.
[21] N.L.S., MS. 7102, Nos. 18 and 19: ' Instructions to Marquis of Tweeddale ' and ' Additional Instructions '.
[22] N.L.S., MS. 7121, Tweeddale to Godolphin, 18 May 1704.

parliament, condemned as a turncoat by most of his old associates and with a makeshift and largely disloyal ministry. Queensberry, furious at being excluded from office, promptly made a pact with the opposition and ordered his minions to thwart the ministry's efforts to raise supply.[23] The session which Tweeddale opened as commissioner on 6 July 1704 proved abortive for the ministry: almost from the beginning he was outmanœuvred. On 13 July Hamilton took the initiative with a resolve that parliament should not proceed to the nomination of a successor 'untill we have had a previous treaty with England in relation to our Commerce and other Concerns with that Nation'.[24] This was a tactical move, not to be construed as a desire for incorporating union in return for free trade. Tweeddale knew well enough what his old comrades had in mind: it was, he wrote to Godolphin, merely ' the most popular handle to throw off the Succession at this time '.[25] Further, they meant to make the terms ' so extravagant as they cannot be yeelded to by England '.[26] In this Tweeddale may have exaggerated a little. Only the committed Jacobites were in principle opposed to a treaty. The Countrymen wished to negotiate some more equitable connection with England, but the furthest they were prepared to go was a federal union. Their main endeavour, indeed, was to preserve and reform the constitution of Scotland.

Tweeddale's unusual honesty commended him to the Court. To the Queen he wrote a frank and dignified account of the session's difficulties in which he declared that bad English policies in the past were mainly responsible for ' the ill temper this natione have been in for some years ', and hinted broadly that no good outcome was possible unless the English ministry and parliament showed a more sympathetic approach to Scottish problems.[27] He even offered to resign—an unprecedented event. Anne and Godolphin, incensed by Queensberry's perfidy and impressed by Tweeddale's candour, continued him in office. Besides, England's situation was delicate. Everything turned on the outcome of Marlborough's daring march to the Danube, but no one could foretell that it was to culminate in a great

---

[23] *H.M.C., Mar and Kellie*, I. 228-9, Queensberry to Mar, 1 August 1704.
[24] *A.P.S.*, XI. 127; Hume, *Diary*, pp. 137-9.
[25] N.L.S., MS. 7121, Tweeddale to Godolphin, 14 July 1704.
[26] *Ibid.*, same to same, 6 August 1704.
[27] N.L.S., MS. 7121, Tweeddale to Queen Anne, 18 July 1704.

victory at Blenheim. In the meantime, the small force in Scotland would have to be disbanded unless supply were granted by the parliament. The need for a supply was imperative and to obtain it Tweeddale was empowered to accept a milder version of the Act of Security. After prolonged debate a very small supply was granted for six months, and in return Tweeddale had to accept the Act of Security virtually in its original form.[28] Not content with this, the opposition pressed other measures; and on 28 August Tweeddale was obliged to close the session, the question of the succession as open as ever. His closing speech admitted his ministry's failure and must have heartened the opposition; for, said he, ' I can assure you no disappointment that Her Majesty hath met with, will in the least alter her gracious disposition towards this Her ancient Kingdom '.[29]

Tweeddale continued in favour and indeed by a belated redistribution of offices late in 1704, the object of which was to rid the ministry of undependables, the New Party had its position strengthened. But its true weakness was that it was committed to carrying the succession, not a treaty; and under pressure from the English Whig Junto Godolphin was obliged to take up the policy of a treaty once more.[30] He needed support, so hotly was he assailed for allowing the Act of Security to pass. The outcome of this furore, and the price he had to pay for Whig support, was the provocative Alien Act. Unless the Act of Security were repealed and either the Hanoverian succession accepted or a treaty in train by Christmas Day 1705, the Queen's subjects of Scotland were to be treated as strangers in England and Scottish exports to England were to be prohibited. Godolphin meanwhile threw out dark hints that if peaceful means failed then force would be used.[31]

In Scotland the Alien Act undermined Tweeddale's ministry. It drove the New Party (or, as it was coming to be called, the *Squadrone Volante*) almost frantic. How could they suddenly reverse their arguments and press for a union? Faced with the prospect of a fall, it was their turn to show lack of principle. Desperately they cast about for allies to shore up their tottering

---

[28] *A.P.S.*, xi. 136-7.   [29] *Ibid.*, xi. 205.

[30] Sir T. Lever, *Godolphin, His Life and Times*, pp. 169-82.

[31] *Jerviswood Corr.*, pp. 22, 28, 122; *H.M.C. 14th Report*, pt. iii, Seafield MSS., pp. 198-207.

administration, turning to Argyll, Hamilton, and even Queensberry—all to no purpose. By January 1705 Seafield was intriguing with Godolphin in an effort to overthrow the New Party.
The *Squadrone* was at odds with itself, most of its members regarding Tweeddale as ' no wayes qualified for his post '.[32] Their
feeble handling of the affair of the *Worcester* merely confirmed the
fall of the New Party. This violent episode was the product of the
resentment still felt at the failure of the Company of Scotland.
Early in 1704 the company's last remaining ship, the *Annandale*,
was seized in the Downs by English revenue officials at the instiga-
tion of the English East India Company. In retaliation the
Worcester, an English vessel, was taken in the Firth of Forth by
agents of the Company of Scotland. That was on 12 August 1704.
On very flimsy evidence, Captain Green of the *Worcester* and his
crew were accused of piracy against the Company of Scotland's
ship *Speedy Return*, which had disappeared mysteriously in the
East Indies in 1703. In March 1705 Green and his men were
tried in the high court of the admiralty of Scotland and found
guilty. The best that can be said is that the accusers believed the
charge to be a true one, though it has since been established that
it was of no substance.[33] A more obvious motive for pressing the
charges against Green and his men was the desire to reimburse
the stockholders of the Company of Scotland by escheating the
Worcester and her cargo. English opinion was convinced that this
was the real motive and agitated for a reprieve, which was granted
by the queen; but the Scottish privy council, overawed by the
mob of Edinburgh, shuffled and prevaricated. Argyll tried to
reprieve Green but was resisted by the New Party. One prominent member of the *Squadrone* wrote cynically: ' Go the
matter as it will, we shall by it have the countrey '.[34] In gaining
the country, they lost the Court. On 11 April 1705 Green and
two of his crew were hanged, the hysteria subsided and the others
were released. The *Worcester* herself was sold for £2,823 and
thereafter plied from Leith.

It was clear to the Court that Scotland required firmer government. What was needed in a commissioner at this time was a
bold heart and ruthless purpose. Argyll, young and ambitious,

[32] *Jerviswood Corr.*, p. 38, Baillie to Johnstone, 16 January 1705.
[33] Cf. Sir Richard C. Temple, *New Light on the Tragedy of the ' Worcester', 1704–1705*.
[34] *Jerviswood Corr.*, p. 66.

allowed himself to be persuaded with lavish promises of rewards: he was to have money and an English peerage. Yet the strange fact is that when he came up to Edinburgh as commissioner in April 1705 nothing was settled. No one knew what the ministry proposed to do in the coming session. Seafield hoped to bring the *Squadrone* into a broad-bottomed administration and to pursue the succession. Argyll would not have this;[35] and in June he pressed the queen to confer office on Queensberry. Anne detested Queensberry and for some time refused to employ him: that, she declared, ' is a thing I can never consent to, his last tricking behaviour having made him more odious to me than ever.' A week later she was reluctantly forced to give way, informing Godolphin that ' it grates my soul to take a man into my service that has not only betrayed me, but tricked me several times, one that has been obnoxious to his own countrymen these many years and one that I can never be convinced can be of any use '.[36] The Old or Court party was back in favour, but its manœuvres were scarcely calculated to lessen opposition. When the session began on 28 June 1705 the majority refused, with studied nonchalance, to consider the recommendations of the queen for settling the succession and initiating a treaty with England.[37] Instead the house spent its time on comparatively trivial domestic matters. Fletcher was still hopefully pressing for limitations, this time in terms of the Claim of Right and so, as he argued, ' not needing the Queen's consent '.[38] At last, on 20 July, Mar, the secretary, succeeded in moving the draft of an act for a treaty with England,[39] although no real headway was made with it until 24 August, after lengthy discussions on a proposed triennial act.[40] The struggle thereafter turned not so much on whether there should be a treaty but on who should negotiate it. The opposition insisted that the estates should elect their own commissioners, and if this point had been carried the attainment of an incorporating union would have proved very difficult, perhaps impossible. The Court was rescued by Hamilton, who on 1 September in a thinly attended house shocked his allies by

[35] See his correspondence at this time, printed in *Intimate Society Letters of the Eighteenth Century*, ed. John, 9th Duke of Argyll, I. 1-12.

[36] G. Davies, ed., ' Letters from Queen Anne to Godolphin ', in *S.H.R.*, XIX. 191-2.

[37] *A.P.S.*, XI. 213-15.

[38] Hume *Diary*, pp. 169-70.

[39] *A.P.S.*, XI. 216.   [40] *Ibid.*, XI. 223.

moving that nomination should be left to the queen.[41]   His
reasons for this remain obscure, though most likely he had made
a deal with the Court through Mar.   At any rate, the ministry
seized the opportunity to clinch the matter with a snap vote,
and on 14 September the parliament was adjourned.

On 27 February 1706 the queen nominated the Scottish commissioners who were to negotiate with their English counterparts
at Westminster.   Naturally, the main body of the commission
was made up of Queensberry and his associates, and therefore
had a marked bias towards an incorporating union.   The Countrymen and the *Squadrone* were pointedly excluded.   Only one
known anti-unionist was named, George Lockhart of Carnwath,
open Tory and not so secret Jacobite.   The English commission,
unlike its predecessor in 1702, also contained a solid core of
' unionists '.   On 16 April 1706 the two commissions began to
deliberate at Westminster, observing the same laborious forms as
in the abortive transactions of 1702-3.   The two bodies sat sepa-
rately and communicated only in writing.   Profiting from the
experience of their recent predecessors, each commission knew
what was possible and what was not.   Indeed, the negotiations of
1706 were largely, as Lockhart asserted, a hollow show,[42] with
any appearance of hard bargaining on the part of the Scots commissioners made largely to secure prestige at home.   Thus, they
countered the demand for an incorporating union with a weak
plea for federalism which they did not sustain.[43]   The Earl of
Stair desired incorporation with England but argued that it
should be achieved in stages, culminating in a union acceptable
to popular opinion.   There was wisdom in his proposals, but
Godolphin saw the fatal flaw in them.   Such a method would
take years, perhaps generations, and events would hardly permit
a gradualist approach.   By 25 April 1706 the Scots commissioners
had accepted the basic proposition of an incorporating union of
the two kingdoms represented by one parliament.   Many matters
of detail still had to be negotiated and some of these took weeks of
involved discussion.   The thorniest problems concerned taxation, parliamentary representation, and questions of law and

[41] *A.P.S.*, xi. 237; Hume, *Diary*, 171; Lockhart, *Memoirs*, 169-72.
[42] Lockhart, *Memoirs*, 209-13; cf. *Carstares State Papers*, ed. McCormick, 743-5,
Mar to Carstares, 9 March 1706: ' you see that what we are to treat of is not in our
choice '.
[43] *A.P.S.*, xi. App., p. 165.

jurisdictions. By 23 July 1706, however, the 25 articles of the Treaty of Union had been agreed upon by the two commissions.

As Great Britain the kingdoms of Scotland and England were to be united, with one parliament and under one flag. It followed, therefore, that the Hanoverian succession was accepted. There was to be complete freedom of trade in the united kingdom and the colonies. Coinage, weights and measures were to be uniform; and, with certain reservations, there was to be one fiscal system. The malt tax and tax on salt were not to be levied in Scotland in the meantime, and an Equivalent estimated at £398,085 10s. was granted to Scotland to offset her future liability towards the English national debt. This Equivalent was to be used to liquidate the national debt of Scotland (principally to pay arrears of salary to office-holders), and as well to compensate the stockholders of the Company of Scotland, which was to be wound up. A smaller equivalent, hypothecated on the increased yield of the revenue, was to be devoted to the promotion of Scottish industry. It was not proposed that the other institutions of Scotland should be suppressed or merged with their English counterparts. The law of Scotland respecting private right was to continue and not to be altered except for the evident utility of the subjects within Scotland; the main law courts were to be maintained, including the heritable jurisdictions. Public law was to be assimilated with that of England, and the courts that served it, notably those of admiralty and exchequer, were to be remodelled. The privy council was to be retained, subject to the united parliament's decision on its future. After some haggling the number of Scotland's representatives was fixed at forty-five for the commons and sixteen elected peers to sit in the house of lords for the duration of each parliament.[44] Nothing was said of the religious establishment in either kingdom.

These were the terms that had to be considered by the two parliaments, and this was the real difficulty in the way of union. It had been easy for the English and Scottish commissions to reach accord; but how would their parent bodies, particularly the parliament of Scotland, react to those proposals? A bitter war of pamphlets was soon being waged in an effort to sway opinion in both kingdoms. Some Scots writers, like Andrew Fletcher and

[44] The full text of the treaty is conveniently reprinted in G. S. Pryde, *The Treaty of Union of Scotland and England*, 1707.

James Hodges, saw in the treaty (which, thanks to Lockhart, was not the well-guarded secret it was meant to be) nothing but a base betrayal. Other writers, like Daniel Defoe and William Paterson, saw in it for Scotland a deliverance and the prospect of a glorious rebirth.[45] In these disputes all the nonsense did not lie on one side and all the best strokes on the other. In general the pro-union authors had the better of the economic arguments, although some of their rosy predictions were wild. The anti-unionists made capital of the fact that the Scots would, if the treaty were accepted, mortgage their future to England. They were aided by the kirk's alarm at the possible dangers involved in union with prelatical England, and in the circumstances these fears seemed justifiable.

It soon became clear that in Scotland the treaty was unpopular, and the ministry was hard pushed to whip up support for the coming session. In an effort to win votes all sorts of inducements were held out.[46] Payment of arrears of salaries to office-holders was made conditional on their supporting the treaty. Partly for this end, a sum of £20,000 sterling sent up from the English treasury was secretly disbursed by the Scottish treasurer, the Earl of Glasgow.[47] Some of the leading politicians were frankly on the make. Argyll, then campaigning in Flanders, refused to return and help out the ministry until he was promoted to a major-generalship. Throughout the session, in short, influence was extensively used; and but for Mar's talent as a manager, the way to union might have proved not just hard but impossible at that time. Early in the session he had difficulty in placating Argyll, who demanded that his young brother, Archibald, should be created a peer—all this with an eye to the future. Only with the greatest difficulty could the Campbells be bought off by Lord Archie becoming Earl of Islay in the peerage of Scotland.

On 3 October 1706 Queensberry as commissioner opened the session. The articles of union were read, and at a second reading on 12 October the storm broke, both inside and outside the

[45] For a useful discussion of the pamphlet literature, see J. Mackinnon, *The Union of England and Scotland*, ch. VIII.

[46] For some examples, see W. Ferguson, 'The Making of the Treaty of Union of 1707', in *S.H.R.*, XLIII. 106-7.

[47] Glasgow later admitted this : *H.M.C., Portland*, v. 114, Glasgow to Oxford, 22 November 1711.

Parliament House. Conscious of the weak forces at its command, the ministry hoped for a rapid dispatch of business and a speedy acceptance of the treaty. The aim of the opposition, on the other hand, was to delay, since its own counsels were divided. Seafield noted that Hamilton, still smarting from being excluded from the commission, was violently opposed to the treaty ' bot knows not how to unite his pairtie '.[48] In view of his recent conduct this was hardly surprising. Then the philippics of Fletcher and Belhaven were overdone and failed to convince the numerous doubters and trimmers. Thus when the first article of the treaty was put to the vote on 4 November it passed by a majority of 115 to 83.[49] This was a smaller majority than had been expected; and, to reduce opposition, on that same day an act to safeguard the established church was proposed. Such an act was needed, for the commission of the general assembly had denounced the proposed treaty. The act guaranteeing the security of the presbyterian establishment was passed on 12 November and declared to be an integral part of the treaty. Thereafter, while the clergy still grumbled and never really cared for union, they ceased openly to oppose it. None the less, widespread popular dislike of an incorporating union remained, sedulously fanned by the Jacobites and the Country Party but existing independently of them. There were nightly mobbings in Edinburgh in which pro-unionist statesmen were threatened and anti-unionists cheered as their country's champions. There was also a good deal of unrest in Glasgow and the west which worried the ministers more than the giddy hooliganism of the Edinburgh mob. It was feared that another Whiggamore Raid for the chastening of the government was hatching, and so 200 dragoons were dispatched to Glasgow to maintain order; but on their withdrawal riots again broke out.[50] There was also the odd affair of Ker of Kersland, who was ostensibly trying to create an alliance between Cameronians and Jacobites but who was probably in Queensberry's pay.[51] However unlikely as close allies, both groups, for quite different reasons, hated the thought of union and might well have co-operated in the negative work of raising the parliament. But Hamilton's

[48] Seafield Letters, ed. P. Hume Brown (S.H.S.), 94, Seafield to Godolphin, 4 October 1706.

[49] A.P.S., XI. 313-15.

[50] H.M.C., Mar and Kellie, I. 344-51. Mar to Nairne, 2 December 1706, and same to same, 7 December 1706.

[51] J. Mackinnon, Union of England and Scotland, 313-15.

inactivity and Queensberry's prompt but unobtrusive preparations prevented any serious disorders.   By December 1706 a
strong English force lay on the border, ready to move at Queensberry's call.[52]

Popular discontent was exploited by the parliamentary opposition, particularly in the production of anti-union addresses.
These addresses seem to have reflected honestly the attitude of
many Scots of all classes, and their terms are worthy of more
consideration than they have generally received.   They condemned an incorporating union and specific articles of the proposed treaty; but they did not condemn union as such.   Those
who have followed Argyll in thinking those petitions fit only to
make kites with[53] would do well to ponder a question that was
put to Mar at the time.   Why did not the ministry bring in
pro-union addresses to counterbalance the anti-union petitions ?
Mar replied that it had been left too late and that few would
look worse than none.[54]   This defect was later noted in parliament, particularly by the Duke of Atholl, who consistently
opposed the treaty.   On 7 January 1707 he stated that ' there is
not one Address from any part of this kingdome in favour of this
Union '; he therefore demanded a dissolution and the summon-
ing of a new parliament ' to have the immediat Sentiments of the
Nation since these articles have been made publick '.[55]   Since
the ministry's purpose *was* to ignore the sentiments of the nation
Atholl's motion was defeated; and the better to secure this end a
proclamation had been issued forbidding people to flock to Edinburgh on the pretext of supporting the addresses.[56]

Voting on the various articles of the treaty varied widely.
The *Squadrone*, which commanded 25 votes, played a crucial
role.   For months after the treaty negotiations were set on foot,
the leaders of the New Party were unable to make up their minds
on this issue.   But by November 1705 Roxburghe was convinced
that the Court was determined to push an act of union through
the parliaments.   He concluded that it might well succeed in the
Scottish parliament: ' The motives will be, Trade with most,

[52] *H.M.C., Mar and Kellie*, I. 353, Nairne to Mar, 10 December 1706.
[53] Lockhart, *Memoirs*, p. 235.   There are three portfolios of these petitions in the
Register House.
[54] *H.M.C., Mar and Kellie*, I. 320, Nairne to Mar, 14 November 1706; and Mar's
reply, 328, 19 November 1706.
[55] *A.P.S.*, XI. 387.   [56] *Ibid.*, XI. 371-2, 27 December 1706.

Hanover with some, ease and security with others '.[57] If this were so, and the New Party could claim no credit for helping to carry the union, then its future would be bleak indeed. Gradually, Roxburghe cleverly steered the majority of the *Squadrone* to his way of thinking. The Court even more cleverly held out powerful inducements to the leaders of the party. They were large stockholders in the Company of Scotland, and this fact had coloured much of their politics. The ministry cunningly encouraged the *Squadrone* leaders to believe that as the nominees of the Company they should have the right to disburse that part of the Equivalent earmarked for its compensation.[58] An undue representation in the sixteen elected peers was also held out as a lure.[59] The *Squadrone*'s support for the union, therefore, was hardly as disinterested or as patriotic as it is often represented.[60] But, quite apart from the attitude of the *Squadrone*, the parliament's response to individual articles varied, some articles making a more general appeal than others. On the second article the opposition could command only 57 votes, thus reflecting general acquiescence in the protestant succession. More popular still was article IV, which conferred freedom of trade; here the opposition dropped to a mere 19 votes—even Lockhart of Carnwath voted for this measure. But this does not necessarily mean that Scotland's main hopes were fixed on the colonial trade. Glasgow, for instance, showed no enthusiasm for this trade and petitioned against union. As in 1702, the economic benefits expected from the union were to derive from communication of trade with England itself and from the rise of Scottish industries, notably fishing, backed by English capital.[61] Most dispute was caused by article XV, which dealt with the Equivalent, and article XXII, which covered representation in parliament. But finally on 16 January 1707 the Treaty of Union was ratified by 110 votes to 67.[62] The rest of the Scottish parliament's life was occupied in sundry items of business of which the most important was the

[57] *Jerviswood Corr.*, p. 138, Roxburghe to Baillie, 28 November 1705.

[58] *H.M.C., Mar and Kellie*, I. 379.

[59] *H.M.C., Mar and Kellie*, I. 367-9, 370-2; and *Jerviswood Corr.*, pp. 188-9.

[60] As, *e.g.*, by G. M. Trevelyan, *Ramillies and the Union with Scotland*, p. 275: ' the disinterested decision of the nobles of the *Squadrone* to support on this great issue [the treaty] the government that had supplanted them '.

[61] A. M. Carstairs, ' Some Economic Aspects of the Union of the Parliaments,' in *Scot. Journ. Pol. Econ.*, II. 61-72.

[62] *A.P.S.*, XI. 404-6.

nomination of the 30 commissioners of the shires and 15 burgess members who were to serve in the united parliament since, contrary to expectation, Godolphin and the English ministers decided against a general election.   In the nominations the *Squadrone* were denied the number of places hitherto agreed with the ministry and this, together with the loss of the handling of the Equivalent, projected them into union in a disgruntled mood. On 25 March the commissioner informed the parliament that ' The publick business of this Session being now over, it is full time to put an end to it '.[63]   He then adjourned to 22 April, but no record exists of any such meeting.   On 28 April 1707 the Scottish parliament was finally dissolved by proclamation [64]— ' the end o' an auld sang ', as the cynical Seafield is alleged to have exclaimed.   On 1 May 1707 the Treaty and Act of Union, which had rapidly passed both houses of the English parliament, came into force.

How to implement the treaty was the problem.   Conscious that as a measure it was not popular in either Scotland or England, Godolphin proceeded warily, hoping for an easy and gradual adaptation.   The Union, therefore, did not at first promote an administrative revolution.   The revenue service was overhauled: a board of commissioners for customs and another for excise were set up and these had to work in conjunction with a new court of exchequer.   In theory the Scottish treasury continued, but it was inactive, it soon became a source of sinecures, and was abolished in 1708.   The secretaries, Mar and Loudoun, continued in office and were of great administrative importance, acting as the channel of communication between the queen and the Scottish privy council.   Godolphin appreciated the manifold uses of the Scottish privy council and wished to retain it.[65]   The grand aim was to manage Scottish affairs quietly, to keep Queensberry and his friends in control, and thus secure their support at Westminster. Among the other rewards showered on him, Queensberry was created Duke of Dover in the British peerage and allowed to sit in the house of lords.   The jealous Hamilton found himself a leader without a following, for the Country party did not survive the shock of 1707 and the Jacobites no longer placed any trust in him.

[63] *Ibid.*, xi. 491.   [64] *H.M.C., Mar and Kellie*, i. 389.
[65] See P. W. J. Riley, *The English Ministers and Scotland, 1707–1727*, ch. ii and *passim*.

In the new dispensation, which was even more closely ruled by patronage and manipulation, there was no place for the ' patriots '. A few of the more substantial of them gradually threw in their lot with the *Squadrone*, which retained a residuum of ' country ' ideas subordinated to unscrupulous tactics. The Jacobites, who in the last Scottish parliament had masqueraded as Cavaliers, still believed that as ' Tories ' they had a parliamentary future. With the Union safely achieved the needs of propaganda were no longer overriding, and Defoe, who throughout the crisis had acted as an English agent in Edinburgh, could accurately describe to Harley the attitude of the Scottish peers: ' The great men are posting to London for places and honours, every man full of his own merit and afraid of everyone near him: I never saw so much trick, sham, pride, jealousy and cutting of friends' throats as there is among the noblemen.'[66] As a consequence, what initially seemed to Godolphin a fairly simple operation turned out to be an impossible one.

The conferring of Scottish dukedoms on Roxburghe and Montrose did nothing to remove the *Squadrone's* sense of grievance, and the party, which stuck together remarkably well (due perhaps to marriage alliances and kinship), arrived at Westminster in a vengeful mood, ready to make a deal with any group in order to hit at the hated triumvirate of Marlborough, Godolphin and Queensberry. They were not insignificant, even by Westminster standards, for they had four seats in the lords and eleven in the commons.[67] Soon they attracted the attention of the Whigs and gravitated into the orbit of the Junto. Since at this time the ministry was in a precarious position and dependent to a large extent on the goodwill of the Whig Junto, the *Squadrone* enjoyed an unexpected success. Marchmont, who was now acting with the *Squadrone*, demanded that, to render the Union more complete (a favourite plea of his), the Scottish privy council should be abolished. The reputation of the council was none of the cleanest and a plausible case could be made for its suppression; but the real objection to the Scottish privy council was simply that it would be used by the Court to influence the parliamentary elections in 1708. The *Squadrone*, therefore, pressed for its abolition before the elections took place, and in spite of opposition from the ministry the measure was pushed through.

[66] *H.M.C., Portland,* IV. 398.   [67] Riley, *English Ministers,* p. 33.

On 1 May 1708 it came to an untimely end, untimely in the eyes of the Court party not merely because of the loss of an instrument of power but because by 1708 the privy council alone gave that party quasi-ministerial status. Henceforth, there was no obvious channel through which patronage could flow. It was a serious loss both politically and administratively, and one that could not readily be made good. The council's impending demise, too, was untimely as far as the security of Great Britain was concerned, for it gave additional scope to the Jacobites which they used to the best of their abilities.

The *Squadrone* acted irresponsibly in this matter, for it was known that the Jacobites were for once engaged in a feasible plot. As early as 1705 the groundwork had been laid by Colonel Nathaniel Hooke, nominally a Jacobite but in reality an agent for Louis XIV. Hooke had met Hamilton and numerous notables, but because of internal dissensions among the Scots plotters and at St Germain the project hung fire. Shortly thereafter, however, the Old Pretender attained the age of eighteen and in the interests of action forced conformity among his followers. He worked hard, as Middleton informed the French minister Torcy, ' avec l'habileté d'un maître ouvrier '.[68] The turmoils in Scotland over the Union revived the interest of King Louis, then hard beset by the genius of Marlborough. Largely owing to the shifts of the untrustworthy Hamilton, nothing came of the plot in 1706, and in the following year Hooke was again dispatched to Scotland to lay a fresh train, this time acting principally through Atholl. In July 1707 the agent took back to Paris the usual glowing report. Louis and his ministers, whose dreams of securing the entire Spanish inheritance were fast fading under Marlborough's hammerblows, decided to make use of a Scottish diversion. The pope, too, was ready to provide money if the French sent troops to reinforce the rebels in Scotland. These would almost certainly have been more numerous than in any other Jacobite rising, far outnumbering the 1,500 troops the government had at command; and if, as was expected, the services of the Duke of Berwick had been secured it would have been a very formidable threat to Anne's government. Berwick, an illegitimate son of James VII by Marlborough's sister, was one of the foremost generals of his

[68] Carte MS., 28 June 1706, 238, fol. 16, cited Jones, *Mainstream of Jacobitism*, p. 71.

time and had already distinguished himself in the service of France, notably in Spain, where he had recently scored a much needed victory at Almanza in April 1707. All went amiss. Berwick was fated never to set foot in Scotland, and command of the French expeditionary force of 5,000 men devolved upon Marshal Matignon. The Pretender caught measles from his sister, thus early in his career justifying his later nickname of 'old Mr Misfortunate'. His 'Declaration to the Scots Nation' was moderate but could with advantage to him have been more explicit. To promise that the settlement of the Scottish church would be left to the votes of a Scottish parliament left much unsaid. As it happened, the venture completely miscarried. In addition to Matignon's troops, the French fleet, under Admiral Forbin, was also to transport arms and equipment for the Scots rebels; but Forbin's navigation was faulty, and the fleet missed its rendezvous with the Jacobites on the southern shore of the Firth of Forth. Ere matters could be mended Forbin was forced to flee before a superior British squadron under Admiral Byng. That was on 24 March 1708, and on 7 April the expedition, sorely buffeted by rough weather, put into Dunkirk. James, who did not lack courage, had begged Forbin to land him in Fife, alone if need be, but Forbin had refused to accept such a responsibility. For the time being the project lapsed, though the French never entirely lost interest in it and a second invasion was planned for the summer of 1710.[69]

If there had been a strong administration in Scotland the Jacobites would have been severely punished; but in its last few weeks of existence the privy council did not stir itself. The ministry, too, was on shifting sands. In February 1708 Godolphin had broken with Harley and the moderate Tories and was thereafter forced to rely more and more on the Whigs. The impending elections were crucial and Queensberry's group pointed out that in Scotland the way of the ministry would be difficult if those involved in the late plot were rigorously punished. In practice, the lord advocate, to the chagrin of some of the English ministers, proved reluctant to prosecute; and the *Squadrone*, in spite of its vaunted 'revolution principles', was ready to ally with the Jacobites. Indeed, such an alliance had already been negotiated by Hamilton, who had been summoned to London during the

[69] Sir W. Fraser, ed., *Melville and Leven*, I. 289-92.

invasion scare to account for his activities. He took the opportunity to make a deal with the Whigs, and this was latterly widened to include the *Squadrone*. In spite of the loss of the privy council the elections were tightly managed. As keeper of the signet, Mar, whose secretaryship had been abolished with the privy council, became for the time being the linch-pin of the new administration. Through the signet patronage flowed and influence could be brought to bear, so that all could see which party enjoyed Court favour. This was necessary, for, as one English observer in Edinburgh noted, ' The difference of the late Elections has perfectly divided the whole Nation and they say here they know not what side to be off '.[70] The contest was hard and only after an involved struggle did the Court party get ten of its listed 16 peers elected. All sorts of malpractice, most of it clumsy since the politicians were feeling their way in a new *milieu*, attended the elections in counties and burghs; but here, too, the ministry emerged victorious. The Queensberry-Seafield-Argyll combine carried 27 seats, while nine went to the *Squadrone* and nine to the Tories.

The repatched ministry was assailed from all sides. In 1709 the house of commons resolved that the law of treason should be uniform throughout Great Britain, thus ensuring that further Jacobite activities in Scotland would not escape unpunished. Scottish M.P.s of all factions resisted the measure; the commons let the matter drop; but it was pressed by the lords. The resulting act served further to disenchant the Scots with the Union. They were satisfied with their own law, which was at once well defined, fair, and relatively humane. Scots law knew nothing of corruption of the blood and the introduction of this doctrine was not welcomed. Nor did the Scots see much virtue in an alien law which its champions could not reduce to an intelligible statute, whose procedures were unfair to the accused, and whose provisions were ferocious. None the less, the substance of the English law of treason was forced upon Scotland, though the opposition managed to wrest some concessions. Forfeiture was to be restricted to convicted traitors, but this concession was not to be operative in the lifetime of the Pretender. The jurisdiction of the high court of justiciary was limited by the introduction of the English system of commissions of oyer and terminer which could

[70] S.P.54/3, No. 31, Francis Philipson to George Tilson, 15 July 1708.

by a writ of *certiorari* oblige the high court to proceed against suspected traitors, though the commission was also competent to try the accused.[71]   Another cause of disgruntlement arose from a series of decisions in the commons whereby the eldest sons of Scots peers, unlike their English counterparts, were ineligible to elect or be elected.   The English, for their part, had found that closer contact with the Scots did nothing to lessen the contempt with which they had long regarded their northern neighbours. The avarice and lack of principle of Scottish politicians were soon notorious.   The house of lords, particularly, became alarmed at the possibility of an inundation of out-at-elbow Scots lords, raised to British peerages by obeying every whim of the ministry and thus occupying permanent seats.

The clue to the understanding of Scottish politics in the remainder of Anne's reign lies in the precarious state of parties in England and the prolonged attempt to negotiate a peace treaty with France.   After 1709 the war became decidedly unpopular in England, due in part to the heavy financial burdens it imposed and in part to the shock of the battle of Malplaquet (September 1709), a pyrrhic victory that cost Marlborough more losses than the French.   Thereafter Marlborough and Godolphin were driven to depend more and more on the Whigs and the Scots members.   In the face of increasingly strong Tory opposition the power of the ministry ebbed.   Harley, dedicated to a speedy peace and bent on forming a moderate Tory ministry which would not exclude other elements, gained an ascendancy with the queen, and on 7 August 1710 Godolphin was deprived of the treasurer's staff.   The victory of the Tories at the ensuing elections put the seal on Harley's triumph but at the same time doomed his policy of moderation.   In Scotland Queensberry had deserted the fallen ministers and he and his group retained office, to the chagrin of the Scottish Tories.   Harley tried to keep in with both Queensberry and his rival Argyll, but was soon under heavy fire from all sides.   He tried to obviate difficulties by seeing to the administration of Scotland himself, largely through the agency of John Scrope, baron of the Scottish exchequer.   In the upshot Argyll was alienated and became a bitter enemy of the new ministry.   From the beginning, too, the Scottish Tories had a

[71] *Statutes of the Realm*, IX. 93-5, 'An Act for improving the Union of the Two Kingdoms'.   It is usually referred to simply as 'the Treason Act'.

clear-cut programme and they refused to acquiesce in Harley's policy of masterly inactivity. They were determined to take advantage of the high church Tory reaction in England in order to release Scottish episcopalians from penal disabilities. And, to add to Harley's discomfiture, Hamilton, who had ably supported him in the elections of 1710, made it clear that the price of continued support was a British dukedom to put him on par with the detested Queensberry.

In Scotland Harley's troubles were not of his own making. The case of James Greenshields, an episcopalian minister who defied the presbytery of Edinburgh, exposed Harley to the wrath of the Scottish Tories. For using the English liturgy and flouting the authority of the presbytery, Greenshields had been imprisoned in 1710 by the magistrates of Edinburgh, whose decision was upheld by the court of session. He then appealed to the house of lords and there in March 1711 the court of session's decision was reversed.[72] This opened up opportunities for the Scottish episcopalians. As Balmerino, the leader of the Scottish Tories in the house of lords, put it: ' We have it in our hand to get presently a Tolleration, or the Act against Baptiseing rescinded, or patronages restored '.[73] It was even hoped that the act of 1695 could be rescinded and full comprehension enforced. In spite of all that Harley could urge against these plans, notably the hostility they would raise in the established Church of Scotland, the Toleration Act and the Patronage Act were passed in 1712. From that moment the ministry of Harley or, as he was created in May 1711, the Earl of Oxford, has borne an ill name with Scottish presbyterians. This fact was later exploited by Argyll, who seized the opportunity to adopt the traditional pose of his house as the kirk's champion. That he had fallen out with the ministry over a ' job ' (he resented Mar being given the secretaryship in 1713) made no odds with the kirkmen. Nor were Oxford's setbacks compensated for by a steady support from the triumphant Scottish Tories, for they too acquired a grievance. They felt badly deceived by the ministry over the question of Hamilton's patent as Duke of Brandon in the British peerage.

[72] George Grub, *An Ecclesiastical History of Scotland*, III. 363.
[73] Reg. Ho., Dalhousie Muniments, 14/352, Lord Balmerino to Harry Maule, 8 March [1711].

Oxford finally gave in to Hamilton's demands; but, in the hope of wrecking the ministry's peace plans, a strong opposition was put up to Brandon's claim to a hereditary seat in the lords. By five votes it was decided on 20 December 1711 that Brandon had no right to such a seat; and, further, it was held that as Duke of Hamilton he could no longer vote in the election of the sixteen elected peers.[74] The Scots lords had regarded it as a test case and hoped that it would open the door for many others. Such a shocking result united the Scots of all factions, and it looked as if Mar's prophecy that an adverse decision would cause the Union to founder might be realised.[75] They presented a memorial to the queen in which they hinted darkly at a possible dissolution of the Union. They threatened Oxford that if satisfaction were not granted they would join with the opposition; and the lord treasurer was worried enough to create twelve new peers to ensure the safety of his government and the passage of the peace pre-liminaries. All the same, Oxford attempted to remedy matters by a fresh decision of the house of lords which should grant some of the Scottish peers a hereditary seat. This, however, came to nothing. The Scots boycotted the house but were soon brought to heel by a threat to their cherished Toleration Bill which came up for a second reading in the lords. The ill effects of the Hamil-ton affair, though, rankled, in spite of every effort by Oxford to humour the Scottish peers.

Oxford tried hard to improve the administration in Scot-land: he overhauled the customs service but possibly was too rigorous in subordinating everything to treasury control. Unfor-tunately, by keeping the administration firmly in his own hands, he angered the Scottish Tories, who had hoped simply to dis-place Queensberry's group. In an effort to fill up the adminis-trative gap left by the suppression of the Scottish privy council, Oxford attempted to set up a commission of chamberlainry and trade which would form a stable base for Scottish administration.[76] It would provide oversight over the royal burghs and would have authority to keep the peace. In fact, like the old privy council it

[74] G. S. Holmes, ' The Hamilton Affair of 1711–1712: A Crisis in Anglo-Scottish Relations ', in *E.H.R.*, LXXXVII. 257-82. Queensberry, cited as a precedent for Hamilton, had died on 6 July 1711, but subsequently his successor was held to be under the disabilities imposed by the Brandon decision.

[75] *H.M.C.*, *Mar and Kellie*, I. 490, Mar to Oxford, 10 June 1711.

[76] Riley, *English Ministers*, ch. XII.

would act as the executive in Scotland, with the lord high chamberlain at its head. It would bridge another dangerous gap left by the Union, namely the separation of administration from general economic policy. The commission had another merit in that it would provide a useful source of patronage in Scotland. In November 1711 the commission of chamberlainry and trade was set up, charged mainly with improving the trade of Scotland and in particular with disbursing the money allocated under article XV of the Union for the advancement of the coarse wool trade. It never really got under way, but the project was revived again shortly before the elections in 1713. The board of trade then protested that its rights were infringed by the commission of chamberlainry, and the latter was allowed to lapse. In many ways this was unfortunate, for Scottish administration badly needed some such co-ordinating body.

In the closing years of Anne's reign Scotland's disappointment with the economic effects of the Union completed the sombre picture. In spite of the optimistic forecasts of the unionist pamphleteers there was no sudden burst of prosperity after 1707. Sundry acts of parliament, indeed, were hostile to Scottish economic interests. Thus a bill intended to promote the Scottish linen interest was wrecked by the Irish linen lobby. And in 1712 it was proposed, in defiance of the Treaty of Union, to apply the malt tax to Scotland. By the end of that year Scottish parliamentary representatives of all parties agreed that the only solution to these ills was repeal of the Union. Argyll, Mar, Lockhart and Baillie, representing every faction, were delegated to inform the queen of this projected measure, which was finally moved by the Earl of Findlater (formerly Seafield) in the house of lords on 2 June 1713. In his speech Findlater itemised the grievances of the Scots: ' the dissolution of the Council, the treason act, the incapacitating the peers—but above all our many taxes, especially the Malt tax bill, and the ruin of our trade and manufactorys '.[77] The motion was only narrowly defeated by four proxy votes; and this episode was not, as it is often represented, merely a shift in the endless manœuvrings of interests and groups to exert pressure on the ministry. The Union was decidedly unpopular and not only in Scotland. In England, too, it

[77] Reg. Ho., Dalhousie Muniments, 14/352, Balmerino to Maule, 2 June 1713.

found few champions, and Swift's doggerel hit off a widespread mood:

> Strife and faction will o'erwhelm
> Our crazy, double-bottomed realm.[78]

By summer 1713 the ministry was rent by internal dissensions: Oxford's policy of drift was too slow for the restless Bolingbroke, who allied himself with the extreme Tories and Jacobites. He himself was neither Tory nor Jacobite but an unprincipled man who cared for nothing except his own advancement. But when Bolingbroke chose he could charm, and the Scottish Tories thought him 'a very generous gentleman and much a friend to Scotland'.[79] In view of his waning popularity, and the strong opposition by Whigs and Hanoverians to the peace proposals, Oxford was obliged to placate the Scots. Mar was granted the office of secretary and Findlater became lord chancellor once more with the right to preside over any court in the country. Oxford, in fact, had to dismantle his centralised system of administration in Scotland in order to hold the support of the Scottish Tories. The commission of chamberlainry still existed on paper only, but the commissioners were kept sweet by having their salaries paid. In this way the opposition in Scotland was countered and the elections of 1713 returned the Court list of sixteen peers; but in the counties and burghs the opposition, provided mainly by the *Squadrone* and the Argyll interest, made a considerable showing. Precise results of the elections for the house of commons are not known but it seems doubtful if Oxford could rely on more than a dozen members from Scotland.[80]

The crisis was fast approaching. The question of the succession, which overshadowed all else, arose in critical form as Bolingbroke steadily undermined Oxford's influence at court. The queen was gravely ill and it became a race against time, not only for Oxford and Bolingbroke but also for the Electress and the Pretender. Oxford, in spite of some apparently incriminating evidence, had no intention of restoring the Stewarts. To be sure, he corresponded with King James in the hope of winning Jacobite votes to shore up his waning influence; but even the gullible exiled court was not deceived. Undoubtedly, too, Oxford paid

[78] *The Poems of Jonathan Swift*, ed. H. Williams, I. 96.
[79] Dalhousie Muniments, 14/352, Balmerino to Maule, 26 May 1712.
[80] Riley, *English Ministers*, pp. 249-51.

the Highland chiefs regularly but this seems to have been an implementation of the policy suggested in the early years of William.[81] The government was paying ' blackmail ', not indenting for future service on behalf of the Pretender, as the embittered Argyll alleged. Additional colour was given to these allegations by the gun-running that went on in the western Highlands and Islands at that time; but the trade flourished in spite of all the government's efforts to suppress it, and no one was more energetic in attempting to stop the traffic in arms than the secretary Mar.[82] None the less, these accusations were accepted at Hanover and they increased the distaste which the electoral house had for the Treaty of Utrecht and those who had helped to negotiate it. In Hanover the treaty was regarded as a gross betrayal of the continental allies—the Dutch, the Imperialists and the Hanoverians.

On 27 July 1714 Oxford was dismissed by Anne, but the elated Bolingbroke had no plans and was unable to form a ministry before the queen died on 1 August. No wonder he lamented: ' The Earl of Oxford was remov'd on Tuesday, the Queen dyed on Sunday . . . what a world is this, and how does fortune banter us '.[83] The Whigs seized the initiative and proclaimed the Hanoverian succession, ready, if need should arise, to back it up with force in both England and Scotland. Bolingbroke, Mar and the others meekly accepted this turn of events and tried vainly to curry favour with George I. Only when they were dismissed, and obviously out of favour with the king, did they discover undying allegiance to the legitimist line. Mar's duplicity is plain to see in his correspondence, private and official. On 9 September he wrote to General Maitland at Fort William urging him to be ready to march upon the clans at a moment's notice, but concluding: ' I hope they will be so wise as not to attempt anything that may disturb our present Tranquility '.[84] A year thereafter he was writing, and acting, to very different purpose.[85] Though there was some Jacobite activity in the

---

[81] *H.M.C.*, *Portland*, v. 121, 122, 129, 216-17.

[82] P.R.O., Mar's Letter-Book, 2, S.P.55/2/28, Mar to Lord Treasurer, 13 May 1714.

[83] *Correspondence of Jonathan Swift*, ed. H. Williams, II. 101, Bolingbroke to Swift, 3 August 1714.

[84] P.R.O., Mar's Letter Book, S.P.55/1.67, Mar to Lt.-Gen. Maitland, 9 September 1714.

[85] John, Master of Sinclair, *Memoirs of the Insurrection in Scotland in 1715*, pp. 15-41.

Highlands the chances are that but for Mar's *volte face* the chiefs would most likely not have stirred, for though the queen's death naturally raised Jacobite hopes and though a considerable opportunity presented itself in the autumn of 1714 it was frittered away by incompetence and lack of leadership. Bolingbroke had no plans and was easily brushed aside by the Whigs, who brought powerful influence to bear on the elections in February 1715. They secured a parliament firm for the Hanoverian interest, and in Scotland that interest was fortified by the engrossment of office by the *Squadrone* and the followers of Argyll. The Whigs then proceeded to take positive steps against the late ministry, and in April Bolingbroke, terrified at the prospect of impeachment, fled to France. James unwisely made him his secretary, in which post he proved more of a liability than anything else. Bolingbroke's indolence left the plotters in Britain uninformed of developments in France, while his arrogance prevented many experienced Irish émigré soldiers from entering the service of King James.[86] Just as disappointing to the Jacobites were the activities of the Duke of Ormonde, who was supposed to raise a rebellion in the west of England; but instead of making for the allegedly disaffected west country the duke, wisely, in August fled to France. The government took prompt measures, and the likelihood of such a rising, on which the main hopes of the Jacobites were pinned, vanished. Foreign aid, too, which was vital, proved hard to obtain. Louis XIV knew that France was exhausted, but for a time he toyed with the notion of giving the Pretender surreptitious help. Pessimistic reports received from Ormonde six weeks before his flight cooled French enthusiasm; and in any event the death of Louis on 1 September shattered any such prospect. The regent Orleans dared not antagonise Britain, whose envoy, Lord Stair, was too vigilant to be hoodwinked; and in fact Orleans impeded rather than aided James' enterprise. The regent even deprived the Chevalier of the services of his half-brother, but the realistic Berwick welcomed this outcome: well provided for in France, he had no wish to risk his all at desperate odds. He drew the correct conclusion from his brother's failure to win support from France or Sweden: James had lost his opportunity, ' for I shall always consider it a folly to think that he will be able to succeed in his undertaking with the Scotch

<hr>

[86] Jones, *Mainstream of Jacobitism*, pp. 104-8.

alone '.[87] The reservation could have been extended, for not all
Scots by any means favoured King James. Whigs and presbyterians,
many of whom cared little for the Union, dreaded the idea of
a popish king and formed themselves into makeshift militia units.
The risings that did take place in Scotland are inexplicable except
on the premise that the rank and file Jacobites were ignorant
of affairs and that the leaders, who were almost as infatuated,
wilfully gambled with the lives of these unfortunates. As Harry
Maule, who was tricked into the rising by his nephew Mar, put it:
' never were men so idly brought in for their lives and fortunes
as we were '.[88]

Yet, all this granted, much could have been done for King
James in Scotland, where dissension was widespread and which
was miserably defended. Not one fortification was in a good
state of defence and none knew this better than the ex-secretary
Mar.[89] In spite of repeated warnings from the lord advocate and
others, the government continued to neglect Scotland, forbidding
the formation of Whig associations (except in Edinburgh) and
omitting the most elementary precautions. A commission of
police was set up in December 1714, but it was for propaganda
purposes rather than anything else.[90] It was designed to clinch
the loyalty of the presbyterians by making for a more popular
exercise of crown patronage; a strict watch was to be kept on
papists and nonjurors; the Highlands were to be bridled; and,
perhaps most significant of all, the commissioners were to disburse
the sums accumulated for the promoting of industries in Scotland
under the provisions of article XV of the Union. In this, as in
most other respects, it failed, for the commission's actual powers
were extremely limited and no substitute for those formerly vested
in the privy council. Finally, the government heeded the Cas-
sandra voices from the north, but its response was ill considered,
and helped, unwittingly, to precipitate Mar's rebellion. An Act

[87] Sir Charles Petrie, *The Jacobite Movement* (1959 edn.), p. 232, quoting from
Berwick's *Memoirs*, II. 199-205.
[88] John, Master of Sinclair, *Memoirs of the Insurrection in Scotland, 1715*, p. 52.
[89] S.P.54/7/No. 11, Sheriff-depute of Dunbartonshire to Duke of Montrose,
2 August 1715: ' My Lord Glencairn being here with 15 men [*i.e.* in Dumbarton
Castle] without one night's meal within the Walls '. Cf. Mar's Letter-Book, I. No. 43,
Earl of Glencairn to Mar, 5 September 1714, on poor condition of the castle and
garrison—' we have not so much as a Boate '. *Ibid.*, no. 36, Colonel Erskine to Mar,
3 August 1714, on feeble state of Stirling castle.
[90] Riley, *English Ministers*, pp. 185-6.

for Encouraging Loyalty, passed on 30 August 1715, was designed to secure lords and vassals; but in the Highlands it had little force. The real mistake, however, was a warrant attached to the act which required a long list of suspects to present themselves at Edinburgh; but those named in it feared that they were marked men and, in desperation, openly joined the Jacobites. The Earl of Mar, known as ' Bobbing John ' on account of his shifty politics, was the self-appointed leader of the rebellion. Unable to win the favour of King George, who pointedly turned his back on him at a levée on 1 August 1715, Mar, fearing imprisonment and dreaming of a dukedom, threw in his lot with the Pretender. He made his way by sea to Elie in Fife, but though the lairds of Fife were Jacobite in sympathy the commons were not and Mar did not tarry there long. He sped north of Tay to his seat at Braemar, where he had consultations with the nobles of the north-east and entered into correspondence with the heads of clans. To his brother Lord Grange he wrote that he had fled to Braemar merely to avoid arrest, that the north-east was quiet and he would do his best to have it continue so.[91] On the 27th he held a *tinchal*, or deer hunt, at which plans for a rebellion were drawn up. Brisk recruiting went on in the north-east, Huntly and the Earl Marischal backing the project; and at the same time Mar was busy persuading the western clans to rise. A thorough politician, he talked big and slurred over the details: England was already in arms, the French were preparing a large invading force, King James himself was at hand, and so on *ad nauseam*. On 6 September the standard of King James was raised at Braemar. Those who best knew Mar, however, were least willing to join, particularly his own vassals and tenants, whom he had to ' force out '. On 9 September he wrote his famous letter to his bailie at Kildrummy, ' Black Jock ' Forbes of Invererman: ' Jocke, Ye was in the right not to come with the 100 men ye sent up to-night, when I expected four times the number. . . . Particularly let my own tenants in Kildrummy know, that if they come not forth with their best arms, I will send a party immediately to burn what they shall miss taking from them .'[92] Such actions were common; and, quite apart from the major campaign that ensued, raid and counter-raid were the order of the day in the Highlands.

[91] S.P.54/7/62, Mar to Grange, 20 August 1715.
[92] Quoted in A. and H. Tayler, *1715: The Story of the Rising*, pp. 43-4.

Mar headed south with a small force drawn mainly from the episcopalian north-east Lowlands, receiving detachments of Highlanders on his route. On 14 September Colonel Hay with a few men easily took Perth for the Jacobites, and a fortnight later Mar made it his headquarters. There he remained, feverishly scribbling lying reports for the consumption of the gullible and waiting, as he alleged, for the clans to come in. Many of them did—Mackintoshes, MacDonalds, Camerons, Athollmen and many others, a formidable turn-out—but still Mar loitered in Perth. He pinned his hopes on all sorts of *coups de théâtre*, most of which misfired. Edinburgh castle was to be taken, but the plot leaked out and the venture failed on 8 September. True, on 14 September Mackintosh of Borlum took Inverness and this, with the activities of Seaforth's Mackenzies, effectively countered the Hanoverian Earl of Sutherland and his presbyterian allies, the Mackays and the Munros. Further risings occurred. On 6 October a handful of Northumberland gentry rose under the command of Thomas Forster, M.P. for the county, who hurriedly received a commission from Mar; and on 12 September a few hundred Jacobites of southern Scotland took arms under Viscount Kenmure. They merely added to Mar's perplexity, for he knew little of their numbers, prospects, or even whereabouts. They should have made no odds, for at this time Mar commanded, at a conservative estimate, well over 10,000 men; but his chronic indecision enabled the government's commander-in-chief in Scotland to contain the rebellion. Argyll had only a small regular force—at its highest less than 4,000—and much of it was of poor quality. The Lowland militia were willing enough but of little use: in Argyll's view ' a Lamb is not more afraid of a Lyon, than these Low Countrey people are of the highlanders '.[93] But Argyll was an experienced soldier; and he knew Mar. He therefore took up position at Stirling, which he saw was the key to the whole situation, hoping that Mar would wage war as he conducted politics—by stealth. He proved to be right. Mar could easily have forced a passage of the Forth; instead his plotter's brain devised a grand envelopment—a veritable Cannae—but for its execution he lacked ability. On 12 October Borlum was sent across the Forth with orders to join the southern rebels and in company with them to attack Argyll from the south while Mar

[93] S.P.54/9/24, Argyll to Lord Townshend, 7 October 1715.

nervously pecked at him in the north. Borlum instead made an attempt on Edinburgh, was beaten off, and ultimately reached the Jacobite gentry of Northumberland and Dumfriesshire who had joined forces and were wandering aimlessly. Borlum encountered them at Kelso on 20 October but found Forster no more fit for command than Mar. He would not hear of attacking Argyll, and he insisted on the combined force entering England, there to raise ' loyal Lancashire '. Although the Jacobites (deserted by many of Borlum's Highlanders) easily scattered the Cumberland militia, the enterprise failed miserably, and they made a humiliating surrender at Preston on 14 November. On 20 October a Jacobite attack was launched on Inveraray in the hope of turning Argyll's flank, but this too failed. At last Mar realised that he must act or watch his army disintegrate. When he did move it was very clumsily. Although his force was superior to Argyll's by over four to one, Mar allowed himself to be outmanœuvred. Argyll occupied the heights above Dunblane and so forced an encounter on Sheriffmuir, where most effective use could be made of his few cavalry. The battle of Sheriffmuir, fought on 13 November, was a comedy of errors. The left of each army was routed, but, thanks mainly to Mar's incompetence, Argyll held the field. The duke was no military genius but, in view of the disparity of the forces engaged, he did well. Argyll knew that he had been lucky;[94] but resolve had made his luck possible, and he deserved better thanks than he received from King George and his ministers. London throughout showed little appreciation of the dangers of the situation in Scotland, and repeatedly the hot-tempered Argyll so informed the king and his ministers.[95]

After 13 November the rebellion was doomed, the more so as Inverness was taken for the Hanoverians by the irrepressible Simon Fraser, now determined to try his luck with King George. This exposed the north-east Lowlands and Highlands to Sutherland's force and drained men from Mar's army for the defence of their own districts. The Highlanders, too, gorged with plunder and none too impressed by their commander, began to with-

[94] S.P.54/10/48, Argyll to Townshend, 14 November 1715.

[95] One example must suffice: S.P.54/8/80, Argyll to Lord Stanhope, 21 September 1715:—' I am sir extreamly surprised that notwithstanding the alarms you have had from hence we have heard nothing either from Lord Townshend or you, and pardon me to say, I am yet more surprised to find by two letters I yesterday received from London, that his Majesties Ministers still persist in thinking this matter a jest . . .'

draw in large numbers. Early in December the Hanoverians were reinforced by 6,000 Dutch troops, and if Argyll had been allowed to parley with the disillusioned rebels all might have been over before the belated arrival of James at Peterhead on 22 December. The Pretender was a brave and honourable man, but he lacked force and made an indifferent impression when he held brief court at Scone. His demoralised army, short of food and munitions, soon had to retreat, firing villages as it went, before the reinforced Hanoverians. On 4 February 1716 James Stewart, a Pretender still, took ship from Montrose for France and a wandering existence. To the best of their abilities his captains followed suit.

3

SOCIAL AND ECONOMIC CONDITIONS FROM THE REVOLUTION TO THE OPENING DECADE OF UNION

The Scotland that was racked by these political troubles cannot be summed up in a few bold generalisations. Its society was in some ways simpler than it now is but in others more complex; for there was then nothing like a national norm and, quite apart from the division into Highland and Lowland cultural zones, regional and even local variations were marked. To add to the general historian's task the social and economic aspects of the period have been neglected, and it is therefore difficult to give in brief compass even the merest impression of the state of the country at or about the time of the Union. Thus, in matters as fundamental as the size and distribution of the population we are forced to rely on guesswork rather than on hard fact. Census returns were unknown, Sir Robert Sibbald's projected description of Scotland was never completed, and it is only by analogy from later figures that it may be deduced that at about the time of the Union of 1707 the total population of Scotland stood at just over one million.[1] It may also be reasonably estimated that of this total four-fifths derived their livelihood from the soil, in itself a most significant pointer to the social economics of that period. Such industry and trade as then existed were small in scale and though of growing economic importance were still of relatively minor social significance. In brief, the land itself was still the main provider and from this basic fact stemmed many of Scotland's difficulties, for, owing to a combination of

[1] G. S. Pryde, *The Treaty of Union of Scotland and England, 1707*, p. 44.

natural and human deficiencies, the soil made niggardly returns and in many parts could do little more than sustain the simplest way of life. Of the total surface area of Scotland only about a quarter was fit for cultivation of even the least rewarding kind. The mountains and high treeless moors could only be used as rough pasture, though the lower slopes of the hills were often cultivated in preference to the water-logged valley floors.[2] The largest county in Scotland, Inverness-shire, consisted mainly of such land and only about one-fortieth of its extent was arable. The central Highland massif was virtually a desert, while the pressure of population in the West Highlands and in the Hebrides was slowly increasing, for there at least the arable soil, though thin and dispersed, permitted the sowing of oats. Even in the Lowlands nature did not appear in its most genial guise. The Southern Uplands, for example, could support only a meagre population; and, before sustained efforts at improvement were made, much of the potentially fertile land in the valleys and howes of the midland belt and the north-east was soured peat-bog. Over the greater part of Scotland in the early eighteenth century the bulk of the population toiled with ineffective implements and primitive methods of husbandry, just as their medieval ancestors had done, to wrest from an ungrateful soil a bare subsistence. They might easily labour in vain. Two bad harvests in succession could result in shortage of victuals, soaring prices, and perhaps even famine, all more or less localised just as the circumstances dictated.[3]

Two factors within the province of man helped to keep agriculture at a low level of production: one was the system of land-holding (which largely determined land use) and the other was the method of husbandry that had been followed from time immemorial. The land law was then, and long remained, feudal in the precise legal definition of that term. Indeed, throughout the eighteenth century it was known simply as ' the feudal law ' and lawyers who specialised in it were called ' feudalists '. This was one of the most important facts about Scottish society, for it moulded the life of the community in a variety of ways. It not only determined the possession and use of land but the main

---

[2] Thomas Morer, *Short Account of Scotland* (1702), noted this: ' 'tis almost incredible how much of the mountains they plough . . .', p. 3.

[3] See T. C. Smout and A. Fenton, ' Scottish Agriculture before the Improvers— an Exploration ', in *Agricultural History Review*, XIII. 74.

structure of society itself, which was still dominated by the land-owning aristocracy. The received ideas that had long held society together were impregnated with feudal notions and the old system, in various stages of decay, was still operative at the Union, heritable jurisdictions and all. Indeed, the latter impediments to sound legal administration were continued under article xx of the Treaty of Union.[4] A major difference between England and Scotland lay in the fact that in the latter no check upon subinfeudation was evolved. There is no Scottish counterpart to the statute *Quia Emptores*, and consequently freehold in the English sense has never emerged. In Scotland proprietors of lands could only be formally infeft feudal vassals, either of the crown (regarded as *ultimus dominus*) or a superior. The survival of udal rights in the old Norse dominions of Orkney and Shetland provided the only exceptions to the rule, and these were few and in many ways dubious. Those in Scotland who held directly of the crown were tenants-in-chief, otherwise known as subjects superior, and for the most part they continued to hold lands by classical feudal tenures—either ward (military tenure) or blench (*anglicé* sergeanty or in some cases socage). But increasingly lands were held in feu-ferm. The feu is difficult to define briefly, since it could appear in many guises: but in essence it can be likened to a lease, which, if the express conditions of grant are observed, may last in perpetuity.[5] It disponed the property but not the superiority, and in certain circumstances the feu could revert by legal action to the superior. The most characteristic feature of feu-ferm was the rendering by the feuar to the superior of a stipulated annual duty, either in money or in kind. On some estates customary tenants, *rentallers* or *kindly tenants*, were to be found, but however important they may have been in some localities (Lochmaben in Dumfriesshire is the oft-cited example),[6] on the national plane they were relatively insignificant. In Scotland the term freeholder occurred but in a radically different sense from its English usage. In Scotland a freeholder was simply a small tenant-in-chief, and by the late seventeenth century the term was used

---

[4] For text see Pryde, *op. cit.*, p. 98.

[5] *Bell's Dictionary and Digest of the Law of Scotland* (1890), pp. 456-8.

[6] While holding from the crown the kindly tenants of Lochmaben were content, but after James VI conveyed the lands to the Earl of Annandale they complained of being oppressed (*A.P.S.*, IX. 210-11, ' Act in Favours of the Four Townes of Lochmaben ').

mainly with reference to the electoral system, the freeholders or barons constituting the county electorate.

In the juridical sense the feudal law of Scotland had distinct merits, notably in that rights in land were scrupulously defined and were precisely recorded in the register of sasines. With charter and sasine to prove his claims the proprietor was in little danger of being denied his rights, whereas the lack of such instruments would cause trouble. In order to serve this ' feudal law ' a precise system of conveyancing had been elaborated by the end of the seventeenth century.[7] For a healthy agrarian society such precision in the law of tenures is indispensable; but ideally the law should be equitable as well as efficient. Here the law of Scotland fell short. It meticulously safeguarded the rights of proprietors but it did little to protect tenants, particularly those— and they were numerous—who had no tacks or written agreements. Even those who held by tack were in a weak position, for their cases would be reviewed in the baron court where the landlord was unlikely to lose by default. Since in most parts of Scotland tenants greatly outnumbered proprietors, this meant that the mass of the farmers had little incentive to tend or improve the land. Their interest was to wring as much as possible from their short leases, many—perhaps most—of which were mere annual verbal agreements. It would have been folly for the tenants, lacking security of tenure, to ditch or drain or carry out even the simplest improvements that common sense might suggest, for to have done so would inevitably have led to rack-renting or eviction. For any given locality only examination of rentals and estate papers can determine the mobility of tenants, but a general view came to be:

> Bouch and Sit,
> Improve and Flit.[8]

The lairds, even if they had the will to improve, lacked the means. Their relative poverty appears from the valuation rolls: in Banffshire in 1690 most of the valuations ranged from £1,200 Scots (£100 sterling) to a mere £20 Scots,[9] while in Angus in

---

[7] Its forms are preserved in George Dallas of St Martin's, *System of Stiles, as now practicable within the kingdom of Scotland* (1697).

[8] James Donaldson, *Husbandry Anatomized* (1697), p. 124. Bouch = botch.

[9] Major James Grant, ' Old Valuation Roll of the County of Banff, 1690 ', in *Transactions of the Banffshire Field Club* (1917–18), pp. 34-51.

1683 the rentals varied from £31 Scots to £2,300 Scots.[10] Neither county could be ranked with the most backward areas of Scotland. Thus the impoverished lairds, even if they possessed (as must often have been the case) first-hand knowledge of the more advanced agriculture of the Low Countries or of England, could do little in the way of emulation. The ill-effects of this all went deep. Lords and tenants should have been partners in the task of exploiting the land, but the records, particularly those of the baron courts,[11] show clearly that any real sense of mutual interests was rare and that in the efforts of these classes to exploit each other the soil was left too much to its own devices.

In these circumstances ' infield-outfield ' husbandry enjoyed a remarkable lease of life.[12] This is the term of art nowadays applied to the variant of open-field cultivation which had evolved in Scotland, though by no means peculiar to Scotland. A similar system had arisen in Ireland and parts of the continent,[13] and traces of it have been discerned in England.[14] In its origin the ' infield-outfield ' system represented a rational effort to farm as effectively as possible where the extent of arable was very limited. As far as tillage was concerned it was in some areas virtually a one-field system with little possibility, therefore, of efficient fallowing. The best arable made up the *infield* which received all the scanty manure available and was under constant cultivation. The steadings were sited near the infield which, significantly, was often referred to as ' the croft ', for in Scots this term could signify continuous cropping.[15] The grain yield of the infield was eked out by occasional cropping of parts of the *outfield* which was mainly used as pasture. (From the late seventeenth century onwards, however, there was a progressive tendency to convert outfield into infield, but the transition was slow, sporadic and localised.) The basic infield-outfield layout was widespread throughout

[10] Alex. J. Warden, *Angus or Forfarshire, the Land and People* (1885), v. 233-51.

[11] *Records of the Baron Court of Stitchill, 1655–1807*, ed. G. B. Gunn (S.H.S.), can be compared with the untypical *Court Book of the Barony of Urie, 1604–1747*, ed. D. G. Barron (S.H.S.). The barons of Urie were quakers and had a highly developed social conscience.

[12] J. E. Handley, *Scottish Farming in the Eighteenth Century*, chs. I, II.

[13] For its occurrence in Europe see Gordon East, *Historical Geography of Europe* (1953 edn.), pp. 104-5.

[14] J. Saltmarsh and H. C. Darby, ' The Infield-Outfield System on a Norfolk Manor ', in *Economic History*, III. 30-44.

[15] *Scottish National Dictionary*, III. 250.

Scotland, though with considerable regional variation in disposition and use: thus the relative proportions of *infield* to *outfield* varied widely, with the outfield generally preponderating. In East Lothian the infield was divided into four brakes or shotts which permitted a simple rotation of crops of pease, wheat, barley and oats. But few parts of Scotland were as naturally fertile as the Lothian plain and in most areas the custom was to alternate oats, the staple food crop, and bere or bigg, a form of barley from which ale or sometimes whisky was made.

In most, if not all, parts of the country the infield was divided into rigs, with intervening baulks of uncultivated soil to act as partitions and perhaps as a rough form of drainage. Farms then rarely consisted of compact units but were more commonly made up of sometimes widely scattered rigs. This was known as *run-rig*,[16] and sometimes, if it occurred on a large scale, as *rundale*. The term *run-rig*, however, came to connote the old pre-improved style of farming; and in this sense it is still useful to speak of ' run-rig ' husbandry. Co-tenancy played an important role in this type of farming, although by the late seventeenth century individual farms were not unknown, more particularly in the better favoured regions such as the estuary of the Forth, the rich Lothian plain and parts of Caithness. But in many, if not most, parts of Scotland, farming was still dependent upon the co-operation of joint-tenants dwelling together in ferm-touns or agricultural hamlets. These were still the most usual form of rural settlement, much more so than villages which are of relatively late growth in Scotland. According to the size of the farm, the nature of the soil and the problem of ploughing it, the joint-tenants might range in numbers from four to sixteen. Indeed, the size of the toun was originally dictated by the size of the plough-team, the ploughgate of 104 Scots acres being related to the area that could be dealt with by a team of eight or ten oxen.[17] This may never have been more than a fiscal calculation and certainly, with the growth of population and the extension of cultivation, the number of ploughs and the size of the touns increased. Such tenants paid rent jointly, each contributing to the extent of his

---

[16] In the precise legal sense *run-rig* applied to land belonging to different proprietors, but the term was more generally used to describe intermixing of strips worked by different tenants (J. Jamieson, *Etymological Dictionary of the Scottish Language*, IV. 80).

[17] *Survey of Lochtayside, 1769*, ed. M. McArthur (S.H.S.), intro., pp. xxxviii-xxxix.

share—a quarter, an eighth, or whatever the exact fraction might
be. They co-operated in ploughing, though rarely without disputes; but each reaped his own harvest and kept the grain.
Traditionally, to ensure fair shares the strips were periodically
reallocated among the joint-tenants. This practice long persisted
in the Highlands, but there is little evidence of it in the Lowlands.

Whatever the variant of run-rig husbandry that was followed,
agriculture in most parts of Scotland was in a poor state even by
subsistence standards. Certainly, in some areas conditions were
above average: Caithness, for example, normally produced a
surplus of grain, and indeed in the year 1695 is said to have
exported 16,000 bolls of victual.[18] But this area was far from
typical, both from the standpoint of natural fertility and estate
management. Isolated examples of this sort cannot invalidate
the general conclusion that Scottish farming was backward and
that rural poverty was widespread. Admittedly, the extension
of corn-lands was a noteworthy feature of late seventeenth-
century Scotland;[19] but its effects may actually have worsened
the condition of agriculture by overcropping of marginal land.
Nor did this necessarily alleviate local shortages in Scotland, since
much of the grain produced was for export. This constituted a
producers' victory over the consumers and represented the
triumph of the landed interest over the crown, culminating in an
act of 1695 not only permitting export of grain but granting a
bounty of eight merks on the chalder.[20]

All things considered, it is hard to avoid the conclusion that the
general picture was gloomy, and particularly so in the Highlands.
The old proverb ' ane to saw, ane to gnaw, and ane to pay the
laird witha' ' summed up the situation of many small farmers at
this time, and indeed in the post-Revolution period the laird's
portion rose. It is clear that in the main grain-producing areas
rent was increasingly paid in victual, a fact that did not pass
unobserved by contemporaries. Fletcher of Saltoun felt that it
led to wasteful farming, for ' The rent being altogether in corn,
the grounds must be altogether in tillage; which has been the
ruin of all the best countries in Scotland '. He concluded that
' the changing of money rent into corn, has been the chief cause
of racking all the rents to that excessive rate they are now ad-

---

[18] J. E. Donaldson, *Caithness in the Eighteenth Century*, p. 21.
[19] Smout and Fenton, *op. cit.*, p. 84.   [20] *A.P.S.*, IX. 458-9.

vanced '.[21] This was not just splenetic hindsight, for surviving rentals tend to bear out the substantial truth of Fletcher's view. A revealing *exposé* of the rack-renting system appears in the ' Rentall of the Barrony of Skirlin for the years 1691, 1692, 1693, 1694, and 1695 '.[22] Throughout these years the ' siller ' or money rent was constant at £1,852 10s. Scots; but the value of victual rent soared. The following summary tells its own tale:

$$
\text{Rent for the years}
\left.
\begin{array}{l}
\text{1691—£2,735 17s. 4d.} \\
\text{1692—£3,988 13s. 6d.} \\
\text{1693—£4,413 7s. 4d.} \\
\text{1694—£4,629 4s. 10d.} \\
\text{1695—£6,411 1s. 6d.}
\end{array}
\right\}
\text{£22,178 4s. 6d.}
$$

The increase was largely due to the rise of the fiars' prices, that is the agreed prices of grain for each year. With such a sustained trend in the market no wonder victual rent was raised, and many landlords must have followed similar courses to that pursued by Lord Strathmore: ' I have brought one Francis Graham in the raws to Alexr. Henderson's roume and raised the rent two bolls of oats '.[23]

The rent structure varied a great deal but the rent was usually composite: so much might be paid in money, so much in victual, and over and above this was exacted *cain* (a stipulated tribute of livestock or farm products, perhaps a wedder or a quantity of butter or cheese). The tenant also usually owed services to the laird—carrying goods (sometimes over considerable distances), cutting and loading peats for fuel, and labour for specified periods in the lord's mains or home farm, often at the very time when his own rigs needed his attention. On most estates, too, the farmers were thirled to the lord's mill and on pain of heavy fines dared not have their grain ground elsewhere. Through the rapacity of the landlord and his minions, the millers, the tenants usually lost on this transaction; and, to add insult to injury, they were obliged to keep the mill in good repair. As Cromwell had correctly noted, all this added up to an oppressive seignorial system not unlike

[21] A. Fletcher, ' Second Discourse on Affairs of Scotland ', in *Political Works* (1732), pp. 157-60.
[22] Reg. Ho., Skirling Writs, No. 198. Skirling is in Peeblesshire.
[23] *The Book of Record, a Diary written by Patrick First Earl of Strathmore, 1684–89*, ed. A. H. Millar (*S.H.S.*), p. 98.

the *ancien régime* in France.[24]   Powerful private jurisdictions were still held and exercised by many of the landlords.   Thus each baron had his court which controlled not only the economic life of the barony but also helped to maintain law and order.   Paternalism could, and often did, soften this hard regime; but paternalism was a shifting quantity, honourably upheld by some landlords only perhaps to be neglected by their successors.

As population slowly but steadily increased, the dangers of such a stagnant system became obvious and the last decade of the seventeenth century drove them home with cruel force.   From 1692 onwards there were poor harvests and severe shortages in the Highlands, and between 1695 and 1699 a succession of bad harvests, caused by wet summers and early frosts, led to a serious famine throughout the entire community.   Ultimately, the privy council was forced to allow in Irish meal and other victuals which were normally rigorously excluded.   It decreed that the girnals should be kept open, it fulminated against forestallers and regraters who sought to profit from the dearth of provisions, and it tried to fix the price of grain.   All was in vain.   As bad harvest succeeded bad harvest, as the price of meal soared and livestock perished, the poor starved to death in untold thousands.   Patrick Walker, the Cameronian chapman, has left vivid, oft quoted, accounts of scenes during the famine, when the living were wearied with burying the dead.[25]   Just as harrowing was the description of the tragedy by Sir Robert Sibbald, M.D., in a pamphlet intended to help the poor by prescribing edible herbs, catflesh, and so on.   Every care should be taken of the poor lest they become desperate and rob the rich, ' And such Considerations ought now to be lai'd to Heart, when the Bad Seasons these several Years past, hath made so much Scarcity and so great a Dearth, that for Want, some die by the Way-side, some drop down on the Streets, the poor sucking Babs are Starving for want

[24] W. C. Abbott, *Cromwell's Letters and Speeches*, iv. 718, the lord protector's speech to the parliament 25 January 1658: said Cromwell, the meaner sort in Scotland while under their great lords were made to work for their living ' no better than the peasants of France '. Cf. Donaldson, *James V to James VII*, p. 350. The Cromwellian administration overthrew the heritable jurisdictions and also curbed the power of the feudal superiors—both reforms ' meet to have been made in better times ', in Clarendon's famous phrase. See J. Hill Burton, *History of Scotland* (new ed.), vii. 59-62.

[25] Patrick Walker, *Six Saints of the Covenant*, ed. D. Hay Fleming, ii. 28-33. Smout and Fenton, *op. cit.*, p. 73, suggest that the Seven Ill Years may have been exaggerated by analogy with the biblical Seven Lean Years; but the point is hardly proved.

of Milk, which the empty Breasts of their Mothers cannot furnish them: Every one may see Death in the Face of the Poor, that abound every where; the Thinness of their Visage, their Ghostly Looks, their Feebleness, their Agues and their Fluxes threaten them with sudden Death; if Care be not taken of them '.[26] The full extent of the catastrophe has never been worked out, but in many parishes the population fell by as much as a half. Nor were the effects confined to rural districts, for Edinburgh and its environs also suffered. Thus, in the winter months of 1696–7 the number of interments in Greyfriars Kirkyard rose significantly.[27]

In addition to the grim death-roll from hunger and disease, the *Seven Ill Years* or *King William's Years* (as the Jacobites maliciously dubbed them) ruined thousands. In parts of the northeast Lowlands tenants threw up their useless farms, some of which reverted to waste.[28] The already numerous ranks of beggars and sorners swelled, increasing at such a rate as to oblige Fletcher of Saltoun to advocate a return to slavery in order to preserve society.[29] Throughout the crisis the Church attributed the famine to the sins and backslidings of the nation, and as a cure recommended fast days! That England also suffered from bad harvests in these years,[30] but that England did not starve, seems to have passed unnoticed except by the earliest advocates of improved agriculture, Donaldson, Belhaven and Fletcher. In 1697, Donaldson, an Edinburgh printer, brought out his *Husbandry Anatomized*; two years later Lord Belhaven published *The Countrey-Man's Rudiments*; and Fletcher in his *Discourses on the Affairs of Scotland* agreed with them in attributing the nation's plight to a bad agrarian system and stagnant agriculture.

Pastoral farming was in little better case than tillage. In relation to the fodder available far too many cattle were kept and this necessitated an annual slaughter at martinmas when the carcases were salted down for winter fare. The stock had to maintain itself mainly on outfield and moor, and on the stubble

[26] Sir Robert Sibbald, *Provision for the Poor in time of Dearth and Scarcity* (1699), pp. 2-3.
[27] *Register of Interments in the Greyfriars Burying Ground Edinburgh*, H. Paton, (S.R.S.), p. vi.
[28] W. Alexander, *Illustrations of Northern Rural Life in the Eighteenth Century*, pp. 44-7.
[29] A. Fletcher, 'Second Discourse on the Affairs of Scotland ', in *Works* (1732), pp. 121-54.
[30] G. N. Clark, *The Later Stuarts*, p. 37.

of the harvest. (The infield, too, was unenclosed and while under crop had to be protected from the cattle.) No artificial grasses or turnips were sown to eke out their sparse diet; in hard winters many died, and only with difficulty could the survivors be carried into the spring pastures. This, a regular task, was known as *the lifting*. The beasts bred, too, by natural selection and their prime quality was hardiness rather than milk-yield or beef-weight; they were small and wiry, and known in England as ' Scotch runts '. In some parts more trouble was taken with them, notably in the West Highlands and Galloway, where pastoral farming was more important than tillage. Indeed, it was on the sale of livestock that these areas largely depended for their livelihood, for from the cash thus raised they were enabled to purchase the all-important meal that they could not grow in sufficient quantity. In the great straths of the Highlands and in the Western Isles the high rainfall produced pastures more lush than in most parts of Scotland, and summer transhumance to the hill pastures, or sheilings, conserved the natural hay of the low-lying meadows. Before the Union, Highland cattle were being sold at Crieff tryst and with the opening up of the English market thereafter the volume of business steadily increased, although until the Highlands were finally pacified the drover's trade was a risky one.[31] Small numbers of sheep, of a stunted variety, were kept by most landholders, but only the Borders specialised in them. A few pigs were kept by most households, and yet, curiously, the consumption of pork is alleged to have been regarded as an English perversion. The Highlanders in particular were supposed to have a horror of swine flesh; but for all this there is little in the way of evidence and it is perhaps best treated as a vague tradition if not an outright old wives' tale.

Yet, such as it was, agriculture remained the most important means of subsistence: as one of its most trenchant critics declared, ' Husbandrie is the Foundation, and Trade the Superstructor '.[32] In the writer's time the superstructure was flimsy and of daunting uncertainty. No reliable trade statistics exist for this period but the general conclusion seems plain: the terms of trade were poor, trade was still largely tied to the old medieval pattern, and it was hard hit by the requirements of the regal union. Thus, in 1667–8

[31] See A. R. B. Haldane, *The Drove Roads of Scotland*.
[32] Belhaven, *op. cit.*, ' Dedication ' (unpaged).

customs on imports raised £317,930 Scots and on exports £66,345;[33] and in spite of vigorous fiscal measures the balance of trade remained adverse at the Union of 1707. It was then calculated that the ratio of population between the two kingdoms was England's five to Scotland's one; but wealth was in the ratio of 38 to 1 in England's favour.[34] That the disparity was so great was due to some extent to Scotland's erratic fiscal policy. The main support of legislation had gone to the wrong industries, and in particular to the woollen cloth industry which had been set the impossible task of rivalling its well-established English counterpart. Encouragement of linen, plaidings and coal would almost certainly have produced better results. Scotland, with a plentiful supply of peasant labour, was well adapted to linen manufacture, but unfortunately standards of weaving and bleaching were low. Coal had long been a source of wealth and ' Scotch great coal ' was in demand both in London and on the continent. In addition to its export, coal was increasingly used as a household fuel (although poor communications limited the domestic trade) and it was used in salt-panning. But though long established, coalmining was, owing to inadequate means of drainage, then restricted to surface seams, tapped either by adit mining or shallow pits. Far and away the most important coal-fields in Scotland were on the Forth, in Fife and the Lothians. The lairds keenly exploited any available coals on their lands, and throughout the seventeenth century output steadily increased. Early in the eighteenth century the introduction of primitive steam-pumps led to the exploitation of the Ayrshire seam. One of the first was installed at Stevenston in 1719, either a Savery or, more likely, a Newcomen engine.[35] Such engines could, however, operate only in shallow pits, in practice few were installed, and the development of the western coal-field was retarded. Other industries fostered in the late seventeenth century were numerous but mostly small in scale and of doubtful permanence.[36] The most flourishing were soap-works and sugar-houses in Glasgow and Greenock; but the whole range covered articles as diverse as pottery and gunpowder, glass and

---

[33] *R.P.C.*, ser. III, VII. 666.   [34] G. S. Pryde, *Treaty of Union*, p. 44.

[35] N. M. Scott, ' Documents Relating to Coal Mining in the Saltcoats District in the First Quarter of the Eighteenth Century ', in *S.H.R.*, XIX. 91.

[36] W. R. Scott, *The Constitution and Finance of English, Scottish and Irish Joint-Stock Companies to 1720*, III. 123-95, assembles most of the extant details of manufactures in Scotland at this period.

leather.   Clearly, Scotland was trying to overcome her trade difficulties by manufacturing as much as possible and so cutting down on imports.   The record can be made to look long and impressive, but the actual achievement was slight: probably the true significance of those developments in the late seventeenth century was that Scots were then serving their apprenticeships in fields they were later to make their own.   Nor, perhaps, would it be quite accurate to describe the economy as stagnant—rather it was nascent, striving to adapt itself to new conditions.

Finance, too, was a problem.   The Scots mint could never provide an adequate uniform coinage and so in Scotland the currency was international, consisting largely of old and debased Dutch and English money.   Gold coinage was rare, silver not as plentiful as once it had been, and as a consequence there was a superfluity of copper coins of somewhat doubtful value.   Bills and bonds circulated freely, and in the absence of banks some of the Edinburgh goldsmiths acted as clearing houses.   In 1695 the Bank of Scotland was founded to alleviate these difficulties; but to begin with it acted as little more than a clearing house, for no deposits were taken, cash credit was unknown, and the Bank was very sparing in its issue of notes.   It was granted a monopoly for twenty-one years, and in fact its position was not seriously challenged until 1727 when the government incorporated the Royal Bank.

It is doubtful, however, if even the most enlightened legislation could have solved Scotland's economic plight, for the simple reason that a large part of the problem lay beyond the competence of the Scottish legislature.   In the seventeenth century the whole pattern of international trade had altered drastically, leaving the Scots stranded high and dry on the old decaying routes.   Their privileged position in the French trade had declined, largely as a consequence of the union of the crowns.   The Dutch trade was languishing, though the staple at Veere survived the Union of 1707 but really existed only on paper until finally wound up in 1799.   Even before the Union the staple was long outmoded and, in spite of the efforts of the convention of royal burghs and the authority of Veere, trade increasingly centred upon Rotterdam. Indeed, in 1688 King James VII was in doubt as to the wisdom of appointing a conservator at Veere and but for the Revolution it seems possible that the staple might have been spared its long inglorious twilight in the eighteenth century.[37] Even before the Union of 1707, in defiance of the laws of both England and Scotland, the beginning of a new trade pattern was fitfully emerging. Despite the navigation laws of both countries, the merchants of the Clyde and the Solway indulged in lucrative but risky trade with England's American and West Indian colonies. And perhaps of even more significance in disrupting the old connections was the growing importance to Scotland of the English market itself. That was the great difficulty: more and more the trade of Scotland existed on sufferance and the risks attached to such clandestine ventures effectively limited its scale. The Company of Scotland, after all, was a desperate attempt to solve this very problem by building markets that would be free from foreign domination. The small number of Scottish-owned vessels was another revealing commentary on this economic malaise. In 1692 the total tonnage was a mere 10,000, of which Glasgow's quota, spread over 15 vessels, was 1,182; and up to about 1718 few Scottish ships were suitable for the transatlantic trade, the merchants of Glasgow and Dumfries being mainly obliged to charter English vessels.[38] The French wars of the reigns of William and Anne had clearly worsened an already bad situation.[39]

In theory, trade (and especially overseas trade) remained the monopoly of the royal burghs and was jealously guarded by their convention, another hoary relic of a past age. But by the late seventeenth century the great days of the royal burghs, and their convention, lay behind them. Trade and industry could no longer be confined to such narrow channels. The power of the royal burghs had been curbed by the crown acting through the privy council, notably in the fixing of prices. The unfree burghs, long held down by the royal burghs, all but turned the tables on their oppressors. In the seventeenth century many of the burghs of barony enjoyed a modest prosperity through the rise of small local industries, and their superiors who profited from this saw to it that parliament would lend a sympathetic ear to their pleas. An act of 1672 bade fair to deprive the royal burghs of their

[37] J. Davidson and A. Gray, *The Scottish Staple at Veere, a Study in the Economic History of Scotland*, pp. 232-3.
[38] H. Hamilton, *The Industrial Revolution in Scotland*, p. 3.
[39] T. C. Smout, *Scottish Trade on the Eve of Union*, pp. 253-6.

privileges, and in spite of another act of 1690 confirming some of
their rights, they never in fact regained their old supremacy in
economic matters.[40]   An exhaustive enquiry into the affairs of
the royal burghs in 1692 showed how severely they had been hit
by the competition of the burghs of barony.   One after another
echoed the mournful dirge: home and foreign trade both in
decay. Perth was a microcosm of their misfortunes. To encourage
trade some Perth merchants had a ship built at Leith, but her
skipper ' runne away with her ' and a cargo valued at £10,000
and never returned from Virginia.[41]   Another common lament,
exaggerated no doubt like much else in these doleful reports, was
of unfair competition from the unfree burghs. Thus Linlithgow
attributed much of its poverty to the illegal enterprise of Bo'ness
and Grangepans. To some extent this was a legitimate grievance, for compared with the royal burghs the unfree burghs
were lightly taxed. The royal burghs, on the other hand, had to
furnish one-sixth of the land tax. This, then, was a factor in the
decay of many of the royal burghs; and indeed the anomaly was
not removed until 1896. But it was not the whole story. Lack of
enterprise, misgovernment and jealousy constrained them to fight
against the new facts of life and to be an impediment rather than
an aid to progress. It was this more than anything else which
defeated the endeavours of the Huguenot refugee, Nicholas
Dupin, to impart vigour and efficiency to the linen trade. Three
acts of parliament of 1693 conferred extensive privileges on the
Scots Linen Manufactory with its main centre of operations in
and around Edinburgh. On the withdrawal of English support
Dupin had to rely on Scottish capital, but the support of the royal
burghs, though promised, was not forthcoming.[42]   By 1707 the
linen trade was in the doldrums.

Notwithstanding their ancient charters and an exalted conception of their status, most of the royal burghs were small. Yet
in spite of their decay and their obscurantism they did not lack
importance within the existing scheme of things. In some ways
they performed vital functions, albeit with varying degrees of
efficiency. True, they no longer monopolised overseas trade, they
were no longer the sole seats of industry, and market facilities

---

[40] G. Donaldson, *James V to James VII*, pp. 392-3.
[41] J. D. Marwick, *Miscellany of the Scottish Burgh Records Society*, p. 60.
[42] W. R. Scott, *Joint-Stock Companies*, III. 162-9.

were increasingly being provided by burghs of barony; but many of the old royal burghs remained important regional centres. Dumfries, for example, already lived up to her proud title of ' Queen of the South '; and Inverness, a small neatly laid out town, was the natural capital of part of the Highlands, profiting in addition from the bridling of that unruly area by garrisons. In the days when a journey to Edinburgh was a test of endurance, Highland gentlemen enjoyed each other's company at Inverness. Again, Aberdeen was the capital of the north-east Lowlands; its port facilities and its two universities made it peerless in this area.

In 1707 there were 66 royal burghs, ranging from Edinburgh with about 40,000 inhabitants and Glasgow with about 12,000 through such intermediate burghs as Dundee, Aberdeen and Perth with about 4,000 each to the small burghs of the East Neuk of Fife with a few hundreds each of population. Edinburgh was far and away the most important; it was the centre for politics, justice, business and culture. The capital was still cramped on its high ridge, in many ways still a medieval town encircled by its walls. Tall French-style tenements filled the space between the castle and the boundary of the Canongate. There was something medieval, too, about Edinburgh's jealousy towards the adjoining unfree burghs of Canongate and Leith. The old city had a life and atmosphere all its own. It was noted even in those unhygienic times for its poor sanitation and unsavoury smells. Manners were rough and ready. Adam Petrie, *stickit minister* and *mess john* (private chaplain), tried to inculcate the lessons of gracious living he had picked up in the course of his duties as a domestic chaplain. His work is heavy, pious, and obsequiously respectful to feudal hierarchical notions. Among the middle grades of society, cutlery and glasses were scarce and served a communal use: hence, adjures Petrie, ' You must drink out of your Glass, that others may not have your blown Drink '.[43] In spite of kirk censures there was raffish life in Edinburgh's taverns and eating houses, where much of the business of the town was transacted. In the first decade or so after the Union a passion for literary and debating societies sprang up, and in these dark howffs in the High Street was engendered something of the spirit that was to give Scotland a brief period of international renown. It is not too fanciful to discern the impact of Edinburgh's peculiar

[43] Adam Petrie, *Works* (1887), *Rules of Good Deportment* (1720), p. 87.

society upon the Scottish Enlightenment of the eighteenth century. Its tall lands housed a cross-section of the entire society, nobles, judges and caddies rubbing shoulders with each other on the common stair. A man of enquiring mind could not live in old Edinburgh without becoming a sociologist of sorts. For a time, however, it looked as if the Union would put a period to the distinctive life of the capital; but the way to London was long, to stay there was expensive, and gradually, helped by the continued business of the law courts, Edinburgh revived to become in the latter half of the eighteenth century one of the leading cultural centres of Europe.

Glasgow, second in rank to Edinburgh, was much more workaday and provincial, still ' a neat little burgh town laid out in form of a cross ' and still dominated by the puritan traditions of the west country. But by the 1720s Glasgow's increasing trade was causing the Reverend Mr Wodrow to predict a day of wrath for so much wealth and carnality. At the time of the malt riots in 1725 Lord Advocate Forbes unconsciously confirmed Wodrow's dark forebodings, giving it as his opinion that ' the tobacco trade has got the better much of the religion of this place '.[44] But in 1743 ' Jupiter ' Carlyle, then a youth at Glasgow College, was bored by Glasgow's excessive piety and lack of diversions. Its manner of living, he found, ' was but coarse and vulgar '.[45] In fact, till almost the end of the eighteenth century Glasgow remained sober and hard-working with few pressing social problems and a negligible crime rate.

On the whole, living conditions in Scotland were poor and the expectation of life was not great. The tradition of housing was lamentable, due to the turbulence of the country's history, its poverty and insecurity of tenure. The average peasant home was built of unmortared stone, sometimes even of clay or turf, and thatched with ferns or heather. It comprised usually one room, had no chimney and lacked adequate ventilation.[46] While the family occupied one end, cattle were tethered at the other. The houses of the more substantial tenant farmers were little more commodious, rarely stretching to two rooms with tiny windows. The burgesses fared better, but even the fashionable

[44] *More Culloden Papers*, ed. D. Warrand, ii. 275.
[45] Alexander Carlyle, *Autobiography*, ed. J. H. Burton, p. 75.
[46] T. Morer, *Short Account of Scotland*, pp. 18-19.

residences of the nobles and wealthy lawyers in Edinburgh were cramped and confined. A superior conception of housing, however, had already moved the nobles to abandon or modify the fortresses of their ancestors and in the seventeenth century some fine mansions were built in both town and country.[47] This trend was maintained by Sir William Bruce of Kinross, who designed such notable mansions as Melville House in Fife, built in 1692 for the Earl of Melville. Bruce's pupil, William Adam, carried on the tradition in the early eighteenth century and Adam's brilliant son, Robert, later achieved international fame. But this welcome change served a small fraction of the total population, and much the greater part of Scotland's people long continued to exist in squalor.

That squalor was gleefully recorded by the few hardy Englishmen who ventured north of Tweed. The miserable inns were described with feeling: they were poky and dirty, and provided ill fare and indifferent service.[48] The charges were just enough, even allowing for the fact that England was not universally served by such splendid hostelries as the Castle Inn at Marlborough and that in the remoter parts travellers complained as bitterly of English inns as they did of Scottish ones. An English traveller of this period, Joseph Taylor, a barrister of the Inner Temple, remarks that the differences between northern England and southern Scotland were slight, and both came under his lash quite impartially. But on entering Scotland a note of trepidation creeps into his account: ' Every one reckon'd our Journy extremely dangerous, and told us 'twould be difficult to escape with our lives.' This possibly reflected the fate of poor Captain Green and the tense atmosphere of 1705. Taylor's person was in no danger but his sensibilities were afflicted. In village and town alike dirt and offensive habits were prevalent, and he found that in the capital ' 'tis a common thing for a Man or woman to go into these closes at all times of the day, to ease Nature '.[49] Prudently, he put up at Snow's hostelry in the Canongate, kept by an Englishman who catered mainly for his countrymen. One who never reached Snow's haven was Sir John Perceval, who in the

---

[47] G. Donaldson, *op. cit.*, pp. 271-2, 395-6.
[48] T. F. Henderson, *Old World Scotland, Glimpses of its Modes and Manners*, ch. VIII, Scottish Inns.
[49] J. Taylor, *A Journey to Edenborough*, pp. 95, 135.

summer of 1701 had set out for Scotland in a mood of high adventure ; but the first Scots inn he entered, at Langholm in Dumfriesshire, so disgusted him that he at once returned home.[50]

Life, if not entirely or uniformly nasty and brutish, certainly tended to be short. The mortality rate was high, particularly among infants. Married women of child-bearing age reproduced with almost annual regularity but few of their offspring lived to maturity. The kirk registers and records of interment must, in spite of the prevailing Calvinistic fatalism, have hidden in their bald announcements much human anguish. The killer diseases were smallpox, tuberculosis, rheumatic fever, and the unspecified but deadly ' fever '. These kept the level of population down, helped no doubt by poor housing, bad hygiene and indifferent diet. For most of the population medical care was non-existent and even those who came within its limited scope could hardly be said to benefit.[51] The upper classes had an almost superstitious belief in the curative power of goat's whey and taking the waters, but probably fresh air and abstention from the bottle were the real sources of benefit. Heroic surgery, often technically competent, without anaesthetics or asepsis killed more than it cured. In the Scotland of that time medical science was in its infancy, for only lately had it gained a footing in the universities, and in the country districts surgeons and physicians were few and far between. Superstition was rife, and if many conceded that the Lord gave and therefore had the right to take away, they were also quick to consult darker oracles in an effort to postpone the day of reckoning. Thus, the old practices of resorting to wells and the use of amulets and charms, which had been subsumed by medieval catholicism, still survived. According to the mood of the moment, witches were either consulted or persecuted. Quackery flourished and even found favour with the kirk—as late as 1730 the kirk session of Shotts in Lanarkshire paid £9 6s. Scots to ' Mr Green the mountebag for couching John Roger's wife's eyes '.[52] Greatest of the mountebanks was John Moncrieff of Tippermalloch from whose cures a best-selling book on self-medication was compiled. His diagnoses were crude and some of his specifics bizarre and disgusting: thus ' Horse-dung, dis-

[50] *H.M.C. Egmont MS.*, II. 206-7.
[51] T. Ferguson, *The Dawn of Scottish Social Welfare*, pp. 10-11.
[52] H. G. Graham, *Social Life of Scotland in the Eighteenth Century*, p. 476, n.3.

solved in Cardums-water, and strained, doth powerfully disperse the Pain and Humour in a Pleurisy '.[53] Moncrieff's popularity was clinched by his piety and acquaintance with scripture.[54] In the Highlands and the Western Isles, an even more ancient form of leech-craft was still practised by certain families, notably the Beatons.[55]

In the capital, physicians of the distinction of Sir Robert Sibbald and Dr Archibald Pitcairn had to compete with quacks like Anthony Parsons, who in 1711 hawked his nostrum ' Orvietan, a famous antidote against infectious distempers, and helps barren-ness '.[56] The quacks usually provided a free show, thus augment-ing the limited entertainments of the town. Not that Edinburgh was entirely void of novelties, for in 1694 James Young's ' House of Curiosities ' had some remarkable displays, such as a machine for producing 15 or 16 copies by pen, a gun of ten barrels that worked like a revolver, a distorting mirror, and a ' Magical Lantern ' whereby pictures of Scaramouche, Actaeon, Diana, and some twenty others ' little broader than a ducatoon ' were magni-fied as big as a man.[57] More or less respectable peep-shows might be allowed, but after the Revolution the drama fell under the ban of the kirk and there was no permanent theatre. Occasionally a company of English players tried their luck and managed to clear some profit before the kirk could deploy its forces. Tony Aston, an English comedian, achieved two such visits, one in 1715 and another in 1726. Plays, too, were sometimes smuggled into musical concerts and ' the prudest might go and enjoy Vanbrugh's " Provoked Husband " and Wycherley's unsavoury " Country Wife " under guise of innocently listening to Corelli's sonatas '.[58]

Few who attended the theatre fully understood the dialogue. The clipped English of the actors fell strangely on Scottish ears, for throughout the Lowlands among all classes spoken Scots still reigned supreme.[59] It grated on English ears: Morer speaks of Scots, however well educated, having ' an unhappy tone ' which gave them away.[60] In spite of the steady increase of anglicising

[53] *The Poor-Man's Physician or the Receits of the Famous John Moncrief of Tippermalloch* (3rd edn., 1731), p. 20. [54] Robert Chambers, *Domestic Annals of Scotland*, III. 54-5. [55] J. D. Comrie, *History of Scottish Medicine*, I. 236.

[56] Chambers, *op. cit.*, III. 260-3. [57] *Ibid.*, III. 100-2. [58] Graham, *op. cit.*, p. 95. [59] See Introduction to *The Scottish National Dictionary*, I. xiii.

[60] T. Morer, *Short Account of Scotland*, p. 14: ' They have an unhappy Tone, which the Gentry and Nobles cannot overcome, tho' Educated in our Schools, or never so conversant with us; so that we may discover a Scotchman as soon as we hear him speak.'

pressures the distinctive Scots speech survived but on the defensive, as James Boswell attests, well into the latter part of the eighteenth century. Yet, homely though his speech may have been, the average Scottish aristocrat was far from ignorant of the world. The grand tour was an established institution and in this period the young Scots laird knew more of the continent than he did of England; and Scots students, particularly of law or medicine, resorted to the Dutch universities where learning, more advanced than any that was to be found in the Scottish colleges, had struck a *modus vivendi* with Calvinism. Scots trading communities had long established themselves in Poland and the Baltic lands, and Muscovy was beginning to draw the Dugald Dalgetties of the age. In Sweden many noble families kept up their Scottish connections, and heads of Scottish noble houses were frequently pestered for flattering pedigrees by Scots soldiers of fortune in the pay of Austria or Prussia. The maxim that ' a' Stewarts are no sib to the king ' was blithely disregarded by these unscrupulous status hunters.

In the Highlands a rather different situation obtained. The Gaelic-speaking area was then much larger than it now is, and the Gaels possibly numbered almost a third of the total population.[61] Erse, or Irish as the Lowlanders called it, was spoken as far south as Arran and round Loch Lomond, in part of Stirlingshire, most of Perthshire, in the Highland parts of Aberdeenshire and some of the upland districts of Moray, Nairnshire and Caithness. But already a sustained assault on this ancient culture had been mounted. The Argyll family had long declared war on it in Kintyre, and the Revolution Church, girding up its loins for the great missionary effort of the eighteenth century, regarded Gaelic as at best a hindrance and at worst an instrument of Satan. The Society for Propagating Christian Knowledge in Scotland, which was founded in 1708, also equated the spread of English with the progress of civilisation.

The glamour of spurious romance cast over the Highlands in the nineteenth century obscures a fascinating but complex society. Ideas of clanship, the dresses and tartans in use, the very names of the people, were far removed from the simple uniformity that appealed to romantic Victorians. This, for example, would have had all Camerons concentrated in one area, uniformly kilted and

---

[61] J. MacInnes, *The Evangelical Movement in the Highlands of Scotland*, p. 10.

tartanned, and reverencing only Lochiel. In point of fact the kilt had developed comparatively late, in the seventeenth century, and was not used in the Western Isles or in Caithness;[62] tartans existed but they were of simple setts and if they distinguished anything it was districts rather than names. The clans identified themselves in war by their plant badges. Surnames were of relatively late date in the Highlands, most persons being known either by patronymics that were almost potted genealogies or by descriptive nicknames. True, by the early eighteenth century the use of surnames of a fixed type was becoming common and there was a strong tendency for clansmen or dependents to adopt that of the chief or landlord. All this has to be conceded; but, even so, clans were stark realities, held together by ideas of kinship fortified by elaborate genealogies in which truth vied with fiction. Social organisation, indeed, varied widely in different parts of the Highlands. In general, it rested upon a blending of clanship and feudalism, the former preponderating in the west and the latter in the east. Thus, it is scarcely accurate to speak of a Gordon clan; but the Campbells, Camerons, Clanranalds, and others in the west cannot be so lightly dismissed. Their origins remain complex and mysterious, obscured rather than explained by the folk-history and oral tradition which too often, to the discomfiture of the historian, have to pass for Highland history.

Yet it may be that the main differences between Highlanders and Lowlanders were the result of recent historical developments. Kinship had once been as strong in the Lowlands but in the sixteenth and seventeenth centuries its strength had declined as new social bonds were forged. At the end of the seventeenth century most Highlanders and Lowlanders were still conscious of having little in common, and indeed that century of strife left behind it a legacy of ill-feeling. The clans, or tribes as Bishop Burnet called them, had become objects of fear to the Lowlander, while the average Highlander held the Lowlander in hearty contempt. Two different conceptions of society confronted each other. That of the Lowlands was struggling out of the old feudal mould; it came to centre more and more upon the individual,

[62] Caithness was not, as generally supposed, entirely Lowland: see N.L.S. MS., 33, 5, 15, 'Sir Robert Sibbald's Collections of Papers in order to the description of Scotland', p. 79: 'The people for the most part, speak both Irish and English', but English predominated in the east and Gaelic in the mountainous west.

and this process had been speeded up by the religious crises of the seventeenth century. 'No bishop, no king' is a hackneyed saying; but after the Restoration it might have been altered significantly and put to new use as 'No bishop, no laird'. By the end of the century Lowland society was unwarlike, satiated with religious strife (though by no means freed from religious bigotry), and eager to improve its material well-being. The Highlands reflected few of these features. If anything the western and central clans were more warlike, if only because of such revealing experiences as the 'Highland Host' of 1678. Indeed, the military tradition of the Highlands entered into a new lease of life, stimulated by the fears of Lowland domination that followed the Revolution.

Thus military tenants seem actually to have increased and prospered. The Highland tacksmen owed their generous leases to the fact that they were expected to supply soldiers at need, and these they secured by sub-letting. Often, too, the tacksmen were cadets of the families of the chief or lord, and were men of substance and culture. At the bottom of the social scale were the small farmers, known by a variety of local names, such as cottars, crofters, or acremen. They lived in 'tounships' in which the divisions of land were often minute, instances of sixteen families living on one ploughgate of land being common. Agriculture was primitive, even by Scots standards; the extent of arable was slight and the Highland economy depended mainly upon cattle and sheep. At the time of the Union there was no industry in the Highlands which would justify comment of even the most antiquarian kind.

Church and education as yet did little to bridge the gap between the two cultures of Scotland. The only bridges were the law and the aristocracy. The law of Scotland ran in both areas, and except in times of war or serious civil dissensions it was applied more often than legend would allow. That this was so is due to some extent to the way in which most of the great men in the Highlands fitted into both societies. At home at Castle Dounie MacShimei dispensed lavish entertainment to his 'cousins', even to the meanest of 'The Name', while in Edinburgh and London the worldly-wise Lord Lovat could ruffle it with the best of them. The Highland chiefs of this period were not invariably patriarchal figures of the cast of Abraham; most of them were well educated, spoke several tongues and had travelled in the world. Only mis-guided romance views them as brigand chiefs, although occasion-ally feuds led them to employ what were to all appearances brigand tactics. But the *creach* or cattle-raid was still regarded as honourable, and the stealing of cattle or even levying of black-mail was not always fairly attributed to the broken men of ' the Rough Bounds ', a district in western Inverness-shire. In 1739–40 there was an outburst of the old anarchy in Ross, when Mackenzies, Rosses, and Munros freely pillaged and abused each other, to the shocked surprise of the lords of justiciary;[63] and in 1743 the caterans harried Badenoch and the north-east Lowland plain.[64]

In both Highlands and Lowlands poverty and its relief remained serious problems. No new principle of poor relief was introduced in the period between the Revolution and the Union, and, in practice, the work of administration devolved mainly on kirk sessions.[65] A rate for relief of the poor could be raised but, on the whole, parishes attempted to avoid this except in times of dire need. The aliment allowed to the poor was slight but together with the charity of relatives and friends it usually pro-vided a bare subsistence. Indeed, family pride and reluctance to ' go on the poor-box ' kept the apparent number of destitute poor at a much lower level than the poverty of the country might well have warranted. Numbers were kept down, too, by the fact that the Scottish system did not concern itself with the able-bodied poor or the hordes of vagabonds and sorners who terrorised the countryside. For them special laws were passed empowering employers to set them to compulsory labour in the manufactories. In this way by virtue of acts of 1606, 1641 and 1661, reinforced by numerous legal decisions, most of the colliers and salters were by the end of the seventeenth century treated as serfs, bound to the pits or to the salt-pans in which they first began to work.

The Scottish system was one of outdoor relief, work houses being unknown until well on in the eighteenth century. Nor was the shunting of wretched paupers from parish to parish as marked

[63] Books of Adjournal, series D, vol. 23, p. 428 ff. *Ibid.*, vol. 24, p. 411, 1 Feb-ruary 1744: ' There of late having been sundry complaints that Perthshire and the Countries lying upon the Borders of the Highlands were greatly infested by lawless persons coming down from these Countries', *i.e.* the Highlands.

[64] W. Alexander, *Northern Rural Life*, p. 66.

[65] For earlier history of the poor law, see G. Donaldson, *James V to James VII*, pp. 398-9.

a feature of poor law administration in Scotland as it was in England, mainly because settlement in Scotland took three years as against forty days in England. None the less, in bad times parishes issued tokens to their own poor and carefully restricted relief to them; and at all times incomers to the parish were scrutinised as to their means. In addition to helping the poor, the kirk sessions devoted what money they could to other charitable works—caring for orphans, hiring surgeons to attend needy patients, or ransoming Christian slaves from the Turks. They also made a point of helping poor students on their way to the universities.

The latter was not surprising since education too mainly devolved upon the church and was as actively promoted in times of episcopacy as of presbytery. The Restoration bishops have been accused of indifference to the ideal of a school in every parish, but the charge is unjust and rests usually on misinterpretation of the evidence. True, in the south-western counties education suffered in the period 1660–88, but this was a by-product of the chronic disorders in that area and cannot rightly be ascribed to episcopal malignancy.[66] In other parts of Lowland Scotland at that same time there was a steady advance in the provision of schools; and when in 1690 an enquiry was made into the religious and political affiliations of the dominies competent to teach Latin, the returns—incomplete though they were—indicated that over wide areas of the Lowlands schools were functioning and that a considerable proportion of them were taught by graduates.[67] The important act of 1696 for settling schools really did little more than reinforce existing provisions: its true importance was that it provided something like an administrative norm for the future. In each parish without a school one was to be set up and the schoolmaster's salary provided by the heritors; if the heritors failed to meet their obligations then the presbytery could have recourse to the commissioners of supply, who were empowered to carry out the provisions of the act.[68] The act was by no means a

---

[66] W. Boyd, *Education in Ayrshire through Seven Centuries*, pp. 35-9, hints at episcopal culpability, thus perpetuating the old tradition which equated presbyterianism with sound educational policy.

[67] D. J. Withrington, ' Lists of Schoolmasters teaching Latin, 1690 ', in *Miscellany of Scottish History Society*, x. 121-42.

[68] *A.P.S.*, x. 63-4. For earlier legislation see G. Donaldson, *James V to James VII*, pp. 262-5.

dead letter, as earlier writers have too often assumed.[69] Indeed, most historians of education have tended to minimise the number and the effectiveness of the parish schools of Scotland in the early eighteenth century.[70] Many schools existed intermittently, often below the level ordained in the act of 1696 but for all that playing important roles in the struggle against illiteracy. All things considered, Scotland's pride in her educational tradition is justified. For a poor country to place such emphasis on education for all (and that was the ultimate aim) was a remarkable phenomenon for the times. The only countries with comparable records were the Netherlands and Prussia, the first, significantly, a stronghold of Calvinism and the latter tinged by it.

All the same, care should be taken to avoid another trap into which credulous historians have fallen—namely, that of exaggerating the merits of the educational system in Scotland. There were many drawbacks and many glaring defects. The schoolbuildings were often rude hovels, tributes either to the poverty or the parsimony of the heritors; the status and remuneration of the teacher were alike low and to eke out a bare livelihood the dominie was often obliged to take on odd jobs such as notary or even grave-digger. The result was patchy, excellent parish schools in some quarters, indifferent to poor in others, and none at all in some. But by the end of the seventeenth century most Lowland parishes had schools of some sort in which boys from most ranks of society were taught together. Girls occasionally attended parish schools but usually either had no formal schooling or were sent to private venture schools. The real educational problem lay in the Highland area which, apart from Argyll, was at the beginning of the eighteenth century almost destitute of schools. It was mainly to remedy this defect that the Scottish Society for Propagating Christian Knowledge was formed at Edinburgh in 1708. In 1711 it settled its first schoolmaster in the remote island of St Kilda and by 1715 it was running 25 schools in the Highlands in which English, arithmetic and church music were taught.[71] But, for various reasons, progress was uphill. Not only were the society's means limited but also its principal ally,

[69] *E.g.*, H. G. Graham, *The Social Life of Scotland in the Eighteenth Century*, p. 420, ' Never was there a wiser law, and never was a law more studiously disregarded '.
[70] As, *e.g.*, J. C. Jessop, *Education in Angus*, ch. IV., esp. pp. 160-2.
[71] John Mason, *A History of Scottish Experiments in Rural Education*, ch. I.

the established church, was unpopular in most parts of the Highlands where, in addition, parishes tended to be large and unwieldy with poor communications adding to the difficulty; besides, Gaelic-speaking teachers were few and this added to the society's troubles. It meant that there was then no viable alternative to education in the medium of English. This created additional troubles, for the Highland aristocracy feared that such an education would undermine their authority, and, not unnaturally, the monoglot Gaels themselves evinced no burning desire to be schooled out of their own language and traditions. Thus, not surprisingly, early results were not encouraging, and it was not until the middle of the eighteenth century that the work of the society began to show visible results.

Most of the burghs had schools on which they lavished attention and in some cases considerable sums of money. Edinburgh and Glasgow each had an excellent burgh school in which the main concern was the teaching of Latin. Long hours and strict discipline were the usual prescriptions, the boys even being forbidden to speak anything but Latin in the school precincts. Despauter's *Latin Grammar*, probably in one of its Scottish editions, was the scholar's vade-mecum until in 1714 it was replaced by the work of a famous Scottish grammarian, Thomas Ruddiman. A curriculum was rigidly enforced, as at the High School of Glasgow where it extended over five years. The first two years were devoted to a monotonous sing-song of grammatical rules; in the third the pupils read from Cicero; in the fourth they tackled Virgil, Ovid, Horace, and selections from George Buchanan; and in the fifth year they studied rhetoric and history from Caesar and Sallust.[72] As well as Latin, English and writing were also taught, but of Greek little or nothing was attempted. Such Greek as was taught in Scotland was left to the universities.

The Scottish universities then numbered five: St Andrews, Glasgow, King's College Aberdeen, Edinburgh, and Marischal College Aberdeen. They had all suffered in the seventeenth century from the politico-ecclesiastical turmoils, all having been repeatedly purged at the dictates of whichever ecclesiastical party enjoyed the support of the lay power. Thus, presbyterians had been weeded out in 1661 and the same fate befell the episcopalians in 1690. Money, too, was scarce and all the colleges were ham-

[72] James Grant, *History of the Burgh Schools of Scotland*, pp. 336-9.

pered by lack of funds. In the late seventeenth century the Scots universities were stagnant, restricted in their teaching and outmoded in thought. In spite of strenuous efforts made by such reformers as Andrew Melville in the sixteenth century, the Scots colleges remained essentially medieval in outlook. Thus the system of regenting was still in use though it was no longer adequate for the more expansive learning of the late seventeenth century. Each regent took a class of students through the entire arts course, teaching each subject himself, in theory if not in practice, for at St Andrews the regents specialised, ' everie one continewing in his awin professioun '.[73] The students were young and often not too well schooled, and the teaching they received at college was often superficial. Instruction was given in Latin and tended to be formal and uninspiring. As a consequence the Scots universities had little or no fame beyond the bounds of Scotland; but they dovetailed remarkably well with the Scots ideal in education. They opened their doors to all ranks of society, and the poor Highland student with his sack of oatmeal begging his way to King's or Glasgow is not just a Scots myth. Most of the students hoped to find a place in the ministry, many were doomed to the drudgery of the parish schools, but in the early eighteenth century other professions were coming more into prominence. Law and medicine became fashionable studies and the more progressive of the universities hastened to cater for the demand. Thus at Glasgow a chair of mathematics was set up in 1691 and a chair of medicine in 1712. In medicine, however, Edinburgh led the way and throughout the eighteenth century easily maintained her supremacy. A medical school had risen outside the university and the activities of the Faculty of Physicians and the Royal College of Surgeons acted as a challenge and a stimulus to the university. In 1705 a chair of anatomy was founded, followed in 1713 by a chair of chemistry. Alexander Monro *primus*, a pupil of the great Herman Boerhaave of Leyden and the founder of a famous professorial dynasty, held the chair of anatomy from 1720: his practical skill and eloquent teaching were soon attracting students from England and Ireland as well as Scotland. In other ways Edinburgh, under the principalship of ' cardinal ' Carstares, broke fresh ground, notably when in 1708 it abolished the outmoded system of regenting. Carstares'

[73] W. C. Dickinson, *Two Students at St Andrews*, p. xxii.

aim evidently was to reorganise the college along Dutch lines, with individual professors responsible for teaching their own subjects. Not until the end of the eighteenth century was this fundamental reform accepted by all the Scottish universities.

Such in outline was the material and cultural state of Scotland in the period between the Revolution and the Union. It reveals a country underdeveloped, poor in its material resources, not devoid of spirituality or idealism but with a culture narrow and confined. Books written and published in Scotland were few and consisted mainly of theological treatises and ecclesiastical polemics. They were poorly produced and abominably printed. The press had fallen on evil days, owing to some extent to monopolist policy. The king's master printer Andrew Anderson received a monopoly in 1671 and ruthlessly exercised his privileges. He at least understood something of his craft, which was more than could be said for his widow who, following his death in 1676, claimed to be sole heiress of his rights. In spite of the atrociousness of her work she long made these claims good, to the exasperation of ambitious and able printers such as James Watson of Edinburgh. Watson tried to improve standards by bringing in foreign craftsmen and machinery; and in 1711 he entered into an agreement with the leading Edinburgh bookseller, Robert Freebairn, in an attempt to prevent Mrs Anderson from securing a renewal of her patent. John Baskett, recently established as queen's printer in England, was a sleeping but by no means inactive partner to the agreement. The confederates managed to obtain the patent but then quarrelled. Freebairn and Baskett tried to deprive Watson of his rights and ultimately made an agreement with Mrs Anderson.[74] The legal wrangle continued for several years but Freebairn forfeited his rights by serving as the Pretender's printer in 1715.[75] Watson, though originally a Roman catholic (his father had been James VII's ' Popish Printer ' at Holyrood) and at heart a Jacobite, kept clear of the rebellion. But he still had to reckon with the doughty Mrs Anderson and Baskett, who in 1716 were granted the coveted patent. The widow, however, died within a few weeks of her triumph and ultimately Watson

---

[74] State Papers, Scotland (P.R.O.), 54/5, No. 41. ' The Case of James Watson, one of Her Majesty's Printers, 1713 '. Watson repeats the charges in his ' History of Printing '; see *Watson's Preface to the History of Printing, 1713* (1913), ed. W. J. Couper, pp. 54-5.

[75] *E.g.,* S.P. 54/10, No. 173.

won his case, despite Baskett's appeal to the house of lords in 1718. Nevertheless, Baskett still caused trouble by attempting to keep Watson's books out of England.[76] All in all, by about 1720 the press had improved, and the day was not distant when Ruddiman and the Foulis brothers were to set exacting standards in printing.

One really significant development of the reigns of William and of Anne was the rise of journalism. Newsletters came into vogue after the Revolution but they were English mainly and had little news value, specialising rather in spreading rumours.[77] James Donaldson, the advocate of improved agriculture, began a new venture in 1699, *The Edinburgh Gazette*. Authority did not welcome criticism and Donaldson's *Gazette* appeared only intermittently for a few years, according to whether its publisher was at liberty or not. Watson was also familiar with the inside of the tolbooth, for he too ventured into journalism, producing *The Edinburgh Courant* (1705), *The Scots Postman* (1708), and *The Scots Courant* (1710). He also catered for a developing taste in literature by reprinting Steele's *Tatler* and some other items then popular in England.

But, as has been well said, in Scotland ' there was little literature to suffer from these troubles '.[78] In part this was because the intellectual climate of seventeenth-century Scotland was hostile to the liberal arts; but the dearth of literature was the product also of a cultural dilemma. Scots as a literary language virtually died in the seventeenth century. Some authors sought refuge in English and others in Latin; but by the end of the century Latin had passed its heyday. Yet well into the eighteenth century Scotsmen of considerable, and sometimes great, abilities quailed before the baffling intricacies of written English and wrote, as they spoke, with trepidation. Two church historians of diametrically opposed views in all else agreed on this. Wrote the episcopalian apologist and subsequent non-juring bishop Sage in 1695: ' It is hard for most Scottish men to arrive at any tolerable degree of English purity. Our greatest caution cannot prevent the stealing of our own words and idioms into our pens, and their dropping thence into our writings.'[79] And as late as 1721 the

[76] W. J. Couper, ' James Watson, King's Printer ', in *S.H.R.*, x. 244-62.
[77] E.g., *Proceedings of the Estates in Scotland* (S.H.S.), 2 vols.
[78] H. G. Graham, *The Social Life of Scotland in the Eighteenth Century*, p. 111.
[79] *Works of Rt. Rev. John Sage*, I. 2.

erudite Wodrow in the preface to his greatest work equally humbly pleads for the tolerance of the English reader.[80]   Later still, David Hume, for all his anglophobia, had friends in England who carefully weeded out the philosopher's scotticisms.   When mind and heart are at variance great prose literature is seldom achieved.   The case was quite otherwise in poetry, for in this department the old Scots tradition survived.   True, it was debased throughout the seventeenth century; but it did not die. In the early eighteenth century it enjoyed a remarkable revival with all classes of Lowland society, inspired no doubt by the frenetic nationalism that was so apparent in the period 1690–1707. Watson, the printer, made a valuable contribution to this by editing an anthology of Scots poetry.[81]   He was an indifferent editor, but he did bring before the public something of the rich old poetry of Scotland.   Minor poets like Hamilton of Bangour and Allan Ramsay kept the tradition alive.

If literature was in poor case, that of the visual arts was even worse, for in many of its branches there was little demand for such works in Scotland.   The existence of numerous painted ceilings—fine though some of them undoubtedly are—scarcely amounts to a high artistic tradition.   What promise there might have been was blighted by the covenanters in their period of power.   They suppressed the ' profane arts ', destroying some fine medieval wood-carvings in the process, and their anti-art tradition took root.   Lack of gear in this world and anxiety for bliss in the next explain best this anti-art tradition and the scarcity of Scottish artists of any note.   The civil wars turned bad to worse, and such painters as late seventeenth-century Scotland produced plied their art in London.   The most notable of these was John Michael Wright (c. 1625–1700) who for a time bade fair to rival Sir Peter Lely.   The rise of Kneller eclipsed Wright, who then applied unsuccessfully for the post of king's painter in Scotland.   In that country a few portraitists struggled on, notably the Scougalls, of whom little authentic is known.   Occasionally patrons lured foreign artists into Scotland, not always with happy results.   For Holyrood Palace in 1684 a Fleming, Jacob de Wet,

---

[80] Robert Wodrow, *History of the Sufferings of the Church of Scotland*, ed. R. Burns, I. xli.

[81] James Watson, *Choice Collection of Comic and Serious Scots Poems both Ancient and Modern* (1706–1711), 3 vols., new edn. in I vol. 1869.

mass-produced portraits of the royal line which ran past all human recollection, each visage bearing a remarkable family resemblance and each costing £1 13s. 4d. More popular was the Belgic Spaniard, Juan Batista Medina, who also worked on the conveyor-belt principle. He was regarded as such an acquisition that he was the last knight created in Scotland before the Union. He founded a school, but his successors, including his son John, did little beyond churning out spurious portraits of Mary Queen of Scots. But in William Aikman (1682–1731) Sir John did tutor one native Scots painter of ability. Aikman, son of an Angus laird, studied at Rome, returned to Edinburgh in 1712, and there set up as a portrait painter. After eleven years he tired of this unprofitable activity and moved to London, where with James Thomson, Mallet, and others he belonged to the first coterie of Scots who managed, more or less successfully, to assimilate themselves to English ways. His best works are probably studies of Allan Ramsay, the poet, and of Sir John Clerk of Penicuik, baron of the Scottish exchequer and Aikman's cousin. In this lean period Aikman's is the one name of note in the meagre list of Scottish painters.

Of the other arts only music held charms for the Scot. Edinburgh society delighted in amateur ensembles, in which attempts to render current fashions nearly always succumbed to the popularity of the old Scots melodies. The taste for these passed to London with William Thomson, an hautbois player, and John Gay made free use of them in *The Beggar's Opera*. St Cecilia's Hall in the Cowgate of Edinburgh (built in 1762) latterly became the recognised mecca of Scots music lovers.[82] Love of song was diffused throughout the whole society and in the later eighteenth century, when the sense of nationality seemed to be disappearing, it was the poetry and music of Scotland which did most to preserve her identity.

[82] D. F. Harris, *Saint Cecilia's Hall in the Niddry Wynd*.

4

RELIGIOUS LIFE, 1689–1761

The bitterness of the strife between presbyterians and episcopalians seriously affected the religious life of Scotland and,
far from being settled by the Revolution, intensified in the
reigns of William and of Anne. It then produced fresh tares of
controversy in which rancour, distortion of fact, and coarseness
of thought and expression distinguished presbyterian and episcopalian alike. Only the most unblushing bias could now choose
between the contestants and find all to laud in one party and all
to condemn in the other. Expediency rather than principle
dominated the minds of the rival publicists. Thus one contemporary episcopalian writer laments that ' the Church of Scotland
is at this time under the Claw of an inraged Lion; Episcopacy
abolished, and its Revenues alienated; the Clergy routed, some
by a form of Sentence and others by violence and popular Fury;
their Persons and Families abused, their Houses ransack'd '. Here
there is some truth, but not the whole truth. The same author,
with a childish naïvete, gingerly skirts the vexed question of
allegiance to King William; he argues that Dundee was forced
to take up arms purely to safeguard his life and liberty; but he
then continues, even more disingenuously, ' if my Lord Dundee
had lived (who was a great Patron of this Clergy) none doubts
but that he had changed the whole State of Affairs in this Nation '.[1]
This slanted approach was imposed by the bitter dilemma in
which Scottish episcopalians found themselves. They wished to
retain control of the church but could not bring themselves to
make timely submission to the new sovereigns. It was not feasible

---

[1] *An Account of the Present Persecution of the Church in Scotland, in several Letters*, (1690),
pp. 1-4.

that William should desert proven allies and take by the hand open enemies; only those deluded by a fanaticism as unreasoning as that which they condemned in the ' Hill People ' could ever have conceived it possible. Whatever the relative strength or numbers of the two parties, William in the last resort could not avoid favouring the presbyterians. The plain truth is that the downfall of episcopacy and the rise of a new presbyterian model were matters of policy rather than polity.

Yet the relative strength of the two parties needs to be considered, for though this did not determine the Revolution Settlement it had its part to play in the long-term problems of the church. Just as at the Restoration, the apologists for each side wildly exaggerated its strength and popularity. William Carstares and other presbyterian exiles in Holland had led William to believe that the Scots were solidly presbyterian at heart and that episcopacy without the support of dragoons would collapse of sheer inanition. This was a distorted view. Over much of the country episcopacy was accepted, and in areas such as the northeast and the greater part of the Highlands that system was revered.[2] South of the Forth presbyterian traditions were at their strongest, but one of the surprises thrown up by the Revolution was the extent and depth of presbyterian sympathies there. The presbyterians were not, as some believe, confined to the southwestern counties, though these undoubtedly formed their main bastion; for in the Lothians and Borders they proved to be the stronger party, and in Fife, Stirlingshire and Argyll they had powerful cadres. They were strong, too, in the extreme north where the Mackays and Munros furnished their principal support. But the division was never as neat and exact as such zoning might suggest. A certain degree of social cleavage blurred the picture. Most of the nobles and a considerable number of the lairds inclined towards episcopacy, whereas tenants and burgesses were more apt to lean towards presbyterianism. It was no accident, therefore, that episcopacy should have been strongest in the conservative north where feudal powers and patriarchal concepts of society proved most durable. In such a society episcopacy struck fewer jarring notes than presbyterianism, which dwelt not so much on human as on divine patriarchy. Significantly, in the south-west

[2] T. Maxwell, ' Presbyterian and Episcopalian in 1688 ', in *Records of the Scottish Church History Society*, XIII. 25-37.

the position was almost reversed. The Duke of Hamilton, for example, found that he could not afford to antagonise the Cameronians and at one point was forced sadly to admit that though the people of Lesmahagow were his tenants he had no authority over them whatsoever. The same lesson had emerged very clearly from the reigns of Charles II and James VII: great landlords in the west Lowlands simply could not be made responsible for the behaviour of their tenants.

From the beginning of the Revolution the struggle was waged for possession of pulpits and control of presbyteries, while latterly it turned on mastery of assemblies. In the winter of 1688-9 the detested curates were rabbled in the south by bands of Cameronians, although presbyterians who had lately accepted King James's toleration also took part in this work. In the chaos of the times the privy council paid little heed to the pleas of the outed episcopal ministers and these unfortunates fared ill. In some cases they were violently abused, especially if found in the possession of Prayer Books. Threats, backed up by beatings, were common; their families might be thrust out of doors in bitter weather, often to throw themselves thereafter on the strained charity of kirk-sessions. Doubtless some of the curates were marked down for such vengeance through being involved, willy-nilly, in the late persecutions; but many of them were blameless and even, in a way, popular. Some who had pleased their congregations well enough were still ousted by wandering bands of zealots, the most formidable of which was said to be a 'Female Rabble'.[3] The curates, indeed, were hated not so much for themselves as for what they represented; and, besides, the opportunity to infiltrate presbyterian ministers into the establishment was too good to lose. A similar policy was followed by the privy council directed by the presbyterian zealot, the Earl of Crawford. The early procedures of the council differed from those of the rabble only in that verbal abuse was substituted for physical. Scandal was the detergent that was to cleanse the church. Presbyterian imaginations, rich in such murky lore, ran riot, convicting Baal's priests of every conceivable excess—moral, doctrinal, or liturgical. 'One was accused because he sometimes whistled',[4] states an episcopal

---

[3] *Case of the Present Afflicted Clergy in Scotland truly Represented* (1690), pp. 39-40.
[4] *An Historical Relation of the late General Assembly, held at Edinburgh, 1690* (1691), p. 10.

pamphleteer, for once contenting himself with bare truth. The most scandalous assertions were recorded but not put to the proof, so that the stigma remained. The fact is that the aim of the presbyterians was to purge the church as rapidly as possible with little regard for truth, law, or justice; and in the process many ministers who were willing enough to conform were deposed.

Such a policy of wholesale purging carried with it its own penalties. Ministers whose education and orders were beyond reproach were in limited supply, and it took the Church of Scotland well nigh thirty years to recover from these self-inflicted wounds. Few presbyterian ministers had the courage to tackle charges in the hostile north where popularity gave a large measure of immunity to the episcopalian clergy. In vain did depleted presbyteries, assemblies and commissions thereof seek to drive out suspect incumbents, who as late as 1707 numbered 165. That mass depositions were hardly likely to promote the religious life of the country weighed not a straw with the dominant party, no more indeed than similar measures had troubled their rivals thirty years earlier. As Burnet put it: ' so apt are all parties, in their turns of power, to fall into those very excesses, of which they did formerly make such tragical complaints '.[5] James Frazer of Brae, one of the few covenanted Highland ministers, justified such conduct on the plea of sacred necessity: ' it was better that the Temple of the Lord did lie sometime unbuilt and unrepair'd, than be reared up by Gibeonites and Samaritans '.[6] On the other hand, the records of the privy council indicate that it was not only the presbyterians who could be considered as the church militant. Many of the curates resisted, though not all of them as violently as Alexander Meldrum of Glendevon in Perthshire who, when ordered to give up his charge to William Spence, armed himself with a pistol ' and threatened to kill and destroy any that should first enter ' the kirk door. He actually wounded one man before he was restrained by a neighbour, whereupon he ' drew at a long whinger or Baganet he had probably under his gown and therewith struck at the said Archibald Blackwood most desperately and furiously '.[7]

Fairer dealing might have reduced many of these problems,

[5] Gilbert Burnet, *History of His Own Times*, II. 561.
[6] *An Historical Relation of the late General Assembly, 1690* (1691), p. 9.
[7] MS. R.P.C., 23 July 1690, p. 299.

but ideal solutions, such as the 'joynt comprehensione of all interests' advocated by Sir James Dalrymple in 1689[8] or the establishment of both presbyterian and episcopalian forms proposed by Viscount Tarbat, were quite chimerical.[9] The gulf between presbyterians and episcopalians was deep, superficial evidence to the contrary notwithstanding. The few moderates on either side might readily have been accommodated, but they were hopelessly swamped by the extremists. So bitter had the contention become that most presbyterians, who in their dread of liturgical forms had already rejected the Lord's prayer, judged episcopalians who used the Doxology to be 'formal and nominal Protestants' with a strong Rome-ward bent. The episcopalians on the other hand, though not bound to a set liturgy, inclined towards the Anglican forms, but not all of them cared for the actual Prayer Book. To them the presbyterians resembled pharisees rather than Christians, and repeatedly they charged presbyterians as a whole, most unjustly, with the antinomian heresy.[10] A few of the crack-brained extremists of the late persecuting times, such as Mickle John Gibb and his covenanted harem, undoubtedly crossed the thin divide between hyper-calvinism and open antinomianism. Antinomians held that they had the assurance of election and were thereby released from the laws; and none condemned the heresy more roundly than orthodox presbyterians. Only credulous ignorance of the kind that Buckle later brought to the subject continues to obscure this fact.[11] In 1648, for example, Samuel Rutherford published a massive tract in which he learnedly refuted the anabaptist and antinomian trends apparent in English independency.[12] Frazer of Brae condemned antinomianism in the treatise on faith which

[8] *Leven and Melville Papers*, p. 8.

[9] *Ibid.*, pp. 125-7.

[10] See *The Scotch Presbyterian Eloquence, or the Foolishness of their Teaching Discovered from their Books*, (edn. 1694). It was an unlucky hit, however, which (p. 13) accused Samuel Rutherford of fomenting antinomianism. For a discussion of this pamphlet see T. Maxwell, 'The Scotch Presbyterian Eloquence, a Post-Revolution Pamphlet', in *Records of the Scottish Church History Society*, VIII. 225-53.

[11] H. T. Buckle, *History of Civilization*, III. Buckle's own bias was reinforced by uncritical acceptance of the prejudices of eighteenth-century Scottish *Moderates*, such as Ramsay of Ochtertyre who (*Scotland and Scotsmen in the Eighteenth Century*, II. ch. VII) consistently refers to the evangelicals as 'the Antinomians'. This bad example was followed by Sir Henry Craik, *A Century of Scottish History*, I. 380-1.

[12] Samuel Rutherford, *A Survey of the Spiritual Antichrist, opening the secrets of Familisme and Antinomianisme*, (1648).

he composed in 1679 while he was a prisoner on the Bass Rock.[13] A more explicit renunciation of the heresy than that of John Livingstone, a good Scots Calvinist, can hardly be found: ' God knows that I would rather serve God on earth, and then endure the torments of the lost, than live a life of sin on earth, and then have for ever the bliss of the ransomed '.[14]

In matters of polity, too, in spite of the retention of the lesser church courts, the episcopal system differed in essence from the presbyterian. From its character at the time, from the mode of appointing bishops and from the powers that they enjoyed, it was more Erastian. Here was a snare from which Scottish episcopacy only painfully extricated itself in the eighteenth century. Only a fixation with forms without reference to functions can regard the two systems as compatible with each other. In theory and in organisation they were poles apart, and in strict logic the presbyterians were right to refuse a so-called compromise which could have had no basis in reality and which must seriously have prejudiced the opportunities so unexpectedly opened up to them by the Revolution.

The erection of a strong presbyterian establishment was the main task to which the dominant party devoted its energies. The purely negative work of purging the kirk was well advanced, thanks to rabble and council, before a general assembly met in 1690. This was a thin gathering, dominated by the restored ' antediluvians ', the survivors of those ejected in the episcopalian purge of 1662. The main purpose of the assembly, which at the king's request acted moderately, was to build anew on the recent acts of parliament restoring presbyterian government and the primacy of the Westminster standards. The commissions for the north and the south which the assembly set up, however, showed no such moderation and continued to harass and deprive episcopalian ministers; already in the summer of 1690 another commission had swept episcopalian scholars out of the universities. Only the regents and masters of the two Aberdeen colleges escaped, owing to the readiness with which they conformed and, probably, the strong local support which they enjoyed. Their failure in the north-east not only embarrassed the presbyterians;

[13] *A Treatise concerning Justifying or saving Faith.*

[14] Quoted in James Walker, *The Theology and Theologians of Scotland chiefly of the Seventeenth and Eighteenth Centuries*, p. 174 (2nd edn. 1888).

it threatened to revive the old quarrel between church and state, for William constantly advised moderation and was as constantly disregarded. Repeatedly, the king through his commissioner to the assembly pleaded for leniency to the episcopal ministers and asked that those willing to make basic submission should retain their livings. In the assembly of 1692 this issue caused a head-on collision, and in despair the commissioner finally dissolved the assembly without naming a date for its next meeting. That important omission was promptly made good by the moderator, thus accepting the challenge implicit in the commissioner's act. It was the king, counselled by his chaplain Carstares—for long the grey eminence of the Church of Scotland—who gave way, though he managed in return to get a vague promise that episcopal ministers prepared to qualify by oath should be accepted by the church. The bargain was ill kept; all sorts of impediments were put in the way of conformist episcopalians; and in 1695 William, in disgust, forbade the assembly to meet. Once more an open breach was narrowly avoided, but the latent struggle continued and received notable expression when in 1698 the assembly repudiated the view that the church was founded on the inclination of the people and acts of parliament. Instead, its commission asserted, ' We do believe and own that Jesus Christ is the only Head and King of this Church '.[15] The interpretation of this doctrine, which was at the root of the difference between presbyterians and episcopalians, had behind it a stormy past and before it lay a troubled future. It could be pushed to singular extremes, but the doctrine itself, of course, was far from singular. It has played an incalculable part in moulding the beliefs and attitudes of a majority of the Scottish people, especially in forging a radical temper which has shown at times scant respect for human institutions while craving some ideal order.

In the reigns of William II and of Anne the Church of Scotland laid the basis of the constitution which was to serve it in the eighteenth and nineteenth centuries and which, with modifications, serves it to this day. Thus, by requiring overtures to be approved by a majority of presbyteries, the Barrier Act of 1697 ensured that general assemblies could not pass hasty or unpopular acts. Then in 1707, after years of discussion, another important act of assembly defined ' the Form of Process ' under which clergy

[15] Quoted in J. Cunningham, *Church History of Scotland*, II. 201-2.

and laity were to be prosecuted in church courts for offences against doctrine or discipline. This act too had a long and useful, if not always popular, life before it. The need for it was manifest, as appears from the numerous other acts which sought to improve religious observance at the time. Efforts were made to secure more reverential attitudes from congregations; people were not to loll, gossip and fidget in time of worship; and the deplorably low standard of psalmody was to be raised. But acts of assembly, like acts of parliament, were often still-born. ' Penny Weddings ', where the guests contributed their mite to the general jollification, were often frowned upon, but their popularity continued. Fiddling and dancing came under the ban, but even the most zealous kirkmen could not find the energy for a sustained assault on these citadels of Satan. Ralph Erskine belonged to the more strictly pious presbyterians, but his love of music was such that he could not for long lay aside his violin. Scots Calvinists were never as uniformly drab as legend has depicted them and Ralph's elders, perfect Davie Deans in all else, were fain to conclude that the minister was a great man and ' nane the waur for his tunes on the wee sinful fiddle '.[16] ' Jupiter ' Carlyle's father was of the old, rigid Calvinist school but he and his colleague Jardine used to scandalise the worldly-wise Jupiter by their buffoonery, such as ' turning the backsides of their wigs foremost, and making faces to divert the children '.[17] The sacrament of the Lord's Supper, never greatly stressed by Calvinist theologians, had long been infrequently observed. This trend was strengthened by the troubles of the Restoration period, when many had stubbornly refused to take communion from conformist ministers but instead resorted to field conventicles. The tradition of infrequent communion continued after 1690. The sacrament was rarely held more than once a year, and, partly to commemorate the sufferings of the faithful conventiclers and partly because of lack of adequate space in church, it tended to be held in the open air, a great gathering (sometimes known as ' the preaching ') to which a team of preachers of some local renown drew the gospel-hungry from miles around, but increasingly drew also the loafers and ne'er-do-weels. The real degradation of such ' Holy Fairs ', however, came in the eighteenth century, to provide Robert Burns with fit subject for satire.

[16] A. R. MacEwen, *The Erskines*, p. 46.   [17] Alexander Carlyle, *Autobiography*, p. 23.

In the reign of Anne the presbyterians in Scotland were very much on the defensive. Their constant dread was of a Jacobite counter-revolution, and after 1707, in spite of the act guaranteeing the Scottish establishment, their unease was increased by possible threats from prelatical England. As the events of 1712 proved, neither fear was unjustified. Three acts of parliament arose out of Greenshields' case, of which the main outlines have already been given. But these acts need to be examined again, stressing this time their ecclesiastical rather than their political implications. The act restoring the Christmas recess in the court of session appears to modern eyes innocent, if not laudable; but to Scots presbyterians it smacked of popery and was indeed contrived as a deliberate insult to their prejudices. The Toleration Act at last secured the right of episcopalian congregations to meet and worship after the Anglican forms; and indeed those who took advantage of this act were obliged to use the English liturgy. To meet the need thus created the English Prayer Book was in that same year printed at Edinburgh. But Scottish episcopalians of the time tended to have a curious ' love-hate ' relationship with the Church of England. Many of them were inordinately proud of their native heritage and had no wish to be considered as mere Anglicans *in partibus*. The Toleration Act did not affect the non-jurors, who in 1712 reprinted for their own use a limited edition of the Scottish Prayer Book of 1637. For long enough many of this dour native stock refused to have any truck with the English liturgy, contenting themselves either with the Scottish Book or with expedients of their own devising. The Toleration Act, then, had the unexpected effect of introducing strife among the episcopalians, whereas its intention had been to divide and perplex the presbyterians. For the latter it had deep, long-term results. It circumscribed the jurisdiction of the courts of the established church, in effect binding to them only those who wished to be bound. From this two main consequences ensued. It led in the long run to a loosening of church discipline. The socially prominent could thereafter sin, and if they were so minded carry on sinning, in spite of the thunders of the presbytery. Thus the continuance of rigid discipline among presbyterians in eighteenth-century Scotland is to be explained on sociological rather than legal grounds: it took strong-minded as well as wayward individuals to fly in the face of entire communities, and strength and waywardness are not exactly synonyms. Then, too, the Toleration Act recognised that the old ideal of one national church brooking no rivals was at odds with the facts. By depriving the established church of the right to discipline all and sundry, it made schism painless and easy. Although devised for mischievous purposes, the act was in itself a just and much-needed measure. That it was a clear breach of the Treaty of Union was unfortunate and led to much bad feeling; but if it had extended its shelter to an even more oppressed minority, the Roman catholics, whether a breach of fundamental law or not, it would today be applauded—and deservedly so. But the good it wrought was quite incidental to its purpose and not an integral part of it.

Its companion piece, the Patronage Act, was equally bad in intention and far worse in practice. Only those hypnotised by the cultural attainments of later eighteenth-century *Moderatism* can make any sort of case for this reactionary piece of legislation. On the specious plea that the terms of the act of 1690 abolishing patronage had not been kept that measure was superseded. The whole justification of the act of 1712 was held to be the failure, in all but two cases, to pay the composition of 600 merks to the deprived patrons of 1690: it therefore restored the powers of the patrons but at the same time, perhaps by inadvertence, it seemed to reserve to the congregations the rights given them by the act of 1690. That is to say, the patron could present a nominee but a majority of the congregation still had the right to dissent from a call, leaving the matter then to be resolved by the presbytery. The purpose of the act was to buttress the local power of the lairds and to check the advance of the popular party in the church. Its effect was to make the patronage question one of the great conditioners of Scottish ecclesiastical, cultural and social history in the eighteenth and nineteenth centuries.

These developments convinced the remnant of the Cameronians that they had acted wisely in steering clear of the uncovenanted, Erastian establishment of 1690. But they, too, had their troubles, produced mainly by divided counsels and earnest contendings on points of conscience. As early as 1689, at the height of the crisis produced by Dundee's rising, dissension appeared over the question of forming a regiment. Only after a great deal of heart-searching did a minority of the Society People

agree to serve in a regiment that became known as the Cameronians, forced, as they saw it, to aid the lesser malignancy against
the greater.   In 1690, their three remaining pastors—Lining,
Shields, and Boyd—glad to escape from their difficult flocks,
defected to the establishment while testifying against its manifest
defects.   The Societies remained in being but lost what little
cohesion a common cause and a common danger had imposed.
Some found an acceptable pastor in John Hepburn, sometime
minister of Urr in Galloway, who in 1705 was deposed by the
general assembly but was restored at the earnest plea of his
congregation in 1707.   Others remained in the wilderness awaiting a worthy minister and eventually found him in 1706 in the
person of John McMillan of Balmaghie.   As a body, however, the
Cameronians were powerful out of all proportion to their numbers,
for the simple reason that some of their criticisms of church and
state were shared by many within the establishment.   In many
parts of the country such people formed prayer societies, usually
because they found fault with the parish minister.   They were
still technically within the establishment but tended to be a focus
for opposition to prevailing trends of which they disapproved.
This was demonstrated in 1712 when at Auchensaugh in Lanarkshire the Cameronians and many sympathisers from the prayer
societies held a great rally, or holy ' wark ', to testify against
toleration, imposition of patronage, oaths, and other recent
backslidings.   In the ' Auchensaugh Declaration ' the Cameronians reiterated their old covenanted claims to be the ' True
Church of Scotland ' and condemned all false doctrines, including
those of the establishment.   How awkward such zealots could be
we learn from the autobiography of Thomas Boston, whose
ministry at Ettrick was harassed by a handful of these earnest
Mucklewraths.[18]   Known sometimes as McMillanites, and after
1743 as Reformed Presbyterians, they were not a proselytising
sect, but were content to perpetuate the tradition of ' the suffering, bleeding remnant '.   After the rise of the Secession, their
appeal declined; and indeed, one section of the Cameronians,
the Hebronites or followers of John Hepburn, rapidly went over
to the Secession.

Most ' Church Histories of Scotland ', unfortunately, live up
to their titles.   They deal mainly with polity and discipline, and

[18] T. Boston, *General Account of My Life*, ed. G. D. Low, pp. 318-19.

rarely venture into the involved subtleties of theology. Even such a fine scholar as A. R. MacEwen could state, with bland dogmatism, that in early eighteenth-century Scotland ' of theology in the strict sense there was none '.[19] This oversimplification has proved a fruitful source of error. It may be granted that Scotsmen made few outstanding contributions to reformed theology in many of its major aspects, though it must not be overlooked that preoccupation with church government itself rests upon a theological base. This point was well understood by both presbyterian and episcopalian divines who on this subject could cite apostolic and patristic sources as learnedly as any. But purely theological controversies which split other churches—such as the Trinitarian controversy—hardly troubled seventeenth-century Scotland. The main Scottish theological interest in that period centred upon the vexed problem of the means of grace, and here some distinctive contributions were made.[20] After the Revolution the overriding primacy of the question of church government tended to wane and conflicts over doctrine became more pressing. To a large extent, this change reflected the general drift of European thought. The philosophy of Descartes and the scientific work of Newton raised serious doubts about the adequacy of the Calvinist (or perhaps one should say ' fundamentalist ') view of the universe. This leaven was already working among some of the more latitudinarian of the Scots episcopalians under the Restoration regime, stimulated by the teaching of the Gregories at St Andrews and unwittingly helped perhaps by the views of Bishop Leighton, who was influenced by the Cambridge platonists. Some of the episcopalians claimed to ' understand the Christian philosophy ' better than their narrow presbyterian rivals;[21] the latter replied that in their zeal for philosophy the ' curates ' clean mislaid the gospels. Here was eighteenth-century charge and countercharge in a nutshell. The assembly of 1690 expressed its concern in the following terms: ' there hath been in some a dreadful Atheistical Boldness against God, some have disputed the Being of God, and his Providence, the Divine Authority of the Scriptures, the Life to

[19] A. R. MacEwen, *The Erskines*, p. 56.
[20] See James Walker, *The Theology and Theologians of Scotland chiefly of the Seventeenth and Eighteenth Centuries*; and John MacLeod, *Scottish Theology in Relation to Church History since the Reformation*.
[21] *An Account of the Present Persecution of the Church in Scotland* (1690), p. 45.

come, and Immortality of the Soul, yea and scoffed at these things.'[22]

To attribute these errors to the episcopalian clergy as a whole was partisan rant; but that beliefs hostile to the old orthodoxy had gained a foothold in Scotland is indubitable. Dr Archibald Pitcairn (an episcopalian, Jacobite, and wit) was a professed deist whose ideas provoked a reply from the Reverend Thomas Halyburton in his *Natural Religion Insufficient*, which was posthumously published in 1714. It is of further interest to note, in view of Scotland's supposed freedom from the deist controversy, that one of the original deistical writers, the Irishman John Toland, had been a student at Glasgow. Such ideas were becoming widespread, and in 1696 (the very year in which Toland published *Christianity not Mysterious*) an act of assembly was passed against them. In that same year an unfortunate student of divinity, Thomas Aikenhead, was cruelly executed for blasphemy, and the ministers of Edinburgh, who had instigated his trial under an old statute reaffirmed in 1695, made no real effort to seek clemency for him. The execution, the last of its kind in Scotland, did nothing to check the progress of new ideas. Even that pillar of presbyterianism, the reverend Mr Hog of Carnock, was in his youth led astray by Cartesian speculations and for a time 'fell headlong into a kind of scepticism'.[23]

In the early eighteenth century, therefore, in Scotland as elsewhere in western Europe, orthodoxy had to brace itself for a struggle with loose or downright heretical doctrines. The weakened establishment, believing itself to be surrounded by enemies, was more than usually apprehensive. The episcopalians stubbornly refused to yield; Roman catholicism was feared to be on the increase in the Highlands; and undoubtedly suspect doctrines were gaining some currency, particularly in the north-east, an area with a curious religious history. This region was for the most part strongly episcopalian and tinged with Roman catholicism; but it was in this unpromising soil that quakerism first took root in Scotland. Among the episcopalians of the north-east, however, there had arisen a mystical tradition which, weary of the ecclesiastical strife of the seventeenth century, stressed the overriding importance of individual piety. But it is perhaps going too far

<hr/>

[22] *Act of Assembly, anent a Solemn National Fast and Humiliation.*
[23] Walker, *op. cit.*, p. 71.

to describe such men as John Forbes of Corse or Henry Scougal as mystics.[24]   The truly mystical element appeared after the Revolution when the episcopalians laboured under persecution. Then the brothers James and George Garden popularised the works of the Flemish mystic, Antoinette Bourignon, who had died in 1680.   Bourignonism was anti-clerical and anti-ecclesiastical, Antoinette holding that ' Church pomp and priestcraft have only served to conceal the simplicities of the Gospel '.[25]   Indeed, she went so far as to describe the pope, bishops and monks as ' the leprosy of Christianity '.   She thought no better of the Reformed Churches, attacking the Calvinist view of predestination as the most pernicious doctrine in Christendom.   Madame Bourignon was a quietist, preaching withdrawal from the vanities of this world and mystical union with God through a confused theology of regeneration in which the prophetess was to act as the ' new Eve '.   For promulgating such doctrines George Garden was deposed from the ministry of the Church of Scotland in 1701, but Bourignonist beliefs spread and found another resting place in St Andrews.   In 1711 ordinands in the Church of Scotland were required to abjure Bourignonism among other heresies, and this requirement continued in force until 1889, although Bourignonism itself, which had also been condemned in 1700 by Bishop Nicholson, the Roman catholic vicar-apostolic,[26] had practically died out by 1714.   Other mystics, however, enjoyed a brief vogue in the north-east, notably Madame Guyon; but with the ruin of the Jacobite episcopalians after 1715 the movement rapidly declined. Undoubtedly, it was stimulated by the dry, talmudic type of religion that was enjoined in Scotland in the period immediately following the Revolution, and it was checked by the rise of a more evangelical outlook in the second decade of the eighteenth century.

A more persistent source of trouble was the vexed question of the precise means of grace laid down in reformed theology.   On the themes of election, regeneration and justification differences of emphasis or interpretation were infinite.   These the scholasticism of the seventeenth century had provided in abundance, but

[24] This is done, albeit cautiously, by G. D. Henderson, *Mystics of the North East* (third Spalding Club, 1934), introduction, *passim*.

[25] See A. R. MacEwen, *Antoinette Bourignon, Quietist*, pp. 50-1.

[26] A. Bellesheim, *History of the Catholic Church of Scotland* (tr. Blair, 1890), iv. 169.

in Scotland heated controversy on this important matter was held over till the eighteenth century. Curiously enough, suspect doctrines flowed from what was normally a stronghold of Calvinist orthodoxy, the university of Glasgow. As we shall see, this paradox had a long and important history in the latter half of the eighteenth century, due largely to the conflicts engendered by the rise of a secular philosophy to which another expatriate Irishman, Francis Hutcheson, contributed so much. To some extent the way was prepared for Hutcheson by John Simson, professor of divinity at Glasgow. Simson was of a speculative cast of mind, an academic *frondeur* intent on building a reputation from dissecting the work of others rather than from any solid contributions of his own. He loved to hover on the brink of heresy, though usually securing for himself safe retreats. His alleged offences were verbal, delivered in scholastic Latin in the course of his lectures, and therefore difficult to prove. His errors, such as they were, were vague and could not be fitted into any recognisable body of thought. Simson, in his cautious way, anticipated the attitudes of the *Enlightenment*; a generation later his activities would scarcely have raised an eyebrow. But in this tense period of transition, it is easy to understand how a man of this laodicean stamp enraged the faithful. In 1714 an evangelical minister, Webster of Edinburgh, forced on a process against Simson, accusing him of spreading Arminian doctrines. A reluctant assembly took the matter up but gladly availed itself of the rebellion of the following year to postpone the trial. Simson in the meantime had declared his adherence to the Confession of Faith and denied all charges laid against him. The evidence was unsatisfactory and the assembly of 1717 was probably right to terminate the case with a virtual acquittal, though warning the professor to be on his guard against ambiguous expressions in the future.

The process against Simson helped to clarify, without helping in any way to settle, latent differences that were emerging in the Church of Scotland. At bottom, all turned upon the theme of redemption. Had Christ died to purchase grace for all or only for the elect? This intricate question had always haunted Calvinist thought, and it was raised in an acute form by the scare over Simson's Arminian teachings. Arminianism stressed free will, thus limiting the range of the unconditional decrees of God;

and it was, therefore, anathema to rigid Calvinists. In an effort to guard against the Arminian danger the presbytery of Auchterarder in 1717 required a probationer to subscribe some additional articles, one of which was, 'I believe that it is not sound and orthodox to teach that we must forsake sin in order to our coming to Christ, and instating us in covenant with God'. The probationer failed to satisfy his examiners, was refused an extract of his licence, and thereupon appealed to the general assembly. On the score of dangerous ambiguity, the so-called 'Auchterarder Creed' was condemned. The judgment was sound, for the proposition was badly framed and could be construed as antinomian. But many of the more zealous preachers (then generally known as 'high-fliers' and later as evangelicals) objected to the stiff line that was taken with their brethren of Auchterarder, in contrast to the leniency that had been shown to Professor Simson. Indeed, the church had not yet heard the last of that bold speculator, whose daring thoughts may well have been stimulated by the discomfiture of the 'high-fliers' of Perthshire.

Thomas Boston, the earnest minister of Simprin, was sorely troubled by these very problems of redemption and justification which the 'Auchterarder Creed', in its clumsy fashion, had sought to resolve. His attitude, like many of the 'high-fliers', was not that commonly, but mistakenly, attributed to Calvin. He was, indeed, reacting against the hyper-calvinism of the seventeenth century, which in its extremest form verged dangerously on antinomianism; but he was also reacting against the legalism that was beginning to appeal to a certain class of ministers. These men were already approaching the later 'moderate' position. They upheld a rather sterile orthodoxy, scouted enthusiasm, and, in spite of formal protests against patronage, were more bent on pleasing the patrons than the congregations. To them theology was heady stuff and the gospel pure and unadulterated dangerous fodder for their flocks. They accepted the formularies of the church as useful expedients for checking errors, but not as vehicles of a living faith. Two approaches so fundamentally opposed were bound to clash sooner or later.

All unwittingly, Boston precipitated the strife by bringing into prominence a seventeenth-century English work which he had picked up in a peasant cot while he was minister of Simprin. He felt that Edward Fisher's *The Marrow of Modern Divinity*, which, significantly, had been balm to Frazer of Brae, met the case and left no further room for confusion about justification and redemption. He recommended it to some friends, who were so taken with it that in 1718 James Hog of Carnock brought it out in a new edition. Thus was born the famous 'Marrow controversy', a bitter dispute of little or no memory now but an important one in its own right as well as in its consequences. The book created a sensation in Fife, where for some years past the synod had been rent by disputes 'touching the covenant of grace, whether it is conditional or absolute'.[27] Principal Hadow of St Andrews, who seems to have cast himself in the role of chief inquisitor into heresies, at once attacked the work, declaring that it was antinomian in its teaching. The attack was carried into the general assembly and in 1720 the book was condemned. A small but stubborn group opposed this decision, only to receive very brusque treatment from the assembly and its commission. The 'Marrowmen' contended that the book had been unfairly condemned, that Hadow had callously ripped passages out of their context, and that the majority in the assembly had not even read the book at all. This is patently true. *The Marrow* was written in dialogue form, with stock characters representing a legalist, an antinomian, and an evangelical. The argument is socratic; the heretics have their say only to be infallibly controverted by 'evangelista'. So far from being antinomian the work was specifically, and convincingly, directed against that heresy. Fisher in his preface made this clear: ' these are they that can talk like believers, and yet do not walk like believers: these are they that have language like saints, and yet conversations like devils; these are they that are not obedient to the law of Christ and therefore are justly called Antinomians '.[28] The book, however, undoubtedly leaned more towards Lutheran than later Calvinist views of justification. Indeed, the system of theology held by Boston and the ' Marrowmen ', the federal or covenant theology, kept predestination very much in the background. A prominent ' Marrowman ', Ebenezer Erskine, like Calvin himself, took the view that predestination was strictly God's business and told his hearers to set it aside

---

[27] Thomas Boston, *A General Account of my Life*, ed. G. D. Low, p. 245.

[28] *The Marrow of Modern Divinity*, ed. T. Boston (17th edn., 1781), p. 21. The book became a standard evangelical work in Scotland and was last published under the editorship of C. G. McCrie in 1902.

as a 'matter with which they have no more concern than with what men are doing in Mexico or Peru '.[29]

Controversies over certain oaths imposed upon establishment ministers further defined the lines of division within the church. From the earliest years of the Revolution Settlement, presbyterian dread of Erastianism gave rise to much uneasiness. Only the diplomacy of Carstares averted a crisis over the refusal of many presbyterian ministers to take the oath of assurance in 1694. The chief source of trouble, however, was the abjuration oath imposed on all ministers by the Toleration Act of 1712. This was an English oath, first imposed in 1701 and intended to ensure the protestant succession and to keep Jacobites out of civil or ecclesiastical posts. When the oath was imposed on Scotland in 1712 no effort was made to recast it to suit Scottish conditions. Many of the presbyterian ministers scrupled to take it, partly because of its Erastian implications and partly because it required them to recognise the claims of the Church of England. The ' scruplers ' quarrelled furiously with the ' clear brethren ', the latter being so called because they felt clear in conscience to take the oath. Again only the suave Carstares, who played a great part in the general management of the church, prevented a rupture. Boston and most of the ' high fliers ' were scruplers and either refused to take the oath or else took it with express qualifications safeguarding the rights of the Church of Scotland. On the accession of George I the oath was again tendered, but this time it was accompanied by a statement that it was not intended to prejudice the rights of the Church of Scotland. Even so, Boston and many of his allies remained ' non-jurors '; and the matter was not finally ended until 1719 when the oath was at last re-phrased to suit the needs of the kirk.

These controversies revealed the emergence of new ideas on the nature of the universal church. All through the troubled seventeenth century, belief in a united national church as part of the catholic church was held tenaciously by both episcopalians and presbyterians. Sectarianism was not native to Scotland and was heartily condemned. Even such extremists as the Cameronians refused to see themselves in any other light but that of ' the suffering, bleeding remnant of the true church of Christ in Scotland '. Schism was regarded with horror. But in the early

[29] A. R. MacEwen, *The Erskines*, p. 38.

eighteenth century the concept of ' one face of a kirk in Scotland ' began to break down. Those who differed from the establishment came to consider themselves for practical purposes as distinct religious communions, although the old theory was preserved by postulating the duty of severance from a false establishment in order to perpetuate the true. This curious hiatus between practice and theory goes far to explain the complicated church history of Scotland in the eighteenth and nineteenth centuries. Such trends were reinforced by the Toleration Act.

A fresh process raised against Professor Simson widened these rifts. In 1726 Simson was summoned by the presbytery of Glasgow to answer charges of Arianism brought against him by an evangelical minister, Coats of Govan.[30] The professor treated the presbytery with contempt, frequently failing to appear or make answer to the charges, on grounds either of ill health or else of irregularities in the presbytery's procedure. The presbytery complained to the assembly of 1727, which set up a Committee of Purity of Doctrine to investigate the case and, incidentally, to keep the presbytery within bounds. Again the charges against Simson were vague and the proof adduced not very conclusive. Some of his students reluctantly gave evidence on certain of the professor's comments in his lectures: Simson apparently was influenced by the views of Samuel Clarke, who had recently caused a furore in England by his anti-Trinitarian views. The Glasgow professor, indeed, was back at his old game of giving original twists to the labour of others. To begin with he seemed to be on safe ground. The doctrinal issues in question were subtle and involved; and the committee appointed by the assembly was ' moderate ' in sympathies and went out of its way to shield Simson from the exasperated presbytery. But in the assembly the high-fliers pressed home the charge and Simson's shuffling became so obvious that the court had to proceed in the matter. The members of the assembly of 1728 came up primed with arguments and counter-arguments, and something not unlike a public disputation of Reformation times took place. Again Simson sought shelter in the Confession of Faith; but his intellectual arrogance offended too many in the assembly for him to get off scot-free once more. Finally, in 1729 he was suspended from

[30] *The Case of Mr John Simson, Professor of Divinity in the University of Glasgow,* (2nd edn. 1727).

teaching but allowed to retain his salary, a sentence which struck the ' Marrowmen ' as monstrous when contrasted with the harsh treatment to which they had been subjected. Ebenezer Erskine, ' the father of the Secession ', referred bitterly to these matters in a sermon delivered in 1742 in which he diagnosed the ills of the Church of Scotland: deism was rife, the gospel was going down before ' the dry sapless harangues of heathenish morality ', and Arianism was abroad ' and appeared before the bar of the Assembly without any becoming censure '.[31]

Patronage troubles filled the cup of bitterness for the high-fliers. It has been held that the exercise of patronage between 1712 and 1730 caused little disturbance; but this view is hardly tenable. Such cases were rarely brought as far as the assembly but they gave rise to bitter resentment among congregations, especially in the southern parts of the country where presbyterianism was most firmly rooted. Until the 1720's, however, the prevailing shortage of ministers masked the uglier features of the system; and the rights of congregations (safeguarded, if somewhat vaguely, by the act of 1712) were generally applied until the late 1720s.[32] The assembly annually protested against the restoration of patronage; but as year succeeded year this became a meaningless face-saving formula. Patrons who deliberately prolonged vacancies by making impossible presentations were indeed curbed by an act of parliament of 1719; but the main tendency was for them to recover more and more power. This stirred up the wrath of congregations, and sometimes an unpopular presentation was blocked by kirk-sessions and presbyteries. In order to resolve such an impasse, in 1729 the assembly provided for special committees to induct unpopular presentees. These became known as ' Riding Committees ', partly because of the way they trampled upon decisions of presbyteries and partly because they were kept busy trotting about the countryside. Such developments added to the bitterness of the strife between evangelicals and legalists; and this further increased as the power and jurisdiction of the church courts came to be questioned, particularly in 1730 when the assembly denied minorities the right of recording reasons for dissent.

The controversy which eventually produced the Secession

---

[31] *The Whole Works of the late Ebenezer Erskine*, ed. James Fisher, III. 51.
[32] A. R. MacEwen, *The Erskines*, ch. IV.

began in 1731. Since 1712 the presbytery had exercised a 'jus devolutum' (that is, the right to appoint in the case of a vacancy where the patron made no effective move within six months of the vacancy occurring). Exercise of the right was loose, each presbytery adopting its own line. By 1730 those few presbyteries with an evangelical bias were to all intents and purposes vesting the right of election in the congregations; but by this time church patronage was closely involved in 'political management', and, not unnaturally, the politicians viewed with disfavour the claims of congregations. Partly to clear up the matter in the interests of smooth administration, but even more to please the political manager, the Earl of Islay, the assembly in 1731 approved an overture restricting election to the heritors and elders. The resulting Act anent Calls of 1732 disappointed many and produced a storm of protest. It made nonsense of the assembly's protest against the act of parliament of 1712, and it was also passed in defiance of the Barrier Act. It was fiercely resisted by a small band of evangelicals headed by Ebenezer Erskine, minister of Stirling. Erskine had himself been a key figure in a notorious case at Kinross which lasted from 1726 till 1732, where he was the popular choice but the patron refused to consider such a firebrand. Erskine was of covenanting stock; his father had been among those ejected in 1662, and both Ebenezer and his younger brother Ralph grew up steeped in the traditions of 'the persecuting times' and the claims for the 'Headship of Christ'. How could such attitudes be reconciled with the sharp practice of the late act of assembly? As Ebenezer bitterly put it, such acts were null 'because Zion's King never touched them with His sceptre, and there is no church authority but what is derived from Him'.[33] To such a man surrender was unthinkable, and by his strongly cherished, if fanatically wielded, principles he was right. Those who have condemned Erskine and the Seceders have done so on no better grounds than to advocate a policy of drift. But churches, like political systems, can drift into very odd waters indeed if no one is willing to put a hand to the helm. The mere fact of resistance worked for the ultimate good of the Church of Scotland, just as the Erskines hoped that it would. And so as moderator of the synod of Perth and Stirling, Ebenezer Erskine fulminated against the act anent calls. On 10 October 1732 he

[33] Quoted MacEwen, *op. cit.*, p. 67.

opened the synod with a slashing attack upon the new measure, concluding his sermon with a biting piece of religious levelling of the sort which has always warred with the oligarchical tendencies of presbyterianism: ' I can find no warrant from the word of God to confer the spiritual privileges of His house upon the rich beyond the poor; whereas by this Act, the man with the gold ring and gay clothing is preferred unto the man with the vile raiment and poor attire.'[34]   Yet he did not advocate secession, although already he had at command all the arguments that would later be used to justify it.   The ' Testimony ' of 1734 was no more than a cogent summary of the tensions of the previous forty years.

Erskine and his followers among the ministers were not numerous, and as the quarrel sharpened some who had previously sympathised with him fell away. As moderator, Ebenezer was rebuked by his synod in 1732, and his appeal to the assembly of 1733 against the rebuke was not sustained. Ebenezer and three of his supporters protested, but the protest was brushed aside— almost literally. It fell from the table, and on being picked up was found to contain some harsh comments on the assembly. This led to the suspension of the recalcitrant four, who, however, retained their livings and the enthusiastic support of their congregations. The dispute then dragged on for seven years, in the course of which various assemblies tried hard to compose the differences that had arisen. That of 1734 even repealed the act anent calls, and two years later a fruitless effort was made to have the patronage act repealed. The situation was peculiar. Ebenezer and his three colleagues had forsworn the courts of the establishment and at Gairney Bridge near Kinross in December 1733 they constituted themselves into a separate presbytery, the Associate Presbytery, though they pointedly disavowed all sectarian or independent ideas. They were joined by Ralph Erskine in 1737. They had, too, the support of numerous ' prayer societies '—embryonic secession congregations, as it turned out— and the sympathy of many laymen and not a few ministers. This was a situation in which to drift would have been fatal, and in 1740 the assembly at last accepted the harsh logic of reality and formally deposed the ministers of the Associate Presbytery.

[34] *The Whole Works of the late Ebenezer Erskine*, ed. J. Fisher, I. 504.   The point is repeatedly made in Erskine's sermons.

Significantly, Ebenezer Erskine's church at Stirling remained deserted for 77 years thereafter; and the Secession, in spite of later divisions and subdivisions, grew into the most formidable body of dissent in Scotland.

By 1742 the Associate Presbytery had twenty ministers and 36 congregations, and by 1745 a synod of three presbyteries—Edinburgh, Glasgow and Dunfermline—was formed. But the strength of the Seceders was actually greater than this and they made inroads into many Lowland parishes in which discontent with patronage was rife. They frequently had to supply sermons in parishes held by *moderate* ministers. As Ebenezer Erskine expressed it to George Whitefield, one of the great apostles of methodism, with whom he had been in correspondence since 1739—'The wandering sheep come with their bleatings to the Associate Presbytery, whereby our work is daily increased'.[35] The evangelical revival headed by John Wesley in England (which was possibly influenced by the works of the Scottish divine Henry Scougal)[36] was maturing into a distinct movement, and in 1740 Wesley ended his period of self-doubt. He broke with the Moravians, and, consumed by evangelical passion for the salvation of England if not the world at large, he formed the Wesleyan society of Methodists. It too, in time, was to be severed from its parent body, the Church of England, and, like the Scottish Secession, was to be rent by schismatic tendencies. These were already in evidence, Whitefield insisting on the Calvinist doctrine of predestination, whereas John and Charles Wesley were drifting towards Arminianism. It was for this reason that, in the letter just cited, Erskine begged Whitefield to ' come over to Scotland and help us, Come up to the help of the Lord against the mighty '. Whitefield came, only to discover that he and the Seceders really had little in common. They made it plain to him that they ' were the Lord's people ' and that his prelatical background was an abomination. The startled Whitefield could not agree as to either of these particulars; he was then gleefully taken up by the establishment ministers who put their pulpits at his disposal. The success of his tour under these auspices led the Seceders to condemn his labours and the wild

[35] Donald Fraser, *Life of Ebenezer Erskine*, pp. 424-7. Letter dated June 1741.
[36] D. Butler, *Henry Scougal and the Oxford Methodists*, ch. VIII. Scougal's *Life of God in the Soul of Man* led to the conversion of the youthful George Whitefield.

frenzies kindled by his glowing eloquence. Thereafter in their
testimonies the Seceders listed, along with the condemned, George
Whitefield and all his acts, particularly ' the Cambuslang wark '.
The religious revival of 1742 at Cambuslang in Lanarkshire was
not initiated by Whitefield but seems to have been the outcome
of the feverish temperature raised by his tour. There was more
than an element of mania about the whole business—shaking,
swooning, and babbling. The news spread and soon a great
gathering of the faithful, the credulous and the incredulous, from
all over Scotland thronged to Cambuslang. The parish minister,
MacCulloch, had to recruit a team of notable evangelicals like
McLaurin of Glasgow (who, incidentally, is said to have delivered
the finest sermon ever heard in Scotland); and finally, drawn by
reports of the phenomenon, Whitefield himself hurried back north
to address the great open-air ' Occasion ' on 11 July, at which
20,000 people were said to be present. Such was the success of
Whitefield's preaching that another mass communion service was
held on 15 August at which an even greater multitude attended.
In Whitefield's own words: ' Such a Passover has not been
heard of '.[37]   But the ' wark ' soon thereafter spent itself. The
Seceders and the Cameronians condemned it as inspired by the
devil; and Ralph Erskine seized the opportunity to condemn
Wesleyan methodism as well. Something, doubtless, must be
ascribed to sour grapes, but in fact Whitefield's appeal to the
emotions was far removed from the style affected by the Seceders.
They, in common with most Scottish presbyterians, aimed at
intellectual conviction rather than invoking pentecostal outpour-
ings of the Spirit, as both Whitefield and John Wesley were to
discover in the course of numerous visits.

The Seceders, indeed, cleaved increasingly to the standards
of the seventeenth century. They celebrated the centenary of the
Solemn League and Covenant by renewing it, and in 1744 they
stored up strife for the future by declaring covenanting to be a
term of communion. They had seceded for religious liberty, only
to inflict upon themselves the shackles of an outworn tyranny.
The confusion of mind thus induced led to division. In 1744 the
more extreme Seceders, led by Alexander Moncrieff and a new
recruit, Adam Gib, held that they could not in conscience take

[37] Quoted by D. Butler, *John Wesley and George Whitefield in Scotland, or The Influence
of the Oxford Methodists on Scottish Religion*, p. 39.

the burgess oath which seemed to entail approval of the established church. The Erskines argued that the point should not be construed too literally, but, for their pains, they were excommunicated by the 'anti-burghers' who formed a separate 'General Associate Synod'. The division was permanent and became known in Secession circles as 'the Breach'. Adam Gib, an able theologian and controversialist but a man of domineering nature, became the shining light among the anti-burghers. Under 'Pope Gib' they became noted for gloom, hair-splitting casuistry, and narrow viewpoints. In spite of a certain prickliness towards the establishment, the 'burghers' under the sway of the Erskines held to the larger vision of catholicity. These differences among the Seceders, and the bitterness they engendered, undoubtedly stood the establishment in good stead. It made objects of fun of the disputants and repelled many who, at bottom, sympathised with the stand made by the Original Secession. One such was Thomas Gillespie, minister of Carnock near Dunfermline, who in 1752 was deposed by the general assembly for refusing to take part in the induction of an unpopular presentee at Inverkeithing. But apart from the manner of his departure from the establishment, Gillespie had little in common with the Seceders. He had been educated partly at Dr Doddridge's famous non-conformist college at Northampton, and there he imbibed some of the liberalism of English dissent. Gillespie in fact had no great reverence for the establishment principle; and he believed in open communion for all protestants, a new and revolutionary concept in Scotland. Gillespie therefore could find no shelter with the Seceders, who believed in an establishment buttressed by covenants. And so he toiled on alone with his small but faithful congregation until in 1760 he was joined by Thomas Boston junior. In 1761 with another minister, Thomas Colier, they formed the Presbytery of Relief, 'for the relief of Christians oppressed in their Christian privileges'.[38] This rapidly grew into a separate presbyterian church, though one which was strongly tinged with liberal independent ideas.

Thus, by the mid-eighteenth century the near unity of the presbyterians in the Revolution Church was broken, and establishment and dissenters were at loggerheads. Within the establish-

---

[38] Gavin Struthers, *The History of the Rise, Progress and Principles of the Relief Church* (1843), p. 160, quoting the minute of the institution of the presbytery, 22 October 1761.

ment differences still remained, though from 1752 onwards the Moderate Party, as it then became called, had a clear ascendancy. For decades thereafter the differences between Moderates and Evangelicals were hidden by the superior strength of the former in the church courts. But in spite of its divisions, presbyterianism held the allegiance of the majority of Scots and was indeed able to profit from the severe disadvantages under which the Episcopal and Roman Churches laboured. These bodies were in decline, owing largely to adverse political conditions and harassing problems of organisation and finance.

For the non-juring episcopalians, the quandary was how to maintain the episcopate, in view of their loyalty to the exiled Stewarts. The right to nominate to sees lay with the sovereign, but here difficulty was piled upon difficulty. The only sovereign recognised by the non-jurors was James Stewart, and he was both an exile and a Roman catholic. No serious effort was made to solve this problem until fifteen years after the Revolution; but in 1704 Archbishop Ross of St Andrews died, leaving only five pre-Revolution bishops. A move of some kind was needed, and finally a makeshift solution was attempted. Presbyters were secretly consecrated as bishops but without royal nomination and so without jurisdiction over specific dioceses. It was hoped that this plan would meet the needs of the church whilst not infringing the king's rights. Two such bishops, Sage and Fullerton, were consecrated in 1705, and two more, Falconer and Christie, in 1709. The gains made under the Tory ministry in 1712, however, were forfeited by the Jacobite rebellion of 1715, in which episcopalians were too obviously implicated. Following an act of 1716 many of their meeting-houses were closed, and in Aberdeenshire especially the presbyterians returned to their old work with a new zeal. Many ' curates ' who still held livings within the establishment were expelled and new and more stringent oaths were required. The penalties for non-compliance with the Abjuration Oath of 1719 were six months' imprisonment and the closing of meeting-houses. Some of the episcopal clergy suffered under these laws, but, inevitably, the persecution has been exaggerated. Its most important effect was probably the rise of episcopal congregations which were careful to keep within the law and dissociated themselves from the non-juring hierarchy. The maintenance of that hierarchy continued to be a problem, and again became critical when in 1720 the last of the pre-Revolution bishops, Rose of Edinburgh, died. The church was then reduced to four bishops resident in Scotland, not one of whom had diocesan jurisdiction. Bishop Rose, in fact, had held the shaky structure together, and his death obliged the episcopalians to confront their difficulties. Again they tried to outflank the problem by adopting a stratagem. They set up a ' College of Bishops ' which was to exercise metropolitan authority over the whole church. The Pretender reluctantly approved the design but requested that in future he should be consulted and not presented with an accomplished deed.

The college did not have a happy history. There were frequent quarrels over elections to bishoprics and later, in 1727, over the question of a primus. The root of the matter was that some bishops exercised what amounted to diocesan authority while others did not. Liturgical controversy, too, broke out over the so-called ' Usages ' question, principally over certain rites connected with the eucharist. These practices had already split the English non-jurors, and the spread of the controversy to Scotland was due to a dangerous fascination felt by some Scottish bishops for their English allies. The question was not so much the validity of the ' Usages ' but rather by what authority they should be approved or condemned. Bishops Falconer, Gadderar and Rattray denied the right of either King James or a majority of the college of bishops to forbid the ' Usages '. Fundamentally, those bishops who held diocesan authority were at odds with those who did not. A peace based on mutual forbearance was patched up in 1724; but the real trouble, the relationship between church and state, continued. King James's main agent, Lockhart of Carnwath, regarded the bishops as no more than political tools. He opposed the appointment of bishops by clergy and laity, and finally his interference became intolerable. The clergy of the diocese of Edinburgh spoke out against these encroachments and called upon the bishops to recover the alleged old rights of the church to self-government. Such a programme could not be carried out at one step, but was only achieved by stages. In 1727 a Code of Canons, which gave the church a workable constitution, was drawn up by the bishops, who profited from the fact that Lockhart had fallen foul of the authorities and had to flee abroad. The most important of the six canons ensured that government of the church should be vested in those bishops who possessed diocesan jurisdiction and that metropolitan authority should lie with the bishop of Edinburgh as vicar-general of the archdiocese of St Andrews. A small remnant of the 'college party' resisted these terms, but the influence of the diocesan bishops prevailed; a concordat was reached in 1731 which, as well as accepting the Canons of 1727, finally ended the 'Usages' controversy. The office of metropolitan was abolished and that of primus made elective, but 'for convocating and presiding only '.[39] Even so, differences persisted and more than once a rupture was only narrowly avoided. Not until 1743 was the constitution faithfully accepted by all in the shape of the Sixteen Canons of that year.

Again all seemed set fair, but again prospects were dashed by episcopalian support for the Young Pretender in 1745. This shattered the frame of the church, so painfully built up in such adverse circumstances. The penal laws were tightened and some of the clergy and laity transported. Fresh disabilities were imposed to keep Scottish episcopalians out of parliament and places of public trust. The non-jurors for a time could not openly flourish, and this led to an increase in the number of qualified chapels. Many of the nobles and gentry gave up episcopacy, finding congenial enough ministrations in an established church increasingly dominated by the Moderates. And in the nature of things it could scarcely have been otherwise. Unflattering as they would have found the comparison, Scots episcopalians after the Revolution displayed all the obstinacy and heroism of the presbyterians of the Restoration period. To dismiss either side as merely fanatical would be misleading. From their different standpoints they fought much the same fight, refusing to allow the church to become the mere plaything of politicians.

The history of the Roman catholics in Scotland in this period is difficult to piece together. The great prospects opened up to them by James VII were never realised and in the eighteenth century their history continued to be that of a missionary enterprise, hampered by ineffective administration and periodic outbursts of persecution. Long before the end of the seventeenth century the harsh penal statutes had virtually extinguished the old faith over most parts of Lowland Scotland. This was secured

[39] George Grub, *An Ecclesiastical History of Scotland*, IV. 7.

by submitting Roman catholics to all sorts of legal inconveniences (notably fining and inability to hold land or public offices) rather than by the shedding of blood. In the eighteenth century their main strength lay in a small area of the north-east Lowlands and in parts of the western Highlands and Islands. Their numbers are matters of conjecture, though they probably did not represent more than 16,500 out of a total population of just over one million.[40] In the Highlands, catholics were most numerous among the MacDonalds, though allegiances tended to shift, due not only to persecution but to the difficulty of providing adequate ministration. For the Roman catholics organisation was an even more intractable problem than for the episcopalians. In the circumstances there could be no question of providing anything like the old episcopal and parochial ministrations. But in 1694 an important advance was made in the setting up of a separate vicariate for Scotland. The first Vicar-Apostolic, Thomas Nicholson, titular bishop of Peristochium, worked personally in the Western Isles in 1700 and reported that he had found numerous Roman catholics on Barra, the Uists and Benbecula. The need was for more priests and, to prevent the high wastage normally incurred by sending promising lads to the seminaries on the continent, a small training centre was established at Scalan in Banffshire in 1714. To begin with, it had a rough passage and in 1726 was obliged to close. In the following year the country was divided into Lowland and Highland vicariates, Bishop Gordon, who had succeeded Nicholson in 1718, taking over the Lowland vicariate, while a product of Scalan, Bishop Hugh MacDonald, the brother of MacDonald of Morar, took over the Highland.

Even such an authoritarian system as the Roman church was affected by the national predilection for ecclesiastical controversy. A group of priests known as ' the pilgrims ' troubled the hierarchy, particularly by its Jacobite activities. The hierarchy wanted the

[40] A rough guide to the distribution of Roman catholics is to be found in ' Lists of Popish Parents and their Children in various districts of Scotland, 1701–05 ; printed in *Miscellany of Maitland Society* (1843), III. 389-440. It was hoped that this information would help to restrain ' the abominable crime of Apostacie ' (*ibid.*, p. 393). Alexander Webster in his ' Account of the Number of People in Scotland. 1755 ', ed. J. G. Kyd, *Scottish Population Statistics* (S.H.S.), p. 77, puts the number of papists at 16,490 out of a total population of 1,265,380. There is no reason to believe that Webster was greatly in error; the number of Roman catholics in the Highlands in the 1760s was reckoned to be 16,500 (R. Macdonald, *Innes Review*, XVI. 218-20).

churchmen to attend to their main business and leave politics
alone, but individual priests openly supported the '45. As a
result Roman catholics were subjected to a fresh outburst of
persecution. Their chapels were demolished, their priests were
arrested, and under heavy pressure some of the leading Highland
catholic chiefs turned protestant, including Clanranald, MacNeill
of Barra and MacDonald of Boisdale. By the mid-eighteenth
century it looked very much as if the catholic faith was on the
verge of extinction, though, *more scottico*, fighting a tenacious
rear-guard action.

Of other Christian denominations in Scotland in the first half
of the eighteenth century little need be said. Baptists, quakers
and congregationalists had gained entry during the Cromwellian
ascendancy but failed to maintain themselves in significant numbers. In the disturbed Restoration period quakerism took root
in Lanarkshire; but it was rigorously suppressed and in 1696
Thomas Story reported of the Hamilton meeting that ' things
were then in a declining condition '.[41] By 1730 quakerism in the
west of Scotland had virtually died out; but in the north-east it
proved more durable. The Aberdeen movement was not large
but it had some eloquent apologists, most notably Robert Barclay
of Urie who wrote a noble plea for toleration.[42] The plea was
vain; in the 1670s quakerism came under heavy persecution, its
spread was checked, and the movement dwindled. Elsewhere in
Scotland it suffered the same fate, due not only to persecution but
also to the rigid concepts of church order which prevailed. Much
the same must be said of congregational independency and baptist
forms. The slow drift towards congregationalism arose really
from dissatisfaction with presbyterianism, for independency provided one outlet from ecclesiastical discipline or tyranny. The
most notable influence here was that of John Glas, minister of
Tealing near Dundee, who came to the conclusion that Christ's
kingdom was purely spiritual and completely separate from the
state. He therefore denounced the covenants and for these
reasons he was deposed in 1728. The Glassites were never
numerous, but they had a wide influence, with their emphasis on

[41] Quoted by J. Torrance, ' The Quaker Movement in Scotland', in *Records of
the Scottish Church History Society*, III. 35. See, too, G. B. Burnet and W. H. Marwick,
The Story of Quakerism in Scotland.

[42] Robert Barclay, *An Apology for the true Christian Divinity, as the same is held forth,
and preached by the People, Called, in Scorn, Quakers, etc.* (1678).

Christian life rather than Christian dogmatics. They practised a spiritual communion, held the Lord's Supper weekly and owing to their 'love feasts' became known as 'kailites'. Through Glas's son-in-law, Robert Sandeman, the sect spread to England and America, where its adherents became known as Sandemanians.[43]   Connected with Glas, too, for a brief space was the eccentric Sir William Sinclair of Dunbeath in Caithness who about 1750 set up at Keiss the first baptist church in Scotland since the Restoration. The baptists, however, made no real progress in Scotland in the first half of the eighteenth century.[44]

Not until the late seventeenth century did Jews first establish themselves in Scotland. In 1665 a converted Jew was employed as a teacher of oriental tongues in Edinburgh; and in 1691 a Jew called David Brown applied to the town council of Edinburgh for permission to trade within the burgh. His request was contested on the grounds that only practising Christians could be granted such privileges. The treasurer, Hugh Blair, defended Brown's application: the Jews, he argued, were not exactly infidels but ' the ancient people of God of the seed of Abraham ' and ' to them belongs the promise '.[45]   David Brown was permitted to live and trade in Edinburgh, but the liberal attitude of 1691 was not maintained. In 1717 the council decided that Jews were, after all, infidels at law, but that law might be propitiated by payment of £100. This was the sum Isaac Queen had to pay for his privilege to trade. Due perhaps to this bigoted and mercenary policy, no further references to Jews in Scotland occur until near the end of the century.

[43] Harry Escott, *A History of Scottish Congregationalism*, pp. 17-42.
[44] G. Yuille, ed., *History of the Baptists in Scotland*, pp. 39 ff.
[45] Quoted from town council records by Rabbi Salis Daiches, ' The Jew in Scotland ', in *Records of the Scottish Church History Society*, III. 198.

5

POLITICS AND THE RISE OF 'MANAGEMENT', 1716–1760

The political history of Scotland in the first half-century of union displays little shape or unity; and this is mainly owing to the dismantling of one system of government in 1707 without care being taken to provide an adequate replacement. In these circumstances, it is not surprising that politics proved tortuous or that at times administration ground to a virtual standstill. Matters have not been helped by the attitudes taken up by later historians. The bad old convention was that Scottish history had come to an end in 1707, according to Robertson ' the union having incorporated the two nations '.[1] More recent historians struggled on into the post-Union period but in somewhat half-hearted fashion, clinging usually to the more romantic aspects of the subject. Only of late years has it been perceived that there thus had arisen a too contracted view of history which ignored the basic facts that the Scottish people did not hurriedly depart the scene in 1707 and that something like a Scottish state, feeble and broken down though it was, survived into the nineteenth century. This ' state's ' composition and functions cannot be explained on English analogies, for, though increasingly subjected to English influence, its roots lay in the period of independent existence.

This is most obviously true of the electoral system operative between 1707 and 1832. The effect of the Act of Union was to give Scotland a new framework within which politics had to be

[1] William Robertson, *History of Scotland during the Reigns of Queen Mary, and of King James VI* (edn. 1794), p. 490.

conducted, but the franchises and the electoral machinery were carried over from the old regime. The outstanding change wrought by the Treaty was the reduction in the number of constituencies from 159 to 45. These were allocated in the proportion of thirty to the counties and fifteen to the royal burghs, a just enough reflection of the social realities of that time. There were in fact 33 counties, but the difficulty was overcome by granting one member each to the 27 largest shires and pairing the six with the smallest electorates—viz. Nairn and Cromarty, Clackmannan and Kinross, and Bute and Caithness. Every other parliament, one of each of the three pairs would be disfranchised: thus Nairnshire would elect for one parliament and Cromartyshire for the next, and so on. A fair distribution of seats among the 67[2] burgh constituencies proved rather more cumbersome, but a modification of the Cromwellian precedent of districts of burghs yielded more or less fair results. In 1707 fourteen such districts were set up, nine with five burghs in the group, and five with four, Edinburgh alone being granted a member to itself. The constituencies created in 1707 endured without change until 1832, and over the same period in both counties and royal burghs the franchises remained unaltered. The basis of the electoral system in the counties was still the act of 1681 which defined the freeholder franchise as being land held of the crown valued at either 40 shillings of old extent[3] or £400 Scots of current valuation. The statute required the freeholders of each shire to meet annually in their head court and charged them with the keeping of the roll of electors. This constituted a basic distinction between Scottish and English practice: from 1681 an official list of county electors existed in Scotland but nothing similar was to be found in England until 1832. In Scotland the all-important matter was to be enrolled as a freeholder, for no one could represent a Scottish shire or vote in its election except an enrolled freeholder. In the royal burghs the right to elect was vested in the town councils, but matters were complicated by the grouping arrangement. To control a district of burghs, it became necessary to secure a majority of the town councils and the delegates whom they sent

[2] There were 66 royal burghs, but until the Union Edinburgh returned two members.

[3] For 'old extent', an obsolete system of assessing the taxable capacity of the second estate, see J. D. Mackie, ed., *Thomas Thomson's Memorial on Old Extent* (Stair Society, 1946).

to parliamentary elections. In practice, therefore, it proved impossible to separate municipal from parliamentary politics.

The most serious defect of the new electoral arrangements was the failure to allow a review jurisdiction to the court of session, the supreme civil court in Scotland. Before 1707 stringent provisions allowing appeals to parliament or, if parliament were not sitting, to the court of session, had kept the system reasonably pure. It is a cardinal error to read back into the pre-Union period the gross malpractices which disfigured Scottish politics in the eighteenth century.[4] Although a propensity for electoral manipulation had long existed, corruption and malpractice quite definitely grew and flourished because of the loosening of legal control over elections consequent on the Union. The house of commons deliberating on contested elections scarcely pretended to judge cases on their merits. Returns were set aside for no other reason than their not appealing to a majority of members; and Scottish election cases, since they often involved intricate legal points from an alien system, received particularly short shrift. The freeholders, therefore, for many years after the Union were at liberty to do just as they pleased. From the Union until 1743, declared Lord Eskgrove in 1790, there was no instance of a man coming before the court of session as a freeholder.[5] This was almost if not quite the truth, Lord Elchies having recorded a few instances of trifling import.[6]

It was in this unregulated era that most of the abuses which afflicted Scottish politics in the eighteenth and early nineteenth centuries evolved. The Duke of Queensberry immediately after the Union was openly rigging elections, largely by means of 'trust conveyances'. In these crude early versions of nominal and fictitious votes, complete disposition of an estate qualifying for a vote was made purely to serve election purposes. Efforts were made to check this abuse by an act 12 Anne (1714), but it did not go far enough. Infeftments had to be registered one year before the writ of election was issued, and in addition each claimant for admission to the roll of the freeholders had to take an oath of

---

[4] Both E. and A. Porritt, *The Unreformed House of Commons*, ii., and R. S. Rait, *Parliaments of Scotland*, vitiate much useful work by failing to note the defects that arose as a consequence of the Union.

[5] Robert Bell, *Treatise on the Election Laws, as they relate to the Representation of Scotland* (1812), pp. 384-6.

[6] Lord Elchies, *Decisions of the Court of Session*, i. s.v. Member of Parliament.

trust and possession. But who could guarantee the honesty of keepers of records ? And besides it took something more substantial than oaths to make eighteenth-century politicians honest. The act had little or no effect, and a similar act of 1734 met much the same fate. Sir Robert Walpole was blamed for the growing corruption—rightly in the sense that he exploited it—and not until he fell from power in 1742 was a really serious effort made to deal with the problem. The result was the act 16 George II (1743) which tried to clean up elections in Scotland by imposing heavy penalties on those found guilty of malpractices. Sheriffs and sheriff-clerks were required to do their duty impartially on pain of fines of £500 sterling for each transgression, a sufficiently severe threat to keep the returning officers in order. A more stringent procedure was laid down for judging applications from claimants, in an effort to prevent cliques from dominating the head courts. A review jurisdiction was conferred upon the court of session, but it was too circumscribed and the judges (partly playing politics but mainly to protect the law from the wild tramplings of the house of lords) confined themselves too narrowly to the express terms of the statute. Thus, the freeholders were still able to manipulate enrolments. Nominal and fictitious votes increased in spite of the act, and indeed developed under sophisticated forms beyond the understanding of any but a Scots lawyer. The more seats in the commons came into demand, the more the lawyers throve on ' the politicks '. As one shrewd eighteenth-century observer noted, ' lawyers are never paid so handsomely as in election causes '.[7] Long before the end of George II's reign Scots county elections might be decided (sometimes years before the writs were issued) by the creation of fictitious votes, shoddy legal manœuvres, the claims of kinship, and the use of influence. In the burghs new patrons of a purely political cast arose, often with no local standing but able and willing to grease the palms of the magistrates and councillors. Here open bribery was the principal weapon employed, although force could sometimes come to the aid of Mammon. A bitter contest in the Northern Burghs in 1742, in which violence and bribery were both prominent, drew forth the lament: ' all elections costs money nowadays '.[8]

[7] J. Ramsay of Ochtertyre, ed. A. A'lardyce, *Scotland and Scotsmen in the Eighteenth Century*, II. 483.

[8] W. Ferguson, ' Dingwall Burgh Politics and the Parliamentary Franchise in the Eighteenth Century ', in *S.H.R.*, XXXVIII. 95.

The history of the sixteen elected peers allowed by the Treaty of Union was pure farce. From first to last, their election at Holyroodhouse was dominated by the current ministry which sent up to Edinburgh a list of the desired peers and, though dissidents might hum and haw, the sixteen returned to the house of lords were usually drawn from the government list. As it was bitterly but truthfully put by the disappointed opposition in 1734, 'it would appear that the said election was rather a nomination by officers of the Crown than an election'.[9] The leading Scots peers, indeed, were little more than ministerial dependents, a large number of them receiving pensions from the Secret Service fund. Thus, for example, in 1721 the Earl of Hopetoun received £3,000 from this source, Marchmont £1,000, and his eldest son, Lord Polwarth, the like amount.[10] The M.P.s were probably just as venal, receiving, according to a partisan but sometimes uncomfortably accurate source, 10 guineas per week from government as a reward for obsequious attendance.[11]

The drift towards 'management' and a system of politics based upon interests was accelerated by the collapse of party. In the last Scots parliament embryonic parties had existed and popular opinion had played a part in politics; but the Union by removing the legislature to London ended virtual representation in Scotland. After 1707 the masses rapidly fell out of touch with parliamentary politics, which became the exclusive preserve of the upper classes. This development strengthened the group interests which already existed, party becoming little more than a term of abuse. True, the *Squadrone* endured but by 1715 it was little more than a territorial interest, located mainly in the south-eastern counties. By that date the old Court party was headed by Argyll and, a significant comment on the trend towards personal politics, known usually as the 'Argathelians'. Indeed, by the early years of George I, parliamentary politics in Scotland had degenerated into a 'spoils system'. The Earl of Islay made no bones about it. To his brother-in-law the Earl of Bute, he described in 1716 the process by which Argyll and he advanced in the world in face of all sorts of opposition and resentment: 'we always judge for ourselves without any prejudice of any side farther than honour and interest joined oblige us. . . .

H.M.C., *Polwarth*, v. 101.   [10] J. H. Plumb, *Sir Robert Walpole*, II. 105.
[11] A. Aufrere, ed., *Lockhart Papers* (1817), II. 139.

Thus Politics is a continuall petty war and game, and as at all other games, we will sometimes win and sometimes loose, and he that plays best and has the best stock has the best chance. . . .'[12] In case Bute missed the point, Islay again explained: ' It is enough that we can maintain an interest with some of both sides without giving up anything we must and ought to maintain, and if I can save myself or my friends by being thought a Mahometan by a Turk, I'l never decline it.'[13] Only the weakened Tories (meaning, in Scotland, Jacobites), held together by common aims, preserved some tincture of party. Yet it was still merely a rudimentary and none too effective ' spoils system ' that existed. Efficiency came gradually as the techniques of management slowly evolved to meet the chronic problems facing government.

In the early years of George I the main struggle was waged between the followers of Argyll and the *Squadrone* and, in spite of accusations of Jacobite complicity that were freely bandied about, it turned on office rather than on principle. By 1715 the Duke of Argyll with his great family and territorial connections was in a strong position, and his personal exertions against the rebels seemed to put the seal on his power. But he was an indifferent politician, and his arrogance antagonised both George I and his English ministers. Argyll also made the mistake of cultivating the friendship of the Prince of Wales and so fell first victim to the curious domestic relationships of the Guelf family. It was impossible to be on good terms with both the king and his eldest son; and in addition Argyll had bluntly criticised the inadequate measures taken by George I and his ministers to suppress the rebellion. When George I withdrew to Hanover for a spell, Argyll demanded that the Prince of Wales should be made sole regent. This indiscretion enabled Marlborough and the *Squadrone* to engineer Argyll's fall from office in the summer of 1716.[14] The king carried the matter further, attempting in the following January to force the prince to dismiss Argyll from his staff.[15] Thus the *Squadrone* secured a monopoly of office but was saddled with the invidious task of dealing with the vanquished rebels.

Neither the lord advocate nor his deputes would take part in the prosecution of rebels and most of these were tried at

---

[12] *H.M.C. Report*, v. (Marquis of Bute), 618. [13] *Ibid.*
[14] *H.M.C., Laing*, II. 188-9.
[15] E. R. Turner, ' The Peerage Bill of 1719 ', in *E.H.R.*, XXVIII. 245.

Carlisle by a commission of oyer and terminer, thus giving offence to many Scots who had no Jacobite leanings, such as the rising young advocate, Duncan Forbes of Culloden. The trials, however, were fair and the punishments were not unduly severe; for only two of the rebel leaders, Lords Derwentwater and Kenmure, were executed and they were tried by impeachment. None the less, the ministry was determined to read the Scots a lesson. Against the advice of the lord advocate, forfeitures were decided upon; and a commission of six, of whom four were English, was set up to dispose of the forfeited estates. The whole subject bristled with difficulties beyond the experience or grasp of English legislators or attorneys; and the commission, unaided by any Scots lawyers of note, was soon enmeshed in an intricate legal system of which it knew nothing. The Scottish exchequer advanced a prior claim on the estates based on the fines imposed on those who had failed to appear in Edinburgh when summoned in August 1715; the court of session was also unhelpful; and the tenants on the estates remained stubbornly faithful to their old lords. In view of all these difficulties, shrewd Scotsmen saw the unlikelihood of making a profit by purchase of the forfeited lands and consequently bids were few. Angered by all this the government appointed a new commission of 13 to expedite matters, but the disposal of the estates still dragged. Finally, an English concern, the York Buildings Company, purchased the bulk of the estates, although in spite of determined efforts at exploitation they were to make little from the transaction. Not until 1725 could the commissioners close their accounts, and it was then discovered that legal fees and other expenses had swallowed up most of the profits, leaving the government with little over £1,000 sterling to offset a great deal of ill will and contempt.

One of Walpole's Scottish correspondents, an Argyll partisan, summed the matter up neatly: the government aimed at punishing misguided individuals, whereas it should have been more concerned to secure the state against further disorders.[16] In fact, none of the measures adopted by the government proved very effective. A rigorous Clan Act was introduced, but efforts to disarm the Highlanders achieved little. Wade's roads (constructed between 1725 and 1737) and the planting of garrisons in the Highlands later proved more effective, but the usefulness

[16] *Culloden Papers*, pp. 61-5. The writer was Duncan Forbes.

of the roads was limited, even from a military point of view. The introduction of independent Highland companies helped to maintain order; but the heritable jurisdictions remained intact and the frictions to which they gave rise did much to preserve the military elements in Highland society. In short, nothing was done to alter social conditions in the Highlands, and there was, therefore, no real reason to suppose that, given the opportunity, the Jacobites would fail to draw further support from this turbulent area. The general distaste of the English for the Scots seemed to be justified when in 1719 the Pretender, after some years of fruitless plotting, managed to enlist the support of Spain. An expedition was dispatched and, though most of it was scattered by bad weather, a small Spanish force was easily crushed at Glenshiel by General Wightman. The problems of Jacobitism and the Highlands then receded into the background but still caused discord and distrust between Scots and English, and, indeed, between Scot and Scot.

Throughout this ungrateful time the *Squadrone* held office, with Argyll in factious and unprincipled opposition. The selfish nature of contemporary politics was blatantly exposed over the Peerage Bill of 1719, moved in the house of lords by Sunderland and Stanhope who thus attempted to make their hold on office unshakeable. The quarrel between George I and his eldest son had become so bitter that the king supported the bill, the effects of which would have been to make the upper chamber a closed oligarchy. The existing number of English peers was not to be increased by more than six, and the sixteen elected peers from Scotland were to be replaced by 25 Scottish peers having hereditary rights to sit in the house of lords. Argyll supported the bill and so did the leaders of the *Squadrone*, Tweeddale and Marchmont being named among the hereditary peers.[17] In other words, those Scottish peers who expected to derive advantages from the bill supported it irrespective of party, but with the rest the proposed measure was unpopular since it threatened to extinguish the slender rights left to them by the Union. All the same, those who held meetings and uttered remonstrances against it were either Jacobites or of Jacobite leanings. As Lord Balmerino, a leading Tory, put it: ' Your Lordship cannot doubt but every

[17] For a list of the peers who were to be added to the sitting sixteen see J. H. Plumb, *Sir Robert Walpole*, I. 276, n. i.

Peer here has the present design in detestation, except such as expect to be of the twenty-five.'[18]   The bill was bitterly opposed in the house of commons and the opposition, ably led by Walpole, scored a complete if unexpected victory.

The *Squadrone* lost ground, partly because it allied itself with one of Walpole's English rivals and partly because it became clear to the ministry that the strongest interest in Scotland was that of Argyll.   After Walpole became first lord of the treasury in 1721, he was driven to this unwelcome conclusion.   He never liked or trusted Argyll, but the situation in Scotland forced him to turn to the Argathelians and particularly to the duke's able young brother, the Earl of Islay, though Roxburghe (a member of the *Squadrone*) retained the post of secretary.   Two factors enabled Islay over the years to perfect the system of management which was painfully emerging and of which he was the chief organiser.   One was the chronic maladministration of Scotland, and the other the difficulty encountered by the king's ministers in maintaining a body of support in the house of commons.   The weakness of the administration explains two unconnected events which are too often lovingly described by historians for their picaresque qualities rather than their deeper underlying significance.   Each concerned lawless acts attributable largely to feeble executive government;   and each, properly interpreted, was an eloquent commentary on the ill-advised abolition of the Scottish privy council in 1708.   These were the Shawfield Riots in 1725 and the Porteous Riot in 1736.

The Shawfield Riots arose as a consequence of the Malt Tax, the history of which in Scotland is mysterious.   It had been pushed through parliament in 1713 in spite of strident Scottish opposition, but apparently some compromise had been reached whereby it was not to be levied, though in the Scots revenue accounts small sums were entered as raised from the Malt Tax, possibly as a blind.   The Tory squires in the house of commons became increasingly disgruntled at the heavy incidence of the land tax and in 1724, in an attempt to provide relief for themselves, they increased the tax on Scots ale by 6d. on the barrel.   Walpole knew this would cause trouble and did his best to soften the blow by altering it to 3d. on every bushel of malt, half the English rate. The Jacobites naturally took advantage of the situation to inflame

[18] *H.M.C., Portland,* v. 579.

national sentiments, and a fierce torrent of abuse rose in Scotland. (Ireland at the same time was in a ferment over Wood's ' Half-pence ', a sordid piece of jobbery that was savagely opposed by Dean Swift in his *Drapier's Letters*.) The disturbance in Scotland was such that the weak administration bent and all but broke. In June 1725 fierce riots occurred in Glasgow and the west, where the main target of the mob was Daniel Campbell of Shawfield, M.P. for the Glasgow Burghs, who was supposed to have sup-ported the act. His house of Shawfield was looted and razed, and ineffective intervention by part of the garrison of Dumbarton led to bloodshed. The really interesting moves, however, took place behind the scenes among the startled officials. Who was to restore order ? In the old days a few lines from the privy council would have been warrant sufficient; but the secretary for Scot-land, the Duke of Roxburghe, did nothing. Roxburghe was closely connected with Carteret, whom Walpole had just dismissed; the duke suspected that he was next to be removed and so he did not exert himself in this affair. The lord advocate, Robert Dundas, had opposed the new tax and for this he was dismissed in May 1725. It was left to his successor, Duncan Forbes, to call in a strong military force under General Wade to restore order in Glasgow and bring the malefactors to justice. The legality of Forbes' actions against the provost and magistrates of Glasgow (who had acted feebly throughout) was called in question. In a letter to Scrope (the doyen of the post-Union administrators in Scotland), Forbes admitted the difficulties under which he laboured: ' It had been a point contested, I mean extrajudi-cially with the Advocates my predecessors, since the abolition of the Privy Council in Scotland, whether they as such had a power of granting warrants of commitment '.[19] Forbes denied that the lord advocates had acted as privy councillors rather than legal officers of the crown. The government upheld Forbes on every count and the magistrates of Glasgow barely escaped prosecution. Instead the royal burgh was fined to compensate Campbell of Shawfield and several rioters were sentenced to transportation.[20]

In August Islay arrived to investigate the whole situation. His report to Walpole went to the root of the trouble, which was

[19] George Menary, *Duncan Forbes*, p. 70.
[20] G. Eyre-Todd, *History of Glasgow*, III. 140-1.

that in Scotland ' by a long series of no-administration, the mere letter of the law had little or no effect with the people '.[21]   To improve matters Roxburghe was dismissed from the post of third secretary and no one appointed in his room.   Working closely with Duncan Forbes, Islay thereafter enjoyed a general over-sight of Scottish affairs and long before Henry Dundas was born became known as ' king of Scotland ', while in the Highlands his principal helper was called ' King Duncan '.[22]   Argyll remained nominal head of the ' party ' but he was a grandee rather than a meticulous administrator; and increasingly the real business fell to Islay.   His lieutenants, Forbes and Andrew Fletcher of Milton, dispensed patronage, blatantly influenced elections, and in general supervised administration.   Here Forbes performed some yeoman service, reorganising the chaotic records and improving the effi-ciency of the courts.   For eleven years Walpole, by these means, achieved his aim of bringing Scotland into ' a position of quiet subordination '.[23]

The pride, greed and avarice of the Campbells, however, created new problems for Walpole in his endless adventure of governing men.   The accession of George II in 1727 made no real change in the political situation, but with each passing year opposition to Walpole and the Argathelians increased.   Wal-pole's Excise Bill of 1733 was lambasted by the opposition in the hope that this might sway the ensuing general election in their favour.   In the course of the struggle Chesterfield, Montrose, Stair and Marchmont were all dismissed from office, so driving them into opposition.   Those hostile to Walpole in both England and Scotland entered into a loose alliance, the main projectors of whose policy were Chesterfield, Pulteney, Stair and Marchmont. But in Scotland Argyll, ably abetted by Islay, carried all before him at this time.   Wrote Andrew Mitchell to Robert Dundas: ' The whole nomination of sheriffs seems to be little more than a list of the sons, sons-in-law, and alliances of those gentlemen whom the D[uke] of A[rgyll] has thought fit to place upon the bench.'[24] More ominously the Duke of Queensberry reported to Stair: ' I am told Lord Islay is taking great pains, being determined to try

[21] W. Coxe, *Memoirs of Walpole* (1798), I. 232.
[22] G. Menary, *Duncan Forbes*, p. 78.
[23] J. H. Plumb, *Sir Robert Walpole*, II. 106.
[24] *The Arniston Memoirs*, ed. G. W. T. Omond, p. 89.

the force of money, promises and threats. . . .'[25] The representation act passed at the end of the session contained a clause disqualifying Scots judges from the house of commons, a measure aimed at Lord Grange, who was one of the leaders of the opposition. In spite of the efforts of the opposition Islay carried the nomination of the government's list of peers, thus winning for himself the nickname of ' congé d'élire '. In the elections to the commons the opposition in Scotland took almost as big a beating, securing only eleven seats. Thus in neither England nor Scotland was Walpole seriously troubled. Attempts to impeach Islay for corrupt practices failed for lack of evidence; the opposition wilted under these disappointments and by 1738 it was despondent and barely active. Lady Murray of Stanhope summed up the situation in a letter to Marchmont: ' I think, as I did, that all your consultations will come to nothing, but Sir Robert outwit you every one '.[26] The poet Pope expressed the same thought in more satirical vein,

> Yearly defeated, yearly hopes they give,
> And all agree Sir Robert cannot live.[27]

Yet in Scotland, at least, Sir Robert's system was already being undermined by an event which could scarcely have been foreseen. In itself the Porteous Riot of 1736 in Edinburgh was a squalid affair, alarming perhaps as an indication of lawless trends in the north but apparently of little political significance. Yet its political significance was to dwarf the immediate effect of outraged shock it caused authority. The affair illustrated the prevalence of smuggling in Scotland and the popularity of the ' free traders '. Two smugglers were arrested and one of them, Robertson, escaped through the self sacrifice of the other, who grappled with the guards while they were hearing their ' hanging verses ' at kirk. The captain of the city guard of Edinburgh, ' Black Jock ' Porteous, was angered by a suggestion that military reinforcements would be needed to ensure a peaceful execution of the remaining prisoner, Wilson. After the execution had been carried out the mob threatened Porteous and his men. Porteous ordered the guard to fire and a few people were killed (the precise

[25] *Annals and Correspondence of the First and Second Earls of Stair*, ed. J. M. Graham, II. 197.

[26] *Marchmont Papers*, ed. Sir G. H. Rose, II. 96.

[27] Alexander Pope, *Poetical Works* (Globe edn., 1956), p. 504.

number is not known) and many wounded. For this slaughter Porteous was tried and condemned but secured a respite for six weeks. The mob rose in well-organised fury, forced the tolbooth and hanged Porteous, all pretty much as Sir Walter Scott has described it in his masterly novel *The Heart of Midlothian*.

The government was furious at this savage act and the contempt for authority that it denoted. Westminster wrongly concluded that the murder of Porteous could not have been committed without the connivance of the civic authorities. A lords' bill, therefore, proposed heavy punishment for Edinburgh and its magistrates. As well, the Nether Bow port was to be demolished, so making it easier for troops to enter the city should a similar outbreak occur in the future. Only strong opposition from the Duke of Argyll removed the more extreme measures from the bill. In the upshot, the provost was deposed and disqualified for life, and Edinburgh was fined.

The true significance of the event was that it precipitated a long-threatened quarrel between Walpole and Argyll. ' Red John of the Battles ' was greedy, corrupt, and patrician; at bottom he despised Walpole as a parvenu upstart. Argyll was too much the monarch in the west Highlands to make a good courtier in London. Islay, the suave dispenser of lavish promises and just enough patronage, stood by Walpole to the end, but from 1736 onwards his brother's allegiance was in doubt. Walpole's reluctant declaration of war on Spain in 1739 gave his numerous enemies in both England and Scotland fresh hope and no one spoke more loudly against the country's unwarlike state than Argyll. For this he was dismissed from office, and he then made common cause with those whom Walpole had discarded or offended, men like Carteret and Pulteney. In Scotland Argyll gathered round him the discontented and the unsatisfied, including the diehard remnants of the *Squadrone* and the Jacobites. In the general election of 1741 Walpole, who was never noted for his tact, learned to his cost what it was to make an enemy of the Duke of Argyll. Despite every effort made by Islay on Walpole's behalf Argyll and his allies made great inroads into the minister's position, capturing nearly half of the forty-five constituencies.[28] This result helped to seal Walpole's fate. Bubb Dodington, one of the

---

[28] *Stair Annals*, II. 273, puts the number of constituencies won by opposition at 30; but J. B. Owen, *Rise of the Pelhams*, p. 5, n. 2, reduces this to 23.

malcontents who had been helping to manage the elections in England, wrote significantly to Argyll on 18 June 1741: 'The elections are over; and our success in them has, I must confess, exceeded my most sanguine expectations. . . . Cornwall gave the first foundation for any reasonable hopes, and Scotland has brought the work to such a degree of perfection, that it would be, now, as criminal to despair of success, as it would have been, before, presumptuous to have expected it.'[29] The new parliament was hostile to Walpole, he failed to produce any victories to placate the national outcry, the ministerialists began to rat (*more scottico* Scots first), and in February 1742 the great minister was forced to resign. He was created Earl of Orford and became, as he put it with considerable false modesty, as insignificant as any man in the kingdom. No one rejoiced more at his fall than the Jacobites. To them he had been a scourge, not so much because of his advocacy of stern punishments for treasonable acts as because of the strength and sanity of his policies. Walpole created a political and commercial system which reduced ' the king over the water ' to sentimental fantasy; but, in areas remote from the great counting-houses of the united kingdom, devotion to the Stewarts was still something more substantial than a dream.

In parliament Walpole had left the triumphant opposition a dubious legacy. For the first time a minister who enjoyed the king's confidence had been forced to resign because of insufficient support in the house of commons. The problem for the late opposition was to win the king's approval and maintain support in the commons. Walpole's heirs proved to be of his own nomination, for his opponents divided into squabbling groups, none of which commanded more than twenty votes in the commons. Carteret, for instance, one of the leading politicians of the time, could count on only seven votes.[30] In these circumstances the representation from Scotland became important out of all proportion to its numbers. By this time it had been proved that strict management could make ' the Scotch interest ' the largest and most stable of all. Argyll had a strong hand to play but lacked the necessary skill. The king detested him; and, mindful perhaps of the ' tyranny ' of one minister who enjoyed the king's confidence, Argyll advocated a ' broad bottom ' administration

[29] W. Coxe, *Walpole*, III. 566.
[30] J. B. Owen, *The Rise of the Pelhams*, p. 77.

which would represent the main interests in parliament. He also wished to maintain himself as the undertaker in Scotland and tried to treat the new Scottish secretary, Tweeddale, as a mere tool. Foiled in both ploys, Argyll resigned. He died in 1743 and was succeeded by his brother Islay, who was better equipped for the cut and thrust of mid-eighteenth-century politics.

Islay was soon reconciled to Henry Pelham and his brother, the Duke of Newcastle, who by 1743 had, with some help from their old master Walpole, emerged as the dominant group. The lesson of 1741 was not lost on the Pelhams and, in their period of power, Scotland became a firm part of the British political structure. In 1747 they would have liked to unburden themselves of Argyll, who wanted to keep Scotland as a separate satrapy; but Argyll was stuck with the ministry and they with him, and until his death in 1761 he became an indispensable, if unloved, prop to succeeding ministries. Newcastle detested him and would have liked to dispense patronage in Scotland himself but he never dared to pick an open quarrel. Argyll was an amateur inventor of gimcracks in mathematics whose most notable invention was the tight system of management which turned the Scottish electorate into one grand ministerial preserve. Individual dissidents like the Earl of Marchmont and his lawyer brother, Alexander Hume Campbell, plotted incessantly against Argyll but to little or no purpose. The only Scot outside the Argyll faction who made his way at this time was William Murray, a brilliant lawyer, who as Lord Mansfield became a great lord chief justice of England. His career, however, was wholly English, proving (according to Dr Johnson) how much might be made of a Scotchman if he were caught young. Newcastle tried to use Mansfield as a counterpoise to Argyll, giving him in 1757 the disposal of Scottish patronage, and later Mansfield supported Lord Bute; but he never made an effective manager. Here his English background and lack of knowledge of the minutiae of electoral politics in Scotland proved to be crippling weaknesses.

By mid-century the Union had become accepted in Scotland as one of the facts of life. One reason was that it seemed finally to be conferring the long-awaited economic benefits; another was that the last stronghold of anti-Union feeling, the Jacobite movement, had been destroyed. The extinction of Jacobitism was a direct consequence of the conflict with Spain which was absorbed in the great European War of the Austrian Succession. War with Spain raised the flagging spirits of the Jacobites, who from 1719 onwards had been reduced to tedious and fruitless intrigue.[31] The exiled court was the victim of wishful thinking and of wild, sometimes dishonest, reporting from its agents. It mistook the current anti-Hanoverianism in England for Jacobite zeal, whereas it sprang really from fear of a foreign policy supposedly dictated by the needs of the Electorate. Muddle-headed Tory resentment at Whig dominance, frequently expressed in Jacobite toasts, was accepted as deathless devotion to the legitimate line; but a contemporary historian accurately described the English Jacobites. ' no people in the Universe know better the Difference between drinking and fighting '.[32] Jacobitism of a more militant type still lingered on in Wales, headed by Sir Watkin Williams Wynn, but there too the old cause was languishing. The catholic Irish were devoid of leadership and in the most cowed phase of their history; and even in Scotland Jacobitism as a fighting creed was on the wane, many Highland chiefs viewing with wary eye the slogans which had undone the men of the '15. Yet simply because each succeeding year thinned the ranks of the dedicated Jacobites, action became the more imperative. Thus on the outbreak of war in 1739 a Jacobite Association was formed and in 1741 it found an able secretary in a young Peeblesshire laird, John Murray of Broughton.[33] He acted as the main co-ordinating link between the association and the exiled court; but matters were complicated by the tall tales of another agent, MacGregor of Balhaldie, who exaggerated Jacobite strength in the Highlands and tried to foment a rising in 1743. The Scottish Jacobites took alarm, fearing, reasonably enough, that just as in 1715 the French would leave the rebels to their fate. Broughton had to go to Paris to seek assurance on this point and to give a more accurate account of probable support in Scotland. The plot then proceeded on a more realistic basis whereby the Pretender's elder son, Charles Edward, was to cross to Scotland, bringing with him 10,000 French troops and adequate supplies of arms and money. Many of the Highland chiefs then entered into a bond, undertaking to bring out their men if these conditions were met. Such an

[31] See G. H. Jones, *The Mainstream of Jacobitism*, ch. v, vi.
[32] James Ray, *A Compleat History of the Rebellion in the Year 1745* (1752), pp. 162.
[33] *Memorials of John Murray of Broughton*, ed. R. F. Bell (S.H.S.), pp. 8 ff.

expedition actually set sail early in 1744, with the troops under the command of Marshal Saxe, but it ran into violent storms and had to put about. So far, there was little fantasy in the project. If such a force had managed to land in Scotland it would almost certainly have been matched in numbers by the local Jacobites. Whether or not the Stewarts were restored, French purposes would have been served by the probability of an ensuing financial crisis in London, especially if this deprived Britain's subsidised allies of money. In this way France might easily have recovered from her defeat at Dettingen in June 1743. These were the cold matter-of-fact calculations which induced the French to support the Pretender and which contributed so much to the hysterical outburst of anti-Scottish feeling in England during and after 1745. The British defeat at Fontenoy in May of that crucial year ironically stood the Hanoverians in good stead by diverting the French from the proposed descent on Scotland.

Charles Edward refused to accept revised French policy and determined to raise a rebellion on his own initiative. He gambled on forcing France to help and lost, but none the less it would be rash to dismiss the '45 as Celtic moonshine, a mere ' romantic but mad fling for a throne '.[34] It had no such appearance in 1745, not to the government, to the rebels, to the general public nor especially perhaps to those who had to pay Jacobite cess. A makeshift army which marched and counter-marched over most of Scotland and much of England, which sometimes evaded and sometimes defeated superior government forces, which levied money and commanded purveys, can hardly be dismissed as a pointless joke. An examination of its recruitment and organisation emphasises the great social and economic cleavages that divided Britain at that period. Nowhere else in the British Isles could such a force have been assembled, for only in the Highlands of Scotland, still veiled and mysterious to the bulk of George II's subjects, were martial attributes still the very stuff of everyday life. There is nothing ' romantic ' in such a bald statement of well-attested fact. Sir Walter Scott in *Waverley*, the greatest of his novels, so far as history is concerned invented little.

Charles Edward lost patience with French equivocation and secretly fitted out a small expedition which sailed from Nantes in June 1745. He and a handful of chosen companions, Irish exiles

[34] C. G. Robertson, *England under the Hanoverians* (15th edn.), p. 98.

mainly, sailed on the *Du Teillay* which had a consort (the *Elisabeth*) carrying 700 troops and supplies. The *Elisabeth* was badly mauled by a British warship, the *Lion*, and forced to return to France, but the *Du Teillay* carried on and landed Charles and his seven companions at Eriskay in the Outer Hebrides on 23 July. The local chiefs were dismayed at the weakness of the Prince's expedition and urged him to abandon the enterprise. Charles was obstinate and finally shamed MacDonald of Kinlochmoidart, young Clanranald and Cameron younger of Lochiel into supporting a rising. Others who had pledged themselves to the cause, such as MacLeod of Dunvegan and MacDonald of Sleat, refused to join on the grounds that the agreed conditions had not been kept. As a result of the defection of these two Highland chiefs the Western Isles contributed little to the rebellion. It drew its strength from two main areas—the central and western Highlands and the north-east Lowland plain. In the main Highland area of recruitment Charles' cause was popular and there is little real evidence of ' forcing out ', although after the collapse of the rebellion this was a favourite plea. But in the north-east Lowlands the Jacobite lairds were forced to use bands of Highlanders to dragoon recalcitrant tenants into joining the Prince. Contrary to current myth, few tried to maintain a foot in both camps; and many who were prevented from joining the rebels, either through their own misgivings or the adroit diplomacy of Lord President Forbes, were at heart Jacobite. Thus, Lovat, that incorrigible old rogue, and Cluny Macpherson were at first non-committal, though Jacobite to the core. The Hanoverians, on the other hand, could rely only on Argyll and his Campbells and on the northern clans such as the Mackays and Munros.

On 19 August Charles raised the standard of his house at Glenfinnan in mainland Inverness-shire. The rebellion made a brisk beginning, the rebels winning some local skirmishes in one of which Cluny was taken and promptly showed his true colours by joining the prince. In the first few months, indeed, the Jacobites scarcely made a wrong move, whereas the government acted indecisively. But even when the remissness of the government is taken into account, the commander in Scotland, Sir John Cope, made a feeble showing. True, his force was small and ill-trained, but if properly handled it should have been able to prevent the rebels from breaking into the Lowlands. Cope should have followed the example of Argyll, who in 1715 doomed Mar's rising by maintaining a strong grip on Stirling. Instead, Cope marched into the Highlands to meet the rebels, but at the last moment he lost his nerve and sought refuge in Inverness, allowing them to slip past into the Lowlands. There the rebels rapidly exploited the situation. On 4 September they took Perth, where many rallied to their standards, including the most important single recruit in Lord George Murray, a younger brother of the Duke of Atholl. Murray was made lieutenant-general and proved to be a commander of genius, greater in many respects than either Montrose or Dundee. The Lowlands in the meantime were in a panic. A volunteer corps was formed to defend Edinburgh but its heart was not in the business; the students and burghers gladly availed themselves of the cowardly behaviour of the dragoons at Coltbridge to scurry off home at first sight of the Highlanders. The capital fell without resistance on 17 September, with most of the government officials in full flight for Berwick. On the 21st the Jacobites completed their hold on Scotland by surprising and routing Cope's army, which had been shipped from Aberdeen to Dunbar, at Gladsmuir or, as the site is better known, Prestonpans. Thereafter, Jacobite recruits poured in but mainly in the shape of late-comers from the north. South of Tay the Jacobite cause was unpopular; there the prince's famous charm made no impression on the predominantly presbyterian countryside. Few indeed, if any, presbyterians took part in the rebellion, which was supported mainly by episcopalians and Roman catholics in the proportions of 70 per cent to 30 respectively.

Secretary Tweeddale was at odds with Argyll, and neither over-exerted himself to put down the rebellion. The English ministers were mystified and, after Prestonpans, distinctly panicky. Newcastle and the lord chancellor both turned to Marchmont for information, only to be informed that 'the country [*i.e.* Scotland] had been sacrificed to party'.[35] Fortunately for the government, the rebels too were troubled by divided counsels. Charles became jealous of Lord George Murray, who had a tactless way of restraining the prince's wild optimism. After some debate, and against Lord George's better judgment, England was invaded. Crisis came after the fall of Carlisle when Charles

[35] *Marchmont Papers*, I. 131.

dismissed Lord George, only to be bluntly told by the Highland chiefs that they would not serve under anyone but Murray. Everything turned upon support from the English Jacobites but as the march south through Cumberland and Lancashire continued it became apparent that no such support was forthcoming. Dissension among the leaders called a halt to the march at Derby. Charles and his Irish favourites demanded an advance on London, which was at that point, 6 December, in the grip of panic. Lord George argued that, with Marshal Wade in the rear and General Ligonier rapidly building up a large force in the midlands, an advance would be fatal. The chiefs agreed with Lord George and on that same day, 'Black Friday', 6 December, Charles sullenly agreed to a retreat. But it was not a beaten army which withdrew into Scotland behind a skilful rear-guard conducted by Lord George, nor was it a beaten army which on 17 January scored a victory at Falkirk over Cope's successor, the brutal and incompetent Hawley. Alarmed at this new setback the government hurried the Duke of Cumberland north with reinforcements.

By the time Cumberland arrived the rebel force was deteriorating. Highland levies had a way of coming and going which cannot actually be described as deserting but which often left the army weak. Supplies, too, were running short. And so, after failing to reduce Stirling Castle, the rebels were obliged to retire into the Highlands, where they fought a series of successful skirmishes. Cumberland meanwhile cautiously edged his way up the east coast. On 16 April 1746 the two armies met on Drummossie Moor, close to the house of Forbes of Culloden. Cumberland's force was well provisioned and well equipped with artillery, whereas the Jacobites were half-starved and many who had dispersed to forage took no part in the battle. On the previous night Lord George had tried, by a desperate night march, to surprise Cumberland as Cope had been surprised; but this proved abortive. The Jacobite general knew that it was madness to engage in such a terrain, but he was overruled by Charles and his Irish favourites who hated the hills and shuddered at the prospect of a guerilla campaign such as Lord George favoured. In a letter to Charles on the day after Culloden Lord George bluntly declared that ' never was more improper ground for Highlanders than that where we fought ';[36] and later still, referring to the

[36] W. Duke, *Lord George Murray and the Forty-Five*, p. 193.

obstinacy of the Prince and his Irish favourites, he concluded, ' We were obliged to be undone for their ease '.[37] Culloden was a slaughter rather than a battle. It was a set piece of the kind familiar to eighteenth-century armies, a battle of limited ma-nœuvre settled by superior fire-power. For an hour the Jacobite line had to endure a heavy cannonade to which it could make no effective reply. When at last the clans charged it was in more ragged fashion than usual; they were held by the bayonet and enfiladed by musket fire. A general rout ensued. The bloody slaughter and ruthless pursuit that followed stemmed from many factors. The Highlanders were regarded as savages, though in truth their conduct throughout the campaign was much more civilised than that of their professional enemies. The rank and file of the Hanoverian army was drawn from the dregs of society and some of the officers were somewhat peculiar gentlemen. And in the early stages of the rebellion they had been repeatedly humiliated by these despised Scots irregulars. Reprisals, there-fore, were the order of the day, with little or no distinction made between innocent and guilty. Some ghastly atrocities were committed and Cumberland, a typical Guelf (who, as Thomas Carlyle declared, ' was beaten by everybody that tried, and never beat anything, except some starved Highland peasants '),[38] earned his nickname of ' the butcher '. He even contrived to insult Lord President Forbes and other loyal Scotsmen who had hazarded their lives and fortunes for George II. Yet far from being a ' Scotch rebellion ', as it seemed to most Englishmen, the '45 was more like a Scottish civil war, a considerable portion of Cumber-land's army itself being Scottish.

Charles fled from Culloden and, after five months of hiding in the Highlands and Islands, escaped to France, thanks to the legendary laws of hospitality of the Highlanders no less than to a romantic devotion to his house. Most of the leaders made their way to the continent, including Lord George Murray. Cluny hid for years on his estate before retiring to France. Old Lovat was taken and the testimony of the prince's secretary, Murray of Broughton, who turned king's evidence, helped to bring him to the block at last. With him suffered the Lords Balmerino and Kilmarnock, Cromartie barely escaping the same doom. As well

[37] Donald Nicholas, *The Young Adventurer*, p. 113.
[38] T. Carlyle, *Miscellaneous Essays*, VII. 161.

as harsh punishments meted out to the rank and file, really effective legislation ensured that no further risings could occur in the Highlands. A rigorously enforced Disarming Act was passed, the tartan and the kilt were proscribed, and the estates of the rebels were forfeited, though this time they remained in the hands of the crown and were administered by an enlightened commission. Much more than Jacobitism died at Culloden. Thereafter the disintegration of the old Highland society, already advanced in some quarters, was accelerated. The patriarchal authority of the chiefs and great territorial magnates was gradually transformed into landlordism. The demilitarisation of Highland life broke the ties of mutual interest and idealised kinship which had bound chiefs and clansmen and paved the way for a new social relationship in which the landlords came to regard their people solely as tenants and cottars. But economic needs and some lingering remnants of the old paternalist regime postponed for half a century, and sometimes longer, the harshest consequences of this social readjustment.

The rebellion also provided the occasion for some much needed administrative and legal reforms ' for rendering the union of the two kingdoms more complete '. Tweeddale's position had become impossible and in January 1746 he resigned from his post of secretary. The office itself then lapsed, partly because of its minor stature compared with the other two secretaryships of state and partly because of the inconvenience and danger of the mystique of management attaching itself to any one office. Management, as Islay had discovered, was best served by persons rather than institutions. Earlier, on the fall of Roxburghe in 1725, Duncan Forbes had rejoiced at the deliverance from ' that nuisance, which we so long have complained of, a Scots Secretary, either at full length or in Miniature. If any one Scots man has absolute power, we are in the same Slavery as ever.'[39] The vacancy thus caused had lasted until the appointment of Tweeddale in 1742 but quite clearly that appointment was an act of expediency; and the mistrust of the office noted by Forbes, and even by Defoe as early as 1711,[40] was by no means allayed.

The opportunity was also taken to abolish the heritable jurisdictions. These were rarely wielded by the heads of clans but in

[39] *More Culloden Papers*, ed. D. Warrand, II. 322.
[40] *H.M.C.*, *Portland*, v. 44 ff.

the Highlands the existence of heritable sheriffs, lords of regality and barons had helped to promote feuds and to debase the administration of justice. Heritable courts still flourished in the north, and, although they were in various stages of decay in the more progressive parts of Scotland, they were, all in all, a drag on administration. Thus in Lanarkshire there existed the heritable sheriffship of the Duchess of Hamilton, eight regalities, and two baronies; and in addition four commissary courts and the magistracies of Lanark and Hamilton.[41] The result was administrative chaos, exacerbated by the ignorance and the sinister interests of the heritable sheriffs. The last hereditary sheriff of Galloway, for instance, had a short way with lawyers and their involved pleas, calling them ' schoondrels ! blethering loons '.[42] Reform here was clearly long overdue, something along the lines which James VII had envisaged but which had been averted first by the Revolution and then by the Union. The time had now come for this particular conflict between private right and public good to be resolved. But the Edinburgh lawyers and politicians did not favour the bill and did their best to sabotage it. Many of the Scots peers protested bitterly against a further encroachment on their rights and put forward preposterous claims for compensation. Argyll opposed the measure, partly because he himself would be stripped of considerable powers but also perhaps, as Hume Campbell hinted, because of the electoral influence that lurked in these private jurisdictions. According to Hume Campbell, ' an heritable sheriffship in a Lord or even a commoner is too great an influence for other freeholders to contest with '.[43] Much of the opposition to the bill in the commons was purely factious and designed to injure the Pelhams, but finally the measure was carried as the Heritable Jurisdictions (Scotland) Act of 1747. All heritable jurisdictions, excepting only that of high constable, were abolished and compensation was to be paid to the holders. Their records were to be handed over to the sheriff courts, which, along with the supreme courts, were reorganised and strengthened to deal with an increased volume of work. Only the baron retained some modicum of his rights: he could still convene his

---

[41] *The Minutes of the Justices of the Peace of Lanarkshire, 1707–1723*, ed. C. A. Malcolm, (S.H.S.), intro. pp. xxix-xxx.
[42] Sir A. Agnew, *Hereditary Sheriffs of Galloway*, II. 263.
[43] *H.M.C., Polwarth*, v. 238.

court but was deprived of jurisdiction in capital cases; and he could try criminal cases only where the penalty might not exceed a fine of 20s. and civil where the sum involved did not exceed 40s. If these had been the only powers left to the barons, their courts would have withered away much earlier than they did. But Lord President Forbes argued that the barons must be allowed diligence (legal procedure to enforce payment) to collect their rents; this was conceded in the act, and probably provided the bulk of the business in the baron courts thereafter. The jurisdiction of the barons has never been abolished but at varying dates in different parts of the country this last remnant of feudal administration succumbed to economic progress and a new social structure. Most had ceased to function by the end of the eighteenth century and those that survived beyond that time did so in the backward Highlands and Islands.

An equally important measure was the Tenures Abolition Act of 1746 which abolished military tenures by converting them into either blench or feu holdings. If lands were held ward of the crown they were converted into blench (at a nominal rent of one penny Scots ' si petatur tantum '), and if held ward of subjects superior they were converted into feus. The conditions of feu were redefined and many of the oppressive and arbitrary exactions abolished: thus, fines for nonentry were standardised at a reduced rate and tacksmen were freed from all services not specified in the tack, saving only thirlage. In its day this was a notable reform, but it may now be regretted that the opportunity was not taken to make a St Bartholomew of feudalism in Scotland along the lines foreshadowed by Cromwell.

None the less, administration as a whole benefited from these reforms. The abolition of the heritable jurisdictions not only extended the scope and improved the efficiency of the sheriff courts but also rendered easier the work of the justices of the peace and the commissioners of supply. The J.P.s have had a chequered career in Scotland and it was not until after the Union of 1707 that they received powers adequate to their supposed functions. An act of 1661 governed the justices for more than a century but it was really the consequences of the Union which gradually conferred on Scots J.P.s some of the powers enjoyed by their English counterparts. The landmarks here were the abolition of the privy council in 1708 and of the heritable jurisdictions in 1747. The loss of the privy council weighed heavily on the J.P.s, who were expected to operate something like a national police system, but the continued existence of the heritable jurisdictions hampered the justices at every turn. Still, in the period immediately following the Union the J.P.s became an accepted and more important part of the administration. They supervised the revenue, adjudicated between masters and servants (usually in favour of the masters) and settled wages, all in addition to their statutory duty to maintain roads, bridges and ferries. In maintaining communications they failed, partly because of the defects of statute labour or commutation and partly because of ignorance of the science of road-making. Indeed, the poor state of most roads in Scotland showed the limited potency of legislation, however enlightened, just as the constancy of human frailty was demonstrated by the royal proclamation which the J.P.s until 1832 annually urged upon the public: ' For the encouragement of piety and virtue and for the preventing and punishing vice, profaneness and immorality '.[44]   Here kirk and state inveighed with one voice against the citadel of Satan; but all too clearly ' auld Nickie-ben ' had the last laugh.

The commissioners of supply for each shire had existed from 1667 when cess based on actual valuation of land was first sanctioned by a royalist regime. The primary task of the commissioners was to settle the value of estates and see to the collection of the cess. This mainstay of public finance was profoundly affected by the Union and not altogether for good. It was treated like the English land-tax but did not have the same effective machinery with which to work. Strict statutory regulation was needed after 1707 but was not provided, and those responsible for the tax found themselves hampered by lack of ' diligence '. The tax fell into drastic arrears but the receiver general for Scotland had insufficient power to force payment, and the reconstituted Scottish court of exchequer ' for the most part . . . pursued a course of inglorious inefficiency '.[45]   Such a clumsy device as the quartering of troops was used but proved more troublesome than effective. The law's uncertainty exposed the troops to legal actions as well as to the wrath of irritated citizens, and by about

[44] *Minutes of the Justices of the Peace for Lanarkshire, 1707-1723*, pp. liv-lvi.
[45] W. R. Ward, *The Land Tax in Scotland, 1707-1798* (reprint from *Bulletin of John Rylands Library*, Sept. 1954), p. 289.

1750 soldiers ceased to be so employed. The receiver general persuaded the barons of exchequer to grant hornings against those who failed to pay cess, but even this move was not proof against the ingenuity of Scots lawyers. The burghs also formed a weak part of the system. The royal burghs were supposed to bear one-sixth of the cess in return for their monopoly of trade, but in a tax based upon property how could one fit in estimates founded on trade? Efforts were made to have the royal burghs assessed on property alone, and a compromise was reached in 1714 whereby three-quarters of the quota was to be so raised and the remainder on trade. Thus, in spite of efforts at reform the fiscal system remained inefficient and actually reached its nadir in the last two decades of the century. This unsatisfactory state of affairs was due to several impediments—to legal defects in the machinery, inadequate staff, and, perhaps most of all, to geographical obstacles. Difficulty of communications is a factor that must always be borne in mind when criticising administration in Scotland.

Yet in spite of their bad financial record the commissioners, who were individually named in the Supply Act, became important elements in local government. In addition to their primary function of levying cess, task after task was heaped upon their willing shoulders. They supplemented the work of the J.P.s on roads and bridges; they helped to see to the provision of schools; they levied ' rogue money ' (usually at 10s. in the £100 Scots of valuation) to maintain jails and bring malefactors to justice. All in all, they came to act as an embryo county council, responsible under their convener for the general business of the shire rather than the administration of its individual parishes. Unfortunately, their efficiency was sometimes impaired by the general rage for politics, and often when a county was seriously divided over its representation in parliament the commissioners took sides and acted corruptly in making valuations in order to create fictitious votes. There is particularly strong evidence of this in the general election of 1768, when numerous processes in the court of session revealed a sorry tale of corruption and maladministration in the shires of Cromarty and Forfar.[46] It is a reminder that the supposed benefits of a corrupt political system are in fact illusory. A diseased electoral system (*pace* all the special pleading about

---

[46] See W. Ferguson, *Electoral Law and Procedure in Eighteenth and Early Nineteenth Century Scotland* (unpublished Glasgow Ph.D. thesis), pp. 59-66.

opening careers to talents, as in the rather exceptional case of Edmund Burke) had a rotting effect on the body politic, and this effect was most evident in administration.

In a limited way much the same criticism must be applied to the court of exchequer, which was supposed to be one of the main co-ordinators of administration after 1707. The court was reconstituted by act of parliament in 1708, retaining some of its old powers but hampered by the adoption of English forms and procedures.[47] The flexibility which had characterised the pre-Union exchequer was lost, and undue respect for alien forms led too often to administrative impotence. That the reconstituted court was from the beginning hybrid in spirit was reflected in its composition. Before 1707 the exchequer was run by a commission whose number was fixed by the crown: there was no sacrosanct tradition which could not be amended or even scrapped. But in 1708 a rigid establishment was set up consisting of one chief baron and four ordinary barons; and their powers as well as their titles were English. In theory the lord high treasurer of Great Britain was first judge in the court, but in practice this right devolved upon the chief baron, of whom the first to be appointed was Seafield. He, however, was soon edged out to make way for an experienced Englishman, James Smith. The most diligent and influential of the early barons was another Englishman, John Scrope, who was a first-rate administrator. It thus became the rule that the judges of the court of exchequer were a mixture of English and Scots, usually with an Englishman as chief baron. There were sound practical reasons for this, as Sir John Clerk of Penicuik, one of the original Scottish barons, explained: ' we were all sensible that to qualify us for being Barons in Scotland we behoved to understand both the Scotch and English Laws, but as this was not to be expected, we did the best we cou'd to learn from one another '.[48]

The exchequer's main purpose was to receive the rents and other feudal renders due to the king, to supervise the sheriffs' accounts, the land tax, and revenue in general. Feudal law, however, was the special preserve of the court of session, which regarded the exchequer as an anglicised upstart, and the jealousy

[47] Sir John Clerk and Mr Baron Scrope, *Historical View of the Forms and Powers of the Court of Exchequer in Scotland* (1820).
[48] *Memoirs of Sir John Clerk of Penicuik, 1676–1755*, ed. J. M. Gray (S.H.S.), p. 71.

thus engendered considerably impeded the work of the exchequer. The judges of the court of session sometimes took a malicious pleasure in deploying their superior knowledge of Scots law to the discomfiture of the barons. Thus, for example, it was found competent to raise an interdict in the court of session on the grant of a deed in exchequer. The exchequer, too, did not escape from the curse of eighteenth-century administration—political wire-pulling and the conversion of offices into sinecures. When Lord Chief Baron Smith died in 1728, one of the barons, Matthew Lant, was promoted through political influence and promptly became an absentee, seldom appearing for more than a few weeks in the year. Lant, in turn, was succeeded in 1741 by another English baron, John Idle, who, while he apparently did not altogether live up to his name, worked to little purpose. Not surprisingly, the exchequer was frequently taken to task by the lord high treasurer but it usually managed to clear itself by casting the blame on other parts of the administration.

A chronic complaint was of the defects of customs and excise. Then indeed ' no crime was so respectable as " fair trading "; none was so widely spread '.[49] Smuggling was accepted by high and low alike and even connived at by judges, not *ex officio* but in their private capacities. Thus, Lord President Forbes frequently deplored the poor state of the revenue and urged the boards of customs and excise to greater efforts; he warmly supported the Excise Bill of 1733; and in a debate in the house of commons in 1735 on the question of increasing the armed forces Forbes supported the motion because ' there was a great need of armed force in Scotland, without which the notorious inclination there to smuggling and cheating the revenue, and to mutiny, and to resist the execution of legal process could not be quelled '.[50] All this was patently true, as the Porteous affair was soon to prove, and Forbes's sentiments did him credit, albeit they were reinforced by concern at so much unfair competition to his family's privilege to distil Ferintosh whisky duty-free; but almost certainly Forbes appreciatively quaffed the fine brandy and claret which Bailie Steuart of Inverness smuggled into the north country.[51] The

[49] H. G. Graham, *Social Life of Scotland in the Eighteenth Century*, p. 527.
[50] G. Menary, *Duncan Forbes*, pp. 101-2.
[51] *The Letter-Book of Bailie John Steuart of Inverness, 1715-62*, ed. W. Mackay (S.H.S.), pp. xxxiii-xxxiv.

excise service was notoriously corrupt, tide-waiters and collectors having a tariff on their remissness as well as on excisable commodities. Thus, in the 1730s William Somerville, a merchant of Renfrew, was daunting the other ' free traders ' on the west coast with vast quantities of Marseilles brandy at ten shillings the gallon. The trade of Scotland increased after the Union, observed Clerk of Penicuik, but the revenue declined mainly because of the rise of smuggling. Before the Union duties were so low that contraband was not worth the risk, but after 1707 high duties led to ' the running of goods into this part of Brittain, which is a practise carried on here both by the English and us and is almost impracticable to prevent because of the convenience and multitude of our ports '.[52]   His argument was clinched by some revealing statistics: the net yield of the customs in 1715–16 was £17,767 but in 1729–30 it had fallen to a mere £6,481; [53] and this was the case in spite of vigorous efforts at reform made by Walpole. So serious was the problem that the court of exchequer could not count upon honest juries and the yield of the customs was ' scarce sufficient to defray the Charge of Management '.[54]   Not for nothing did English politicians, as they wasted their energies trying to impose new and more profitable taxes, lose patience with the conniving Scots. But as with the Malt Tax, so with the Window Tax of 1747 the administration practically gave up in despair.[55]   To paraphrase Dr Johnson, the Scots were not a taxable people.

On the whole subject of law and administration Lockhart of Carnwath vaunted, with considerable exaggeration but some justification, Scotland's ' happy Constitution of Government, well digested Laws, and regular Courts and Forms of Justice '.[56]   The happy constitution was a fledgling, but apropos of the law as a system of jurisprudence he was not so wide of the mark. By 1707 Scots law had pretty well assumed its characteristic shape and

[52] Clerk of Penicuik Muniments (Reg. Ho.), Box 113, MS. 2703, ' General Observations on the two Branches of the Revenues of Scotland the Customs and Excise '.

[53] *Ibid.*, Box 113, MS. 2760, ' Abstract of the General Account of the Customs in Scotland from Michaelmas 1715 to Michaelmas 1731 '.

[54] *Ibid.*, Box 119, MS. 3141, ' Dissertation by Sir John Clerk on events which led to the union '.

[55] *Memoirs of Sir John Clerk of Penicuik*, ed. Gray, pp. 206-7.

[56] George Lockhart, *Memoirs* (edn. 1714), p. 389.

the main courts had their established procedures and traditions,[57] facts which were acknowledged in the Treaty of Union. At various epochs the law of Scotland had been dominated by different influences, each one of which made important contributions; for Scots legalists were great borrowers rather than originators and increasingly they drew upon Roman law, initially through the canon law but in the sixteenth and seventeenth centuries from the civil law itself. In the seventeenth century, statutes and the work of the great institutional writers, Viscount Stair and Sir George Mackenzie of Rosehaugh, completed the process. By 1707 the law of Scotland was a distinct entity, neither Roman nor English but displaying many of the best features of these two great seminal systems. It used Roman principles freely in harmonising its various parts, and one useful consequence of this was the fusion of law and equity: in Scotland there was no need for separate equity courts to testify to the failure of common law. The Scots were not so bound by rigid forms, mainly because they displayed little veneration for antiquity. Their great concern was with function, and each generation of lawyers willingly scrapped the unserviceable parts of its inheritance. As a result, ' there is an agreeable lack of dead wood in almost every branch of the law '.[58]

In 1707 the law of Scotland was distinguished by its consistency and simplicity, reducible, as by Mackenzie,[59] to one slender and remarkably lucid volume. The land law was strongly feudal in conception, characterised by a remarkable precision and fortified by a sound system of registration of which the main pillar was the register of sasines. The law of property was complicated, dominated mainly by Roman principles. The law regulating personal relations—such as husband and wife, or parent and child—was permeated by canonist ideas. Provision for dependents was adequate and fair, and in Scots law it was not possible for the father, however irate, to cast aside the erring son with the proverbial English shilling. In the case of bastardy the law was enlightened for its times: legitimation by subsequent

[57] On Scots law and its development consult *An Introduction to Scottish Legal History* (Stair Society, 1958); W. M. Gloag and R. C. Henderson, *Introduction to the Law of Scotland*; and an excellent brief conspectus by A. Dewar Gibb, *Preface to Scots Law* (3rd edn., 1961).

[58] A. D. Gibb, art. ' Scots Law ', in *Chambers's Encyclopaedia* (edn. 1955), XII. 311.

[59] Sir George Mackenzie, *Institutions of the Law of Scotland* (1684).

marriage had long been accepted. The so-called 'irregular marriage' had a good grounding in canon law; and after the Reformation marriages could be dissolved by divorce without the need of a special act of parliament. Towards debtors, too, the law of Scotland was kinder than was its English counterpart. Imprisonment was not the automatic fate of the debtor as it tended to be in England. Diligence was strictly defined—that is, legal seizure of goods of a defaulter culminating in 'cessio bonorum'. Though eighteenth- and nineteenth-century English common lawyers showed marked contempt for this supposedly barbarous legal system, any list of the enlightened features of the law of Scotland would be a long and creditable one, as generations of reform-minded English lawyers have since handsomely acknowledged by the sincerest form of flattery. The weakest part of the Scottish civil system in 1707 was mercantile law, due largely to the relative economic backwardness of the country. The mercantile law was really built up in the eighteenth century and freely availed itself of English practice, although contract retained some specifically Scottish features. But, as has been well said: 'The mercantile law of Scotland, as of other lands, tends to be cosmopolitan'.[60]

The supreme civil court in Scotland, guaranteed as such by the Treaty of Union, was the court of session. By article xix of the Union no Scottish cases were to be cognoscible in English courts, and 'the auld fifteen', as the judges of the court of session were jocularly called, continued through their acts of sederunt to regulate the court and its procedures. A prominent feature of the court was its stubborn adherence to principle in reaching decisions and its dislike of binding precedents; but by the end of the eighteenth century it was paying increasing deference to the stultifying English doctrine of *stare decisis*, whereby the judge became little more than a walking index of decisions. The process of anglicisation was aided by the appellate jurisdiction of the house of lords, first exercised in 1708, though without any express warrant of the Treaty of Union. The exercise of this assumed jurisdiction during the eighteenth century forms one of the most lamentable chapters in the history of Scots law. Significantly, the library of the house of lords did not at this period contain so much as a line of Justinian;[61] and, not surprisingly,

[60] A. Dewar Gibb, *A Preface to Scots Law* (3rd edn., 1961), p. 113.

[61] A. Dewar Gibb, *Law from over the Border, a short account of a strange jurisdiction*, p. 15, citing P. C. Yorke, *Life of Lord Chancellor Hardwicke*, ii. 481.

sound decisions from Edinburgh were overturned by their learned lordships at Westminster in an atmosphere compounded of ignorance and levity. Of the various English influences to which the law of Scotland has been subjected in the post-Union period, the most pernicious was that of the house of lords, worse by far than the influence of statute or the anglicising trends of the late eighteenth- and early nineteenth-century institutional writers, Hume and Bell. The law officers of the crown for Scotland usually saw to it that legislation did not seriously clash with Scots law, and the institutionalists at least clung to the idea of codification which had been the dream of Scots jurists in the 'golden age' of the seventeenth century.

Thus the laws were, as Lockhart claimed, well digested; but there was one glaring exception. For some obscure reason the criminal law of Scotland has never been as well defined or enlightened as the civil law.[62] Unlike the law of England it showed scant regard for the liberties of the subject. *Habeas corpus*, or any equivalent procedure, was unknown in Scotland (and so remains to this day), and an act of 1701 against wrongous imprisonment was so qualified as to be almost worthless. Torture was commonly used to obtain information until the Revolution and even thereafter its use was not absolutely prohibited, although the case of the Jacobite plotter Neville Paine reflects more discredit on King William than on the reluctant legal authorities in Edinburgh. This harsh authoritarianism was stimulated by Roman law, in which the safety of the state came first and the rights of the individual a poor second. Moreover, the supreme criminal court, the high court of justiciary, which was created in 1672, was arbitrary in its procedures and sometimes savage in its punishments. Juries were virtually hand-picked by the judges, and even after 1707 social undesirables were transported often with scant regard to either law or justice.[63] The saddest and most frequent crime encountered in the records of the justiciary court, the Books of Adjournal, stemmed from religious fanaticism. This was concealment of pregnancy culminating in infanticide. In 1690 a statute made this offence capital; but, far from deterring, it had

[62] For a general treatment, see Sir J. H. A. Macdonald, *The Criminal Law of Scotland* (5th edn., 1948).
[63] For instances, see R. Chambers, *Domestic Annals of Scotland*, III. 115-16.

no other effect than to butcher demented females. On this whole subject there is much sound law, history and humane sentiment in Scott's account of the trial of poor Effie Deans. Another black spot, proceeding from the same source, was the continued belief in witchcraft, trials for which continued until 1727 but latterly confined to private courts. More generally, the anachronistic heritable jurisdictions probably accounted for some of the other peculiar features of the criminal law. The subject, however, has never been properly explored.

Yet the criminal law of Scotland was not without its redeeming features. The list of capital crimes was long but did not increase in the eighteenth century to the same fearsome length as in England. In Scotland, too, prosecutions were directed by the lord advocate and irksome private prosecutions were virtually unknown. And the faculty of advocates zealously upheld the tradition that no person should be tried for his life without benefit of counsel, a marked contrast to the state of affairs in England where felons were expressly denied such benefit. But, unhappily for Scotland, English influence was most marked where it was least needed—in civil causes—and took a long time to soften the harsh criminal law.

6

SOCIAL AND ECONOMIC TRENDS, 1707–1815

Historical perspective has been distorted by equating the eighteenth century with the Agrarian and Industrial Revolutions, for these terms of art have too readily supplied glib solutions for complex and long-drawn-out problems. They suggest norms where there were none; and in fact the post-Union period was marked by drifts and trends rather than by grandiose projects. This was very much the case with developments in agriculture which were essentially piece-meal and localised, conforming to no one predetermined pattern. Marginal improvements were possible within the old system, and in particular the heavy use of lime could yield startling if temporary rewards;[1] but, on the whole, such attempts in the late seventeenth and early eighteenth centuries only succeeded in defining the limitations of run-rig. One of the earliest lessons grasped by the innovators was that run-rig and sustained improvement went ill together. By the mid-eighteenth century concepts of ideal husbandry did indeed act as a general stimulus, but conditions varied so widely from region to region, and even from estate to estate, that normative development rarely proved practicable. The trends were set by differences of soil and climate, by the attitudes of lairds and tenants, by the availability of capital or credit, and by the state of communications and of markets.

The impetus to improvement was heightened after 1707 by the permanent opening of the English market to Scottish products

[1] A. Fenton, ' Skene of Hallyard's Manuscript of Husbandrie ', in *Agricultural History Review*, xi. 65-81.

and particularly black cattle.   Not surprisingly, the earliest improvements were carried out to serve the cattle trade which brought much needed currency into the country;   and these usually embraced the extension and enclosure of pastures and efforts to sow artificial grasses to eke out natural fodder.   Shortly after the Union the sixth Earl of Haddington was experimenting in this way on his Berwickshire estate, and he also anticipated the later improvers by bringing in skilled farmers from progressive districts in England.[2]   Such experiments were at first confined to the southern counties of Scotland, notably Berwickshire and Galloway, since they were best placed to avail themselves of the English market.   In Galloway Gordon of Earlstoun and Viscountess Kenmure were early enclosers, and by Whitsunday 1723 many of their neighbours had followed suit.   Small farms were swept into large units, entailing numerous evictions; and, as well as this, enclosure of parks and commons deprived the peasants of customary rights of pasture.   The more substantial of the dispossessed emigrated to America but many remained in their native land, homeless and desperate.   In 1724 two farmers refused to be evicted.   The countryside as a whole sympathised with them, including some of the lairds and parish ministers.   The evicted formed themselves into bands and aided by Billy Marshall, chief of the Galloway gipsies and a deserter from the Greys, they ranged up and down the Stewartry throwing down the hated dykes.   Some of the ' Levellers ', as they were called, published a manifesto at Kirkcudbright in which they condemned the lairds and declared for an agrarian democracy.   Their sentiments were caught in such folk-art as the following ballad, which clearly owes much to the psalmist:

> Against the poor the lairds prevail
> With all their wicked works,
> Who will enclose both hill and dale,
> And turn corn-fields to parks.
> The lords and lairds they drive us out
> From mailings where we dwell;
> The poor man cries, ' Where shall we go ? '
> The rich says, ' Go to hell! '[3]

[2] James E. Handley, *Scottish Farming in the Eighteenth Century*, pp. 145-6.
[3] Quoted in Sir Herbert Maxwell, *A History of Dumfries and Galloway* (1896), p. 304. The poem, known as ' The Levellers' Lines ', was once widely current in the south-west.   For a fuller version of it, see W. Mackenzie, *History of Galloway*, (1841), II. 395, n.

It seems clear that the Cameronian spirit was still at work, for the parish of Irongray, that old stronghold of the covenant, turned out fifty well-armed horsemen to aid the peasants, who were equipped for the most part with forks and flails. The military had to be called in, and only after a struggle were the Levellers put down. Many of them were transported; but, in spite of this, similar outbreaks occurred in Wigtownshire. Not until the 1740s were enclosures fully accepted in the south-west.

As the demand for Scotch beef grew, however, improvements aimed at increasing supply became more widespread. The trade in cattle, indeed, came to be one of the staples of eighteenth-century Scotland, and not the least part of its importance was the prominent role which the Highlands played in it. All over the Highlands and Islands cattle were reared, most of them to be driven south to the great trysts at Crieff or Falkirk, and then many of them south again to the lush pastures of south-east England and ultimately the slaughterhouses of Smithfield. From the fine pastures of Islay alone, it was estimated in 1772 that some 1,700 animals were exported annually. The extensive use of shielings or hill pastures[4] enabled most parts of the Highlands to contribute their quota, and by the close of the century the greater part of the 100,000 beasts driven annually into England were reared in the north. This sustained demand was due mainly to the growth of London and the requirements of the army and navy. When the trade was at its height during the Revolutionary and Napoleonic Wars prices sometimes rose as high as £18 to £28 per head.[5] But even before the collapse of the market in 1815 the rearing of cattle in the Highlands was being seriously challenged by sheep. The clamour for wool in England about the middle of the century led to the gradual introduction of large flocks into the Highlands, and from about 1759 onwards Linton sheep were displacing cattle and Lowland farmers displacing Highlanders in parts of the north. Their progress was slow but steady, and by the end of the century sheep predominated in much of Perthshire and Argyll. Largely at the instance of Sir John Sinclair, the Cheviot breed was introduced and from the close of the eighteenth century this aggravated an already serious

---

[4] Victor Gaffney, ' Summer Shealings ', in *S.H.R.*, xxxviii. 20–35.
[5] For a full account of the cattle trade, see A. R. B. Haldane, *The Drove Roads of Scotland*.

social problem in the Highlands. Here and there population was already declining; but the massive Clearances which shattered the old social framework and initiated the process of depopulation in the area as a whole took place mainly in the very different milieu of the early and middle nineteenth century.

The pioneer work in tillage was carried out in the Lothians, notably by John Cockburn of Ormiston in East Lothian. Building on the foundations laid by his father, Adam Cockburn, the lord justice-clerk, and applying the lessons which he gained while he was M.P. for his county from 1707 to 1741, Cockburn transformed his estate. He abolished run-rig, laid out his land in compact farms and granted carefully selected tenants long leases which itemised a strict schedule of improvements that had to be maintained: fields had to be enclosed, drained, marled or limed, and a specified rotation of crops followed. Not content with this, he rebuilt the village of Ormiston and spent considerable sums to improve the local economy. An enthusiast rather than an entrepreneur, Cockburn over-extended himself and in 1748 he had to sell his estate. An equally enthusiastic, but more cautious and successful improver, was Sir John Clerk of Penicuik in Midlothian. Clerk, a baron of exchequer, felt himself conscience bound to lay out the money he drew from his official salary in improving his lands and providing work. About 1730 he forced his ' Tennants at Pennicuik to divide their Lands, for till now all of them were in Run-Rig. This I found a very difficult matter, for that few Tenants cou'd be induced to alter their bad methods of Agriculture.'[6] This was the experience of most of the early improving landlords, and was neatly summed up by Sir Archibald Grant of Monymusk, who declared: ' Peter the First of Russia had more trouble to conquer the barbarous habits of his subjects, than in all the other great improvements he made.'[7]

Slow and difficult though the work was, it gathered momentum. If, as has been well said, in the eighteenth century ' agriculture became a passion in Europe, as well as in England ',[8] in Scotland it became almost a mania. In 1723 a ' Society of Improvers in the Knowledge of Agriculture ' was set up in Edinburgh and this body acted as a nation-wide stimulus,

[6] *Memoirs of the Life of Sir John Clerk of Penicuik*, ed. J. M. Gray (S.H.S.), pp. 136-7.
[7] Quoted Handley, *Scottish Farming in the Eighteenth Century*, p. 161.
[8] D. George, *England in Transition*, p. 81.

investigating all sorts of problems and disseminating propaganda through its energetic secretary, Robert Maxwell of Arkland in Galloway.   Among the lairds interest in the subject quickened, catered for by a large and growing literature.   Early in the field was Mackintosh of Borlum, the Jacobite brigadier who whiled away the tedium of imprisonment by writing *An Essay on Ways and Means for Inclosing, Fallowing, Planting etc.*, which was published in 1729.   By the middle of the century agriculture had become an intellectual passion with many Scots lairds and was even beginning to engage the interest of the more substantial tenants.   Two treatises which greatly helped to mould opinion were those of Adam Dickson and of Lord Kames, the judge.[9]   Yet of the actual *work* of improvement only a bare beginning had been made and progress was not really rapid or widespread until after 1760. Partly this was due to the inertia of many of the lairds, partly to their lack of capital, and partly to the strict entails which fettered so much of their land.   In 1770 lord advocate Montgomery's Act, ' to encourage the Improvement of Lands in Scotland held under Settlement of strict Entail ', enabled proprietors of such estates to grant long leases and to undertake extensive improvements while debiting to their successors part of the outlay of capital.   The rise of banking and a liberal system of credit speeded up the process of improvement, as did the accumulation of capital from commerce and professions.   Urban growth, by providing large markets, also stimulated the zeal for agrarian change.   Thus, the wealthy merchants of Glasgow were by the 1760s helping to transform the agriculture of Clydesdale, while the growth of the city exercised an influence on the whole of the agricultural south-west.   Similar effects were produced in the south-east by the increasing population of Edinburgh and the wealth of the legal profession.   Farming in East Lothian was geared up to the requirements of the metropolis, market gardening playing a prominent part.

In the last quarter of the eighteenth century agrarian improvements were being zealously pursued from the Solway to the Moray Firth, not excluding parts of the Highlands such as the straths of Perthshire.   But the extent and depth of improvement

[9] Adam Dickson, *Treatise of Agriculture* (1762–69, and 2nd edn. 1785); Henry Home, Lord Kames, *The Gentleman Farmer, being an attempt to improve agriculture by subjecting it to the test of rational principles* (1776).

must not be exaggerated. The great Statistical Account of Scotland, parish by parish (compiled in the 1790s), reveals that the process in Lowland Scotland was far from complete. Some parishes were still lurching on in all their old torpor while contiguous parishes were fashioning new economies. Even where improvements were well advanced much remained to be done. The old ridges long persisted, partly as an aid to drainage, and in most areas they were only gradually levelled out in the early nineteenth century. In the eighteenth century drainage was superficial and not always very effective, and much land could not properly be utilised until after the introduction of tile drainage in the 1820s. Thereafter ridge cultivation gradually went out of fashion.[10] Implements had also improved but in many areas there was a time-lag between the invention of, say, Small's swing plough and its extensive use.

By 1815 Lowland agriculture in all its variety had been transformed, the booming war years promoting yet one more burst of energy. A new class of farmers had emerged, men who were prepared to accept agriculture as a science and a farm as a business venture. Various agencies encouraged the growth of this professional outlook. The old Society of Improvers seems to have died out in 1745; but in 1784 the Highland Society was formed at Edinburgh and as the Highland and Agricultural it exerted an incalculable, and permanent, influence on Scottish farming, though its first show was not held until 1822. Edinburgh, too, both as city and university did much to encourage scientific agriculture. Modern chemistry had from the beginning strong connections with the soil; and at Edinburgh such notable scientists as Cullen, Black, and Francis Home helped to spread knowledge of agricultural chemistry. The science of botany was also making some contributions, especially with the discovery of the elements of plant physiology on which Kames took care to secure expert counsel.[11] Matters were sufficiently well advanced in 1790 to justify Sir William Pulteney endowing a chair of agriculture, and shortly thereafter William Dick established a veterinary college in Edinburgh which as the ' Dick Vet.' won considerable fame. The fearsome energy of Sir John Sinclair of Ulbster in Caithness also helped to change the agrarian economy of

---

[10] A. Birnie, ' Ridge Cultivation in Scotland ', in *S.H.R.*, xxiv. 194-201.
[11] Nan and Archibald Clow, *The Chemical Revolution*, ch. xxi.

Scotland; he was influential as editor of the first Statistical Account and as president of the board of agriculture, which his pertinacity caused to be set up in 1793. The dramatic rise in the total rental of Scotland is the most revealing commentary on all this activity. In 1783 it was estimated at about £1½ m., by 1795 it had risen to £2 m., and by 1815 it had reached £5½ m.[12] Doubtless part of this increase was attributable to inflation, but most of it was due to improvement.

By 1815 the distinction between infield and outfield, which was still valid in many parts in the 1790s, was obliterated in Lowland Scotland. In 1814 no less than 140,000 acres were sown with wheat, and, with the price standing at 126s. the quarter, even marginal land was used for grain cultivation. The most productive tillage area was East Lothian, which was favoured by nature with a light soil and a fairly sheltered position. By 1815 it was a region of large farms, ranging from 200 to 500 acres, all neatly laid out; and the steam engine was actually being put to more effective use in these grain factories than in almost any other Scottish industry of that time. East Lothian was an exhibition of skilled farming which drew experts from two continents. The English agricultural writer Curwen rhapsodised over its excellence of soil and management, which ' exceeded anything he had ever witnessed in any part of Great Britain '.[13] Wherever conditions were favourable high-farming of the Lothian type was followed—most notably in parts of the Borders, the Howe o' the Mearns, and the Laigh o' Moray. Elsewhere ' mixed farming ' was the rule, combining grain and pasture in varying proportions, the particular balance struck giving a district its character. Thus in the moist climate and green pastures of the south-west dairy farming prospered, particularly in Lower Clydesdale and North Ayrshire which, in order to meet the growing demands of Glasgow, specialised in the production of milk, butter, and cheese. Needless to say, the quality of all these commodities had improved enormously: butter and hair was no longer a Scotch delicacy. North of the Forth, apart from a few exceptional areas, the degree of improvement was markedly less than in the south, since the heavy

[12] J. E. Handley, *The Agricultural Revolution in Scotland*, pp. 170, 242. A reasonable estimate for earlier periods is not practicable because of the composite nature of rents and inadequate information on the various localities. For the first time the Statistical Account made such information available.

[13] Quoted in J. E. Handley, *Scottish Farming in the Eighteenth Century*, pp. 286-7.

soils could not be effectively drained until better methods were introduced in the nineteenth century.   But already Aberdeen-shire and the low country of the north-east were evolving superior strains of beef stock, and in the Borders, as well as in many parts of the north, sheep-runs were efficiently and profitably conducted.

The social effects of these changes are difficult to summarise, mainly because of wide local variations.   Thus in Berwickshire they seem to have led to an increase in population, whereas in East Lothian they tended to cause depopulation.   So much was this the case that by 1800 the high farmers of East Lothian had to rely upon migratory harvesters, drawn at first from the High-lands and latterly from Ireland.   On the whole (apart from the isolated incident of the Galloway Levellers) the breakdown of the old social order in Lowland Scotland does not seem to have caused great hardship.   Partly this was due to the slow and irregular pace at which the changes were effected, and partly it was because those displaced from the land were readily absorbed by the rise of industries, with the consequent formation of villages and the growth of the towns.   And so in Lowland Scotland the term ' agrarian revolution ' touches no chords in the folk-memory. There is no vestige in Burns' works of the ' Deserted Village ' theme, or of the bitter lamentations that later anathematised the Highland Clearances.   The simple truth seems to be that the benefits of agrarian improvement were shared by all classes of Lowland society.   The landlords' increased rents led to the build-ing of gracious new mansions, designed in many cases by the famous Robert Adam himself.   A prodigious number of trees were planted for reasons partly utilitarian and partly aesthetic. Grant of Monymusk is said to have planted 50 million trees, and most improvers did indeed plant by the million.   Interest in gardening, which had been increasing ever since the Restoration, reached its peak in the late eighteenth century.   The lairds were keen to beautify their policies;[14] and thus encouraged, the Scots gardener (personified by Scott's canny Andrew Fairservice) [15] won international repute.   Musselburgh and other parts of the Lothians became famous for horticulture; cottage gardening

[14] Cf. *Letters of John Cockburn of Ormiston to his Gardener, 1727–1743*, ed. James Colville (S.H.S., 1904) ; E. H. M. Cox, *History of Gardening in Scotland*, pp. 98-9.
[15] Scott, *Rob Roy*; A. Carlyle, *Autobiography*, p. 362, noted the prevalence of Scots gardeners in England.

became generally more popular, and the range of vegetables and flowers increased. The weavers of Paisley were noted for their passion for flowers, and excelled in growing pinks and carnations, selling their plants as far afield as London.[16]

The new style farmers were no longer content with the hovels which their predecessors had shared with their beasts. Substantial stone houses and byres replaced the ' auld clay biggin ', to which no false sentiment was then attached. The cottages of farm and estate workers also underwent a modest transformation. In spite of spiralling prices the real wages of agricultural labourers increased over the period; their diet was better, famine was unknown and, but for the bad war year of 1799, by the end of the century all but unthinkable. Better living conditions led to marked improvement in health and vigour. Little wonder, then, that Sir John Sinclair and his team of reporters could adopt such smug airs and foresee an even brighter future. If the statistics that they handled with such loving care had applied to the whole of Scotland their optimism would have been more than justified; but, as they well knew, north and west of the Highland Line a very different state of affairs existed.

To some extent this reflected a growing population problem. In the eighteenth century population increased generally, but in the Lowlands this posed few serious difficulties. The demographic structure is hard to reconstruct mainly because of inadequate data, though Scotland can stake a fair claim to have produced the first reasonably accurate enumeration of population. This was the work of the Reverend Alexander Webster, minister of the Tolbooth church in Edinburgh and a curious character who managed to be one of the leading lights among the High-Fliers or Evangelicals and at the same time a noted bon-vivant, known from his deep potations as ' Dr Bonum Magnum '. Aided by the mathematical genius of the reverend Dr Robert Wallace, minister of West St Giles, Edinburgh, he was mainly instrumental in persuading the general assembly of 1743 to accept an annuity Fund for the Widows and Orphans of the Ministers of the Church of Scotland, a scheme which helped to make actuarial history. Wallace was interested in population and published in 1753 *A Dissertation on the Number of Mankind in Ancient and Modern Times* in which he

[16] For horticulture generally, see E. H. M. Cox, *loc. cit.*; and J. A. Symon, *Scottish Farming, Past and Present*, ch. XXVI.

anticipated many of the arguments later used by Malthus. He also criticised as being too high the latest estimate of Scotland's population, which put it at 1,500,000. Webster's *Account of the Number of People in Scotland*,[17] which was completed in 1755, reckoned the total population to be 1,265,380. In spite of his workmanlike methods it is safer to regard it as an account rather than a census, since the returns which Webster received from his main sources of information, the Scottish Society for Propagating Christian Knowledge and the parish ministers of the established church, were by no means uniformly precise or exhaustive. He may, therefore, in many instances have used a calculus of his own devising;[18] but, give or take a little, his final result was probably not far out.

A recent breakdown of Webster's findings into regions is of great interest:[19] 51% lived north of Tay, 37% in the midland belt and parts of the south-west, and 11% in the Borders and Galloway. But Mr Kyd's division into *Highland, Central*, and *Lowland* areas must be cautiously interpreted, since about half of the population he assigns to his Highland section belonged to the traditional Lowlands. Even so, it is clear that a fair proportion of the total population (something of the order of 30%) can safely be assigned to the Gaelic-speaking Highlands and Islands. Throughout the eighteenth century the rate of increase was maintained, and this was particularly true of the Hebrides and the west coast, where in some areas, notably in the Uists, population doubled in the period 1755 to 1811. In the north and west Highlands, increasing numbers threatened to thrust 'the whole economy on to the Malthusian margins'.[20] This 'population explosion', encouraged by widespread potato cultivation, was one of the basic features of the intractable Highland problem of the late eighteenth and early nineteenth centuries.

Highland society was conservative but far from uniform or static. Even before the shock of the unsuccessful rebellion of 1745 and the government policy of 'thorough' that followed it, the old social and economic order was decaying in some parts of the

---

[17] J. G. Kyd, ed., *Scottish Population Statistics including Webster's Analysis of Population, 1755* (S.H.S.).

[18] For the formula which Webster may have used, see D. J. Withrington, 'The S.P.C.K. and Highland Schools in Mid-Eighteenth Century', in *S.H.R.*, XLI. 90-1, n. 5.

[19] Kyd, *op. cit.*, p. xviii.   [20] Malcolm Gray, *The Highland Economy*, p. 60.

Highlands. The second Duke of Argyll had already employed Duncan Forbes to enquire into conditions on his lands in Mull and Tiree; in 1737 Forbes reported that the agricultural methods used were wasteful and that the tacksmen exercised a pernicious influence, oppressing the sub-tenants with onerous duties and resisting all attempts at improvement. The remedy suggested by Forbes, and accepted by the duke, was to remove the tacksmen and to grant the sub-tenants leases in which rents and services were carefully specified.[21] The house of Argyll maintained and extended this policy: the Campbells led the way in abolishing run-rig and in commuting labour services for small money payments.[22] Another innovator was Daniel Campbell of Shawfield who, with the inflated compensation wrung from Glasgow in 1725,[23] purchased Islay. He and his successors virtually revolutionised its agriculture: by the 1780s the island was exporting 5,000 bolls of meal instead of as hitherto having to import annually some 3,000 bolls.[24] Clearly, the decline of clanship after 1746 gave a great impetus to such movements, leading particularly to the slow elimination of the old style tacksmen. The chiefs and great landowners conformed to new standards of social prestige, based not upon fencible men but on money and the conspicuous consumption that money alone could provide. But it is important to note that, even so, many Highland landlords in this period were loth to reduce the number of their tenants and dependents. This was due partly to sentiment and partly to the dictates of current economic theory, for if industries were to be introduced to the Highlands then a plentiful source of cheap labour was deemed necessary. Indeed, so far from enforcing or even encouraging emigration, whether to America or the Lowlands, many Highland landlords in the eighteenth century opposed it. The essential point is that in the period between 1750 and 1815 there was a good deal of muddled thinking which gave rise to more optimism than pessimism. Wherever the terrain permitted, a conscious plan of agrarian improvement, aimed at building viable farms and a steady displacement of the sub-tenants and their uneconomic holdings, would probably have proved to be the best solution. But this could not be squared with the passion for retaining

[21] G. Menary, *Duncan Forbes*, ch. XI.
[22] Gray, *op. cit.*, p. 67.   [23] See p. 142.
[24] H. Hamilton, *Economic History of Scotland in the Eighteenth Century*, p. 78.

population, and as a consequence genuine agricultural improvements, as against mere innovations, were restricted to a few areas on the fringe of the Highlands—to parts of Argyll, Perthshire, and the north east Highlands.

The industries that were expected to transform the economy of the Highlands failed to do so. Fishing had its advocates and numerous schemes were tried, but the Highland crofter-fisherman could not compete with the highly capitalised professional fleets from the Clyde or the north east coast; and, in any event, by far the greater part of the profits made by Highland fishers went to the landlord in extortionate rents. So, too, with the production of kelp, which was in great demand at the end of the eighteenth century. The Revolutionary and Napoleonic Wars cut off foreign supplies of barilla and ' pot-ashes ', and kelp became a main source of alkali, fetching high prices until 1815. In many coastal areas of Scotland the gathering and burning of seaweed became a profitable occupation: the estimated output for a good year was 20,000 tons selling for nearly £200,000.[25] Much of this was produced in the Highlands and Islands where peak production in 1810 yielded 7,000 tons, with the best quality selling at about £20 the ton. Regarded at first as a godsend, kelping soon exhibited some bad features. As one contemporary observer noted: ' the great body of seafaring Hebrideans are now metamorphosed into slavish kelpers ', while the rapacious landlords took an extortionate share of the profits.[26] Kelping also needed a large labour force and undoubtedly contributed to the congestion of population in the Islands; again, it had an adverse effect on peasant agriculture, both through insufficient cultivation and loss of sea-ware as manure. After 1815 the kelp industry rapidly declined, partly because of competition from Spanish barilla but mainly because the chemical industry had solved the problem of mass producing soda.[27] In a much reduced form kelping continued as a source of iodine. By 1815 the economy of the Highlands rested on a flimsy basis, and thereafter the illusions that had blinded so many to stark reality were rapidly dissipated, forcing many of the landlords to revise their views about the desirability of a teeming population and the need to curtail emigration.

[25] Sir John Sinclair, *Analysis of the Statistical Account of Scotland* (1826), Pt. II, p. 344.
[26] J. Macdonald, *General View of the Agriculture of the Hebrides* (1811), p. 140.
[27] A. and N. Clow, *The Chemical Revolution*, p. 107.

There was nothing new about Scots seeking abroad the gear denied them at home, for in relation to its resources Scotland had for centuries produced a surplus population.   In the early eighteenth century Ulster continued to siphon off some of the surplus population of south-western Scotland, especially after the Ulstermen had begun their great transatlantic migration in 1718. This rendered even more perplexing to the American colonists, and later historians, the problem of distinguishing ' Scotch-Irish ' from Scots.   The problem remains, largely because of the continued and lively interchanges in the eighteenth century between Ulster and Scotland, which arose not simply from ties of blood but also from strong church and educational connections.   Many so-called ' Scotch-Irish ' who migrated to the American colonies were natives of Scotland taking advantage of organised means of emigration which existed in Ulster earlier than in Scotland.   Even so, the Ulstermen in the North American colonies by 1776 greatly outnumbered the Scots, probably in the ratio of 150,000 to 50,000. Some of the early eighteenth century Lowland Scots emigrated as indentured servants; but in the 1770s bad years in Scotland led to organised settlement, as by the Inchinnan Company (officially known as The Scots-American Company of Farmers) in what was to become Caledonia County, Vermont.   But of the emigrant Scots most were Highlanders, though the role of the Jacobites who were transported after 1715 and 1746 has been exaggerated, for at most under a thousand actually set foot in the colonies.[28] To these could be added the unknown number ' kidnapped ' by some unscrupulous individuals in the Hebrides, notably Norman Macleod younger of Bernera who raided Skye and Harris for men to sell in the plantations,[29] and the similar nefarious activities of Aberdeen magistrates.[30]   Really heavy settlement of Highlanders began with the disbanding of Highland regiments at the end of the Seven Years' War, and their glowing accounts of colonial life provided most of the ' pull ' for their kinsmen at home.   In this way areas of settlement in North America became linked with certain parts of Scotland.   Emigrants from the Uists and Barra favoured Prince Edward Island where a colony of Roman catholic Gaels was established; other Hebrideans from Skye and the

---

[28] I. C. C. Graham, *Colonists from Scotland*, p. 45.
[29] A. Cunningham, *The Loyal Clans*, p. 464.
[30] Joseph Robertson, *The Book of Bon-Accord* (1839), pp. 86 ff.

Inner Isles settled Cape Breton; while the people from Argyll, Ross and Sutherland preferred the Carolinas. The process was speeded up by developments in the Highlands, notably by the changed status of the tacksmen. Increasingly the landlords demanded that the tacksmen should pay economic rents, but in many instances these terms were refused. The tacksmen usually managed to prevail upon their sub-tenants to remove to America, there to reproduce the old society with the tacksmen no longer middlemen but proprietors in their own right. Highland settlement, therefore, was community settlement. All that was asked of America was land in which the Gael could live as his fathers had lived.

In the period of the American Revolution such conservatism stood the Highlanders in ill stead, for most of them, unlike the Lowland settlers, supported the cause of King George. Consequently, after 1783 they formed a large proportion of the United Empire Loyalists who were resettled in Canada. When the fever of emigration again hit the Highlands in the wake of bad harvests in 1782–83, it was to Canada that the bulk of the emigrants made their way. Government set its face against the movement: again and again Henry Dundas condemned emigration, and most of the great Highland landlords agitated against it.[31] The manpower problem which confronted the army and navy during the long wars from 1793 to 1815 strengthened these attitudes, and at one point Henry Dundas even toyed with the fantastic notion of reviving the clan system in the Highlands so as to maintain a large military reserve in that area. It was partly from a similar motive that the forfeited estates had been restored in 1784 to their former proprietors or their successors.[32] But in spite of increasing wealth, the state of the economy by 1814 was parlous enough to justify the gloomy forecasts of Patrick Colquhoun who in a notable book argued that only planned emigration could prevent the formation of a large destitute population.[33] Thereafter the official attitude changed, and from being an evil to be avoided emigration came to be regarded as a positive good, to mother country and colony alike.

[31] See, *e.g.*, Helen I. Cowan, *British Emigration to British North America* (2nd edn., 1961), pp. 14, 19.
[32] H. W. Meikle, *Scotland and the French Revolution*, p. 83.
[33] Patrick Colquhoun, *Treatise on the Wealth, Power, and Resources of the British Empire* (1814).

Almost as chequered as the fortunes of agriculture in the eighteenth century were those of industry and commerce. In the years immediately following the Union, the manufactures of Scotland were hard hit by the open competition which was the necessary corollary of free trade with England. The woollen cloth trade, which had been so cosseted in the late seventeenth century, virtually collapsed, and the linen trade was too defective in its techniques to make much headway in the English and colonial markets. As it was plaintively put circa 1720, though with some exaggeration: ' There is nothing hinders Scotland from being a Trading Nation but the want of goods to export '.[34] For years the convention of royal burghs plagued the government with memorials and petitions on the crying need to improve manufactures in Scotland. Article XV of the Treaty of Union, which had promised to allocate money to stimulate the coarse wool trade of Scotland, was frequently invoked; but not until 1727 did the government implement this article. Two acts of parliament embodied most of the convention's recommendations. One act, passed in 1726, laid down strict regulations governing the production of linen, recommending the use of better flax seed and improvements in the various processes involved in manufacture, and insisting, on pain of fines, that linen should be stamped by an official stamp-master. The other act, in 1727, set up the Board of Trustees for Manufactures to disburse the money that had accumulated since 1707. The strict letter of Article XV of the Treaty of Union was not enforced, and the board was allowed to use its discretion in allocating the accrued sum of about £30,000 to help the most promising industries. The board worked on three-year plans which had to be approved by the king in council.

The first such scheme, drawn up in 1727, allocated £6,000 of which £2,650 was granted to the linen trade, a like sum to the herring fisheries, and a mere £700 to the original beneficiary, the moribund coarse wool industry.[35] The board sought to encourage improvements in every branch of the linen industry, offering premiums for the growth of flax and for the introduction

---

[34] Quoted (from a petition to the house of commons against laying a duty on Scotch linen) by H. Hamilton, *Economic History of Scotland in Eighteenth Century*, intro., p. xiii.

[35] See R. H. Campbell, ed., *State of the Annual Progress of the Linen Manufacture 1727–54*, intro., pp. vi–vii.

of better methods of scutching and heckling, processes that prepared the flax for spinning. Both scutching and heckling were at that time laboriously carried out by hand; and other ancillary processes to the production of finished linen, bleaching and dyeing, were also primitive. At considerable expense and trouble, the finer linens had to be sent to Holland to be bleached and dyed. In spite of the slow, uphill nature of the work, the board did a remarkable job. It brought in skilled weavers from Flanders and Ireland; it caused scutching and heckling machines to be introduced; and it encouraged the laying out of large bleach fields. The industry was certainly not revolutionised, but gradually it responded and there was a notable increase in production. In 1728 just over three million yards were produced, and by 1733 this figure had risen to nearly five millions. Too much should not be made of such statistics, for, all too clearly, the troubles of the industry continued, as the board realistically perceived. Scotch linen was mainly of the coarse category and of lower quality than its main rivals, the products of Germany and Ireland. In Scotland production was hindered by shortage of flax and, as the agrarian improvements spread and flax ceased to be a profitable crop, the linen industry became increasingly dependent on imports from the Baltic. All in all, perhaps the most notable development in the early part of the century was the rise of a fine linen industry in Glasgow and Edinburgh. In spite of the gloomy prophecies of the Reverend Robert Wodrow, who equated luxury products with moral decadence, from 1725 onwards the fine linen industry of Glasgow prospered and at Paisley there stemmed from it an important thread industry.

Such progress notwithstanding, Scottish linen continued to compete poorly in the English and colonial markets. The Scottish producers attributed this to unfair advantages enjoyed by foreign manufactures, particularly where the colonial markets were concerned, in that English merchants were allowed substantial 'drawbacks' on foreign linen intended for immediate re-export. A good case could be made for this view, and finally in 1742 the Bounty Act (which with intermissions was operative until 1832) redressed the balance by granting a bounty on the export of British linens. After the passing of the Bounty Act, linen played an increasingly important part in the expanding commerce between the Clyde and the American colonies where rough linen was much in demand. In 1746 another stimulus was provided by the setting up of the British Linen Company, whose primary object was to promote the marketing of Scottish linen, especially in America and Africa; but soon the company (which, in spite of its name, was purely Scottish) embarked on banking activities, extending credit to the manufacturers through numerous local branches. In spite of these improvements, the greater part of the industry continued to be run on ' cottage ' lines, only the fine industry of the west achieving real concentration. Spinning and weaving were still done by hand, and it was only towards the end of the century that lint mills became common. By that same period, weaving was rapidly becoming a full-time and well paid occupation. Spinning tended to predominate in the north-eastern counties while elsewhere (notably in Perth, Forfarshire and Lanarkshire) weaving took precedence. Weaving required more skill and capital than spinning, and thus it was natural that weavers should concentrate in the main commercial centres. In 1778 there were about 4,000 handlooms in and around Glasgow, Paisley had 1,360, and Dundee about 2,000. By that time, too, further improvements were transforming the finishing processes, particularly bleaching and dyeing. In 1749 Dr Roebuck pioneered the use of vitriol in bleaching, and, with Samuel Garbett, set up a large vitriol works at Prestonpans. James Watt, that great all-rounder, in 1786 adapted the French chemist Berthollet's process for bleaching by chlorine; and another Scot, Charles Tennant, improved the process by the introduction of chloride of lime in 1798. Perth became a notable centre for bleaching, which, with dyeing, became a leading industry in its own right, an important by-product of the so-called ' chemical revolution ', in the creation of which Scotsmen played no mean part.[36]

It has already been remarked that the growing commerce of Glasgow with the American and West Indian colonies stimulated the industries of Scotland as a whole. Such trade was not new but after 1707 it was free to expand, though at first hampered by lack of capital and of adequate shipping. In the first decade of Union ships had to be chartered from the port of Whitehaven in Cumberland. Up to 1728 the trade fluctuated, but overall there was fairly steady expansion, especially after 1718 when Clyde-

[36] A. and N. Clow, *The Chemical Revolution*, chs. I, VI.

owned shipping played the major part in the trade. On a much reduced, but locally important, scale the Solway also participated in the colonial trade. Soon the Scots were providing fierce competition for their main English rivals—Whitehaven, Liverpool and Bristol—and by 1721 the English Virginia merchants were complaining bitterly to parliament of the unfair trading of the Scots. It was alleged that they constantly evaded the customs, helped by the corruption of the local customs officers. There was truth in these allegations, but, as the treasury on investigation discovered, it was a universal truth and just as applicable to the English ports. The customs service in Scotland was nevertheless purged, and in 1723 new officers were appointed to the ports of Greenock and Port Glasgow. In 1722 total imports of tobacco had been 6½ million lbs, but by 1725 they had dropped to 4 million. The decline was not necessarily due to reform of the customs, for these were years of general depression following the failure of the South Sea Bubble; and when trade revived Glasgow's advantages again became apparent. The route to and from the Clyde was easier and safer than that used by the English ports, the Scots merchants were accommodating in the matter of debts, and, living frugally, they managed to undercut their rivals.

From being simple and leisurely in the first 30 years of the Union, the trade underwent a rapid change in the period after 1740. In the earlier phase it really consisted of casual trading, with captains of ships acting as commercial agents; but, as the demand for tobacco grew, a more complex organisation developed, based on the use of resident factors in the plantations. This so-called 'factorage system' was organised more successfully by the 'tobacco lords' of Glasgow than by their rivals. The Scots factors were shrewd and pertinacious, apt to use their countrymen who willingly responded by passing on information, thus helping the Scots merchants to snare the planters with easy credit and so secure liens on future crops. In the process they became highly unpopular in the colonies and by the eve of the American Revolution the Scots were regarded as an insufferable blight, which may help to account for the loyalty of some of them to King George.

By the 1760s Glasgow had a stranglehold on the trade, and its growing commerce dynamised the economy of Scotland. The trade figures bring this out clearly. In 1764 trade with North America came an easy first, followed by trade with the

West Indies, then on a much diminished scale came trade with Scandinavia. The connection with Holland had declined; but tobacco had revolutionised Scotland's balance of trade with France, for the great bulk of the Clyde's cargoes was for immediate re-export in the form of raw leaf and the main customers were the farmers-general of France. All in all, the importance of tobacco to the trade and industry of Scotland in the eighteenth century is difficult to exaggerate. In 1771 no less than 46 million lbs. of tobacco was imported into Glasgow; and, to meet the needs of the colonists for barter goods, the industries of Scotland were increasingly stimulated. Thus in that same year two million yards of coarse linen were exported to the colonies; and herrings, delft, leather goods, wrought iron, paper, and a host of minor but by no means insignificant articles also figured in the trade. It has been suggested that the importance of the colonial trade has been overstressed,[37] but the facts of the case are hard to establish. That the transatlantic trade was vulnerable and rested on the maintenance of ' the old colonial system ', that it faltered during the American Revolution and could not be restored on the old lines after the colonies gained their independence in 1783, should not obscure its basic importance in its heyday. It built up strong commercial traditions (compare, for example, the activities of Robert Bogle, a typical Glasgow tobacco lord, with those of the Company of Scotland); it led to the accumulation of capital (and it has to be remembered that much of the outstanding debt of the planters was recovered before 1776); and directly or indirectly it stimulated the entire economy. Such benefits more than offset the problems posed by the collapse of the American trade. Indeed, in many instances it was the profits of the tobacco trade which thereafter made possible ventures into new and profitable fields.

After 1783 the West India trade rapidly recovered, for in addition to the old staples of sugar and rum there was a rising demand for cotton. The contraction of markets brought about by the collapse of the tobacco trade was overcome in a surprisingly short time by the phenomenal rise of the cotton industry.[38] Until the last quarter of the eighteenth century cotton fibre was not put to any great use, although from the early part of the century fine Indian cotton textiles, such as muslins and calicos, were finding

[37] By R. H. Campbell, *Scotland since 1707: the rise of an Industrial Society*, p. 46.
[38] W. R. Scott, ' Economic Resiliency ', in *Econ. H.R.*, II. 291-9.

their way into Scotland. By 1730 a mixed cotton-linen cloth was being produced, mainly for handkerchiefs, in the centres of the fine linen industry in the west.[39] This trend was encouraged by the rise of cotton fustian manufactures in Manchester which depended on Scots linens. When raw cotton became plentiful and cheap, the cotton industry in Scotland was naturally grafted on to the fine linen industry.[40] The availability of capital at low rates of interest and the rise of power-spinning expedited the process, one which helped ultimately to revolutionise not only the means of production and the organisation of the industry but also the structure of society itself. The establishment of mills demanded high capital investment and led to the rise of a factory system, compact and well organised, rather than duplication of the old diffuse cottage system which still predominated in the pure linen trade. Such concentration contributed to the growth of an industrial proletariat, opening up new and deeper social gulfs than had hitherto existed. Not that the wage earner was new; but in agriculture and in the coalfields paternalism frequently offset exploitation. In the fiercely competitive world of cotton manufacture paternalism was at a discount. The cotton spinners, especially after the introduction of steam-powered machines in 1792,[41] were subjected to almost military discipline: in consequence, they soon had an unsavoury reputation for violence. The weavers, too, were affected by this new industry but in a different way. New techniques vastly increased the productivity of the spinning side of the industry, but weaving long lagged behind. More and more handloom weavers were needed to maintain a balance, leading eventually to over-crowding: the ill consequences of this were not seen in the eighteenth century but added much to the growing pains of an industrial society in the early nineteenth.

The first cotton mill in Scotland, powered by a water-wheel, was set up at Penicuik in Midlothian in 1778, to be followed a year later by one at Rothesay in Bute. Within the next few years similar establishments sprang up at Paisley and Johnstone in Renfrewshire, East Kilbride in Lanarkshire, and various other locations where water power was available. Cotton spinning on

[39] H. Hamilton, *Economic History of Scotland in the Eighteenth Century*, p. 161.

[40] Miss G. M. Mitchell, ' The English and Scottish Cotton Industries: a Study in Interrelations ', in *S.H.R.*, XXII. 101-14.

[41] W. H. Marwick, ' Cotton and the Industrial Revolution in Scotland ', in *S.H.R.*, XXI. 213.

a really large scale began in 1786 when the New Lanark mills, set up by David Dale in partnership with Arkwright, began to produce. Within a decade they were employing over 1,300 hands, with Dale as sole proprietor. In some ways he was typical of the new type of entrepreneur, a capitalist manufacturer pure and simple; but he was untypical in that he did not separate his religious views from his economic activities and he tried, though with only limited success, to treat his workers humanely. Soon others of this economic type, though not so burdened by social conscience, were active from the Dornoch Firth to the Solway. The Buchanan brothers built a large cotton mill at Deanston in Perthshire, and they later took over and extended a muslin factory at Balfron in Stirlingshire. James Finlay and Company grew into a large combine, acquiring one after the other of the pioneer mills, except New Lanark which passed in 1799 to Dale's son-in-law, Robert Owen, who used it not merely as a means of production but also as a fit subject for social experiment. In general, conditions in the mills were harsh and to augment the reluctant labour force children were ruthlessly exploited. Owen tried to run a model mill on lines both profitable and humane, restricting the number of hours worked by children and providing the rudiments of education.

The initial phase of what was later to be called ' the Industrial Revolution ' thus had its most dramatic effects in the main textile industries, cotton and to a lesser extent linen, which by 1803 accounted for 64 per cent of Scotland's exports. But steady, if slow, progress was also made in the coal-mining industry. In the first half of the eighteenth century the lairds themselves continued to exploit their coal-heughs, as did Sir John Clerk of Penicuik in Midlothian and the Wemyss family in Fife. Improved techniques and more complex mining, however, led in the later eighteenth century to the lairds leasing mineral rights to coal companies. The rise of Glasgow's trade, and the industries associated with it, stimulated production in Lanarkshire and Ayrshire; but extracting these difficult measures was dependent on the introduction of efficient steam-pumps. One of the first in Scotland was installed at Elphinstone colliery in Stirlingshire about 1720; but this type of engine was cumbrous, none too reliable, and, while the patents were in force, extremely expensive.[42] Not until the second half of

[42] R. Bald, *A General View of the Coal Trade of Scotland* (1812), pp. 20-3.

the eighteenth century were improved Newcomen or Watt engines widely used, and even so, they had their serious limitations.[43] Another inhibiting factor was that sinking shafts was done by hand until about the middle of the eighteenth century when gunpowder, an extremely inefficient explosive, was first used for blasting.   In short, although coal mining was expanding at a rapid rate in the late eighteenth century, the industry was still in its palaeotechnic stage.   But due to the rise of other industries such as iron-smelting, brewing and distilling, glass-manufacture and lime-burning, the demand for coal was steadily increasing. This created a problem: the new industrial complex that was emerging relied upon coal, but the mining industry was still ill-equipped to keep pace with demand.   Much of the east coast of Scotland still depended upon Newcastle for coal, although in part this may have been attributable to unfair discrimination against the Scots sea-borne coal trade.[44]   But it was probably owing even more to the technical difficulties that impeded exploitation of the richest coal measures in Scotland.   Deeper shafts entailed hardships and risks: the problem of keeping the workings clear of water remained, and to this were added the dangers of poor ventilation, firedamp, and 'fa's' brought about by faulty timbering.   Throughout the eighteenth century, too, the coal industry of Scotland was hampered by an inadequate labour force.

By the early eighteenth century most colliers, in both east and west,[45] were in a condition of serfdom.   This is the clear tenor of numerous legal processes for the recovery of runaways: in the 1730s and '40s such cases increased as coal-masters, eager to expand, fought for a share of the limited supply of labour.   The colliers were not, as Henry Cockburn stated, 'literally slaves',[46] for they could own property, associate in benefit societies, and they could, and did, agitate by legal means to improve their lot. Rather, as Bald correctly held, they 'were under a most severe servitude: [and] were accounted *ascripti glebae*'.[47]   They were tied to the pits in which they were first *arled* (*i.e.* accepted earnest

---

[43] See C. Singer, ed., *History of Technology*, IV. 81-2.

[44] T. S. Ashton and J. Sykes, *The Coal Industry of the Eighteenth Century*, pp. 228-9.

[45] J. U. Nef, *Rise of the British Coal Industry*, II. 163, implies that serfdom scarcely operated in the west.   This was certainly not so in the eighteenth century.

[46] H. Cockburn, *Memorials of His Time* (edn. 1910), p. 70. So, too, R. Page Arnot, *A History of the Scottish Miners*, p. 3.

[47] R. Bald, *Coal Trade of Scotland*, p. 73.

money) and their labour was bought and sold with the property. Frequently, coal-works were advertised for sale in the Edinburgh press, with the colliers and bearers listed among the assets.[48] By the middle of the eighteenth century, this vicious system was failing to supply adequate labour and many coal-owners were forced to employ free colliers on strict yearly contracts. How far these men maintained their liberty is problematical, and so too is the extent to which they influenced the degraded but by no means spiritless serfs. But not only economic pressures operated against serfdom: a new climate of opinion was arising which was beginning, faintly it is true, to question man's inhumanity to man. Thus, in 1757 a case was brought before the court of session to determine whether a negro slave, bought in Virginia, could be regarded as a slave in Scotland. ' The Lords appointed counsel for the negro, and ordered memorials. . . . But during the hearing in presence, the negro died; so the point was not determined.'[49] Certain it is that from the early 1760s, possibly as a faint echo of ' Wilkes and Liberty ', the collier serfs became restive. The coal-masters took alarm at this and met in Edinburgh to concert measures for maintaining serfdom.[50] But that the masters were struggling against growing opposition appeared in another interesting case which came before the court of session in 1770. A negro slave brought from the West Indies by his master was baptised in Wemyss: he took the name of the officiating minister, Spens, and became popular locally. He applied to the court of session for his freedom and seemed set to win his case when, unfortunately, the master died and the case collapsed. The really significant feature is that the colliers, salters—who also suffered from bondage—and farm labourers of the parish of Wemyss subscribed for Spens's defence.[51] In the next few years the colliers were actively campaigning on their own behalf, their cause strengthened by Lord Mansfield's decision of 1772 in the case of the negro Somerset that on English soil no man could be deemed a slave. If no man on English soil could be anything but free, was

---

[48] See A. S. Cunningham, *Mining in the Kingdom of Fife*, pp. 11-12, for an example from the *Caledonian Mercury* for 24 January 1770.

[49] *Faculty Collection of Decisions*, II. No. xxxiv, 4 July 1757: Robert Sheddan against A Negro.

[50] H. Hamilton, *Economic History of Scotland in the Eighteenth Century*, p. 369, citing *The Edinburgh Evening Courant* for 11 March 1762.

[51] A. S. Cunningham, *Rambles in the Parishes of Scoonie and Wemyss*, p. 155.

any man on Scottish soil to be considered less than free ? The case was cogently put and advanced another step by the manumission of a negro Joseph Knight in 1775 by decision of the court of session.[52]

In 1775 the coal-owners conceded that serfdom had outlived its usefulness, though a few of them opposed the Emancipation Act that was passed in that year. The preamble to the act stated quite bluntly that the main reason for its existence was the impossibility of maintaining an adequate supply of labour while serfdom remained to scare off potential recruits. The measure, however, was half-hearted. Instead of abolishing the evil, it sought to overcome it by degrees. The serfs were to be liberated in stages and only on application to the sheriff courts. Not until 1778 were the first collier serfs freed from bondage; and, in spite of their relatively high wages, they promptly deserted the mines for agricultural labour or the factories. The demand for coal, however, continued to rise steadily, and in an attempt to attract recruits a further Emancipation Act of 1799 abolished serfdom entirely. This led to a fresh exodus from the industry and not until after 1815 did a severe general depression provide the coal-mines of Scotland with an adequate labour force.

In other respects the Act of 1799 did not work the wonders fondly expected of it. It said nothing about conditions of labour, and increasingly women and children were drawn into the mines as bearers. This was a consequence of the era of more intensive mining that was beginning, as the problem of transporting the hewn coal from the face to the pit-bottom was magnified. In the coal-fields of Scotland with their difficult measures and steep dips, this opened up to women and children a hell on earth. Often they were related to the colliers for whom they laboured and even so their lot was hard; but harsh beyond all description was the fate of the ' fremit ' bearers, women labourers who were no kin to the colliers and who were cruelly exploited. In the older, shallower pits of the eastern coalfields (where female labour had long existed) they even carried the coal in creels up successive galleries to the surface: ' and such is the weight carried, that it frequently takes two men to lift the burden upon their backs '.[53]

---

[52] R. Chambers, *Domestic Annals of Scotland*, III. 453-4.
[53] Robert Bald, *General View of the Coal Trade*, ' Inquiry into the Condition of those Women who carry Coals under Ground in Scotland, known by the name of Bearers ', p. 131.

It was estimated that a woman bearer might daily haul to the surface about 36 English hundredweights of coal, all for 8d. a day wage. In the deeper pits the labour involved in carrying coal from the wall to the pit-bottom was almost as great. The female bearers usually began to work at the age of seven, some continuing to labour until they were almost fifty. No wonder a contemporary observer described their condition as ' worse than Egyptian bondage ',[54] and deduced that from it sprang much of the social evils—improvidence and drunkenness—that characterised mining communities.

The increasing demand for coal in the last quarter of the eighteenth century was due in part to the rise of the iron industry. In the early eighteenth century iron smelting played an insignificant part in the economy of Scotland, and, such as it was, it depended upon English capital and expertise cashing in on Scotland's wood supply. The country was by no means as treeless as Dr Johnson concluded, for in parts of the Highlands extensive forests existed. They accounted for the otherwise inexplicable locations of furnaces in the early eighteenth century, for at that time the iron industry still relied upon charcoal and the Highland forests usefully supplemented the rapidly dwindling woods of England. Thus, furnaces were built at Invergarry in Inverness-shire in 1729, and later at Taynuilt (1753) and Furnace (1775) in Argyll. But these ventures were small in scale and their products, rather highly priced and not of the best quality, were mostly disposed of in England. In the main ' their experience was an expensive demonstration of the futility of establishing an industry in the Highlands, remote from the source of raw materials and also from markets '.[55] Changes then gradually taking place in the techniques of iron production rendered more certain the failure of such projects. These technological improvements turned upon the discovery of the great English iron-master, Darby of Coalbrookdale, that coke was just as satisfactory a fuel for smelting as charcoal. Slow and piecemeal though the development was, coal came to play an ever greater part in the iron industry and this led to a re-zoning of the furnaces. In the second half of the eighteenth century proximity to coal outweighed most other considerations, and this was clearly revealed in the setting

[54] Bald, *op. cit.*, p. 142.
[55] H. Hamilton, *Economic History of Scotland in the Eighteenth Century*, p. 191.

up of the famous Carron Ironworks near Falkirk in 1759. The selection of Carron was determined by the availability of coal and ironstone, adequate water supply to drive machinery, and the possibility of sea-transport. All these considerations were carefully pondered by the three partners to the undertaking, two of whom, significantly, were English, for most of the building materials, machinery and skilled labour had to be brought from England. Dr Roebuck was a chemist and long familiar with Scotland and its potentialities; Samuel Garbett was a Birmingham manufacturer with wide business experience; and the solitary Scot involved was William Cadell, a merchant of Cockenzie on the Firth of Forth. In its origins, therefore, Carron was very much an Anglo-Scottish venture, as indeed were the pioneer works at Invergarry and Taynuilt. By 1766 the Carron Company had four furnaces in blast and was producing a variety of goods, ranging from nails at the Cramond works, which had been acquired in 1759, to casts of all kinds including cannon. With the last, after a sore technical and financial struggle, the company finally made its name, producing a superior naval gun, the carronade, which was much in demand during the American War of Independence.[56]

Possibly inspired by Carron's bold venture other projects appeared, notably at Dalnotter in Dunbartonshire in 1769[57] and at Wilsontown in Lanarkshire ten years later. Small firms like Dalnotter relied on imports of Swedish bar iron, until the rising cost of this material forced them to purchase bar iron locally. To meet this demand, the Clyde Iron Works was set up at Tollcross near Glasgow in 1786. A year later at Cleland in Lanarkshire the Omoa iron-works were established, and in 1788 Muirkirk in Ayrshire was chosen as another site because of its rich coal and ironstone deposits.[58] Most of these concerns were to some extent interlocked through the principal shareholders. Thus, the original Muirkirk Company was connected with the Smithfield works, which had been set up in Partick as far back as 1738, and with the more recent Dalnotter company. Clearly, the industry was expanding but hardly at a phenomenal pace. In 1796 there

[56] For details of this important concern, see R. H. Campbell, *Carron Company*.
[57] G. Thomson, 'Dalnotter Iron Company, an Eighteenth Century Scottish Industrial Undertaking', in *S.H.R.*, xxxv. 10-20.
[58] J. R. Hume and J. Butt, 'Muirkirk 1786–1802. The Creation of a Scottish Industrial Community', in *S.H.R.*, xlv. 160-83.

were sixteen blast furnaces in Scotland; but, on the whole, the industry lagged dangerously in the rear of developments in England. It was nothing like as highly organised; its techniques were dated, and the introduction of Watt's improved steam-engine and the puddling process of Henry Cort was slow. In short, the iron industry in Scotland was being built on new and more productive lines, but in the late eighteenth century this process was merely in its initial stage. Whether there were to be any later stages would depend on improved technology within the trade itself; and, not least, on a transformation of communications and transport.

In many parts of the Lowlands serious efforts were made to improve the roads in the second half of the eighteenth century. With the commissioners of supply usually taking the initiative statute labour was commuted, and acts of parliament were obtained authorising the setting up of turnpike trusts; but the expense was crippling and the turnpike roads that were constructed varied greatly in quality and usefulness. The science of road-making was still in its infancy and the work of such a notable pioneer as John Loudon McAdam did not revolutionise road surfaces generally until the early nineteenth century. The improved roads of the late eighteenth century, therefore, were of real but limited importance. Agriculture in the area favoured by good roads benefited most of all, and the cart, hitherto a rarity, became common. Marl and lime could more easily be transported and markets were rendered more accessible to farmers. The problem of travel was considerably eased. For long enough, if a sea-route was not available, travellers went on foot or horseback, and some found private coaches to be all but useless luxuries, as Lord Lovat discovered when in April 1740 he set out with his two daughters to travel from Beauly to London in his own coach. In spite of frequent calls on the services of wheelwrights and carpenters, the coach repeatedly broke down, and when after eleven days of hideous jolting the party reached Edinburgh the coach was a wreck. Lovat probably chose the worst possible route for his experiment, for roads in the Highlands were unspeakably bad. But they were poor in Scotland as a whole, as the absence of public coach services testified. Project after project collapsed on the dangerous roads, a fate that seems to have been shared by various attempts to provide a service between Edinburgh and Glasgow.

Curiously enough, at a time when its bad roads precluded all possibility of regular and extensive use of coaches, Scotland became famous for coach-building. In 1738 John Home returned to Edinburgh from London where he had served an apprenticeship as a coach-builder. He set up in business and seems to have anticipated the modern concept of mass production, for he greatly increased his output by assigning different parts to various craftsmen and then assembling the coaches. The quality of Home's work was first rate and he soon built up a large export business, with brisk custom all over Europe, to the discomfiture of the leading centres of the industry, London and Paris. But about the middle of the century, Home found a small but growing market for his coaches in Scotland. From 1749 a stage-coach plied regularly, if slowly, between Edinburgh and Glasgow. It took twelve hours to cover 46 miles and this slow pace was maintained until in the 1780s improvement of roads led to the rise of fast mail services.[59] The mail service was instituted in Edinburgh in 1786 and cut the time to London to sixty hours, a journey which hitherto had taken a month and sometimes longer. Edinburgh became the hub of the coaching services in Scotland, with regular runs to London, Carlisle, Aberdeen, Dumfries and Stirling. By the end of the century, too, numerous services were radiating from Glasgow. Even so, the hey-day of coaching did not come until the early nineteenth century; in 1800, there was still no coaching service north of Tay and not until 1806 was there one from Perth to Inverness. It could not have been otherwise, for in many parts the north was virtually roadless. No serious effort was made to supplement the relatively useless and largely abandoned military roads until after 1803 when a Commission for Highland Roads and Bridges was appointed. It showed its wisdom by committing the work to the capable hands of Thomas Telford, the son of a Dumfriesshire shepherd and one of the greatest civil engineers in an age of great engineers. In spite of the daunting magnitude of the task, Telford triumphantly overcame all difficulties. Neither niggardly doles from parliament, the hostility of the lairds, the inertia of Highland labourers, or the rugged terrain could overcome this indomitable southern Scot. By 1820 he had completed 875 miles of good roads and well over 1,000 bridges, some of them, like the bridge at Dunkeld, works of

[59] L. Gardiner, *Stage Coach to John-o'-Groats*, ch. 4.

art.[60] Telford also produced numerous noble bridges and canals in England, as well as such masterpieces as the Dean Bridge in Edinburgh. His friend, the poet Southey, sometimes playfully dubbed Telford ' Pontifex Maximus ', and at others ' Colossus of Roads ', both hyperbolic puns richly deserved.[61]

The improved roads also made possible a more regular and efficient postal system. In 1741 there were 106 post-towns in Scotland, but by 1791 the number had grown to 164. From about the middle of the century mail began to be delivered by horsemen to the principal places in Scotland, but the bulk of the mail was still carried by loitering foot boys. ' The condition of the roads however in Scotland, would not admit of any thing like rapid travelling ';[62] and the carrier between Edinburgh and Selkirk, covering a mere 38 miles, took a fortnight to complete the return journey. In spite of the laws, cadgers and casual travellers carried a large proportion of the mails. But as the roads improved in the latter part of the eighteenth century, so did the delivery of mail. A notable achievement was the setting up of a penny-post in Edinburgh by the remarkable Peter Williamson, who as a boy had been kidnapped in Aberdeen and shipped to the colonies. So successful was Williamson's venture that government bought him off with a pension and took over the penny post.

Growing in importance though they were, the roads could not cater for the needs of the coal and iron industries. Efforts had long been made to ease the problem of coastal collieries by the construction of wooden-railed wagonways, the earliest of which, from Tranent to Cockenzie, dates from 1722. By the end of the eighteenth century many of the collieries on either side of the Forth were served by wagonways.[63] Iron works, too, made use of them, as at Carron where in 1766 a line was built from the iron-works to Carronhall pits. From about 1768 onwards iron rails were being introduced in England, but they were slow to be laid in Scotland, the first iron track there dating from 1810. Until the 1830s traction was supplied by horses, although in 1816 a steam locomotive was tried out, with disappointing results, for the Duke of Portland's ' Kilmarnock & Troon Railway '. This

[60] A. R. B. Haldane, *New Ways Through the Glens*, ch. 8.
[61] S. Smiles, *Lives of the Engineers: Life of Telford* (1874), pp. 245, 305.
[62] T. B. Lang, *An Historical Summary of the Post-Office in Scotland* (1856), p. 13.
[63] G. Dott, *Early Scottish Colliery Wagonways* (1947).

line was opened in 1812 and proved of importance not only to the coal industry but to the economic life of the neighbourhood as a whole. It was, in fact, a miniature prototype of the later railways.

But the most important improvement in communications in the late eighteenth century as far as industry and commerce were concerned was the construction of canals.[64]   Such projects had long been considered.   Charles II, for example, who was interested in science, appreciated the strategic value of a ship canal linking the Forth and the Clyde. During the Seven Years' War, the ravages of French privateers and men-o'-war revived interest in the scheme; and later the strategic motive strengthened the plan for a canal through the Great Glen.   But, in the event, it was economic pressures that led to the cutting of the major canals in Scotland.   As early as 1724 Defoe noted that the merchants of Glasgow had established warehouses at Alloa on the Forth in order to facilitate transport of tobacco from the Clyde to the continent, and indeed in the previous year the first survey of a possible Forth-Clyde canal was made, mainly to serve the interests of the tobacco merchants.   Thirty years later the project was taken up by the Board of Trustees for Manufactures who engaged the services of the foremost civil engineer of the day, John Smeaton. The route recommended by Smeaton—from the river Carron to the Yoker Burn just below Glasgow—was substantially that which was later followed in the construction of the Forth and Clyde canal.   The commercial interests fought for a Shorter Canal Bill but after years of bitter wrangling they were defeated.   Typical of all these early ambitious ventures at canal building, the costs were underestimated and in 1773 the work came to a halt because of financial difficulties.   The canal was then navigable from Grangemouth to Kirkintilloch, and shortly thereafter it was extended by a short branch as far as Glasgow.   Finally, with government assistance, the canal was carried to Bowling on the Clyde; it was opened to navigation in July 1790 and the following May a ship (happily named *The Experiment*) sailed from Dundee to Liverpool via the new canal in the then unprecedented time of four days.   In 1790 authority was also granted to form a junction with the Monkland Canal, which had originally been designed to serve purely local purposes.   It was built to open up the rich

[64] E. A. Pratt, *Scottish Canals and Waterways*; H. Hamilton, *Economic History of Scotland in the Eighteenth Century*, ch. VIII, pp. 234-45.

Lanarkshire coalfield and so to break the extortionate monopoly of the Glasgow coal-masters.   Glasgow town council commissioned James Watt to survey a route from the Airdrie–Coatbridge area to Glasgow; work began in 1770 but was delayed owing to the financial crisis caused by the American War of Independence. The Monkland Canal did not pay until in 1792 it was connected to the Forth and Clyde.   The resulting complex—Forth–Clyde and Monkland Canals—was far and away the most important of the numerous canal projects undertaken in Scotland.   It enabled the rich coal and iron deposits of Lanarkshire to be carried both east and west; it eased the general commerce of the whole country, and it even conferred a boon on travellers by instituting passenger services.   Passenger service was increased and became very popular after 1822 when the Union Canal joined Edinburgh to the Forth and Clyde Navigation.   At its height in 1836 this service, which was in every way preferable to the stage coaches, carried nearly 200,000 passengers.

There were numerous other canals of local importance, such as the Inverurie joining the place of that name to Aberdeen, and the Paisley–Glasgow canal.   But the two other canals of limited national importance, apart from the Forth–Clyde complex, were in the Highlands.   The Crinan Canal was first projected by the Trustees of the Forfeited Estates to give the fishers of the north-west easy access to markets in Glasgow.   Here again the indefatigable James Watt[65] was employed to make the survey, and later, under different auspices, the Crinan route which he mapped out was followed.   Construction began in 1793 under John Rennie, and, after the inevitable financial troubles, it was completed in 1801.   Unfortunately, the costs had been too severely cut, the work was not up to standard, and the history of the Crinan Canal was one of lost opportunities.   It was taken over by the state in 1848, but the emergence of large steam-ships diminished its usefulness.   A white elephant of even greater proportions was Telford's ' Caledonian Canal ', a marvellous feat for its time but one which also suffered from cheese-paring and faulty construction.   Begun in 1804, it was not completed until 1822; the winds funnelled through the Great Glen made it difficult for sailing ships, and steamers preferred the long voyage round Cape

[65] Smiles called him, with some reason, ' the greatest of engineers ';   S. Smiles, *Lives of the Engineers: Early Engineering* (1874), intro., p. xviii.

Wrath to the high charges levied in the canal. Thus, the volume of traffic was never as great as had been expected, and it had no such galvanising effect on the Highlands as the Forth–Clyde complex had on the Lowlands.

In sum, the economic development of Scotland in the eighteenth century is best regarded as constituting the so-called ' take-off ' phase, making possible the emergence of an industrialised society. The actual achievement of industrialisation, however, was the work mainly of the nineteenth century. Not only did this tend towards urbanisation but also towards the creation of villages,[66] designed sometimes for agricultural purposes, sometimes to serve the cotton industry and latterly, increasingly, the coal and iron industries.

[66] For this see Hamilton, *Economic History of Scotland in the eighteenth century*, ch. 1.

7

EDUCATION AND CULTURE IN THE EIGHTEENTH CENTURY

Few major subjects in the history of Scotland remain so ill understood as the state of her schools in the eighteenth century. Some authorities elide the problem by maintaining that ' educationally, Scotland has been described as the happy woman who has no history '.[1] But there *is* a history, and in some ways a noble history, though it still awaits its historian. Wide generalisations have been made on narrow grounds and judgments have swung violently from extremes of praise to equally uncritical condemnation.[2] When every allowance is granted for backwardness in some areas, it seems clear that progress was being made towards realising the ideal of a school in every parish and that some of the parish schools were remarkably good. It is scarcely conceivable that the golden age of Scottish culture could have occurred in a country which set little store by its schools. Nor can the burgh or grammar schools claim all the prominent old boys, for such eminent scholars as William Robertson the historian and Thomas Reid the philosopher were products of the

[1] Quoted in H. M. Knox, *Two Hundred and Fifty Years of Scottish Education, 1696–1946*, p. xi.

[2] Thus J. Kerr, *Scottish Education: School and University from Early Times to 1908*, p. 179, considers that for more than 150 years after 1696 Scotland was ' in the van of educated nations '; and even more emphatic is E. E. B. Thompson, *The Parliament of Scotland, 1690–1702*, p. 146: ' Her educational system was perfect of its kind, and more admirable still, it was universal in its operation '. Resiling from these untenable positions, J. C. Jessop, *Education in Angus*, concludes, p. 162, that ' Our educational pre-eminence was a mere supposition ' and that under the parochial system Scotland was only ' A Half-Educated Nation '. But Dr Jessop founds too much on the records of one presbytery.

parish schools.[3] Yet, undeniably, the parish schools laboured under great difficulties. The sheer size of some of the Highland parishes made the scheme impracticable. How could one school serve the parish of Gairloch in Wester Ross, which measured thirty-two miles by eighteen ? ' In the great extent of this parish . . . there is no school but the parochial, by which means the rising generation suffer much, and are wholly neglected, having no access to the benefit of instruction.'[4] Matters were not helped by the various interpretations to which the act of 1696 was subjected. In some parishes the provision of one ' legal ' school, conforming to all the requirements laid down in the act, was regarded as mandatory, while other parishes rejected this view in favour of erecting several schools, humbler in scope, as need required. The Society for Propagating Christian Knowledge, an important auxiliary in the fight against illiteracy, favoured the concept of a ' legal ' school in each parish and refused to aid parishes which failed to provide them.[5] By its rigid attitude, the society may unwittingly have inhibited the development of educational facilities in many large and unwieldy parishes. This apart, the society's record was excellent, particularly in the Highlands where it carried out some extremely interesting experiments in practical education. The rebellion of 1745 underlined the need for educational facilities in that area and the society found a welcome ally in the commission for the forfeited estates. Together they set up many joint ventures, supported at times by the board of manufactures, in which the aim was to teach not only reading and writing but also useful trades such as weaving, spinning, and agriculture.[6] Most of the ventures were shortlived but should not be dismissed as outright failures, for ' the enterprise of the Board of Manufactures, of the S.P.C.K. and of the Forfeited Estates Commissioners exerted an influence upon social conditions which gradually permeated the community '.[7]

In the later eighteenth century further defects in the act of

[3] J. Strong, *History of Secondary Education in Scotland*, p. 123, n. 1.

[4] O.S.A., III. 92.

[5] D. J. Withrington, ' The S.P.C.K. and Highland Schools in Mid-Eighteenth Century ', in *S.H.R.*, XLI. 89-99.

[6] For a full account see John Mason, *A History of Scottish Experiments in Rural Education*, ch. 1. For a bitter, but only partially justified, criticism of the work of the society, see John Lorne Campbell, *Gaelic in Scottish Education and Life*, pp. 50-56.

[7] J. Mason, *op. cit.*, p. 64.

1696 became glaringly apparent. The salaries granted to school-masters under the act were too low, but in spite of representations made to the general assembly in 1748 and again in 1782 no increases were allowed. As a result, in many areas the dominies struggled on as best they could on what were little more than labourers' wages. Inevitably as opportunities for alternative employment increased the abler men, often graduates, drifted away from teaching into clerkships in the service of the East India Company or of large merchant houses. Nor were the inadequate salaries the only burden under which the schoolmasters laboured. General working conditions were poor, and often the parish school was a miserable hovel with earthen floors on which the pupils scrawled their letters and numbers. One such in Aberdeenshire in the early nineteenth century was a mere hut thirty-four feet by fourteen with walls six feet high, and ' along each side stood a flat table or desk with a form attached to each side, so that the scholars sat facing each other '. The master sat in the middle, listening to his flock dutifully intoning their lessons but never asking questions or offering explanations.[8] Every morning the scholars arrived each with his peat to fill the room with much smoke and little heat. This was bad; but as against it could be cited examples of well-run parish schools in which the art of teaching reached a high level. Thus, whilst condemning the general standard of teaching in Ayrshire in the 1780s, Dr Mitchell excepts from his strictures ' my own Latin teacher, Mr David Allison, parochial schoolmaster of Beith '.[9] Allison had never been to college and was largely self-taught, ' but he possessed energy, enterprise and enthusiasm in no small degree ' and later became a successful teacher in the High School of Glasgow. Then the young Robert Burns was fortunate in his schoolmasters, and especially in John Murdoch. Murdoch was educated at Ayr burgh school, he had studied at Edinburgh University, and in 1765 he returned to Ayr to look for a post. Burns's father and a few neighbours pooled their resources to engage his services. He proved an excellent teacher and as well as expounding the Bible and catechism he introduced the boys to a wide range of literature, later teaching young Robert the rudiments of French.[10]

[8] J. Kerr, *Scottish Education*, p. 204, quoting from Dr Findlater's *Reminiscences*.
[9] ' Memories of Ayrshire about 1780 by the Reverend John Mitchell, D.D.', in *Miscellany of S.H.S.*, 3rd ser., VI. 275.
[10] Franklyn Bliss Snyder, *The Life of Robert Burns*, pp. 41 ff.

The parochial system was not perfected and to the end the great vision of 1560 was never realised; but more honest endeavour went into the attempt than historians sometimes allow, and by the end of the eighteenth century most parishes, Highland[11] as well as Lowland, had schools of some sort. As one authority concludes: ' There was much more schoolbuilding and schoolkeeping in eighteenth-century Scotland than has commonly been allowed.'[12] The presbyteries tried hard to make the heritors do their duty under the act of 1696 but frequently the commissioners of supply had to be called in to enforce its provisions.[13] In many cases, however, it proved impossible to collect the money due from landlords and tenants.[14] But it is difficult to generalise on this subject, for some great landowners took a pride in the local schools and helped them to the best of their abilities. Ayrshire, for example, was blessed in this respect, each of its three historic divisions enjoying the patronage of a prominent family. The Earls of Eglinton were active in Cunningham, the Earls of Loudoun in Kyle, while Carrick benefited from the Fergussons of Kilkerran.[15] Of many other areas much the same tale could be told; but in such variable circumstances any given parish school was apt to have a chequered history, flourishing in one generation only perhaps to decline in another. Not until 1803 was parliament convinced that reform was needed, and in that year an act was passed to remedy the defects in the parish schools. The schoolmaster's salary was increased to a minimum of 300 merks and a maximum of 400, and in addition the heritors were required to provide him with a dwelling house. The houses were modest two-roomed structures, but even so many of the lairds were scandalised at being mulcted ' to erect palaces for dominies '.[16] The problem of the overlarge or overpopulous parish was also tackled by expressly permitting the appointment of two or more teachers. It was a sensible act as far as it went, but the proposed reforms were belated and did not really meet the requirements of the times. New social conditions obtained in many parts of Scotland,

[11] John MacInnes, *The Evangelical Movement in the Highlands of Scotland*, pp. 234-5.
[12] Withrington, *op. cit.*, p. 99.
[13] For numerous instances see J. A. Russell, *History of Education in the Stewartry of Kirkcudbright, from Original and Contemporary Sources* (1951), *e.g.*, p. 24.
[14] *O.S.A.* XXI. General Appendix, 308.
[15] William Boyd, *Education in Ayrshire through Seven Centuries*, p. 100.
[16] Henry Cockburn, *Memorials of His Time* (edn. 1910), p. 179.

and the country's needs could not be met by patching up the old limited parochial system.   It has to be remembered, however, that the political scare of the 1790s left the upper classes doubtful of the wisdom of education for ' the lower orders of society ',[17] and thus the act of 1803 perhaps represented all that was feasible at that time.

Towards the end of the eighteenth century, too, a more secular attitude towards education was arising and this had some important effects.   For one thing, the control exercised by the established church was increasingly challenged, as in the Bothwell case of 1792.   Here the minister clashed with a majority of the heritors over the appointment of a teacher, the minister taking exception to the dominie's lack of Latin.   The presbytery upheld the heritors but on appeal to the synod the minister won.   The schoolmaster, threatened with dismissal, took his case to the court of session which found the church courts incompetent in this matter and set aside the synod's decision.   The matter did not rest there, for on further appeal the house of lords reversed the court of session's judgment and declared that power of review lay with the ecclesiastical and not the civil courts.   The kirk's triumph was shortlived, for the act of 1803, whilst apparently upholding the claims of the church, in practice seriously undermined them. The act gave the presbytery control of the parish school and its judgments were to be final; but it also allowed the civil courts to review the formality of the presbytery's procedure.   If the presbytery did not have the benefit of sound legal advice, its decisions could easily be nullified on trifling technicalities.   In fact the powers exercised by the presbytery after 1803 were much diminished, ' and from this time down to 1861 it possessed but a shadow of its ancient jurisdiction '.[18]   In other ways the kirk's authority was declining, notably in its relations with the burgh schools. This was an old source of controversy but by and large the town councils controlled the burgh schools, though keeping constant guard to repel encroachments by the presbytery.   By the end of the eighteenth century the church was on the defensive and no longer absolutely insisting that burgh schoolmasters had to subscribe the Confession of Faith as a condition of appointment.[19]

[17] Henry Cockburn, *Life of Lord Jeffrey*, I. 68.
[18] J. Strong, *Secondary Education in Scotland*, p. 102.
[19] James Grant, *History of the Burgh Schools of Scotland*, pp. 91-2.

The spread of presbyterian dissent made this a vexed question, though it did not become critical until after the Disruption of 1843.

In other ways the burgh schools adopted more secular attitudes, in many instances revising curricula to include modern languages, mensuration and other subjects then coming into favour. A few burghs went so far as to set up entirely new schools known as Writing or Commercial Schools in which the emphasis was placed on such useful subjects as book-keeping and arithmetic. The first such appeared at Dumfries in 1723, and its example was followed in Stirling in 1747, Banff in 1762, and Paisley in 1781.[20] The reaction against the exclusive use of classics as a means of education was strengthened by the rise of the *Realschulen* in Germany, by the influence of the Enlightenment, and by the needs of an increasingly commercial economy. The movement culminated in the founding of academies, the first of which, Perth Academy, was founded in 1761; it was devoted mainly to science and all the teaching was given in English.[21] This proved to be a very influential venture and it soon had imitators at Dundee in 1786, Inverness in 1788, Elgin and Fortrose in 1791, Ayr in 1794, and Dumfries in 1802. The academies were set up by private subscription and were therefore independent of the town councils. The reaction against the classics had gone too far, however, and led to counteraction. Edinburgh Academy was founded in 1824 as a classical school, but by this time a new element had crept in which was alien to the Scottish educational tradition. Edinburgh Academy was built to accommodate ' the better class of boys ', the first open break with the old Scots tradition of sons of lairds and sons of hinds being schooled together.[22] But in fact for upwards of a century the sons of the nobles and the gentry had been more and more dispatched to the miscalled English public schools. Thus in 1715 Clerk of Penicuik sent his son to Eton ' with the advice and concurrence of the Earl of Galloway and the rest of his Mother's friends '. The object was utilitarian rather than social: Clerk hoped that the boy would master English

---

[20] J. Strong, *Secondary Education in Scotland*, p. 160.

[21] For its curriculum see Strong, *op. cit.*, pp. 161-2.

[22] Contrast this with Henry Brougham's glowing eulogy of the High School of Edinburgh whose great merit was that ' men of the highest and lowest rank of society send their children to be educated together '. Quoted in James Grant, *Old and New Edinburgh* (1882), II. 114.

and so be able to profit from the opportunities opened up by the Union, but unfortunately John junior died young.[23]   Sir John, though, thought little of the English universities, sending his sons to Edinburgh.   By the end of the eighteenth century other considerations were prevailing;   more and more upper-class Scots boys attended the English public schools and many of them went on to one or other of the English universities.   The result was to create a chasm in Scottish society which persists to this day and which divides an anglicised upper class from other sections of the nation.

The worthy baron of exchequer reasoned well, for in the eighteenth century the universities of Scotland won for themselves a unique place in the world of learning.   Many causes helped to bring this about.   It may be attributed in part to the decline of religious fanaticism and the strong worldly good sense of the Moderates, in part to reforms in the universities such as the changeover to the professorial system or the use of English, and in part it was the consequence of a wider mental horizon stimulated by closer contact with England (yet with most of the old continental influences still strong).   Only unhappy St Andrews made but a minor contribution to this period of exciting and high achievement.   Its story is a doleful one.   In 1727 it seemed to Defoe that St Salvator's college was ' looking into its Grave '.[24] Efforts at improvement were made, notably by the union in 1747 of the colleges of St Salvator and St Leonard; but this wrought no miracles.   Not one new chair was founded in the United College until 115 years after its formation;[25] and in 1773 Dr Johnson found St Andrews ' pining in decay and struggling for life '.[26]   At the end of the eighteenth century under Principal Hill, the leader of the Moderates, corruption and nepotism were the rule; and St Andrews, which had a chair of medicine but no medical school, seriously embarrassed Edinburgh and Glasgow by selling M.D. degrees.   Aberdeen's two colleges, though inferior to Glasgow and Edinburgh, managed to contribute something to the intellectual ferment of eighteenth-century Scotland.   Some of the famous Gregory dynasty, which supplied men

[23] *Memoirs of Sir John Clerk of Penicuik*, ed. J. M. Gray, pp. 86-7, 98-9.

[24] R. G. Cant, *The University of St Andrews, a Short History*, p. 87.

[25] *University of St Andrews. Handbook of the United College*, p. 15.

[26] Samuel Johnson, *Journey to the Western Isles of Scotland*, ed. R. W. Chapman (1951), p. 8.

of genius from the mid-seventeenth to the nineteenth century,[27] were active teachers of medicine at King's College; and John Gregory, who held a regentship in philosophy until his resignation in 1749, was followed in that post two years later by his cousin Thomas Reid.[28] Reid was a noted teacher at King's until in 1764 he succeeded Adam Smith in the chair of moral philosophy at Glasgow. Marischal College also played a part; it had in George Campbell a philosopher of real attainments, and in Thomas Beattie one who in his time enjoyed a greater name in literature and philosophy than he deserved. That the feud between the two colleges hindered their progress was well understood at the time, but repeated efforts at union merely increased the disharmony.[29]

At Glasgow ' the reforms of 1727 ushered in a period which must rank as one of the most brilliant in the history of the University ',[30] though there were drawbacks to offset the inspired teaching of Francis Hutcheson of the chair of moral philosophy, of William Cullen in medicine, or of Adam Smith. These were all great men and devoted teachers; but some of their colleagues fell far short of their calibre. The professors as a body enjoyed too much power and wasted too much time on petty intrigues. Some of them gained their places by wire-pulling and then either lectured intermittently and atrociously or not at all. Thus William Cross, the professor of civil law from 1746 to 1750, shuffled out of lecturing altogether; but between 1761 and 1801 John Millar in the same chair showed what zeal allied to genius could do. His fame drew students from all over Britain; his classroom was overcrowded, the students eager, expectant, waiting, according to the poet Thomas Campbell, ' as for a treat '.[31] In the circumstances of that time wire-pulling and nepotism were inevitable but did not invariably lead to bad results, although sometimes the blessings were mixed. Thus in 1743 William Leechman was elected to the chair of divinity largely through the

[27] See Agnes Grainger Stewart, *The Academic Gregories.* They furnished teachers for St Andrews, Aberdeen, Edinburgh, Oxford and Cambridge.

[28] Philip Spencer Gregory, *Records of the Family of Gregory,* p. 51, suggests that Reid was Gregory's immediate successor; but this is disproved by A. Campbell Fraser, *Thomas Reid,* p. 42.

[29] R. S. Rait, *The Universities of Aberdeen, a History,* pp. 342 ff.

[30] J. D. Mackie, *Short History of Glasgow University, 1451–1951,* p. 185.

[31] A. Dewar Gibb, in *Fortuna Domus,* p. 163.

influence of his friend Hutcheson; as a professor Leechman exercised a liberalising influence, but as principal from 1761 onwards he was autocratic and not entirely above board in his handling of the university finances.

Glasgow shone in philosophy and mathematics, her fame secured by such scholars as Hutcheson, Smith, and Robert Simson who from 1710 to 1760 held the chair of mathematics. The emphasis that came to be placed on mathematics was to stand the west of Scotland in good stead, providing as it did an indispensable aid to technological development. After all, James Watt was loosely attached to the college and was in a sense a protégé of Joseph Black.[32] Not so favoured by fortune was Glasgow's medical school. It began promisingly enough about the middle of the century and it had, but could not hold, distinguished men like Cullen and Black. William Cullen held the chair of medicine at Glasgow from 1751, but four years later, disgusted with the stultifying professorial intrigues, he moved to the professorship of chemistry at Edinburgh, where he had already studied for two years. In 1766 Black followed suit, succeeding Cullen who had switched to the chair of institutes of medicine or, as it would now be called, physiology.[33] The propensity of Glasgow professors to intrigue and wrangle was personified in John Anderson, professor of natural philosophy from 1757 to 1796, who managed to fall foul of everyone and who bequeathed a sum of about £1,500 to found a university more forward-looking than his *alma mater*. In it the professors were to be carefully supervised and not ' be permitted, as in some other Colleges, to be Drones or Triflers, Drunkards, or negligent in any manner of way '.[34] Money was too scarce to permit the realisation of the scheme, but in the nineteenth century Anderson's College became the centre of a flourishing medical school, and the bequest also contributed to the development of the Technical College.

Edinburgh's attainments in arts were respectable but hardly outstanding. In the middle years of the eighteenth century it could offer no names to rival those of Hutcheson, Smith, or Reid; but in Dugald Stewart, who succeeded Adam Ferguson as professor of moral philosophy in 1785, it had a remarkable teacher. Stewart was not an original thinker, rather ' a professor of philo-

[32] J. D. Mackie, *op. cit.*, 218-20.   [33] J. W. Cook, in *Fortuna Domus*, pp. 280-1.
[34] J. D. Mackie, *op. cit.*, pp. 211-12.

sophical deportment ';[35] but as one of his many enthusiastic students claimed, ' there was eloquence in his very spitting '.[36] Then in Colin Maclaurin, who in 1725 secured the chair of mathematics largely on the recommendation of Isaac Newton, Edinburgh possessed a mathematician of the first rank. Even so, the arts faculty was not as strong as it might have been. The town council displayed little wisdom in regulating this side of its college's activities, notably in refusing to consider David Hume for a chair; and, in common with most of the Scottish universities, the college was weak in classical learning. Greek tended to be regarded as the exclusive preserve of the university and the professors taught it only at an elementary level. The great classical tradition which survived in England in spite of ' port and prejudice ' found no real home in Scotland. Some frustrated Greek scholars attributed this loss to presbyterian hostility to profane culture; Professor Dalzel of Edinburgh, referring to the proficiency of English Hellenists, once enviously remarked: ' if it had not been for the confounded Solemn League and Covenant, we would have made as good longs and shorts as they '.[37] Then, too, the bulk of the students were boys in their early teens, and the reforms of the early eighteenth century had some unexpected drawbacks in that the professors did not, or could not, maintain the same discipline as the old regents. ' Laureation ' went out of fashion and few took degrees in arts. Rather more healthy were the developments in law where Edinburgh clearly surpassed its rivals, capitalising on the fact that it was the chief legal centre in the country. By the end of the first quarter of the eighteenth century the faculty of law, or laws as it was then known, was firmly established; and annexed to it was a novel venture, a chair of universal history. This, the first of its kind in Britain, made a promising start under Charles Mackie,[38] but was latterly treated as a sinecure.

Edinburgh's real claim to fame rested on its great medical school, the propagator ' of the best medical teaching in the English-speaking countries of the world '.[38a] And here, as in law,

[35] *D.N.B.* (edn. 1909), XVIII. 1172.

[36] Henry Cockburn, *Memorials of His Time* (edn. 1910), p. 23.

[37] Quoted in G. Davie, *The Democratic Intellect*, p. 204.

[38] L. S. Sharp, ' Charles Mackie, the First Professor of History at Edinburgh University ', in *S.H.R.*, XLI. 23-45.

[38a] C. Singer, *Short History of Medicine*, pp. 140-2.

external pressures forced the pace of development, for its story
' cannot be separated from the history of extra-Academical
Medicine as practised and taught in the City '.[39]   There was
already in existence a promising medical school, buttressed by
the Royal College of Physicians and aided by the Royal College
of Surgeons, before the university created its own school.   The
rivalry that ensued was not always friendly but it was entirely
healthy, each school acting as a stimulus to the other.   Monro
primus, the university professor of anatomy from 1720 until
1758, soon acquired a great reputation.   He worked in close
harmony with Lord Provost George Drummond and together
they enabled the university medical school to expand and improve.   They were largely responsible for the establishment of
the Royal Infirmary—an indispensable aid to clinical teaching
of which full use was made from 1746 onwards.[40]   Later, Cullen's
abilities as a clear and forceful lecturer further enhanced Edinburgh's name, and so did Black's reputation as a researcher.   By
the end of the eighteenth century, Edinburgh was firmly established as one of the leading medical centres of Europe.   Its degrees
were prized and the number conferred (all of them earned) grew
steadily from a mere half dozen or so per annum in the 1730s to a
steady fifty by the end of the century.   By that time indeed
medicine had come to be considered, like gardening, as a peculiarly Scottish art;   and this view was not unwarranted.   In all
probability the greatest natural genius Scotland produced in her
golden age in the eighteenth century was John Hunter (1728–93),
who established himself in London as a first-rate surgeon and
pioneer of natural science.[41]   Born on a Lanarkshire farm, poorly
educated, ill read and inarticulate, his ability to explore and
observe has left an indelible mark in medicine and biology.   His
advice to his favourite pupil, Edward Jenner,—' Don't think.
Try it '—was typical of the man and his method.   Hunter was
trained by his elder brother William who made some striking
contributions to obstetrics.

   Though the universities played an important part in diffusing
the culture of eighteenth-century Scotland, they cannot be held

[39] Sir A. Grant, *The Story of the University of Edinburgh*, I. 292-3; J. D. Comrie,
History of Scottish Medicine, I. ch. XIII.

[40] Grant, *op. cit.*, I. 305-6, 317; Comrie, *op. cit.*, I. 306-7.

[41] There is an exuberant but reliable account of him in John Kobler, *The Reluctant
Surgeon*.

solely responsible for the remarkable outburst of intellectual activity which distinguished that age. Many lines of force can be traced, but any likely resultant would have to be regarded as tentative. There were, in fact, not a few old and familiar aspects of Scottish society which contributed to, and made possible, the dynamic movement known as the Enlightenment. Calvinism, that bogeyman of the *avant garde* from David Hume's day to our own, was an intellectual system of theology which in rigorously logical fashion covered both God and man. More than a few attitudes later regarded as typical of the Scottish school derive from Calvinist theology; but it also imposed certain limits on the philosophers, for though the decline of church authority loosened the hold of theology over philosophy the church was still a powerful social agency. Even under the benign rule of the Moderates it was a case of ' thus far and no further ', as David Hume was to discover. Some of the philosophers, unlike Hume, were eager to salvage what they could from the old theology, in one or other of its forms, and to harmonise it with the new modes of thought. It was on this base, indeed, that Thomas Reid's philosophy of ' common sense ' rested. Then, too, the law of Scotland exerted an obvious influence on the Scottish philosophers of the eighteenth century, many of whom were as well versed in Stair as in Hobbes, Shaftesbury, Locke, or the French ' philosophes '. That law was philosophical in its bent; it put its faith in principles rather than in collections of dry precedents; and it too ranged far and wide over the condition of man. Hume, Ferguson and Stewart on such topics as marriage and divorce do little more than popularise the law of their country.[42] The traditions, conventions and customs of their native land also influenced their thought. One and all they rejected the social contract theory. To men still steeped in ideas of kinship the social contract must always have appeared as a fanciful notion. Adam Ferguson, himself a Highlander, knew that the so-called primitive society was in fact complex and bound by ties of blood; in insisting that ' mankind are to be taken in groupes, as they have always subsisted '[43] he reasoned well within his own experience.

[42] Cf. Stair's *Institutions of the Law of Scotland* (ed. G. Brodie, 1826), I, Bk. i, Tit. IV, Conjugal Obligations.

[43] Gladys Bryson, *Man and Society: The Scottish Inquiry of the Eighteenth Century*, p. 44, quoting from Adam Ferguson, *Essay on the History of Civil Society*.

And since experience was the touchstone of their system this is significant. The very first point that David Hume, such a supposedly detached thinker, made in his fragment of autobiography was that he came of a good family;[44] and in one of his famous essays he states categorically, ' Man, born in a family, is compelled to maintain society from necessity, from natural inclination, and from habit.'[45] These were the conceptions, and above all the insistence on the group rather than the individual, which made the Scottish philosophers of the eighteenth century the parents of modern sociology. In addition, there was something in their times which made such inquiries possible. The Union of 1707 created conditions which raised them above mere factious dispute. Hume fancied himself a Tory, but this did not cause any bitter strife with those like Robertson who fancied themselves to be Whigs. The practice of politics in Scotland after the Union had become a boisterous game rather remote from everyday life. The would-be parliamentarians might berate each other, but the intellectuals knew that no great principles were involved in the antics of corrupt burgh managers and retailers of airy freeholds. In an older Scotland the intellectuals would have been forced to take sides, since issues of considerable moment might have depended on the unprincipled shifts of the politicians. But in eighteenth-century Scotland the philosophers could engage in debates which were models of their kind, were charitably conducted and such as to advance understanding of the themes concerned. It is remarkable that when by the end of the century practical politics again embraced principles philosophy rapidly declined. Finally, ideas ignore boundaries. The eighteenth century generally was fertile of ideas and no narrow conceptions of nationalism fettered them. The culture of any people, indeed, is largely an acknowledgment of its debts. On the whole, the Scottish philosophers were empirical and tried to employ the methods of Francis Bacon and Isaac Newton; yet they were eclectic and in many ways they ' were representative and typical of the thought of the century '.[46]

The career of Francis Hutcheson illustrates the origin and

[44] David Hume, *History of England* (edn. 1812), I. ' My Own Life ', p. v.

[45] David Hume, *Essays, Moral, Political, and Literary*, ed. T. H. Green and T. H. Grose (1875), I. 113, ' Of the Origin of Government '.

[46] Gladys Bryson, *Man and Society, passim, e.g.* p. 176.

foreshadows the later development of philosophical thought in eighteenth-century Scotland. Hutcheson, born in 1694 at Armagh in Northern Ireland where his father was a presbyterian minister, studied at Glasgow under Gershom Carmichael in philosophy and John Simson in divinity. Simson exercised a powerful influence on Hutcheson, whom he won over to liberal or latitudinarian views. Ultimately Hutcheson corresponded with Samuel Clarke and came to hold that rational enquiry was the only useful method in either theology or philosophy. In 1725 he published *An Inquiry into the Original of Our Ideas of Beauty and Virtue*, which was followed in 1728 by his *Essay on the Nature and Conduct of the Passions and Affections, with Illustrations upon the Moral Sense*. Hutcheson also owed much to Shaftesbury, particularly his belief that benevolence is the criterion of morality. As a philosopher his fame has not endured: his real greatness was as a teacher. From 1729 when he became professor of moral philosophy at Glasgow until his death in 1746, his attractive lectures, delivered in English, influenced not only young philosophers like Adam Smith but also a whole generation of embryo divines. A far greater thinker, David Hume, soon eclipsed Hutcheson as a philosopher. Born in 1711, the younger son of a Merse laird, Hume dedicated himself to thought and literature and, in spite of penury, refused to train for law or any other profession but that of letters.[47] He published in 1739 his *Treatise of Human Nature*, following it up in 1741-2 by *Essays Moral and Political*; in 1748 appeared his *Philosophical Essays concerning the Human Understanding*, and by 1751 he had pretty well completed his work in speculative philosophy. His starting point was the doctrine of Locke that all knowledge is derived from experience of particular facts. Hume founded on experience and by a marvellous, though tricky, logic he reduced everything to mental impressions. The end product was scepticism and a system of morality based on no very solid grounds. The orthodox did not take kindly to these theories, and their hostility twice cost him a chair of philosophy, once at Edinburgh and again at Glasgow. Partly because of this unpopularity and misrepresentation but mainly because in his philosophical work he had reached an impasse, Hume turned to history. It was a natural enough

---

[47] For a full account of Hume's extraordinary career see E. C. Mossner's monumental *Life of David Hume*.

transition, for Hume, laying great stress on experience, looked to history to furnish data, following the well-known eighteenth-century dictum that history was 'philosophy teaching by examples'. There seemed, therefore, to be scope for a philosopher-historian and in fact Hume came to regard himself as primarily a historian. He deceived himself, for it is as a supreme philosopher that he still intrigues the world. As a man, too, he was unusual: brimful of good sense and good nature, at times childishly sensitive but a generous and loyal friend, David Hume knew that life was greater than philosophy. If Scotland had existed for no other purpose than to produce such a man then her rigorous past could be justified; and Hume, though in a sense a citizen of the world, was conscious of his debt to his own country.

Hume's speculations have excited philosophers from his time to our own. Reacting against him, Thomas Reid in his *Inquiry into the Human Understanding* (1764) mounted an assault on the prevailing psychology of sensationalism. Reid distinguished between the brain which receives impressions and the mind which produces ideas. Reid, in short, rejected the conclusion that 'ideas' were separate entities; for him the universe still existed, and God ultimately regulated all. In spite of some serious philosophical flaws in his argument, the 'common sense' philosophy was eagerly accepted, and after Reid found notable exponents in George Campbell, Dugald Stewart, and (residually perhaps) Sir William Hamilton (1788–1856). In the late eighteenth and early nineteenth century it became very influential, especially in France and the United States of America.[48] But though psychology occupied a prominent part in the *Scottish Philosophy* it by no means embraced the entire scope of the subject. Philosophy was not then as limited in content as it is now: it ranged over and bound together a wide variety of subjects, impinging on theology, physics, mathematics, politics, and the nature and functions of society. All these matters philosophers may still consider but in a self-conscious fashion that was foreign to the Enlightenment. Most of the eighteenth-century Scottish philosophers, well armed for the fray by their college training, touched naturally on all of these topics, and a few achieved their reputations in subjects which have since parted company with their parent, philosophy.

[48] See Henry Laurie, *Scottish Philosophy in its National Development*; and S. A. Grave, *The Scottish Philosophy of Common Sense*.

Adam Smith (1723–90) would not have dreamt of regarding himself as anything but a moral philosopher, though he has every right to be considered the founder of the new science of political economy. Smith's great book, *The Wealth of Nations* (1776), was simply an extension of certain aspects of his course of lectures on moral philosophy, and a strong moral influence pervades it (though not overtly treated). It is a serious error to confuse Adam Smith with the later Manchester school, the true begetters of 'economic man' and the 'dismal science'. David Hume also made some striking contributions to the development of economic thought, and indeed political economy was largely the off-spring of the Scottish Enlightenment. The term was first popularised by the Jacobite Sir James Steuart who in 1767 published his *Inquiry into the Principles of Political Economy*; and later the subject was advanced by the Whiggish Earl of Lauderdale's *Inquiry into the Nature and Origin of Public Wealth* (1804). In its early days economics was very much a 'Scotch science'.

A lesser figure than either Hume or Smith, but still an influential one, was Adam Ferguson (1723–1816). His *Essay on the History of Civil Society* (1767) has been variously estimated, favourably in America but on the whole unfavourably in England.[49] He was not a great thinker, but that did not prevent him from becoming the father of modern sociology. There were many others of lesser note who caused a stir in their time, notably the two acute but eccentric court of session judges, the Lords Kames and Monboddo, whose jealous feuding added spice to philosophy, and John Millar, who extended and deepened the pioneer work of Ferguson. Most of these men of letters were contemporaries and kept up a lively social intercourse in which claret vied with good talk. Their very conviviality was a large part of their culture; it aided scholarship, and it set ideas freely circulating. Most of them, and especially Hume, were generous in their appraisal of the works of others, and when they disagreed it was usually with a suavity and urbanity that did credit to them all. The only real exception to this was the malignant Gilbert Stuart, a social and constitutional historian, who was ravaged by egotism and jealousy.

49 W. C. Lehmann, *Adam Ferguson and the Beginnings of Modern Sociology* takes a favourable view; but H. J. Laski, *Political Thought in England from Locke to Bentham*, (edn. 1955), p. 116, dismisses Ferguson as a 'pinchbeck Montesquieu'.

History also had its place in the philosophy of the Enlightenment, and in this branch of study eighteenth-century Scots played no mean role. As David Hume declared: ' I believe this is the historical age and this the historical nation '.[50] There was justification for such a belief in that the Enlightenment gave historians something that had long been wanting—a standpoint and a rounded sense of values. Their technical defects they turned into virtues, for their limited scholarship preserved unity of theme and enabled their philosophy to make cool assessments. Their works, therefore, were above all readable and soon captured a large public. Voltaire is usually regarded as the greatest of the rationalist historians of the eighteenth century and the founder of the school; but, in fact, David Hume was an independent thinker both in philosophy and history. The two subjects, Hume believed, were closely connected, for his outlook and methods as a historian were governed by his philosophy, though there is no need to invoke metaphysics to explain why he wrote his *History of England* (1754–62) ' as the witches say their prayers—backwards '.[51] This was accident rather than design. (Oddly enough exactly the same thing happened a century later to Hume's biographer, John Hill Burton, with his *History of Scotland*.) Hume began with the seventeenth century for the best possible reason, because it interested him. His intention was to limit himself to that period, but when the first volume was published in 1754 he was so hotly assailed for his sympathetic treatment of Charles I that he had to take up the Tudors to justify his interpretation of the struggle between king and parliament. He then rounded his work off with two volumes covering events from the Roman invasion to the close of the middle ages. It only makes sense if the reader follows the same sequence, for Hume had little true feeling for history and no sense of continuity. As an illustration of the attitudes of the Enlightenment Hume's ' History ' has value, though historians do not now regard it as a good example of their craft—for them it suffers from too much philosophy and too little history. Hume paid scant heed to sources and did not trouble to control his prejudices. The famous style is there but it

[50] *Letters of David Hume to William Strahan*, ed. G. B. Hill, p. 155, Letter XLII, Hume to Strahan, August 1770. For a modern assessment, see D. B. Horn, ' Some Scottish Writers of History in the Eighteenth Century ', in *S.H.R.*, XL. 1-18.

[51] *Letters of David Hume to William Strahan*, p. xxix, n. 3. The *bon mot* belonged to Horne Tooke, philologer and radical.

sometimes disappears in a medley of subordinate clauses and bad syntax. In form, curiously, the ' History ' consists of a bald political narrative, with little consideration of social, economic, or cultural factors; and like most eighteenth-century rationalist historians Hume had a contempt for the middle ages which he did not bother to hide. Thomas Warton gave the game away when he wrote, ' We look back on the savage condition of our ancestors with the triumph of superiority '.[52] Thus Hume on the Anglo-Saxons tells us more about Hume than he does about the Anglo-Saxons. The rationalists also had a contempt for religion which they invariably dubbed ' fanaticism ' or ' superstition '; and, as Adam Smith put it, the philosophy of the Enlightenment was intended to be ' the great antidote to the poison of enthusiasm and superstition '.[53]

To a less obvious extent these characteristics were shared by William Robertson, the foremost historian in eighteenth-century Scotland. Robertson, the leader of the Moderate party in the established church and principal of Edinburgh University, had considerable merits. He worked as much as possible from original sources, manuscript as well as printed; he gave full references and added illustrative appendices, since he realised that his sources must support his arguments; and his style was lucid and elegant. These qualities appeared at their best in his *History of Scotland* (1759), which was a remarkable book for its time and probably the best ' national ' history then in existence. Robertson wrote much and won a great reputation, especially with his *History of the Reign of Charles V* (1769) and his *History of America* (1777). His influence was apparent in the work of Thomas Somerville, also a Moderate, who wrote rather dull narratives on the reigns of William and of Anne but who showed some skill in the use of manuscripts. Gibbon, too, was fired with the ambition to equal the names of Hume and Robertson; and when he produced his mighty *History of the Decline and Fall of the Roman Empire* it was the praise of the two leading Scottish historians that he prized most. The Romans also engaged the attention of Adam Ferguson whose *History of the Progress and Termination of the Roman Republic* (1782) became a widely used

---

[52] Quoted J. B. Black, *The Art of History*, p. 28.
[53] Adam Smith, *Wealth of Nations*, ed. Edwin Cannan (6th edn., 1950), II. 281; cf. *ibid.*, 272-3.

manual. Ferguson, however, could not match Gibbon in depth of knowledge or force of exposition, and these defects, with his chronic moralising, seriously weakened his work. But like Gibbon he knew how to turn his military experiences to account and his treatment of campaigns, for example Zama,[54] is first rate. This kind of rational literary history, since it appealed to the public, soon had numerous camp-followers, and some of the best works of this kind in English were written by Scots. Tobias Smollett was quick to cut into Hume's market with his journalistic *History of England* (1757), which showed most of the vices and few of the virtues of the school. Robert Henry, a minister of the Church of Scotland, produced yet another *History of England* (1771–93), covering the period from the Roman invasion to the death of Henry VIII, in which attention was given to social and economic matters, though the research was superficial and the conclusions facile. A. F. Tytler (later a judge of the court of session as Lord Woodhouselee) was for a time professor of universal history in Edinburgh; unlike most of his predecessors he lectured regularly, and in 1801 he published an expanded version of his lectures as *Elements of General History*. An effective populariser was the Scots clergyman John Adams, who among numerous other ventures published a digest of Kames, Monboddo, and Montesquieu entitled *Curious Thoughts on the History of Man* (1789). He also abridged Gibbon's *Decline and Fall* into two moderate volumes, and on the whole he did it all so well that ' one is rather surprised at the attractive and modern character of Adam's books than inclined to carping criticism '.[55]

The impression is sometimes given that all the eighteenth-century historians belonged to the philosophical or rationalist school, but this was not the case. In Scotland other approaches to history were well established before the philosophical methods of the eighteenth century had been worked out. Few people think of Gilbert Burnet as a Scot or even seriously consider his work as a historian, most preferring the easier course of dismissing him as a mere tattler. Yet even apart from his great essay in ' contemporary history ',[56] Burnet was a serious scholar who well

[54] Adam Ferguson, *History of the Progress and Termination of the Roman Republic* (edn. 1783), I. 163-6.

[55] T. P. Peardon, *The Transition in English Historical Writing, 1760–1830*, p. 56.

[56] Gilbert Burnet, *History of His Own Time*, 1st edn., I (1723), II (1734); thereafter various editions.

knew the worth of sources. To the modern student, however, by far the most interesting of eighteenth-century Scottish historians was Robert Wodrow, the much-maligned author of *The Sufferings of the Church of Scotland*. There was nothing philosophical about the pietistic Wodrow and his style is not likely to lead to addiction. He was a propagandist but not a maimer of truth, and his real significance lay in the techniques that he employed. As he remarked, ' It is with pleasure that I observe a growing inclination in this age to have historical matters well vouched, and to trace up facts to their proper fountains, with a prevailing humour of searching records, registers, letters and papers written in times we would have knowledge of'.[57] Wodrow followed the precept of the ancient historian Josephus who advocated that history should be written from records. In short, the technique used by Wodrow is precisely that which was later advanced by Leopold von Ranke; and in spite of moralising and occasional credulity Wodrow's *History* was the best produced in eighteenth-century Scotland. It is still in use, for not only is it a storehouse of original material but it contains the finest account in print of the complex opening years of the Restoration.

The record tradition, moreover, did not die out. It continued to make valuable contributions to knowledge but mainly by the editing of original documents. Notable among the collectors and editors was James Anderson, author of the *Diplomata Scotiae* published in 1739 by the grammarian Thomas Ruddiman who himself printed two volumes of *Epistolae Regum Scotorum*. Anderson was influenced by the great French record scholar Mabillon, whose influence was also apparent in the work of Father Thomas Innes who appended many original documents to his famous *Critical Essay on the Ancient Inhabitants of the Northern Parts of Britain or Scotland* (1729). Others again edited texts of chronicles and memoirs, like the quarrelsome Walter Goodall who in 1759 published an edition of John of Fordun's *Scotichronicon* which has not yet been superseded. All this effort made little appeal to the Enlightened, but in the later eighteenth century a more professional approach again began to assert itself. It is evident in such works as Lord Hailes's *Annals of Scotland* (1776–79), which broke with the philosophers in specialising in medieval history. The renewed interest in sources also appeared in Sir

[57] R. Wodrow, *History of the Sufferings of the Church of Scotland*, ed. Burns (1828), I. xxxix.

John Dalrymple's *Memoirs of Great Britain and Ireland* (1771–88); in James Macpherson's *Original Papers, Containing the Secret History of Great Britain, from the Restoration to the Accession of the House of Hanover* (1775); and in the antiquarian George Chalmers's *Caledonia* (1807–24). John Pinkerton went further, protesting against opinionated philosophy and insisting that ' history is a science, and must like other sciences have rules peculiar to it '.[58] His ' scientific ' prejudices proved almost as misleading as Hume's opinions, though to be fair to Pinkerton he undertook difficult ' dark age ' researches. Thus, by the end of the eighteenth century, history was coming to rely more and more on hard evidence and the prevailing mood was that which in the early nineteenth century was to serve the history of Scotland well in the publications of the Maitland and Bannatyne clubs.

Such activities demanded a more efficient press and book trade than Scotland could hitherto provide, and yet up to the middle of the eighteenth century there were only four printing houses in Edinburgh, none of them distinguished.[59] True, a high standard of workmanship was set by Thomas Ruddiman, the learned grammarian, antiquary, and Keeper of the Advocates' Library, who in 1728 was appointed printer to the college of Edinburgh. He specialised in producing good text-books for the use of schools and colleges, a long-felt want which had necessitated the import of books from Holland. The requirements of the lawyers also furnished steady business for the Edinburgh printers, since written pleadings were the rule in the court of session and each year some 90,000 quarto pages were run off as Session Papers,[60] ' the best paid work which a printer undertakes '.[61] The established church and the Seceders also supplied useful business; and in the last quarter of the century rapid advances were made. By 1779 there were twenty-seven printing establishments in the city, most of which produced sound work. The one outstanding Edinburgh printer of the time, however, was William Smellie who set up the second or Edinburgh edition of Robert Burns's *Poems* in 1787. He also had the distinction of being the first editor of the *Encyclopædia Britannica*, which began its long

[58] John Pinkerton, *An Enquiry into the History of Scotland, preceding the Reign of Malcolm III or the year 1056*, 2 vols. (1789), I. xxiv-xxv.
[59] Hugo Arnot, *History of Edinburgh* (1779), pp. 437-8.
[60] *A Printing House of Old and New Edinburgh, 1775–1925*, anon., N.D., p. 39.
[61] *Letters of Sir Walter Scott*, ed. H. J. C. Grierson, I. 97.

career in Edinburgh, appearing in instalments over the years
1768–71. The number of booksellers slowly increased, though in
the eighteenth century Edinburgh trailed in the wake of London.
Allan Ramsay senior was the pioneer of the book trade and has
some claim to have operated the first circulating library in
Britain from 1725 onwards. And the émigré Scots who so aroused
Samuel Johnson's ire were active in the London book trade,
though with his usual inconsistency the great doctor had nothing
but praise for their services to literature. In the late eighteenth
century many of the leading London booksellers were Scots,
such as Andrew Millar and Alexander Donaldson, and William
Strahan who published Gibbon's *Decline and Fall*. In alliance
with the Edinburgh printers they were a menace to London
booksellers who tried by means of associations known as ' congers '
to control the book trade in Britain. The Scots, meanwhile,
persistently challenged the Copyright Act of 1709 by bringing out
cheap pirated editions of books. The battle of the books raged
on and off for over thirty years before Donaldson triumphed by
a decision of the house of lords in 1774, which upheld the Scots
contention that there was no perpetual copyright at common law
to eke out the fourteen years granted by the act of 1709. This
decision was a stimulus to the Scottish printers and by the end of
the century Edinburgh had become a leading centre for printing
and publishing. Its great days, however, lay in the early nineteenth century when Archibald Constable was the first to break
the monopoly of the London publishers.[62] At that time more
printing was being done in Edinburgh than in all the other cities
of the United Kingdom put together, London excepted.

But the finest printing ever produced in Scotland issued from
Glasgow in the work of the printers to the university, Robert
and Andrew Foulis. Robert, the elder brother, was largely self-
educated. He was trained as a barber but became a keen student
of the classics, and had the good fortune to win the sympathy
of that great teacher and good man, Francis Hutcheson. The
brothers were keen collectors of manuscripts and fine books,
visiting among other parts of the continent the Scots College at
Paris where they were warmly received. Father Thomas Innes,
a member of the college, approved of them as scholars but

[62] F. A. Mumby, *Publishing and Bookselling, A History from the Earliest Times to the
Present Day* (edn. 1930), p. 254.

deplored their latitudinarian ' aversion to persecuting any for their different sentiments in religious matters '.[63] This was the very essence of Hutcheson's teaching and throughout it informed the work of the Foulis press. Robert Foulis was grieved by the low condition of the press in Glasgow, which mainly turned out ill-written, and worse printed, sour religious tracts. He hoped to stimulate demand for literature of a more cultured kind, and when in 1741 he was appointed university printer he began immediately to produce editions of the classics which were distinguished for the accuracy of their texts and the beauty of their type. Probably their greatest achievement was the magnificent folio edition of Homer (1756–58), on which every care was lavished, the text being closely scrutinised six times. No literary or technical flaws, however minute, were allowed to go uncorrected, even though this meant frequent reprinting of entire sections. But, as has been well said: ' This is the way in which really great work is done; it is not the way in which dividends are earned '.[64] The dividends slumped, however, not through any failure of the press but because in 1754 Robert Foulis threw himself ardently into a new venture—the setting up in Glasgow of an Academy of Arts. It anticipated the Royal Academy by almost fifteen years, but proved too ambitious and too costly. Foulis over-extended himself, public assistance was not forthcoming, and when he died in 1776 he was heavily in debt. His business died with him, for his son Andrew lacked ability; but the fame of Robert Foulis's work endured and high-quality printing remained a feature of the trade in Glasgow.

Eighteenth-century Scotland added much to the literature of knowledge, but its contributions to the literature of power were also substantial. The revived interest in the vernacular continued and, in the opinion of some good judges,[65] culminated in the poetry of Robert Fergusson (1750–74), who wrote in a pure, idiomatic, and pointed Scots. His descriptive poems of Edinburgh life, such as ' Leith Races ' or ' The Daft Days ', catch the scene to perfection. He was not as limited in range as sometimes represented, for he could draw rustic scenes with equal insight.

[63] Quoted by James Maclehose, *The Glasgow University Press, 1638–1931*, p. 155.
[64] J. Maclehose, *op. cit.*, p. 178.
[65] Sydney Goodsir Smith, ed., *Robert Fergusson, 1750–1774*; the best edition is *The Poems of Robert Fergusson*, ed. M. P. McDiarmid, 2 vols. (1954–6), with valuable introductions.

His 'Farmer's Ingle' is a truer poem than Burns's rather contrived
'Cottar's Saturday Night'. Fergusson died all too young, leaving
behind him a sizeable output of genuine poetry and a haunting
enigma. Could he really, as some have suggested, have changed
the course of Scottish literature by raising the vernacular into a
literary language? It seems unlikely, for at that time the whole
drift of Scottish life was towards closer assimilation with England.
In any event, technically flawless though Fergusson's art was it
lacked the power which made Robert Burns (1759–96) not only
the poet of Scotland but also the poet of humanity. Burns has
been made to suffer unfairly for the excesses of his hero-worship-
pers and the frustration of the modern makars. Much that he
wrote was vapid and should never have been printed; but there
is no rubbish in the Kilmarnock and Edinburgh editions of 1786-7,
which he himself carefully supervised. His range was wide and
he shone in no less than three separate kinds of poetry. In satire
he was strong and coarse, yet amazingly subtle, qualities which
merge to make an unforgettable portrait of 'Holy Willie'; 'Tam
o' Shanter' is one of the finest narrative poems in any dialect of
English; and, as a noted critic has bluntly put it, 'Burns was the
greatest song writer Britain has produced'.[66] He is also one of
the most popular and widely read poets that Britain has produced.
Shakespeare apart, no other British poet has been translated into
so many languages; nor is this due to current political sympathies, for Burns was widely translated in the nineteenth century.[67] The universal appeal is due largely to the poet's character,
to the peasant traditions of Scotland (Highland as well as Lowland), and the claims of freemasonry, all of which the genius
of Burns fused into a simple but deeply felt humanity. He is
interesting from other points of view, notably his insatiable
curiosity about people: this made him, next to Chaucer, the
historian's poet *par excellence*. In a series of sharply etched vig-
nettes he depicted his country, in most of its aspects, at the time
of its transition from a semi-feudal community into a bustling
industrial society, and because most countries have made, or are
making, just such a transition he remains topical.

Less well known but equally striking was the work produced
in Gaelic. Here matters are complicated by the fact that

[66] David Daiches, *A Critical History of English Literature*, II. 827.
[67] William Jacks, *Burns in other Tongues* (1896).

' literature ' is largely a misnomer, since much of the best of the
Gaelic poetry of that time was still being carried in oral tradition.
The old bardic school based on Ireland had virtually ceased by the
early seventeenth century and in Scotland there rose a modern
colloquial tradition which, stimulated by Jacobitism, reached its
peak in the eighteenth century. Alexander Macdonald (c. 1700–
c. 1770) is usually regarded as the greatest of modern Gaelic
poets, and in 1751 his work had the distinction of being the first
to be printed. But he had close rivals in Duncan Ban McIntyre
(1724–1812);[68] and Iain MacCodrum (1710–96);[69] and the
religious verse of Dugald Buchanan (1716–68) was not only of
great social significance in the Highlands but of much higher
merit than is usual in that genre. Gaelic poetry differed in
purpose and structure from most west European models; the
language was rich, descriptive, and pointed; and the feeling
for nature was strong. The poets held an honoured position in
Celtic society and their works played a great part in the lives of
Gaelic-speaking people: in a sense they were the true Highland
dominies, robbing illiteracy of its worst consequences. Their
fame, however, was and has remained local, though in a curious
way something of the tradition in which they worked came
to exert a powerful influence on European literature. This was
through the mediation of James Macpherson (1736–96), who
exploited a growing interest in primitive poetry by producing
what purported to be translations of an alleged ancient epic
Fingal (1761) which was followed by *Temora* (1763), and the whole
collected as *Ossian* in 1765. At once a tremendous controversy
ensued, men of letters taking sides as nationality or prejudice
dictated. Macpherson was accused of fraud and for long this was
the accepted verdict, though it now seems possible that he may
have worked in good faith.[70] He certainly consulted old manuscripts which contained pieces of Ossianic ballads, going back
perhaps to the sixteenth century, but of an epic no trace whatsoever. However contrived and however turgid, Macpherson's
work certainly had an extraordinary vogue and helped to give
rise to romanticism.

The literature, however, that was most highly regarded in

[68] See a very useful edition with translations, *The Songs of Duncan Ban Macintyre,*
ed. Angus Macleod.   [69] *The Songs of John MacCodrum,* ed. William Matheson.
[70] Derick S. Thomson, *The Gaelic Sources of Macpherson's ' Ossian '.*

'polite' society was that of the so-called Augustans who purged themselves of Scotticisms and fitted as far as they could into the mood and conventions of eighteenth-century English literature. The two greatest names here are undoubtedly those of the poet James Thomson (1700–48) and the novelist Tobias Smollett (1721–71), both of whom, significantly, moved to London. Thomson, a Borderer, was trained for the ministry but his deistic leanings dictated escape into literature. In England he at once made a name for himself with his poem *Winter*, published in 1725 and subsequently expanded to *The Seasons*. He was influenced by Milton but also reacted to the work of Sir Isaac Newton, though underlying both was the strong feeling for nature typical of Scots literature. In an England that was becoming weary of stylised treatments of the countryside 'Thomson was the first to make Nature his theme' and his popularity was matched by his influence.[71] He impressed not only contemporary and later poets but also the great English landscape painters, Constable and Turner, who used excerpts from *The Seasons* to describe their works. But Thomson had to pay for writing in a 'second' language, for his diction was pompous and obscure. He also wrote lifeless dramas, most of which were mere vehicles for political satire on Sir Robert Walpole, Thomson having thrown in his lot with the opposition. Of his dramas only one appalling line is now remembered, ' Oh Sophonisba! Sophonisba Oh!' As unlike Thomson as he could well be was Tobias Smollett. Whereas the poet was indolent and easy-going, the novelist was full of ferocious energy. His first work, *Roderick Random* (1748), a novel of incident rather than of plot, drew largely on his experiences in the navy and gives vivid, if savage, pictures of eighteenth-century life. *Peregrine Pickle* (1751) was in much the same vein; but his last work *Humphrey Clinker* (1771) shows a mellower and more discerning art, and, incidentally, contains an intriguing account of Edinburgh life. Again unlike the anglicised Thomson, Smollett remained a fiery Scottish patriot of the type of Fletcher of Saltoun. There were many lesser figures in this Augustan style, such as David Mallet and Henry Mackenzie, and, of course, a major one in James Boswell, biographer of Samuel Johnson and diarist extraordinary. Boswell is interesting in that he suffered acutely from the anxieties which afflicted men reared in one culture who

[71] Douglas Grant, *James Thomson, Poet of ' The Seasons '*, p. 100.

tried feverishly to assimilate themselves to another. His touchiness, his crawling, his snobbery, his boasts, and his self-pity, nearly all arose from this social malaise. By Boswell's time the great dread was not of Scotticisms in writing but of uncouth Scottish pronunciation. Dr Johnson might say 'Who's for poonch lads?'; but late eighteenth-century Scottish men of letters had to learn to put a curb on their tongues. To help them, in 1761 the Irish actor Sheridan lectured in Edinburgh on correct English usage, and some of the efforts made by his pupils were not just ridiculous, they were pathetic. Henry Cockburn, writing on the judges Eskgrove and Braxfield (who had forgotten more Scots law than Cockburn was ever to learn), dwells lovingly on their uncouth tongues; but Cockburn's friend Francis Jeffrey had triumphed to the extent that he spoke with a mincing English accent and could scarcely understand broad Scots, a dubious attribute in a Scottish advocate.

In art eighteenth-century Scotland made some notable contributions. Allan Ramsay (1713–84), the son of the poet, was trained partly in Italy and at first painted in the baroque style, but latterly he struck out in a simpler line of his own which made him the first portrait painter of real distinction produced in Britain. But he too was forced to work in London, although he retained a close link with Scotland through his friendship with David Hume and others. Ramsay indeed was the typical man of the Enlightenment, an accomplished scholar and amateur philosopher as well as artist.[72] Latterly he was eclipsed by Reynolds, a more imaginative painter; but Reynolds, who was not noted for acknowledging his debts, gave himself away in the most telling manner by taking over Ramsay's techniques. Later, too, in Scotland Ramsay's work was overshadowed by that of Henry Raeburn (1756–1823), though the trend of recent criticism has been to upgrade Ramsay. Between them Ramsay and Raeburn have left us a splendid pictorial gallery of the eighteenth century, including most of the leading politicians, authors, and judges. The work of Sir Robert Strange (1721–92), the Jacobite, who was one of the foremost engravers of his time, also deserves to be remembered; and a Scottish painter of great reputation in his day was David Wilkie (1785–1841) who concentrated on homely social themes rendered in the Dutch style.

[72] Alastair Smart, *The Life and Art of Allan Ramsay*.

The drama, meanwhile, was slowly and painfully winning a place for itself in Scotland. In 1736 Allan Ramsay senior ventured to open a regular theatre in Carrubber's Close in Edinburgh, but within six months the hostility of the church made use of a new act of parliament to have it closed. Under various pretexts plays continued to be staged and in 1752 John Lee was brought from Drury Lane to manage the Canongate Concert Hall. He was skilled in his craft and did much to raise the status of the theatre, but in the end he was unscrupulously defrauded by his backers, headed by Lord Elibank and others.[73] By this time the stage was becoming popular, to the chagrin of the traditionalists who joyfully took up the challenge implicit in the production of the Reverend John Home's tragedy of *Douglas* in December 1756; the more so as Home and his friends had taken such a prominent part in disciplining those like Thomas Gillespie who had objected to a high-handed system of church patronage. The dramatist gave up his living and beat a prudent retreat to London, where his lifeless declamations enjoyed some success. One of his friends, Whyte, minister of Liberton, escaped with a light sentence, on the naïve plea that while in the theatre he had concealed himself to avoid giving offence. ' Jupiter ' Carlyle was also libelled but he fought back and put his enemies to rout. The victory lay with the Moderates and thenceforth the theatre was free to develop as best it could. By 1759 the Edinburgh stage was beginning to attract short visits from leading London performers like Samuel Foote, and, two years later, Mrs Bellamy. In 1762, however, a gang of religious zealots fired the theatre in Glasgow at which Mrs Bellamy was to appear and she lost her valuable wardrobe. In spite of such an event the broad current was towards tolerance and, indeed, when the great Sarah Siddons appeared in Edinburgh in 1784 ' during the sitting of the General Assembly, that court was obliged to fix all its important business for the alternate days when she did not act, as all the younger members, clergy as well as laity, took their stations in the theatre on those days by three in the afternoon '.[74] In Glasgow the same change gradually took place and by the end of the century, except by the strictest dissenters, plays were regarded as innocent amusements.

[73] James C. Dibdin, *Annals of the Edinburgh Stage*, p. 79.
[74] Alexander Carlyle, *Autobiography*, pp. 322-3.

All too evidently it was not just the drama that caused unease among orthodox Calvinists. Eighteenth-century Scotland was a cultural battleground and only the dominance of the Moderate party in the established church from about the middle of the century onwards prevented large-scale heresy hunts. Thus in 1755 and 1756 David Hume and Lord Kames were bitterly attacked in general assemblies but on each occasion were saved by the tact of their friend Robertson who led the Moderate party from 1762 until 1780. Robertson was a realist. He knew that the trend of the age was secular, that the powers of the church had been curtailed, and that no good would come from theocratic delusions. But on the other hand, while he accepted patronage, he carefully dissociated himself, and as far as possible his party, from political management. Clergymen were thus free to contribute to the general culture of the times, but they were not encouraged to regard their livings as sinecures. In a way, the Moderates were essential to the maintenance of presbyterianism in Scotland by obliging it to conform to the general temper of the eighteenth century and thus helping to dispel its reputation for political subversiveness. But in terms of the well-being of church and nation a high price had to be paid for this service. Robertson's policy took no stock of new and disturbing social conditions. He believed that dissent should be not only tolerated but encouraged, so as to rid the Church of Scotland of its unruly members. In practice such a policy was too often illiberal and was aimed at securing the dominance of a party rather than the good of the church. Thus, the Relief Church, like the Wesleyans in England, had originally no wish to sever connections with the parent body, but a series of harsh decisions by the Moderates turned the Relief Presbytery from an ally into an embittered enemy. Yet in many areas, due to social and economic change, there was need for more churches. The law made the setting up of new parishes difficult, but still the Relief Church, active and enthusiastic in forming new congregations and eager to maintain a link with the establishment, was rebuffed. The bigotry of the Moderates was repaid in just measure, for, unlike the Seceders, the Relief placed no great emphasis on the establishment principle and it was from this body that voluntaryism emerged in the early nineteenth century. In other ways Moderate policies failed mainly because of excesses. Robertson and his party accepted patronage and regarded the claims of congregations with a mixture of fear and contempt. Gradually by decisions of church courts they reduced the call from the congregation, which was vaguely implicit in the act of 1712, to a mere form. Quite clearly, when statutes were infringed in a way that met the approval of the dominant political class they were not to be treated as sacrosanct, though the future would reveal just as clearly that the converse did not hold. Finally in 1784, infuriated by renewed agitation against patronage, the general assembly, then dominated by Robertson's successor as leader of the Moderates, George Hill of St Andrews, omitted to instruct its commission to petition parliament for repeal of the act of 1712. From 1736 until 1783 that had been an annual form. Under Hill Moderatism took on ugly features, becoming little more than the Dundas interest at prayer, with nepotism and pluralism the main order of service.

With theology the Moderates had little concern, although Robertson stubbornly resisted demands for the abolition or loosening of the Westminster Standards. There was truth in the stinging satire of John Witherspoon, an evangelical Church of Scotland minister, who, disgusted with lukewarm Moderatism, emigrated to America to become a noted teacher at Princeton and later a signatory of the Declaration of Independence. Infuriated by the high-handed actions of the general assembly of 1752 in expelling the blameless Gillespie, Witherspoon in 1753 published his *Ecclesiastical Characteristics* in which he quipped, ' The Confession of Faith, which we are now all laid under a disagreeable necessity to subscribe, was framed in times of hot religious zeal; and therefore it can hardly be supposed to contain anything agreeable to our sentiments in these cool and refreshing days of moderation '.[75] In so far as the Moderates valued the Confession it was as an aid to church discipline rather than to salvation. Most of them in their sermons copied the elegant but empty rhetoric of Hugh Blair, the most fashionable preacher of late eighteenth-century Edinburgh, whom in 1762 the grateful town council elected to the recently created chair of rhetoric and belles lettres. Their sermons were polished essays enjoining good works, kind thoughts, and social order. Hell fire had gone, but with it too had gone the saving mysteries of the Christian faith. Rational religion was the natural companion of rational philosophy and rational history,

[75] John Witherspoon, *Works* (edn. 1805), VI. 162-3.

and under the Moderates the seeds of unbelief were spread in Scotland, not deliberately or systematically, but simply as a consequence of the laodicean views of the dominant party in the kirk. The tradition established by Hutcheson and Leechman had also by the 1780s led to the rise of Socinianism (particularly in the old covenanting area of the south-west), the very fate which had already overtaken the bulk of the English presbyterians. In 1786 something of all this appeared in a work by Robert Burns's friend, the Reverend William McGill of Ayr, whose *Practical Essay on the Death of Jesus Christ* soon became suspect. The book was a pedestrian effort, rational in intent but confused in argument, and its theology was thin and meagre. It was a muddled examination of the Atonement, Arminian in tendency, though in places it could be construed as Arian or Socinian. In 1789 McGill was arraigned as a heretic, but on recanting he escaped with a mild censure. The Evangelicals within the establishment and the Burgher Seceders kept up a bitter attack on him; but they too were affected by the spirit of the age. No denomination escaped entirely the effects of the Enlightenment. The Popular or Evangelical party in the Church of Scotland was by the late eighteenth century no longer ' high flying ' and had in many ways accommodated itself to Moderatism. Its leaders John Erskine and Sir Henry Moncrieff were as polished and acceptable in society as Jupiter Carlyle or George Hill; but long before the Moderates recognised the significance of the new social order that was emerging, the Evangelicals sensed the problems that it brought in its train and particularly the threat posed by presbyterian dissent. The Seceders, too, were racked by disputes as to the place of the covenants in a country which was fast ceasing to bear any resemblance to the Scotland of the mid-seventeenth century. Influenced perhaps by the acts of their brethren in America, both Burghers and Anti-Burghers divided over this question, a New Light section in each church arguing that the covenants had to be seen in a historical perspective and not accepted as literally binding, whereas the Old Lights placed the covenants on par with the Confession of Faith. At bottom, the struggle was really a transition from establishment to voluntary principles, the New Lights arguing that church and state should be separate, a doctrine which rigid adherence to the Solemn League and Covenant would nullify.[76]

[76] D. Scott, *Annals and Statistics of the Original Secession Church*, p. 81.

In 1799 the Burghers split into two rival synods, generally known as New Light Burghers (officially the Associate Synod) and Old Light Burghers (Associate Presbytery or Original Burghers). The more conservative Anti-Burghers, no longer as rigid as in the days of ' Pope ' Adam Gib, were similarly divided in 1806 into Old Lights (Constitutional Associate Presbytery) and New Lights (General Associate Synod). These divisions notwithstanding, the Seceders steadily increased their numbers.

Methodism, in spite of many tours undertaken by the indefatigable John Wesley, failed to prosper in Scotland. Whitefield, who was intent on making Christians rather than Methodists, was much more successful. His Calvinism was more acceptable in Scotland than Wesley's Arminianism; and, besides, Whitefield shrewdly forecast that Wesley's efforts to form Methodist Societies in Scotland were foredoomed to failure. Though five Wesleyan preachers were ordained in 1785–86, organised Methodism had little or no hold in Scotland. Doctrinal argument, and not oratory alone, was what moved Scottish audiences. Wesley came to this realisation at last: ' They knew too much ', he admitted, but added slyly, ' therefore they could learn nothing '.[77] But in the last decade of the eighteenth century there arose a new type of evangelism, which aimed at combating the social problems thrown up by the quickening economic life of Scotland. It was strengthened by similar developments in England, particularly by the emergence of the ' Clapham sect ', an influential body dominated by William Wilberforce who in 1797 gave a classic exposition of its aims in his *Practical View of Christianity*, which was later described as ' the bible of evangelicalism '. The main champion of the new movement in Scotland, Robert Haldane of Airthrey, a retired sea-captain, attributed his spiritual awakening to the shocks produced by the French Revolution and like Wilberforce was keenly alive to the dangers of radical atheism. For society to be preserved it had to be Christianised, and if this task was beyond the moribund establishments then they would have to be reinforced by enthusiastic lay skirmishers. Haldane and his brother James hoped to work with the establishment; but in a bitter debate on foreign missions in the general assembly of 1796 the Moderates made it clear that they had no time for such projects, particularly as they had lately been promoted by suspect

[77] B. Dobrée, *John Wesley*, p. 131.

bodies which held dangerous political views.[78] The Haldanes
formed a missionary society at Edinburgh, but their efforts were
regarded with contempt by the establishment. They set up
sabbath schools, but these were condemned as seminaries of
sedition. In 1796 James took part in a missionary tour of the
north, in which the main preacher was the Reverend Charles
Simeon of Cambridge; and in May of the following year James
preached to the colliers of Gilmerton before, in July, setting off
on a missionary tour with another lay-preacher. As well as
preaching in pulpits when they could and in the open when
none were available, they assailed the shortcomings of establishment and dissenters alike. In January 1798 the Haldanes founded
and largely financed 'The Society for Propagating the Gospel
at Home', which was pledged to undenominational evangelism.
They could count, however, on the support of a handful of
evangelical ministers in the Church of Scotland, notably Greville
Ewing and George Cowie of Montrose. A Tabernacle was set up
in Edinburgh, and in the summer of 1798 they obtained the
services of Rowland Hill of Surrey Chapel in London, a pithy if
rather eccentric preacher. Hill's vocation, like that of John Knox,
craved plainness of speech, and his comments on the religious
state of Scotland contrasted sharply with the nebulous bumbling
of the Moderates. Thus his published account of his tour increased the unpopularity of the new movement. He found fault
with all the presbyterian denominations except the Relief, cas-
tigating in particular the Church of Scotland in which ' too many
I fear can subscribe the most explicit Calvinism, and preach the
grossest Arminianism '.[79] The presbyterians replied by forbidding the use of their pulpits to any but their own ministers, and
unworthily smeared the Haldanes with jacobinism. These
charges were indignantly rebutted by Hill in a series of addresses
written in the course of a second tour of Scotland in 1799.[80] From
this point onwards the work of the Haldanes gave rise to independent sects. Scottish congregationalists and baptists really derive

[78] D. Mackichan, *The Missionary Ideal in the Scottish Churches*, ch. IV.

[79] Rowland Hill, *Journal Through the North of England and Parts of Scotland with Remarks on the Present State of the Established Church of Scotland and the different Secessions therefrom* (1799), p. 111.

[80] Rowland Hill, *A Series of Letters, occasioned by the late Pastoral Admonition of the Church of Scotland, as also their Attempts to Suppress the Establishment of Sabbath Schools* . . . (1799).

from this movement, though each body lays claim to an earlier but extremely tenuous history. True, the followers of John Glas, forming a sect from 1730 onwards, showed certain features of congregationalism, and rather more were displayed by the Old Scots Independents who came into existence in 1768, to be followed a year later by the Old Scotch Baptists.[81] These were all tiny bodies and of very limited significance. The Tabernacle Churches set up by the Haldanes were the true foundation of congregationalism in Scotland, though to begin with their polity was vague and the real work of organisation was to be carried out later by Greville Ewing. In spite of petty and malicious harrying by kirk and state the new movement caught on, and even made an impact on the Highlands. Tabernacle Churches there were few, but the idea of lay-preaching fitted well into Gaelic society and gave rise to ' the men ', a body of devoted itinerant preachers who wrought a remarkable transformation in many parts of the Highlands. In 1808 the Haldanes became baptists and many of the congregationalists followed them into the baptist church. But in spite of these new denominations drawing some away from the Seceders and the Relief, presbyterian dissent remained far and away the most serious threat to an establishment which at the close of the eighteenth century was being forced, reluctantly, to take stock of its position.

The end of the eighteenth century found the fortunes of the non-juring episcopalians rising after a dismal period of official disfavour and petty persecution. They were able to settle their liturgy by 1764, more or less on the lines advocated by the Usagers. In the same period discipline and administration were improved by bishops who directly supervised their dioceses, such as Robert Forbes, Bishop of Ross and Caithness, who has left an interesting account of his activities in the north of Scotland.[82] Still, in 1784 there were only four Scottish bishops and not more than forty clergy, and for the most part they were confined to the north and north-east of Scotland. But the status of the church was improving and its standing was further raised in 1784, when Scottish bishops consecrated Samuel Seabury, an American who

[81] See James Ross, *A History of Congregational Independency in Scotland*; and George Yuille, ed., *History of the Baptists in Scotland*.

[82] *Journals of the episcopal visitations of Robert Forbes*, ed. J. B. Craven. Forbes collected the Jacobite memorabilia known as *The Lyon in Mourning*, ed. H. Paton (S.H.S.), 3 vols.

was refused consecration by the Church of England. A decisive change came when, on the death of Charles Edward in 1788, nearly all the clergy at last decided to acknowledge the Hanoverian dynasty. They were thus able to benefit by an act of 1792 which removed the special disabilities on presbyters ordained by Scottish bishops and made it possible for them to qualify for toleration on certain conditions, one of which was acceptance of the Thirty-Nine Articles of the Church of England. The next step was to bring gradually into the fold the ' qualified chapels ' which had been set up on the Anglican model to escape the stigma of Jacobitism and disloyalty. The general result was to give a much more English character to the Episcopal Church in Scotland. The effects of English education, too, were beginning to reinforce the latent sympathy which many of the aristocracy and the gentry had long harboured for episcopacy, and after 1792 (when its loyalty was no longer in question) the Episcopal Church gradually received converts from the upper classes.

The history of the Roman catholics in Scotland in the late eighteenth century was not dissimilar to that of the episcopalians. Catholics, too, were harried after the '45, many of the bishops and priests being forced to flee the country. Pressure was brought to bear on the main catholic chiefs and many of them lapsed from their faith, though they found great difficulty in getting their people to emulate them. The failure of the ministrations of the church undoubtedly reduced the numbers of its communicants; and it is noticeable too that in the early phase of Highland emigration, in the 1770s and 1780s, a considerable proportion of the emigrants were Roman catholic. But gradually more favourable conditions obtained (again largely due to the extinction of Jacobitism) and it seemed that tolerance was to be the order of the day. In England a bill reducing the discrimination against Roman catholics was passed in 1778 and such a measure for Scotland was favourably received by the general assembly. Unfortunately, the Moderates, who favoured it, for once underestimated the bigotry of their fellow presbyterians. Immediately the cry of ' no popery ' was raised, a Protestant Association was formed and carried on vigorous propaganda, riots in Glasgow and Edinburgh alarmed the authorities, and the bill was withdrawn. The outbreak of the French Revolutionary War, however, showed that the old fears about the loyalty of Roman catholic subjects were groundless, and in 1793 an act was passed, largely through the diplomacy of Bishop Hay, which relieved Roman catholics from the worst of the penal disabilities under which they laboured but still treated them as second-class citizens excluded from public office. By 1800 the numbers and distribution of Roman catholics in Scotland were beginning to change. The main strength of the faith still lay in parts of the Highlands and the north-east; among native Lowland Scots it was still almost non-existent; but already a stream of Irish Roman catholics was entering south-west Scotland and in the course of the next half century it was to leave its mark on Scottish society and transform Scottish catholicism.

History is not cricket, and centuries as such have no claim to any peculiar virtue. But in the period of time just surveyed every aspect of Scottish life was being subjected to change—sometimes slow, sometimes rapid, but seemingly inexorable. Furthermore, it was revolutionary change, not a mere shift of emphasis within the same system. It affected material conditions, these in turn brought social change, and contingent on this, but not absolutely dependent on it, there arose new beliefs and new values. It would be idle to try to account for changes of this magnitude by any simple formula; and it would be worse than useless to assign primacy to economic, social, or religious factors. To do so would be to ignore the all-important point that society is a complex entity to which nothing simple or self-contained ever happens. Everything has repercussions, be it the introduction of the potato or the rise of the Anti-Burghers. On the 1st of January 1801 the full implications of the changes wrought in eighteenth-century Scotland still remained to be worked out.

8

POLITICS IN THE LATE EIGHTEENTH CENTURY: THE CHALLENGE TO THE OLD REGIME

The so-called ' classical age of the constitution ' when powers were clearly distributed and checks evenly balanced is a fiction, for throughout the eighteenth century the rights of king, houses of parliament, and law courts, were the subject of a hidden struggle. That struggle erupted most dramatically in the first twenty-five years of the long reign of George III, not because the king wished to be a despot but rather because of the very uncertainty of the constitution. Though overlaid by factiousness and much special pleading on all sides, the fundamental point at issue in the crisis of 1782–84 was whether the house of commons could force a ministry upon the king. In 1782 the house had apparently demonstrated the converse, that the king's confidence could not sustain a ministry which did not command the support of the commons.

Yet George III's reign began peaceably enough. The half-dreaded purge of the ministry did not take place, if only because the young king was eager to carry on the Seven Years' War and, conscious of his own inexperience, was at first hesitant in the exercise of his powers. The old Duke of Newcastle remained in office, but soon began to complain that he was not being con-sulted. Nor was it at first regarded as unreasonable that the Earl of Bute, the king's former tutor, should be brought into the ministry in March 1761 as secretary, acting with Pitt. Bute was honest, a man of culture and ability, but he was vain and lacked experience of either politics or administration if one discounts a brief appearance as a representative Scots peer and his tenure of the groomship of the stole. Shortly thereafter the ministry disintegrated and a new one had to be fashioned. In October 1761 Pitt resigned in a tantrum after differences with his colleagues over the question of peace or war with Spain; and in May 1762 Newcastle after numerous slights gave up office, refusing to cut ' a contemptible figure in business '.[1] Bute became first lord of the treasury and head of the ministry, with as his main object the making of a reasonable peace with France. This was accomplished, but shortly after its conclusion Bute fell victim to the rancour of the times and thankfully resigned in April 1763, hoping that his retirement would ' remove the only unpopular part of Government '.[2] In the scurrilous campaign against Bute, and against Scotsmen in general, John Wilkes first caught the public eye. By 1763 the problem was to weld together a stable ministry—something that was desired by both king and parliament but which for long enough seemed a chimera. Thus, on the fall of Bute, George Grenville struggled to hold a patchy ministry together in the face of violent criticism from Newcastle's friends under the Marquis of Rockingham. Despairing of the obstinate Grenville, who lectured interminably and drove hard bargains, the king in 1765 turned to Rockingham, who tried to form an all-party ministry on the model of the Pelhams. William Pitt's cloudy vision of non-party government led to Rockingham's failure and to increasing ministerial instability, nominally under Pitt but in reality under the indolent Duke of Grafton. In these years, too, the quarrel with the American colonies waxed and waned, creating an atmosphere of increasing tension and distrust. The problem of government seemed to be solved, however, when Grafton retired in 1770 and Lord North became head of a ministry which enjoyed the favour of the king and the support of a majority in the house of commons. The first few years of this ministry saw a return to Newcastle's policy of placating interests and nursing constituencies; but from 1775 North was faced with the troubles which culminated in the revolt of the American colonies.

[1] G. W. T. Omond, *Arniston Memoirs*, pp. 172-4, Duke of Newcastle to Lord President Dundas, 5 June.
[2] *A Prime Minister and His Son: from the Correspondence of the 3rd Earl of Bute and of Lt. General The Hon. Sir Charles Stuart, K.B.*, ed. Mrs. E. Stuart Wortley, p. 49.

With British politics in such an upheaval it is not surprising that affairs in Scotland should have been equally confused. The tight management of the previous reign relaxed, helped by the death of Argyll in 1761 and the failure of a comparable figure to emerge. Bute was Argyll's nephew but was not successful in management; he tried to fill the gap with his brother, James Stuart Mackenzie, but in this sphere Stuart Mackenzie had neither experience nor talent. In Rockingham's short-lived ministry in 1765 Newcastle tried to control Scottish affairs through the head of the judiciary, but Lord President Dundas wisely refused to play politics.[3] North in his turn had the good fortune to light upon a natural successor to Argyll in the lord president's half-brother, Henry Dundas. It is in itself a significant commentary on the social changes of the later eighteenth century that the man who was to wield virtually undisputed power in Scotland sprang not from the great aristocracy but from one of the increasingly important smaller landed families with strong legal and administrative backgrounds. In the conditions of the earlier eighteenth century Henry Dundas, in spite of his considerable abilities, could have been little more than an understrapper to some great man of title.

Following family tradition Henry Dundas trained as an advocate but his active period at the bar was brief. In 1766 at the age of twenty-four he was made solicitor-general, and when in 1774 he judged the time right he calmly used the family interest in Midlothian to oust the sitting member, who had already agreed that Dundas had a ' natural interest ' in the county which he would not dispute.[4] Dundas was promoted lord advocate in 1775, and his chief concern thereafter was to extend his electoral influence in Scotland and so increase his bargaining power with the ministry. He was no innovator and contributed little to the art of management, contenting himself with adroit use of the existing foundations and extending them as opportunity offered. He began with a vague attachment to so-called 'Whig principles', but this phase was shortlived and failed to survive the needs of electoral manipulation. In all this Dundas was old-fashioned and, even at the outset of his career, rather behind the times. The great questions

---

[3] Omond, *Arniston Memoirs*, pp. 176-7.
[4] Holden Furber, *Henry Dundas, first Viscount Melville*, p. 5; Omond, *Arniston Memoirs*, pp. 183-4.

raised by the American Revolution, and even the philosophical enquiries into the nature of society that were so typical of the Scottish Enlightenment, posed no problems to his closed mind. Indeed, it is possible to read and re-read his voluminous correspondence and not once light upon anything that resembles an *idea* let alone an ideal. Everything was judged in terms of power or expedience, though personally he was tolerant and large-minded, with a bluff sociable manner that made him genuinely popular. He believed in religious freedom, but only so long as it did not threaten his electoral interests. He was a strong speaker of the brisk ' no nonsense ' school who could still indulge in sophistry and near-nonsense when occasion demanded. Dundas, in short, was the complete eighteenth-century politician, out of season and run to seed. At the height of his powers he straddled Britain like a colossus,[5] but this was due largely to the circumstances of the times in which he lived. Neither as lawyer nor administrator nor statesman can he be compared with Duncan Forbes; but his long tenure of numerous offices and a voluminous correspondence have led predictably to the usual imposing biographies. It is, therefore, all the more necessary to make the clear point that, appearances notwithstanding, Henry Dundas did not engross the politics of Scotland in the last two decades of the eighteenth century. ' Harry the Ninth ' was the uncrowned king not of Scotland but of the Scottish electors and their hangers-on.

Events conspired to challenge the existing political system: in particular the repercussions of the American War (1776–83) affected Scotland no less deeply than England, but in Scotland they found different expression. To begin with, the war was generally popular and regarded as a just assertion of the rights of the crown and the imperial parliament. Little sympathy was shown for the colonists, not even by the merchant interests which deplored the loss of trade caused by the conflict. Certain of the Seceders passed resolutions pleading for conciliation but they represented a small minority. Dundas opposed every such attempt and in February 1778 even the king, obstinate champion of his rights though he was, complained of the lord advocate's activities, stigmatising him as a pest.[6] The hint was not lost on

---

[5] J. A. Lovat-Fraser, *Henry Dundas*, p. 42: ' He stood like a Colossus with one foot in London, and one in Edinburgh '.   [6] *Ibid* p. 5.

Dundas, who became a more or less consistent supporter of North. But the consequences of the defeat at Saratoga—the alliance of France and Spain with the United States and a dismal series of reverses for the British—caused Dundas again to alter his attitude. By 1780 the war was unpopular mainly because of its ill success, and the ministry laboured under an increasing load of criticism. North's amiable slackness irritated Dundas, not least perhaps because the prime minister had failed to heap offices and rewards on the lord advocate. In particular, Dundas was disgruntled at not being granted the keepership of the Scottish signet for life.

Moreover, the ominous cry had been raised that the ministry's troubles were all attributable to corruption and mismanagement. This was exaggeration; but none the less there was substance in the charge. The Reverend Christopher Wyvill was already urging the freeholders of Yorkshire to demand moderate parliamentary reform to correct abuses in government, while at the same time in London and Middlesex more radical claims were being advanced. The core of the parliamentary opposition, the Rockingham Whigs, flirted with the reformers but at bottom the Rockinghamites were opposed to reform of representation. Their panacea was 'economical reform', fervently advocated by Edmund Burke, the object of which was to break the supposed power of the crown by abolishing sinecures and controlling the king's civil list. The ministry, harassed by these troubles—by the stalemate in America, by the League of Armed Neutrals, and by the Volunteer Movement in Ireland—sought to take advantage of a brief triumph in Georgia to dissolve parliament in the hope of gaining support in a new house of commons. The general election of 1780 did not quite reproduce the old-style campaign dominated by the treasury in co-operation with local electoral interests.[7] Measures, and not just men, were in debate and in many of the English constituencies this fact was apparent: for instance, the number of contested elections was appreciably higher than had been the case in 1761 or 1768. But these changes hardly affected the Scottish constituencies, most of which the clerk of the treasury, John Robinson (a skilled manager in the government interest) might have bracketed with the stewartry of Kirkcudbright and

[7] For a penetrating analysis of the elections of 1780, see I. R. Christie, *The End of North's Ministry*, pp. 116 ff.

Roxburghshire as ' the same to government whoever succeeds ', or ' whichever way a friend '.[8]

For want of any better prospect Dundas, in spite of his discontent, supported North. He could hardly have thrown in with the Rockinghams and he knew only too well that Dundas without ministerial support would have made little impression on the Scottish constituencies. Twenty of the 45 constituencies were contested, and in the end 41 out of the 45 Scottish M.P.s supported the ministry. This remarkable feat enhanced the value of Scots political management to government and did much to account for Dundas's extraordinary career. The administration, in short, was driven to rely on the closed English constituencies and the well-drilled phalanx from the north. In 1780 Dundas personally controlled 12 of the 41: his aim thereafter was to extend his interest and so appreciate his value to government. The times were chaotic, and any consistency shown by Dundas in the prolonged crises of the next four years was more or less thrust upon him. He believed that the war was lost and ought to be ended: by 1780 most reasonable minds had so concluded. Cornwallis's surrender at Yorktown in November 1781 forced North to think along the same lines. Dundas pressed for the dismissal of those ministers, like Lord George Germain and Lord Sandwich, who still believed in the war. He managed to secure the dismissal of the incompetent Germain but failed with the abler Sandwich. The great problem was the king's obstinate determination to fight on, and finally in March 1782 North gave up the unequal struggle and resigned. Rockingham formed a ministry in which the pliable Dundas continued to serve as lord advocate, and when the new prime minister died within a few weeks Dundas continued to serve under Lord Shelburne. Shelburne was beset by difficulties, particularly by the jealousy of Charles James Fox, and he recognised Dundas's value by heaping offices upon him. Thus Dundas received the coveted signet for life, was made treasurer of the navy, and was admitted to the privy council. In February 1783 Shelburne was brought down by the so-called unnatural coalition of Fox and North. In fact, ever since 1780 all sorts of coalitions had been bruited and this one was no more unnatural than many that had been suggested, particularly by Dundas, who was fertile of such schemes.[9] By 1783 Dundas had committed himself to

---

[8] Christie, *op. cit.*, p. 69, citing Windsor MSS.   [9] Furber, *Dundas*, pp. 14-15.

William Pitt the younger, to whom George III turned in a desperate but unsuccessful effort to avert a ministry dominated by the apostate North and the detested Fox.

These involved constitutional crises not only determined the career of Dundas but helped to dominate Scottish politics for the next forty years; for if Dundas could have worked with Fox he would almost certainly have retained the office of lord advocate and with it the lasting resentment of George III. As it was, Fox could not abide Dundas; and in August 1783 Dundas was replaced as lord advocate by Henry Erskine. But though apparently out of the game Dundas was well placed, for he could now openly align himself with the younger Pitt and make the final break with North. All this ensured the ready sympathy of the king, who personally cared nothing for the insensitive Dundas. Furthermore, the very question which was to ruin the coalition ministry proved advantageous to Dundas. The administration of the East India Company's territories had become a complex problem, which had been tackled but not solved by North's Regulating Act in 1773. Corruption and misgovernment in the East continued, and from 1781 onwards Dundas had made a close study of these problems. By 1783 he was regarded as an expert on the subject and he proved of considerable service in attacking the measures proposed by Fox. These were embodied in two bills, one of which aimed at depriving the East India Company not only of political control but of the disposal of its vast patronage. Some such act was needed, but Fox's bill exposed him to the charge of seeking for his own faction an even greater source of political corruption than the crown patronage which he had so often condemned. The company raised a hue and cry, and George III seized on the pretext to bring down the hated coalition by having the house of lords reject the bills.

Dundas's knowledge of Indian affairs, no less than his political expertise in Scotland, made him one of the mainstays of the ministry formed by the younger Pitt in December 1783. 'The schoolboy' prime minister was fiercely assailed by the office-less and outraged opposition, and there is no doubt that in this trying period he found Dundas a valuable support. It was Dundas, too, who largely drafted the India Bill which Pitt introduced and passed in 1784. The main feature of the bill was the setting up of a board of control for India which regulated the political aspects of the company's affairs and had considerable influence over its patronage. From the beginning Dundas was the most prominent member of the board, and in time this enabled him greatly to increase his political strength in Scotland.[10] The wealth of the Indies had been diverted from 'Carlo Khan' (as Fox was dubbed in a famous cartoon of the day) to the political manager of Scotland. One of the older historians of British India summed the matter up pithily: 'All parties when in opposition declaim against the increase of ministerial patronage—all parties when in office labour to add to its extent'.[11] Dundas's first act in his new office was to 'perpetrate a foul job',[12] granting payment to the alleged creditors of the Nabob of Arcot. He continued in this fashion to the end. For example, it was chiefly owing to Dundas that in 1803 the ministry annexed the entire patronage of Ceylon.[13] It should, however, be said that in recommending appointments in the company's service Dundas was careful to ensure that his obvious predilection for his countrymen was offset by a reasonable standard of efficiency on their part.

Dundas's skill as a political manager contributed appreciably to Pitt's victory in the general election of 1784. As far as the English constituencies are concerned 'the rout of Fox's martyrs' remains a highly controversial subject, on which it is safe to say the last word has yet to be written. Some historians see it almost as the classical general election of the old system, with management settling the issue;[14] but the more recent trend of opinion has been to emphasise the decisive influence of public opinion, representing outrage at the immoral Fox–North coalition and representing, too, the need for reform.[15] Fox had flirted with the parliamentary reformers, but in 1784 it was Pitt who had their confidence. As far as the Scottish constituencies are concerned the question hardly arises. There the conventional means of

[10] Walter Scott later referred to 'command of the Board of Control, which is in a manner the key of the corn-chest' for Scotland—H. J. C. Grierson, ed., *Letters of Sir Walter Scott*, II. 276.

[11] E. Thornton, *The History of the British Empire in India* (1859), p. 304.

[12] Thornton, *op. cit.*, p. 182; J. Marshman, *History of India* (1876), p. 214.

[13] Thornton, *op. cit.*, pp. 304-5.

[14] Notably W. T. Laprade, ed., *Parliamentary Papers of John Robinson* (Camden Society, 1922); and Laprade, 'Public Opinion and the General Election of 1784', in *E.H.R.*, xxxi. 224-37.

[15] Mrs E. George, 'Fox's Martyrs; the General Election of 1784', in *T.R.H.S.*, Fourth Series, xxi. 133-68.

' influence ' prevailed virtually unchallenged; and though Dundas was far from being at the zenith of his power he outstripped all possible rivals, securing 22 out of the 45 seats.

While Dundas was thus skilfully making his way, other developments were beginning to undermine such a system of politics. From 1768 onwards that great parrot-cry of the eighteenth century, a perfected constitution, was increasingly suspect. Moved perhaps by the bold escapades of John Wilkes, Lord Buchan in 1768 startled Scots politicians by a vigorous condemnation of the mode of electing the sixteen peers. He put himself forward as a candidate ' free and independent of every influence whatsoever ', and he protested vehemently against ministerial influence which reduced ' the election . . . to a mere ministerial nomination, at once disgraceful to the community and subversive to the freedom of Parliament '[16] Nothing came of the agitation, but Buchan was persistent and his strictures encouraged others to look critically at various aspects of the existing system. The numerous and unblushing scandals associated with the general election of 1768 reinforced these trends. The court of session, horrified not only at the corruption of elections but also at the falsification of administrative records, made a determined assault on electoral abuses and notably on fictitious votes. The judges allowed special interrogatories to be put to suspect freeholders, only to have this useful expedient declared *ultra vires* by the house of lords in 1770. Yet it was notorious that by this time the creation of ' airy freeholds ' had robbed the county representation of any vestige of reason, and that in the royal burghs parliamentary elections were carried by open bribery which it was apparently beyond the competence of the courts to check.[17] It is not surprising, therefore, that though the American War was initially popular in Scotland its ill-success should have raised demands for reform.

In the 1780s these demands came entirely from the ' political nation ' and those on the fringe of it. Such movements as arose were not popular and were in no sense radical or democratic. Scotland had no real counterpart to Wilkes or Wyvill and, as the latter discovered, the resemblances between the Scottish reformers

---

[16] A. Fergusson, *Henry Erskine*, pp. 194-5.
[17] W. Ferguson, ' Dingwall Burgh Politics and the Parliamentary Franchise in the Eighteenth Century ', in *S.H.R.*, xxxviii. 104.

and his Yorkshire Freeholders' Association were superficial and illusory. The minority of the Scottish freeholders who pressed for reform desired nothing more than the curbing of glaring abuses, chief of which was the fictitious vote. As early as 1775 a bill for this purpose had been introduced and was even supported by Lord Advocate Dundas; but it was lost and Dundas never again toyed with the subject. None the less, stimulated by the ferment in England, in 1782 some of the Scottish freeholders returned to the charge. In April the commissioners of supply of Inverness-shire passed a resolution against the splitting of superiorities to make votes, a practice which complicated the work of the commissioners. Shortly thereafter the freeholders of Moray passed similar resolutions, and in June the justices of the peace of Caithness followed suit. A general meeting of reformers was called in Edinburgh at which 23 out of the 33 Scottish shires were represented. This body could be said to represent the genuine freeholders, who wished to reduce the power wielded by the nobles and other great landowners who could create votes by dividing superiorities. From this group Wyvill expected strong support in his difficult campaign, but in the result he was disappointed. The movement was too narrowly based to make much headway; and its failure to evolve any radical solutions precluded popular sympathy. Its grievances were largely personal and could be met on that level. And so it fell out. In 1790, when a new drive was made against fictitious votes, the rolls of many counties were purged, thanks to a belated decision of the house of lords; and in face of the radical agitations then starting up, most freeholders became pillars of the existing constitution. The renegades were few and their brief careers of little import.

Those who demanded reform of the royal burghs were more radical and more tenacious, if only because the notorious corruption then rife in the burghs was no matter of abstract theory but could affect the prosperity of every resident in the burghs. The town councils were closed oligarchies beyond any control: rarely did burgh treasurers go through the motions of book-keeping and the records that do exist usually have sorry tales to tell. Often the common good was systematically plundered, burgh lands were feued to interested parties for nominal duties, debts were contracted and unaccounted for, arbitrary ' rates ' were imposed, and the parliamentary franchise was in many cases a marketable

commodity for the behoof of the councillors. In these abuses—
and many others too numerous to list—there was nothing new.
But they were increasing and so was the gravity of the problem
that they posed. They were beginning to constitute a threat not
only to the royal burghs but to the country as a whole. Their
adverse effects on individual burghs is easy to appreciate. For
example, the depletion of the common good of Inverness from the
equivalent of £3,000 per annum at the beginning of the eighteenth
century to a mere £500 by the 1780s clearly wrought the burgh
nothing but harm.[18] That at the same time Perth was £20,000
in debt was also, clearly enough, not in the public interest.[19] But
this cancerous corruption had wider effects: it helped to retard
the progress of industry. Entrepreneurs were not keen to risk
their capital in the royal burghs, where hydra-headed corruption
and the archaic powers of the craft incorporations might well
between them bring ruin. It was easier, less expensive, and less
dangerous to negotiate feus with country lairds.

Many of the merchant class in the royal burghs were all too
aware of these dangers, and the economic views of Adam Smith
strengthened their uneasiness. In addition, new social theories
were in the air to which Smith and other Scottish philosophers of
the time contributed. If not the first sociologists, they were at
any rate keenly aware of the complex nature of society: their work
therefore tended to demonstrate the inadequacy of a system of
government based on feudal principles which no longer accorded
with social realities. A bourgeois middle class may not have been
new, but never before in the history of Scotland could merchants,
lawyers, professors and doctors preen themselves as ' men in the
middle ranks of life who generally constitute the majority of every
free community '.[20] Yet this category of men, steadily increasing
in wealth and importance, had little or no voice in government.
Individuals might ingratiate themselves with great electoral
interests, but as a group they were not represented in parliament
and might indeed even be excluded from the government of the
royal burghs. Doubtless there were counterparts to all this in the
England of that time; but what might be local and haphazard in

[18] A. Fletcher, *Memoir concerning Origin and Progress of Burgh Reform in Scotland*
(1819), Pt. III, p. 56.
[19] Fletcher, *ibid.*, p. 68.
[20] *Caledonian Mercury*, 28 December 1782, Letters of Zeno, number II.

England was in Scotland depressingly uniform. The demands for reform that arose were not doctrinaire: they drew heavily on the current situation and little if at all on the American declaration of independence. Burgh reform in Scotland was inspired by the same general ferment which gave rise to the Irish Volunteer movement and the Yorkshire Freeholders' Association. With government so discomfited and corruption and ' virtual representation ' alike discredited, it was the obvious time to agitate for change. The movement was initiated by Thomas McGrugar, a wealthy Edinburgh burgess, who in December 1782 and January 1783 published in the *Caledonian Mercury* his *Letters of Zeno*. He particularly criticised the representative system, with special reference to Edinburgh, where at most no more than twenty-five persons were involved in electing the M.P. Zeno, however, advanced no pleas for democracy: he held that ' the dregs of the populace are disqualified by ignorance and hebetude ', and that their interests should be protected by the knowledgable, virtuous, and propertied middle class. The *Letters* struck a ready chord, and in 1783 a committee dedicated to burgh reform, both as regards parliamentary representation and internal government, was set up in Edinburgh. The movement spread rapidly throughout Scotland, and in March 1784 a convention of delegates was held in Edinburgh in which 33 of the 66 royal burghs were represented.

For the most part the local groups of the movement were composed of merchants; but the standing committee which co-ordinated policy was dominated by lawyers. Most prominent among them were some young advocates—notably Archibald Fletcher (himself of humble origin), Henry Erskine (an aristocrat but with the reforming zeal of his elder brother, the Earl of Buchan), John Clerk of Eldin, and, tribute to the utter iniquity of burgh administration, Lord Gardenstone, a judge of the court of session. Unfortunately these reformers acted under the delusion that the merits of their case would lift it above party politics. In justice to them, the factiousness of politics at this time confused all such issues. Pitt was accepted as the champion of reform and Fox regarded as a trimmer. But even so the failure of the Scots burgh reformers to support Wyvill, who then had Pitt under considerable pressure, was a bad error.[21] Even before the defeat

[21] I. R. Christie, *Wilkes, Wyvill, and Reform*, pp. 174, 212.

of Pitt's motion for limited parliamentary reform in 1785 the burgh reformers in Scotland had lost heart and had relinquished a draft bill intended to reform the parliamentary representation of the royal burghs. This they did in order to concentrate on a bill dealing with internal abuses in the burghs. Their main recommendations were extension of the franchise to all resident burgesses and the holding of the annual elections in all the burghs on the same day. This would effectively break the existing oligarchies, but to safeguard the purity of administration the electors were also to appoint seven auditors of accounts and the court of session was to be granted a review jurisdiction over them.[22] The project roused no interest in the Scots parliamentary politicians, and even George Dempster, who had the reputation of being upright and independent, refused to introduce the bill in the commons. Dempster may not have deserved his reputation: in 1767 he had been indicted for bribery in a burgh election at Cupar but the case lapsed on a question of competency.[23] Only after some delay and difficulty did the bill find a sponsor in Richard Brinsley Sheridan, playwright and M.P. Sheridan was a considerable orator but a poor house of commons man and under his advocacy the bill failed to make any progress, in spite of two judicial decisions which proved to the hilt the contentions of the reformers. In 1784 the court of session decided in a case concerning Nairn that non-resident councillors were illegal, but this judgment was overturned by the house of lords; and in 1787, in a test case from Dumbarton, the Scottish court of exchequer found that unlike the pre-Union exchequer it did not have the power to review burgh accounts. But, properly, the barons of exchequer rejected the plea that such powers of review lay with the convention of royal burghs, since this body was art and part with the corrupt municipal regimes. The ludicrous pass was reached where *custom*, however tainted, was put on par with positive law. Sheridan, naturally, made use of these decisions to reinforce his arguments, but Dundas had become a committed anti-reformer and he had no difficulty in stifling Sheridan's pleas.

Indeed in these years Dundas was steadily expanding his electoral power and, in so doing, making full use of the defects of

[22] H. W. Meikle, *Scotland and the French Revolution*, p. 22.
[23] *Letters of Sir Walter Scott*, XII. 463; *Letters of George Dempster to Sir Adam Fergusson, 1756–1813*, ed. James Fergusson, pp. 65-7.

the existing system. In 1784 he was strongest in Midlothian and the surrounding counties, and his main ally at this point was the Duke of Buccleuch. One of the bases of Dundas's power, in fact, was a series of accommodations with great local interests and this tactic was particularly important in the earlier part of his career. Thus, his conquest of the north turned upon an alliance with the Duke of Gordon. Otherwise, he used the old, well-established techniques of influence—dispensing patronage and promoting compromises favourable to his interest. By these means his electoral power grew, spreading into county after county and burgh after burgh. In the summer of 1788 he informed Pitt that the political outlook in Scotland was 'very favourable'; and though they bravely put the best face on it, the supporters of Fox, headed by Henry Erskine, were more or less forced to the same conclusion by a political survey which they carried out in that same year. It anatomised the electoral interests in the Scottish counties and charted the inroads made by Dundas.[24] In October 1789 Dundas could vaunt to Lord Grenville that 'a number of circumstances concur in my person to make me the veritable cement of the administration ',[25] and the general election of 1790 did nothing to contradict his boast. Actual contests were few (nine in the counties and seven in the burghs) and at the end Dundas controlled 34 out of Scotland's 45 M.P.s.[26] But by this time the securing of such results by such methods constituted a challenge to men of independent mind. Robert Burns was not a systematic politician any more than he was a systematic theologian but he had the knack of hitting off the viewpoint of the common man.

> Let posts an' pensions sink or soom
> Wi' them wha grant 'em:
> If honestly they canna come,
> Far better want 'em.[27]

Underlying the *fausse bonhomie* of most of Burns's political verse there was deep contempt for the politicians of his time and not least for ' the slee Dundas '.[28]

---

[24] *The Political State of Scotland in 1788*, ed. Sir Charles E. Adam, *passim*.
[25] *H.M.C., Fortescue* (1892), I. 534.
[26] Furber, *Dundas*, p. 228.
[27] R. Burns, *Poetry*, ed. Henley and Henderson (1896), I. 27, ' The Author's Earnest Cry and Prayer '.
[28] R. Burns, *Poetry*, ed. Henley and Henderson, I. 249.

Unnoticed or ignored by the professional politicians, the society which had largely stood aside from parliamentary politics was in process of dissolution. Economic and social changes were forcing people into new situations in which the old answers had little relevance. The result was social antagonism and a new truculence on the part of ' the labouring poor '. Here and there in the Old Statistical Account which was produced in the 1790s observant ministers remarked this strange phenomenon. Thus the minister of Wigtown noted with approval that ' a spirit of independence in the progress of opulence has arisen especially among the more substantial part of the people '.[29] Such an indulgent view was unusual; and, on the whole, those who benefited from ' the taciturn regularity of ancient affairs '[30] dreaded the aspiring insolence of the lower orders which as early as 1787 had manifested itself in hitherto all but unknown strikes or ' combinations '. In that year the weavers of Glasgow demanded higher wages and when their demand was refused a riot followed, to suppress which the military were forced to fire, killing or seriously wounding about half a dozen people.[31] What in the earlier eighteenth century would have been dismissed as a mere mob was rapidly becoming a mob with a purpose, a deliberate but necessarily violent form of political expression. In many urban areas, too, the old preoccupation with ecclesiastical affairs was yielding to political disputation, and the popular mind (which in Lowland Scotland was remarkably literate) was no longer confined to scripture and the commentaries of such Calvinist divines as Boston or the Erskines. Somewhat later Alexander Somerville could jest that his father's favourite book, *The Marrow of Modern Divinity*, ' might not be in all respects a substitute for a marrow bone '.[32]

In Britain, as in most parts of Europe, the French Revolution was the catalyst which activated latent antagonisms into violent reactions. But, to begin with, the Revolution was well received by all classes. To the statesmen it appeared as an inexpensive means of bridling Bourbon pretensions, and Pitt rejoiced at the prospect of years of peace in which to pursue economic and administrative reforms.[33] Most politicians, with the exception of

---

[29] *O.S.A.*, XIV. 483. [30] John Galt, *Annals of the Parish*, ch. XXIX.
[31] Meikle, *op. cit.*, p. 64.
[32] A. Somerville, *Autobiography of a Working Man*, p. 17.
[33] *Parliamentary History*, XXIX. 826.

Edmund Burke, inclined to this view. The upper-class political reformers were entranced by the apparent vindication of their claims in a country lately a byword for despotism. Thus Samuel Romilly recorded his joy at this unexpected deliverance and looked forward to the renovation of Europe. In Scotland there was scarcely a dissentient voice, with the older generation of intellectuals, as represented by the historian William Robertson, for once at one with their juniors. Only James Beattie, philosopher and poet, struck a sombre note, reserving his plaudits till the national assembly in Paris ' had given proof of ability in legislation, as well as of zeal in levelling '.[34] No such doubts assailed the labouring poor, to whom events in France came as a revelation. Their discontents were local and their knowledge of national and foreign affairs limited; but the great doctrines of the Revolution made a strong appeal to the egalitarian values which had long co-existed in Scotland with feudal institutions. And that appeal was powerfully enhanced by the ability of Burns to speak both to and for the common man. ' A Man's a Man for a' that ' embodied not only the age-old unpolitical democracy of peasant Scotland but also the Rights of Man.

These early views were too simple and the Revolution too complex for this happy state of harmony to endure. The triumph of the third estate in France, the downfall of privilege, the fettering and subsequent tragic extinction of monarchy led to fierce controversies in Britain. In 1790 Edmund Burke published his *Reflections on the Revolution in France* in which he defended the old order as a system hallowed by time and sanctified by prescription. His attacks on the revolutionists were hysterical, ill-informed, and at first rather derided; but, Cassandra-like, much that he predicted came to pass. Men of property lost their early enthusiasm, and the statesmen were disturbed by the emergence of new forces which threatened to overthrow not just the old Balance of Power but the old powers themselves. In the course of the years 1791–92 the bulk of the upper classes sought refuge in Burke's passionate rhetoric, while the diminishing ranks of upper-class and middle-class reformers availed themselves of James Mackintosh's reply to Burke, *Vindiciae Gallicae*, which appeared in 1791. Mackintosh was a young Scot who had tried both medicine and law none too successfully and who was launched on a moderately successful

[34] M. Forbes, *Beattie and his Friends*, p. 245.

political career by this controversy. He later repented of his early democratic sympathies (as so many in his situation did) and became a fulsome adulator of Burke. A far more formidable opponent of Burke was Thomas Paine, whose *Rights of Man* drove home some hard truths about the inadequacy and the corruption of the existing constitution in Britain. Paine, an Englishman, was a practical man, an experienced political pamphleteer on behalf of the colonists in the American Revolution, which his tract *Commonsense* may have helped to bring about. He was a journalist rather than a philosopher or rhetorician, and in short the complete antithesis of Burke. But for these reasons his pamphlet was the more popular, especially since his dogmatic assertions were laced with both wit and humanity. Thus he disposed of Burke's emotional outburst: ' He pities the plumage but forgets the dying bird '.[35] Paine, in fact, is a neglected but forceful political writer who was far less negative in his ideas than is commonly supposed. For custom and prescription he had little regard, and he easily punctured Burke's absurd notion that the Revolution of 1688 bound all posterity. In Paine's view governments which took no stock of natural rights were tyrannous, and monarchy ' is the popery of Government; a thing kept to amuse the ignorant, and quiet them into taxes '.[36] Later he describes monarchy as ' the master-fraud which shelters all others '.[37] High in the list of such frauds he put a so-called constitution which made a mockery of the principle of representation. His views on this subject give a fair example of his style: ' As to the state of representation in England, it is too absurd to be reasoned upon. Almost all the represented parts are decreasing in population, and the unrepresented parts are increasing. A general Convention of the Nation is necessary to take the whole state of its Government into consideration.'[38] He derided the idea of the corrupt political oligarchy reforming the system on which it flourished. A free political association of the entire people should, he argued, elect a general convention to carry out the work of reform. These were intoxicating ideas, not just by American or French analogies

---

[35] T. Paine, ed. R. Carlile, *Political and Miscellaneous Works*, 2 vols. (1819), I, ' Rights of Man ', Pt. I, p. 24. E. P. Thompson, *The Making of the English Working Class*, ch. IV, brilliantly discusses Paine's influence.

[36] *Ibid.*, ' Rights of Man ', Pt. II, p. 38.

[37] *Ibid.*, Pt. II, p. 57.

[38] *Ibid.*, Pt. II, p. 54 n.

but also because of the patent truth of many of his strictures on the corrupt state of British politics.

Paine also had a social message. He believed that war was the curse of the age and that it was a necessity to corrupt monarchies. He further believed that rational governments would forswear war and put the money thus saved to good social use. Poor people with families would be exempt from taxation; there would be an allowance of £4 per annum for every child under fourteen; education would be free for all; and old age pensions should be granted ' not of the nature of a charity, but of a right '.[39] These ideas, and the appeal they made to contemporaries, cannot be lightly dismissed. Because of the cocksure unsophisticated way in which he exposed political and social abuses his works sold briskly, to the extent of over 200,000 copies of *The Rights of Man* by the end of 1793. The sale was actually stimulated by a royal proclamation against the work in May 1792, and it seems to have been particularly sought after in Scotland, possibly even penetrating into the Highlands in a rough Gaelic translation.[40] Thomas Telford, a promising young engineer, was so carried away by Paine's *Rights of Man* that he made use of his patron Sir William Pulteney's frank to send a copy of the work back to his native Eskdale, galvanising the ' Langholm patriots ' to disturbances of the peace.[41]

In Scotland the division between reformers and conservatives was deep, lasting, and bitter. ' Everything rung, and was connected with the Revolution in France; which, for above 20 years, was, or was made, the all in all. Everything, not this or that thing, but literally everything, was soaked in this one event.'[42] Debating societies and radical political associations spread rapidly and were by no means restricted to the towns and weaving villages. There was a remarkable increase in the number of newspapers and a revolution in their contents. In 1782 there were only eight newspapers in the whole of Scotland, mainly of local interest and unenterprising in their views; by 1790 there were 27 and most of them had become intensely political, championing one side or the other. Their numbers continued to

[39] *Ibid.*, Pt. II, ch. v.
[40] P. A. Brown, *The French Revolution in English History*, p. 90.
[41] S. Smiles, *Lives of the Engineers—Thomas Telford* (1874), p. 143.
[42] Henry Cockburn, *Memorials of His Time*, ed. H. A. Cockburn (1910), p. 73.

increase and after 1792 government subsidised certain sympathetic organs.[43] By that time many could hold, with George Dempster, that ' The horrors of this French Revolution sicken me at the human race and have corrected a good deal of my democratical spirit '.[44] Indeed, as early as 1791 conservative opinion, under the influence of John Reeves in England, was organising itself along the lines pioneered by the radicals. Loyalist associations were formed to counter the activities of their radical counterparts. Such was the Edinburgh Goldsmiths' Hall Association which came into existence in December 1792. It was designed to check the most formidable of the democratic associations in Scotland, the Societies of Friends of the People, which had mushroomed from the summer of 1792. Unlike its English namesake, the Friends of the People in Scotland was a popular and not an aristocratic body, resembling rather the London Corresponding Society which had been founded in January 1792 largely through the influence of an *émigré* Scots shoemaker, Thomas Hardy. A leading light in the Glasgow association, inaugurated by a meeting at the Star Inn on 3 October,[45] was a young advocate, Thomas Muir of Huntershill. A few upper-class reformers belonged to and held office in the association (notably Colonel Dalrymple of Fordell, Colonel Macleod of Macleod, and Lord Daer), but their main concern seems to have been to advise only constitutional measures and to restrain the hot-headed advocates of violence. This was a hopeless endeavour, for violence was implicit in the head-on clash of opposed ideologies.

Violence indeed was initiated by the supporters of church and state who connived at the Birmingham riots in July 1791 in which dissenting meeting-houses were destroyed. The government all but openly approved of such activities and the lord advocate went so far as to hope that the good people of Edinburgh would treat unitarians in the same way, hinting that authority would not be over-zealous in dealing with culprits.[46] The mob of Edinburgh failed to oblige: instead of rabbling dissenters, it celebrated the king's birthday on 4 June 1792 by burning Henry Dundas in effigy and throwing a riot in the cause of reform. In spite of military intervention (which a mere disturbance directed against

---

[43] H. W. Meikle, *Scotland and the French Revolution*, pp. 86-9.
[44] James Fergusson, ed., *Letters of George Dempster to Adam Fergusson, 1756-1813,* p. 222.   [45] Meikle, *op. cit.*, p. 92.   [46] *Ibid.*, p. 197, n 3.

' dissenters ' would hardly have entailed), disorder prevailed for three days.[47] The leaders of the mob escaped detection and the lord advocate had to rest content with two very minor figures, Alex Bertram and Alex Lochie, described as ' servants ', who were tried in the high court of justiciary. Bertram was acquitted, but Lochie, who was defended by Thomas Muir, was found guilty and sentenced to fourteen years' transportation.[48] The great debate which shortly afterwards arose about the legality of transportation in such cases would seem, in the circumstances, to have been pointless.

Undoubtedly, a tense situation existed in 1792. The radical associations were numerous, Paine's work was spreading, and many of the societies were issuing hotly phrased pamphlets of their own. The sense of crisis caused by theoretical objections to the existing regime was heightened by the economic hardships of the time. The Corn Law passed in 1790 was meant to be permanent, unlike its numerous predecessors, and thus raised resentment and alarm. In addition, it was ill thought-out and poorly administered, dividing Scotland into four main areas without regard to fertility or needs. A bad harvest in 1792 sent the price of bread soaring, while in parts of the Highlands the introduction of sheep was leading to large-scale evictions. A minor disturbance in the north in July was attributed by Lord Adam Gordon, the commander-in-chief in Scotland, to the creation of great sheep runs. Government, in short, had every reason to exercise caution, but instead it embarked upon a series of state trials in an effort to intimidate its critics. Dundas as home secretary played a key part in this offensive which began with prosecutions in England of which the most notable was that of Tom Paine. Duly warned, Paine had fled to France where he was actually elected to represent Calais in the national assembly. In December 1792 he was tried in his absence and, in spite of an ingenious defence by Thomas Erskine, was found guilty of seditious libel. The policy seemed to justify itself and Dundas wrote glowingly to the Earl of Hopetoun, ' The tide here is completely changed; all levellers are drooping their heads, and my only fear now is that they may proceed to any excesses on the other side '.

---

[47] H. W. Meikle, ' The King's Birthday Riot in Edinburgh, June 1792 ', in *S.H.R.*, VII. 21-8.

[48] Reg. Ho., Books of Adjournal, ser. D, vol. 46, 16 July 1792. Lochie had his sentence remitted and was released, 6 February 1793.

Pitt and he were now so sure of their ground that they had ordered similar prosecutions before the quarter sessions in January. He concluded, ' I never was proud of being a minister before but I do feel gratified in being one of those who I do think by their timely interposition of vigor and spirited measures have raised their country from despondency '.[49] The same ' vigor and spirited measures ' were soon applied in Scotland, where an odd situation was developing. Every effort at reform by parliamentary means had been rebuffed, but the leaders of the Foxite Whigs, Henry Erskine and Archibald Fletcher, refused to co-operate with the extreme radicals. Thomas Muir tried hard to win over Fletcher in the hope of securing the burgh reformers, but Fletcher was not to be moved. Of Muir and his ideas he said: ' I believe him to be an honest enthusiast, but he is an ill-judging man. These violent reformers will create such an alarm in the country as must strengthen the Government. The country is not prepared to second their views of annual parliaments and universal suffrage.'[50] The truth of all this was soon apparent; and yet the proposition could be put another way: the irresolution of the upper-class reformers left the field wide open for the extremists.

On 11 December 1792 the Friends of the People in Scotland, determined to force matters, held a general convention in Edinburgh. It was attended by 160 delegates drawn from societies scattered throughout Scotland, although owing to the poverty of many country branches the representatives of the Edinburgh and Glasgow societies predominated. Serious divisions were soon evident between upper-class leaders like Colonel Dalrymple and Lord Daer on the one hand and on the other the self-appointed tribune of the people, Thomas Muir. For the most part the moderates prevailed and the resolutions passed on parliamentary reform were mild enough to meet the approval of Henry Erskine. Muir, however, could not be restrained from reading to the delegates a fiery address from the Society of United Irishmen, which, in the opinion of Dalrymple, ' contained treason or at least misprision of treason '.[51] This gave the government an excuse to move against the ' jacobins '. Already it was making use of paid

---

[49] *H.M.C., Hope Johnstone* (Report xv, 1897), App., Pt. ix. 132.
[50] Mrs. Eliza Fletcher, *Autobiography*, p. 65.
[51] Meikle, *Scotland and the French Revolution*, p. 108; also App. A, Minutes of Proceedings of the First General Convention . . ., p. 245.

spies and soon had a full report of the proceedings, including the contents of this wild address. Muir, in fact, was already a marked man and the work of the convention merely confirmed the opinions of him already held by the lord advocate. On the last day of the convention occurred a curious little incident which establishes some important points and which was to have unexpected repercussions. At this time the Goldsmiths' Hall Association was acquiring signatures to a loyalist address and, in order to demonstrate their belief in peaceful and constitutional measures, Muir and many of the radical delegates signed the resolutions, each adding after his name the words ' delegate of the Society of the Friends of the People '. When this was discovered their names were promptly deleted.

On 2 January 1793 Muir was arrested but on securing bail he left for London, there to publicise his grievances at a reform meeting. His prolonged absence, first in London and then latterly in France, where he went to intercede for the life of Louis XVI, led to his outlawry and delayed his trial until the autumn. In the meantime the law had proceeded against lesser offenders, such as the well-known Edinburgh chemist and litterateur James ' Balloon ' Tytler, who failed to appear and was outlawed. Next, three printers, accused of attempting to suborn the soldiers in Edinburgh castle, were found guilty and each sentenced to nine months' imprisonment. Thus far, the trials were fairly conducted and the punishments reasonable. But these were political trials in the fullest sense and they failed to produce the desired political effects. So far from being cowed, the jacobins held another general convention in Edinburgh in May 1793. The moderate delegates were outnumbered and outmanœuvred; and under the influence of a fire-brand from Glasgow, John Sinclair, the proceedings were tumultuous. The inevitable spy was present and the home office soon possessed a full report of the convention's activities. Muir's circuitous return from Paris by way of Ireland, where he made contact with the United Irishmen, was a relief to the government. He was taken on his arrival at Stranraer and kept under close arrest, although latterly he must have been allowed a certain amount of liberty, for on 30 August, when the case against him opened, displeasure was expressed at his keeping the court waiting.[52] The indictment contained three

[52] T. J. Howell, *State Trials*, XXIII. 118.

main charges: exciting disaffection by seditious speeches, circulating Paine's *Rights of Man*, and reading and defending the address of the United Irishmen in the first general convention in December 1792.

Muir's trial has a place of its own in the legal history of Scotland and an even more special one in folk-lore. So much partial history, if not total myth, has enveloped these state trials that it is hard now to recreate anything like the authentic atmosphere in which they were conducted. Certainly, however, under the dominating lord justice clerk, Braxfield, Muir's trial was far from impartial and was in many respects at odds with most modern concepts of justice. Yet the matter was not as simple as generations of Whig commentators, headed by Henry Cockburn,[53] have made it appear. Cockburn exaggerated the misconduct of Braxfield (whose behaviour was in fact closely paralleled by that of Lord Kenyon in the corresponding English trials) and minimised the foolhardiness of the panel, Thomas Muir. Not only the prosecution but also the defence can be seriously criticised. This need not have been so, for Henry Erskine, who was dean of the faculty of advocates and a fine pleader, offered Muir his services on the sole proviso that he should have complete charge of the defence. Muir refused and Erskine withdrew, prophesying that the panel would convict himself by making wild harangues which would establish the one thing needful for the prosecution to establish, namely intention. And so it fell out. Muir handled his case atrociously, failing to challenge the relevancy of the indictment at the proper stage. The evidence against him was weak and even the testimony of the crown witnesses (with one exception and that a suspicious one) could have been turned to the panel's account. An able defence might also have invoked the spirit of Fox's Libel Act of 1792, whereby it was left to the jury to decide whether a libel, if established, were seditious or not. Even though the jury was selected by the judges according to custom, and even though the jurors actually chosen were all members of the Goldsmiths' Hall Association and obviously prejudiced against the panel, a properly conducted defence might have so exposed the feebleness of the prosecution's case as to make a verdict of guilty too absurd to be practicable. This, after all, was the measure of the achievement of Henry Erskine's brilliant

[53] See H. Cockburn, *Examination of Trials for Sedition in Scotland.*

brother, Thomas Erskine, in the not dissimilar English trials of this period: and it is significant that on the one occasion in these trials when an accused person accepted Henry Erskine's services the lord advocate was obliged to drop the charges.[54] Muir had a good case but it was thrown away. His long impassioned speech in his own defence was greeted with spontaneous applause, deservedly, for it was a moving and convincing political speech; but as a legal defence it sealed his fate. One of the judges, Lord Henderland, in his summing-up referred to ' the indecent applause which was given to Mr Muir last night '; to the judge's mind this merely proved ' that the spirit of sedition had not yet subsided '.[55] In Braxfield's summing-up no attempt was made to separate political opinions from judicial duties: he instructed the jury to take into account the prevalence of disorders and the real risk of anarchy. As a personal reaction to the times this was far from peculiar. Even former democrats had been shocked by the wanton September Massacres of 1792 in Paris in which men, women and even hapless orphans had been brutally murdered. It has also to be borne in mind that in February 1793 the French Republic had declared war on Britain. But in strict law these considerations had no place in court and Braxfield's harangue was indefensible. In the lord justice clerk's view it appeared that Muir's chief offence, and that a heinous one, had been his attempt to promote ideas of reform among the lower orders who were nothing better than *canaille*. Muir's witnesses were indeed contemptuously dismissed as ' a rabble ', unpropertied and therefore rightless. For the old judge, political science was simplicity itself. He held that: ' A government in every country should be just like a corporation; and, in this country, it is made up of the landed interest, which alone has a right to be represented; as for the rabble, who have nothing but personal property, what hold has the nation of them ? '[56] This was a crude parody of Burke's none too subtle argument, and indeed the real case that was being decided was Burke *contra* Paine. As a consequence Muir was

[54] For Charles Sinclair's case, see *State Trials*, XXIII. 778-802; Cockburn, *op. cit.*, II. 34-40 has a singularly malicious account of it, since Erskine's triumph gave Cockburn's views on these trials a very hard knock. On no evidence at all, Cockburn dismissed this intriguing case by alleging (on hearsay) that Sinclair had made a deal with the lord advocate, whereby he would turn government spy if the case against him was dropped.

[55] Howell, *State Trials*, XXIII. 232.   [56] *Ibid.*, 231.

found guilty and sentenced to fourteen years' transportation to the new penal colony at Botany Bay.

The sentence passed on Muir was certainly harsh, heavier perhaps than even the jurors relished, and it caused a public outcry. The Foxite Whigs raised the matter in parliament, but since there was no appeal to parliament in criminal cases there was little that could be done. Fox made some cutting remarks on the judges, but could not move Dundas. Indeed, another renegade to his class, the Reverend Thomas Fyshe Palmer, was already in the toils. In the opinion of Lord Advocate Robert Dundas, Palmer, an English unitarian minister of Dundee, was ' the most determined rebel in Scotland '.[57] He was tried for sedition at Perth in September 1793 and sentenced to seven years' transportation. But these severe examples still failed to deter. The associations continued to agitate and the one noticeable effect of the trials was to forge stronger bonds between the English and Scottish radicals. In the upshot, the Friends of the People in Scotland and the London Corresponding Society decided to show their contempt for the notorious ' Scotch trials ' by holding an all-British convention in Edinburgh. It was summoned for 29 October 1793 but made no headway until the arrival of the English delegates on 19 November. Possibly because of a healthy fear of spies little is known of its actual deliberations, but it seems to have planned underground activities in the event of government action. And indeed the delegates tried to carry on after being ordered to disperse; their determination led to the arrest of the leading men in the convention. Scott, editor of a radical news-sheet, the *Edinburgh Gazetteer*, fled; the case against Charles Sinclair, a delegate from the London Corresponding Society, was dropped; but Skirving, Margarot, and Gerrald were tried and found guilty in trials which closely followed the pattern set by that of Muir, down even to the sentences. Joseph Gerrald, who represented the London Corresponding Society, defended himself nobly, on occasion even moving the pity of the judges; Maurice Margarot, another of the English delegates and a conceited coxcomb, drove Braxfield almost berserk; but, with a rare impartiality, each received the same sentence, fourteen years' transportation to Botany Bay. And so it fared also with William

[57] Meikle, *Scotland and the French Revolution*, p. 129, citing H.O. Scottish Correspondence, 2 August 1793.

Skirving, secretary of the Canongate Society of Friends of the People.

At the time their hard fates excited so much attention that in 1796 successful efforts were made by American sympathisers to rescue Muir who then had a remarkable odyssey: he was transferred to a Spanish vessel, wounded in a fight with Royal Navy ships, and eventually found refuge in France. There he was fêted and used by the Directory for propaganda purposes, in particular the reforging of old links with the United Irishmen. Muir died in January 1799 and was buried at Chantilly. Gerrald and Skirving had already died in the penal settlement in March 1796. Palmer served his time but died at Guam in 1802. Of those who in later years were to be canonised as the Edinburgh Martyrs only the egregious Margarot lived to set foot in Britain again. In 1812 he returned to Edinburgh, according to one version,[58] as bumptious as ever, eager to talk over old times with the judges and jurors who had sent him down under. Alas, they were all gone except one juror to whom Margarot gave a supper. It must have been a curious affair, for so fleeting are political allegiances that in the interval between their meetings Margarot had become a Tory and the juror a Whig. It is a good story, told with Cockburn's usual zest, but unfortunately other evidence demonstrates that Margarot remained as radical as ever. On his return to Britain he tried to renew contacts with his old comrades of the British convention, and may even have supported the struggle of the Glasgow weavers in 1812.[59]

This second tussle with authority in 1793 proved decisive and thereafter most of the radical associations disintegrated. In 1794 government struck hard, suspending *habeas corpus* in England and its none-too-close analogy in Scotland, the act of 1701 against wrongous imprisonment. In this overheated atmosphere the so-called 'Pike Plot' caused further panic. Pikeheads were discovered in Edinburgh which were alleged to have been ordered by the British convention: a desperate conspiracy was apparently uncovered which aimed at a revolutionary coup in Edinburgh but which had tentacles reaching into the industrial west. The

[58] H. Cockburn, *Examination of Trials for Sedition in Scotland*, II. 33.
[59] H. W. Meikle, *Scotland and the French Revolution*, p. 219; M. Roe, 'A Radical in two Hemispheres', in *Bulletin of Institute of Historical Research*, XXXI. 68-78, puts the best possible case for Margarot.

plot was wildly exaggerated by the government, and as a result in August 1794 Robert Watt and David Downie were tried for high treason. This necessarily entailed a change in procedure, treason being cognoscible in the first instance by a special commission of oyer and terminer. With a reasonable case for once, the political manager took care to exclude Braxfield and appointed temperate judges to the commission. The trial was fair by any standards and, though the government's account of a widespread plot hardly stood up in court, the evidence against Watt was sufficient to condemn him. He was an odd product of his times, a government spy who had gradually been converted to reform and ended up with more extreme views than the reformers themselves. He was found guilty and hanged at the tolbooth of Edinburgh. Downie was a Roman catholic and belonged to a small catholic republican group which was highly embarrassing both to the catholic hierarchy and to the government who were then busy cementing an alliance against revolutionary France. Largely because of this Downie was regarded as a ' dupe ' and pardoned.[60]

The scare raised by the Pike Plot was immense and as a result local authority was reinforced by the appointment of lords-lieutenant of counties on the English model who were to be aided by the sheriffs-principal. Their purpose was to suppress internal disorders and prepare to meet threatened invasion from France. The main forces at their command were the new volunteer companies which were rapidly growing at this time. In spite of intensive agitations during the Seven Years' War and the War of American Independence (when the renegade Paul Jones—né John Paul of Kirkbean in the stewartry of Kirkcudbright—had harassed the coast of his native country in 1778–9), Scotland unlike England had no militia. Even Ireland was granted a militia in 1793, but Scotland had to make do with the volunteers, who were carefully selected so as to exclude those of jacobin sympathies. In effect the companies were mainly recruited from the upper- and middle-classes. The young Walter Scott and the Edinburgh Light-Horse were untypical only in that most companies were of foot. Recruiting was brisk and by the middle of 1796 the volunteer companies were established in many parts of Scotland. Many disillusioned or nervous reformers, like the poet Burns, expiated their past

[60] Rev. W. J. Anderson, ' David Downie and the Friends of the People ', in *Innes Review*, xvi. 165-79.

errors in the finery of the volunteers. The few Whigs who refused to conform were ostracised and discriminated against. Thus Archibald Fletcher, the mainstay of the burgh reformers, found briefs hard to come by; and in 1796, for daring to attend a meeting of protest against the repressive sedition and treason bills, Henry Erskine was deprived of the office of dean of the faculty of advocates which, even on the admission of his enemies, he had graced for the past eleven years. Tradesmen of democratic sympathies were denied credit at banks which normally were, if anything, all too accommodating, and workmen suspected of holding subversive views were dismissed and blacklisted. But in spite of feverish efforts to shore it up, the old political structure was never again secure. The ideas of 1792 had struck deep and the bogies they conjured up terrified the Tories, as the followers of Pitt and Dundas had come to be called. A small desperate minority of reformers continued to meet in secret, adopting the name of United Scotsmen and clearly inspired by the revolutionary society of United Irishmen. One of its leaders, George Mealmaker, was arrested in November 1797 and tried for sedition. His past was against him, for he had been arrested twice before, once in connection with Fyshe Palmer's activities and again in connection with Watt's conspiracy; but each time he had slipped through the net. Government was also alarmed lest the chronic discontent in Ireland (which issued in actual rebellion in the summer of 1798) should spread to Scotland, and so Mealmaker was transported for fourteen years to Botany Bay. In July 1799 an act was passed suppressing various radical societies, and by 1802 the last feeble remnant of the United Scotsmen seems to have gone into voluntary suspension.

The uneasy atmosphere of these times was also illustrated by the militia riots of 1797. The war was then going very badly for Britain (not least perhaps because of the inefficiency of Henry Dundas, who since 1794 had acted as secretary at war); the strain on the army was severe, and in an effort to supplement the regular regiments Scotland at long last was granted a militia. The boon was neither wisely conceded nor kindly received. The militia was intended for service in Scotland only, but on just this score some of the fencible regiments had already been grossly deceived. The Militia Act was also resented as a class measure, since those of the upper-classes who were not enrolled as volunteers could hire substitutes to take their places in the militia drafts. Terms of pay were not bad (1s. 1½d. per day), but this point was at first obscured and when the act became operative in August 1797 ' Scotland went stark mad as if it had been hit by Corsica '.[61] To the authorities this was just one more proof of ' jacobinism ' at work: ' I am satisfied,' wrote Henry Dundas to the Duke of Portland, ' that the Advocate is right in believing that Jacobinism is, to a certain extent, at the bottom of it.'[62] Certainly, here and there, radicals did fan the discontent but for the disorders that arose the chronic bumbledom of government was mainly to blame. All over Scotland the poor dominies, who as session-clerks kept the parish registers on which the drafts were to be based, were terrorised and their precious records frequently destroyed. The holding of a census to facilitate balloting led to worse riots. Alarmed by these reactions, the government took the trouble to explain the terms of the act and in some areas, notably Renfrewshire which was usually a radical hot-bed, good management prevented disorders. Where the authorities were ham-fisted there was serious trouble, most notably at Tranent in East Lothian where the colliers—an exploited but spirited race—formed the hard core of the resistance. There rioters clashed with troops hastily summoned from Haddington and the exasperated soldiers ran amok. They scoured the neighbouring countryside, wounding or killing all they came upon, including a boy of thirteen who was murdered in a field by a dragoon.[63] A schoolboy, Adam Blair, was twice for no good reason viciously sabred and left for dead. Unfortunately for the authorities, he survived to become a minister and prominent church historian who in 1835 testified that ' I shall never, while I retain my senses, forget the bloody work at Tranent '.[64] In this disgraceful affair eleven people were killed and many wounded, but the lord advocate worked diligently to prevent any prosecutions. Nor was he prepared to condescend on the pillaging and robberies carried out by the troops in the wake of this famous victory. It was only by such methods

[61] J. R. Western, ' Formation of the Scottish Militia in 1797 ', citing Sir G. Elliot's letter of 30 August 1797, in *S.H.R.*, xxxiv. 4.

[62] Quoted Meikle, *Scotland and the French Revolution*, p. 185.

[63] J. Sands, *Tranent* (1889), p. 85; J. Miller, *The Lamp of Lothian* (1844), ch. xix, p. 320.

[64] Miller, *op. cit.*, p. 321. Blair became minister of a United Associate Synod church at Ferryport-on-Tay, and in 1833 published *The History of the Waldenses*.

that resistance was overcome and the militia grumblingly accepted. But what success the act enjoyed was due mainly to the power of the great Highland landlords, who bade fair to break the monopoly of the German flesh-brokers and raised regiment after regiment, though in some cases with difficulty. Resentment still smouldered in the Lowlands, and in October 1799 there was a riot against a militia draft at Bathgate in West Lothian. Henry Erskine defended the accused—colliers again—and managed to secure a verdict of not proven.[65]

These, and similar occurrences, produced in Scotland an ambivalent attitude to the armed forces. Until the end of the eighteenth century Scots did not share the ingrained anti-militarism of the English. They continued to take a pride in their martial traditions and one welcome aspect of the Union of 1707 was the way in which it consolidated the new prospects for Scots soldiers ushered in by William's wars. In the early eighteenth century the army was in its infancy but, while regimental history is fluid and often highly suspect, it appears that by Marlborough's prime the full complement of traditional Lowland Scots regiments had emerged. Names and numbers have changed repeatedly since, but all the Lowland regiments were present, if only in embryo, at the siege of Namur in 1695.[66] That soldiering was still a major Scots occupation was evident at the battle of Malplaquet in 1709 where in addition to the Scottish units of the British army there were present several regiments of mercenaries in the Dutch service. Indeed, the United Provinces maintained a Scots Brigade until 1783; but from about 1750 it had recruiting difficulties due largely to George II's refusal to countenance the enrolment of Jacobite refugees, who were thus obliged to soldier mainly in the service of France or Austria.

Until the formation of the Black Watch by the amalgamation of the Independent Companies in 1739 the Scots regiments were all Lowland, although they drew many of their recruits from the Highlands. For many years the Black Watch was the sole Highland regiment, but its fine performance at Fontenoy in 1745 and the no less remarkable prowess of the Jacobite clans in that same

---

[65] A. Fergusson, *Henry Erskine*, p. 404.
[66] In later nomenclature, and with earliest feasible origins, they were: Royal Scots (1633); Scots Guards (1642); Royal Scots Fusiliers (1678); Royal Scots Greys (1681); King's Own Scottish Borderers (1689); and Cameronians (1689).

year ensured that, in the words of the elder Pitt, government eventually had to seek ' for merit wherever it was to be found '. During the Seven Years' War soldiers were badly needed and as a result four Highland regiments were raised for regular service, one of which, Fraser's, served under Wolfe at the taking of Quebec. The regiments were disbanded in 1763, two of them in Canada. In that same war Pitt tried to make up for Scotland's lack of a militia by raising fencible regiments for home defence. Two such were formed in 1759 (the Argyll Fencibles and the Sutherland Fencibles, significantly areas where sympathies had been Hanoverian rather than Jacobite). Between 1759 and the end of the century 26 fencible regiments were used, all of them Highland and bearing suitable territorial titles; a few favoured more romantic designation such as the Caithness Legion (1794) and the Ross and Cromarty Rangers (1799). In the Revolutionary and Napoleonic Wars the fencibles played an important role as feeders to the line regiments, which were also increasing in number. In the American War of Independence several Highland regiments were raised for regular service, notably Macleod's Highlanders (the nucleus of the Highland Light Infantry) and the progenitors of the Seaforths and Gordons. By 1800 all the Scottish regiments, Lowland and Highland, were established, and by the end of the epic series of Napoleonic wars each had an established reputation and a jealously guarded tradition.

Quite apart from their exploits in the field these military units played a large part in Scottish life in the eighteenth and nineteenth centuries. They contributed to the maintenance of national sentiment, and the use by the Highland regiments of ' the garb of old Gaul ' actually gave a new and unexpected impetus to that sentiment. The Gaels, from being viewed as barbarous nuisances, became regarded as in some ways the very embodiment of Scotland. The kilt and the bagpipes acquired popularity where hitherto they had enjoyed none. The new cult was mawkish and often at variance with the facts of Scottish life, whether Highland or Lowland, but its effects were none the less real and lasting. Most of the regiments acquired local connections, which were prized, and their effects on the populace as a whole are incalculable. Certainly, interest in their deeds broadened the horizons of peasant Scotland and especially so perhaps in the remoter Highlands. It was soldiers, no less than tacksmen, who blazed the trail to Canada; and exotic names like Ticonderoga or Seringapatam (however mauled in Scots or Gaelic) opened up new dimensions to minds hitherto confined to neighbouring parishes and the place-names of the Bible. This very influence Burns captured with rare fidelity in his 'Jolly Beggars ',[67] with its bragging son of Mars and his tales of the Heights of Abram and the Moro, and, even more significant, its spirited song of ' John Highlandman ':

> With his philibeg, an' tartan plaid,
> An' guid claymore down by his side,
> The ladies' hearts he did trepan,
> My gallant, braw John Highlandman.

A host of incidents could thus stir the blood and titillate national pride, incidents often rendered larger than life to contemporaries and posterity by the remarkable literacy of so many of the Scots recruits. The Irish figured just as prominently in these wars and added to their established reputation as fighting men, but their lack of letters stood them in ill stead with a news-hungry public. The Scots soldiers knew how to broadcast their fame and a series of drum and trumpet sagas counteracted the tedium of the everyday life of their kinsfolk:[68] the vile-tempered David Baird storming Seringapatam in 1799; Sir John Moore's skilful retreat and hero's death at Corunna in 1809; the charge of the Greys and the Gordons at Waterloo—all these, and many other incidents, were gratefully absorbed into the folk-lore of Scotland. What they could not do, however, was to erase the memory of the bitter years when the army was used at home for less laudable purposes. Pride in the Scottish regiments continued all through the nineteenth century, but it was often tempered by a degree of cynicism about the ends to which they were employed.

[67] Burns, *Poetry*, II. 1-19.
[68] See, for example, Sergeant Joseph Donaldson's suggestively titled *Recollections of the Eventful Life of a Soldier in the Peninsula*; Alexander Somerville, *Autobiography of a Working Man*, p. 188, puts the matter bluntly: ' it was the writing quite as much as the fighting of the Scotch regiments which distinguished them '.

9

THE STRUGGLE FOR REFORM,
1800–1832

The 'Revolutionary horror', as Cockburn called it,[1] held the reformers in check for a decade, and only by degrees did the Whigs manage to oppose the Tories without incurring accusations of subversion. But by 1802 the worst of the upper-class Whigs' ordeal was over although merchants and workmen for long thereafter dared not avow reform principles. The peace of Amiens of March 1802 created a slightly more relaxed atmosphere, and in the following October the *Edinburgh Review* made its first appearance. It began as a bold *jeu d'esprit*, an effort on the part of its young Whig projectors to counteract the tedium of their blighted careers and perhaps to recapture some of the glory of the age of Hume and Adam Smith. The leading spirits were Francis Jeffrey, a briefless advocate, Francis Horner, a promising young economist, Henry Brougham and Sidney Smith, all of whom chafed under the narrow restrictions imposed by patriotic Toryism. From the beginning the *Review* enjoyed a great vogue, partly because it took a moderate line in politics and partly because the time was right for such a novel venture in journalism. Walter Scott, a firm Tory, was much taken with the *Review* and shrewdly noted that its success was largely owing to the fact that ' it is entirely uninfluenced by the Booksellers who have contrived to make most of the other reviews mere vehicles for advertising and puffing of their own publications or running down those of their rivals '.[2] The publisher, Archibald

---

[1] H. Cockburn, *Memorials*, p. 96.
[2] Grierson, ed., *Letters of Sir Walter Scott*, II. 102-3.

Constable, gave a free hand to Jeffrey, the first effective editor, who saw to it that contributors were handsomely paid. Thus the *Edinburgh* attracted some of the best writers of the time: its anonymous reviews were sprightly, outspoken, and highly critical, cultivating an amusingly omniscient style. The *Edinburgh Review* became, in fact, one of the great moulders of public opinion in early nineteenth-century Britain, and especially perhaps of middle-class opinion.[3]

But considerable though the *Review's* early influence was it did little at first to undermine the hegemony of Dundas and his powerful interest. Nor were the younger Whigs well received by the grave seniors of their party headed by the Earl of Lauderdale, a humourless economist, and Henry Erskine, whose blithe spirit had been crushed by the harsh politics of his times. In these circumstances it was natural enough that some of the leading early reviewers, notably Brougham and Horner, should have given up Scotland as an unrewarding desert and removed to London to push their fortunes. Brougham, a brilliant but unprincipled gad-fly, burned with ambition and at this time the Tories could have won him over with a grant of office;[4] on the failure of his hopes he became a *frondeur*, loosely attached to the Whigs but with strong radical connections. Brougham thereafter deliberately used the *Review* to advance his prospects and often injected political polemics into his contributions. But overall, these were mere pinpricks: the Whigs in their various fragments scarcely amounted to a worth-while opposition, far less to an alternative ministry. While George III lived and had possession of his faculties the cause of the Foxites seemed doomed. Even Pitt's resignation in 1801, over the king's failure to accept Roman catholic emancipation as the natural corollary of the Irish Union, opened up no prospects for Fox and his friends. This was as true of Scotland as of any other part of the United Kingdom, for, notwithstanding the resignation of Dundas at the same time, his interest continued to support the weak Tory ministry formed by Henry Addington. Since the economic situation was bad and the nation's finances deranged, Addington's policy of peace and retrenchment strengthened his position. The peace of Amiens, therefore, was generally popular and was acclaimed by the

---

[3] See John Clive, *Scotch Reviewers: the Edinburgh Review, 1802–1815.*
[4] A. Aspinall, *Lord Brougham and the Whig Party,* p. 13.

Whigs; but Napoleon's imperialism and the outbreak of a fresh war with France in May 1803 again forced the Whigs into the unpopular position of denouncing war as a shabby Tory trick to monopolise office. Addington was an indifferent war-time prime minister and Pitt was soon obliged to resume office; but when he tried to form a broadly based coalition the Foxites raised their terms too high. The Whigs thereafter degenerated into mere satellites of the Prince of Wales, who used them to further his unsavoury and ill-judged schemes, and who finally ditched them when he became Prince Regent in 1812.

In Scotland the most significant political event of these years was undoubtedly the impeachment of Henry Dundas, who had been created Viscount Melville in 1802. Melville supported Pitt's return to office in 1804 and by way of reward became first lord of the admiralty; but, unfortunately for Melville, Addington's passion for economy had already set on foot an investigation of that notorious source of corruption and in March 1805 the report of the commission of enquiry brought to light malpractices ' in the office of the Treasurer of the Navy which did not redound to Dundas' credit '.[5] By the standards of the eighteenth century the faults were venial and would hardly have caused comment in the heyday of that prominent looter, Henry Fox, the father of Charles James. But times had changed and Melville's numerous enemies eagerly pressed their advantage. The facts were simple enough: as paymaster to the navy, Alexander Trotter, a Scot, had used public funds to speculate on his own behalf and apparently Dundas had connived at this. The navy did not lose thereby, since the principal sums involved were replaced, nor did Dundas himself gain; but the squalid details could be used to blacken the character of Pitt's administration and indeed were so used even by Napoleon.[6] The matter could not be hushed up and Melville was impeached. He was forced to resign and though he was acquitted by his peers in April 1806 he never again held office. None the less, he retained much of his political influence in Scotland until his death in 1811. His Whig nephew by marriage Henry Cockburn loyally minimised the charges against

[5] Holden Furber, *Henry Dundas*, p. 149.

[6] J. A. Lovat-Fraser, *Henry Dundas*, p. 96. On 2 May 1805 Napoleon wrote to Barbé Marbois: ' Faites faire un petit pamphlet sur l'affaire Melville pour montrer l'immoralité de M. Pitt et du gouvernement Anglais '.

Dundas but eloquently testified to the effect of such a fall on Scotland, ' where people could scarcely believe their senses '.[7] Scott lamented his patron's hard fate (not unmindful of the cloud that it threatened to cast over his own hopes of comfortable office),[8] but perked up sufficiently to regale a celebration dinner at Melville's acquittal with some atrocious verse.[9] Scott's unwonted bitterness in these lines may have reflected the horror of the Tories at the coalition ministry headed by Fox and the Duke of Portland.

The so-called ' ministry of all the talents ' (1806–07) was in fact narrowly based and not particularly talented. Fox was already a dying man and the coalition did not long survive his death in September 1806. But shortlived and weak though it was, it helped to make the position of the Tories uncomfortable. The abolition of the slave trade and a plan for reform of the court of session were sufficient to render ludicrous the Tory ideal of standing for ever on the *status quo*. Reform of the court of session was long overdue. A single lord ordinary sitting in the Outer House could not cope with the growing volume of business, and the Inner House, consisting of the other fourteen judges, was also overworked and frequently driven to making snap decisions. As a result many dissatisfied litigants appealed to the house of lords, and the lords did not relish having to wrestle with the involved details of an alien system of law. Walter Scott as early as 1802 believed that the Tories should have seized the opportunity to undertake much needed legal and administrative reforms, so dispelling the dangerous notion that they were averse to reform of any kind;[10] but with many of his fellow advocates he opposed the bill introduced by the coalition government to reform the court of session. The Whigs wanted to divide the court into three chambers and to set over them a court of review to winnow out frivolous or unsatisfactory appeal cases, thus reducing the burden on the house of lords. The coalition fell before the bill could be passed and in the event Melville's son and successor as political manager was responsible for reform of the court of session. This was achieved on less thorough lines than

<hr/>

[7] Henry Cockburn, *Memorials of His Time*, p. 204.

[8] Grierson, ed., *Letters of Sir Walter Scott*, I. 273-4, 282.

[9] Walter Scott, *Poetical Works* (Oxford edn. 1904), ' Health to Lord Melville 1806 ', pp. 708-9.

[10] Grierson, ed., *Letters of Sir Walter Scott*, I. 127.

had been envisaged by the coalition: in 1808 the court was reorganised in two divisions.[10a] Scott hoped that his policy had at last been adopted, but though further legal reforms were considered little was achieved and that little grudgingly conceded to public pressure. Such, for example, was the introduction of a jury court for civil cases in 1816, and in 1825 reform of the Scottish criminal jury system. Legal reform, therefore, gained the Tories little credit.

In that same year 1808 Napoleon's invasion of Spain led to a trenchant article in the *Edinburgh Review* which was to have an important influence on British politics. For some time, partly to suit the needs of Brougham, the *Review* had been edging away from its initial cautious policy. Increasingly, too, through a new contributor, James Mill, it began to adopt some of the views of Jeremy Bentham, the father of ' philosophic radicalism '. Undoubtedly, these trends were strengthened by the fall of Melville; but at the same time care was taken to condemn the democratic radicalism advocated by William Cobbett. Jeffrey slashingly reviewed Cobbett's works, and Cobbett in turn referred to the reviewers as ' northern leeches '.[11] The new Whiggism that was being pushed by the *Review* was not, then, democratic: Jeffrey made it clear that he believed in oligarchy but in an enlightened reforming oligarchy. Nor was the Whig party at this point keen on parliamentary reform, which was not a pressing issue at elections; instead the Whigs raised the old cries against the power of the crown. A heavy defeat in the general election of 1807 confirmed them in these attitudes, and their main efforts were devoted to ' economical reform ' designed to cut down sinecures and bridle the use of patronage.[12] This form of argument, however, as the younger and more progressive Whigs saw, was illogical. Under the defective system of representation only very exceptionally could there be pressing election issues; but it did not therefore follow that such issues either did not exist or were of little moment. The younger Whigs, in fact, were dissatisfied with their seniors,

---

[10a] For details consult Green's *Encyclopaedia of the Laws of Scotland*, v. 3 ff. The act of 1808 created a first division and a second division; these have been retained, but in 1825 the practice of having an Outer House and an Inner House was restored. In 1830 the number of judges was reduced to 13, five sitting as an Outer House, while each division of the Inner House had four judges.

[11] Clive, *Scotch Reviewers*, p. 86.

[12] Michael Roberts, *The Whig Party 1807–1812*, pp. 229-35.

who during the coalition had acted in an aloof and autocratic manner. Jeffrey feared a recrudescence of old-style grand Whiggery on the Rockingham model, which, if allowed to develop, would antagonise the middle-class and working-class radicals. Jeffrey was too intelligent not to perceive the dangers of such a course. His view was that the Whigs could only prosper by making an alliance with the more restrained radicals; such an alliance might hold out double benefits by enabling the Whigs to defeat the Tories and at the same time hold the masses in check. The first hint of such a scheme (which took many years to mature) appeared in an article in the *Review* on ' Don Pedro Cevallos on the French Usurpation in Spain '. The rottenness of Spanish political life was exposed, but exposed too were the defects of the British constitution. The article, the joint work of Jeffrey and Brougham, raised a furore of criticism and abuse, with the Tories only slightly more incensed than the leaders of the Whigs. Jeffrey could not retreat and by 1809 he was cautiously advocating an alliance between Whigs and radicals.[13] In other ways, too, the *Review* was influential, notably in developing the economic ideas of Adam Smith to suit a new age.

That times were changing, even if institutions and governments were not, was clear enough in other walks of life. In 1805 the rigid proscription of all but staunch Tories in the universities received a blow when the chair of mathematics became vacant at Edinburgh. The best candidate was John Leslie who was supported both by the uncommitted *savants* and the town council—a rare concurrence. The local Moderates, however, saw in the appointment of such a candidate a serious threat to their position. Not only would it reduce the number of offices that they could monopolise but it would also bring into prominence an open and forthright mind. Proscription suited well a party more interested in power than in learning: the well-being of the universities was a secondary consideration and there can be no doubt that the intolerance of these times hastened the decline of the great tradition built up in the eighteenth century. On flimsy grounds the Moderates attacked Leslie as an atheist, and paradoxically, but quite sincerely, he was defended by the Evangelicals.[14] After a

[13] *Edinburgh Review*, xiv. 298 ff.

[14] H. Cockburn, *Memorials*, p. 186 ff; I. D. Clark, ' The Leslie Controversy, 1805', in *Records of Scottish Church History Society*, xiv. 179-97.

bitter struggle, in which numerous pamphlets kept the public informed of murky manœuvres, Leslie was appointed. His case was important from many points of view and not least because of the bad light it cast on the Moderates. Though their majorities in the church courts continued for many years to be unassailable, in practice from 1805 onwards the Moderates, who were scarcely to be distinguished from ecclesiastical Tories, were on the defensive. They could no longer pose as the party of culture or of intellectual liberty, and increasingly the Evangelicals appealed to the more progressive of the young probationers in the church. The great Thomas Chalmers is himself the prime example of this switch of allegiances: the young Chalmers began as a typical Moderate but by 1811, after years of groping, he definitely emerged as a dedicated Evangelical.

The views of the labouring classes, as they were then called, are harder to determine. History (or rather historiography) has a short way with village Hampdens who leave no memorials behind them. But it seems probable that the attitudes of the so-called ' lower orders ' were mixed, and possibly confused. The mendicant Edie Ochiltree, one of the ripest products of Scott's genius, felt in *The Antiquary* that he had as much stake in the land as the greatest laird. A good deal of evidence can be adduced to suggest that some such sentiment was widespread. Domestic dissension was one thing, but the threat of a French invasion was quite another. It is probably significant that not a few of the radicals who were tried in 1817 had served in the volunteers or in the militia during the wars.[15] On the other hand there must have been many who like John Younger, the shoemaker of St Boswells, maintained the radical cause and only reluctantly participated in ' the more extensive measures to be adopted for the defence of our *gentry's* precious island '.[16] Younger, like many others, joined the volunteers only to escape the militia draft. He was born in 1785 at the ferm-toun of Longnewton in Roxburghshire which was later swept away by agrarian reform. He was poorly schooled but like his fellow Borderers, James Hogg (the Ettrick Shepherd) and the polymathic John Leyden, he was a lifelong student. His radicalism was confirmed by close study of the works of Robert Burns who ' became to me like a modernized

---

[15] Such, *e.g.*, as Alexander McLaren and Thomas Baird; Howell, *State Trials*, XXXIII. 6, 12.   [16] John Younger, *Autobiography*, ch. XIX *passim*, e.g., pp. 220-1.

prophet or a pocket oracle '.[17]   Interestingly enough, Younger, who belonged to the new rural proletariat, had no high regard for the works of Scott, which he likened to 'a mere low bagatelle of literary flummery '.[18]   The judgment seems severe, but coming from one who had nearly starved to death in the famine of 1799 it is understandable.   To Younger, Scott was landlordism incarnate and landlordism was already a *bête noire* of Scottish radicalism.

Contrary to the rarefied arguments of statistical economists, past and present, these were hard times for the labouring classes. Trade fluctuated violently, prices soared and wages fell, and in these circumstances the Corn Laws were bitterly resented by both manufacturers and workers.   The sufferings of the handloom weavers were particularly severe.   From being the aristocracy of labour, literate and thoughtful,[19] many of them were reduced to destitution, for in the period between 1800 and 1808 the wage of the average weaver fell by nearly a half.   The industry was unregulated and in 1808 the English and Scottish weavers made common cause in an effort to secure a bill to fix minimum rates.[20] Glasgow became the great centre of agitation and there in 1809 an Association was established.   It failed, to some extent because of the Combination Acts,[21] but mainly because the weavers were widely dispersed and consequently difficult to organise.   Napoleon's Continental System and the rival British Orders in Council ushered in even worse times, leading to numerous bankruptcies in 1810 and a disastrous fall in wages and employment in 1811. In spite of the obvious distress this caused, parliament refused to loosen, far less abolish, the Corn Laws.   In Scotland, however, there were no actual disorders, such as the machine-breaking activities of the ' Luddites ' in England.   Rather, despairing of new legislation, the Glasgow weavers, ably led by Alexander

[17] J. Younger, *Autobiography*, p. 218. He also states that Burns ' confirmed my former suspicion that the world was made for me as well as Caesar '. Alexander Somerville in his *Autobiography of a Working Man*, pp. 86-9, also testifies to Burns's importance as one of the inspirers of Scottish radicalism.

[18] Younger, *Autobiography*, p. 193.

[19] One example must suffice: M. Blair, *The Paisley Shawl* (1904), p. 46, notes that many of the weavers of Paisley subscribed to journals, established book societies and amassed libraries which rivalled those of ministers and professional men.

[20] Donald Read, *Peterloo, the Massacre and its Background*, p. 20.

[21] J. L. Gray, ' The Law of Combination in Scotland ', in *Economica*, VIII. 332-50, shows that the Combination Acts of 1799 applied only in England and Wales, but that in Scotland the same effects were achieved by a construction of the common law.

Richmond, fell back on the old. Under the terms of a Scottish act of 1661 they petitioned the magistrates to fix fair rates of wages. Reluctantly, the magistrates complied, but the employers appealed to the court of session, where the workmen's case was successfully pleaded by Jeffrey and Cockburn.[22] The employers flouted the decision and the court of session apparently lacked power to enforce it. The fault lay with the government and nothing showed it up in a worse light than the aftermath of this decision. The weavers went on strike and were promptly coerced: their leaders were arrested and convicted but Richmond, on the advice of counsel, Jeffrey and Cockburn, absconded rather than face the certainty of imprisonment or the possibility of transportation.[23] The real enormity of government lay in its repealing the act on which the decision of the court of session had been based. The point was clearly taken: in spite of the government's repeated eulogies of the law and the constitution, law itself was mocked by the Toryism of that age. This incident, and others, were neither overlooked nor forgiven and do much to explain the weakness of Conservatism in Scotland after 1832.

Thanks largely to these developments political radicalism revived. In parliament a radical group emerged headed by Sir Francis Burdett: it was far from extreme and remained loosely, if at times precariously, attached to the Whigs. Far more significant was the development of popular radicalism in the country, encouraged by such irrepressible veterans as Major Cartwright, who, together with Burdett, was in 1812 largely responsible for the creation of the Hampden Club. In that same year Cartwright may have conducted a lecture tour in Scotland with the object of setting up local Hampden Clubs, but for this the evidence is vague. However that may be, he was certainly at this time in correspondence with radical groups in the west of Scotland.[24] This was an extremely important development. It

[22] *Faculty Collection of Decisions*, 1810–19, No. CXCI, 27 June 1812, William Fulton and others, Operative Weavers of Glasgow, against David Mutrie and others, Master Manufacturers there.

[23] A. B. Richmond, *Narrative of the Condition of the Manufacturing Population; and the Proceedings of Government which led to the State Trials in Scotland* (1824), p. 39; Cockburn, *Memorials*, p. 311.

[24] Cockburn, *Memorials*, p. 296, states that Cartwright held successful meetings in Scotland in 1812 but of this there is no corroboration in F. D. Cartwright, *Life and Correspondence of Major Cartwright* (1826), 2 vols.; there is, however, evidence of liaison between Cartwright and the Glasgow reformers, II, p. 50.

brought about a conjunction of the old theoretical objections to the constitution, of which Cartwright was an indefatigable if none-too-learned exponent, and the pressure of economic and social grievances. In 1813 the existence in Edinburgh of a depressed proletariat which differed markedly from the eighteenth-century mob was demonstrated in the ' Tron Riot '.[25]   The middle-class held aloof from such activities, and indeed heartily condemned them; but the waning of its attachment to Toryism was being revealed for all that. The Tories had made the mistake of mixing politics with business and the chartered banks extended credit only to those of sound constitutional views. As a protest against this the Commercial Bank was founded in 1810—the protest implicit in its very title.[26]   Then, too, burgh politics were as corrupt as ever and mounting municipal debts caused bitter resentment, especially among the well-to-do merchants who were excluded from the government of the royal burghs. Middle-class restlessness first found expression in a public meeting held in Edinburgh in July 1814 to advocate the abolition of West Indian slavery. The first great public meeting to be held in Scotland for over twenty years, it showed that the lines along which Scottish politics were to move over the greater part of the nine-teenth century were clearly drawn before the peace of 1815, for it intertwined radicalism both secular and ecclesiastical. Sir Harry Moncrieff, leader of the Evangelical party in the estab-lished church, presided, and 10,000 signatures to a petition against slavery were obtained. Clearly, by the close of the war the public apathy on which Toryism flourished was fast disappearing.

These problems were intensified by the peace of 1815. The government gave little or no thought to adapting a ' siege economy ' to the needs of peace and as a result both agriculture and industry suffered. During the war years intensive farming forced even marginal land under the plough, but by the end of 1815 the artificial boom had collapsed. A policy of rigid protec-tion staved off complete disaster but could not prevent a long depression, in which, however, the mixed agrarian economy of Lowland Scotland proved more buoyant than that of most parts of Britain.[27]   Nevertheless, the state of agriculture long continued

[25] Laurance J. Saunders, *Scottish Democracy, 1815–1840*, p. 88.
[26] Anon., *Our Bank, The Story of the Commercial Bank of Scotland, 1810–1941*, ch. I.
[27] J. A. Symon, *Scottish Farming: Past and Present*, ch. x.

bleak and uncertain, and the landlords and farmers soon formed a powerful 'agricultural interest' which could vex Whig and Tory alike. In the Lothians the farm labourers did not fare too badly, but in less favoured areas the rule was long hours of hard work for a bare subsistence. The law favoured the masters, and though agricultural workers tried spasmodically from as early as 1805 to secure better conditions their efforts were no more success-ful than those of the weavers.[28] Hardest hit of all were the small tenants in the Highlands. As we have seen, in that area popula-tion was soaring, and in many parts holdings were being divided into minute lots. The rising price of wool induced many land-lords to turn to a deliberate policy of clearing the land of people to make way for Cheviot sheep. The collapse of the cattle trade and the decline of kelp confirmed this tendency. In the name of improvement, and under the sanction of the law, many bewildered Highlanders were driven from their homes. In Strathglass from 1801 onwards the Chisholm was evicting his 'clansmen'; and about the same time the crazed Glengarry, deep sunk in debt, began to clear his lands. The most notorious of the Clearances began in Sutherland in 1807 in the parishes of Farr and Lairg. Directed by the superintendent of the Marquess of Stafford's estates, James Loch, the Sutherland Clearances continued in 1814 when Patrick Sellar brutally evicted the people of Strathnaver. Robert MacKid, the sheriff-substitute of Sutherland, attempted to bring Sellar to book, but Sellar was acquitted and MacKid ruined. There was little resistance, the people were leaderless and stunned, the clergy for the most part siding with the lairds. The news leaked out and some caustic comments were passed, to counter which Loch produced in 1820 an elaborate but by no means candid or convincing defence.[29] According to Loch, all was done for the best; the people had been idling uselessly on the hills, which sheep could profitably graze; the landlord out of beneficence granted them holdings on the coast where fishing could eke out crofting. Loch's work was simply an application of current economic thinking to the rural scene.

It is difficult to assess the Clearances, surrounded as they are by bitter feelings. That the population of the Highlands and

[28] George Houston, 'Labour Relations in Scottish Agriculture before 1870', in *Agricultural History Review*, VI, Pt. I, 27-41.

[29] James Loch, *An Account of the Improvement on the Estates of the Marquess of Stafford*.

Islands needed to be reduced scarcely admits of argument; but the methods employed to secure this end were too often heartless and indefensible. As early as 1805 the Earl of Selkirk had examined the problem and concluded that only planned and assisted emigration to the colonies could provide a humane solution.[30] The earl sponsored such settlements, notably on the Red River in Manitoba in 1814; but the few ventures that were promoted, mainly to Canada, scarcely scratched the surface of the problem. Most emigrants had to shift for themselves and suffered a good deal of hardship. The Clearances continued, extending to the Hebrides, though not, significantly, to Lewis where the Seaforth family, impoverished though it was, refused to evict. Most of the landlords indeed, unlike the wealthy Staffords, were relatively poor and faced difficult, perhaps insoluble, problems. In the long run the net result was extensive depopulation, the concentration of wealth in fewer hands, and an implacable resentment which is as fierce today as it was at the time of the actual Clearances. However regarded, however palliated, it is not a pretty story; and when the question of the Clearances again came before the public in the 1840s it added to the ill reputation of landlordism and thus further strengthened the base of Scottish radicalism.

Trade and industry also suffered in the unwonted peace. Partly this was because some industries, especially textiles, had over-expanded and failed to adjust to demand; partly the recession was attributable to the financial chaos left by the war; and it was compounded by a revolt of the European countries which refused to be treated as dumping grounds for British manufactures. Already on the continent a reaction was beginning against Adam Smith and his successors; it was reinforced by the strident nationalism which Napoleonic imperialism had helped to provoke. The movement culminated in the work of the German economist, Friedrich List, and his insistence on national political economy. Radicalism throve on such dislocations and their attendant hardships. In the summer of 1815 old Major Cartwright held well-attended meetings in Scotland and as a consequence numerous Hampden Clubs were formed.[31] The deepening depression increased radical activity. By 1816 many were unemployed and

[30] Earl of Selkirk, *Observations on the Highlands of Scotland.*
[31] Cartwright, *Life and Correspondence of Major Cartwright,* II. 109 ff. for his activities in Glasgow, Dundee and Aberdeen.

the provisions of the poor law, which was hopelessly thrown out of gear by the new hard facts of life, proved totally inadequate to their needs. A growing flood of Irish immigrants aggravated the problem. In despair the depressed weavers and cotton spinners turned more and more to political agitation. One such group in the manufacturing districts in and around Glasgow had the misfortune to enlist the help of Alexander Richmond. Richmond is an enigma. He had begun his working life as a weaver and had championed the weavers' cause in 1812. After a brief interval as an outlaw he had given himself up and, the affair of the strike having somewhat blown over, was imprisoned for a month. On his release he set up in business, aided by Jeffrey and Cockburn, and for a while he prospered. But Richmond had been marked down for treatment of a different sort by Kirkman Finlay, M.P. for the Glasgow district of burghs. Finlay was a great cotton manufacturer who combined this role with that of merchant prince: he had been one of the main contrabandists who undermined the Continental System and when this lucrative if risky venture ceased he pioneered the illegal trade with the Far East which eventually broke the East India Company's monopoly.[32] Finlay lived in terror of revolution, which at that time seemed to threaten to devour Europe. In 1816 he became a self-appointed suppressor of revolutions and co-operated with the home secretary in building up an intelligence system to counteract the radicals. He renewed contact with Richmond who impressed on Finlay the terrible straits of the poor and induced him to raise a relief fund. By degrees Richmond was inveigled into Finlay's system and finally information provided by him led to the arrest of several weavers. Later, Richmond ' The Spy ' was anathematised by liberal opinion as the fomenter if not the only begetter of these troubles;[33] but he was probably as much a victim as those who were arrested.

Quite apart from Richmond's activities the troubles existed and there was a conspiracy of sorts, the by-product of a great meeting at Thrushgrove Field in Glasgow on 29 October 1816. In an effort to prevent informing, the conspirators (who do not seem

[32] George Eyre-Todd, *History of Glasgow*, III. 434 ff. For the leading part played by Scots in the Far East in the early nineteenth century, see M. Greenberg, *British Trade and the Opening Up of China, 1800–1842*.

[33] The egregious Peter Mackenzie consistently took this line in his rambling *Reminiscences of Glasgow and the West of Scotland*, I. 109 ff.

to have been very numerous) had to take a strict if somewhat schoolboyish oath, disregard of which was supposedly to be punished by death.   Such a threat may not have been entirely idle, however, for already industrial Glasgow was winning for itself a reputation for violence.   At any rate, Richmond penetrated this little circle and told Finlay about the oath.   The information was speedily dispatched to the lord advocate, Alexander Maconochie, who made melodramatic use of it in his maiden speech in the house of commons in February 1817.[34] The house was then debating whether or not to suspend *habeas corpus* and Maconochie's revelations clinched the issue.   *Habeas corpus* was suspended and, urged on by the home secretary Lord Sidmouth (the former Addington), Maconochie prepared to prosecute some of the alleged plotters.   Alarmed by the trend of events in England, which in June 1817 led to Jeremiah Brandreth's rising in Derbyshire and the subsequent exposure of the activities of ' Oliver ' the spy, the government became still more anxious to secure convictions in Scotland.[35]

The so-called ' state trials ' of 1817 in Scotland misfired disastrously and their chief effect was to increase distrust of the Tory government and its agents.   But they were creditable to the law and to the judges who, though for the most part Tories, did not allow their politics to influence their judicial acts.   This plainly appeared in the first trial, that of Alexander McLaren, a weaver, and Thomas Baird, a grocer, which took place at Edinburgh in March 1817.   Both the accused lived in Kilmarnock; they were both respectable men; and both had served in the volunteers during the·war, Baird holding a captain's commission.   By 1816 McLaren, a skilled operative, had to toil fifteen hours a day for a pittance of 5s. per week, while others less skilled could only earn 3s.   Hard times and governmental indifference led them to take part in radical meetings at one of which on 7 December 1816 McLaren delivered a speech.   He lamented the woes of the people and urged that a petition should be sent to the Prince Regent; but if this were disregarded then, McLaren concluded, ' to Hell with our allegiance '.   Baird, a member of the committee set up to prepare the speeches for publication, was accused of inserting

---

[34] Hansard's *Parliamentary Debates*, xxxv. 728-30.
[35] E. Halévy, *History of the English People in the Nineteenth Century*, ii. 28-9 ; more fully dealt with in R. J. White, *Waterloo to Peterloo*.

some inflammatory passages and of selling numerous copies of the resulting pamphlet in his shop. At the outset of the trial it was established that the spirit of Fox's libel act of 1792 should apply: namely, that the jury should decide not merely whether the facts alleged by the crown were true but also whether these facts entailed a seditious libel.[36] The accused were well represented, Clerk of Eldin appearing for McLaren, and Jeffrey and Cockburn for Baird. The evidence, such as it was, upheld the lord advocate's charge and in spite of an eloquent and able speech by Jeffrey, which showed how nebulous the law relating to sedition was, the panels were found guilty and sentenced to six months' imprisonment. The sentence was so unexpectedly mild as to be tantamount to a defeat for the crown. Even Cockburn declared himself content with the conduct of the trial, which he described as ' the first perfectly fair trial for sedition that Scotland had ever seen '.[37] But from the point of view of the ministerialists it was unsatisfactory. Where were all those desperate jacobins that Lord Advocate Maconochie and Kirkman Finlay had described to the house of commons ?

Richmond's information suggested a way out of the difficulty: the Glasgow conspirators should be unmasked, thereby justifying the government and all its works. The first of them to be charged with the capital offence of administering unlawful oaths were William Edgar and John Keith. Here the law, a statute of 1812, was even more obscure than in the case of sedition and the defence counsel easily routed the lord advocate and his depute. Maconochie, in fact, was an indifferent lawyer and could not even draw up formal indictments. He attempted grapeshot charges, containing both treason and sedition; but the bench agreed with defence counsel's objection that this procedure was unwarrantable.[38] The first indictment against Edgar failed and his trial was postponed. In fact, Edgar was never tried, for a later case, that of Andrew McKinlay, undermined the whole shaky structure on which the lord advocate prosecuted. In the interval there was ripe farce in the shape of the trial of Neil Douglas. Douglas had begun his long and varied career as a Relief Church minister and

[36] Howell, ed., *State Trials*, xxxiii. 13.

[37] H. Cockburn, *An Examination of the Trials for Sedition in Scotland*, ii. 191.

[38] Howell, ed., *State Trials*, xxxiii. 270, Lord Reston: ' the prosecutor has no right to pass from his libel, to the effect of making us consider a new one, without the authority of the Court '.

had been a notable member of the British Convention in 1793. He never lost his belief in the necessity for political and social reform, but by degrees his Calvinism changed to Arminianism and he became pastor of a small universalist church in Glasgow.[39] By 1817 he was regarded as one of the town's worthies, a bold and entertaining preacher whose eloquence frequently outsoared his understanding. On 26 May 1817 Douglas was tried at Edinburgh for sedition, accused of having in the course of one of his sermons compared George III to Nebuchadnezzar who had been ' driven from the society of men for infidelity and corruption '. If true, this was an unfeeling description of George III's mental illness, though a strong case could have been made for Douglas bracketing the Prince Regent with Belshazzar as ' a poor infatuated wretch, or a poor infatuated devotee of Bacchus '. For added measure Douglas had apparently castigated the house of commons where ' seats were sold like bullocks in a market '. The preacher's furious Highland delivery had confused the informers, and the evidence adduced against him was weak. For Douglas it was argued that he was in fact lecturing on the Book of Daniel and could scarcely do so without touching on such prominent characters as Nebuchadnezzar or Belshazzar, however seditious the prosecution might find certain parts of the Old Testament. Maconochie did not appear in this case but if anything the Solicitor-General Wedderburn proved even more inept than his superior. The case for the prosecution was botched and Jeffrey skilfully availed himself of Wedderburn's tirade to secure a verdict of not guilty.[40]

All this time the lord advocate had been racking his brains to frame an indictment against McKinlay. The patience of the cabinet was wearing thin and awkward questions were being raised in the house of commons, even by Kirkman Finlay, who scathingly denounced the lord advocate's incompetence.[41] At the third attempt Maconochie's indictment satisfied three of the five judges and on 19 July McKinlay was at last tried for administering unlawful oaths. The trial had a dramatic dénouement. Jeffrey, as counsel for the accused, dreaded the testimony of John

---

[39] G. Struthers, *History of the Relief Church* (1843), ch. XXII, and App. X.
[40] Howell, ed., *State Trials*, XXXIII. 633 ff.; Cockburn, *Examination of Trials for Sedition*, II. 192 ff.
[41] *Hansard*, XXXVI. 1078-81.

Campbell, a weaver who had been arrested and held *incommunicado*; but Campbell's testimony astonished the entire court, including counsel for the defence, who had no prior knowledge of it.[42] To the bench's customary opening question, ' Has anybody given you a reward, or promise of a reward, for being a witness?',[43] Campbell replied in the affirmative and pointed out as the person who had approached him the advocate-depute. The judges disallowed Campbell's testimony; but the prosecution fared little better with its other witnesses, and the case collapsed. The libel against McKinlay was found not proven and he was freed along with others held on similar charges. Maconochie was now a liability to the government, which in 1819 solved the problem by making him a judge of the court of session under the title of Lord Meadowbank.

This fiasco was a serious setback to the government and an encouragement to reformers of all shades of opinion. A reforming press had meanwhile come into existence which developed Jeffrey's scheme of a union of reformers and of which the main organs were *The Dundee Advertiser* (founded as early as 1801), *The Aberdeen Chronicle* (1806), and, most powerful voice of all, *The Scotsman* (1817). The need for burgh reform was more glaring than ever: on this issue the most radical and the most moderate of reformers could agree and in 1817 the long-dormant burgh reform association revived its activities, still directed by Archibald Fletcher. A new tactic was employed, aiming at reforming the town councils by poll elections. At Montrose an irregular election was deliberately contrived in order to secure the benefit of a poll warrant, which was reluctantly granted by the lord advocate in 1817. Montrose was thus able to rid itself of the old corrupt oligarchy and start afresh. Other royal burghs hastened to avail themselves of the same procedure but the government, alive to the danger, refused further poll warrants.[44] Here was yet another example of the Tory government's contempt for law, since proof of malpractice at burgh elections had hitherto inevitably led to the issue of a poll warrant.[45] This denial of legal right was even applied to Aberdeen which was a notorious seat of corruption. In May 1819, however, Lord Archibald Hamilton

---

[42] Cockburn, *Memorials*, p. 318.

[43] Howell, *State Trials*, xxxiii. 584.

[44] Meikle, *Scotland and the French Revolution*, pp. 225-6.

[45] For procedure by poll warrant see Alexander Wight, *Rise and Progress of Parliament* (edn. 1806), i. 356 ff.

succeeded in moving a parliamentary inquiry into the Scottish burghs and its subsequent report proved that corrupt practices had bankrupted Edinburgh, Aberdeen, Dundee and Dunfermline.[46]

The introduction of police acts for the burghs had already exposed the weakness of the Tory position. The growth of the towns required extended powers—for security, cleansing, lighting, and so on—but even the Tories had to admit that to grant further powers to the existing town councils would simply multiply abuses. Thus the earliest of Edinburgh's police acts in 1805 vested such powers in a popularly elected commission, and in 1817 the commission's right to control the superintendent of police was established. The 'police system', therefore, was a small but growing democratic enclave surrounded by irresponsible oligarchy. The continued existence of corrupt burgh administration helped to undermine Toryism in Scotland and turned the burghs after 1832 into impregnable Liberal bastions.

A brief revival of trade eased political tension,[47] but by 1819 bad times and ill tempers had returned. In that year England was disturbed by massive demonstrations which in August led to tragedy at ' Peterloo '.[48] The ' massacre ' was approved by the government which seized the opportunity to pass further repressive legislation, the so-called Six Acts. Even the normally cool and collected prime minister, Lord Liverpool, lost his head. Wherever they looked the Tories saw plotters and their fears seemed to be confirmed by the desperate Cato Street conspiracy—hatched, not unknown to the government, between December 1819 and February 1820—which aimed at liquidating the cabinet. Walter Scott babbled wildly about 50,000 blackguards ready to rise in arms in Northumberland and commended the spirit of the Highland chiefs who were ready to furnish another ' Highland Host ' to preserve society.[49] Thomas Carlyle, who was then in Edinburgh, took a different view of the situation, regarding it as much ado about nothing.[50] Yet while Scott grossly exaggerated,

---

[46] *Parliamentary Papers*, 1819, vi, *passim*.

[47] Halévy, *History of the English People in the Nineteenth Century*, II. 30 ff.

[48] Donald Read, *Peterloo, the Massacre and its Background*.

[49] J. G. Lockhart, *Life of Sir Walter Scott* (edn. 1902), VI. 141, 149, 153; Grierson, ed., *Letters of Sir Walter Scott*, VI. *passim*, *e.g.*, W. Scott to Cornet W. Scott, 28 December 1819.

[50] J. A. Froude, *Life of Carlyle*, I (1903), 73-4. Cockburn, *Memorials*, pp. 342-5, agrees with Carlyle. Says Cockburn, ' Edinburgh was as quiet as the grave, or even as Peebles '.

Carlyle's satirical humour minimised the danger. Not only was radical literature, such as Wooler's periodical *The Black Dwarf*, being widely disseminated, but numerous local radical unions were also springing up in the manufacturing counties of the west with a central committee in Glasgow. There a plot of some kind was undoubtedly being hatched which its projectors hoped would be co-ordinated with risings in England; but it was scotched by the arrest of its leaders in February 1820. After that date the government knew that there was little danger of a serious outbreak, but it gladly availed itself of a mysterious incident that diverted Glasgow on 2 April 1820. Bills were placarded calling upon the people to support a provisional government. To help the new ' government ' (which failed to materialise) the weavers went on strike, but the expected *sansculotte* hordes did not appear. Possibly egged on by government agents a few men rose in arms. A small band from Strathaven in Lanarkshire, which included an old jacobin James ' Perley ' Wilson, marched on Glasgow; but on the outskirts they could not find the promised reinforcements and dispersed quietly to their homes. Some of the Calton weavers trudged eastwards to join up with some non-existent English rebels who were said to be marching to seize the Carron Ironworks; but at Bonnymuir near Falkirk the Calton rebels were scattered by cavalry. Thus ended the mysterious so-called ' Radical War ' of 1820. Forty-seven prisoners were tried for treason by a commission of oyer and terminer, and of these three— Wilson, John Baird and Andrew Hardie—were executed.

In spite of apparent successes, by the end of 1820 the position of the government was beginning to deteriorate. Either the state was in grave danger, in which case repression could be justified, or it was not. From 1820 onwards the middle-class was no longer convinced of the imminence of revolution and, increasingly, members of this class demanded reform. The new mood showed itself in some curious ways. George IV's treatment of Queen Caroline stirred up opinion against the ministry and led to large public meetings such as that held at the Pantheon in Edinburgh on 16 December 1820. The ostensible aim of the meeting was to protest at the ministry's treatment of the queen but its real purpose was to create a working alliance between the Whigs and the middle-class democrats. In helping to fashion such an agreement Adam Black, a prominent Edinburgh bookseller, played an important part.[51]   Here Scotland was in advance of England, where the Whig leadership, in spite of Brougham's furious tactics, still vacillated, torn between jealousy and dislike of the Tories and dread of the masses.   In Scotland, on the other hand, the Edinburgh reviewers had captured the leadership of the Whig party, and Jeffrey and Cockburn were respected and trusted by the workers whose interests, it was felt, they had championed in court.   The term ' liberal party ' was commonly used in Scotland and with some justification.   Signs of a changed or changing climate were many, from Jeffrey's election as rector of Glasgow university at the end of 1820 to the bitter newspaper war of the early twenties.   Alarmed at the growing influence of the Whig and radical press, which even heavy taxation failed to check, the Tories had gradually set up organs of their own.   Thus in 1809 the *Quarterly Review* was set up to counteract the *Edinburgh*, and in 1817 *Blackwood's Magazine* appeared to offset the *Scotsman*.   The conflict was waged venomously on both sides, producing two fatal duels as well as much rancour.

In such an impassioned atmosphere the old genteel system of politics was foundering.   The electoral system again came under heavy attack.   In 1823 Lord Archibald Hamilton, one of the leading Scottish Whig members, drew the attention of the house of commons to the defects of county representation in Scotland. He showed that the electors were a mere handful of the population—2,889 to be precise.[52]   He proved that elections depended upon malpractice and legal chicane.   Lord Archibald made no bones about it: he had been returned for Lanarkshire since 1802 and had held the seat at the last contest in 1820 because he had created or bought more fictitious freeholds than his rival.   And, he contended, in no other way could it have been done.   To all this the Tories could only make the feeble reply that the county franchise in Scotland had been settled in 1707 and could not thereafter be amended without breach of the Act and Treaty of Union.   The house was not convinced by this argument and Lord Archibald's motion was defeated by a mere 35 votes.[53]   While the Tories had to fall back on such desperate arguments the Scottish Whigs were drawing up detailed plans of electoral

[51] A. Nicolson, *Memoirs of Adam Black*, pp. 65-7.
[52] *Hansard*, n.s., IX. 615, 2 June 1823.
[53] *Hansard*, n.s., IX. 611-44.

reform; from 1821 onwards this was one of the main employ-
ments of T. F. Kennedy of Dunure, M.P. for the Ayr Burghs.[54]

In this work the Whigs had the tacit co-operation of the
working-class radicals, who after 1820 renounced violent methods
as unprofitable. The repeal of the Combination Acts in 1824,
through the efforts of Joseph Hume (radical M.P. for the Montrose
Burghs) and Francis Place, led to a decline in political activities
on the part of the workers, who turned instead to trade-union
activities. Some trade unions had existed, illegally, before 1824
but in a very weak condition. The strongest and most militant
was that of the cotton-spinners, who already had acquired an
unsavoury reputation in Glasgow. The Glasgow cotton-spinners
helped to jeopardise the workers' newly won rights by embarking
on a long and violent strike, thus affording the ultra-Tories an
opportunity to whittle down the workers' freedom.[55] Still,
much energy was diverted into the building-up of trade unions,
although on the whole this activity produced indifferent results,
largely because many trades were not sufficiently developed to
maintain unions and the difficulties of organisation were too
great.

After 1825 latent divisions in the Tory party came to the
surface as the ultra-Tories led by Lord Chancellor Eldon were
increasingly challenged by more progressive men like George
Canning, William Huskisson, and the young Robert Peel. In
their different ways each of these gifted statesmen attempted to
deal with the actual situation, trying hard to escape from the
strait-jacket that had been fastened on their party by the ultras.
After Castlereagh's suicide in 1822 Canning, a less-skilled diplo-
matist but a much greater politician, expounded the more liberal
foreign policy devised by his predecessor but with an éclat that
Castlereagh could never have attained. Huskisson made a start
on a more enlightened economic policy, while Peel was learning
administration the hard way in Ireland. But they were pulling
in different directions and in the end they helped to disrupt their
party. The question of Roman catholic emancipation deeply
divided the Tories and after the retirement of Lord Liverpool in
1827 it could no longer be burked. Liverpool's successor, Canning, was known to favour emancipation and the ultras would not

[54] H. Cockburn, *Letters on the Affairs of Scotland* (1874), pp. 9, 258 ff.
[55] N. Gash, *Mr Secretary Peel*, pp. 348–51.

serve with him. Canning, therefore, had to patch up a ministry of Tory and Whig moderates; in this he might have failed but for the fierce energy of Brougham who saw in this situation a wonderful opportunity to destroy ultra-Toryism.[56] Rather than lend himself to the support of catholic emancipation, even to stave off the more dreaded parliamentary reform, the second Viscount Melville resigned—and with him ended the classical regime of management in Scotland. Oversight of Scottish affairs went to the Whig Lord Lansdowne, with Kennedy of Dunure and James Abercromby acting as his chief assistants. In the event Canning died before policy had been properly defined, far less implemented, and his short-lived ' piebald administration ' remains a political enigma. None the less, it had shattered the united Tory front; only with difficulty, and at the bitter cost of repealing the Test and Corporation acts in 1828 and carrying Roman catholic emancipation in 1829, did the Duke of Wellington's ministry survive for two troubled years. The Tory majority was reduced in the general election of 1830, but though the ministry had lost its grip on Scottish opinion the system made genuine representation impossible. As it was bitterly put, in Scotland ' men would enlist under Beelzebub's banners, if he were First Lord of the Treasury '.[57] Already the country was in a fever of excitement, an excitement that had been intensified but not created by the July Revolution in France. In the towns and in the countryside the masses were organising in ' political unions ' whose members, known as ' unionists ', raised variants of the old demands for annual parliaments, adult suffrage and the secret ballot.[58] To all but the most obstinate Tories the stark alternatives seemed to be reform or revolution.

Wellington's ministry fell in November 1830; and not without a struggle Earl Grey, with the help of the Canningites, formed a Whig administration. As a reformer Grey had long since cooled; but the needs of the moment forced parliamentary reform on him, though he and his colleagues made it clear that their main concern was to enfranchise the middle-class. Their ideas were broadly

---

[56] A. Aspinall, *Lord Brougham and the Whig Party*, pp. 141 ff.

[57] *The Scotsman, or Edinburgh Political and Literary Journal*, 1830, p. 729, 17 November 1830.

[58] See W. Ferguson, ed., ' A Renfrewshire Election Account, 1832 ', in *Miscellany of Scottish History Society*, x. 218, for objects of the Renfrewshire Political Union formed on 3 December 1830.

those of James Mill: the middle-class was well-to-do, responsible, and educated, and only by granting its members representation as allies of the old governing class could the constitution be saved from democratic threats. Such democratic measures as universal suffrage and the secret ballot were not favoured by the Whig reformers. Their ideal, and they were human enough to believe that their measures would realise it, was a constitution cured of its grossest defects and operated by a progressive and enlightened oligarchy. Their problem was to retain the support of the democrats for such a programme and so enable the Whigs to resist the opposition of the Tories. Somehow the unlikely alliance held firm, temporarily cemented by the epic struggle which lasted almost two years and in the course of which the opposition of the house of lords twice, in April 1831 and again in May 1832, brought down the Whig government. In these critical months the main contest was naturally fought over the Reform Bill for England and Wales, to the comparative neglect of the proposed bills for Scotland and Ireland.[59] The Scottish bill was never properly debated and this perhaps helps to explain some of its peculiar features. The government's intention was clear enough, for Francis Jeffrey, then lord advocate, ' gloried in making the avowal that no shred or rag, no jot or tittle of the old system was to be left '.[60] So well did the Scottish Whigs succeed, in their own estimation at any rate, that Henry Cockburn, the solicitor general, wrote complacently that the Reform Act gave Scotland ' a political constitution for the first time '.[61] This, though it rested on much bogus history, was, in the circumstances, a pardonable exaggeration. The bill itself grew piece-meal, shaped mainly by Jeffrey, Cockburn and Kennedy.

The changes that were finally made in the constituencies were reasonable and in view of the franchises accepted could scarcely have been more extensive. The number of county constituencies remained at thirty, but the old ' pairs ' were abandoned and where necessary fusion took place, as in Ross and Cromarty. The principle of districts of burghs was retained but amended to serve new needs. Thus, Edinburgh was granted an additional member; Glasgow was withdrawn from the Clyde burghs to return two M.P.s of its own; and such large royal burghs as Aberdeen,

[59] See N. Gash, *Politics in the Age of Peel*, ch. 2.
[60] *Hansard*, 3rd. ser., VII. 536.   [61] H. Cockburn, *Journal*, I. 13.

Dundee, and Perth were also drawn out of their districts and granted a member each. The monopoly of the royal burghs was broken by the recognition that ' parliamentary burghs ' were to include such large non-royal burghs as Paisley and Greenock which became one-member constituencies, while other non-royal burghs such as Falkirk and Kilmarnock were added to existing districts of burghs. In all, the number of burgh constituencies was increased from 15 to 23 (a significant commentary on the process of urbanisation) and throughout the basic £10 householder franchise was uniformly applied. The act also ended the parliamentary influence of the town councils and direct voting replaced the old system of delegation. At one stroke, from being centres of reaction the burgh constituencies became the most dynamic part of the new representative system in Scotland.

In the counties the intention of the Reform Act (Scotland) was, granted the limitations imposed by its sponsors, equally good, but muddled thinking and bad drafting vitiated the act. Many of the concepts on which this part of the act rested were at variance with Scots law and some of its clauses were confused.[62] As a consequence the county franchise was ill defined. The effect of the act was to abolish old abuses and inadvertently to make new ones possible: a measure designed to abolish fictitious votes merely served to bring their price down. The provisions made for tenants also led to abuses. Tenants were entitled to be registered as voters if they had a life lease, or one of not less than 57 years' duration, on property valued at £10 per annum; or if they had a lease of not less than 19 years on property of annual value of £50; or, irrespective of the length of the lease, where a *grassum* of not less than £300 had been paid. Sub-tenants, whatever the value of the property concerned, were not enfranchised. Worst of all its drawbacks, the act gave tenants the vote without the safeguard of the ballot and thus put them in political bondage to their landlords. The adoption of the English system of open nomination and polls led to the development of election techniques long familiar in some English counties. Soon the magnates were mustering their cohorts and voting was done very much by estates. The tenant who defied his landlord was subjected to all sorts of pressures, culminating on the expiry of his lease with summary

[62] W. Ferguson, ' The Reform Act (Scotland) of 1832: Intention and Effect ', in *S.H.R.*, XLV. 105-14.

eviction. These malpractices became widespread in the Scottish counties and indeed were in evidence at the first reformed election itself in December 1832. Even Cockburn remarked this unexpected development in Midlothian and drew the obvious conclusion when he wrote to Kennedy, ' Lord what they are doing in the County! Were it known, the Ballot would be triumphant '.[63] In spite of this, and in spite of fumbling with new techniques, the Whigs scored a great victory in the general election of December 1832, winning 43 out of the 53 Scottish seats.

Limited though it was in its aims and mangled though it was in execution, the Reform Act (Scotland) was more revolutionary in its effects than the corresponding English measure. The old electoral machinery was scrapped; the head courts ceased to operate; the court of session lost its jurisdiction in franchise cases, and instead the sheriffs were made responsible for the running of the new registration courts. By December 1832 the electorate had increased from 4,500 to 65,000, and in the next few years the number of voters rose owing to late registrations and artificial creations. Yet considerable though the changes were, the parliamentary system was still too remote from the needs of a society in the throes of protean regeneration. By regarding the work of parliamentary reform as well and finally done, the Whigs merely deluded themselves. That sometimes uncanny guide to his own times, Henry Cockburn, divined this when he predicted, at the very time of the passing of the Reform Act, that ' In a few years the Whigs will be the Tories, and the Radicals the Whigs '.[64] He himself was destined to evolve somewhat, for though he did not become a Tory his zeal for reform diminished.

[63] H. Cockburn, *Letters on the Affairs of Scotland*, p. 437. There is plenty of evidence that such practices were not restricted to Midlothian. Cf. Reg. Ho., G.D.22.2–158, Cunninghame Graham Muniments.

[64] Cockburn, *Journal*, I. 32.

10

THE LIBERAL TRIUMPH, 1832–1886

The period in British history between 1832 and 1886 was saturated in politics, and in some ways this was particularly true of Scotland. With society undergoing rapid change at nearly every level and with improved communications drawing the country closer together, all sorts of problems which formerly would have been treated at the local level came to centre upon parliament. At the same time local conditions continued to colour such general issues as the reform of institutions, extension of the franchise, repeal or maintenance of the corn laws, and the status of trade unions; they also helped to determine attitudes to a wide range of projects for social reform, such as public health requirements, shorter working hours, and educational facilities. For good measure, the church question erupted once more, and this time it had strong political motivation and produced diverse social consequences. The spectrum was too wide to be covered by the existing political parties, neither of which was broadly enough based to comprehend all these problems or well enough organised to formulate clear-cut programmes. Thus this crowded period is difficult to reduce to order, though to suggest that its essence was disorder would be clear exaggeration. Slowly the tangential forces were resolved; and by the end of the period a stronger conception of party made possible fuller control of an enlarged, and subtly changed, electorate. In spite also of increasing cultural assimilation, Scotland for most of her inhabitants retained much of her individuality, and her outstanding problems —concerning church, poor law, education, or public health— differed in substance from their English counterparts. Few politicians grasped this fundamental fact; and statesmanship of even the highest order, as embodied in the career of Sir Robert Peel, could founder when attempting to settle Scottish problems on misleading English analogies.

The political aspirations and ideologies of the period were rough hewn by social and economic changes, the significance of which at the time was not invariably clear. Thus the distribution of population was radically altered, partly by a slow and sporadic process of resettlement which had begun in the late eighteenth century, and partly by the dramatic population increase of the early nineteenth century. By the 1830s areas of hitherto restricted population (like the shires of Lanark, Renfrew and Ayr in the western and the Lothians, Fife and Angus in the eastern Lowlands) came to contain a higher and higher proportion of the total population. Reinforced by the subsequent predominance of industry, which was mainly located in these areas, and by the continuing process of depopulation in the Highland counties, this trend was maintained all through the nineteenth century. It was strikingly illustrated by the growth of some Lowland towns: in the ten main Scottish towns in 1851 only 47% of their swollen populations were native-born.[1] Glasgow's rate of growth was staggering, and in proportion to the total populations of Scotland and England exceeded that of London. Such rapid expansion was due in no small part to immigration, and from about 1820 a large number of Glasgow's new residents were Irish-born. The developing economy of Scotland—and England too—proved an irresistible lure to the depressed Irish, and by 1841 the Irish-born constituted 5% of the population of Scotland, concentrated most heavily in Glasgow, the western coalfields, Edinburgh and Dundee. In some ways they were an economic asset, providing a hard-working mobile force of unskilled labour. Gangs of Irish ' navvies ' did yeoman service in all sorts of construction projects, particularly canal and railway building; and, in addition, the Irish provided a reserve of seasonal harvest workers. But they also acted as cut-price labour in the mines, where they were frequently employed as ' black-legs ' to break strikes, and they added to the miseries of the handloom weavers by swamping with cheap labour that already overcrowded trade.[2] Economic

---

[1] D. F. Macdonald, *Scotland's Shifting Population, 1770–1850*, p. 13.

[2] Walter Scott could make acute assessments of the contemporary scene: he recognised the good qualities of the Irish but also their defects as cheap labour. Cf. Lockhart, *Scott*, IX. 261-3.

rivalry gave rise to bitter resentment, especially in the coalfields of Lanarkshire, though seasonal harvesters (both Highland and Lowland) also had a legitimate grievance at being supplanted by Irish workers. The economic resentment, however, might well have been lost in a common struggle for improved conditions of labour but for the fierce religious antagonisms roused by the settlement of a large Roman catholic population in a strongly protestant country. The resulting prejudices and tensions long continued and have left their mark not only on church history but on education and, indeed, on modern Scottish society as a whole.[3]

A further conditioning factor in politics was the economic growth of the early and mid-nineteenth century, which was attributable mainly to a revolution in iron production. During the Napoleonic wars the infant iron industry had stagnated, partly because of trade fluctuations but mainly because of inhibiting technological problems. The basic defect was the low coke yield of Scottish coals, which caused high production costs; had transport difficulties been solved in the crucial post-war period (1815–1830) then almost certainly the Scottish iron industry would have been beaten on its home ground by its more progressive English and Welsh rivals. With providential suddenness the position changed: the invention of the ' hot blast ' process by James Beaumont Neilson in 1828 and its rapid adoption in Scotland cut costs and raised productivity. Not only did Neilson's process permit raw coal to be used instead of coke but it also enabled the Scottish iron industry to utilise the abundant supplies of native blackband ironstone, the possibilities of which as a source of ore had been demonstrated by David Mushet in 1801. Between 1828 and 1838 the industry made great progress: new furnaces were set up and production increased by over 500 %.[4] The large coal and ironstone deposits of the parishes of Old and New Monkland turned that part of Lanarkshire into the main centre of the iron industry. The period of greatest expansion was from 1835 to 1870: in 1835 there were 29 furnaces in Scotland with an annual

[3] See J. H. Handley, *The Irish in Modern Scotland*, *passim*.
[4] H. Hamilton, *Industrial Revolution in Scotland*, p. 173; R. H. Campbell, ' Investment in the Scottish Pig-Iron Trade, 1830–43 ', in *Scottish Journal of Political Economy*, I, e.g. 233: in 1830 production of pig-iron was 37,500 tons, or 5% of U.K. production, but by the 1840s it had risen to just under 400,000 tons, or 25% of total British production. See Campbell, *Scotland since 1707*, p. 121.

output of 75,000 tons, but by 1869 there were 158 furnaces producing 1·15 million tons. By the 1870s not only had the productivity of individual furnaces increased but the industry had grown to vast proportions and interlocking interests ramified through the entire range of ' heavy industry '.

The iron industry, in turn, was dependent upon plentiful supplies of coal. In the period after 1815 coalmining entered on an intensive phase, owing partly to increased demand and partly to the more efficient steam-powered pumps available to keep the workings dry. As improved methods permitted the sinking of deeper mines to exploit the rich but difficult measures of Lanarkshire and Ayrshire, the centre of gravity of this vital industry slowly shifted from east to west. By the 1870s nearly 70 % of the Scottish output came from the western coalfield;[5] production in the Forth area also rose but at nothing like the pace set in the west. By the 1830s the south-west was fast becoming the main centre of industry in Scotland and the next half-century confirmed its predominance. And in the words of a noted economic historian: ' Coal was king '.[6] Coal in ever greater quantities was needed for the ironworks, for shipyards, railways, factories of every kind which were swinging over to steam power, for the production of gas as an illuminant, and, not least, coal as an important item for export. There is no thorough history of this essential but highly diverse industry, and there are no firm details of capital investment or technical processes. But it can be said that in spite of cyclical slumps the coal industry prospered until the 1860s, and wages overall compared favourably with those earned in other occupations.

Wages apart, the coal was wrought at a fearful cost. In spite of the backbreaking nature of the work and the dangers of deep and intensive mining, child and female labour increased in the pits of Scotland; and particularly in the east, where the colliers themselves forced their women and children to work, conditions were atrocious. Until the commission on mines reported in 1842[7] neither the state nor the public showed much concern about

[5] W. H. Marwick, *Scotland in Modern Times*, p. 74.

[6] Hamilton, *Industrial Revolution in Scotland*, p. 190.

[7] *Parliamentary Papers*, 1842, xvi, Children's Employment (Mines), report by R. H. Franks. Franks stated (p. 387) that ' a picture is presented of deadly physical oppression and systematic slavery, of which I conscientiously believe no one unacquainted with such facts could credit the existence in the British dominions '.

this: for example, little is said of bad labour conditions (and that little most coyly phrased) in the *New Statistical Account*.[8] The commission's report was a horrifying document and led to the passing of Lord Ashley's act prohibiting the employment in mines of females of any age and boys under ten. But not until 1861 did parliament attempt to lay down safety regulations for the industry, and the Mines Act of that year was a paltry beginning. Coal-mining, in fact, was one of the worst monuments to *laissez-faire*; it was reckless of social havoc and yet its unfettered capitalism showed little of the technical efficiency that latter-day devotees have read into ' Manchesterism '. Little wonder, then, that in the coalfields the ' class war ' had a starkness that was by no means universal in an increasingly capitalist economy. The troubles of the Scottish colliers did not fall away with serfdom, for in the primitive rows and drab villages of the coalfields the new style capitalist often proved more of an exploiter than the old style paternalist. Even though some paternalist attitudes survived, notably in the provision of schools,[9] it is not surprising that the colliers should have been pioneer trade-unionists, operating clandestinely as early as 1817, and that with the growth of the industry they took a prominent part in the rise of the trade union movement.[10]

Vital to these developments in coal and iron was the improvement of communications and particularly the advent of railways. These were designed primarily to serve the needs of the coal industry, and the pioneer lines evolved quite naturally from the earlier colliery wagon-ways.[11] The first Scottish railway properly so called was the *Dalkeith and Edinburgh*, opened in 1826 but not fully mechanised until 1845. More important as a nucleus of later networks was the *Monkland and Kirkintilloch*: it also dated from 1826 but by 1832 was mainly operated by steam locomotives. The *Monkland and Kirkintilloch*, with later extensions to Ballochney and Slamannan, speeded up the exploitation of the coal and iron deposits of Old and New Monkland. In 1848 these lines were

[8] See, *e.g.*, *N.S.A.*, II. 189, Gladsmuir parish: ' There are employed at the Penston coal-works 50 colliers, 30 women putters, and 26 boys. . . . A collier and his putter throw out, at an average, fifteen load of coals per day, which is equal to 4s. 4½d.' Nothing is said of actual working conditions, for which see Franks, *op. cit.*, p. 459.

[9] William Boyd, *Education in Ayrshire*, ch. VI; A. Bain, *Education in Stirlingshire*, ch. VIII.   [10] R. Page Arnot, *History of the Scottish Miners*, ch. II.

[11] George Dott, *Early Scottish Colliery Wagonways*.

amalgamated as the *Monkland Railways*, and in 1865 they combined with the *Edinburgh and Glasgow* line, which in that same year appeared in new and larger guise as the *North British*. The nucleus of the *N.B.*'s great rival, the *Caledonian*, can be traced to another early western line, the *Glasgow and Garnkirk* (1831), which, unlike the *Monkland and Kirkintilloch*, began in open competition with the canals. Larger views were forced on the infant Scottish railways when in the late 1830s the major English lines were poised for an assault on Scotland. If this advance had succeeded it would have had significant, and perhaps harmful, effects on an economy that was still Scottish in more than name; but by a supreme effort the invaders were beaten off and Scottish interests were able ' to draw out on a large scale and in bold outline, a comprehensive scheme of railways in their new development as the grand highways of national and international communication '.[12] The cut-throat competition that characterised the early history of the Scottish railways was by no means as wasteful as is sometimes alleged. Duplication of lines was not serious at a time when, for industrial purposes, roads were of little significance; and the changing locations of coalmining could more easily be served by the laying of branch lines than by canal cuts. Fierce railway competition not only favoured the economy but also benefited the public by an efficient and keenly priced form of transport. Nor were the benefits solely economic. In easing communications between the country's component regions, the railways had incalculable social consequences,[13] although in some instances railroad construction had a depressing effect, particularly in hitting at the coastal trade of some of the smaller ports. In certain areas, however, the rise of steam navigation was of greater importance, and most obviously so in the case of the islands of Scotland. Thus the Northern Isles were well served by steamships from Aberdeen and Leith, operated mainly by a concern which developed in 1875 into the North of Scotland line; and the west coast and the Hebrides were covered by various companies which in 1851 were merged in the MacBrayne line. On the Clyde, the railway companies also ran their own steamers.

[12] W. M. Acworth, *The Railways of Scotland*, p. 38.
[13] Duncan Campbell, *Reminiscences and Reflections of an Octogenarian Highlander*, pp. 532-5, describes the surprisingly wide effects of railway construction in the Highlands after 1860.

Important to communications, industry and commerce was the shipbuilding industry which rose on Clydeside in the first half of the nineteenth century. The growth of this industry was the most dramatic economic achievement of that period, a triumph for individual enterprise gratefully drawing on the advantages provided by the coal and iron industries and ceaselessly battling against nature.[14] The River Clyde was not naturally suitable for shipbuilding, and only a massive programme of excavation and constant dredging enabled it to compete with its main rivals, the Mersey and the Thames. On the Clyde shipbuilding was virtually a new industry, for in the eighteenth century it had been overshadowed by the output of the American colonies, though Scott and Sons had been active at Greenock since 1711. The loss of the American colonies provided a stimulus for the native shipbuilders and in the first two decades of the nineteenth century the industry entered an experimental phase, contributing considerably to the development of steam-power, notably with Henry Bell's *Comet* which was built in 1812 by John Wood of Port Glasgow. The rise of Glasgow as a leading centre of the coal and iron industry stimulated interest in steam; for a time Scott of Greenock took the lead but from the 1830s many small yards were established nearer Glasgow, concentrated mainly at Govan on the south bank and Whiteinch on the north. By the mid-century the main shipbuilding centres on the Clyde were Govan, Whiteinch, Dumbarton, Renfrew, Port Glasgow and Greenock, with Govan and Whiteinch the more progressive.

Many pioneers contributed to the growth of the industry, but the greatest and most influential of these was Robert Napier.[15] A typical ' self-made ' man of the early nineteenth century, his yard and engineering shop became virtually schools of shipbuilding, and most of the men who succeeded on the Clyde could be described as his apprentices. Thus Charles Randolph and John Elder, who together in 1852 founded the nucleus of the Fairfield Company (1885), were protégés of Napier's. Elder was a brilliant engineer; his improved engines first made possible long-distance voyages under steam, provoking the sailing ship to a last superb effort. Yet though the triumph of the iron-hulled steamship was clearly

[14] J. Shields, *Clyde Built: A History of Shipbuilding on the River Clyde*; C. R. Fay, *Round About Industrial Britain*, ch. 7, ' The Clyde '.

[15] J. Napier, *Life of Robert Napier*.

foreshadowed in the '50s, its supremacy was not confirmed until the opening of the Suez Canal in 1869; indeed, the Clyde yards also turned out not a few of the famous clipper ships that fought such a gallant fight in the '60s and '70s. The *Cutty Sark*, built by Scott and Linton of Dumbarton in 1869, was launched to compete with another famous clipper, the Aberdeen-built *Thermopylae*. Aberdeen was a flourishing shipbuilding centre, sometimes credited with the invention of the clipper design and certainly famous for its fast sailing ships. It had a long tradition behind it, deriving largely from the needs of the fishing industry but branching out to meet the demands of commerce. By the '60s Aberdeen-built wood-cum-iron hulled clippers were of the first quality, and the industry was employing about 1,000 hands. Dundee, too, was an early starter with iron-hulled vessels but was unable to maintain the pace set by the Clyde; about 1840 the same fate overtook Leith, though both east coast ports continued to play an important part in the production of coastal vessels, and as shipping centres.

The rise of heavy industry in the period 1830 to 1870 was fortunate, for the Scottish textile manufactures were already faltering, particularly the overspecialised cotton trade which by 1840 was suffering from intense competition from Lancashire. By the '50s the Scottish cotton industry was organised throughout on factory lines and thereafter the numbers engaged in handloom weaving, long a distressed occupation, steadily dwindled, apart from those employed in the highly skilled Paisley shawl trade. Mechanisation came too late; the Scottish cotton industry continued to stagnate, and the shortage of raw materials during the American Civil War (1861–65) dealt it a crushing blow. Linen also suffered in the nineteenth century. In the early decades of the century it was hampered by inadequate supplies of flax, and latterly by heavy competition from Manchester. As a result, in some areas linen gave way to allied manufactures, such as jute and linoleum: by 1850 Dundee had earned the nickname of ' Juteopolis ' and Kirkcaldy had begun its long career in floor-covering. Dunfermline, long famous for its fine table-linen, was fortified by the introduction of jacquard looms in 1825 and became the most prosperous centre of the linen trade. In the same period a highly efficient woollen textile industry, specialising in the production of tweeds, was built up in the Borders, principally at Hawick, Galashiels and Innerleithen. Many other industries of local importance evolved in this same period: a good example is furnished by Shetland hosiery, which was popularised by Queen Victoria shortly after her succession and has remained fashionable ever since.   An important industry of a different type was paper-making, which was located mainly in Midlothian to meet the growing demands of the Edinburgh printers but which also thrived in Fife and Aberdeenshire.   In spite of fervent temperance crusades brewing and distilling also rapidly expanded in the nineteenth century, Edinburgh, for example, becoming not only a main centre of the brewing industry but of whisky blending as well.

These manufactures depended on mass importation of raw materials, and, as a consequence, in the nineteenth century Scotland became not only a leading shipbuilding but also a great shipping country.   Many famous shipping lines originated either in Scotland or through the energy of Scottish entrepreneurs. Thus Robert Napier was one of Samuel Cunard's partners in founding the Cunard line (1840), and it was Napier who supplied the earliest ' cunarders '.   The White Star line began at Aberdeen in 1825, and in 1837 a Shetlander, Arthur Anderson, was the main begetter of the Peninsular Steam Company, the precursor of the Peninsular and Oriental.[16]   The Allan line of Glasgow began in the emigrant trade but latterly branched out into general transatlantic service.   On a rather different plane Denny's of Dumbarton, a leading shipbuilding firm, built up strong overseas connections, particularly with Burma and South America.[17]   In the opening up of the Far East, too, Scotsmen played a leading part;[18] Kirkman Finlay's pioneer work was carried a stage further by the growth of mammoth houses, such as Jardine, Matheson and Co., which drove a thriving trade with China in Indian opium and was largely responsible for the Opium War of 1840–42.   Other Scottish based or Scottish financed enterprises of this kind were later active in Africa and Australasia.

Rapid growth on this scale was afflicted by the then dimly understood trade cycle, a phenomenon which also played a significant role in politics.   Sustained radical political activity

---

[16] J. Nicholson, *Arthur Anderson, a Founder of the P. and O. Company*, ch. III.

[17] W. H. Marwick, *Scotland in Modern Times*, p. 114; A. B. Bruce, *William Denny*, ch. XIX.

[18] Michael Greenberg, *British Trade and the Opening up of China, 1800–42*, pp. 37-8.

tended to coincide with trade depressions, since slump conditions militated against industrial action. The main cycle can be roughly plotted: from 1825 until about 1831 there was depression, followed by a boom which ended in the late '30s to usher in a bad decade, after which came a long period of steady expansion which lasted until the late '70s. In this prosperous mid-Victorian period, Britain became ' the workshop of the world ', the main exporter of manufactured goods, the leading overseas investor, and the financial regulator of world trade. Her national income and standard of living rose substantially. But much of the improvement in conditions of life and labour was due not so much to legislation as to ' self-help ', the virtues of which were incessantly extolled by Samuel Smiles, second most famous son of Haddington. The state's principal contribution was the encouragement of such diverse forms of self-help as friendly or benefit societies, savings banks (pioneered by the Reverend Henry Duncan as parish minister of Ruthwell in 1810), trade unionism and the beginning of collective bargaining, and not least the growth of the co-operative movement which culminated in the formation of the Scottish Co-operative Wholesale Society in 1868. But in spite of improvements stemming from these activities, certain social problems proved intractable. The general standard of housing in Scotland had long been poor, and in the early nineteenth century it was worsened by overcrowding in the industrial towns. The census of 1861 revealed that almost a third of Scotland's population lived in one-roomed dwellings, a considerable number of which were windowless. Partly because of a shortage of suitable building land and partly because of the feuing system, the old style of many-storied tenement buildings was favoured in this period, and they were hastily constructed with little or no regard for sanitation or public health. In the slum areas of the expanding towns there was seldom an adequate water supply. New buildings rapidly fell into decay, becoming as iniquitous sinks as ' the Happy Land ', a notorious slum of old Edinburgh, in which want, disease and alcoholism produced appalling mortality rates. Glasgow, indeed, has been described, justly, as ' possibly the filthiest and unhealthiest of all the British towns of this period '.[19] Infant mortality rates were very high, particularly among the working

---

[19] M. W. Flinn, ed., Chadwick's *Report on the Sanitary Condition of the Labouring Population of Great Britain*, pp. 10, 99.

class, and in 1850 slightly more than half the deaths registered were of children under five years of age.[20]

Life was not uniformly grim, or so predictably short, in the more prosperous districts of the cities and in the smaller less industrialised towns.[21] The public health question of that period is, in fact, a puzzling one. In some ways Scotland, with her flourishing medical schools, can claim an honourable niche in the development of social medicine: the provision of hospitals and of insane asylums, for example, had increased in the late eighteenth century. It is hard to avoid the conclusion that in the early nineteenth century there was a breakdown, not only because the existing machinery of government was overtaxed but also because society itself became deranged. The rights and duties of the individual were still stressed, as by Samuel Smiles, at a time when the individual counted for less and less, dominated as he was by forces that he, as an individual, could not possibly control. Out of the ashes of *laissez-faire* (not quite the meaningless abstraction that modern commentators assume[22]) a new sense of community and of social responsibility had to arise. It has been shrewdly put another way: Scotland's ' industrial development during the Victorian Age suggests the successful elaboration of means towards an end unknown and unconsidered '.[23]

For these unhappy developments the economic and social theories then current must share a large part of the blame. The power of the Malthusian devotees of the dismal science in the early nineteenth century has not been exaggerated: even such a kindly man as Henry Cockburn could ask himself, 'are not millions of starving people the necessary occasional sloughs of a very manu-facturing nation?'[24] Poverty was regarded as both a sin and a crime, the relief of which called for the most careful handling lest the evil infect the body politic. The philosophy only broke down when typhus, cholera, tuberculosis and other diseases spread from the teeming slums into the well appointed suburbs. In spite of

[20] D. F. Macdonald, *Scotland's Shifting Population*, p. 95. The exact figure was 50·85%, as against 32·3% for Paris which was also reckoned to have a bad bill of health.

[21] For example, between 1820 and 1830 the royal burgh of Cullen in Banffshire was, to its great improvement, completely rebuilt (*N.S.A.*, XIII. 342).

[22] M. W. Flinn, ed., *Chadwick's Report*, pp. 38–43, tends to minimise the effects of *laissez-faire*; but his case is not entirely convincing.

[23] W. H. Marwick, *Economic Developments in Victorian Scotland*, p. 231.

[24] H. Cockburn, *Journal*, II. 5.

periodic panics the local authorities, weighed down by inertia and lacking adequate powers, could do little. The cause of public health in Scotland was further retarded by mistakes on the part of the advocates of reform. Professor W. P. Alison and his supporters became obsessed with the poor relief problem and believed that the prevention of destitution would lead to a substantial improvement in public health. Unlike the English reformer Edwin Chadwick with his ' drain-pipe mania ', the Scottish reformers underestimated the importance of strictly hygienic considerations which, if unimproved, would still wreak havoc even if the last pauper were rehabilitated. As a result, really sustained efforts to improve public health were not made until the 1860s. A major advance was the act of 1855 permitting Glasgow corporation to pipe an adequate water supply from Loch Katrine; and, typically, this measure had been opposed by private interests for over twenty years. The appointment of Medical Officers of Health in Edinburgh in 1862 and in Glasgow in 1863 led to increased powers, and began the long assault on the slums that has continued ever since.[25] Similarly, the maltreatment of children in the factories (which has been curiously overlooked in Scotland) yielded only to steady pressure, from the pioneer work of Robert Owen through Richard Oastler's agitation in the early 1830s to the tardy implementation of Fielden's act of 1847.[26] As corporate bodies the churches played no consistent part in these movements; but it is noticeable that Free Churchmen seem to have been more inclined to advocate social reforms.

Quite clearly, neither Whigs nor Tories could provide answers to the numerous problems thrown up by such pell-mell change. Indeed, in the period between 1832 and 1867 the two parties were largely at the mercy of conditions that were frequently beyond their comprehension and of events that were beyond their control. It would be misleading, therefore, to label one party progressive and the other reactionary, for in certain matters the Conservatives showed more awareness of the needs of the times than did the Whigs or, as they were often described in Scotland after 1832, the Liberals. On the whole the Liberals were devotees of Manches-

[25] J. H. Brotherston, *Observations on the Early Public Health Movement in Scotland*.
[26] J. T. Ward, ' The Factory Reform Movement in Scotland ', in *S.H.R.*, XLI. 100-23.

terism and exponents of that remorseless economic creed. They tended to be institutional reformers with scant regard for social legislation, and such badly needed measures as factory reform were championed by Tories rather than Liberals. The politicians were also hampered by the constitution, which, far from being perfected in 1832, represented a posting-stage between oligarchy and democracy, and as such was difficult to operate efficiently. Influence still played a part but a part that was steadily reduced by reform of the civil service, which progressively whittled away the amount of patronage that could be purveyed. As John Young, the parliamentary secretary of the treasury (known, significantly, as the ' patronage secretary ') put it in 1844: ' the patronage of the Treasury does not afford the means of providing for one in a hundred of the persons recommended for appointments in Scotland '.[27]

The Whigs owed their triumph in the first reformed general election largely to their grip on the burghs, where the mass of the new middle-class electors were anti-Tory. They were also well entrenched in the northern counties, but the Tories (who, significantly, never again officially used that label in Scotland but styled themselves Conservatives) were stronger in the southern counties. Political warfare, however, was no longer confined to the two major parties, and even in the first reformed elections the Whigs were under fire from the democratic radicals, who stigmatised the Reform Act as a gross betrayal. Many Whig candidates were hotly assailed on such issues as extension of the franchise, shorter parliaments, and the secret ballot. Further reforms carried by the Whig government did nothing to appease the working-class radicals. As Thomas Carlyle acutely remarked, the Whig ministry's programme was like a Barmecide feast at which the hungry millions were ' bidden fill themselves with the imagination of meat '.[28] The burgh reform acts of 1833, which ended the hegemony of sinister interests in the royal burghs and created an enlarged municipal electorate of £10 householders, made a necessary prelude to honest and efficient local government; but, like the emancipation of the slaves, such measures did not meet the demands for political and social reform nearer home which dominated working-class politics. Nor was it simply a

---

[27] Quoted in N. Gash, *Politics in the Age of Peel*, p. 351.
[28] T. Carlyle, *Chartism*, ch. IX.

question of extending the franchise, for, as one of the early historians of the working-class movement noted: ' Political reforms were certainly valued because of their abstract justice, but they were also looked upon as a means of securing a better social position for the humbler classes '.[29]

Organisation was the main problem for the unenfranchised workers. They had lost faith in the Whigs and were doubtful of the middle-class radicals, some of whom, however, provided leadership and inspiration in the early stages of chartism. Chartism was the product of frustration. The People's Charter, with its famous but by no means novel six points,[30] was drawn up by the London Working Men's Association as an expression of political idealism, but soon gained widespread acceptance as a platform for immediate action. In 1838–39 chartist branches proliferated in the north of England and in Scotland; nor were they confined to the industrial areas. It is doubtful, however, how far the term ' Scottish chartism ' may legitimately be employed, for chartism was neither national nor nationalist. Despite the use of common slogans, chartism was essentially a regional phenomenon and its main centres strove to realise different millennia.[31] These characteristic features were as well marked in Scotland as in England. Controversies between ' physical forcers ' and ' moral suasionists ' divided the chartists of Glasgow and Edinburgh, the Glasgow chartists advocating physical force ideas which Edinburgh pointedly renounced. Too much should not be made of these differences: the point was largely tactical, and the motto ' peaceably if we may, forcibly if we must ' represented the views of most chartists.[32] A more likely explanation of the inability of Glasgow and Edinburgh chartists to co-operate is to be found in the very different backgrounds of the two areas: Glasgow was more proletarian and suffering from industrial depression and unrest, whereas the Edinburgh chartists were dominated by fairly prosperous artisans. All in all,

[29] R. G. Gammage, *History of the Chartist Movement, 1837–54* (ed. 1894), p. 9.
[30] They were: annual parliaments, universal male suffrage, equal electoral districts, the removal of the property qualification for membership of parliament, secret ballot, and the payment of M.P.s.
[31] A. Wilson, ' Chartism in Glasgow ', in *Chartist Studies*, ed. A. Briggs, pp. 249–287. This account can be usefully compared with L. C. Wright's *Scottish Chartism*, which tends to overstress the Scottishness of the movement.
[32] Briggs, *op. cit.*, p. 302.

chartism in Scotland was less embarrassed by a lunatic fringe than was its counterpart in England; Feargus O'Connor and Bronterre O'Brien, the Irish demagogues who ousted the moderate English leaders at a farcical National Chartist Convention held in London and Birmingham in 1839, never won much acclaim in Scotland. Their wild arguments and visionary schemes made little appeal to the Scots who, as Wesley had already found, cared more for logic than for appeals to the sentiments. Like Thomas Carlyle, the chartists in Scotland plumped for education as the sovereign remedy for much of Britain's ills. Nor were they indifferent to the other great questions of the time. They keenly debated the non-intrusionist issue; and it was largely in an effort to hold their rank and file that chartist leaders condemned the non-intrusion-ists and even set up chartist churches to maintain social orthodoxy. It was an interesting experiment: the chartist churches were based on primitive Christianity, relying upon simple appeals to the New Testament, and their principal object, none too success-fully achieved, was to wean the working class from evangelicalism and the emphasis that it laid on the life to come. No precise answer to the problem of working-class attitudes to religion in this period is possible. Many members of that class were already indifferent to the churches if not actively opposed to them; many sided with the voluntaries who, in that same distracted decade, were pressing for disestablishment; but, equally, the Ten Years' Conflict which led to the Disruption struck a responsive chord in many working-class households.

After 1848 chartism faded away, having apparently failed. Yet, though not one of the six points was then carried, failure would scarcely be a just verdict on chartism; for, in spite of its crankiness, it cannot be dismissed as a ripe example of Victorian melodrama. In the long run chartist activities helped to under-mine the political system set up in 1832; and, more important, chartism acted as a demonstration-school for working-class political organisation. Its lessons were not lost on later generations of working-class politicians, who insisted on the necessity for unity of aim and clarity of purpose.

The feverish decade between 1835 and 1845 was also disturbed by controversies over the corn laws. The middle-class radicals, eager to introduce free trade, pressed for repeal of the corn laws; but both the great landlords and the humble tenant farmers were equally adamant for their retention, and in Scotland the Whigs, who were supported by many landlords and farmers, were particularly vexed by this question. In the 1830s this became one of the most fiercely debated issues and bade fair to undo the Whigs. Indeed, after 1839 the activities of the anti-corn-law league embarrassed Whig and Tory alike. Richard Cobden, the leading figure in the league, lectured in Scotland in 1842–3 and was everywhere heard with enthusiasm, deriving support even from the chartists. He concluded that ' Scotland is fairly up now, and we shall hear more in future from this side of the Tweed '.[33] His lieutenant, John Bright, was also much in demand; and, indeed, it was Bright's brother-in-law, Duncan McLaren, who was destined to become the living voice of Scottish middle-class dissenting radicalism. McLaren embodied the dictum that dissent was the soul of liberalism. The leaguers triumphed when in 1846, faced with the Irish famine produced by the failure of the potato crop, the Conservative prime minister Peel abolished the corn laws, thereby shattering his party and ruining his own political career.

The Whig attitude to ecclesiastical questions in the 1830s also raised a storm, for one of the problems which increasingly coloured elections was that of patronage in the Church of Scotland. It was an issue from 1832 onwards; but the Whigs refused to grasp it. For as long as possible they left the Scottish church controversy on one side, but their approach to the Irish church question raised temperatures all round. They proposed to reduce the revenues of the established but unpopular Church of Ireland and to devote the money thus saved to the training of Roman catholic priests on Irish soil. In view of the magnitude of the Irish problem what the Whigs proposed was modest, not to say timid, but their programme roused a storm of bigotry, especially in Scotland. In the general election of 1835 the Whigs lost ground, mainly because of the scare over ' Irish popery ' which cost them Inverness-shire and seriously reduced their votes in Ross and Cromarty. By the late 1830s there were distinct signs of widespread disillusionment with the Whigs and some prospects of a Conservative revival.

From this difficult situation the Whigs were rescued not by

[33] J. Morley, *Life of Cobden*, 1. 252. A flourishing branch of the anti-corn-law league was even founded in Shetland, on which the corn laws bore particularly harshly: J. Nicholson, *Arthur Anderson*, ch. vii.

any virtues of their own but by Conservative folly. All three established churches in Britain were alarmed by the new radical trend in politics and dreaded the rise of a secular state. Catholic emancipation had undermined the theory of establishment and raised in a peculiarly vexed form the question of the relationship between church and state. The tractarians in England and the non-intrusionists in Scotland differed in theology and in polity, but their reactions to this one problem were remarkably similar. Both stressed the divine origin of the church; both acknowledged its responsibility to the state; but both denied that the church, as the body of believers, could ever be regarded as a creature of the state.[34] The so-called Ten Years' Conflict, however, which ended in the Disruption of 1843, was not simply a battle between church and state; it was, in part, a by-product of a bitter controversy which first blew up in 1829 stimulated by Roman catholic emancipation. Horrified by the prospect of Roman catholic voters who might demand that the Roman church should be established in Ireland, many of the Scottish dissenters raised a clamour for disestablishment. The *voluntaries*, as they were called, argued that the churches could preserve their spiritual independence only by following the American example of complete separation from the state. Only thus could the Church of Scotland rid itself of the millstone of patronage and dissenters be freed from the hated annuity tax[35] which helped to provide stipends for established ministers, and only thus could ' popery ' be checked since the voluntary contributions on which it could count were meagre. The main seedbed of voluntaryism in Scotland had been the Relief Church but by 1829 large numbers of Seceders, forsaking the rigid covenanted views of the founding fathers, adopted the voluntary position. The establishment and the dissenters were caught in a vicious circle. In the crowded urban areas where the old parish ministrations had virtually broken down, the dissenters were rapidly making headway against the establishment. This

---

[34] Cf. W. E. Gladstone, *The State and its Relation with the Church* (1838), p. 4: ' The union is to the church a matter of secondary importance. *Her* foundations are on the holy hills. Her charter is legibly divine.' Chalmers, in addressing the general assembly of 1839, sharpened the point of this argument: ' She [*i.e.* the church] did not make over her liberties to the State, at the time when she entered into fellowship with it, in this new character of a National Establishment—she only made over her services.' W. Hanna, *Memoirs of Thomas Chalmers*, IV. 108.

[35] J. B. Mackie, *Life of Duncan McLaren*, I. ch. IX.

goaded the evangelical section of the established church into an ambitious programme of church extension, which in turn alarmed the dissenters. New establishment churches which were freed from patronage and did not make heavy financial demands on congregations would furnish dissent with very stiff opposition indeed. The dissenters made up their minds to fight and, as chance would have it, the Reform Act armed them for the fray. One of the act's effects was to enfranchise a large number of voluntaries, who made no secret of their intention of using the franchise to exert political pressure on behalf of their own schemes.[36] In the latter part of 1832 voluntary associations sprang up all over the country and in 1834 a Central Board of Scottish Dissenters, with Duncan McLaren as chairman, was formed. In the troubled decade that followed, some of the fiercest and bitterest strife was between the voluntaries and the established church evangelicals. This was significant because it inflamed the question of Erastianism, the merest breath of which, since it played into the hands of the voluntaries, became intolerable to the Evangelicals and non-intrusionists in the established church.[37]

The Ten Years' Conflict, then, was not, as it is sometimes made to appear, just an example of the supposed Scottish passion for minute controversy over abstruse principles. The whole place of the church in modern society was what was being contended for, and it raised serious questions about the constitution and powers of the state. Patronage, in fact, served as a focus for deeper controversies. Open strife began in the general assembly of 1833 when the Evangelicals, most of whom did not desire the abolition of patronage, attempted to regulate the system so as to restore to congregations the rights held to be implicit in the statute of 1712. Only thirty-three Evangelicals demanded abolition.[38] But public, as distinct from clerical, opinion was so roused on this matter that the bulk of the Evangelicals in the assembly could not accept the shrewd proposal put forward by their leader, Thomas Chalmers. Chalmers was a great preacher, a strong champion

---

[36] John Brown, *What ought the Dissenters of Scotland to do in the Present Crisis?* (1840), pp. 6-9; Mackie, *op. cit.*, I. 169 ff.

[37] D. Woodside, *The Soul of a Scottish Church or the Contribution of the United Presbyterian Church to Scottish Life and Religion* (n.d.), ch. IV; T. Brown, *Church and State in Scotland, a narrative of the Struggle for Independence from 1560 to 1843*, lect. VI.

[38] Thomas Guthrie, *Autobiography*, I. 175. A year later 42, mainly from the north, voted for abolition and were jocularly referred to as the 42nd Highlanders.

of the establishment principle and a doughty enemy of the voluntaries; but in spite of his insistence on pastoral care and his own work at St. John's in Glasgow, he was an academic rather than a politician.   Chalmers wished the church courts to restore the call by liberal construction of the somewhat hazy act of 1712; in this way disputes could be settled in the church courts without incurring any danger of a collision between church and state. The plan was sound; but it was too tame for a generation which, influenced by Thomas McCrie's recent biographies of Knox and Melville,[39] was eager to testify against the defections and backslidings of the times.   Chalmers was obliged to support another measure (famous later as the Veto Act) which bound presbyteries to absolute acceptance of objections made to a presentee by a majority of heads of families.   The Moderates were not wholly opposed to it; but they rejected both the veto and another proposal which would have granted ' chapel ' ministers, that is those serving chapels of ease or extension churches, the right to sit in church courts.   The Chapel Act would have ended the long reign of the Moderates, and it is significant that to this measure they were more consistently hostile than they were to the veto.

In 1834 the Evangelicals had a working majority (owing, perhaps, to the effects of reform of the burghs on the return of representative elders) and the two rejected measures of the last session became acts of assembly.   Though the Veto Act had been approved by the lord advocate and the lord chancellor (presumably legal opinion of some weight) it was bitterly assailed by a Moderate elder, John Hope, dean of the faculty of advocates. Hope argued that it was *ultra vires*, and that by contravening the statute of 1712 the church was invading the province of the state. In practice, the veto procedure worked well, and the legal disputes which convulsed the country from 1834 onwards were test cases brought on the advice of Hope.[40]   The first such arose in 1834 when a rejected presentee at Auchterarder, Robert Young, refused to accept the presbytery's decision and raised an action in the court of session.   This ' appeal to Caesar ' was without precedent and, apart from opening up a very uncertain situation at law, it led to a notable hardening of the attitude of the Evangelicals, who

---

[39] For the quite extraordinary effects of McCrie's works see W. Wilson, *Memorials of Robert Smith Candlish, D.D.*, p. 27.

[40] Hugh Watt, *Chalmers and the Disruption*, ch. 12.

had to suffer the exultant taunts of the voluntaries. The voluntaries made no secret of the fact that they were well pleased at the difficulties piled on the Church of Scotland.

At no time in these cases did the Evangelicals dispute the court of session's right to adjudicate on temporalities, but they steadily refused to accept that the civil courts had the power to regulate spiritual matters. The judges themselves were divided, and most of them had strong personal sympathies: as Lord Cockburn admitted, ' passion sometimes invades the Bench; and when it does it obstructs the discovery of truth as effectually as partiality can '.[41] Thus Lord President Hope, father of the dean of faculty, was an extreme Moderate and a convinced Erastian; Lord Medwyn was an episcopalian, well known for his detestation of presbyterians and covenants; Moncrieff was a devout Evangelical; and Jeffrey and Cockburn sympathised with the non-intrusionists, though lamenting from time to time the melodramatic utterances of some of their leaders. It is not, therefore, surprising that the court did not reach a decision until March 1838, when by eight votes to five it found in favour of Young. If this decision was a blow to the non-intrusionists, the *dicta* of some of the judges were catastrophic. In the majority view the Church of Scotland was strictly governed by statute and her courts had no powers beyond those specifically conferred by acts of parliament. Appeal to the house of lords brought no comfort to the non-intrusionists. Brougham, who as lord chancellor had welcomed the Veto Act in 1834, now had the effrontery to condemn it. He was supposed to understand Scottish questions (which he rarely did) and his speech did much to confirm English politicians in the belief that in Scotland they had to deal with theocratic madmen. Not only Brougham but also the Whig party won little credit from the Scottish Church question. Lord Melbourne's interest in theology did not extend to Scotland, whose homespun religion did not appeal to his languid fancy. His ministry, too, was weak and divided, and as a result the efforts of the Whig government in 1839–40 to promote through Lord Aberdeen a compromise which would give presbyteries the right to adjudicate on vetos were half-hearted. When they fell from power in 1841 the Whigs left a series of controversial issues to be tackled by the Tory ministry headed by Sir Robert Peel, of which the greatest was the problem

[41] H. Cockburn, *Journal*, II. 41.

of the corn laws and not the least the Scottish Church question. Unfortunately, Peel was already obnoxious to the non-intrusionists, for when home secretary he had used crown patronage to maintain the hegemony of the Moderate party.[42]   Chalmers, himself a Tory, hoped against hope that the new ministry would set matters right; but the rank and file of the non-intrusionists were under no such illusions.   Many of the patrons were Tories, and a Conservative ministry was hardly likely to legislate against its own supporters in favour of their opponents.   It was, therefore, no surprise when in 1841 another compromise measure sponsored by the Duke of Argyll broke down.

Any prospect of a peaceful solution was dashed by the bitterness raised by other legal cases, in particular that of Marnoch in Strathbogie which began in 1837.   In the course of the prolonged wrangle that followed, the presbytery was split; seven of its members were willing to defer to the court of session and induct an unpopular presentee, Edwards, while four members of the presbytery were equally insistent on applying the Veto Act.   The court of session and the general assembly stubbornly adhered to their positions, and the result was a head-on clash.   The assembly suspended the seven for failing to comply with the laws of the church and the court of session interdicted ministers from proclaiming the suspension in the presbytery of Strathbogie.   In January 1841 the induction of Edwards took place amid riotous scenes, and the following year's assembly deposed him in spite of an interdict served by a court of session messenger-at-arms.   By 1842 an impasse had been reached.   Peel and his home secretary, Sir James Graham, were further confirmed in their determination to yield nothing to the non-intrusionists by the rise of a ' middle party ' in the Church of Scotland.   This consisted of Evangelicals who withdrew from the non-intrusionist party either through disgust at the fulminations of some of its leaders, such as Candlish, the party's real tactician, or else through fear of a rupture. Fortified by the utilitarian John Austin's rigid views on sovereignty and firm in the belief that it was their duty to preserve the state from a band of crazed zealots, Peel and Graham rejected ' The Claim of Right ' drawn up by the assembly of 1842.   This was certainly an uncompromising document: it claimed complete spiritual independence for the church, and while most of its

[42] T. Guthrie, *Autobiography*, I. 66-7.

arguments were sober its conclusion was badly phrased and could be construed as setting the church above the state.[43]   For the non-intrusionists the last straw was provided by the decision in the Stewarton case in the early spring of 1843.   It condemned the Chapel Act as *ultra vires*, deprived chapel ministers of full ministerial status, and, by denying them representation in the courts of the church, was bound to strengthen the Moderates at the expense of the Evangelicals.   In spite of all this, the politicians believed that firmness would win the day.

The general assembly of 1843 gave them a shock.   Instead of a secession by a few hot-heads, of some 1,200 establishment ministers over 470 withdrew, taking with them as many elders, numerous dominies, most of the overseas missionaries, and altogether nearly 40 per cent of the Church of Scotland's communicants.   Most of the Disruptionists suffered heavy initial material losses but their sacrifice won them admiration in many quarters, even among the dissenters, though it is important to notice that the Free Church which resulted from the Disruption stood on establishment principles.   As Chalmers, the first moderator of the first general assembly of the Free Church of Scotland, declared: '. . . though we quit the Establishment, we go out on the Establishment principle; we quit a vitiated Establishment, but would rejoice in returning to a pure one . . . we are not Voluntaries '.[44] The Free Church's disruption from the state probably saved the Church of Scotland from a worse fate.   It checked the drift towards Erastianism, and it contained the growing threat posed by the voluntaries.   Voluntaryism was the common cause which enabled a majority of the Seceders and the Relief Church to unite in 1847 as the United Presbyterian Church of Scotland.   If this church had provided shelter for non-intrusionist refugees from the establishment, the Church of Scotland would have been on a lee shore indeed.   The Free Church, bitter though it was against the ' Auld Kirk ', interposed a useful buffer between the establishment and the voluntaries.   Nor did the Free Church regard itself as in any way schismatic.   Indeed, in point of doctrine and worship Scottish presbyterians were still at one, though during the next half-century the impact of German liberal theology was to shatter their spiritual unity.

[43] The Claim of Right is printed in Robert Buchanan, *The Ten Years' Conflict*, II. 471-85.   [44] Hanna, *Chalmers*, IV. 348.

For Scotland the Disruption was the most momentous single event of the nineteenth century, and its repercussions were felt not only in most departments of Scottish life but overseas as well. By 1850 the Free Church rivalled the Church of Scotland in Canada, Australia and New Zealand; and it had a strong influence on the continent, notably in France and Switzerland where it stimulated the formation of free evangelical churches.[45] At home it virtually sealed the fate of the old poor-law system of which, ironically, Chalmers had been the stoutest champion. He had tried to preserve the old system of parochial relief based on family responsibility and self-help; he had written weighty answers to the criticisms of reformers like Professor W. P. Alison (a disciple of Dugald Stewart) who argued that in the new conditions of life and labour a compulsory assessment for poor-relief was inevitable; and between 1819 and 1823 Chalmers had conducted a notable experiment in St John's parish in Glasgow to refute the need for an assessed rate, but its results were, if not illusory, at least suspect. As one of his helpers in St John's, William Collins, later a famous publisher, confessed: they could deal with honest poverty but did not know 'what to do with immorality and drunkenness'.[46] The Disruption made the old poor law unworkable, and in 1845 a new, but far from revolutionary, act was passed. Under it, the established church was deprived of its powers in this sphere; but the parish remained the unit of administration, and parochial boards (comprising kirk sessions, heritors, and elected representatives of the ratepayers) dealt with poor relief, under the loose oversight of a central board for general supervision.[47] Outdoor relief remained the rule, and assessment, though increasingly common, was permissive and not mandatory. In 1846, 420 parishes were assessed and by 1894 the number had risen to 840. The new poor law was not the answer to the problem of destitution: improvement came rather from the long period of relative prosperity in the mid-Victorian age.

In education, too, the effects of the Disruption were felt, for,

---

[45] J. R. Fleming, *A History of the Church in Scotland 1843–1874*, pp. 31-5, 66.

[46] Quoted by William Logan, *The Moral Statistics of Glasgow*, p. 26. Chalmers' own account is in his '*The Sufficiency of a Parochial System without a Poor Rate*,' in *Works*, XXI (1840), 92-149.

[47] A. C. Cormack, *Poor Relief in Scotland*, ch. XIII. The statute was appallingly drafted and frequently nonsensical; and, like previous acts, it made no provision for the able-bodied unemployed.

partly to avoid the parish schools controlled by the establishment and partly to provide for the 400 teachers who had seceded in 1843, by 1851 the Free Church had built 712 schools. To some extent because of the problems created by the Disruption the principle of state aid, which had begun on a minute scale in the 1830s, was extended; and after 1847 schools that were judged efficient, whatever their origin, received a modicum of financial aid. Thus, the Disruption led to a much needed expansion of educational facilities, but at the same time it emphasised that the unplanned educational structure was entering on a chaotic phase, with too many schools of various types and qualities and no real co-ordinating supervision. Matters appeared at their worst in the slums of the industrial towns where the children of the poor were often neglected, many of them starving and homeless. In 1845 the governor of Edinburgh prison proposed to set up an industrial school on the lines of the 'Ragged Schools' opened in Aberdeen four years earlier by Sheriff Watson: the governor revealed that in the past three years 740 children under fourteen years of age had been committed to prison, and of these 245 were under ten.[48]   The challenge was taken up by the Reverend Thomas Guthrie, a prominent Free Churchman who became 'the Apostle of the Ragged School Movement'. In spite of some bigotry displayed (Guthrie would not allow Roman catholic teaching in his schools although many of the children were Irish catholics), the movement stirred the public conscience and helped to end the iniquity of neglecting and then imprisoning delinquent children. (But not until the 1860s did the work of William Quarrier in Glasgow lead to the formation of 'The Orphan Homes of Scotland'.[49]) Guthrie was a realist: he believed that the problem could be solved only by state intervention and that the ragged schools were merely temporary measures to cope with a desperate situation. Just how bad the situation was can be judged from the fact that in 1853 it was estimated that 'barely two thirds of the children who ought to be at school are in attendance on any school in Scotland'.[50] This was exaggerated; but the problem undoubtedly was growing. The slow but sure trend

[48] T. Guthrie, *Autobiography*, II. 113-14.
[49] A. Gammie, *William Quarrier and the Story of the Orphan Homes of Scotland* (n.d.).
[50] Sir James Kay-Shuttleworth, *Public Education, as affected by the Minutes of the Committee of Privy Council from 1846 to 1852*, p. 371.

was towards a national system supervised by the state, and in 1861 this was reinforced when the established church lost its legal powers over the parish schools. Increasingly rules were laid down by government inspectors. The ground was thus well prepared for the Education Act of 1872 which set up a national system under a newly created Scotch Education Department. Popularly elected school boards were given wide discretion in running the public schools. The qualifications and status of teachers had also gradually improved, starting with the pioneer work of David Stow (later another Free Churchman) in Glasgow in 1828 which led to the setting up of training colleges.

For the universities, too, this was a period of searching reappraisal. Scots academics could pride themselves on the fact that when in 1828 the University of London was founded, in some respects it followed the Scottish model; but already in 1826 certain aspects of that model had been called in question by a royal commission which recommended that Scotland should adopt English practice and favour classics and mathematics rather than philosophy and science. These proposals were resented as an attempt to impose English ' élitist ' values on an essentially democratic system, and no action followed on the report. But the dilemma remained and cannot simply be explained in terms of the opposition of traditionalists to anglicising innovators. The Scottish system, which was barely adequate in eighteenth-century conditions, was by the nineteenth century increasingly unsatisfactory. Scholarship in nearly every field of knowledge was becoming deeper and more particular: how long, then, could the Scottish universities, teaching at a very general and often superficial level, retain any kind of reputation? Confidence in the old Scottish system was undermined, and this process was accelerated rather than caused by the Disruption and its disorganising effects on the universities. As one authority puts it, ' by 1850 the disintegration had spread to the educational system, profoundly disturbing the intellectual balance of the Universities '.[51] Repeal of religious tests in 1855 was merely an obvious symptom of the trouble. A royal commission of 1858 further reflected the declension of Scottish confidence. Its recommendations for more specialised teaching were given point by the civil service examinations,

---

[51] G. E. Davie, *The Democratic Intellect: Scotland and her Universities in the Nineteenth Century*, p. 289.

which were geared to the English system and in which Scottish-trained candidates fared ill. The Scots, then, would either have to bring their universities into line with the English universities or accept virtual exclusion from the civil service. Even so, there was a strong conservative opposition, headed by Professor W. E. Aytoun, and the commission was obliged to suggest a compromise: the ordinary degree was to be retained and to be obligatory before students could proceed to the suggested new honours degree. The compromise was not very happy, and a good deal of contention went on until in 1889 an act of parliament acceptable to most shades of opinion was passed. Under it both ordinary and honours degrees were recognised and the choice was left to the discretion of students advised by the professors. The new honours structure that emerged was, for the most part, a carbon copy of the existing ' Oxbridge ' model: for example, the new honours classes in history all closely resembled the Oxford prototype.

Finally, not the least important effect of the Disruption was the accession of strength that it brought to the Liberals, for after 1843 much the greater part of the Free Church vote went consistently to that party. This appeared in a very striking form in the general election of 1847 in the northern Highlands, where the landlords had long dictated politics to their tenants. On this occasion, in spite of widespread detestation of free trade, the Tory landlords could not dragoon their tenants into voting protectionist, *i.e.* Conservative. The Free Church question crushed the Conservative candidates, the more so as many lairds had for a time after the Disruption harried and persecuted the Free Churchmen, denying them building sites and forcing them to worship on the bare hillsides.[52] In the face of the bitter opposition raised to them, the Conservatives found it hopeless to venture to the polls and in constituency after constituency the Liberals were returned unopposed. As Hugh Miller, self-taught geologist and brilliant editor of the non-intrusionist *Witness* newspaper, had predicted in 1842: ' Conservatism, too, may give up at least the northern Highlands as a political field whenever it pleases '.[53] The Whig landlords, on the other hand, ingratiated themselves with the Free Church, granting it every facility that was in their power to give. The only Highland county to adhere to Conservatism after

[52] Thomas Brown, *Annals of The Disruption* (ed. 1893), *passim*.
[53] Hugh Miller, *The Headship of Christ* (1861), p. 413.

1847 was Inverness-shire. In the burghs the Free Church vote made the Liberals virtually impregnable, and it was rare indeed for a Conservative to win a burgh seat before the Liberal-Unionist split of 1886.[54]

An unexpected result of the turmoils of the early Victorian age was a revival of Scottish nationalism. In the early decades of the nineteenth century it had looked as if the idea of Scotland was about to perish, a victim of the British chauvinism roused by the Napoleonic Wars. The drift towards North Britain was arrested by the great popularity of the works of Burns and Scott. P. F. Tytler's monumental *History of Scotland* (published 1828–43) stressed the heroic aspects of Scotland's struggle for existence in the middle ages, and, thanks to a growing vogue for history, it reached a wide public, thus strengthening the revival of national sentiment. That sentiment had also been roused by the bitter closing stages of the Ten Years' Conflict.[55] The anglicising policies of the Scottish Whigs, the eclipse of Scottish by Irish interests, and a growing fear that, in spite of material progress, Scotland was fast losing her own ethos, all contributed to the development of a rather self-conscious nationalism. The countervailing force was strongly represented by Thomas Carlyle (1795–1881), who, while retaining a strong personal affection for Scotland, in his works identified himself with England and things English. The same attitude can be discerned in that quintessential Scot, David Livingstone (1813–72), for whom Britain was an unknown concept: it was to create Christian English colonies that he thrust into the Dark Continent. These two great men, like many of their lesser countrymen, suffered from an element of cultural schizophrenia. Loss of confidence led to a virtual collapse of Scottish culture: literature degenerated into mawkish ' kailyard ' parochialism and painting into uninspired ' ben and glen ' romanticism. Loss of confidence was also evident in jurisprudence, and the long and distinguished line of Scottish institutional writers ended in the anglicising Whig George Joseph Bell (1770–1843).

[54] The only Conservative victories in the burghs in this period were: Falkirk Burghs 1841, 1847, 1852; Haddington Burghs 1841; and Inverness Burghs 1832, 1835, 1837. Cf. T. Wilkie, *The Representation of Scotland*.
[55] T. Brown, *Annals of the Disruption*, pp. 69, 76.

Yet in this period all was not lost : what Victorian Scotland lacked in the arts she made up for in the sciences.[56] The Edinburgh medical school was at the pinnacle of its fame, and Scotsmen made some striking contributions to the rise of scientific medicine.[57] The great tradition outlasted the nineteenth century and was not confined to Edinburgh and Glasgow, for Aberdeen latterly produced some famous figures.[58] Nineteenth-century Scotland was also noted for engineers and scientists, two of whom stand pre-eminent—Kelvin and Clerk Maxwell. William Thomson, Lord Kelvin (1824–1907), had a powerful if facile intellect which enabled him to make fundamental contributions to many aspects of physical science. Since his death he has been rather downgraded, but not altogether justly. Basically, Kelvin's world was that of the engineer; his real significance was the way in which, to his own profit, he acted as a bridge between science and industry. It was the misfortune of Scotland, which with the setting up of the Andersonian University in Glasgow in 1796 had pioneered technical education, that Kelvin's initiative was not maintained. The object lesson was not lost on Germany or the United States. Kelvin was one of the greatest of applied scientists; but he lacked the finer intellectual qualities of the pure scientist displayed by James Clerk Maxwell (1831–79). As has been cogently said, ' Maxwell's genius, like that of Newton and Faraday, was timeless; Kelvin's was of his day '.[59] The judgment is perhaps less than fair to Kelvin; but it neatly pinpoints the significance of Clerk Maxwell. He belonged to the well-known landed family of Clerk of Penicuik, his father having adopted the Maxwell name for purposes of inheritance. Clerk Maxwell was the outstanding mathematical physicist of the nineteenth century, and it is on his equations for the evaluation of electro-magnetic phenomena that modern physics rests. And, curiously, in a time of growing scepti-

[56] A. G. Clement and R. H. S. Robertson, *Scotland's Scientific Heritage*, chs. 4, 5.

[57] Most notably Sir Charles Bell (1774–1842), brother of the jurist George Joseph Bell, and a great neurologist; Robert Liston (1794–1847), one of the foremost surgeons of his day, and James Syme (1799–1870), probably the greatest; and, of course, Sir J. Y. Simpson (1811–70), famed not only as a pioneer anaesthetist but also as obstetrician and gynaecologist.

[58] Chiefly Sir Patrick Manson (1844–1922), ' the father of tropical medicine ', and his disciple Sir James Cantlie (1851–1926).

[59] Sir John Randall, ' Aspects of Maxwell's Life and Work ', in C. Domb, ed., *Clerk Maxwell and Modern Science*, p. 22.

cism, Maxwell, like Newton and Faraday before him, was deeply religious.

The reputation won by Scotsmen in science, however, did little to enhance the culture of their country. This is far from being a singular case, for science stands independent of national contexts. Methods and results are all—whether those of a Scot like Manson or a Japanese like Noguchi matters little. For good or ill, therefore, science cannot nurture the irrational bonds that make nations. The rise of a scientific outlook, indeed, hastened the decline of the specifically Scottish intellectualism which throughout the eighteenth century had without conscious effort sustained the concept of a Scottish nation.

The decline of a specifically Scottish culture, which had been based on native educational and intellectual traditions, coincided with a change in Scotland's status within the United Kingdom. For over a century after 1707 management had preserved something like a separate Scottish administration; but with the passing of management after 1827 and increased centralisation Scotland came to be treated as a province rather than a partner. Just as in education, there was need for change, for no good would have come of maintaining the antiquated machinery of government; but, again as in education, the innovations were unhappy. Thus the old inefficient boards of customs and excise were swept away, only for other and no more efficient boards to proliferate.[60] It came to be believed that Scotland's influence at Westminster had diminished and that governments were now more concerned to placate Irish rather than Scottish interests. Gradually, there arose a widespread feeling that Scotland was ill-used. The movement to which this feeling gave rise is usually dismissed as a romantic Tory reaction; but though Tories played a leading part in its activities, it was broadly based and non-party. The Irish repealer agitations of the time served as a goad rather than an example, and perhaps Mazzini's views on national self-determination struck a sympathetic echo in Scotland.[61] More obviously, the methods of the anti-corn-law league were copied in a

[60] J. B. Mackie, *Life of Duncan McLaren*, II. ch. XX

[61] It is odd that one of Mazzini's first and closest friends in his London exile was the aged Mrs Archibald Fletcher, widow of the burgh reformer—Mrs Fletcher, *Autobiography*, p. 230 ff. Mazzini also contributed papers on chartism to Tait's *Edinburgh Journal* (Bolton King, *Life of Mazzini*, p. 93). The Risorgimento captured the popular fancy in Scotland, with Garibaldi cast in the role of William Wallace.

propaganda campaign carried out in some of the leading Scottish newspapers in 1852, with the brothers John and James Grant playing the parts of Cobden and Bright. James, the leading spirit, was a prolific romantic novelist of the school of Scott. He professed Tory and even Jacobite beliefs, but in practice he knew how to make a cunning blend of patriotic themes, uniting in one national cult the hapless Mary, Queen of Scots, and the stern Knox. The campaign was conducted with uncommon skill. From such trifles as Garter King's contemptuous treatment of Scottish heraldry, the Grants in innumerable letters under a variety of pseudonyms broadened out into an itemised catalogue of Scotland's grievances. They were stimulated by the taunts of *The Times*, the irreverent satire of *Punch*, and the ponderosities of the superior *Scotsman* (no longer radical but rather the mouthpiece of the prim Whig establishment of Edinburgh).

The Grant brothers found numerous supporters, and in 1853 an Association for the Vindication of Scottish Rights was founded. The significance of this body, which was promoted by many sections of Scottish opinion, has rarely been recognised.[62] Its president was the Earl of Eglinton (providing *Punch* with some good jousting material based on the absurd Eglinton Tournament of 1839), and two prominent members were the Dukes of Hamilton and of Montrose. The association was not the creation of the Tory romantic W. E. Aytoun, professor of rhetoric at Edinburgh, although Aytoun wholeheartedly supported it. It was warmly backed by most of the town councils in Scotland, by several of the county commissions of supply, and by many professional bodies. The outcome of numerous well-attended public meetings was over fifty petitions to the government, demanding that Scotland should no longer be left to the ministrations of an overworked lord advocate loosely supervised by the home secretary, that a Scottish secretary should be restored to head a reformed and separate administration, that Scotland should receive a larger share of parliamentary representation (71 M.P.s as against 53), and that she should enjoy a more just proportion of United Kingdom expenditure. That the Union of 1707 had been carried by bribery and that its provisions had been scandalously broken was a common point of departure; and yet the association indignantly

---

[62] Sir R. Coupland, *Welsh and Scottish Nationalism*, gives, pp. 281 ff., an inadequate account.

repudiated the allegation that it was a ' repealer ' movement. As one of its supporters, the high Tory sheriff of Lanarkshire, the historian Sir Archibald Alison, declared: ' We do not wish the dissolution of the Union—we do not deny its benefits—we wish to carry out the Union in its true spirit—and we wish to obtain that justice for Scotland which the Union promised, which the English promised; but which we have not yet received '.[63] Indeed, the Tory associates gratefully seized the opportunity to have a dig at the anglicising Whigs; and at the same time they hoped that redress of some outstanding grievances would prevent the emergence of a genuinely separatist movement. The Grants skilfully kept the pot boiling, adding something for every taste. Thus the radicals sympathised with the association, since its demands fitted in with their passion for clockwork efficiency. Moreover, it afforded them an opportunity to hit out at the careerist Edinburgh lawyers, whose proverbial selfishness impeded Liberalism in Scotland. Efforts were made to enrol the industrialists and these succeeded surprisingly well, for in the early 1850s there were few government orders for the Clyde shipyards and Scottish harbours received little government help. Insistence on the need to extend the franchise elicited some working-class support but not enough to counteract the strong incentive to make common cause with English and Irish workers. Even thus early it was clear that a sense of working-class solidarity precluded any serious nationalist commitments.

The movement's case was strong, and indeed in some ways unanswerable. The disbursement of public revenue told its own story.[64] London and Dublin received large grants for the maintenance of charitable or police institutions, but Edinburgh got nothing. Expenditure on navy and army installations in England was lavish but meagre in Scotland, which dreaded—or affected to dread—a Russian invasion. Famine relief in the Highlands in 1846–7 following the failure of the potato crop had to be met

[63] *Report of the First Public Meeting of the National Association for the Vindication of Scottish Rights, held in the Music Hall, Edinburgh, on the Evening of November 2, 1853* (1853), p. 22. But Alison does not seem to have been deeply committed to the movement; at any rate there is no reference to it in his *My Life and Writings*. He made a practice of addressing public meetings in order to increase his ' moral influence ' (*op. cit.*, II. 89), and he may have joined the association for this purpose.

[64] Strikingly summarised in a pamphlet by Robert Christie, *Injustice to Scotland Exposed, in a Letter to the Scottish Representatives in Parliament* (1853).

from local resources, to the impoverishment of many of the lairds; this was a painful contrast to what had happened in Ireland. The Clearances, in the same breath, were condemned as brutal and anti-social—propaganda, as usual, showing scant regard for logic. And so it went on, a crowded list, not forgetting the iniquitous malversation of the revenues of the bishopric of Orkney to help light the streets of London. These charges were never answered, for, in many instances, answer there could be none. Many of them were self-evident truths culled from parliamentary papers. So much was this the case that Scottish M.P.s were furious at the exposure of negligence on their part, and, like the chartists, the associates won no support in parliament. The excitement of the war in the Crimea, however, diverted public attention; the system seemed to have triumphed; and in 1856 the association dissolved. But, as in the case of chartism, failure is hardly a sufficient verdict on its brief but hectic existence. There has scarcely been a single position later advocated by Scottish nationalists, of whatever complexion, that was not anticipated by some members of the association. That body restored the idea of nationhood, of which the most interesting spokesman was the political scientist Patrick Edward Dove, who advocated responsible nationalism as the indispensable basis for internationalism.[65] It exposed the dangers of over-centralisation and parliamentary congestion, the ill effects of which it described almost a century before governments were prepared to listen. Duncan McLaren, the dissenting-radical-voluntary lord provost of Edinburgh, supported the association in its brief span; and from 1865 onwards McLaren, as M.P. for Edinburgh, championed most of its aims, thereby winning for himself the title of ' M.P. for Scotland '.

McLaren's career typified in many ways the frustration of middle-class Manchester style radicalism, with its passion for constitutional reform, its resentment of privilege whether lay or ecclesiastical, its belief in free trade and unfettered capitalism, and its inability to form a party which could turn its hopes into acts of parliament. Ever since the passing of the municipal reform act of 1833 McLaren had been active in local politics; and as bailie, treasurer, and ultimately lord provost (1851–4) of Edinburgh, he

---

[65] *Report of the Great Public Meeting of the National Association for the Vindication of Scottish Rights in City Hall, Glasgow, on the Evening of December 15, 1853*, p. 19.

helped to restore the capital's shaky finances and put its administration on a sounder basis. At the same time he championed the voluntaries, pressing particularly for the abolition of the hated annuity tax. Like his brother-in-law John Bright, McLaren, an ' advanced liberal ' or radical, was at odds with the Whig oligarchy. By the '40s this hostility was deep-rooted in Scotland and the opposition to T. B. Macaulay in Edinburgh is merely a prominent instance of it. He was tormented by voluntary radicals who wished him to act as their delegate in the house of commons, and such was the persecution that Macaulay dared not attend church in Edinburgh for fear of offending some or other of his constituents.[66] He refused to abase himself and in 1847 was defeated by a voluntary candidate, Charles Cowan, who also later sympathised with the National Association. It is significant, too, that some Free Church voters were paying little more than lip service to the establishment principle and making common political cause with the voluntaries. The alliance was slow to mature but in spite of resistance from the leaders of the Free Church it waxed in strength, providing Scottish radicalism with a formidable and popular cause from which McLaren derived much of his influence.

McLaren was fortunate, too, in becoming an M.P. in 1865, just at the time when the period of political confusion ushered in by the fragmentation of the Conservatives after 1846 was drawing to a close. This period had seen numerous unstable cabinets, with the clashing groups skilfully if mischievously manipulated by such atavists as Lord Palmerston and Lord John Russell.[67] By the late '60s the groups were being subsumed into more or less committed political parties, the Conservatives headed by Benjamin Disraeli and the Liberals by William Ewart Gladstone. Even before this happened the need for further extension of the franchise had long been generally accepted, Disraeli sponsoring a bill in 1859 only for it to be defeated over trifles. By the late '60s it was merely a question of chance as to which party would pass a second Reform Act. After prolonged debate on the franchises it fell to Disraeli, with Liberal help, to carry an act in 1867. The case which McLaren put to Disraeli for Scotland, and which was in part accepted, was essentially that which had been advocated by

---

[66] G. O. Trevelyan, *Life and Letters of Lord Macaulay* (ed. 1889), pp. 467-73.
[67] Sir L. Woodward, *The Age of Reform* (2nd ed., 1962), ch. IV.

the defunct National Association. But the number of Scottish constituencies was increased to only 60 instead of the 68 demanded, probably because Disraeli was concerned at the weakness of Scottish Conservatism. The extension of the franchise was not as great as the radicals had hoped, and the secret ballot was not introduced until 1872; but in spite of its defects the Reform Act of 1867 accelerated the re-emergence of organised parties with definite programmes. An unexpected, but obvious enough result, was the further undermining of the chaotic administration headed by the lord advocate; for parties that had to devise programmes to win votes were bound when in office to attempt to turn their promises into acts, and though reform in Scotland was meagre, it imposed a burden which the existing administration could not carry.

The second Reform Act strengthened the Liberal hold on Scotland; but the failure of Gladstone's first and greatest ministry (1868–74) to take stock of Scottish grievances caused resentment. The mouthpiece of this discontent became the brilliant, if somewhat petulant, young Lord Rosebery who saw, quite rightly, that it tied up with another pressing problem, namely the inadequacy of local government. Rosebery was the more concerned in that Scotland, the most consistent of the Liberal bulwarks, was being assiduously courted by Disraeli, who was heartened by the relatively good showing made by the Conservatives in the general election of 1874. In that year he tried to popularise the Church of Scotland, which was largely Conservative in political sympathies, by abolishing patronage. This was justified on many accounts: the cry for disestablishment was steadily mounting; indeed, in that same year of 1874 a majority of the Free Church declared for disestablishment and concerted measures with the voluntaries; and, besides, the Church of Scotland itself had for years protested that the Benefices Act of 1844, which allowed congregations to protest against presentees but left presbyteries to decide on the merits of each case, was unworkable. In other ways Disraeli tried to breathe life into the moribund Conservative party in Scotland, notably by new directives given in 1876; but through over-reliance on the landlords, the most detested class in the community, these plans bore little fruit.[68]

[68] B. L. Crapster, 'Scotland and the Conservative Party in 1876', in *Journal of Modern History*, XXIX. 355–60.

The exciting politics of the '70s and '80s were relished to the full in Scotland, an eager public following every lunge and parry in the personal duel between Gladstone and Disraeli. In many Scottish homes Gladstone became a household god; and yet, in spite of this curious devotion to an English High Churchman, all was far from well with the Liberal party in Scotland. Electorally, it seemed invincible; but it was torn by inner dissensions. The old feud between Whigs and radicals continued. Religion and politics dictated an ambivalent attitude to the crucial Irish question, in which genuine sympathy for a downtrodden people had to contend with detestation of Roman catholicism. There was also discontent with the way in which the Irish nationalists at Westminster had usurped the part formerly played by the Scots. Rosebery put it in a nutshell: ' But I confess I think Scotland is as usual treated abominably. Justice for Ireland means everything done for her even to the payment of the natives' debts. Justice to Scotland means insulting neglect. I leave for Scotland next week with the view of blowing up a prison or shooting a policeman....'[69]

The Irish example—terrorism apart—was not without its effect in Scotland. The disestablishment of the Irish Church in 1868 undoubtedly stimulated the demand for disestablishment in Scotland, which reached its peak in the '80s and was raised in parliament in 1882. In that same year the crofters in the Highlands and Islands, who had been groaning for years under an oppressive agrarian regime, followed the example set by the Irish Land League.[70] The crofters complained of insecurity of tenure, of frequent evictions, and of the excessive rents which were demanded for their minute and ill-favoured holdings. The so-called ' Battle of the Braes' which took place in Skye in April 1882 epitomised the situation: some of Lord Macdonald's tenants protested at the loss of pasture rights, refused to pay rents, and resisted ejection. In that same month the Highland Land League was formed, following propaganda activities by the Irish Land League in Glasgow. One of the leaders of the Highland league was Dr G. B. Clark, later a prominent Fabian, member of the Scottish Home Rule Association, and in 1887 Keir Hardie's political mentor. Rebuffed by the Liberals, the Highland Land

<hr />

[69] Rosebery to E. Hamilton,? May 1882, quoted R. R. James, *Rosebery: a Biography of Archibald Philip, Fifth Earl of Rosebery*, p. 130.

[70] See D. W. Crowley, 'The Crofters' Party, 1885–1892', in *S.H.R.*, XXXIV. 110–26.

League successfully exploited the third reform act of 1884 by running crofters' candidates in the general elections of 1885 and 1886. In 1885 Clark himself was returned for Caithness, and three other candidates succeeded in crofting counties, in spite of heavy opposition from the Liberals, the Church of Scotland and the Free Church. The Crofters' Party anticipated the rise of labour political organisations, but it was essentially reformist and lacked a specific ideology. The passing of the Crofters' Act in 1886, which gave security of tenure, and the work of a commission empowered to fix fair rents, took the force out of the Highland Land League, and it was soon reabsorbed into the mainstream of Liberalism.

The land agitation undoubtedly antagonised most of the great Whig landlords, many of whom, like the Duke of Argyll, became hostile to Gladstonian Liberalism. The Liberal government's fumbling response to the crofters' grievances had also given point to the renewed agitation for an overhaul of the machinery of government in Scotland. Rosebery headed this campaign but found it difficult to get Gladstone to share his sense of urgency. Reluctantly in 1881 Gladstone made Rosebery an under-secretary of state responsible for Scottish affairs to the home secretary. The experiment failed; and, in his usual forthright fashion, Rosebery described it as ' unworkable ' and resigned in 1883. He was too impetuous, for the government was promoting a bill which aimed at the establishment of a new administrative agency to be known as the Local Government (Scotland) Board.[71] This failed: the demand was for a full secretary of state for Scotland. The third reform act of 1884, which raised the number of Scottish constituencies to 72 and went a considerable way to establishing adult male suffrage, increased the difficulties confronting the Liberals, almost hamstringing their legislative programme. The government was unpopular: the occupation of Egypt had disgruntled the radicals, and the old quarrels between them and the Whigs grew more bitter. These tensions were as strong in Scotland as elsewhere, and efforts to improve party organisation merely accentuated them.[72] The long predominance of the Liberals had led to weak organisation presided over by the Whiggish east. As a

[71] H. J. Hanham, ' The Creation of the Scottish Office, 1881-87 ', in *Juridical Review*, (n.s.), x. 205-44.
[72] D. Savage, ' Scottish Politics, 1885-6 ', in *S.H.R.*, XL. 118-35.

corrective to this in 1876 the West and South of Scotland Liberal Association was founded; it was mainly radical in sympathy, unlike the East and North of Scotland Association which was formed in the following year. With some trouble a merger was effected in 1881, but this made little difference to the party at large. The old feuds continued, and indeed grew sharper as the government limped to its inglorious close June 1885. Finally, in September following the example set by Joseph Chamberlain in England, the Scottish radicals formed the National Liberal Federation of Scotland. The Federation put forward a radical programme, demanding church disestablishment and reform of parliamentary procedure, of the house of lords, of the land system, and of local government. Gladstone had taken Scottish Liberalism very much for granted and was perplexed at these developments. He refused to accept disestablishment, knowing that in the long run this would constitute a threat to the Church of England, to which he was devoted. No compromise seemed possible and deadlock ensued. Both in England and in Scotland Liberal strength was dissipated by numerous double candidatures, and as a result of the general election of 1885 the Conservatives, aided by a pact with the Irish Nationalists, continued office.

Though weak and short-lived, Lord Salisbury's first ministry passed the bill creating a Scottish secretary; but the act did not entirely satisfy public opinion in Scotland, for the new minister was not a secretary of state and did not, therefore, have cabinet rank. Even so, attempts were made to circumscribe his powers, the home office and the treasury both proving obstructive. The Scotch Education Department, long dominated by anglicisers, was reluctant to break its close ties with its English counterpart; and the lord advocate was keen to preserve as much of his powers as possible. The far-sighted Salisbury refused to be dominated by departmental bumbledom; and by an act of 1887 (passed in Salisbury's second administration) these differences were settled in favour of the Scottish office, which, however, was based not in Edinburgh but at Dover House in Whitehall. The lord advocate became a purely legal officer, not indeed subject to the Scottish secretary but obliged to work in close liaison with him. Almost from its inception the Scottish office pretty well corresponded to the home office, particularly in its responsibility for the maintenance of public order and the regulation of the police. It also controlled various agencies—such as those dealing with poor law, education, lunacy—and its powers were gradually extended by further reforms.   In 1888 the so-called Goschen formula was drawn up by the chancellor of the exchequer of that name, whereby another of the grievances raised by the National Association was met.   In proportion to her contribution to United Kingdom revenue, Scotland could claim her share of budgetary grants: the Goschen formula was that Scotland was due $\frac{11}{80}$ths of any sum allocated to England and Wales.   Salisbury's ministry, in fact, was not taken up entirely with foreign affairs, as later historians have tended to suggest.   In 1889 county councils were established in Scotland (one year after their English counterparts); democratically elected by the ratepayers, the councils took over numerous *ad hoc* functions from the commissioners of supply, justices of the peace, and lesser bodies.   The Burgh Police Act of 1892 further strengthened local government by ending conflicts between police commissions and town councils, which, under the terms of the act, were no longer allowed to overlap.   These developments in local government extended the authority of the Scottish secretary, for he was charged with general oversight of the system. The Scottish office had, in fact, become ' by the end of the century, the real heart of the executive government of Scotland '.[73]

To return to the pressing issues of 1885, Salisbury's acceptance of ' devolution ' in Scotland may have strengthened Gladstone's hope that the Conservatives would abandon their traditional policy of coercion in Ireland and make some move in the direction of home rule.   This, he was convinced after long years of wrestling with the Irish problem, was the only hope for a peaceful and durable relationship between Ireland and the rest of Britain. Through an indiscretion on the part of his son Herbert, those views were made prematurely public, and the Tories joyfully resigned, leaving Gladstone to work whatever miracles he could in the face of their opposition and the bitter reaction of strong sections of the Liberal party which felt that they had not been properly consulted in the elaboration of such a revolutionary policy.   Gladstone failed to carry his Irish Home Rule Bill, and the elections that followed in 1886 resulted in a triumph for unionism and a Conservative government pledged to fight home rule to the last.   Sections of the Liberal party broke away as

[73] G. S. Pryde, *Central and Local Government in Scotland since 1707*, p. 20.

Liberal-Unionists. By and large the Irish question confirmed an imminent split in that the Whig magnates withdrew from the Liberal party; the loss of the radical leader Chamberlain, too, was already foreshadowed by his bad relations with Gladstone.

In Scotland the Unionist secession was a strong but by no means fatal blow to the Liberals: none the less, the Liberal majority in Scotland of 52 in 1885 was in 1886 cut to 14, when no less than 17 Liberal-Unionists were returned. The Unionist vote was heaviest in Glasgow, where, significantly, anti-catholic feeling and Orangeism were strongest. The Conservatives, co-operating with the Unionists, returned 12 members. The dissenting ecclesiastical radicals, however, mostly remained faithful to Gladstone but had no success in trying to force him to accept their programme. In the Highlands the Leaguers took the place of the seceding Whig landlords as the hard core of the party. Indeed, so far from destroying the Liberal party in Scotland the Irish home rule controversy of 1886 could be said to have rendered it more homogeneous and more vigorous. It also had the effect of stimulating nationalist aspirations and led to the founding in 1886 of the Scottish Home Rule Association: thereafter home rule ' all round ' became an accepted feature of Liberal party beliefs. Nor did the Liberal-Unionists merge with the Conservatives. Many of them later changed their minds and returned to the Liberal fold, while the convinced Unionists maintained organisations of their own which observed the time-honoured political division of east and west. Finally, partly as a result of the shock of 1886 the Liberal party moved to the left, but not far enough or quickly enough to satisfy the needs of the new mass electorate.

11

THE END OF AN ERA, 1886–1918

By the mid-1880s the material and moral condition of the bulk of the Scottish people was in process of rapid change, much of it brought about by economic trends that had been gathering momentum for decades. Thus the dominance of heavy industry was an established fact, and one which carried social and political as well as economic implications. It confirmed the re-zoning of population in Scotland, whereby more and more of the total population was concentrated in the south-west and centre. By 1911 the ten main industrial counties held 79·4% of the total population, while the eight crofting counties had a mere 8%. Of the principal occupations, agriculture and textiles had relatively declined, and by 1901 the greatest employer of labour was the heavy industry complex—that is, coal-mining, iron and steel, shipbuilding and engineering. Thus, Scotland's prosperity came increasingly to depend on heavy industry, which was the part of the economy most vulnerable to growing international competition and to the vagaries of the trade cycle. From 1870 to 1914 the most rapidly expanding industry was shipbuilding which entered a new phase in 1879, when William Denny of Dumbarton launched the first steel-hulled ocean-going vessel. Within a decade the bulk of Clyde production was of steel-hulled steamships, the clippers rapidly falling out of favour in the '90s. Naval rivalry between Britain and Germany stimulated production, and in 1913 a record tonnage was launched. Yet the Clyde's most dynamic period lay in the past, when her shipbuilders and engineers had contributed much to the development of the marine steam engine. In retrospect, ominous significance can be seen in the fact that in the rise of the diesel engine (first patented in 1892) Clyde engineers played no part.

There were disquieting trends, too, in the coal and iron industries, where international competition was most severely felt. By the 1880s the Scottish iron industry had lost many of its advantages: the supply of blackband ironstone was virtually exhausted and ore had to be imported from Spain, thus increasing costs; Lanarkshire splint coal was also depleted; and the transition to the production of high grade steel, difficult in Britain as a whole, proved particularly troublesome in Scotland.[1] When some degree of success was achieved, there remained in Scotland the added drawback that steel production was overdependent on shipbuilding. The closely allied coalmining industry reflected these difficulties all too faithfully. The best seams then workable were nearing exhaustion, competition was keen (especially, though not exclusively, from Germany), prices and markets were uncertain, and the industry was harried by disputes, strikes, and intermittent unemployment. Yet in spite of these facts, heavy industry cannot be described as completely stagnant. To some extent, these were the normal ups and downs that afflict any industrial system and should not be regarded as necessary causes of the bleak years that followed the Great War of 1914-18.[2] In the period now under discussion, between 1886 and 1914, no little part of the trouble lay in the chronic pragmatism of management, which riveted many firms to the worthy but outmoded standards of Samuel Smiles and prized 'self-help' beyond science or technology. Failure to develop a modern system of education must shoulder part of the blame, particularly the failure to provide adequate science teaching in schools and universities. The Universities (Scotland) Act of 1858 and its successor of 1889 transformed the government of the universities, sweeping away many cumbrous anachronisms; but the reconstituted universities were slow to introduce new subjects like science and engineering. Yet such as they were, these changes have been deplored as betrayals of the Scottish tradition, though in fact they erred by too timidly extending that tradition. No one

[1] D. L. Burn, *The Economic History of Steelmaking 1867-1939*, passim.
[2] W. A. Lewis, *Economic Survey 1919-39*, p. 79: 'Stagnation before 1913 was relative; after 1913 in the export trade, it was absolute'. Cf. S. B. Saul, *Studies in British Overseas Trade 1870-1914*, pp. 41-2; and S. Pollard, *Development of the British Economy 1914-50*, p. 53.

was more conscious of this than R. B. Haldane, a leading Scottish Liberal politician who devoted much of his time to campaigns for more effective general and scientific education on the lines pioneered in Germany.[3] More than half a century later, and in a new set of pressing circumstances, Haldane's vision is still far from realisation. So it would seem but rough justice to heap all the blame on his contemporaries.

For agriculture the '80s also ushered in a time of trial, occasioned by the so-called ' Prairie Corn Crisis ' which swamped the market with cheap American and Canadian grain. The resulting depression lasted until 1914 and was most acutely felt in the wheat growing areas; but Scotland, by virtue of its traditional mixed farming, escaped the worst of it.[4] In the areas where grain farming prevailed (the Lothians, Fife, Angus and Perthshire) intensive organisation enabled the farmers to weather the storm, while in the north-east the main emphasis was placed on beef production, and in the south-west on dairying. Hardest hit of all were the small farmers and crofters of the Highlands and Islands. They had lately been granted security, the powers of the landlords having been circumscribed by legislation; but no such brake was applied to the depression, the effect of which was to continue the long process of depopulation. The landlords were able to profit by letting grouse moors or deer forests, to make way for which the sheep-runs were destroyed. In the period from 1883 to 1912 the extent of deer forest in the Highlands more than doubled. In sum, by 1911 agriculture had long ceased to be the main occupation in Scotland, and in that year gave employment to less than one in twenty of the population. The change was significant, but again care has to be taken not to draw exaggerated conclusions. The older ' feudal ' society was not altogether destroyed. Scotland was still a country characterised by great estates which in many parts held virtually self-contained communities, such as that presided over by the fifth Earl of Rosebery at Dalmeny.[5] The contrast between such a community and that which existed in the stone canyons of Glasgow was startling. Doubtless economic hardship and social grievances existed in these rural enclaves; but they

[3] R. B. Haldane, *Autobiography*, *passim*.

[4] J. A. Symon, *Scottish Farming Past and Present*, ch. XII.

[5] The Marquess of Crewe, *Life of Rosebery*, contains many illuminating insights into life at most levels on a great estate.

were muted, and on the whole the better-run estates upheld an archaic way of life that seems to have satisfied its partakers. Though an undoubted force in Scotland, the strength of this older form of social organisation is difficult to estimate since it consisted of individual units and could not, in the nature of things, present a united front. Socially, however, the great landed estates tended to be bulwarks of conservatism, though not necessarily in the narrow party political sense.

It would be a mistake, however, to imagine that only the material conditions of life were in flux. In the new situation obtaining after the Franco-Prussian war of 1870, the position of Britain as a first-class power was declining; and by the 1880s the cocksureness of the mid-Victorian period was eroded by doubt. Foreign and imperial questions weighed heavy: was the extension of an already world-wide empire a sufficient substitute for a foreign policy; anyway, for what purpose did that empire exist, and how was it to develop? A new race of imperialists, stimulated by Disraeli, sought to settle these questions—men as diverse as Joseph Chamberlain, the fifth Earl of Rosebery, Sir John Seeley and Sir Charles Dilke. Scotland they found a difficult field for their labours. There, in spite of the hysterical trumpetings of the press, existed a powerful core of radical ' little Englandism ' and a cynical refusal to plaster material needs with moral whitewash. For many of the Scots the empire denoted objects rather than ideas—places to go, to explore, to exploit, proselytise or settle. Except among the anglicised upper class the empire had little of the quasi-religious significance which seemed to appeal to all classes in England. Thus, the rise of Liberal Imperialism, headed by Rosebery, did nothing to strengthen the Liberal party in Scotland. On the contrary, imperialist leanings probably helped to undermine Scottish Liberalism.

Of fundamental importance to the conditioning of thought were the religious trends of the late nineteenth century, not least of which was the expansion of Roman catholicism due mainly to Irish immigration. Hitherto the Roman Church had claimed the support of a minute percentage of the population and was restricted to a few areas in the Highlands and Islands, with a notable enclave in the north-east Lowlands. By the late nineteenth century all this had changed and catholicism was firmly established in the industrial and commercial centre of Scotland, its communicants in 1871 numbering 300,000. Apart from having to brave the hostility of a predominantly protestant country (which often resulted in dismal outbursts of bigotry), the Roman Church was rent by internal problems. There was a long feud between the hierarchy, which derived exclusively from the old ' Scots catholics ', and the rank and file, priests as well as congregations, who were either of Irish birth or Irish descent. A bitter saying of the time epitomised the problem: ' Paddy sows and Sandy reaps '. While ' the Hielan' clique ', as the Irish dubbed their opponents, engrossed power the contention lasted; but by the end of the century the Scoto-Irish were infiltrating positions of authority, and this the ' old catholics ' had to accept. For the catholics a major step forward was the assumption by the bishops of Scottish territorial titles in 1878; oddly, the most bitter opposition to this move came from the Episcopal Church, which regarded itself, after the Anglican fashion, as the true representative of the medieval *ecclesia Scoticana*. Nevertheless, by the 1880s the Roman catholic community was firmly established and well organised, an integral, if disliked and maligned, element of Scottish society. Quite naturally this produced catholic attitudes to politics, education, and social and economic problems. Again, naturally enough, these were coloured by the Irish question. In response to Irish pressure, too, catholic worship in Scotland was transformed; it lost the old puritanical austerity of the days of proscription and placed more emphasis on ceremonial. The change was wrought mainly through the devoted labours of Bishop James Gillis (1802–64), who was born in Montreal and educated in France.[6] As well as meeting the needs of the Irish this transformation was probably in part a deliberate effort to counteract the secularist trend of the times, not dissimilar to that which slowly and with difficulty permeated with tractarian ideas the Episcopal Church in Scotland.

The tractarians laid great stress on apostolic succession and sacramental rites, views which were already deeply rooted in the old non-juring areas north of Tay but which were long condemned in the southern parts of Scotland, where the great concern of episcopalians was the closest possible identification with the establishment in England.[7] As long as the hierarchy of the

---

[6] P. Anson, *The Catholic Church in Modern Scotland*, pp. 124-8.
[7] W. Perry, *The Oxford Movement in Scotland*, pp. 36-51.

Church of England condemned the allegedly Romeward leanings of the Puseyites, so long did the episcopal hierarchy in Scotland reject them. Their most strenuous opponent in Scotland was Bishop Wordsworth of St Andrews: he detested tractarianism, and feared in addition that it might militate against his own dream of a union, on more or less episcopal terms, of the Episcopal Church and the Church of Scotland.[8] Trouble ensued when a Scottish Pusey appeared in the person of Bishop Forbes of Brechin, who in 1860 was tried and admonished for promulgating false doctrine concerning the real presence and the eucharistic sacrifice.[9] The strife in the Episcopal Church produced some paradoxes. The real anglicisers were not, as popularly supposed, the high churchmen but were rather those of low church views, like Bishop Wordsworth, who deliberately suppressed the old and extremely interesting Scottish liturgy in favour of the English. Bishop Forbes and his brother George, a noted liturgical scholar, did not live to witness the triumph of tractarianism, which they identified with the old Scottish non-juring tradition. They were mistaken, however, in equating this with seventeenth-century Scottish episcopacy, which was thoroughly protestant and had no reservations about the meaning of protestantism. In spite of these growing pains the Episcopal Church made considerable advances in nineteenth-century Scotland. Its main strength derived from its attractiveness to the anglicised upper class educated at English public schools. Many of the great landed proprietors became generous patrons of the Episcopal Church, but this did not enhance its appeal to the masses. Outside the north-east, where it was genuinely popular, it had to struggle against traditional prejudices which regarded it as little more than a Roman chapel of ease. Puseyism and its appeal to the well-to-do or the aesthetic did nothing to soften these prejudices. Where the Episcopal Church did find popular support in the industrial areas it was largely of an embarrassing and inhibiting character. Such support came from some of the Irish Orangemen, originally adherents of the Church of Ireland, whose rabid anti-popery outdid even that of the staunchest Scottish presbyterian. The Episcopal Church rose

---

[8] Wordsworth has had a good press in the ecumenical atmosphere of the mid-twentieth century; but the merest perusal of his *Public Appeals in behalf of Christian Unity with reference to the Present Condition of the Church of Scotland* (2 vols., 1886) shows it to be a somewhat sour *eirenicon*.

[9] W. Perry, *Alexander Penrose Forbes, Bishop of Brechin*, pp. 78-110.

above these local difficulties, and its sense of isolation ended when it became a recognised province of the world-wide Anglican communion, represented as such at Lambeth Conferences from 1867 onwards.

In this troubled period it was not only Roman catholics and Anglicans who found themselves obliged to re-examine the foundations of their zions: the presbyterian churches too were shaken by the scientific materialism of the new age, and, though the champions of Calvinism fought a long and stubborn fight, by the end of the nineteenth century in divinity schools and in many pulpits the iron faith was suspect. An aura of puritanism survived, but as an intellectual system Calvinism collapsed. This was certainly one of the most significant and least understood of the revolutionary changes wrought in nineteenth-century Scotland; and, as in the case of the Church of England, doubts as to the validity of the Calvinist position antedated the onslaught of German historical scholarship. The beginning of the end was noted by Thomas Carlyle, who in 1844 referred to ' bare old Calvinism under penalty of death'.[10] Earlier still, in the 1820s, John Erskine of Linlathen, a layman and an amateur theologian, had rejected the rigid doctrine of predestination and pointed the way towards an appealing but unreasoned universalism. Erskine inspired a new and more spiritual outlook in some of his younger contemporaries, including the wayward genius Edward Irving who charmed the great of London but not the presbytery of Annan which in 1833 deposed him from the ministry. Irving then founded a separate sect, the Catholic Apostolic Church, in which intellect was subordinated to emotion. The predictable result followed: the speaking of tongues and a frenzied quest for a new pentecost. Much healthier was Erskine's influence on another young minister of the Church of Scotland, John McLeod Campbell. In 1830 he too was deposed because of suspect views on the atonement. McLeod Campbell developed and formulated his beliefs in his great work, *The Nature of the Atonement and its relation to the Remission of Sins and Eternal Life* (1856). In it he examined and rejected the main interpretations of the Calvinist doctrines of predestination and election. Deriving much of his inspiration from Luther (in this resembling the ' Marrowmen '), Campbell roundly concluded that ' salvation otherwise than

[10] *Correspondence of Emerson and Carlyle*, ed. Slater, p. 357.

through the atonement is a contradiction '.[11] The laboured style and obscure diction of Campbell's work did not prevent a slow but eventually widespread acceptance of his ideas. He wrote in the old literal scriptural tradition, and in the 1870s, when the higher criticism was brought to bear, his rejection of Calvinism roused great interest. The revolt against Calvinism extended even to the United Associate Synod, from which in 1841 the Reverend James Morison was deposed for his universalist beliefs. Ten years later Morison founded the Evangelical Union, which became one of the main congregational churches in Scotland and a notable disseminator of universalism. A striking indication of the extent to which the old faith had lapsed is that shortly before Morison's death in 1893 almost 2,000 influential ministers and laymen of the United Presbyterian Church, which had subsumed the Seceders from whose fold Morison had been thrust half a century before, presented him with an address in which the fault of the Associate Synod was freely admitted.[12]

By the '80s the advanced thought of the age was hostile to Christian orthodoxy, and particularly so to the Calvinist system of theology. Its old ally, the 'Scotch philosophy of common sense', whose last great exponent was Sir William Hamilton, had been ousted from the universities by Hegelianism. Science was giving rise to a new cosmology that was difficult to reconcile with the old, and the rationalist biblical scholarship that was emanating from Germany was causing heart-searching in Scotland. In 1880 a joint volume of *Scotch Sermons* was issued which fairly posed the dilemma and was on this account fiercely assailed. One of the authors, the Rev. W. S. Macfarlane, in his contribution rejected or appeared to reject such dogmas as the fall of man and original sin, on the grounds that they were unhistorical and could not be reconciled with the concept of evolution enunciated by Charles Darwin. Such doubts were not entirely new but hitherto they had either been suppressed or very timidly stated. As early as 1845 Robert Chambers had written an anonymous work, *Vestiges of Creation*, which anticipated, though in no very scientific style, the germ of the doctrine of evolution. Such a distinguished amateur geologist as Hugh Miller, a noted Free Churchman, to the end of his life subordinated the testimony of the rocks to the

[11] John McLeod Campbell, *The Nature of the Atonement*, p. 29.
[12] W. Adamson, *Life of Rev. James Morison, D.D.*, pp. 415-16.

Book of Genesis. In 1847 he published *Footprints of the Creator*, a refutation of Chambers's work: but the tensions produced by the attempt to reconcile science and religion may have had some bearing on Miller's mysterious suicide in 1856. A later Free Churchman, Henry Drummond, in his *Natural Law and the Spiritual World* (1883) sought to harmonise the old faith with the new science, but with more acclaim than success. As biblical scholarship undermined the view of the Bible as a single inspired revelation, the perplexities of the orthodox increased. Thus, in the same year, 1881, in which Macfarlane had to submit to the general assembly of the Church of Scotland, another embattled scholar, W. Robertson Smith, was, after years of controversy, suspended from teaching for holding that the Bible was in fact an accretion. Smith, a professor in the Free Church College at Aberdeen, had considerable support in his own communion and in the United Presbyterian Church, both of which were then strongholds of ecclesiastical liberalism. The U.P. was particularly prominent in the attack on the Westminster Standards, but in 1878 Fergus Ferguson of Glasgow went too far and was tried for heresy. None the less, the old system was weakening, and by the end of the nineteenth century the Westminster Standards were as tattered and torn as the Thirty-Nine Articles of the Church of England. Nor was it simply outmoded confessions that stood in danger of rejection: belief itself seemed at hazard.

At the same time that these theological and scholastic changes were taking place, a liturgical movement was gradually and just as inexorably transforming the worship of presbyterian Scotland. This movement was not synchronised with the theological or scholastic changes and was indeed in some ways a revulsion against the latter. It stemmed rather from the Victorian obsession with medievalism, so apparent in the ecclesiastical and general architecture of the period. Significantly, it first revealed itself in the introduction of stained glass windows in Glasgow Cathedral in 1854. The plain fact is that the puritan regime was faltering, and of this the most obvious sign was the decline of church discipline. Robert Lee of Greyfriars, the stormy petrel of the liturgical movement, was hauled before assemblies in 1859 and again in 1864–7, accused of conducting an Anglican style service, permitting organ music, and other innovations. He went on his way regardless and was largely the inspirer of the Church Service Society which was formed in 1865. If Lee's brethren had not been seriously troubled by similar aspirations he could hardly have escaped so lightly; by the end of the century his once daring experiments were common form in most parts of Scotland, their acceptance hallowed by the effective use of the organ made by the American evangelists, Ira D. Sankey and Dwight L. Moody, in their triumphant tour of 1874. Clearly, in the late nineteenth century a time of crisis had come, a crisis of a kind beyond the imaginings of men like Patrick Walker or the early Seceders. The rock on which Scottish presbyterianism had stood for centuries fell before the onslaught of the scientific spirit of the nineteenth century. The intellectuality of its faith, once its great strength, was now a grievous weakness; for it had rejected sacramentalism and so could not stress a mystic means of grace as a solatium. The sanctity of the Sabbath and the habit of churchgoing remained; but undeniably religion was no longer the very pith and core of Scottish life.

It is not surprising that in this sombre atmosphere the presbyterian churches began to think in terms of unity rather than of division. From the early '60s there had been intermittent discussions between the Free Church and the United Presbyterian Church, in which the main bond had been growing dislike of the Establishment. Protracted delay was caused by the bitter opposition of a group within the Free Church which rigidly identified itself with the men of 1843. This group, strongest in the Highlands, was ably marshalled by Dr James Begg. On grounds of dogmatics, in 1893 an extremist section of this minority broke with the Free Church to form the Free Presbyterian Church. When in 1900 union between the majority of the Free and the United Presbyterian Churches gave rise to the United Free Church, another minority, again concentrated mainly in the north, elected to carry on as the Free Church. It claimed to be the true Free Church, and, as such, entitled to all the possessions of the old Free Church. The claim was rejected by the court of session, but by a surprise judgment of the house of lords the decision was overturned. Parliament in the interests of equity had to legislate, and these proceedings added bitterness to an already sour situation. In the event the Free Church and the Free Presbyterians have preserved the Calvinist tradition by reasserting the values of the seventeenth century. They stood firm on the establishment principle, and indeed this was one of their main quarrels with the U.P. Church which was largely voluntary in outlook. The cry for disestablishment, however, died down. After 1886 many of the U.P. laity became Unionist in politics and highly critical of disestablishment, so much so that they formed a Laymen's League, the object of which was ' to declare against Disestablishment and the secularizing of the endowments of the Church '.[13] The league also advocated presbyterian reunion in Scotland. In fact the old hostility between the established and the larger dissenting presbyterian churches was waning in the face of the growing threat from the materialist philosophies that seemed to be triumphing everywhere. The unions already formed by the daughter churches of the various Scottish presbyterian denominations in the colonies also acted as a challenge and a stimulus. In the '90s prominent members of the Church of Scotland had discussed union with leading United Presbyterian and Free Churchmen, and from 1907 onwards negotiations were resumed between the establishment and the United Free Church. In spite of difficulty in reconciling attitudes on the relationship of church and state, by 1912 it looked as if a greater union was in the offing; but the outbreak of war in 1914 shelved this proposal, though not, as in the case of other matters so postponed, to the Greek kalends.

These developments had a powerful, if slow, solvent action on politics, the ultimate effect of which was to take religion out of politics. More immediately, the enlarged electorate created by the third reform act of 1884 posed some awkward problems to Liberals and Conservatives alike. Each party desired to secure the working man's vote, but neither was prepared to legislate in his favour. And in the severe depression of the late '70s and early '80s the cry for improved conditions and higher wages was growing in volume. The '80s became the seed-time of socialism in Britain, characterised by the appearance of some small but vigorous bodies such as the Scottish Land and Labour League. The league, largely the creation of an Austrian socialist exile settled in Edinburgh, Andreas Scheu,[14] was in 1884 affiliated to the Marxist Social Democratic Federation. By 1886 some working class electors were growing doubtful of the Liberal Party, which was in a sense the party of the capitalists, with its principles deep rooted

[13] D. Woodside, *Soul of a Scottish Church*, p. 211.
[14] H. Pelling, *Origins of the Labour Party 1880–1900*, p. 26.

in *laissez-faire*. Then, too, the leadership of the party in Scotland was weak: the Earl of Rosebery was popular but too patrician, too much of a Whig grandee, to capture the imagination of the horny-handed. He was interested in local government, and was later a leading Liberal-imperialist (he first coined the phrase ' commonwealth of nations '); but at no time in his long but uneven career did he display any sustained interest in social reform.[15] There was no one in the Scottish Liberal hierarchy to attempt the role that Joseph Chamberlain had essayed in England. The defection of the Unionists in 1886 might have led to a Liberal Party rejuvenated by a labour, or even socialist, radical wing; but by 1888 this vision had ceased to tantalise the leaders of the new left that was emerging.[16]

The original intention of much of the new left had been to clarify and extend the existing ' Lib-Lab ' arrangements under which a handful of M.P.s sat in the labour interest by courtesy of electoral pacts with the Liberals. This principle was detested by out-and-out socialist organisations such as the small but influential Social Democratic Federation, whose aim was to make socialists rather than M.P.s. As against this there was a growing body of opinion which insisted on the primacy of parliamentary representation and demanded that it should take precedence of doctrine. The great architect of this social-reformist, as opposed to doctrinaire socialist approach, was James Keir Hardie. Born in Lanarkshire in 1856, the illegitimate and unacknowledged son of a miner, Hardie suffered much in a childhood stifled by poverty, scant education, and hard dangerous toil in the mines from the age of ten. He was intelligent and read as widely as he could; but of the works of Karl Marx he knew little and cared less. His socialism was untheoretical and based on feeling rather than intellectual analysis: his mentors were Robert Burns,[17] Thomas Carlyle (whose radicalism was more apparent to Hardie's than to subsequent generations), and the gospel. Hardie's mother and stepfather had given up religion and the boy was brought up as an atheist; but in his teens he accepted a simple but satisfying view

[15] R. B. Haldane, who belonged in the '80s to a group of young Liberal M.P.s interested in social problems, noted that Rosebery was indifferent to these. Haldane, *Autobiography*, p. 100 ff.

[16] W. Hamish Fraser, ' Scottish Trades Councils in the Nineteenth Century ', in *Bulletin of Society for Study of Labour History*, XIV. 11.

[17] W. Stewart, *J. Keir Hardie, a Biography*, p. 19.

of Christianity which he took into the Evangelical Union rather than from it. He claimed that socialism was the embodiment of Christianity in the industrial sphere, and much the same concept was rendered by Beatrice Webb as ' the flight of emotion away from the service of God to the service of Man '.[18]   For many, social reform became the new faith, and indeed Labour Churches rose to serve it.   Hardie first came into prominence as a trade union organiser; but, important as he always believed trade unionism to be, he soon reached the conclusion that a greater need was for parliamentary representation.   By 1887 he was rapidly losing faith in the Liberal Party, and in May of that year he was calling for a separate and distinct labour group in parliament.

Shortly thereafter Hardie stood as a candidate for North Ayrshire and in his speeches he put the Liberal party on trial. He did not go to the polls; and when in 1888 he again came forward at a by-election in Mid-Lanark it was on a pure labour platform, though he still retained a tenuous link with the Liberals.   Lack of funds, defective campaigning, and the hostility of the Irish catholic home rulers led to another defeat.   The lessons gained were pondered and applied.   Hardie became the great exponent of organisation and was largely instrumental in the founding of the Scottish Labour Party in 1888.   This shortlived enterprise, a coalition of various small labour and socialist groups, made little progress, most working class electors continuing to put their trust in the Liberals.   Thus, for years, labour politics seemed to be little more than an interesting diversion, a form of theosophy to fill the blank left by non-attendance at church.   But under the indomitable Hardie, and such inspired propagandists as H. H. Champion and Robert Blatchford in England, the new cause made steady progress, and there was a marked upsurge of interest when in 1892 Hardie was returned for the working class London constituency of South West Ham.   The result was largely a fluke, attributable to dissensions within the local Liberal association; but even so, it was a decisive event, for Hardie, borrowing his tactics from Parnell, became a skilled parliamentary *frondeur*, using the house as a medium for propaganda.   His efforts on behalf of the unemployed highlighted crying social evils which both Liberals and Tories would have preferred not to publicise.

In many ways Hardie symbolised his times, and not least some

[18] Quoted H. Pelling, *Origins of the Labour Party*, p. 152.

of its contradictions. He was a Christian but opposed to what he called 'churchianity'; a socialist but sceptical of the dogma of class war; a sentimentalist but shrewdly practical in his conduct of affairs; and a saint whose idealism did not preclude a liking for power. He was, and remained, a staunch believer in home rule for Scotland as well as Ireland; but his public career demonstrated that parish pump politics were not enough. This was typical of his time, for it is remarkable how little Scotland and its problems figured in the speeches and memoirs of the leading Scottish politicians of that age. From the political point of view Scotland was becoming little more than a nursery for Westminster. After 1892 Hardie was of even more significance in England than he was in Scotland, and it was largely owing to his influence that the Independent Labour Party was formed at a conference held in Bradford in 1893. Its main constituents were the Scottish Labour Party, the Marxist Social Democratic Federation, and numerous small local associations pledged to the return of labour members. Initially, the I.L.P.'s main strength was concentrated in the north of England and, to a much lesser degree, in southern Scotland. In deference to trade union susceptibilities, the new organisation's socialism was not vaunted and found no place in its title. Nor was the idea of permeating the Liberal Party with socialist activists entirely given up. There was point in the statement later made by one of the I.L.P.'s foremost recruits, Ramsay MacDonald: 'We didn't leave the Liberals. They kicked us out and slammed the door in our faces.' [19] Power, in fact, proved hard to come by, and the chief significance of the early I.L.P. was as a propaganda machine.

As far as representation in parliament was concerned labour was still nowhere. At the general election of 1892 the Liberals with the aid of the Irish Nationalists scored a narrow victory, though their hold on Scotland (50 seats out of 72) still seemed impregnable. Conservatism, in spite of the furore over home rule, continued to make a relatively poor showing in Scotland: its main prop was still the unpopular landed interest, strengthened by the seceding Whig Unionists, and relying increasingly for drive and ideas on the urban Liberal-Unionists. Real accessions of strength were the Liberal-Unionist newspapers *The Scotsman* and *The Glasgow Herald*; but Unionism in Scotland was significant

[19] Quoted in H. Pelling, *Origins of the Labour Party*, p. 238.

mainly for the much needed artificial respiration that it gave to moribund Conservatism. The Liberal-Unionists, however, failed to maintain a mass following, and by the end of the century they had become mere auxiliaries of Conservatism. Glasgow, thanks to its militant Orange element and to the determination of its industrialists not to disrupt the U.K. economy on which they depended, soon became the main bastion not only of Unionism but of Conservatism as well. Yet the Liberal-Unionists stubbornly refused to merge with their old enemies and, as in England, maintained a separate organisation until 1912. When the two organisations merged in 1912, such was the Tory image in Scotland that it was the Unionist label that survived. This was realistic, for the Scottish Conservative tradition, which exercised Disraeli, continued to dismay Austen Chamberlain, who saw clearly that it held out few hopes for the future.[20]

Hamstrung by the opposition of the house of lords and by Rosebery's weak leadership, the Liberals suffered a crushing defeat in the general election of 1895. In Scotland the Conservatives and Unionists carried 33 out of the 72 seats. In Britain as a whole the I.L.P. ran 29 candidates; not one of them was returned but the working class vote seriously embarrassed the Liberals, who were forced to rely increasingly on the Irish Nationalists. The dissipation of the strength of the Liberal Party, rather than the supposed attractions of imperialism, was probably the main reason for the decade of Conservative rule that followed. The South African War further divided the Liberals, Rosebery and the imperialists supporting it as just and necessary while the radical wing, led by Sir Henry Campbell-Bannerman, opposed it and condemned the methods used to subdue the Boers. The khaki election of 1900 exposed these divisions but, significantly, did not appreciably increase government strength. For whatever it was worth, by 1906 the jingoistic fever had subsided; the Liberals had patched up their differences; and the Conservatives were in disarray, rocked by a bitter controversy on whether or not free trade should be abandoned in favour of imperial preference.

In the meantime prospects of independent labour representation had been enhanced by gathering hostility to trade unionism. The trade unions were accused of restrictive practices which

[20] Austen Chamberlain, *Politics from the Inside*, pp. 156, 196-8.

impeded the country's ability to compete with its industrial rivals. A parallel situation already existed in the United States, where the formation of trusts had led to embittered labour relations. In Britain the employers showed a tendency to emulate their American counterparts, and this, together with a growing uneasiness concerning their legal rights, forced the larger unions into politics. In 1899 the Trade Union Congress voted, reluctantly, for negotiations to secure ' a better representation of the interests of Labour in the House of Commons '.[21] Scotland led the van in this movement, partly because the comparative weakness of its unions made their members more politically minded; and in 1897 a Scottish T.U.C. was formed to take a more active part in politics. The S.T.U.C. together with the I.L.P. played the major role in creating in 1900 the Scottish Workers' Parliamentary Election Committee, which anticipated by some weeks the more famous Labour Representation Committee set up in London. Early relations between the two committees were not easy. In 1906 the Scottish committee adopted the title of Scottish Labour Party; but the pull of England was too strong and by 1909 it was merged in the L.R.C., the nucleus from which the Labour Party developed.[22] The rise of the Labour Party was further accelerated by the effects of the Taff Vale judgment of 1901, whereby the trade unions were deprived of their imagined immunity from tort. This led the large unions to support the L.R.C., and their funds could thus be tapped to finance electoral campaigns and to support Labour M.P.s. In Scotland the Liberals, too, were awakening to the realities of the situation and their Chief Whip, the Master of Elibank, constantly urged co-operation between Liberals and labour, on the grounds that radical electors would otherwise secede to the extreme camp ' and what was once the life-blood of Liberalism . . . be dried up '.[23] In retrospect Haldane, who maintained close contact with the Fabians, deplored the failure of the Liberal party to move far enough to the left at this time; but, as it was, sufficient was done to justify an electoral compact, and in the general election of 1906 the rewards were reaped. For many reasons the ten years' dominance of the Conservatives had rendered

---

[21] Quoted by Philip P. Poirier, *The Advent of the Labour Party*, p. 74.
[22] W. H. Marwick, *Labour in Scotland*, p. 19; W. H. Marwick, *Scotland in Modern Times*, p. 151.
[23] P. Poirier, *Advent of the Labour Party*, p. 182.

them unpopular and they were badly worsted at the polls. The Liberals won a large majority; but by far the most significant feature of the election of 1906 was the progress of the L.R.C. It ran 50 candidates of whom 29 were returned, but of these only two sat for Scottish constituencies. Another 24 members sat as 'Lib-Labs' or trade union representatives. As *The Scotsman* bitterly remarked: 'Socialist Labour—the curse and danger of Continental politics—is the death's head that grins down derisively on the triumph of the Radicals; it may before long turn their rejoicing into wailing.'[24] As prophecy, it proved to have a certain validity.

The new premier, Sir Henry Campbell-Bannerman, a Scot who insisted on the title, could be described as the first radical prime minister. He had been a pro-Boer and this was reflected in the constitutional settlement that gave rise to the Union of South Africa in 1908. He was not doctrinaire but was prepared to sanction any reforms for which a good case could be made. Thus, in addition to grappling once more with the involved question of home rule for Ireland, the Liberals under Campbell-Bannerman were willing to examine a wide range of questions. This quiet, ailing Scotsman (he died in 1908 and was succeeded by H. H. Asquith) gave the Liberal party new purpose and made possible one of the great reforming ministries of twentieth-century Britain. Though its programme evolved rather piecemeal, owing largely to the opposition of the house of lords, and had its limitations (most notably perhaps in refusing to consider votes for women), it was in startling contrast to the inept domestic policies pursued by the late Unionist ministry under A. J. Balfour. Balfour was the Rosebery of the Tory party: a man of radiant intelligence who none the less seemed to embody the philosophy of doubt on which he wrote so graciously but vaguely. The Unionists were slow to perceive the crucial importance of the social legislation put forward by the Liberals. In the second Salisbury administration, Joseph Chamberlain had campaigned for old age pensions but imperial questions diverted his energies and nothing came of his schemes. When in March 1906 a bill proposed to feed needy schoolchildren at government expense, Unionist bankruptcy was exposed. The Tories admitted the evils of unemployment, but

[24] *The Scotsman*, Monday, 15 January 1906, leader, p. 6.

they attacked the proposed remedy as too costly and as an invasion of parental responsibility!

The Liberal ministry was beset by great difficulties, not least by the high expectations which the electoral triumph of 1906 had raised in radicals, socialists and Irish Nationalists. The details belong to British history in the widest sense.[25] They would include: the lengthy duel with the house of lords which ended in the Parliament Act of 1911, whereby the primacy of the commons was assured, the duration of parliaments was cut to five years, and payment of M.P.s (of vital importance to the Labour party) was introduced; the introduction of old age pensions and unemployment benefit, and the beginning of organised medical care; and the painful climax of the Irish question, when a Home Rule bill, negotiating the new legislative channels, was hampered by a threatened revolt of Unionist Ulster, aided and abetted by leading members of the Conservative and Unionist party. The one important piece of legislation exclusive to Scotland arose out of the government's controversial land policy and was passed mainly by the insistence of the Scottish Secretary, Sinclair. That was the setting up of the Land Court in 1911, with competence in matters relating to smallholders, crofting being technically abolished:[26] it proved to be one of the very few successful public bodies operating in the Highlands, although the encouragement of small-holding came to little in practice. By 1912 there was widespread disillusionment, either at the speed or slow pace of reform, and a tendency arose towards violent unparliamentary action. This was true not only of the Irish question but also of industrial relations and the mounting demand for votes for women. It is hard to find any specifically Scottish attitude to these problems, though such an attitude perhaps existed towards home rule.

Apart from fierce controversies between Unionists and Liberals, many champions of the measure in Scotland insisted that it must entail home rule ' all round ' and not just favour the Irish. Unionist opposition to home rule was based on the need for imperial unity, and was buttressed by a superficial reading of nineteenth-century history, with its illusion of progress and the

[25] R. C. K. Ensor, *England from 1870 to 1914*, chs. XII, XIII.
[26] I am indebted to Dr John Brown for allowing me to read an advance copy of his forthcoming article in *S.H.R.*, ' Scottish and English Land Legislation 1905–11 '. In 1955 a new Crofters Commission was set up.

absorption of small states by larger units which were equated with nations. The Unionist candidate in the Glasgow St Rollox by-election of 1912 summarised this viewpoint: ' it [*i.e.* home rule] would not work. The whole progress of civilisation had been towards building up nations, and not towards their separation.' [27] Certain aspects of government policy towards Ireland caused resentment in both Unionists and home rulers in Scotland, notably the expensive land programme initiated by Balfour. If great estates were an admitted evil in Irish life, why were great estates in Scotland to be regarded as social blessings? If Scotland were to be granted home rule would it be in the same handsome manner as the boon that, under the terms of the Parliament Act, the government was trying to confer on Ireland? Even staunch Scottish home rulers were unhappy about this question. To placate them, Asquith in introducing his Irish Home Rule Bill in 1912 declared that it was the first instalment of home rule all-round; and, indeed, a Scottish Bill was actually in its second reading when the outbreak of war in August 1914 shelved the project. The extent of the demand for home rule in Scotland at this time has been variously estimated. Bonar Law, the leader of the Conservatives, regarded it as factitious; but, like many politicians, Bonar Law could see only what he wanted to see. The demand for home rule seems to have been widespread, its most consistent support coming from the Scottish segment of the Labour movement. That it was coloured by the Irish Nationalist movement is not open to doubt; but, as we have seen, the germs of it considerably antedated Parnell's activities.

The other problems that harassed the Liberal government from 1910 onwards had few specifically Scottish features but did have significant Scottish nuances. Industrial unrest had various causes, of which perhaps the chief was despondency at the slow growth of Labour representation in parliament and consequently tardy and inadequate social legislation. Compared with German and French socialism, the movement in Britain seemed inchoate and powerless. Yet in these years socialist propaganda was permeating the mass of working men, especially in the west of Scotland where Keir Hardie's example had produced a crop of fiery young orators. One of the I.L.P.'s most assiduous speakers was the youthful James Maxton, who survived the wrath not only of

[27] *The Scotsman*, Monday, 19 February 1912, p. 9.

school boards but also of catholic Irish Nationalists and militant Orangemen. These arch-enemies owned a common foe in the socialists, whose meetings they regularly converted into riots. At this time, too, another young Glasgow schoolteacher, John Maclean, was establishing himself as the main disseminator of Marxism in Scotland.

To complicate matters, other views—industrial unionist and syndicalist—gained some currency in Scotland, particularly after the founding of the Socialist Labour Party in Glasgow in 1903, for a section of it was much influenced by the ' industrial union-ism ' advocated by the American labour leader Daniel de Leon. After 1908 the views of the anarcho-syndicalist section of De Leon's International Workers of the World, an American organisation, caused some stir in labour circles. Syndicalism proper had perhaps an even stronger influence among the workers in the engineering and mining industries after 1910, when the watchword became ' Workers' control of industries '. The official labour movement, in both its political and industrial sectors, gave a frigid reception to ideas which condemned both nationalisation and existing unions. Industrial unionists and syndicalists feared that national-isation would simply perpetuate capitalism, leaving the workers still mere ' wage slaves ': their own ideas, hazy though they were, envisaged ' workers' control ' as a step towards the transformation of society.[28] Labour, in fact, was in a dilemma. The revival of radicalism bade fair to undermine parliamentary socialism; existing trade unions, especially the craft unions, had acquired an odour of sanctity; and yet socialist doctrines were stirring the masses. The situation forced the emergence of millennarian ideals; and syndicalism, vague and ill defined though it was, made con-siderable appeal to the colliers. The importance of coal, and the peculiarities of the industry, made the general strike an attractive weapon. Thus, in these years there were frequent strikes and bitter conflicts in the coalfields, in the course of which violence and the destruction of property were far from unknown. A common, but not very convincing, contemporary explanation attributed these disorders to the ungovernable tempers of the numerous Poles and Germans employed in Scottish mines. Thus, the Poles were blamed, unjustly as it subsequently appeared, for

[28] Branko Pribićević, *The Shop Stewards' Movement and Workers' Control, 1910-1922*, ch. I.

a riot at Tarbrax Colliery near West Calder when the colliery was wrecked and the engine-house burned.[29]

The remaining domestic problem that bedevilled Asquith's cabinet was the rising demand for the enfranchisement of women. It was the logical culmination of the emancipation movement which had begun in mid-Victorian times, had been blessed by John Stuart Mill but not by W. E. Gladstone, and had thereafter gathered momentum, winning position after position until the chief obstacle that remained was the vote. The feminist question was a particularly difficult one: it cut across normal party lines and was supported or reviled by politicians of both main parties. The suffragists' most consistent supporters were the socialists, and notably Keir Hardie, who was a personal friend of the veteran Mrs Pankhurst and her daughter Christabel. The agitation swelled after the great Liberal victory of 1906, but the demand for adult female suffrage was difficult to concede in the absence of adult male suffrage. Mrs Pankhurst and her militant Women's Social and Political Union cared nothing for soft answers and embarked on a campaign of refined but diabolical ingenuity. Liberal ministers were heckled and terrorised, and when the government introduced a bill to grant male adult suffrage Mrs Pankhurst and her followers adopted still more violent methods. The agitation in Scotland was nothing like as extreme as it was in England. In Scotland many of the suffragists were Liberal and did not wish seriously to embarrass the government.[30] The social differences between the two countries also contributed to this result. The movement was largely lower middle class, deriving its strength from urban centres; but in Scotland the middle class was nothing like the potent force that it was in England. These facts, coupled with a Pauline view of man as the predominant partner, made Scotland an indifferent recruiting centre for the militants. The main strength of the movement was concentrated in Edinburgh, where its champion was Dr Elsie Inglis, who in 1906 promoted the Scottish Federation of Women's Suffrage Societies.[31] On the whole the Scottish suffragists, like Dr Inglis, pinned their faith on peaceful propaganda and deplored the violent tactics of the extremists. Later, as the struggle inten-

---

[29] *The Scotsman*, Friday, 8 March 1912, report, p. 7.
[30] Christabel Pankhurst, *Unshackled: The Story of how we won the Vote*, p. 85.
[31] Lady Frances Balfour, *Dr Elsie Inglis*, pp. 82–110.

sified, there were some arrests in Scotland, followed by hunger-strikes and forced feeding; but there were not many instances of this kind, and the disturbances were nearly always sparked off by Mrs Pankhurst's electric oratory.

Unknown to the general public, to the opposition in parliament, and even to members of Asquith's cabinet, a new factor loomed over these domestic broils. This was the unavowed but growing commitment in foreign policy which swung Britain away from ' splendid isolation ', and which made her in effect an integral part of the Entente. The naval competition with Germany from 1908 onwards was merely the outward sign of this new alignment; its real substance was a secret military understanding with France. The murder of the Austrian Archduke Franz Ferdinand at Sarajevo on 28 June 1914, the feverish diplomatic activity that followed and culminated in war between France and Russia on the one side and Germany and Austria-Hungary on the other forced Britain to keep her commitments. The violation of Belgian neutrality by the Germans enabled the Foreign Secretary, Grey, to justify to the country at large, and to the great majority of his party, the path on which Britain was already set. The Labour movement, however, was split on this issue, the majority of the parliamentary party and the trade union leadership supporting the government while a strong minority led by Keir Hardie and Ramsay MacDonald opposed the war. The feuding Irish groups also for a time suspended operations in order to help the war effort against Germany. The history of the four years of bitter struggle that followed cannot be summarised here; but its effects on Scottish society must be considered.

The Great War, of course, had cataclysmic effects on the entire world, on belligerents and neutrals alike. The endless lists of killed, wounded and missing afflicted Scotland as it did the other belligerent countries, the loss of young manpower hitting with cruel force the already underpopulated areas of the Highlands and Islands. In other ways, the new conditions created by the war had adverse long-term effects for Scotland. Among the many things that perished in August 1914 was the era of Samuel Smiles which, for all its defects, had enabled Scotland to take a commanding place in trade and industry. The new conditions established by the war were to prove all but fatal to Smiles' native land: in 1914 the Scottish economy was a reality, but by the 1920s the phrase, while still in use, could be taken to mean only a depressed sector of a none-too-robust British economy. There is irony in the fact that a superb effort during the war years made the Scottish economy virtually its own executioner.

A common, and perhaps exaggerated, criticism of the Scottish economy in the pre-war period is that it was overdependent on heavy industry and that little or no effort was made to diversify. This view takes little stock of the fact that heavy industry, in spite of increasing challenges from abroad, was still in a relatively strong position; and in any case efforts were made to diversify, such as the setting up of the large Singer sewing-machine factory at Clydebank in the early 1880s. Nor were the possibilities of the manufacture of motor-cars entirely ignored.[32] First in the field was the Arrol-Johnston Company located successively at Glasgow, Paisley and Dumfries; William Beardmore's, the iron company, followed, and the most permanent of these early companies, the Albion. But the naval competition with Germany, stimulating as it did the complex of heavy industries which had its apex in shipbuilding, made these ventures seem little more than novelties at a time when the demand for cars was still limited and the principle of mass production had still to be proved in practice. Nor would it have been as easy as some critics seem to imagine to switch from heavy to light industries. The whole issue, in fact, has been obscured by hindsight and partial considerations.

During the war the heavy industries of the west of Scotland were utilised to the full, and were, in fact, grossly overexpanded in the shipbuilding and engineering sectors. In several vital respects the Clyde played a leading role in Britain's war effort. Since it provided a safe harbour, it had to handle a vastly increased volume of shipping; and its great shipbuilding industry, also enhanced by its strategic position, turned out warships of every known type from battle-cruisers to minesweepers. As well as this, after 1916 the Clyde greatly contributed to the replacement of merchant shipping losses caused by the German submarine campaign; and, throughout, it repaired many damaged vessels, though the Tyne and the Forth were the main scheduled areas for this type of work. By the end of the war streamlining of methods had given the Clyde shipyards a vastly increased productive capacity. Scotland also produced munitions, having two out

[32] R. H. Campbell, *Scotland since 1707: The Rise of an Industrial Society*, pp. 243-48.

of the twelve British areas of production. In January 1916 there were almost 250,000 munition workers in the Clyde area:[33] this number, of course, included workers in the engineering and ship-building industries; but even so it illustrates the gigantic effort that was being made in a country dominated by heavy industry in which there were few light-engineering plants, such as Singers, for easy conversion. Clydeside was actually the single most important munitions centre in Britain—a fact that is often overlooked.

All this effort depended on the maintenance of supplies of coal and iron. In Scotland the coal industry faced great difficulties, initially through the loss of overseas markets, and throughout because of a shortage of skilled manpower. As in Britain generally, the enlistment of colliers in the first flush of patriotic fervour was unrealistically high. By August 1915, 26·8 % of Scottish miners (and these the youngest and fittest) had, in the current phrase, 'joined the colours'. The oncost workers who replaced them were unskilled, and production fell. Not until the enlistment of colliers was prohibited in June 1916 and many of those already in the army re-directed to the mines was the problem contained. Coalmining also suffered much from the chronic transport prob-lems of the time. The railways were controlled by the government and their resources in Scotland were deployed for two main purposes: the supply of the shipyards of the Clyde with steel and other basic materials, and the maintenance of the Grand Fleet at Scapa Flow. For other purposes rolling stock was in short supply, and at one time owing to scarcity of wagons coal was piling up at the pit-heads. The coal industry of Scotland was gravely debili-tated by the war effort, and its pre-war level of production has never been restored.

Steel and iron, on the other hand, which were facing hard times in 1913–14, received a powerful artificial stimulus from the war. The main problem was the maintenance of supplies of hematites, imported chiefly from Spain, and here again the great difficulty was transport. To augment supplies of ore even the inferior ironstone deposits of the island of Raasay were pressed into service, worked largely by German prisoners of war. In spite of these difficulties the output of the furnaces increased, though less forge and foundry iron was produced than in 1913.

[33] B. Pribićević, *Shop Stewards' Movement*, p. 110.

The steel section of the industry expanded, but its increased output was due not merely to the addition of new plant but also to
a lowering of quality.   Worse, in these years of siege-economy
American steel was making great inroads into Scotland's established markets in Japan and Australia, and by 1916 the export
trade to the colonies and to neutral countries had practically
ceased.   This was another ominous trend that was never reversed.
But largely because of additions to plant, amalgamation and
rationalisation (characterised by the growth of Colville's of
Motherwell which in the course of the war acquired not only
ironworks, steelworks and collieries but also an interest in the
Harland and Wolff Shipbuilding company), ' the iron and steel
industries of the West of Scotland emerged from the war considerably changed in their productive potentialities '.[34]   In short, the
effect of the war was to accentuate the existing imbalance of the
Scottish economy and this, coupled with the loss of old markets
and the financial stringencies caused by the war, was to contribute
dolefully to the bleak post-war years.

The war also left its mark on agriculture.   By 1914 Britain
had for long been dependent on massive imports of foodstuffs, and
following the Prairie Corn Crisis of the 1870s much arable land
had been converted to pasture, though the process was nothing
like as marked in Scotland as in England.   Because of lack of
shipping, however, by 1916 a new policy was initiated.   The
government set up committees with considerable executive powers
and the farmers (hampered by shortage of horses as well as
labourers) were guaranteed minimum prices for wheat, oats and
potatoes to encourage them to plough grasslands.   Much rank bad
farming was not only permitted but encouraged in order to secure
quick returns.   In Scotland the acreage under crop increased between 1916 and 1918 by more than 21% which, in view of the
difficulties, represented a considerable feat.   The elasticity and
efficiency of farming methods in Scotland ' enabled the food production campaign to be carried on in Scotland with much less
trouble and expense to the nation than in England '.[35]   Still,
the desperate expedients of wartime cannot properly be described
as improvements, and the end of the war found the agricultural
industry exhausted and run-down.

[34] W. R. Scott and J. Cunnison, *The Industries of the Clyde Valley during the War*, p. 70.
[35] J. A. Symon, *Scottish Farming Past and Present*, p. 220.

In retrospect it is apparent that the Great War of 1914–18 was, in fact, the major force in shaping the history of Scotland in the twentieth century, for important as its effects were on the economy they were not limited to that sphere. In politics the Byzantine intrigues which led to the fall of Prime Minister Asquith in December 1916 also in the event split and weakened the Liberal Party. This was of special significance to such a Liberal stronghold as Scotland had been, the more so as left-wing socialism in Scotland was at the same time strengthened by the strain of war conditions. It was in this period that the label ' Red Clydeside ' became a journalistic cliché. Throughout the war, in spite of numerous handicaps, labour relations in the coal, iron and steel industries remained surprisingly good; but of the Clyde shipyards and engineering shops there is a very different tale to tell. These industries were plagued by problems arising from ' dilution ', that is the use of semi-skilled labour in a way that normal trade union practice would not have sanctioned. The majority of the parliamentary Labour party and the official trade union hierarchy endorsed dilution as essential to the prosecution of the war, but a movement arose on ' the shop floor ' which militantly opposed these measures, protesting bitterly against the relaxation of existing union agreements, the high cost of living (particularly soaring rents) and, latterly, conscription. Tempers flared when early in 1915 the engineers on the Clyde went on strike, demanding the immediate settlement of a wage claim. The strikers were condemned as revolutionaries and traitors, and the patriotic press fiercely lampooned them in such pathetic lines as ' Tommy Atkins at the Front ', in which Tommy after throwing away his rifle on receipt of the news finally:

> ' picked up me ole gun; me bit of iron, too:
> I'm jist a common soldier, so I've got to see it through.
> An' if they lets us down at 'ome, and if 'e reads I died,
> Will 'e know 'e 'elped to kill me—my brother on the Clyde ? '

It is doubtful if these stirring lines would have impressed such hard core left-wingers as William Gallacher, David Kirkwood, Emanuel Shinwell and others, even if they had been addressed to them in the racy argot of Private Spud Tamson of the ' Glesca Mileeshy '. All unconsciously, too, the doggerel posed the dilemma: were the workers to be subjected to military-style discipline, with the government acting as general staff and the employers as sergeant-majors? This was one of the large issues raised by war which Asquith's government fumbled. In the course of the strike the official union organisers were by-passed by the shop stewards, who emerged from comparative obscurity to seize the leadership of the working class movement. Gallacher, one of the leaders of the militants, a Marxist and a member of the British Socialist Party, poured scorn on the syndicalist idea, which he regarded as 'sectarian'. But his account of the movement is coloured by bolshevik sympathies: according to him a revolutionary situation existed but was vitiated by lack of revolutionary leadership.[36] In fact, syndicalist leanings were more in evidence than bolshevism, and pacifism rather than any inclination to armed insurrection. The movement contained an amalgam of left-wing opinion opposed to capitalism and the war that was allegedly being waged for profits. Divergences of doctrine were wide and caused basic weaknesses in the leadership. All the same, both government and country as a whole were seriously perturbed by the repeated alarms on the Clyde labour front, especially after the split between the unions and the shop stewards widened and resulted in the formation of the Clyde Workers' Committee, whose primary aim was opposition to the Munitions of War Act and the conditions of labour it imposed. As minister of munitions, Lloyd George in December 1915 tried to charm the dissidents with his famed Celtic eloquence, only to be rebuffed by the members of the committee and howled down by the rank and file. The introduction of conscription in 1916 increased opposition on the Clyde and caused the government to take a short line with agitators. Left-wing papers were suppressed, and those most closely associated with them, including Gallacher, were arrested and imprisoned. Other leaders of the movement, including Kirkwood, were deported and forbidden to appear in Glasgow; and on charges of sedition John Maclean and James Maxton were imprisoned. Of the leaders only John Wheatley and Emanuel Shinwell—the most intelligent—escaped the net. These repressive acts seem merely to have increased the prestige of the committee, and its principles spread to other industrial areas in Britain. Indeed, something like a United Kingdom organisation was built up and caused some concern to the government in the closing stages of the war. Matters were not helped by the fact that the quasi-revolutionary

[36] William Gallacher, *Revolt on the Clyde, passim.*

agitations were solidly based on genuine grievances as to pay and social conditions.

The effects of the war, indeed, were many and varied. Virtual control of essential industries by the government gave point to the socialist demand for nationalisation, a demand hitherto derided as visionary. In the great crisis of the war, private enterprise and individual effort proved inadequate either to supply recruits for the armed forces or the munitions on which they depended. In many ways the war acted as a catalyst. For example, it re-inforced the trend towards union of the two main presbyterian denominations in Scotland by demonstrating just how little in practice separated the two churches. With ministers in short supply owing to the needs of the armed forces, the Church of Scotland and the United Free Church interchanged pastors and few congregations noted any difference. Similarly, the war forced to a conclusion the tentative steps taken since 1872 towards an integrated national system of schools. These had entailed a gradual shift of emphasis away from the parochial structure to-wards larger units. In 1902 Balfour's Education Act had replaced English school boards by county and borough councils, but similar attempts in Scotland found the weight of tradition too great. Under an Education Act of 1908 the parish continued as the main administrative unit, and the powers of school boards were extended. The obvious need was to gear up the administration of education to the system of local government that had evolved, based on county and burgh councils, and in 1918 a major step was taken towards this end. By the great Education Act of 1918 the school boards were replaced by elected Education Authorities, one for each county, and one for Edinburgh, Glasgow, Aberdeen, Dundee and Leith. Recently there has been a tendency to deplore the passing of the school boards, which have been invested with all sorts of virtues. The boards undoubtedly gave good service but they were open to 'sinister interests', whether from the right or the left of the political spectrum, and they could not be fitted into a truly national system. Professionalism was growing, notably in the provision of teacher training, and *ad hoc* school boards, however well intentioned, could not meet the new conditions that were developing. The supervisory powers of the Scottish Education Department (as it was henceforth to be known) were increased, and the department, basing itself on Edinburgh rather than

Whitehall, needed stronger subordinate agencies than school boards could provide. The 1918 act also solved, in a simple but satisfactory way, the vexed problem of denominational schools which still plagues other countries; under it all state-aided schools were brought within the ambit of the Scottish Education Department and the appropriate Education Authority; teachers in denominational schools had to meet the requirements of the department but such schools were free to manage religious instruction in their own way. On the whole, this simple exercise in logic has worked remarkably well, in spite of residual prejudices, and has done much to foster a more tolerant atmosphere in a country once harried by religious bigotry.

Another question to which the war hastened a solution was that of the enfranchisement of women. On the outbreak of war the government and the suffragettes concluded an armistice; and, in fact, much of the diluted labour of the war years was provided by women: they drove trams, they worked in munitions factories and even in heavy engineering shops. The leader of the Scottish suffragists, Dr Elsie Inglis, used her organisation to found hospital units. She herself served with great courage in Serbia and, after the overrunning of that country in 1915, with Serb units in Russia. There, in difficult and latterly chaotic conditions, Dr Inglis literally worked herself to death. Against such testimony even Lloyd George, an arch-anti-feminist (in politics, anyway), could not stand out, and the Representation Act of 1918 which granted adult male suffrage also conferred the franchise on women of thirty and over. Ten years later another act completed the process by introducing adult suffrage irrespective of sex.

The Armistice of 11 November 1918 thus confronted a radically changed Britain with totally new conditions. After four feverish, devastating years it was a new Europe, beset by new problems, that had to turn to the difficult path of peace. As part of that process Scotland was to discover some uncomfortable truths— social, economic, and political.

12

BETWEEN TWO WORLD WARS, 1918–1939

The transition from war to peace was hard, not only in terms of economic and administrative difficulties but also in terms of basic human attitudes. It took almost two decades to convince government and business circles that the world of 1914 had vanished. On the other hand, socialists, even of the most tepid kind, understood this, but read far too much into it. The great experiment initiated in Russia in November 1917 was to be extended round the globe: progressive elements were not to stand on its coming but actively to prepare. These two views could not be reconciled, and the resulting conflict created havoc in the inter-war years. In Britain, Scotland provided one of the earliest forums for this bitter debate. Thus in December 1918 an attempt was made to convert the Trades Council of Glasgow into a working soviet.[1] The main inspirer of this movement was the fervent Marxist crusader John Maclean, who had been praised by Lenin as a socialist ' who put the idea of revolutionary struggle against imperialist war into life '.[2] The bolsheviks appointed Maclean soviet consul in Great Britain; for this dangerous eminence he was arrested in April 1918 and sentenced to five years' imprisonment. With the war ended, the government relented, and Maclean was released on 3 December 1918; he stood for Gorbals in the ensuing general election but, like most left-wing candidates, was severely defeated. Disillusioned with the bolsheviks, the nationalist streak in him predominated, and in the last five years

[1] *The Scotsman*, 18 December 1918, p. 5.
[2] T. Bell, *John Maclean, a fighter for freedom*, p. 67.

of his troubled life (he died in 1923) he tried, impeded by poor health, to create a Scottish Workers' Republican Party which should blend the ideals of Marx with those of Sinn Fein. Maclean was not purely a visionary, but had a practical bent as well and helped to found the Scottish Labour College. He has been variously estimated, some regarding him as more than a little mad;[3] and his influence has been minimised by more conventional socialists. Whatever the exact truth, the intriguing figure of Maclean cannot be lightly dismissed, for to the unsophisticated masses of the socialist movement in Glasgow he became a legend, a symbol of integrity and incorruptibility.

It was not only left wing extremists like Maclean who were shocked by the results of the ' Coupon Election ' of December 1918. They came as a severe blow to Liberals and Socialists of all hues. Only seven Labour members were elected in Scotland, and only six non-coalition Liberals, Asquith himself being rejected by East Fife. Labour's equivocal war record told against the party, though the election of William Graham for the unpromising central division of Edinburgh showed what could be achieved by an outstanding candidate.[4] Of the Scottish extremists only Neil McLean was returned for Govan, while in England Ramsay MacDonald himself was defeated. Disappointment with the general election results helped to give a new lease of life to the syndicalist ideas of the pre-war years. More important perhaps in sparking off the troubles of 1919 was the effort of the shop stewards' movement to stage a *coup* which would render more difficult the resumption of leadership by the official trade unions. The moment seemed propitious, for the post-war boom on Clydeside was of remarkably short duration, and by the end of 1918 unemployment was rising significantly. To restrain it, Gallacher and the Clyde Workers' Committee pressed for a 30-hour week; but Shinwell as president of the Glasgow Trades Council regarded this as unrealistic, and successfully insisted on a 40-hour week demand. In January 1919 this led to strikes in many parts of Britain, notably in Glasgow, Edinburgh, and Belfast. The government was alarmed, not only because of the known bolshevik sympathies of many of the leaders—such as Gallacher—but also because of doubts as to the loyalty of the police and the armed

[3] See correspondence in *The Scotsman*, various issues of December 1965.
[4] T. N. Graham, *Willie Graham*, ch. VIII.

forces. Such alarm was unjustified, but before the matter was put to the test the authorities could hardly know that. The test came in Glasgow when on Friday 31 January there was a riot in George Square in which the red flag was ominously flaunted. The right wing press shrieked of the coming terror, and responsible statesmen, including the ex-coalition Labour politician J. R. Clynes, condemned the strike as dangerous and unpatriotic. The situation was misread on every hand. Violence erupted, but not because of a revolutionary plot: it was unwittingly touched off by the outnumbered and understandably nervous police attempting to clear tram lines. Yet something like a revolutionary mood had brought together these restless thousands. Gallacher later contended that a revolutionary atmosphere existed but was dispelled through lack of skilled leadership. It may have been so; but his corollary to this belated awareness (that a march on Maryhill Barracks would, in true Petrograd fashion, have brought out the troops in support of their fellow workers) was pure fantasy.[5] All the same, the government, plagued by the bolshevik bogey, seems at the time to have taken such a possibility seriously. Troops were rapidly drafted into the city, strategic points were guarded by armed sentries, and tanks were held in reserve in the Meat Market. Had the government but known its Glasgow it could have saved public money, for the day after the riot the strike leaders had no forces to command: their rank and file were all venting their fervour, revolutionary or otherwise, at football matches. The strikers were beaten, the 40-hour week was denied, and the shop stewards' powers rapidly declined. Of the main leaders only Gallacher and Shinwell were imprisoned for 'incitement to riot'. Kirkwood had a lucky escape: he was able to produce photographic evidence proving that, far from inciting the crowd, he was trying to pacify it when he was felled by a police truncheon.[6]

Further labour troubles were in store, however, particularly in the coalfields where the report of the Sankey Commission of 1919, with its reluctant advice to nationalise, sharpened antagonisms on both sides of the industry. Government control of the mining industry was relinquished in 1920, to some extent because of the staggering losses incurred by the Scottish pits. Scotland's once great coal industry had indeed fallen on evil days, owing in

[5] W. Gallacher, *Revolt on the Clyde*, pp. 233-4.
[6] D. Kirkwood, *My Life of Revolt*, p. 174.

part to bad management such as had virtually ruined the central coalfield and in part to a fall in demand. The export market was lost at precisely the same time that, with the end of the post-war boom, the need for capital goods at home began to slacken. The coal-owners insisted that the only remedy was longer hours and reduced wages, and this led to a long and bitter strike in 1921. The owners won, but the condition of the industry continued to deteriorate. It fell far behind its main continental competitors, particularly in the important matter of haulage. The contrast was startling: whereas in 1913 output per man shift in the U.K. was slightly higher than that of the Ruhr or Holland, in the period 1913-38 it increased by over 60% in the Ruhr and over 100% in Holland to the U.K.'s paltry 13%. Faced by such a bleak future, the miners reacted bitterly.

Heavy industry in general was damaged by the policy of ' squeezing Germany till the pips squeaked '. Confiscated German shipping sold for a fraction of the cost of new ships, and once the replacement boom was over the shipyards were brought to a virtual standstill, heavily reducing the demand for steel and coal. By 1922 there were over 80,000 unemployed in Glasgow alone. ' Rationalisation ' ensued—that is, the merging of firms to elimi-nate competition and so control the market. This demonstrably worked against Scotland's interests, particularly the merging in 1923 of the Scottish railways in larger London-controlled U.K. lines. The London, Midland and Scottish Railway absorbed those inveterate rivals the Caledonian and the Glasgow and South-Western, while the London and North-Eastern Railway Company took in the North British and its subsidiaries. So far so good: all could be justified in terms of imposing economic jargon. Not so easy to justify was the transfer of locomotive building and repair work from the hard-hit west of Scotland to the north of England. From this, and other blows, the great locomotive engin-eering industry of Glasgow and Kilmarnock never fully recovered. As a contemporary remarked, ' there is a five-word phrase which brings a terror all its own to the hearts of Scottish people: *The Southward Drift of Industry* '.[7] The exponents of the dismal science justified it as the inevitable concomitant of ' rationalism '.

In the financial turmoil of the post-war era a distinct Scottish economy ceased to be a reality: control lay elsewhere. In a

[7] G. M. Thomson, *Scotland That Distressed Area*, p. 3.

wider view, the 1920s represented a period of lost opportunity when Britain, clinging to the standards of the past, failed to adjust to the new economic facts of life[7A]. London strove to remain a great financial centre and banking was regarded as of greater importance than production. To maintain confidence in the £ Britain returned to the gold standard in 1925 but at an unreasonably high valuation which helped to price British goods out of world markets. A more realistic policy would have concentrated on renewing plant and switching to producer goods to meet the new export demands; but any such developments were inhibited by the continued acceptance of outmoded *laissez-faire* economic theory. Liberals and Socialists were as ill-equipped for the challenge as the Conservatives, their panaceas scarcely venturing beyond schemes of public works to reduce unemployment. These were general British economic problems, but in Scotland they appeared in their starkest form. Before 1914 Scotland had been heavily dependent on exports and was accordingly dealt a severe blow by the general disruption of world trade thereafter. As Britain's share of world exports steadily declined, the main locations of heavy industry—Clydeside, Tyneside, South Wales, and Belfast—became centres of persistent depression. From contributing 12·5% of the net industrial output of the U.K. in 1907, Scotland was by 1924 producing 10·9%.[8] Nor was it only heavy industry and its ancillaries that suffered. The Baltic market for Scots fish was never recovered, and the fishing industry, which had been expanding before the war, thereafter steadily contracted. In many parts of the country, and not just in the industrial west, unemployment became a major and persistent problem.

Because of economic difficulties, emigration, always a marked feature of Scottish life, increased in the interwar period; in the decennium 1921–31 nearly 400,000 Scots emigrated, and in spite of a high natural increase rate the total population of Scotland in 1931 was 40,000 less than it had been in 1921. In

---

[7A] S. Pollard, *The Development of the British Economy 1914–50*, p. 98, cogently sums up: ' It was the tragedy of British industry in the inter-war period that the shift had to be made too quickly, that few were aware, until the 1930's, of its necessity, and that it had to be carried out not only in the midst of a world depression, but in the midst of a particularly difficult time for Britain's old staple export industries, owing to a change in the terms of trade, a restrictive monetary policy until 1931 and an open home market, until 1932, in a world of rampant protectionism '.

[8] J. Gollan, *Scottish Prospect*, p. 5.

1931 the total population was 4,842,980; by 1951 it had risen to 5,095,969. The drain on Scottish population has continued and is undoubtedly one of the really serious problems confronting the country in the second half of the twentieth century. It has been authoritatively stated that ' No country on the continent of Europe has lost such a high proportion of her people as Scotland '.[9] In this period the depopulation of the north-west was further accentuated, and correspondingly there has been a drastic decline of the Gaelic-speaking population. In 1891 there were over 250,000 Gaelic speakers, but by 1961 the number had fallen to just over 80,000, the overwhelming majority of whom were bilingual. The Outer Hebrides now constitute the largest Gaelic-speaking community.

The deepening economic gloom lent point to vigorous socialist propaganda and enabled the Labour group to make sensational gains in the general election that followed the collapse of the coalition in 1922. True, with 347 M.P.s the Conservatives scored a convincing overall victory, Labour running second with 142, and the seriously divided Liberals mustering 117 (60 for Asquith and 57 for Lloyd George). In Scotland the story was markedly different. There the Unionists had opposed the ending of the coalition and in the general election they aided the ex-coalition Liberals. As a result of their labours the Unionists held 15 seats, the National Liberals 14, the Independent (Asquithite) Liberals 14, and Liberals (Lloyd George) 3. The real surprise was the return of 29 Labour M.P.s and one Communist; but the advance of the socialists was still mainly confined to the urban and industrial areas. Their greatest triumph was in Glasgow where the I.L.P., vigorously generalled by John Wheatley and Patrick Dollan, won 10 out of a possible 15 seats. It was this great victory in 1922 which loosed the so-called ' Clydesiders ' on Westminster, headed by Wheatley and his young acolyte James Maxton. The Clydesiders never constituted a homogeneous group, either in terms of human temperament or of geography. Kirkwood was returned for Clydebank (which is ' Clydeside ' but not Glasgow), Shinwell for Linlithgowshire, and Thomas Johnston for West Stirlingshire.

At Westminster the wild Caledonians were awaited with a mixture of alarm and curiosity. They did not disappoint their

[9] J. G. Kyd, *Scottish Population Statistics*, intro., p. xxii.

electors. Scornful of tradition and ceremonial, their interventions were apt to be unparliamentary, and were indeed too often crude and unwitty. Maxton was a clear and striking speaker but he had still to learn the art of parliamentary repartee. On 27 June 1923, in the course of a speech attacking the parsimonious policy of the Scottish Board of Health, he was suspended for describing as a murderer a Tory M.P. who supported cuts in child welfare. There was Bismarckian contrivance about the whole affair. Maxton genuinely lost his temper, but a demonstration of some sort had already been planned, though pinned to no specific issue. Wheatley and another Clydesider, Campbell Stephen, repeated the offensive remark and suffered the same fate. In the rumpus Shinwell was called a Jew, and Buchanan, who rounded on Shinwell's baiter, was suspended for questioning the impartiality of the chair.[10] The scene was not as squalid as a bald description can make it appear, for the Conservatives in that parliament had in their ranks an undue proportion of ' hard-faced City gents ', and these patriotic profiteers went out of their way to goad the uncouth Clydesiders. To their surprise, the Clydesiders found that the friendliest and most courteous members of the house of commons were Bonar Law and Stanley Baldwin. The escapade did the individual M.P.s concerned no harm with their constituents, who expected fighting representation; but it seriously strained the unity of the parliamentary Labour Party. Ramsay MacDonald had been elected to its leadership mainly by the votes of the Scottish group. This was done from mixed motives, partly in recognition of his anti-war stand and partly to defeat Clynes, who was anathema to the left. MacDonald, however, was a sensitive soul and was soon as pained by the ructions of the left as the most staid Tory or Liberal.

Party politics were in as confused and drifting a state as the economic condition of the country. It was probably the principal achievement of Stanley Baldwin, the Conservative premier, that he managed, perhaps of no set purpose, to realign the political forces within the country on more or less two-party lines. To secure a mandate for a mildly protectionist policy he went to the country in December 1923, with results unforeseen and far reaching. The Conservatives secured only 257 seats, Labour 192, and the Liberals, reunited behind Asquith by the threat to their

[10] *Hansard*, CLXV, 2381 ff. George Buchanan was Socialist M.P. for Gorbals.

cherished ideal of free trade, numbered 158. In Scotland the swing to the left was again even more pronounced: Labour won 35 seats, the Unionists 16, and Liberals 23. And ominously, Labour was no longer virtually confined to the industrial west but was making inroads into the mining areas of the east as well. The Highland constituencies remained faithful to the Liberals, and the agricultural counties of the south to the Unionists. The Liberals were placed in a dilemma. A successful Labour government might hasten their own party's demise; but unsporting opposition might have the same effect. Since Labour was also anti-protectionist, the Liberals reluctantly decided to support MacDonald's government. It seemed reasonable, for with a minority government MacDonald was constrained to play safe, in spite of the agitation of the ' revolutionary ' left. In any event his party's lack of experience obliged him to lean heavily on ex-Liberals such as Haldane, as lord chancellor, Charles Trevelyan, president of the board of trade, and the famous barrister, Patrick Hastings, as attorney-general. The only left-winger to secure office was John Wheatley who became minister of health. That the imbalance was forced upon the prime minister weighed nothing with the more extreme socialists, even though matters were so bad that MacDonald had to have recourse to the extraordinary device of a Tory ' non-party ' lord advocate for Scotland, H. P. MacMillan.

Yet in the beginning hopes ran high. Many of the Labour electors confidently expected a social if not political revolution which would abolish unemployment and every form of social injustice. The I.L.P., reorganised by the dynamic Clifford Allen, hopefully began to churn out programmes as well as propaganda. A cold douche was applied by the Yorkshireman Philip Snowden, who as chancellor of the exchequer dedicated himself to saving the nation's brass. Failure to check, never mind abolish, unemployment led to bitter chagrin. The government's conformity to such traditional etiquette as court dress caused it to be stigmatised as ' a bloody lum hat Government like a' the rest '.[11] In fact, MacDonald's cabinet had the haziest grasp of economics, socialist or any other kind. The prime minister, not yet wreathed in clouds of mixed metaphors, set a bad example by mellifluously droning away about ' the delicate mechanism of international

[11] John Paton, *Left Turn!*, p. 168.

trade '.[12]   Nor was the ire of the left damped down by the astonishing fact that the one clear success of MacDonald's cabinet was Wheatley. This self-educated Lanarkshire ex-miner was a man of extraordinary parts. Through his Catholic Socialist Society, in spite of heavy clerical opposition, Wheatley had played a large part in swinging Roman catholic votes to Labour in Glasgow, and for years he had led the Labour group in Glasgow town council. He was also a successful publisher whose motto was, ' There can be no Socialism in business under Capitalism: the man who thinks differently is not in business long '.[13] Wheatley's important Housing Act reflected not only his socialist ideals but also his sound grasp of business. The scheme was realistic, based on close co-operation between government (central and local) and the building industry. Wheatley handled its passage through parliament brilliantly, to MacDonald's amazement. Had it been allowed to run its projected course, Wheatley's Act might well have solved a social evil that was particularly felt in Scotland. Little or no provision had been made for local authority housing before 1918. Glasgow and some other large cities had been granted limited powers to deal with the appalling problem from 1866 onwards. However, by 1913 Glasgow had built a mere 2,000 houses and these were on the old tenement pattern, simply reduplicating the bad old single-end and double apartments. Much the same can be said of Aberdeen and the other larger burghs: housing, as an issue, was not resolutely faced until after 1918 when matters were complicated by a serious shortage of accommodation. Neville Chamberlain had toyed with the problem, by-passing local authorities in favour of cheap, and inferior, private building. Unfortunately, Wheatley's act was curtailed in 1926, local authorities were seriously hampered as a result, and what looked like a massive onslaught in the late '30s turned out to be a mere holding operation. It has been noted that in Aberdeen combined efforts of local authorities and private enterprise between 1919 and 1939 ' did little more than mitigate the acuteness of the housing shortage '.[14] Give or take a little, the judgment is of general validity and applies equally well to Glasgow, Dundee, Edinburgh, and many other parts. In the whole Highland area,

[12] R. W. Lyman, *The First Labour Government*, p. 152.
[13] Paton, *Left Turn!*, p. 148.
[14] *Third Statistical Account of Scotland, Aberdeen*, p. 123.

for example, only 4,000 new houses were built in the inter-war period.

Paradoxically, the one other bright spot in the government's indifferent record ensured its fall. MacDonald acted as foreign secretary and as such did well; but in attempting to negotiate a much needed trade treaty with Soviet Russia he came too near success for Lloyd George's liking. The bolshevik bogey was resurrected, and by ill luck government ineptitude handed the opposition a gift in the shape of the Campbell case. J. R. Campbell, as temporary editor of the communist *Workers' Weekly*, printed an article that was held to be seditious. Hastings, the attorney-general, was not much of a lawyer and less of a politician. He initiated a prosecution but dropped it when he learned from Maxton, the ' conchie ', that Campbell had had a distinguished war record! The opposition seized its opportunity and pushed it unscrupulously. MacDonald, worn out and sickened by the abuse of his left-wing critics, fumbled the matter, thus precipitating his government's fall.

The Campbell case posed in blatant form the dilemma that had confronted the Labour movement since the foundation of the Communist Party of Great Britain in 1920. In Scotland John Maclean had denounced the C.P. as a mere tool of the Kremlin; but in spite of this rebuff the Scottish contribution to the new party was considerable. Gallacher's sturdy individualism was overcome by personal contact with Lenin, who had lampooned him in his stinging pamphlet *Left Wing Communism an Infantile Disorder*.[15] Unable to resist the blandishments of the great revolutionary, Gallacher returned to Scotland determined to follow Lenin's instructions that a united British Communist Party should be formed and that it should use classical bolshevik tactics of infiltration.[16] Every vestige of anarcho-syndicalism and of sectarianism was to be eradicated, the Labour movement was to be courted, and parliament was to be undermined from within. Not without difficulty, for there was some pressure for maintaining a separate Scottish party, Gallacher succeeded early in 1921 in persuading the majority of the Scottish Communist Party to join

[15] V. I. Lenin, *Selected Works* (1947), II. 615-18, in which Gallacher is praised for his zeal but flayed for his naïve tactics.

[16] W. Gallacher, *Revolt on the Clyde*, pp. 251-3, and more fully in its sequel *Rolling of the Thunder*, ch. 1.

the C.P.G.B.,[17] and Arthur Macmanus, another Clydesider, became its president. The Labour Party, alarmed by these developments and not unaware of Lenin's plans, refused a request for affiliation, although individual communists could still belong to Labour Party local branches or even be returned to parliament as Labour M.P.s. As the C.P. was steadily ' bolshevised ' (to the ultimate discomfort of the Clydeside comrades Macmanus, Bell and Gallacher) this created an awkward predicament for the Labour Party. In Scotland the C.P. was weak: its forerunner, the shortlived Scottish Communist Party, had boasted of 4,000 members but probably had in fact a mere 200.[18] Electorally, the Communists made no progress. Their one member in this period in Scotland was Walton Newbold who sat briefly for Motherwell from 1922 to 1923; but their discipline and tenacity made them formidable beyond their numbers. And, of course, their activities (which could easily be exaggerated) furnished excellent propaganda for the parties of the right. Conservatives and Liberals rarely missed an opportunity to equate ' socialism ' with ' bolshevism '.

The Campbell case afforded such an opportunity and may indeed have inspired the mysterious, but almost certainly spurious, ' red letter ' which purported to be from Zinoviev, head of the Comintern, to Macmanus, president of the C.P.G.B. If the Zinoviev letter was to be believed, the C.P. was to carry out a thorough programme of subversion in Britain, using the Labour party as a dupe. Quite apart from the bombshell of the Zinoviev letter and MacDonald's feeble reaction to it, the Labour movement was ill prepared for the general election of October 1924. The government had been uninspiring, there was a growing rift between right and left, and many stalwarts of the I.L.P., headed by Wheatley and Maxton, were suspicious of the Labour Party leadership. For its part, the right of the movement was bent upon securing the radical Liberal vote, and this the *gaucheries* of the left made exceedingly difficult. The result was a great Conservative victory (414 seats); but Labour (with 151) again formed the main opposition, the Liberals returning a bare 42. In Scotland the swing to the right was not so marked as in England and Wales, though still substantial. The Unionists won 38 seats,

---

[17] H. Pelling, *The British Communist Party: a Historical Profile*, ch. 1.
[18] T. Bell, *Pioneering Days*, p. 195.

making gains at the expense of the Liberals who managed to return only 9 members. The socialists secured 27. Clearly, the most significant result of the general election of 1924 was the decline and fall of the once great Liberal Party.

Baldwin's leisurely if not devious policy seemed to complete the rout of Labour, both politically and industrially. Unemployment continued to defy remedy; and the coal industry's troubles culminated in the ' general strike ' of 1926. Under the militant leadership of A. J. Cook—Welsh evangelical turned Marxist—the miners refused to accept cuts in wages and managed to secure the backing of many other unions, notably those of the railway and transport workers. The I.L.P., swinging steadily to the left under Wheatley and Maxton, was ready to support the strike; but it was mismanaged and the I.L.P.'s services were not requisitioned. After a week of stoppages and effective countermeasures by government in May 1926 the strike was called off, to the decent relief of MacDonald and the other leaders of the Labour and trade union movement. Only the miners carried on the bitter, hopeless struggle. The I.L.P. was infuriated, especially at the ease with which the Conservative government introduced and passed a more stringent Trade Union Act outlawing the ' general strike ' and obliging trade unionists to ' contract in ' rather than ' out of ' the levy for Labour party funds. From that point onwards the sporadic sniping between the I.L.P. and the Labour Party developed into open hostilities.

Baldwin's approach to the general election of May 1929 was too easy-going. His election address actually held up the export of British broccoli to the continent as a sure portent of the solution of Britain's economic problems; but in point of fact these problems were increasing rather than diminishing. The balance of payments was still some £100 million in Britain's favour, but the surplus was accounted for by ' invisibles '—shipping revenue, insurance, and banking. The gap between imports and exports was steadily widening—broccoli or no broccoli. Both the Liberal and Labour parties showed some awareness of these pressing economic problems and their social sequelae, but neither party could put forward any precise plans. Labour was returned as the largest single party with 289 seats to the Conservatives' 260 and the Liberals' 58. Again the Scottish results leaned more heavily to the left, Labour winning 38 of the 74 constituencies, Unionists 22, and Liberals 14.

MacDonald's second cabinet was constructed on pretty much the principles of 1924, except that Wheatley was excluded. The only I.L.P. members of note, both admitted to minor office, were Shinwell and Tom Johnston, both of whom were fighting the leftward tendencies of Wheatley and Maxton. The exclusion of Wheatley was MacDonald's idea, both Snowden and Henderson arguing that it would be wise to include him if only to placate the left.

Like its predecessor, the second Labour government had no luck. As a minority government it was again dependent on the Liberals. No sooner was it in office than the great depression of 1929 began, sparing Britain its worst effects at first but still pushing up the rate of unemployment. MacDonald found to his dismay that he depended not only upon the approval of Lloyd George but also on that of John Wheatley, M.P. for Shettleston. Indeed, the opposition of the Wheatley-Maxton group was more dangerous to the government than that of the Conservatives, who were divided over the old free-trade versus protection issue. The I.L.P. caucus was in fact making a bold bid to dictate to the parliamentary Labour Party, and like most enthusiasts they were genuinely bewildered when their assaults provoked retaliation. Too late Wheatley saw the danger, but he collapsed and died in May 1930 before he could prevent a head-on collision. Within weeks of his death the caucus virtually formed a separate group in parliament, bound not by the parliamentary Labour Party's decisions but by those of the I.L.P. conference. Backed, however, by most M.P.s of the I.L.P. group, the Labour party retaliated and there then ensued almost two years of bitter and at times sordid struggle. Maxton's inept leadership must bear a large part of the blame, as even his close associates in the struggle later acknowledged, though in guarded terms.[19] When in August 1931 MacDonald and some of his closest colleagues, panicked by the financial crisis, entered into a National government with Conservatives, a few Liberals, and some of the parliamentary Labour Party, it proved no anodyne to the left. The Labour Party, regrouping under Arthur Henderson, saw plainly enough that a sizeable if not major contribution to MacDonald's 'apostasy' had been made by the refractory neo-marxist caucus that wielded, none too scrupulously, the central organisation of the I.L.P. Reconciliation proved impossible, and in 1932 the break

[19] John Paton, *Left Turn!*, ch. 11, ' False Prophet ', pp. 287-315, 399, and *passim*.

between the Labour Party and the I.L.P. was completed. The I.L.P. rapidly faded into insignificance, especially after a costly and revealing flirtation with the Communists. The Labour Party slowly recovered its strength, emerging as a more cohesive and disciplined, if somewhat more prosaic, organisation.

In the circumstances it is not surprising that in the general election of October 1931 the National government scored the greatest electoral victory ever in British history. Conservatives, National Labour, and National Liberals among them took 533 seats, Labour a mere 52, and the independent Liberals 6. The National government was in essence a Conservative government, though MacDonald continued as prime minister. That there was something spurious about the crisis that had produced it was suggested by a remarkably empty king's speech at the opening of the new session. If the financial crisis was as desperate as had been alleged, surely it would have called for a bold remedial programme. There was none such. The one major step achieved, imperial preference, proved to be a paper shield in a world by then devoted to economic nationalism. Lack of policy and absence of drive allowed the depression to linger over Britain, and particularly Scotland, for longer than it did in other countries. It may be that the very magnitude of the National government's majority—comfortably renewed in 1935—inhibited any sense of urgency in dealing with social and economic problems. The drift of population and industry to the Midlands and south-east of England and the continuing prosperity of these areas also obscured the issues. The result was one of the most miserable chapters in the story of Scotland.

The steel and shipbuilding industries had struggled through the '20s hampered not only by the fluctuations of world trade but also by their own ageing plant and obsolescent techniques. Shipbuilding failed to keep pace with new methods of production and in particular neglected the growing importance of welding. The industry was weakened too by the increasing debility of the Scottish steel industry, occasioned largely by a decline of pig-iron production which led to overdependence on imported pig-iron and scrap. In these circumstances, the location of the steel and iron industry, once so favourable, was disadvantageous: the need was for a completely integrated new plant situated on the navigable Clyde. Such a scheme, recommending Renfrew as the site, was submitted in 1929 by the American expert, Henry Brassert, but it was turned down in favour of partial renovation of the old inland sites. Throughout the '20s these two basic industries—steel and shipbuilding—though stagnant could not be said to be absolutely depressed; but by 1931 they were in the grip of a deadly depression, the end of which none could foresee. The rusting hull of No. 534 in John Brown's shipyard at Clydebank symbolised the waste and frustration of these bitter years. When work on the *Queen Mary* was at last resumed in 1934, it was thanks largely to the ceaseless prodding of David Kirkwood. Nor was the depression restricted to the heavy industries; Dundee found it increasingly difficult to compete with cheap Indian labour, and the jute trade languished; and, apart from quality wool products, the textiles as a group suffered similarly. By 1933 over 30% of insured persons in Scotland were unemployed, and many of those in employment had no security. It is fashionable now to claim that the depression was marginal, that its effects were local, temporary, or in some way restricted; but to the regions mainly afflicted these philosophical reflections have little relevance. The depression has left a deep scar on Scottish society.

Central Scotland in 1934 was classed as a ' special ' or ' development ' area, in which new light industries were to be induced to settle. The first industrial estate opened at Hillington near Glasgow in 1937, but the new light industries did not cure the depression. That was accomplished by the rise of Adolf Hitler to power in Germany and Britain's slow agonising drift from collective security to defensive re-armament; and, paradoxically, re-armament was seriously hampered by the drift of key workers away from the uncertainties of the vital heavy industries. During the depression these had undergone rationalisation and financial integration: thus, Colville's merged with Dunlops to form a virtual steel monopoly, while in shipbuilding the financial structure became extremely complex and ramified into related industries throughout the U.K. It would have been well for the country if economic streamlining had accompanied these financial rationalisations. The blunt fact is that it did not. When every allowance is made for the grave difficulties of these years, Scottish entrepreneurs showed remarkably little initiative. Their main concern seems to have been to shuffle the blame on to their grandfathers. But as has been well said, the pontificating captains of industry of the inter-war period were not, as they liked to assume, the accusers but rather the accused: men like Sir James Lithgow or Lord Maclay ' have not a prerogative of wisdom and common sense. They have a record of failure and decline. They are facing a charge, summoned to give an account of their stewardship, to explain how and why, under their guidance, the welfare of their country has been so gravely and so uniquely damaged.'[20]

It is obvious now, and did not altogether escape notice then, that while Scotsmen continued to play a leading role in politics Scotland did not. Bonar Law, MacDonald, Wheatley, Maxton, and even Macmanus and Gallacher (covering the political spectrum) were all figures of note but in a United Kingdom rather than a Scottish context. In politics, as in economic affairs, the trend was towards centralisation and standardisation. One notable means of national self-expression was lost by the collapse of the Liberal Party, for the Scottish Liberals had never tamely accepted orders from London. The Scottish Unionists, on the other hand, though they had all the trappings of independence, had never really evolved policies of their own, and centralisation was a boon to them. They remained content to underwrite Conservative programmes with the mere addition of a few homespun examples. The Labour movement had a more troubled transition to the centralised monolithic structure that emerged after 1932. Roughly speaking, for most Scottish socialists the more left they were the less nationalist in outlook. Internationalism, which was a prominent feature of left-wing thinking, softened the decline of Scottish influence. Apart from John Maclean, there was little sign of national consciousness among the Communists and indeed much interesting evidence to the contrary. The Glaswegian Tom Bell, describing his visit to Moscow in 1921, marvelled that he, ' a worker from insular little England ', should have lived to see such glory.[21] The rumbustious Gallacher had a deep affection for the proletariat of Clydeside and the mining area of West Fife, but for Scotland itself—past or future—he apparently felt little or nothing. John Paton, a devoted I.L.P. organiser, loved London, which he regarded as a deliverance from the ' kailyaird ' atmosphere of his native Aberdeen or the crude realities of Glasgow.[22] Maxton cared passionately for the well-

[20] G. M. Thomson, *Scotland That Distressed Area*, pp. 64-5.
[21] T. Bell, *Pioneering Days*, p. 231.   [22] J. Paton, *Left Turn!*, pp. 180 ff.

being of the people of Scotland (indeed, for people anywhere) but his nationalism appeared only in fits and starts, consisting usually of outbursts of platform rhetoric drawn from him by his audience. Thus in April 1924 at a Scottish home rule demonstration in St Andrew's Hall in Glasgow he proclaimed his ambition to make 'the English-ridden, Capitalist-ridden, landlord-ridden Scotland into a Scottish Socialist Commonwealth '.[23] The very language, so reminiscent of Scottish presbyterian dissent, was diagnostic of the theological concept of politics which deeply coloured left-wing thinking, with its concern for orthodoxy and the creation of a world-wide communion of believers. Others, notably Tom Johnston, the Reverend James Barr and David Kirkwood, were less visionary and more practical. They felt strongly about Scotland and were not ashamed to appear as patriots of a sort that rather went out of fashion in the '20s. They were concerned about the 'here and now', and were not in the least excited by the promise of future utopias. Their practical bent enabled them to shrug off charges of parochialism. They confidently looked to their records and were justified in doing so, for in terms of actual achievement they eclipsed not only Wheatley, Maxton and their Scottish colleagues of the left but those of all other parties as well.

The Great War and the recognition of the principle of nationality at Versailles stimulated the home rule movement, which was again affected by the Irish struggle. Almost as influential was the weakness of the administration revealed by the strains of war. The congestion of parliament, the ill effects of which the Scots had denounced for well over half a century, was by 1918 a generally acknowledged fact, and ways and means of relieving the load on parliament were considered by a Speaker's Conference in 1919. Two views emerged: one body of thought recommended the setting up of area Grand Councils rather on the model of the Scottish Grand Committee which had functioned fitfully since 1894; the home rulers refused to accept this and countered with a demand for a federal constitution for the U.K. with subordinate parliaments for Ireland, Scotland and Wales. But as one authority concludes: ' the cause of " federalism " in England was dead as soon as Englishmen understood what it meant '.[24] In other words,

[23] G. McAllister, *James Maxton: the Portrait of a Rebel*, p. 152.
[24] Sir R. Coupland, *Welsh and Scottish Nationalism*, pp. 330-1.

English nationalism was the least publicised but most potent of all in Britain. Federalism was not quite dead, however, for the Irish treaty of 1921 realised it in the shape of the Ulster parliament. The value of this working model was soon apparent and agitation for a similar boon continued in Scotland. In 1924 a federal home rule bill was introduced by George Buchanan, socialist M.P. for Gorbals, and supported by the entire Scottish Labour representation. MacDonald, who like Keir Hardie had before the war been a confirmed home ruler, professed sympathy with the bill; so did the Liberals, but in the face of Conservative and Unionist hostility the prime minister deemed it prudent to let the matter drop. Yet the practical case for home rule was too strong to be ignored. A particularly bad episode in 1925 made even the Conservatives ponder the situation. An expensive and time-consuming farce was enacted at Westminster over an inquiry into a proposed bill to extend Glasgow city boundaries. The tribunal was composed of English M.P.s who knew little of Scotland and nothing of the legal quiddities involved. Scots advocates as ' expert witnesses ' had a field day, collecting inflated fees for the most trifling services. The cost was estimated at £200,000: an expensive, but by no means isolated or singular, lesson in the need for devolution.[25]

The Conservative answer was to upgrade the Scottish secretary to a full secretary of state in 1926, and two years later this was followed by a reorganisation of the three offices (health, agriculture and prisons) for which the secretary was responsible to parliament. This policy of piecemeal reform culminated in 1939 in the removal of the various Scottish departments from Whitehall to St Andrew's House in Edinburgh. Thereafter, Scotland had all the appearance of a separate administration, though how far this was a reality could be debated. Connected with these developments was the other notable Conservative reform of this period, that of local administration. A system that would operate efficiently at all levels in a country as diversified as Scotland has proved far to seek, for what works well in industrialised urban areas is apt to have little relevance in a depopulated countryside. For the Highlands and Islands the system that evolved in the nineteenth century, with the emphasis on boards and *ad hoc* local bodies, was promising; but in fact it worked no wonders owing largely to lack of co-ordination and of effective liaison with the

[25] T. Johnston, *Memories*, pp. 62-3.

central government. By the Local Government (Scotland) Act of 1929 the parish councils and similar bodies were abolished and authority vested in larger units, either in county or burgh councils. Four of the largest burghs (Glasgow, Edinburgh, Dundee and Aberdeen) were ranked as counties and received oversight of the full range of local government, including health, education, and police. The larger burghs retained considerable functions, but the small burghs were divested of authority except for housing (then a comparatively minor charge), lighting, and cleansing. The concentration of power in larger units looked workmanlike at the time, but before long some obvious cracks appeared in the new structure. Some of the county authorities, especially those in the north and west, simply did not have the resources efficiently to discharge their functions, even when income from rates was supplemented by grants from the central government.

But administrative reform and mild devolution could not stem the upsurge of national feeling. The Local Government Act of 1929 (by obliterating the really local in favour of centralised control of larger units) may well have fanned resentment. Nationalism also was powerfully influenced by a literary revival (headed by C. M. Grieve, better known by his pen name, Hugh MacDiarmid), which sought to create or re-create a distinct Scottish culture. George Douglas Brown's savage novel *The House with the Green Shutters* (1901) had already effectively demolished the pawky 'kailyaird' school of the late nineteenth century. The post-war nationalist authors continued in this iconoclastic vein: MacDiarmid, in particular, soon became a controversial, astringent writer, almost as good in denunciatory style as his countryman Thomas Carlyle. The movement created a remarkable literature in 'Scots' of some sort or another, either the synthetic 'Lallans' or a thinly disguised current vernacular: it also, however, stressed the Celtic aspect of things Scottish and had an appreciable effect on Gaelic literature and general interest in that language. Later, in the '30s, Leslie Mitchell (also better known by a *nom de plume*, Lewis Grassic Gibbon) brilliantly made use of native Scottish themes in his novels, using a contrived but haunting Anglo-Scots. This rising national consciousness was reflected in the Government of Scotland bill introduced by the Reverend James Barr in 1927. The bill was talked out amid wild scenes, and its loss undoubtedly precipitated the emergence of the National Party of Scotland in 1928.

The National Party was a fusion of at least four small bodies: the Scottish National Movement, the Scots National League, the Scottish Home Rule Association, and the Glasgow University Scottish Nationalist Association. Its main begetter was a young Glasgow solicitor, J. M. MacCormick, who, like many other nationally minded Scots socialists, had given up the I.L.P. in despair. He was aided by such home rule veterans as R. E. Muirhead and R. B. Cunninghame Graham. The aims of the party were ill defined, most contending for ' Ulster ' status but not a few for complete severance from England. Certainly, the party's 1932 manifesto went far beyond Barr's bill, and so alarmed the Unionists as to call forth a counter manifesto, signed by leading industrialists, warning of the economic dangers of separation. With nearly 400,000 unemployed in Scotland in that year it was hard to envisage a worse fate; and for a time it looked as if the Nationalists might make a considerable impact on politics. But the fate of their early candidates in 1929, scant votes and lost deposits, proved to be an accurate forecast of the party's electoral role. Indeed, not to forfeit the deposit came to be hailed as a victory, as in Oliver Brown's candidature at East Renfrewshire in November 1930. The one unexpected triumph was the election of the novelist Compton Mackenzie to the rectorship of Glasgow University in 1931. In spite of some support from the press, particularly Lord Beaverbrook's *Scottish Daily Express*, the movement was unable to advance beyond a promising start. Scottish voters are slow to change their minds, and, while some of the arguments used by the Nationalists (particularly over economic grievances) commanded wide sympathy, certain aspects of the party's activities inhibited its progress.

Nationalist extremists were feared and derided; the movement's left wing bias upset Scots of conservative views; and the old religious bigotry was pressed into service. On the whole, the Nationalists were mainly protestant, and few Roman catholics (apart from Compton Mackenzie) were identified with the party. Yet unscrupulous Unionists alleged that it was a ' popish plot '; MacCormick (a Scots presbyterian) was repeatedly described as an Irish catholic,[26] and the old brainless war-cry that ' Home Rule means Rome Rule ' was raised. As applied to Scotland, this was the most arrant nonsense, and indeed some Scots Roman

[26] J. M. MacCormick, *The Flag in the Wind*, pp. 51-3.

catholics feared that home rule might result in a protestant despotism. But that these were real inhibitions was proved by the rise in 1932 of a small right wing Scottish Party which derived from a breakaway group from the Cathcart Unionist Association in Glasgow. This body, disillusioned with Conservative indifference to Scotland's plight, adopted a moderate home rule programme, attracting the support of the Duke of Montrose, Sir Alexander Macewan, Professor A. Dewar Gibb of the chair of Scots law at Glasgow University, and other rightist nationalists. Not until the National Party had purged its extremists was it able to promote a merger with the Scottish Party in 1934, and then no great results ensued. The resulting Scottish National Party continued to be faction-ridden and failed to make any real electoral progress. The Unionists were more confirmed than ever in their opposition to home rule. The Liberals were in disarray, committed to everything but answerable for nothing. The Labour Party seemed to be pledged to home rule, but it escaped notice at the time that the leader of the party in 1937 gave only the most vague lip service to his party's commitments.[27]

The stresses and strains of the inter-war years also left their marks on the religious life of the community. Marxism and rationalism fostered the growth of unbelief, or to be more precise offered alternative beliefs. The vague agnosticism which had so worried churchmen in the late nineteenth century was reinforced, if not replaced, by militant atheism. Especially in the presbyterian churches some alarm was occasioned by a tendency for attendance to become more irregular, although all denominations had to face this problem. The sabbath continued to be observed but usually in some pharisaical form which sanctioned Sunday 'excursion trains' but not organised games or cinemas. Yet, except for the traditionalist areas dominated by the Free Church in the Hebrides, step by step the churches gave way on this once sacrosanct issue. By the late '30s Sunday golf or the Sunday cinema were by no means unknown. In this perplexed age, with its economic insecurity and its materialist beliefs which could sanction all sorts of profane diversions, the churches seemed to have little to offer the unemployed or the exploited. Conscious of this, the churchmen had to look to their defences; before these

[27] C. R. Attlee, *Labour in Perspective*, p. 154, refers in the most casual way to the need for 'decentralisation' in Scotland and Wales.

new terrors old antagonisms softened. As was well said: ' Giant Pagan, in his modern guise of secularising materialism, is an enemy more to be dreaded than Giant Pope '.[28] Yet the Roman Church continued to be reviled and denounced. Dark fears were entertained of its increasing numbers, of the alleged illiteracy, improvidence, and even criminality of much of its flock. Its clergy were stigmatised as dull bigots, devoid of learning or scholarship. By some peculiar logic, these prejudices were often reconciled with bitter attacks on the Education Act of 1918 and particularly its provision for Roman catholic education. It is noticeable, however, that most of this hostile criticism came from specifically ' anti-popish ' bodies, such as the Orange order or the Protestant Institute. These organisations had no monopoly of bigotry, and certain Roman catholic organs and publicists retorted in kind. On the other hand, the bitterness between presbyterians and episcopalians steadily waned, though in the inter-war period pleas for union were little regarded. Talks were held over the period 1932-4, but they did not advance beyond rather vague statements of mutual goodwill.

The heightened ecumenical spirit of the post-war years gave a new urgency to union negotiations between the Church of Scotland and the United Free Church. Throughout, the Church of Scotland clearly favoured the project, but delay was occasioned by a determined though fair-minded minority in the United Free Church which contended for the full voluntary position. Headed by the Reverend James Barr, the voluntaries refused to be placated by an act of parliament of 1921 which freely conceded spiritual independence to the Scottish establishment. The endowment problem remained; the heritors haggled over the settlement of the teinds; and it took four years of patient labour to resolve the issue. That the legislature had given up the Erastian views that had contributed so much to the troubles of the past was proved again in the act of 1925 which gave the establishment full financial control. In fact, the last vestige of parliamentary control was removed from the Church of Scotland, which achieved ' establishment ' on uniquely favourable terms.[29] The very fact of establishment, however disguised by clever formulas stressing 'recognition',

[28] J. R. Fleming, *The Church in Scotland 1875-1929*, pp. 150-1.
[29] R. King Murray, ' The Constitutional Position of the Church of Scotland ', in *Public Law* (1958), pp. 155-62.

offended the voluntaries and the struggle continued. Barr was by this time a Labour M.P., and, deriving support from the latent anti-clericalism of many of his socialist colleagues, he managed to fight a hard rearguard action in the house of commons. This notwithstanding, the two churches were steadily moving towards union, presbytery after presbytery declaring satisfaction with the proposed terms. Mindful of the aftermath of the union of 1900, the churches took care to obtain favourable legal opinion on property rights, and at last the union was consummated in 1929. The churches rejoiced, the press rejoiced, but no emotive aura surrounds the year 1929 such as still clings to the year 1843. A small minority carried on the United Free Church but in no embittered spirit. Their struggle was not in vain, for it led to the clarification of issues which badly needed to be defined and not just buried in some wordy ' compromise '.

By this time another religious community had established itself in Scotland which, though small, was of some significance. By the end of the eighteenth century the practice of discriminating against Jews had died out and by the opening decades of the nineteenth century a small Jewish colony, which had a synagogue and a burial ground, flourished in Edinburgh. Its members derived mostly from Germany, and so did the bulk of the even smaller congregations which settled in Glasgow and Dundee. For the most part these early Jewish immigrants were merchants and fairly substantial businessmen; but the pogroms in Russia at the close of the nineteenth century swelled their numbers with humbler folk such as tailors, craftsmen, and itinerant salesmen known in Scottish-Yiddish as ' trebblers '. The Glasgow community, heavily concentrated in the Gorbals, became the largest in Scotland, numbering by the mid-1920s about 20,000 souls and having ten places of worship. The precise influence of the Jews on Scottish society is hard to assess but is real enough for all that. They have been, and are, prominent in the garment trade, retail business, warehousing, and so on. In high finance they have produced Sir Isaac Wolfson, head of Great Universal Stores, whom long residence in England has not robbed of pride in his native Glasgow. They have graced the professions that Jews traditionally favour—notably law and medicine. A popular and respected figure in Edinburgh from 1919 until his death in 1945 was the Rabbi Salis Daiches, whose great object was to harmonise

Scottish and Jewish traditions; and, indeed, one of his sons, Professor David Daiches, is now a leading authority on Scottish literature.

It would be too much to claim that anti-semitism is or has been non-existent; but none the less relations between Jew and gentile in Scotland have been remarkably good. In the 1930s, when Fascism was causing disturbances in some parts of England, in Scotland it found no footing, apart from extremely small and quite insignificant cells. There were no street battles in Glasgow, such as took place in London and other large English cities. Probably this tolerant atmosphere can be attributed to the smallness of the Jewish population: yet something is due to the fact that as ' the People of the Book ' the Jews and their beliefs have a fascination for a country much of whose religion was deep rooted in Scripture.[30] Enough of the old Calvinism remains to prevent the Jew being regarded as an entire stranger, nor does the Jew in Scotland see himself as such. Freemasonry has helped to form a bridge between Jew and gentile, the Lodge Montefiore playing an important part in Jewish life in Glasgow, while in Edinburgh Lodge Solomon contains both Jewish and gentile members.

Such, in bald outline, was the condition of Scotland in what proved, unfortunately, to be the interwar period. When on 3 September 1939 Great Britain declared war upon Germany, the decision was accepted in Scotland with rare unanimity. Unlike the first world war the second was regarded by virtually all as just and necessary, and this time no qualifications were admitted. Through six long checkered years sacrifices of every kind were patiently borne—by those at the work bench and in the home no less than those in the armed services—to further what was felt to be a crusade but one devoid of romance.

[30] David Daiches, *Two Worlds: an Edinburgh Jewish Boyhood*, pp. 6, 127.

13

THE SECOND WORLD WAR AND AFTER

At the outbreak of war in September 1939 Tom Johnston, then Labour M.P. for West Stirlingshire, was appointed regional commissioner for Scotland charged with the organisation of civil defence. His knowledge of the country and his impatience with red tape soon marked him out as an administrator of high quality. Churchill was on the lookout for such men, and early in 1941 he insisted on Johnston becoming secretary of state for Scotland. They were two of a kind, and just as Churchill demanded wide powers for the conduct of the war so Johnston would settle for no less in the running of Scottish affairs. He demanded a 'council of state' for Scotland,[1] consisting of all the living ex-secretaries. Churchill admired the 'non party' spirit in which the project was conceived; but, historian that he was, he did not much like the Cromwellian ring of its common title or the fact that it resembled a separate government in embryo. Still, he was for whatever would work, and in the end he consented. Johnston and his council were given what virtually amounted to a free hand, and the result was illuminating. For the duration of the war, the supposed propensity of Scots to quarrel among themselves was stilled. Party postures were given up in favour of getting on with the job, and on most matters of consequence the council acted with a surprising degree of unanimity. This appeared most evidently in a scheme for hydro-electric development in the Highlands, which Johnston had long cherished and which was warmly recommended by an enquiry headed by an energetic and patriotic judge, Lord Cooper. All sorts of objections were

[1] Its official title was 'Scottish Advisory Council of ex-Secretaries', but it was nearly always referred to as the 'council of state'.

advanced then and later, mainly from industrial concerns which feared such an exercise in state capitalism and from unprogressive lairds,[2] categorised by Johnston as ' grouse moor lamenters '. The council stood firm, none more so than the Unionist members, and the North of Scotland Hydro-Electric Board was set up by act of parliament in 1943. In many other ways the thrusting Johnston left his mark. In 1942 he helped to create the Scottish Council on Industry, designed to establish liaison between government and industry; and not without difficulty he managed to promote a separate Scottish Tourist Board. At the secretary's instance, too, Scotland was the first part of the U.K. to operate rent tribunals. He utilised civil defence facilities to pioneer a miniature but highly successful health service in the Clyde valley, and by the end of the war the scheme had been extended to cover much of Scotland. When every allowance is made for the unusual latitude that he enjoyed, Tom Johnston still emerges as easily the greatest of secretaries of state for Scotland. Both the man and his methods were widely appreciated. A colleague in the wartime cabinet has left a revealing description of him working at this level: ' One of the most able men in the technique of getting his own way at cabinet committees was Tom Johnston, the Secretary of State for Scotland. He would impress on the committee that there was a strong nationalist movement in Scotland and it could be a potential danger if it grew through lack of attention to Scottish interests. ... Time has proved that his energetic enthusiasm, even in wartime, was amply justified.'[3] It was perhaps unfortunate for Scotland, though no great misfortune for Johnston himself, that he withdrew from active political life at the end of the war and turned to directing the hydro-electric board where he again rendered great service. Without serious loss of reputation, he could scarcely have served as secretary of state under the terms imposed by the Labour prime minister, C. R. Attlee, whose party had scored a massive victory in the general election of 1945. Under Attlee's government, the Scottish office soon fell from the heights it had attained during the war. It has not risen since.

The second world war, like the first, had profound effects on

[2] T. Johnston, *Memories*, pp. 150, 174 ff.
[3] Lord Morrison, *Autobiography*, p. 199. In stating that his ' energetic enthusiasm ' was amply justified the author refers to the measures carried out by Johnston and not to the alleged dangers from Scottish nationalism, which Morrison dismissed, perhaps mistakenly, as a mere subterfuge.

Scotland: in spite of the skilled advocacy and administrative expertise of Johnston, the demands of war had again strained the country's resources. The real damage inflicted stemmed from failure to maintain the programme of diversification of the economy. Coal, steel, iron, and the products of heavy industry were again at a premium; and by 1945 the heavy industries of Scotland employed 25% of the insured population as against 16% in the summer of 1939. It is pointless to criticise the priorities imposed by the struggle against Nazi Germany and its allies; but the long-term drawbacks have to be considered. As well as emphasising shipbuilding and the production of a wide range of heavy engineering, more might have been done to establish on a permanent basis such new light industries as the manufacture of aircraft and motor vehicles. A little was done in this way but in half-hearted fashion; and, in general, Scotland ' suffered a really raw deal as regards new factory construction during the war '.[4] Only 32 government factories were built there, and this was to have serious consequences once the problems of reconversion to peace-time production arose. In fact, dispersal of industry in the U.K. as a whole was not great, owing largely to the difficulty of moving massive plants. The tendency rather was to reinforce existing industries and so minimise the problems of assembling or retraining the necessary labour force.[5] The effects of the war in diversifying the old stagnant areas, therefore, were marginal.

Scotland, however, had one considerable advantage when at the end of the war reconversion had to be tackled. Apart from the heavy aerial bombardment of Clydeside in March 1941, war damage was negligible compared with that inflicted on England. But the exigencies of the total situation prevented any real exploitation of this advantage. Lack of development capital and a strict system of controls hampered private enterprise; the rigid priorities applied favoured the basic heavy industries—coalmining, steelmaking and shipbuilding. Most of the promising new ventures, such as the manufacture of aircraft and motors, came to an end in the first difficult years of peace, and only after a struggle was the Rolls-Royce engine factory retained at Hillington in Glasgow. The southward drift of industry and men was resumed and continued, in spite of government white papers skilfully

[4] John Gollan, *Scottish Prospect*, p. 11.
[5] M. P. Fogarty, *Prospects of the Industrial Areas of Great Britain*, ch. 11.

compounded of strictures on the past and pious hopes for the future. The archetype of a number of virtually identical white papers on Scottish economic prospects was issued in 1947. In it the sins of the Tory pre-war past were exposed, and the certainty of a prosperous future under Labour was held out. Every sector of the economy was to be transformed, from the sterile crofts of the Outer Hebrides to the tottering coalmining industry of the midland valley. The grand aim was to provide 155,000 more jobs than had existed in 1937.[6] New factories were to spring up in the Development Area (a euphemism for the old ' special area ' in the locations of heavy industry in the west) and new industries were to be persuaded to fill them. New towns, like East Kilbride, were to serve this second and more humane industrial revolution. As for the Highlands, the crofters were to receive more substantial aid, forestry was to be extended, much needed new housing provided, and a Highland Advisory Panel (in the event, devoid of any real powers) was set up under the chairmanship of Malcolm MacMillan, Labour M.P. for the Western Isles. The only substance in this woolly Highland section was provided by the activities of the hydro-electric board,[7] which, however, in the first fine rapture of nationalisation only narrowly escaped being swept into the newly created bureaucratic empire of the electricity boards. As a post-war vision of a brave new Scotland all this was intoxicating; but as a blueprint for action it suffered from being unrealistic. This was noted at the time: Gollan remarked that ' the really serious situation exists that mass unemployment can develop in Scotland ';[8] and *The Scotsman* criticised the white paper for too optimistically ' counting chickens before they were hatched—and some of the eggs may be addled '.[9] Apart from the new towns, all that emerged in practice were some industrial estates, such as those at Newhouse near Glasgow and Kingsway near Dundee. These were welcome in themselves but fell far short of the job target set by the economic survey.

There was, in fact, a vicious circle. Coal was desperately needed and so was steel, but both these industries were too debilitated to render profitable returns on investment. The unpalatable truth obscured at the time was that the coalmining industry of Scotland was on its last legs. The Lanarkshire field, once so rich,

---

[6] Cmd. 7125, *Industry and Employment in Scotland*, p. 10.
[7] *Ibid.*, pp. 20-1.   [8] *Scottish Prospect*, p. 25.   [9] *The Scotsman*, 4 June 1947.

was virtually exhausted, and the grandiose plans for development in the Lothians and Fife rested on unsound geological and economic premises. Considerable capital investment in the Fife coalfield was lost, notably at Rothes Colliery. In many industries oil had already displaced coal and its advance was not to be halted by nationalisation of the stricken coal industry. The money lost in nationalising coal might have been more fruitfully deployed in promoting growth industries. Steel looked healthier, but in fact its plant was still out of date and poorly integrated. In the vital post-war years, when there was a seller's market for all kinds of heavy engineering products, steel proved inadequate for the needs of heavy industry. By 1947 some experts were openly advocating nationalisation as the only solution to the industry's problems. Thus, William Stewart, a former director of Stewarts and Lloyds, stated publicly that the industry was organised as a cartel and was as such more interested in the maintenance of high prices than in the economies of scale.[10] None the less, the steel industry was vital to the economy, and, unlike the ramshackle coal and railway concerns, it had real potential. It is perhaps unfortunate that its period under nationalisation from 1950 to 1951 was so brief as to be inconclusive, whether considered in terms of the industry's well-being or the rationale of public ownership. Since 1951 it has not in the least benefited from being treated as a political shuttlecock. As for shipbuilding (which had expanded to maximum capacity during the war on the Clyde and in Leith and Dundee as well) it too was seriously hampered by shortage of coal and steel. The real problems of the shipyards, however, were masked for the better part of a decade—1945 to 1955—owing to the replacement boom. The yards were slow to accept modern techniques; in most the slovenly layout that had been inherited from the nineteenth century was complacently retained, oblivious of the streamlining and mechanisation that had been pioneered in the United States and elsewhere during the war. Labour relations also perpetuated the outmoded tradition of the founding fathers of trade unionism: ' one union one job ' was still the cry, resulting in numerous demarcation disputes. Yet there was no shortage of work into the early fifties, and this was also true of the locomotive building industry. It was something of a fool's paradise, for it depended on a temporary situation. While the nations devastated

[10] Quoted Gollan, *op. cit.*, pp. 44-5.

by war were slowly restoring their economies, Britain could appear to prosper by simply standing still. But the war-shattered nations did not obligingly adopt the British habit of thinking in Victorian terms or rebuilding on Victorian lines.

The policies of the Labour government involved centralisation; and, in the opinion of some good judges, the result was over-centralisation. The nationalisation of coal, railways, road transport, gas, electricity and for a brief period steel, crashed on regardless of the peculiar problems that afflicted certain areas of the U.K. and notably Scotland. As Walter Elliot, a witty Conservative politician, phrased it: 'for Scotland, nationalisation means denationalisation'. Real power gravitated more and more towards Westminster and Whitehall, a development that proved to be of dubious advantage not only to the economy but to the practice of democracy. The socialist secretaries of state for Scotland, first Joseph Westwood and then Arthur Woodburn, dutifully accepted their diminished roles. The change in emphasis did not pass unnoticed or uncriticised, nor were the critics all political nationalists by any means. The Scottish Labour party conference of 1947, normally a quiet enough affair, had its peace disturbed by some sharp calls to the government to keep the supposed Labour commitment on home rule. This had no effect other than to encourage the Scottish Nationalists who, elated by the return of Dr Robert MacIntyre for Motherwell at a by-election in April 1945, had held high hopes of the general election of 1945. These hopes were dashed, for in the general election the party made an extremely poor showing. Dr MacIntyre, who in the brief period of his membership of parliament had played a vigorous but unconventional role, failed to retain his seat; and no other Nationalist candidate came within measurable distance of success, most of them forfeiting their deposits.

The Scottish National Party was going through an extremely difficult phase, and, riven with internal disputes, it was unable to make much capital of Scotland's troubles. The party had become almost a joke, notorious for its factious disputes and the wild utterances of some of its best known adherents. Much of this stemmed from an acrimonious division in 1942 when the moderates, William Power and John MacCormick, were defeated by the activists headed by Douglas Young, a Greek scholar and modern makar. Young had been imprisoned for refusing conscription, not, needless to say, because of any sympathy with Hitlerism (which, as a left-winger, he loathed) but simply on the grounds that only a Scottish government could requisition his services. His election to the chairmanship seemed to the moderates to cast the party in a dangerously unpatriotic light; MacCormick, too, by this time had almost a proprietorial interest in the party, and he resented the defeat of his nominee, Power. MacCormick, rather huffily, and Power, reluctantly, withdrew with their supporters to form a new body called Scottish Convention. They did so under considerable provocation, for their critics lacked manners. The break was violent and led to over a decade of squabbling, especially among the activists within the S.N.P. Internal strife and crude electioneering techniques doomed the S.N.P. to another round of forfeited deposits and endless sneers at the follies of 'Scotnattery'. For a time it seemed that the Scottish Convention would serve the nationalist cause better by other means. Its tone was moderate, studiously non-party, and it had a broad appeal. In 1947 the convention called together a 'Scottish National Assembly', which was well attended and represented most sections of opinion in Scotland. It even included some members of the Unionist party, and *The Scotsman*, though Unionist in sympathies, went so far as to describe it as 'the most representative gathering of its kind ever brought together in Scotland'.[11] The national assembly demanded parliamentary devolution but failed to impress either Prime Minister Attlee or Scottish Secretary Arthur Woodburn. The latter, stung by increasing criticism of his conduct of affairs, became a strong opponent of home rule. A brief white paper of 1948, which appeared shortly after the assembly's delegates had put their case to Mr Woodburn, curtly rejected an enquiry into the question of devolution.[12] This spurred the convention on to new efforts, and MacCormick hit upon the idea of a modern national covenant. The terms of the covenant carefully stressed loyalty to the crown and, somewhat ambiguously, bound its signatories 'within the framework of the United Kingdom to do everything in our power to secure for Scotland a Parliament with adequate legislative authority in Scottish affairs'.[13] Within a week of being launched

[11] *The Scotsman*, 24 March 1947.
[12] Cmd. 7308, *Scottish Affairs: Memorandum on Government Proposals*, p. 4.
[13] J. MacCormick, *The Flag in the Wind*, p. 128 (text of the covenant).

in October 1949 the covenant had 50,000 signatories, by December the number had risen to over 400,000, and in the end it totalled almost two million. This was certainly significant—but of what exactly was the rub. Both Unionists and Labour were for a time alarmed; but as by-elections revealed that the ' covenanters ' had not altered their voting habits the two major parties soon reverted to their old passive attitudes where Scotland was concerned. Yet the covenant movement, though it was rapidly to lose momentum in the mid-1950s, did have some importance, if only by stressing the claims of Scotland. For many the Labour Party's image was tarnished, not only by its inadequate handling of post-war problems but also a seemingly cynical betrayal of pledges on devolution, further aggravated by increased centralisation.

In the general election of February 1950 Labour's majority was drastically reduced, though as usual the swing in Scotland was much less than in England. Labour held 37 Scottish seats in 1945, 3 went to the moribund I.L.P., the Unionists secured 32, independents 2, and Liberals nil. In 1950 the results were Labour 37, I.L.P. nil (the I.L.P. members had joined the Labour party), Unionists 32 and Liberals 2.[14] The reaction was carried further in the general election of October 1951 when for the first time the two major parties tied with 35 seats each, while the Liberal Jo Grimond for Orkney and Shetland was the sole Scottish representative of this once great party. A Conservative administration took office on an avowedly anti-socialist programme which stigmatised nationalisation and planning. To begin with, the loosening of controls had some beneficial effects, but before long the Tories were to regret their blanket condemnation of planning. The plain fact was that Britain's economic malaise could not be cured by even skilful adaptations of nineteenth-century panaceas. But in the 1950s votes seemed to be more important than economic solutions, and the winning of votes became an end in itself. Budgets were openly manipulated to woo electors, and illusory booms were carefully staged to coincide with general elections. The Conservative government's victory in 1955 seemed to confirm the soundness of these tactics and to vindicate its faith in private enterprise. For the first time the Unionists won a majority of the Scottish constituencies, 36 out of 71. The return to Baldwinism

[14] An act of 1948, by abolishing the university seats, reduced the number of constituencies in Scotland from 74 to 71.

seemed to answer well enough; but in reality by the mid-1950s all was far from well. The basic heavy industries in Scotland continued to stagnate,[15] and by 1955 the shipyards were beginning to suffer from overseas competition. The new light industries, free to develop where they would, studiously avoided Scotland and other languishing areas, adding to the congestion of south-east England. The only real advances made in Scotland at this time were by the introduction of American subsidiaries, and by the spontaneous development of the petro-chemical industry at Grangemouth. The old bogey of unemployment appeared once more with the Scottish figure running consistently at double the English rate. In many industries, too, wage rates in Scotland were appreciably lower than in England, though this was to some extent offset by lower rents in Scotland. Only agriculture was on a relatively stable and prosperous basis, partly owing to government subsidies but more to increased mechanisation and skilful utilisation of assets. Scotland's gross agricultural output in 1950–51 was one-eighth of the U.K. total, which, considering the poor to indifferent quality of much of her soil and the vagaries of the climate, is a remarkable tribute to the Scottish farmer. Specialties such as the development of superior strains of potatoes and of beef stock also added considerably to the gross national product. Important social changes accompanied this modern agricultural revolution. The number of owner-occupiers has increased and, apart from the crofting areas, the most influential rural class in Scotland is now that of the capitalist farmer.

In the general election of 1959 the Conservative victory did not extend to Scotland where Labour took 38 seats to the Unionists' 32, with Mr Grimond still ploughing a lone Liberal furrow in Orkney and Shetland. But the Conservative policy of free enterprise and a somewhat inane election slogan, ' You've never had it so good ', were increasingly criticised, particularly in Scotland where the fiscal policy of ' stop-go ' (alternate deflation and reflation) was condemned as hostile to real economic growth. The government at first tended to brush aside deputations from various sectors of Scottish industry, sometimes with uncomplimentary remarks on their ' defeatism '. But the criticisms did not abate, nor were they confined to the government's political opponents. In a discreet way the Scottish Council for Development and

---

[15] For details see A. Cairncross, ed., *The Scottish Economy*.

Industry could be outspoken enough, as was evident in its Toothill
Report on the Scottish economy.[16]   The report found that the
incidence of unemployment in Scotland, whilst by no means as
desperate as it had been in the 1930s, had risen steadily from 1957
onwards.   On the whole, this rather pontifical document followed
the often expressed advice of the council to avoid alarmist talk
lest prospective investors or industrialists should be scared off;
but beneath its veneer of bland optimism it high-lighted some of
the most disturbing features of Scotland in 1960–61.   Scottish
management was condemned as too cautious and lacking adequate
training.   On the other hand, the report held that industrial relations in Scotland were by no means as bad as rumour made out.
The main defects of the economy were itemised: the inability of
the old heavy industries, which still formed the indispensable base,
to adapt to new circumstances, and the failure to introduce
science-based industries.   The report rejected further devolution,
somewhat gratuitously (since it was not in its terms of reference),
on the grounds that the Scottish economy was so inextricably
bound up with that of the U.K. that separate economic policies
would be unworkable.   Yet the Toothill report did not evade the
very real problem that this raised: it recognised that a major difficulty in the U.K.'s situation was regional differentiation, and that
it was self-defeating to submit regions of slow economic growth
to fiscal policies designed for the booming south-east of England,
The report therefore recommended consideration of some such
economic plan as had lately been adopted in France, ' into which
regional policies are integrated '.[17]   It concluded, honestly if not
very helpfully: ' If there is a panacea for Scotland's economic
problems we have not found it '.[18]

The Conservative government's awakening to the underlying
significance of the situation came too late.   Economic stagnation
was not confined to Scotland; the north of England and the west
were also in trouble, and so were Ulster and South Wales. Clearly,
to regard midland and south-eastern England as a norm for the
U.K. could no longer be justified.   What was good for that area
was obviously bad medicine for less prosperous parts.   But short
of planning what could be done?   The government clearly did

---

[16] *Inquiry into the Scottish Economy 1960–61: Report of a Committee appointed by the
Scottish Council (Development and Industry) under the Chairmanship of J. N. TOOTHILL*
(1962).   [17] Toothill Report, p. 170.   [18] *Op. cit.*, p. 181.

not know. In the summer of 1961 a solution was sought in
belated application for membership of the European Economic
Community, an issue on which the electorate had never been
consulted and never seemed likely to be consulted. As far as can
be judged Scottish opinion tended to be favourable, believing that
entry to the common market might open up new and improved
economic prospects, and not in the least dreading absorption or
loss of identity. There was probably a degree of complacent
ignorance in this attitude: but certainly the proposal did not
rouse the same passions in Scotland that it did in England. It
was pointed out that Scotland had had stronger links with the
continent in the past and that these had left their mark on legal
concepts and traditions. Indeed, Scots lawyers, smarting from
centuries of English contempt for the ' barbarous Scotch system ',
eagerly looked forward to burying the sacrosanct English common
law whilst Scots law happily adapted itself to the continental
Roman system; and, bursting to win fresh laurels, the University
of Edinburgh eagerly set about founding a centre of European
Studies. It was a chimera: the lengthy negotiations at Brussels
ended in January 1963 when President de Gaulle of France
rejected the U.K. application, to the anger of the other members
of the community and British complaints of Gallic perfidy. Evidently, there was no panacea for the troubles of the Conservative
administration, which was struggling from the summer of 1963
onwards in a morass of desperate expedients and unwelcome
domestic scandals. Of the Conservative prime minister it has
been said, ' Had Job been a politician his ill-luck stories would
have paled into insignificance beside those of Harold Macmillan'.[19]
On grounds of ill-health Mr Macmillan gave up the premier-
ship, to be succeeded after a prolonged struggle by Sir Alec
Douglas-Home, formerly Earl of Home, who under the terms of a
recent act had renounced his peerage. Sir Alec's brief spell as
premier coincided with the return to a planned economy.

In the pre-planning period of Conservative administration
John S. Maclay as secretary of state for Scotland had been
heavily, though in many respects unfairly, criticised for inertia.
In fact, he did some important background work, persuading
industry that Scotland was neither as black nor as red as it was
painted. Though the ablest of Tom Johnston's successors, Mr

[19] *Annual Register* (1963), p. 30.

Maclay could not dictate cabinet policy. His successor (from July 1962), Mr Michael Noble, Unionist M.P. for Argyll, was fortunate enough to enter office when ' Conservative planning ' was introduced as the nostrum for Scotland's ills. The Conservative plan for Scotland that finally emerged was somewhat tentative and incomplete. It applied only to central Scotland and aimed at promoting growth areas for new industries rather than resuscitating the old. At the same time, it was indicated that the needs of other areas were under consideration and that eventually plans for their development would be forthcoming. The older industries were not entirely neglected, and after a great deal of political pressure a much needed steel strip mill was sited at Ravenscraig near Motherwell. This was essential to the establishment of a car industry, which made a promising start with a B.M.C. plant at Bathgate and a Rootes factory at Linwood near Paisley. But this was offset by the depression in shipbuilding, six of the 25 Clyde yards having been forced out of business; and transport problems were a further complication. The nationalised British Railways had suffered severely from road competition, their own efficiency was suspect, and in 1961 Dr Richard Beeching was brought over from Imperial Chemical Industries to investigate the state of the railways. His report in March 1963 showed that many lines in Britain were either unnecessary or hopelessly uneconomic. The doctor prescribed some radical surgery, the effect of which would have been further to depress the north and the south-west of Scotland. Local opinion was outraged and soon organised into pressure groups, which contended that Dr Beeching's conclusions were based on inadequate data and that the entire question needed to be reviewed not just in terms of accountancy but of social economics as well. There was substance in the argument, for Britain's malaise too easily confounds economics and cost accountancy. Furthermore, the existing roads in the areas of proposed closure—and indeed to some extent in Scotland as a whole—are not up to modern requirements. Mr Noble had a harassing time, but he did manage eventually to secure a partial suspension of the operation. The construction of the road bridges over the firths of Forth and Tay also began under the Conservatives, but detracting from the credit claimed by the politicians was the long gestation of these projects, which had been mooted for over thirty years.

Mr Noble put a cheerful face on things, constantly referring to jobs ' in the pipeline ', which, unfortunately, stubbornly refused to emerge at the Scottish end. This defect was ruthlessly exposed by Mr Noble's opposite number on the Labour front bench, Mr William Ross, M.P. for Kilmarnock, who conveyed the impression that he had a firm grasp not only of the problems but of the answers as well. And answers were badly needed; for undoubtedly in the period 1962–4 there was much disillusionment with both major parties in Scotland. The Liberals and Scottish Nationalists—both pledged to home rule—were attracting more sympathy than hitherto. The pragmatic approach of the Liberals appealed at a time when the ideologies of Socialists and Unionists had both been tried and found wanting. The S.N.P., too, had managed to slough off its wilder elements, and the party was busy elaborating a sober and, given its premises, sensible programme. In 1962 the membership of the S.N.P. was about 2,000, but by 1964 it had risen to over 20,000 with many new branches spread over most parts of Scotland. The Nationalism of the 'sixties was obviously more broadly based than hitherto, deriving support from most sections of the community.

Too much perhaps should not be read into it, but in fact the general election of October 1964 was won and lost in Scotland. There the Unionists were heavily beaten, holding only 24 seats; Labour secured 43, gaining three from the Unionists, while the Liberals won three Highland constituencies (Caithness and Sutherland, Ross and Cromarty, and Inverness-shire) bringing their total to four, shortly thereafter increased to five when a Liberal won Roxburgh and Peebles at a by-election. Clearly, the Unionists were out of favour. Their biggest humiliation occurred in West Lothian where an S.N.P. candidate, Mr W. Wolfe, polled well, taking second place to Labour. In six years the Scottish Tories had lost 13 seats and had suffered dangerously reduced majorities in others. Some of this was attributed to faulty organisation, which had defied all efforts at remedy from 1960 onwards. The Eastern and Western Divisional Councils went their own ways, stubbornly resisting efforts to impose central authority on them. The sharp reverses of October 1964 forced the divisional councils to capitulate. Early in 1965 they were abolished and replaced by five regional groups under the firm control of a Scottish Conservative Central Office. The old Unionist label was on the way out. The aim was clear: as Mr Edward Heath, who became leader of the Conservative party shortly after the general election, stated in a tour of Scotland in September 1965, such a Tory debacle ' must not happen again '.[20]

The Labour government, however, with Harold Wilson as premier, had to struggle on with a narrow majority of four, the swing to his party not having been as great in England and Wales as it was in Scotland. Mr Ross became secretary of state for Scotland, but puzzled many by long weeks of unwonted silence. He finally emerged metamorphosed, radiating the bland optimism which he had so recently denounced in his Tory opponent; and Mr Noble, for his part, became nothing if not critical. It was a deft quick-change act, the humour of which was noted and appreciated by the press. It was suspected, too, that Mr Ross could not produce his plans too quickly because of the magnitude of the problems which, according to his own recent utterances, had to be faced; and besides it was well known that Mr Noble had had further plans in view. The first instalment of a new deal for Scotland was a Highland Development Council;[21] but apropos of it, one incongruous feature was soon apparent. The North of Scotland Hydro-Electric Board, which almost alone of government sponsored bodies had a record of success, was soon fighting for its life. The Dick-Campbell report concluded that hydro-electricity, as compared with coal-fired generating stations, was uneconomic;[22] but since the troubles of the coal industry were not considered by the enquiry, many felt that the case against the hydro-electric board was overstated. Moreover, the estimates on which the Dick-Campbell report was based were alleged to be erroneous, and so far this charge does not seem to have been rebutted. The South of Scotland Electricity Board, a bureaucratic but not notably successful or popular body, was poised to take over. All the old arguments against the hydro-electric board, word for word those which Tom Johnston had contemptuously swept aside twenty years earlier, were resurrected. Probably the most signifi-

[20] Reported in *The Scotsman*, Thursday, 16 September 1965, p. 13.

[21] The necessary legislation was passed in August 1965—*Annual Register* (1965), p. 52.

[22] *Scottish Development Department: Report of Public Inquiry into North of Scotland Hydro-Electric Board's Constructional Scheme number 39 (Fada-Fionn Project) and Constructional Scheme number 39 (Laidon Project)* (October 1965). It is usually referred to as the Dick-Campbell report.

cant political development of this sterile period was the way in which public opinion rallied to the defence of the hydro-electric board. Bureaucracy had to retreat, and, for the time being at least, the hydro-electric board was spared. Quite apart from its ability to generate electricity, the board was the one body with experience and skill on which the newly instituted development council could rely.

Then in January 1966 appeared the much heralded Labour 'Plan' for Scotland.[23] Its pedigree was clearly Toothill out of the white paper on industry and employment of 1947. Generally, it received a warm welcome, though with some truth Mr Noble described it as 'most emphatically not a national plan. It is a dull and longwinded document on the Scottish economy.'[24] Certainly, its descriptive and diagnostic passages could not claim the charm of novelty, nor would its literary merits have stimulated its sale. But these are the hallmarks of the *genre*, and it would be unfair to assess the 'Plan' on these grounds alone. It pinpointed the obvious economic ills of Scotland and its prescriptions made sense. The older industries had to be streamlined and modernised. Loss of jobs in this sector of the economy had to be countered by massive retraining and redeployment for new growth industries, notably cars, electronics, and so on. Except for the Edinburgh, Leith and Portobello Employment Exchange areas, the whole of Scotland was to be treated as a development centre in which investment grants of 40% would be available for new industrial enterprises. Over the projected period it was forecast that public investment in Scotland would total nearly £2,000 million. Two essential objects were to create more work to lower the dangerously high rate of emigration and also to attempt to revive certain declining areas such as the Borders and the north-east. The Highlands and Islands, as usual, came off worst in the white paper: the Highland Development Council was expected to attend to the needs of that area, though the plan clearly implied that the main hopes for its future lay in the extension of forestry (with paper pulp mills such as that recently set up at Fort William) and tourism. As a declaration of intent, all this was admirable; the real question that remained to be answered was whether it could be implemented. As a plan it deserved the warm welcome

[23] Cmd. 2864, *The Scottish Economy 1965 to 1970, a Plan for Expansion.*
[24] As reported in *Scottish Daily Express*, 27 January 1966.

that it received, but acclaim must wait on achievement. It may be long withheld, for the budget of 1967 was, in the opinion of many expert commentators, the epitaph of the famous ' Plan '66 '.

Indeed, from its very inception the omens for the government's economic plan could never have been described as bright, for in 1965 the coal and shipbuilding industries in Scotland had received severe jolts. Throughout the 1950s coal output had steadily declined while costs had soared. In desperation the government forced the coal board to take drastic steps to eliminate uneconomic pits and at the same time conserve the labour force. The Scottish Division of the National Coal Board in 1962 reviewed the situation and forecast the closing of 27 pits by 1965. The miners had by this time lost confidence in the board and its pronouncements, particularly since in that same year each region had to charge ' economic prices '. This meant that the hard-hit Scottish mines had to sell coal at 15s. a ton higher than other more favourably placed regions in the south. Competition from other fuels increased, and by 1965 the Scottish mines were incurring heavy annual losses. The government again exerted pressure on the coal board, which introduced a plan for massive contraction of the U.K. industry. Of Scotland's 71 remaining pits 23 were scheduled to close by 1970, and the fate of another 13 was uncertain. An additional increase of 10s. in the ton on Scottish coal was imposed. The board put a brave face on things: by 1970 production was expected to rise to over 40 cwt. per man output and the efficient remaining pits would produce 13 to 14 million tons of coal in 1970–1. But even if this target were to be reached, how many consumers would remain, apart from the coal-fired electricity generating stations, and could even these absorb heavy increases in costs? Colville's, the giant of the Scottish steel industry, had no doubts about their own attitude in a harshly competitive world. Faced with the increased cost of coal, they announced that wherever possible they were converting to oil. The drive for smokeless zones has also diminished the domestic consumption of coal. In face of all this, the miners, unimpressed by the coal board's optimism, lobbied persistently, but with little effect, for a stay of execution until such time as alternative employment could be provided for the affected areas. Should, as seems most likely, the national development plan of 1966 turn out to be just another political incantation, then many of the older mining areas will be left derelict.

That same year 1965 produced a crisis in shipbuilding, of which Scotland has about a third of the U.K.'s capacity, based mainly on the Clyde. Since the late 1950s demand had steadily fallen off: in the period 1950–4 the U.K. share of world launchings was 31% but ten years later it had dropped to 13%; and in that same decade Scotland's share of U.K. launchings fell from 38% to 34%. The Clyde yards had kept going by 'micawberism', accepting unprofitable tenders in the hope that something would turn up to stave off bankruptcy. That the overall situation was poor was well known but no one expected the collapse of Fairfield's of Govan, a modernised yard which had enjoyed a fair amount of admiralty custom. The contraction of the Royal Navy forced Fairfield's to accept unremunerative orders for merchant ships, and by October 1965 the firm stood on the verge of liquidation. The government was pressed to intervene, but some econo- mists argued that it would be folly to prop up an inefficient member of a dying industry. On the other hand, a case could be made for preserving a modernised yard and finally in December the shipyard (but not its engineering associate, Fairfield-Rowan) was reprieved by a new consortium based on private enterprise, government support, and trade union co-operation. This was a forward-looking policy which if successful would do more than save Fairfield's. It could well contribute to the renovation of this still important, and perhaps even vital, industry. Other shipyards on the Clyde have had and still have serious difficulties: the unexpected collapse of Fairfield's raises the question of just how bad the situation really is.

The publication of the report of the Geddes Committee on shipbuilding in March 1966 clarified the problems facing the U.K. industry and made some valuable constructive suggestions. It stated roundly that the industry was not only vital but, if the right steps were taken, had real growth potential. A Shipbuilding Board should be set up to co-ordinate construction; the main shipyards (those capable of building vessels of over 5,000 tons burden) should be grouped into larger units, two such groups being recommended for the Clyde, one covering the lower and the other the upper reaches of the river. The policy put forward by Geddes was one of rationalisation, but this time rationalisation was to be accompanied by the introduction of better techniques and business methods. Labour relations would have to be improved, and it was recommended that the unions concerned in shipbuilding should be amalgamated so that no more than five unions should be involved. Flexibility of labour was urged and an end to demarcation disputes. Government aid (but definitely not nationalisation) was recommended during the period of reconstruction to tide the industry over any short term difficulties caused by such revolutionary changes. If the report were implemented, the Geddes committee felt that the major work of reconstruction ·could be carried out by 1970, when the industry ought to be able to compete with its Swedish, German and Japanese rivals. The report was generally well received, but again there was misgiving about the practicability of its recommendations. For one thing, the Geddes report urged that the steel-makers should grant a discount to the shipbuilding industry; but the Scottish steel industry, faced with problems of its own, felt unable to comply. Whether a nationalised steel industry would be any more accommodating is a moot point which may shortly be resolved one way or the other. The government, however, seemed determined to help the shipbuilding industry, by proposing to set up a Shipbuilding Industry Board with powers to extend credit facilities up to £200 m. But as yet all this is in its initial stages and its possible effects cannot be gauged.

The virtuoso performance of Mr Wilson in governing without an effective majority ended in March 1966 and he and his main rival, the leader of the opposition Mr Edward Heath, went to the country in what was admitted on all sides to be a dull campaign. Both Labour and Conservative parties stressed the need to safeguard sterling, to modernise Britain and to take it into Europe. The latter issue was muffled, and indeed to many the parties seemed to speak with one voice except in the matter of recrimination. Throughout, the opinion polls suggested a strong swing to Labour, and after the actual poll on 31 March Labour was indeed returned with a clear majority of 97. In Scotland the swing to Labour was not as marked as it was in the English midlands or Wales; but in spite of some electoral apathy the Labour party continued to forge ahead. The Scottish results were: Labour 46, Conservatives 20, and Liberals 5. But perhaps the most interesting feature of the general election of 1966 in

Scotland was the progress made by the Scottish National Party. The Nationalist vote more than doubled; in three seats their candidates came second, and in most of the 23 constituencies in which S.N.P. candidates stood (many of them for the first time) they polled well, gaining over 5,000 votes in eleven of them and saving 13 deposits. This may not have been the breakthrough triumphantly proclaimed by the Nationalists, but it was a considerable improvement on previous performances and one that opened up interesting prospects. If Labour policies fail, the Nationalists might conceivably make further progress. Their performance at the Pollok by-election in March 1967 and their astonishing victory at Hamilton in the following November confirm this possibility.

And indeed the Labour government, like its much criticised Tory predecessor, found it easier to diagnose Britain's ills than to cure them. Within months of being returned, Prime Minister Wilson—pragmatically swallowing his recent promises—was forced to change his policies. He was pledged never to use the discredited Tory fiscal device of 'stop-go'; but when a voluntary incomes policy failed and inflation continued, in July 1966 the government introduced more massive deflationary measures than any attempted in ' the thirteen wasted Tory years '. It was a feat of considerable legerdemain. Both employers and trade unions were coerced by a government armed with dictatorial powers, the like of which had been unknown in peace-time since Peterloo. Alarmed Scots were assured that their country would be sheltered from the bleak blast: exactly how was not made clear. Predictably, unemployment rose, though the figures did not tell the entire story, for the greatest annual exodus for many years—nearly 50,000—put a more or less respectable gloss on them. Resentment was keen, and in April 1967 Mr Ross spoke with more force than conviction to an unresponsive S.T.U.C. Only a bold *coup*, apparently, could restore the government's prestige. Mr Wilson, who had hedged his common market bets with his usual adroitness, now suffered a total conversion. Europe, after all, was the answer, and in May it was decided that a fresh approach should be made for membership of the E.E.C. The powerful all-party market lobby rejoiced, the anti-market members of the government and of the parliamentary Labour Party maintained a discreet silence, and the British people—giddy with all these somersaults—scarcely knew what to make of it all. Noticeably, however, opinion in Scotland was by no means as favourable to the move as it had appeared to be in 1961, for a widespread opinion, most strongly held by the Nationalists, was that Scotland should have been consulted and that in the event of joining the Community she should have a vote in its councils. On this whole question, neither side produced deep or convincing answers. The Beaverbrook press campaigned against joining the Market; and the University of Edinburgh, aided by a providential windfall, hastily revived its plans for a Centre of European Studies. President de Gaulle then further endeared himself to British chauvinists by pointing out that in essence nothing had changed since the last British application. Clearly, there was some great significance in all this; but exactly what only the future may reveal. Amid this gloom and uncertainty, the Scottish Council for Development and Industry produced a report which claimed that Scotland's export record was better than that of any other part of the U.K. Unfortunately, no one quite knew what to make of the council's statistics or the conclusions that might validly be drawn therefrom. But that the U.K. was in poor case was proved in November 1967 when the £ had to be devalued.

Future historians may well puzzle over the paradox that in an age of economic stagnation social conditions should, on the whole, have shown a marked degree of improvement. Paradoxical or not, it is in no way mysterious. Indeed, the obvious need for social reforms has contributed to the economic problem by absorbing a large proportion of the gross national income and by requiring even more. The bad debt inherited from the past now has to be paid. Of these longstanding social problems housing still remains the greatest, and though much has been done since 1945, as much again remains to be done. In rural parts the problem seems to be on the way to solution. The grim miners' ' raws ' have mostly disappeared, the broken-down unhealthy farm cottages are rapidly being replaced by attractive council houses, and in the Highland and Islands the old traditional hovels are slowly diminishing in number. But in some areas this long overdue social revolution has come too late. Thus, in the parish of Ardnamurchan, where living conditions have greatly improved since the end of the second world war, ' The present community is happy and contented, but there is room for a larger population, and it is felt that, if some industry were introduced, many of the exiles might return '.[25] The same could be said of too many rural parishes in Scotland, Lowland as well as Highland; but it is debatable whether these improvements, if introduced earlier, would have prevented depopulation. Improved transport, particularly from the early 1920s by motor buses and cars, has merely speeded up the exodus, and of the exiles few return. Many of them, in fact, contribute to the chronic housing problem in the county towns and cities of Scotland. In spite of herculean efforts at rebuilding, aided by a policy of overspilling some of the population into new towns, Glasgow still has a massive slum problem and will have for the foreseeable future. Like Glasgow, Aberdeen had until lately its Gallowgate; and some serious social problems— due mainly to overcrowding and inadequate sanitation—still lurk behind the handsome exterior of this imposing city. Much the same is true of Edinburgh, where the town council has been repeatedly criticised for inertia. Dundee reproduces the Glasgow picture on a smaller scale.

The housing problem is not simply a matter of bad living accommodation, unpleasant as that can be; it contributes to Scotland's indifferent bill of health. That Scotland has one of the poorest public health records of any so-called advanced country is not generally publicised. Tuberculosis was a scourge until the 1950s, when new methods of treatment curtailed its ravages. To this extent matters have improved; but no false optimism should be allowed to obscure the established facts. Scotland has a very high mortality rate from ' chest diseases ', and enjoys the unenviable distinction of having the highest known incidence of death from lung cancer—due partly to atmospheric pollution and perhaps to the very ' Scotch ' habit of smoking cigarettes to the last possible puff. The incidence of coronary thrombosis is appreciably higher than in other countries; the reason is unknown, though diet may be a factor. Infant mortality remains higher than in England and Wales;[26] and, to the concern of the public health authorities, rickets, supposedly banished, is reappearing in Glasgow. Mental illness and alcoholism are said to be of higher incidence in Scotland, but in these cases the statistics may reflect

[25] *Third Statistical Account of Scotland, Argyll* (1961), p. 142.
[26] See *Annual Report of Registrar General for Scotland* (1964), ch. 7, Infant Mortality, p. 42, for a most revealing table.

a better than average standard of medical care. None the less, Scotland's bill of health obviously needs close attention. Poor housing, unemployment, relatively lower wages and, in some cases at least, faulty diet probably all contribute to these bad results. A factor of considerable importance, too, is the perpetuation of the slum mentality in what should be adequate accommodation in some of the new housing schemes. As in many other countries, abuse of amenities and anti-social behaviour of all kinds present very serious problems. How far education can supply remedies is debatable.

Educational problems in Scotland are as acute as elsewhere in the U.K., though they differ in substance from the controversies that rage in England. In Scotland the question of comprehensive schooling raises few temperatures. For one thing, the idea of comprehensive schools combining junior and senior secondary activities is not alien to Scottish tradition, although it tends to be opposed by honours graduate teachers who believe that everything should be subordinated to the supply of students for the universities. The relative absence of conflict on this issue in Scotland stems from the fact that there the national system of schools is much more homogeneous than it is in England and Wales. There is not in Scotland the same sense of social cleavage or deprivation at school level. Indeed, there is a strong body of opinion which favours a return to the even more democratic traditions of the past and which regards the ' fee-paying schools ' as anomalies. In Scotland the fee-paying schools are the nearest equivalent to the English grammar schools, but they do not play anything like the important over-all role of their English counterparts. Outside Edinburgh and Glasgow they are of little account; and only in Edinburgh, an increasingly anglicised city, are they objects of almost superstitious veneration. Of ' public schools ' in the peculiar English sense there are very few, and on the whole Scottish opinion does not favour them. The root of the objection to boarding schools seems to lie in a strong sense of family and the feeling that it is unwise to separate young children from their parents. The fact that in the Highlands and Islands children often have to board away from home for secondary schooling is resented, but criticisms are shrugged off by officialdom.

Educational controversies in Scotland, therefore, do not really flourish on accusations of snobbery and counter-accusations of inverted snobbery. The pressing problem is really an administrative one, and in particular how to maintain an adequate supply of teachers. The teaching body is much more professional than it is in England; a far higher percentage of entrants are university graduates and all have to be certificated, that is they have to undergo a period of training in one or other of the nine colleges of education.[26a] Since the end of the second world war the teachers feel that their professional standing has been impaired; they complain of loss of status, relatively low earning power, slow promotion, and an accumulation of clerical work heaped on them by social welfare schemes, none of which they condemn except in so far as they waste valuable and increasingly scarce trained manpower. The administrators put forward ' dilution ' as an answer (that is, the use of uncertificated teachers), but this is steadily resisted by the teaching associations. The main representative of Scottish teaching opinion is the Educational Institute of Scotland (founded in 1847), though of recent years its activities have seemed too staid for many teachers and as a result there has been a proliferation of associations most of which represent only segments of the profession. This has led to some militant talk and has occasioned a poor press for the teachers as a whole. They are, in fact, attempting to do the impossible, namely to educate their masters, the politicians. The teachers also suffer from the disadvantage of having to fight a war on two fronts, on one side against the local education authority and on the other against the Scottish Education Department and its ultimate chief, the secretary of state for Scotland. Thus in spite of considerable expenditure on new and better schools, there is a serious prospect of the educational machine breaking down. The school population has risen—aided after April 1947 by the raising of the leaving age to 15—and the flow of recruits into teaching has steadily diminished, many graduates finding jobs either in industry or the civil service. Classes are in many instances overcrowded, reducing teaching to a mockery. In Glasgow the serious shortage of teachers, especially honours graduates in science and mathematics, has reached crisis proportions, some children receiving only part-time education, and the matter is of fluctuating concern in most urban

[26a] There are seven non-denominational colleges located in Edinburgh, Glasgow, Aberdeen, Dundee, Ayr, Falkirk and Hamilton; and two Roman catholic colleges, one in Edinburgh and the other in Glasgow.

areas, only Edinburgh escaping the blight. In spite of the known facts, the Labour government elected in March 1966 adheres to its policy of raising the school-leaving age to 16 in 1970. Objections are airily swept aside—just as in the 'comprehensive' project— even though most educators feel that this can lead only to the collapse of full-time education or to a farcical parody of it enacted by untrained amateurs operating mindless machines. The growing popularity of the fee-paying schools (a noticeable feature of the post-war period) is a reflection of the unpalatable truth, so persistently glossed over by politicians both local and national, that all is very far from well with the public schools.

In higher education also the last twenty years have witnessed great changes, not all of which may be regarded as improvements. The old Scottish Leaving Certificate was based on the conception of broad rather than specialised education. Specialisation was held to be more properly the task of the universities, and even there only for those students who could show sufficient ability to profit from taking honours degrees. It was probably a mistake to give up this essentially modern concept to fall sheepishly into line with English usage which was already under heavy criticism.[27] The pace has been forced by the changes made in the Scottish universities since 1945. The ordinary degree with its wide spread of subjects has been robbed of much of its value and is now in danger of being pretty well superseded by a wide variety of honours degrees which can, in many instances, be regarded as soft options. Of recent years the ridiculous situation has arisen in which students unable to meet certain basic requirements of the ordinary degree of M.A. (a language or a science subject usually) have insisted on studying for honours degrees and, in spite of protestations to the contrary, this has not in the least enhanced the standards of many so-called 'honours schools'. The universities in Scotland are, in fact, no longer distinctively Scottish and are at the moment developing into curiously unsatisfactory hybrids. Much of this can be attributed to the unduly large proportion of their staffs who are the products of English education. Those who are prepared to adapt their outlook contribute powerfully to the well-being of the universities in Scotland, not only in terms of their academic abilities but also in

---

[27] For a recent searching criticism of over-specialisation in English schools, see F. S. Dainton, 'The Swing away from Science', in *The Listener*, 18 May 1967, pp. 645-7.

terms of fresh vision; but too many react like doleful birds of passage stranded in hyperborean parts. That Glasgow is not Bristol, or Edinburgh Birmingham, closes the matter in too many otherwise well-stocked minds; and querulous Scottophobia is by no means unknown.

The number of universities in Scotland has doubled of recent years: to the traditional four (St Andrews, Glasgow, Aberdeen and Edinburgh) have been added two 'technical universities' by the upgrading of the Glasgow Royal Technical College in 1964 and the Heriot-Watt in Edinburgh in 1965. By some curious atavism the Glasgow 'Tech.' was metamorphosed into the University of Strathclyde; but this romantic lead has not been followed by the Heriot-Watt, which simply became the Heriot-Watt University. After years of pressure and debating, the site of a completely new university foundation went to Stirling in 1964: its first students matriculated in 1967. The aim here was to be experimental, though exactly on what lines or with what prospects of success are hardly as yet clear. Again after years of discussion Queen's College Dundee, part of the University of St Andrews, was upgraded to full university status as from October 1967. In the meantime, the older universities had not, as casual reading of the press might suggest, been idle. They have, in fact, borne the brunt of the required expansion and will probably continue to do so, though under present conditions the strain on some departments becomes intolerable. The grand object seems to be to create as many student places as quickly as possible, and at the least possible expenditure. Between 1962 and 1966 Scotland's student population increased by 12,000, making a total of 32,000, and still applicants have to be turned away. At the same time research is to be promoted in all its forms, and in most faculties provision for research students has been improved.

Other aspects of the situation of the universities in Scotland cause disquiet. Quite clearly, and rightly, they are not confined to taking Scottish students, any more than the ancient four had ever been. But in the past twenty years a higher proportion of the English population seeks entrance to the universities, and an increasing number of them are admitted to those in Scotland. Within reason this is a welcome and highly beneficial development, but if carried too far it has results that are good for neither the students nor the institutions concerned. Some critics have alleged that where this so-called cosmopolitanism exists the students break up into provincial groupings, and even if only partly true this would be an absurd negation of any reasonable idea of a university. Yet other critics are alarmed lest the new cosmopolitanism should unfairly discriminate against Scottish candidates for admission. There is certainly something to be watched here, since holders of Scottish Certificates of Education have little hope of gaining admission to English universities where other criteria are applied. If the universities in Scotland were to bring their entrance requirements into line with those of the universities in England—and there is such a tendency—then this could result in unfair discrimination against Scottish applicants. Already charges of this kind have been made, and rebutted; but clearly this is a matter that calls for careful, and candid, scrutiny, particularly since some of the universities in Scotland now deal with admissions through a central body, the Universities Central Council for Admissions. The point can be made quite plainly: the universities in Scotland exist to serve the United Kingdom, and to a lesser extent, the world as a whole, but not to the point of rendering disservice to Scotland. In this connection, it is important to remember something that nowadays tends to be overlooked in view of increasing dependence on exchequer grants. The Scottish universities are the inheritors and transmitters not only of tradition in the abstract sense but also in more concrete terms of stone, mortar and material benefactions of all kinds. They can, and should be, improved without losing their distinctive character, for it is from their democratic, rather than Oxbridge élitist, traditions that the modern university in the English-speaking world derives.[27a] Should they become merely northern extensions of the English idea of a university (of which there are numerous excellent examples), it would be an expensive and frivolous waste of the kind that Britain can ill afford.

The religious life of Scotland since the end of the second world war has experienced some unexpected developments which, though coloured by Scottish conditions, are clearly responses to a much wider situation. On the whole, in the inter-war period

[27a] Significantly, in planning the democratic Open University (formerly provisionally called 'The University of the Air'), which is to commence in 1970, Miss Jennie Lee, minister for the arts, concludes that it should be 'modelled more on the Scottish or the American system than on the English one'. Cf. *The Scotsman*, 19 September, 1967.

Christianity had given all the appearance of losing ground. Partly because of faltering belief (in the old sense of belief as a basis of life) and partly because of changing patterns of community life, the church was no longer the social force that it had been. The humanist movement seemed to be predominating. But after the war (and perhaps to some extent because of it) the churches rallied. An extension programme carried the churches into the new housing estates in Glasgow and elsewhere, and in many of them a more classless form of pastoral activity evolved which led to vigorous congregational life. Both the Church of Scotland and the Roman Catholic Church could testify to the reality of faith renewed in better surroundings. The challenge was also taken up in other ways, particularly by the adoption by the Church of Scotland of organised evangelism on the American 'hard sell' model. The best known experiment of this kind was the 'Tell Scotland' crusade which from 1947 onwards was vigorously directed by a young Glasgow minister, Tom Allan. Much of the dynamic of all this activity was supplied by the fact that ' the issue which is most stirring the mind of the Scottish Churches at present is " the menace and challenge of Communism " '.[28] Not only Roman catholics were alarmed by this. The 1948 general assembly of the Church of Scotland condemned Communist oppression as an ' offence against the Christian doctrine of God and man . . . done in the name of an ideology that categorically denies them '.[29] The gradual disillusionment of many who initially supported the aims, but knew little of the practice, of Communism, weakened the secularist movement (which by the late 1950s was clearly on the defensive), and to that extent the position of the churches was strengthened.

The whole trend of modern life, however, prevented the churches from returning to their old confident postures. Militant atheism was not the only enemy: creedless indifference and hedonism disguised as ' a new morality ' could not lightly be ignored. Then again, the Christological emphasis of current theological trends condemned the divisions of Christianity. Thus the ecumenical movement, which had existed since 1910 but which before 1939 had made little progress, became after 1945 an increasingly potent force. Its roots went deeper than most observers could see, for it built on strong if unofficial foundations.

[28] John Highet, *The Churches in Scotland Today*, p. 173.   [29] Quoted in Highet, *loc. cit.*

However much denominations might differ in creed or polity, in discharge of their duties the clergy were already co-operating, promoting various social welfare measures. Sometimes this was done through local government representation, but more often simply by priests and ministers interesting themselves in matters of common concern. The flocks might quarrel, but the pastors tended to co-operate. The tendency to co-operate was even more marked in the foreign mission field. The doctrinal laxness of the Church of Scotland, however, proved a bar to further presbyterian union, for the Free Presbyterians and the Free Churchmen clung to Calvinist orthodoxy, while the United Free Church continued to reject the state connection. One small achievement, though it had a venerable significance, was the return of the remnant of the United Original Secession Church to the establishment in 1956. There have been negotiations with congregationalists and others, but interest has centred mainly on the possibility of union with episcopalians.

The rapprochement between presbyterians and episcopalians was initiated, in a fortuitous way, in England when in 1946 the Archbishop of Canterbury urged a fresh and more energetic approach to the English Free Churches. But, clearly, if the Church of England and the Presbyterian Church of England could be reconciled this would open up wider possibilities. The general assembly of the Church of Scotland agreed in 1947 that the question of intercommunion between the Church of Scotland and the Church of England merited full discussion. This view was endorsed by the Lambeth Conference of 1948 and led to joint conferences of representatives of the two churches, with representatives of the Episcopal Church in Scotland and the Presbyterian Church of England acting, to begin with, as observers. The evolution of a united Church of South India which subsumed its founding denominations, including Anglican and presbyterian, acted as an incentive. Not enough attention, however, was given to the fact that the Anglican Churches for an interim period refused to hold intercommunion with the Church of South India which, in other respects, was held up as a model worthy of emulation. It seemed to many that the ecumenists were forced into rather devious courses. Their tactics were gradualist: constitutional union did not head the proceedings, but was to lie over until such matters as order and communion were settled. This was a sound approach, but it had the unfortunate defect of making the negotiators appear disingenuous. The necessity of an episcopate to the Anglicans was well known, and had indeed been stressed by the Archbishop of Canterbury in his famous sermon of 1946: *pace* the experiment in South India, he declared, the Church of England 'cannot submit itself to any constitution convenient for these islands unless it is one which in principle its related Churches can also adopt for themselves '.[30] To convinced presbyterians, and notably the National Church Association, this foredoomed the talks. The subsequent discussions were closely scrutinised by a party which regarded the introduction of bishops (however defined) as hostile to the past traditions and present interests of the Church of Scotland. This probably represented the majority view and increasingly the ' ecumaniacs ' were stigmatised as a narrow academic clique, on the most charitable interpretation out of touch with feeling in the Church of Scotland and on the less charitable view bent on emerging as the new episcopate. The Scottish press, on the whole, did not incline to charitable views; but, in fairness, the difficulties under which the joint conferences laboured seemed to give substance to the charges. Interim reports to the general assembly were necessarily tentative and difficult to pin down to any specific theme. A franker approach might not have been any more successful, but at least it might have minimised the atmosphere of uneasy suspicion which was engendered and which led to charges of devious plotting.

The publication of the joint report[31] in 1957 produced an explosion. The report recommended that in the interests of unity the Church of Scotland should consider the adoption of a form of episcopacy, thus resolving the outstanding difficulty of the validity of presbyterian orders and paving the way to intercommunion. Each presbytery was to have ' a bishop-in-presbytery ' chosen ' from its own membership or otherwise '.[32] In the beginning the

[30] *Relations between the Church of England and the Church of Scotland, a Joint Report* (1951), Appendix I, text of a sermon preached before the University of Cambridge by the Archbishop of Canterbury, pp. 18-19. The plea was for intercommunion rather than constitutional unions, but still (p. 20) non-episcopal churches were asked to try the episcopal experiment ' on their own ground first '.

[31] *Relations between Anglican and Presbyterian Churches* (1957). The Presbyterian Church of England and the Episcopal Church in Scotland were fully represented in the discussions which gave rise to this report.

[32] *Op. cit.*, p. 25. But in a pamphlet, *Church Unity: Question and Answer on the Conversations* (1957), published for the general assembly's committee on church relations (p. 7) this point is rendered: ' Each Presbytery would have a Bishop-in-Presbytery, chosen by itself '.

bishops-in-presbytery would be consecrated by representatives of the presbytery and by bishops from one or more of the episcopalian churches. The bishop was to preside over the presbytery and exercise pastoral oversight over its clergy. The bishops would be constituent members of the general assembly which was to remain the supreme authority, 'although decisions on doctrine and constitutional matters might well have to require their consent'. The Church of England, for its part, would introduce an office akin to that of the eldership and a wider and more effective lay representation in the church assembly. The stated aim was not 'one single " Church of Great Britain " but rather a " Church of England " and a " Church of Scotland " in full communion with one another; nor do they involve a uniformity of life and worship throughout these Churches '.[33] The aim was union between the Church of Scotland and the Episcopal Church in Scotland, and a similar union in England between establishment and Presbyterian Church. Such a scheme, in Scotland at any rate, would have had to solve great, if not insuperable, problems, posed from both presbyterian and episcopalian sides. Those who supported the report pointed out that bishops in the reformed Church of Scotland were not unprecedented, and that they might play an important part in the running of the church, which had become excessively bureaucratic. In particular the authority of the bishops might resolve, or even prevent, the unseemly wrangles that sometimes split kirk-sessions.

Such arguments were of little avail. To those who believed in the presbyterian system of government and the parity of ministers the 'Bishops' Report' was anathema, and as such it was fiercely assailed. Criticism of the report was widespread and did not come only from the membership of the Church of Scotland. The press was hostile to the project, the *Scottish Daily Express* in particular acting as a platform for the opposition. But to credit the newspapers with the creation of this opposition seems farfetched: they merely reported, and commented on, a piece of hot news. Indeed, that the report should be attacked, pretty much on the grounds on which it was attacked, was entirely predictable, since it undoubtedly advocated a very large departure from the traditions of Scottish presbyterianism. Nor was this all: it was widely feared that the provisions of the report if imple-

[33] *Relations between Anglican and Presbyterian Churches*, p. 23.

mented would in the long run have changed both the doctrine and worship of the Church of Scotland. This may, or may not, have been all to the good; but to imply, as the report did, that no such changes were likely seemed to many unconvincing. After prolonged and at times bitter discussion,[34] the report was rejected by the general assembly of 1959. Anglican-presbyterian talks have continued, but presbyterian insistence on the validity of their orders has protracted matters.[35] Gradually, the negotiators have found some common ground, and the idea of a 'covenant' to enter into unity has been suggested; and the general assembly of 1966, by a narrow majority, agreed that the discussions should continue. But many members of the Church of Scotland do not favour a unity which requires fundamental change in the government of their church; and a matter that has been ignored, but which might prove troublesome, is that under the terms of the act of 1921 the maintenance of presbyterian government is enjoined. Any change proposed might require statutory sanction; but whether, in the face of strong opposition, any government or political party would espouse such a cause seems doubtful.

The ecumenical movement, however, continues, and has indeed extended to the Roman Catholic Church which hitherto had stood aloof. The brief but historic pontificate of John XXIII (1958–63) made the Roman Church more ecumenically minded and at the same time encouraged a reforming mood within the church. It is too early yet to assess the outcome of Pope John's initiative, but certainly it has led to closer relations between the Roman church and other denominations. Scarcely otherwise could the moderator of the general assembly in March 1962 have made a courtesy call on the pope. At a lower, but possibly even more significant level, in Scotland meetings between prominent ecclesiastics of all persuasions have become common, and the growing sense of comradeship between protestant and catholic is almost startling. Yet, inevitably, to diehards on either side this amity is in itself a cause of complaint. It seems to confirm the worst suspicions of the protestant opposition to the ecumenical movement that it is a Romeward trend, that the aim is to undo the Reformation and to reunify Christendom under the authority of

---

[34] But not all adverse discussion was bitter—see, e.g., *Glasgow Speaks: a reply to the Joint Report on Anglican-Presbyterian Relations* (1959) which is a courteous, sober, and considered appraisal of the report by the presbytery of Glasgow.

[35] *The Anglican-Presbyterian Conversations* (1966).

the supreme pontiff. On the other hand, conservative catholics see in the ecumenical movement an attempt to subvert and destroy their faith. Hostile attitudes have been stiffened by the archbishop of Canterbury's formal visit to the pope in March 1966 and the policy of rapprochement that was then proclaimed. Old prejudices die hard, and the way to church unity is littered with obstacles. Yet churchmen, both clerical and lay, on the whole welcome the new catholicity of spirit, though they differ as to its significance. Some, clearly the minority, regard division as sinful and feel that divisions should be healed at any cost. Many are of the belief that charitable co-operation is the essence of true unity, while others again see positive benefits in the various Christian traditions and warn that unions built on sacrifice of principle can hardly be expected to promote Christian brother-hood. On this important question the churches are not of a mind; but in spirit they are closer than they have ever been.

The situation of its churches faithfully reflects that of the Scottish people: jolted from old certitudes and groping for new beliefs. Whether there is a Scottish nation today depends largely on the definition of nation that is employed. It is, however, surely a matter of some consequence that most Scots consider themselves as belonging to an ancient and historic nation, although the terms 'nation' and 'national' are loosely employed, sometimes to denote Scotland and sometimes the United Kingdom. Yet, on balance, a shift of emphasis in favour of Scotland and things Scottish can be detected, if only as a riposte to tasteless and wholly inaccurate English usage which would substitute the part for the whole. Scots lawyers are no longer apologetic about the law of Scotland and nowadays tend rather to overpraise its mani-fest virtues. The Union with England, which was regarded as the ark of the covenant a century ago, is not now generally regarded as sacrosanct, and this more questioning attitude un-doubtedly has been reinforced by the changed situation in which the United Kingdom now finds itself. The passing of empire, the eclipse of the commonwealth, and a half-century of economic decline have put a very different face on things. It is an effort now to recall that Glasgow once prided itself on being the second city of the British Empire and performed considerable juggling feats with population statistics to prove it. Now, all has changed, and the essence of the new situation seems to be uncertainty.

The hub of the problem would seem to be, as Dean Acheson (a former American secretary of state) put it in December 1962, that England had lost an empire and failed to find a role in the world. The analysis was sound and deserved more consideration than the howl of jingoism that greeted it in Britain. But English nationalism, which is real enough though it assumes various disguises, can only with difficulty adjust itself to new realities. The Scots have this considerable advantage: they have retained the mentality of a small nation, and, realistically, see no profit in what many regard as the continuing delusion of Great Britain as a world power. If, the argument runs, economic and social regeneration is to be sacrificed to such a phantasm, then radical, and perhaps even desperate, expedients may have to be adopted to make Scotland's continued existence feasible. Whether the will to survive as a nation exists, or whether it could successfully assert itself, are deep questions that admit of no answer.

Postscript, 1977

The decade that has passed since this book was first published has done little to resolve these issues but much to intensify them. Labour's performance from 1967 to 1970 was curiously mixed. The hoped for 'technological revolution' failed to materialise; full employment remained an ideal rather than an achievement; the weakened pound had to be propped up by overseas borrowing; prices were rising and so too were demands for increased wages, raising the spectre of inflation; but skilful management of the Exchequer by Roy Jenkins improved the reserves, and for six months in 1969–70 the balance of trade figures showed a surplus. But in the ensuing general election of June 1970 the Conservatives, confounding the opinion polls, won an unexpected but decisive enough victory. True, they did not fare so well in Scotland. There the most unusual development, though rather overlooked at the time, was the growth in the S.N.P. vote. The Nationalists, however, won only one seat, the Western Isles taken by Donald Stewart from Labour, while Labour recaptured Mrs Ewing's seat at Hamilton from the S.N.P.

The warning implicit in the Scottish results was not lost on Mr Heath. Already, in the wake of a Conservative party committee report of March 1970 recommending a Scottish Convention, he had repeated the call for moderate devolution he had first raised at Perth in 1968. He was to do so consistently; but devolution, though widely discussed in Scotland, did not really loom large on the British political scene until after the publication of the Kilbrandon Report on the Constitution in October 1973, in which the majority recommendation was that a directly elected legislative assembly should be set up for Scotland and an executive assembly for Wales. The prime minister again advocated devolution—not necessarily on the Kilbrandon model, which went far beyond the rather vague Conservative commitment. Mr Heath got little real support from his own party which became steadily more confused over the entire issue. Point, however, was given to the premier's warning by the victory chalked up for the S.N.P. by Mrs Margo MacDonald at the Govan by-election on 8 November 1973: but since the S.N.P. threat still seemed to be aimed at Labour, the Scottish Conservatives were lulled into a sense of false security. Anyway, Mr Heath's major priorities had been putting the economy right and negotiating entry into the E.E.C., a fresh application for entry having been made by the previous government.

Success with the E.E.C. was as marked as failure with the economy. After prolonged negotiations, a somewhat rambling public debate and a fierce parliamentary struggle, the United Kingdom finally joined the Common Market, in company with the Irish Republic and Denmark, on 1 January 1973, adding a new and in many ways incalculable dimension to British affairs. But the United Kingdom joined the E.E.C. with an economy that was still stagnant, hampered by an antiquated industrial structure and bedevilled by ever-worsening industrial relations. The last problem was not new; it had, for instance, been raised, only to be fudged, by the preceding Labour Government; and Mr Heath's efforts to solve it in the end ruined his government. His wages policy was unpopular, particularly because of failure to curb rising prices, and more troublesome still was the Industrial Relations Act of 1971. This act, which aimed at imposing a system of legal arbitration, caused strife with the trade unions. The bad economic climate also led to liquidations and 'sit ins', such as the one at Upper Clyde Shipbuilders, an ill-fated consortium created on the Geddes' plan which, in spite of government support, was forced into liquidation. Such events added to the bitterness of the strife with the trade unions which had no inhibitions about taking on a Conservative government. The miners' strike in February 1972 was of a peculiar violence, and later it was the N.U.M.'s ban on overtime in the winter of 1973–4 that helped to bring the country virtually to a standstill. Mr Heath's opponents in his own party blamed him for calling a general election rather than refusing to give in to intimidation. His was the more realistic view, for to have held on might have ruined not just the Conservative government but the country itself. Besides, it was an extremely complex as well as difficult situation, which only a mandate could resolve. The government had a case; and so, too, had the miners.

Their industry had been steadily run down and they had fallen in the wages scale. Oil seemed to provide the fuel base for a modern economy; but a sudden, if not altogether unexpected, development transformed the situation. The possible disruption of Middle East oil supplies, together with drastic price increases, following the Arab-Israeli War of October 1973, put coal at a premium and placed the workers in a supposedly dying coal-industry in a powerful position. The miners, aided by the railwaymen and electrical power engineers, were not slow to press their advantage. Their initial weapon, a ban on overtime, was difficult to counter, and the government's dilemma was soon clear. A 'wages explosion', which seemed unavoidable if union demands were met, might, together with the oil problem, boost the inflationary spiral to catastrophic proportions. The confrontation was stark and bitter. The left blamed the ills of the country on inept and arrogant government; the right repudiated the charge and called for national unity to counter the menace of trade unions manipulated by subversive elements. Whatever the exact truth of the matter, the 'three day week' of the early days of 1974 showed that a very grave crisis was building up. A mandate from the country, a concept previously scornfully dismissed by the pro-Europeans in the debate over the E.E.C., suddenly became a necessity.

In Scotland, perhaps even in the United Kingdom as a whole, the outstanding outcome of the general election of February 1974 was again the progress made by the S.N.P. The Nationalists won seven seats, mainly at the expense of the Conservatives, and polled 21% of the Scottish electorate. Various reasons were advanced for this, notably loss of faith in the two major parties and in policies that had been repeatedly tried and found wanting. The vigorous campaign waged by the S.N.P. on North Sea Oil also played a part. The finds, the bulk of which lay under Scottish jurisdictional waters, were far greater than government had made out, and according to the S.N.P. 'Scotland's oil' could turn an independent Scotland into a rich and prosperous country. But, the argument continued, if it was exploited as U.K. oil, Scotland might end up as the only oil-rich country to be impoverished. The debate on the subject went on long after the election, and Shetland, around which the major fields were located, took a United Kingdom rather than 'Scottish' line. Whatever is to be made of these arguments, the discovery of North Sea Oil had this salient effect: it seriously dented the old contention that a self-governing Scotland could not possibly be viable in the economic sense.

The overall result of the elections of February 1974 was a virtual stalemate. Conservative attempts to negotiate a coalition with the Liberals failed and a minority Labour administration was formed. As well as making peace with the trade unions and having to tackle the deepening economic crisis, Mr Wilson's third government came from the beginning under mounting pressure to grant devolution, particularly from a small group of Scottish Labour M.P.s headed by James Sillars, the M.P. for South Ayrshire and erstwhile 'Hammer of the Nats'. A growing Scottish dimension in British politics was obvious; but the government responded cautiously.

Caution was apparently justified by the failure of the S.N.P. in the local elections in May 1974. But these were not very good indicators, for local government was being launched into a new and as yet untested phase. The whole structure was being altered as the result of a Conservative act of 1973 which was based, with modifications, on the Wheatley Report of 1969. The report recommended the scrapping of many small units of local government, counties and burghs alike, and the setting up of a few large 'all purpose' regions with a lower tier of district councils. These changes injected yet another contentious element into Scottish politics. The regions, and particularly Strathclyde which covered most of the West of Scotland, were regarded by many as potentially remote, bureaucratic and wasteful. Their virtues could only at that early stage be conjectural; but not the least of the virtues of the regions to anti-devolutionists was that they seemed to pre-empt the need for devolution. The Conservatives, uneasy about their party's vague commitment to devolution and fearful that devolution might slide by degrees into separatism, in time became enmeshed in the endless pros and cons of such arguments. On devolution Labour fared little better. The Scottish Council of the Labour Party adopted a rigidly unionist stance (later peremptorily reversed on orders from London), while the S.T.U.C. consistently pressed for devolution.

In the general election 'of October 1974 the Labour Party committed itself to setting up a directly elected single-chamber Scottish assembly with considerable, though unspecified, powers. The aim obviously was to improve Labour's quest for a majority and dish the Conservatives who were still fumbling the devolution issue. Partly, too, the move was designed to scupper the S.N.P., but here success was limited. The S.N.P. polled 30% of the Scottish vote and emerged with 11 seats. Again the Conservatives suffered most severely from the S.N.P. assault, but the Nationalists also ran Labour close in many traditional socialist strongholds in the broken-down industrial west. There followed for the two major parties a harrowing nightmarish experience. Labour had only an overall majority of three, and since support from the Scottish and Welsh Nationalists and the Liberals was desperately needed so too was action on devolution. The plain fact was, however, that the majority of Labour M.P.s, apart from a few Scottish members, were either indifferent to devolution or vehemently opposed to it. The government, well aware of the gathering problems, finally issued a White Paper in November 1975. The White Paper offered a legislative assembly with executive powers for Scotland and an executive assembly for Wales where Nationalist pressure was not so strong.

The proposals had a mixed reception, some holding that they went too far and others that they did not go far enough. No major economic powers were to be given to the Scottish assembly, which was to operate on a block grant from Westminster. Real control of the recently set up Scottish Development Agency was to lie with the Secretary of State and the cabinet at Westminster. The Secretary of State's role was apparently to wane in some respects, the assembly running the rule over St Andrew's House, but to wax in others. On these and other grounds, divisions of opinion in the two major parties became wider and more obvious, producing some odd bodies that operated under a variety of curious titles. The S.N.P. was left, as usual, *tertius gaudens*. The party, as such, cared little for devolution and its response was largely tactical; but gradually some members of the S.N.P. saw devolution as not only desirable in itself but potentially useful as a posting stage to independence. Labour's position remained delicate: how to draw up a bill that would satisfy enough M.P.s to vote for it and yet not play into the hands of the separatists? By doing nothing, the S.N.P. was still making the running, and eventually some members of the Labour Party in Scotland took the alarm. In December 1975, after vainly attempting to secure further powers for the assembly, especially on economic affairs, they formed a separate Scottish Labour Party which was soon joined by two Scottish Labour M.P.s, James Sillars and John Robertson. Following the failure of efforts to heal the breach the dissidents were expelled from the Labour Party, though the Labour government still relied heavily on the S.L.P.'s two parliamentary votes.

As for the Conservatives, their unease about devolution became more marked after Mrs Margaret Thatcher replaced Mr Heath as party leader in February 1975. Anyway, events seemed to have swept remorselessly past the Douglas-Home Report of 1970, and the Conservatives became increasingly divided over devolution. This was particularly the case when strong opposition to any kind of devolution arose among many English Conservative M.P.s who by then had to grapple with this new word. The clearest expression of the fundamental cleavage came at the stormy Scottish Conservative Conference held at Perth in May 1976. In the end, after tumultuous debates, the party was apparently left committed to a directly elected assembly shorn of any substantial powers; though many Tories obviously dissented.

To some extent confused attitudes all round resulted from the slow pace of the government's programme. Deferring legislation for a year because of a crowded programme did not help. Opposition, too, hardened, and not just from the Conservatives, when the government's intentions were debated in January 1976. The slow evolution of the draft bill, and the sporadic and increasingly bitter debate, turned vague fears into entrenched positions as the bogey of separatism loomed larger and larger and as the economic situation of the country got worse with the rate of inflation, and of unemployment, steadily rising. To many devolution seemed irrelevant in the face of a threatening economic maelstrom. Apart from such considerations, the bill that finally came up for discussion in November 1976 was open to criticism on many counts. It sought to deal simultaneously with Scotland and Wales; it was so poorly drafted as to give rise to the suspicion that it was merely a propaganda exercise; it got tepid support from the government and even less from the supporters of the government. Even the Liberals, long-time champions of home rule, found it unacceptable. Efforts to improve the bill, and efforts to scuttle it, came from all parts of the House. In general the debates were very bad, some of the contributions reeking of vintage *Punch*. In the end a half-hearted approach by the government led to the bill being lost on 22 February 1977 when Labour dissidents and exasperated Liberals voted with the opposition against the crucial time-table motion.

Shortly thereafter the new Liberal leader, David Steel, made a pact with the government to see the country through the continuing economic crisis, and part of the price of Liberal support was to be a better and more strongly promoted government bill on devolution. But whether the parliamentary Labour Party and its allies can successfully support the separate bills proposed for Scotland and Wales remains to be seen. The prospect of an improved economy, with North Sea Oil at full flow, could yet abort devolution, but whether such an eventuality would solve the U.K.'s constitutional problems, no small part of which reside at Westminster, seems open to debate.

BIBLIOGRAPHY

As in the preceding volume, the place of publication is not given except in the case of rare works, and for volumes published by clubs or societies the date of publication is omitted.

I. Works of Reference

There is no comprehensive bibliographical work of reference. The nearest approach is G. F. Black, *A List of Works in the New York Public Library Relating to Scotland* (1916), a splendid compilation, but, as well as being now dated, it was never, as its title makes clear, a complete bibliography. Fortunately for students of Scottish history, the tendency to equate British with English history is not displayed by bibliographers. Godfrey Davies, *Bibliography of British History, Stuart Period, 1603–1714* (1928) has a section on Scotland; and Stanley Pargellis and D. J. Medley, *Bibliography of British History, the Eighteenth Century, 1714–1789* (1951), gives an even fuller coverage. Clyde L. Grose, *A Select Bibliography of British History, 1660–1760* (1939), also pays reasonable attention to Scotland. Three brief select bibliographies on general Scottish history are serviceable: two of them are produced by the National Book League—H. W. Meikle *et al.*, *Scotland, A Select Bibliography* (1950), and J. D. Mackie, *Scottish History* (1956)—and one, *Scottish Books* (n.d.), by the Saltire Society.

C. S. Terry, *Catalogue of the Publications of Scottish Historical and Kindred Clubs and Societies . . . 1780–1908* (1909), and its continuation up to 1927, by C. Matheson (1928), remain indispensable aids. The official list of record publications (H.M.S.O.) should also be consulted. For manuscript sources M. Livingstone, *A Guide to the Public Records of Scotland* (1905), and J. M. Thomson, *The Public Records of Scotland* (1922) are not much help for this period: the annual lists of accessions to the Register House printed in *S.H.R.* are more useful, and the National Register of Archives (Scotland) can aid in tracing manuscripts still in private hands. The National Library of Scotland, *Catalogue of Manuscripts* (2 vols., I, 1938, and II, 1966), furnishes a clear guide to a growing collection which covers more facets of Scottish life than do the official records. The most useful reference works for legal and administrative history are: G. Brunton and D. Haig, *Senators of the College of Justice* (1832); G. W. T. Omond, *The Lord Advocates of Scotland* (2 vols., 1883); and, more generally, *Sources and Literature of Scots Law* (Stair Soc.). J. Foster, *Members of Parliament for Scotland* (2nd edn., 1882) is idiosyncratic but useful; it can be checked against *Parliamentary Papers*, LXII, pt. ii (1878), *Members of Parlia-*

ment, 1705–1874. Both should be supplemented, if not superseded, by the *History of Parliament* project, but so far only the period 1754–90 has been covered (in 3 vols., 1964). A separate project dealing with the Scottish parliament is in train. C. S. Terry, *An Index to the Papers Relating to Scotland, published by the Historical Manuscripts Commission* (1908) is of limited use: the guide volume (XXII) in the *H.M.C.* series is much more efficient.

For economic history, use can still be made of W. R. Scott, *Scottish Economic Literature to 1800*(1911) ; and W. H. Marwick has compiled bibliographies of subsequent writings in three articles in the *Economic History Review*, III, 2nd ser. IV, and XVI. The N.L.S. has bound them into a volume, with addenda.

For local history A. Mitchell and C. G. Cash, *Contribution to the Bibliography of Scottish Topography* (2 vols., S.H.S.), still provides the best guide. It is continued by P. Hancock, *A Bibliography of Works relating to and on Scotland, 1916–50* (1960). F. H. Groome, *Ordnance Gazetteer of Scotland* (6 vols., 1882–5), is not only a guide to the topography of Scotland but is in effect a late-Victorian statistical account. Regrettably, there is no historical atlas of Scotland, but the following works can be used: *County Atlas of Scotland* (1831), and J. Bartholomew, ed., *Survey Atlas of Scotland* (1912).

For family history the best guides are: M. Stuart and J. B. Paul, *Scottish Family History* (1929); J. P. S. Ferguson, *Scottish Family Histories held in Scottish Libraries* (1960); and *Scottish Family Histories, A List of Books for Consultation in Edinburgh Public Library* (2nd edn., 1955). G. F. Black, *The Surnames of Scotland* (1946), often gives essential information, though it is stronger for earlier periods.

The *Dictionary of National Biography* has articles on most Scottish notables of the period, but they are sometimes of poor quality. This applies even more to W. Anderson, *The Scottish Nation* (3 vols., 1863), and to R. Chambers, *Biographical Dictionary of Eminent Scotsmen* (3 vols., 1868–70). J. B. Paul, *The Scots Peerage* (9 vols., 1909–14), is a first class work of reference but now a little dated. It can be checked against the latest edition of G. E. C., *The Complete Peerage*. For the ministers of the established church, H. Scott, *Fasti Ecclesiae Scoticanae* (7 vols., new edn., 1915–28), is the great source; two additional volumes have been added: VIII (1950), containing corrections and a continuation to 1914, and IX covering the period 1929–54 (1961). Related, but less exhaustive, works are: *Annals of the Free Church of Scotland, 1843–1900* (ed. W. Ewing, 2 vols., 1914); and *The Fasti of the United Free Church of Scotland, 1900–1929* (ed. J. A. Lamb, 1956). As an elementary guide, M. B. Macgregor, *The Sources and Literature of Scottish Church History* (1934), has its uses.

II. GENERAL

(i) *Primary sources. The Acts of the Parliaments of Scotland* (12 vols., 1814–75) remains indispensable right up to the conclusion of the record in 1707. *The Register of the Privy Council* has not been published beyond 1689 and must for subsequent events be consulted in MSS. in Register House; but a further printed volume is shortly expected. As a source, however, it is of diminished importance after 1689, thus faithfully reflecting the constitutional changes brought about by the Revolution. The published volumes of *State Papers* (*Domestic*) often contain valuable material bearing on Scotland, but they also peter out in the reign of Anne. After 1707 information on Scottish affairs is to be found in the records of the British parliament: *The Journals of the House of Commons*; *The Journals of the House of Lords*; *Cobbett's Parliamentary History* (1806–20), and its continuation, *Hansard's Parliamentary Debates*. Statutes are another important source and may be found in *Statutes of the Realm*, and from 1797 in the annual volumes of *Public General Statutes*. There is a convenient collection, *Public General Statutes affecting Scotland* (3 vols., 1848), covering the period 1707–1848. For the nineteenth and twentieth centuries *Parliamentary Papers* constitute a rich source: consult the official *Indexes to Reports, 1801–1900* (n.d.); P. and G. Ford, *Select List of British Parliamentary Papers, 1833–99* (1953); and by the same authors, *A Breviate of Parliamentary Papers, 1900–54* (3 vols., 1957–61).

Legal records of importance include: The Books of Adjournal, the MS. record of the high court of justiciary (in Register House); and *Session Papers*, which are the printed pleadings before the court of session. Also of importance are the decisions of the court of session, the most useful guide to them being W. M. Morison, *Dictionary of the Decisions of the Court of Session* (27 vols., 1801–16). There is fuller reporting in *The Faculty Collection of Decisions* (21 vols., 1752–1825) and its continuations up to the present time. Considerable information is contained in *The State Trials*, ed. Cobbett, continued by Howell (XI–XXXIII, 1811–20).

For information on the tenure of land, the Register of Sasines (MS., Register House, with printed abridgement from 1781) is virtually infallible—a magnificent record. The records of the commissioners of supply are rather fugitive but their valuations are, when available, very important sources. For the operation of the electoral system before 1832, the following treatises should be consulted: A. Wight, *The Rise and Progress of Parliament* (1st edn., 1784; 2nd edn., 2 vols., 1806); R. Bell, *Treatise on the Election Laws . . . Scotland* (1812); A. Connell, *Treatise on the Election Laws of Scotland* (1827); and Thomas Thomson, *Memorial on Old Extent*, ed. J. D. Mackie (Stair Soc.).

MS. ecclesiastical records are now being concentrated in Register House; and the Roman catholic archives at Columba House, Edinburgh, are also very important.

(ii) *Secondary works*. The older general histories are weak on the post-Union period. Most of them, like those of J. H. Burton (8 vols., new edn., 1897), and of A. Lang (4 vols., 1907), end in 1748. W. L. Mathieson's work tails off at 1843. P. H. Brown (III, 1909) also draws to a close in 1843, but the library edition (1911) goes up to 1910. On the whole, Hume Brown's treatment of the nineteenth century is sketchy. An attempt at a more comprehensive treatment was made by A. Macrae, *Scotland from the Treaty of Union with England to the Present Time, 1707–1907* (1907), but it is slight. Sir Henry Craik, *A Century of Scottish History from the days before the '45 to those within living memory* (2 vols. 1901), is dull and prolix, with a strong Conservative bias. G. S. Pryde, *Scotland from 1603 to the Present Day* (1962), is the best general account; but it is uneven, some periods—notably the seventeenth century—receiving skimped treatment while the later chapters on the nineteenth and twentieth centuries are sluggish with statistical details. A more lively introduction is the same author's revised edition of R. S. Rait and G. S. Pryde, *Scotland* (1954). T. Johnston, *History of the Working Classes in Scotland* (1922), is a pioneer work marred by partisanship.

Little help is to be found in general histories of England or Britain (the precise title usually makes little difference to the contents); but the relevant volumes in the *Oxford History of England* furnish necessary background. C. L. Mowat, *Britain Between the Wars, 1918–40* (1955), and A. F. Havighurst, *Twentieth Century Britain* (2nd edn., 1966) do not consider Scotland, but none the less advance dogmatic opinions.

There is no satisfactory general work covering the Highlands. W. C. Mackenzie, *The Highlands and Islands of Scotland: a Historical Survey* (1949), is superficial on the modern period. W. R. Kermack, *The Scottish Highlands: a Short History, c. 300–1746* (1957), is sound but very brief, particularly for the period 1689–1746. A Cunningham, *The Loyal Clans* (1932), goes up to 1746 but is prolix and repetitive. One of the best works is still J. Browne, *A History of the Highlands and of the Highland Clans* (4 vols. 1838), but it is dated both in matter and in manner.

For economic developments the best general account is R. H. Campbell, *Scotland since 1707: the Rise of an Industrial Society* (1965), which supersedes J. Mackinnon, *The Social and Industrial History of Scotland from the Union to the Present Time* (1921). Much useful information is embodied in W. H. Marwick's brief *Modern Scotland* (1964). I. F. Grant, *The Economic History of Scotland* (1934), gives a convenient synopsis of the modern period; and there is value still in J. Mackintosh, *The History of Civilization in Scotland* (4 vols., 1892–6). Agriculture is well covered by J. A. Symon, *Scottish Farming, Past and Present* (1959), which is particularly good for the period 1689 to the present time. E. H. M. Cox, *A History of Gardening in Scotland* (1935), is written by an expert; and so is M. L. Anderson, *A History of Scottish Forestry* (2 vols., 1967), a work of massive research.

For the constitution R. S. Rait, *The Parliaments of Scotland* (1924), remains the standard work, but it is misleading on the eighteenth century. M. R. McLarty, ed., *Source Book and History of Administrative Law in Scotland* (1956), consists of thumb-nail sketches of various aspects of administration and has little to do with 'administrative law' in the legal sense. *An Introduction to Scottish Legal History* (Stair Soc.) is indispensable. A. Dewar Gibb, *Preface to Scots Law* (4th edn., 1964), lucidly expounds the leading features of Scots law, and this is done more fully by T. B. Smith, *The United Kingdom: the Development of its Laws and Constitutions: Scotland* (1955). W. I. R. Fraser, *An Outline of Constitutional Law* (2nd edn., 1948), covers the subject as it affects Scotland. For specific points, reference should be made to Green's *Encyclopaedia of the Laws of Scotland* (17 vols., 1926–49) ; to W. M. Gloag and R. C. Henderson, *Introduction to the Law of Scotland* (4th edn., 1946) ; and to *Bell's Dictionary and Digest of the Law of Scotland* (ed. G. Watson, 1890).

There are many works dealing with aspects of ecclesiastical history but no wholly satisfactory general account. J. H. S. Burleigh, *A Church History of Scotland* (1960), is compendious but not at its best in the post-Revolution period. A. J. Campbell, *Two Centuries of the Church of Scotland, 1707–1920* (1930), has an establishment bias. F. Goldie, *Short History of the Episcopal Church in Scotland* (1951), is succinct but rather tails off. P. F. Anson, *The Catholic Church in Modern Scotland* (1937), gives the main outlines but is rather an erratic introduction. Numerous articles in the *Innes Review* (1950–   ) are preparing the way for a better appreciation of Roman catholic history. This apart, the study of ecclesiastical history has obviously declined in the past half century. It is fortunate that some of the older works wear remarkably well and are still worth studying. R. H. Story, ed., *The Church of Scotland: Past and Present* (5 vols., n.d., *c.* 1890), consists of essays by various contributors on different aspects of the church—constitutional, liturgical, etc.—and is still valuable, although inevitably some of the contributions are now outdated. J. Cunningham, *The Church History of Scotland* (II, 1882), gives a sober appraisal up to the Disruption: the standpoint is presbyterian but not partisan. G. Grub, *Ecclesiastical History of Scotland* (4 vols., 1861), is a scholarly, comprehensive work which also goes up to the middle of the nineteenth century and is particularly valuable for its elucidation of the complex history of the episcopalians after the Revolution. A. Bellesheim, *The History of the Catholic Church of Scotland* (tr. D. O. Hunter-Blair, 4 vols., 1887–90), gives perfunctory treatment to the post-Revolution period. W. Forbes Leith, *Memoirs of Scottish Catholics during XVIIth and XVIIIth Centuries* (2 vols., 1909), prints some interesting material but does not always handle it critically enough.

Other denominational histories of value are: J. McKerrow, *History of the Secession Church* (1839); G. Struthers, *History of the Relief Church* (1843); G. B. Ryley and J. M. McCandlish, *Scotland's Free Church* (1893); N. L. Walker, *Chapters from the History of the Free Church of Scotland* (1895); M. Hutchison, *History of the Reformed Presbyterian Church in Scotland* (1893), which deals with the Cameronians up to 1876; D. Woodside, *The Soul of a Scottish Church or the Contribution of the United Presbyterian Church to Scottish Life and Religion* (n.d.); G. Yuille, ed., *History of the Baptists in Scotland* (1926); G. B. Burnet and W. H. Marwick, *The Story of Quakerism in Scotland* (1952); and H. Escott, *A History of Scottish Congregationalism* (1962).

J. Macleod, *Scottish Theology* (1943), is the only attempt at a comprehensive discussion of reformed theology but is diffuse and poorly arranged. J. T. MacNeill, *History and Character of Calvinism* (1954), devotes some space to Scotland. H. F. Henderson, *The Religious Controversies of Scotland* (1905), describes leading heresy trials in the eighteenth and nineteenth centuries.

There is no thorough general history of education in Scotland, which is surprising in view of the longstanding interest in the subject and the abundance of materials. The best of a rather indifferent lot is probably J. Strong, *History of Secondary Education in Scotland* (1909). Other general works worth consulting are: J. Kerr, *Scottish Education: School and University from Earliest Times to 1908* (1913); and H. M. Knox, *Two Hundred and Fifty Years of Scottish Education 1696–1946* (1953), which, however, is rather thin and general. There are some good specialised studies, notably: J. Grant, *History of the Burgh Schools of Scotland* (1876), a mine of undigested information; J. Mason, *A History of Scottish Experiments in Rural Education, from the Eighteenth Century to the Present Day* (1935), which deals largely with the work of the S.S.P.C.K.; and J. L. Campbell, *Gaelic in Scottish Education and Life* (1945), which is illuminating, though partisan. There are also local studies of varying merit: J. C. Jessop, *Education in Angus* (1931), seems determined to do a Lytton Strachey on the myth of Scottish pre-eminence, but only partly succeeds; I. J. Simpson, *Education in Aberdeenshire before 1872* (1947), is a scholarly appraisal; and W. Boyd, *Education in Ayrshire Through Seven Centuries* (1961), is very good on the post-Revolution period, as is A. Bain, *Education in Stirlingshire from the Reformation to the Act of 1872* (1965). M. B. Dealy, *Catholic Schools in Scotland* (1945), grapples unsuccessfully with a notoriously difficult subject.

The universities have fared better. Two studies by R. G. Cant cover St Andrews: *The University of St Andrews: A Short History* (1946), and *The College of St Salvator* (1950). Glasgow is well represented by J. D. Mackie, *The University of Glasgow, 1451–1951: A Short History* (1954). R. S. Rait, *The Universities of Aberdeen* (1895), deals with King's College and Marischal College. Sir A. Grant, *The Story of the University of Edinburgh* (2 vols., 1884), remains the best general account; a brief but cogent treatment is D. B. Horn, *A Short History of the University of Edinburgh 1556–1889* (1967). The aims and constitution of the universities are discussed by A. Morgan, *Scottish University Studies* (1933).

Scottish literature has been studied in fits and starts, a fact that is clearly evident in writings on the subject. The generally accepted standard, J. H. Millar, *A Literary History of Scotland* (1903), is vigorous but outdated; the same author, *Scottish Prose of the Seventeenth and Eighteenth Centuries* (1912), gives copious extracts. T. F. Henderson, *Scottish Vernacular Literature: a Succinct History* (1900), deals only with poetry; acute and lively, it makes little of the eighteenth century. G. Gregory Smith, *Scottish Literature: Character and Influence* (1919), consists of essays on various topics, most of which now seem jejune. A few items of interest are to be found in *The Cambridge History of English Literature* (VOLS. IX–XIV, 1912–16). A revival of interest in the subject has led to better fare. J. Speirs, *The Scots Literary Tradition* (1940, 2nd edn., 1962), is a pioneer essay in the modern style. K. Wittig, *The Scottish Tradition in Literature* (1958), is compendious (it glances at Gaelic) but its interpretations are sometimes forced. D. Daiches, *A Critical History of English Literature* (II, 1960), devotes some space to Scottish literature, giving a stimulating introduction to the eighteenth-century material. D. Craig, *Scottish Literature and the Scottish*

People, 1680–1830 (1961), is good on literature but weak on social history. J. Kinsley, ed., *Scottish Poetry, a Critical Survey* (1955), deals largely with the period covered in this volume.

There is no scholarly up-to-date treatment of Gaelic literature. Perhaps the best available works are still: M. Maclean, *The Literature of the Highlands* (edn. 1925), which concentrates on the development of modern Scottish Gaelic; and D. Maclean, *The Literature of the Scottish Gael* (1912). There is a highly condensed but good introduction to the subject by Derick Thomson in *Encyclopædia Britannica*, xx (edn. 1964).

Many insights into social and cultural history can be obtained from J. G. Fyfe, *Scottish Diaries and Memoirs, 1550–1843* (2 vols., 1927–42), which contains lengthy extracts.

Dramatic art has no great history in Scotland and consequently its literature is slight. The best work is still J. C. Dibdin, *The Annals of the Edinburgh Stage, with an account of the Rise and Progress of Dramatic Writing in Scotland* (1888). Other arts are better covered. J. L. Caw, *Scottish Painting, Past and Present, 1620–1908* (1908), is an important, but dated, pioneer work. S. Cursiter, *Scottish Art to the Nineteenth Century* (1948), is much slighter. I. Finlay, *Scottish Crafts* (1948), is a brief general introduction. H. G. Farmer, *A history of Music in Scotland* (1947), stands alone. On costume S. Maxwell and R. Hutchinson, *Scottish Costume* (1958), is a good elementary outline; J. Telfer Dunbar, *The History of Highland Dress* (1962), has become a standard.

Architecture, on the whole, has been well served. I. C. Hannah, *Story of Scotland in Stone* (1934), is an introductory survey; J. Stirling Maxwell, *Shrines and Homes of Scotland* (1937), is readable and informative; and J. Dunbar, *The Historic Architecture of Scotland* (1966), though by no means exhaustive has the great merit of considering ' housing ' rather than just historic edifices.

Scotland's contribution to the rise of medical science has not yet been the subject of a fully worthy history. The spade-work was done by J. D. Comrie, *History of Scottish Medicine* (2 vols., 1932), but it is a poor synthesis. C. H. Creswell, *The Royal College of Surgeons of Edinburgh* (1926), is a collection of historical notes; and D. Guthrie, *The Medical School of Edinburgh* (1959), is too brief; a fuller picture emerges from the numerous other writings of Dr Guthrie. T. Ferguson, *The Dawn of Scottish Social Welfare* (1948), and the same author's *Scottish Social Welfare, 1864–1914* (1958), are interesting but poorly arranged.

III. FROM THE REVOLUTION TO THE UNION—1689–1707

(a) Political

(i) *Primary sources.* For the Revolution the most revealing sources are: Balcarres, *Memoirs touching the Revolution in Scotland* (Bannatyne Club); *Leven and Melville Papers* (Bannatyne Club); *Proceedings of the Estates in Scotland* (2 vols., S.H.S.); *Carstares State Papers* (ed. McCormick, 1774); *Annandale Family Book*

of the Johnstones, Earls and Marquises of Annandale (ed. W. Fraser, 2 vols., 1894);
Culloden Papers, 1625–1748 (1815); *More Culloden Papers, 1626–1704* (ed. D.
Warrand, I, 1923); *Chronicles of Atholl and Tullibardine* (5 vols., 1908). Two
later works incorporate a good deal of official records: Sir J. Dalrymple,
Memoirs of Great Britain and Ireland, 1681–92 (2 vols., 1771–3); and J. (' Ossian ')
Macpherson, *Original Papers containing the Secret History of Great Britain, 1660–
1714* (2 vols., 1775).

For the Highlands, the main printed sources are: H. Mackay, *Memoirs*
(Bannatyne Club); *Memoirs of Sir Ewen Cameron of Lochiel* (Maitland Club);
and *Papers Illustrative of the Political Condition of the Highlands of Scotland, 1689–96*
(Maitland Club), an essential, though somewhat misleading, source for the
Massacre of Glencoe.

The Company of Scotland and the Darien Scheme are well covered by:
Darien Papers, 1695–1700 (ed. J. H. Burton, Bannatyne Club); and *Darien
Shipping Papers* (ed. G. P. Insh, S.H.S.).

For the Union of 1707, the chief sources are: *Carstares State Papers* (ed.
McCormick); *Memoirs of Sir John Clerk of Penicuik* (S.H.S.); Sir David Hume
of Crossrigg, *Diary of the Proceedings in the Parliament and Privy Council of Scotland,
1700–1707* (Bannatyne Club); *Correspondence of George Baillie of Jerviswood,
1702–1708* (Bannatyne Club); H.M.C. *Mar and Kellie* (VOL. I, 1904); H.M.C.
Portland (VOL. IV, 1897); *Seafield Correspondence* (S.H.S.); *Seafield Letters*
(S.H.S.). George Lockhart of Carnwath, *Memoirs Concerning the Affairs of
Scotland from Queen Anne's Accession to the Throne . . . to the Union* (1714), is
heavily biassed but, in spite of the author's strong Jacobitism, still indispensable.

(ii) *Secondary works*. There is no adequate general account of the reign of
William II. The best is still W. L. Mathieson, *Politics and Religion*, II (1902),
and the same author's *Scotland and the Union, 1695–1747* (1905); but both
books have serious shortcomings, partly attributable to the disjointed treatment favoured by their author. A suggestive article is J. Halliday, ' The Club
and the Revolution in Scotland, 1689–90 ', in *S.H.R.*, XLV.

Interest has focussed mainly on Glencoe, and this has produced much
unscholarly writing—such as J. Buchan, *Glencoe* (1933), and J. Prebble, *Glencoe* (1965), both of them journalistic and highly subjective. Not particularly
deep, but more sensible, is D. J. Macdonald, *Slaughter under Trust* (1965). But
on the whole, the best general account is still T. B. Macaulay, *History of
England* (ed. C. H. Firth, VOL. v, 1914). J. Paget, *New Examen* (1st edn., 1861,
2nd edn., 1934), which seeks to controvert Macaulay's view, quibbles
ingeniously.

There are several good works on the Darien episode: F. Cundall, *The
Darien Venture* (1926), based largely on Spanish sources; F. R. Hart, *The
Disaster of Darien* (1930); and G. P. Insh, *The Company of Scotland* (1932),
which, though in some ways the most complete study, suffers from a cloying style.

Numerous secondary works deal with the Union, but many of them are vitiated by bias or determinist views. Daniel Defoe, *History of the Union* (1709, 2nd edn., 1786) is quite unreliable and has misled generations of historians. J. Bruce, *Report on the Union* (2 vols., 1799), contains a valuable appendix of original documents. The fullest and fairest work is still J. Mackinnon, *The Union of England and Scotland* (1896), but it is now dated. P. Hume Brown, *The Legislative Union of England and Scotland* (1914), is scholarly, but, for all that, a marked pro-Union bias can be detected. This is even more obvious in G. M. Trevelyan, *Ramillies and the Union with Scotland* (1932), and in G. S. Pryde, *The Treaty of Union of Scotland and England, 1707* (1950), which, however, has the unusual merit of seeing the Union not as a *fait accompli* in 1707 but as a continuing process. D. Nobbs, *England and Scotland, 1560–1707* (1952), deals mainly with the seventeenth century. The interpretation of the achievement of Union in 1707 is at the moment in a state of flux, some indication of which appears in W. Ferguson, ' The Making of the Treaty of Union of 1707 ', in *S.H.R.*, XLIII, and in P. W. J. Riley, ' The Formation of the Scottish Ministry of 1703 ', in *S.H.R.*, XLIV.

(b) Social and economic

(i) *Primary sources.* The social and economic history of the period between the Revolution and the Union remains to be written, though there is abundant material in official records, estate papers, and burgh records. For agriculture, there are numerous rentals, of which there is a collection in Register House. Much can be gleaned also from Sir Robert Sibbald's MS. in the National Library of Scotland. A. Symson, *A Large Description of Galloway*, though not printed until 1823, was written at Sibbald's prompting, and there are several such accounts for other parts of the country in the Sibbald MS. W. Hamilton of Wishaw, *Descriptions of the Sheriffdoms of Lanark and Renfrew, compiled about 1710* (Maitland Club), is also invaluable and shows how important were the small feuars in that area. Several volumes published by the Scottish History Society amplify the picture, notably: *Records of the Baron Court of Stitchill, 1655–1807* ; *Court Book of the Barony of Urie, 1604–1707*; and *The Book of Record, a Diary written by Patrick, First Earl of Strathmore, 1684–89.* Contemporary treatises on agriculture are also important: J. Donaldson, *Husbandry Anatomized* (1697); Lord Belhaven, *The Countrey-man's Rudiments* (1699); and A. Fletcher of Saltoun, ' Second Discourse on the Affairs of Scotland ', in *Political Works* (edn. 1732).

For trade, the best sources are the publications of the Scottish Burgh Records Society, particularly *The Miscellany* (1881). *Minute Book of the Managers of the New Mills Cloth Manufactory, 1681–90* (S.H.S.), is a unique source, with an illuminating introduction by W. R. Scott.

(ii) *Secondary works.* The pioneer work was done long ago by W. R. Scott in several articles: ' The Fiscal Policy of Scotland before the Union ', in *S.H.R.*, I; ' Scottish Industrial Undertakings before the Union ', and ' The Woolcard Manufactory at Leith ', in *S.H.R.*, II. He consolidated and extended his work in *The Constitution and Finance of English, Scottish and Irish Joint Stock*

Companies (3 vols., 1910–12). T. C. Smout, *Scottish Trade on the Eve of the Union* (1963), is an important study based on customs records and more general than the title might suggest. Valuable information is to be found in two old compilations, which give copious extracts from sources: George Chalmers, *Caledonia* (8 vols., new edn. 1887–1902); and R. Chambers, *Domestic Life of Scotland* (III, 1861). An interesting biography of Chalmers, an industrious eighteenth-century antiquary, is G. A. Cockcroft, *The Public Life of George Chalmers* (1939).

(c) *Ecclesiastical*

The ecclesiastical history of this period has also been neglected. The outlines are given in R. H. Story, *Life of William Carstares* (1874), though it is badly dated. The first-fruits of what promised to be a more thorough exploration are two articles by the late T. Maxwell: ' Scotch Presbyterian Eloquence: a Post Revolution Pamphlet ', in *Records of Scottish Church History Society*, VIII, and ' Presbyterian and Episcopalian in 1688 ', *ibid.*, XIII.

IV. The Eighteenth Century
(a) *Political*

(i) *Primary sources.* The main official sources, State Papers Scotland, Series II (S.P. 54-57) are still in MS.: similarly with Home Office papers, from 1782. Printed sources for the first half of the eighteenth century tend to be scattered and of very unequal value. Apart from H.M.C. publications (for which see Report XXII), the following are the most informative: *Lockhart Papers* (ed. A. Aufrere, 2 vols., 1817); *Marchmont Papers* (ed. Sir G. H. Rose, 3 vols., 1831); *Annals and Correspondence of the First and Second Earls of Stair* (ed. J. M. Graham, 2 vols., 1875); and *Letters of Lord Grange, 1731–41*, *Miscellany* III (Spalding Club).

For Jacobitism see Dorothy A. Guthrie and Clyde L. Grose, ' Forty Years of Jacobite Bibliography ', in *Journal of Modern History*, XI. As they ruefully remark: ' lost causes frequently have feline vitality, and bibliographically they nearly always do '. There is a vast amount in print, primary as well as secondary; for the bulk of the former category the Scottish historical clubs are mainly responsible. For the '15 the chief source is John, Master of Sinclair, *Memoirs of the Insurrection in Scotland* (Abbotsford Club), the work of a disillusioned rebel; most of the available material is extensively quoted in A. H. Tayler, *1715: The Story of the Rising* (1936). *Historical Papers relating to the Jacobite Period, 1699–1750* (New Spalding Club), deals mainly with the North East Lowlands, and other publications by the same club add details. Lord Elcho's bilious *Short Account of the Affairs of Scotland, 1744–46* (ed. E. Charteris, 1907), does for the '45 what the Master of Sinclair did for the '15; and the indefatigable Taylers, *1745 and After* (1938), again display most of the available material. Numerous volumes published by the S.H.S. deal with Jacobitism, of which the following are outstanding: *A List of Persons concerned in the Rebellion of 1745*; *The Jacobite Attempt of 1719*; *The Lyon in Mourning*, 3 vols.; *Itinerary of Prince Charles Edward*; *Memorials of Murray of Broughton*; *Origins of the '45*; and *Prisoners of the '45.* A useful guide to Jacobite material should be the National Library of Scotland's forthcoming, *Shelf Catalogue of the Blaikie Collection,* consisting of pamphlets, broadsides, etc.

On the broader plane of politics, *Arniston Memoirs* (ed. G. W. T. Omond, 1887) contains useful material for the reign of George III; and so does *Letters of George Dempster to Sir Adam Fergusson* (ed. J. Fergusson, 1934). *The Political State of Scotland, 1788* (ed. Sir C. E. Adam, 1887), analyses the electorate in the Scottish counties. Further details occur in *The Parliamentary Papers of John Robinson* (ed. W. T. Laprade, Camden Society). Two later *Political States,* 1790 and 1811, have the merit of covering the royal burghs as well as the counties, but are inferior in other respects.

The eighteenth century was the heyday of diarists and autobiographers— for which see Fyfe, *op. cit.* The following are the most rewarding: A. Carlyle, *Autobiography* (ed. J. H. Burton, 1860); T. Somerville, *My Own Life and Times, 1741–1814* (ed. W. Lee, 1861); H. Cockburn, *Memorials of His Time, 1779– 1830* (ed. H. A. Cockburn, 1910); and Mrs Eliza Fletcher, *Autobiography* (1876).

(ii) *Secondary works.* Scottish historians have long suffered from the Carlylean delusion that 'history is but biography writ large'. Most of the resulting works, however, reveal the defects of this pathetic fallacy, and in particular they frequently lack balance. But for the first half of the eighteenth century the following are of some service: G. W. T. Omond, *Andrew Fletcher of Saltoun* (1897), brief but pointed and not entirely superseded by W. C. Mackenzie, *Life of Andrew Fletcher* (1935); nor is J. H. Burton, *Life of Duncan Forbes* (1847), altogether routed by G. Menary, *Duncan Forbes* (1936); and J. H. Burton, *Simon Fraser* (1847), is still worth reading in spite of the fuller study of the same subject by W. C. Mackenzie (1908).

The only attempted general synthesis of the eighteenth century is W. L. Mathieson, *Scotland and the Union, 1695–1747* (1905), and the same author's *The Awakening of Scotland, 1747–97* (1910). It is a trenchant but now rather old-fashioned work. Of more specialised works, P. W. J. Riley, *The English Ministers and Scotland, 1707–1727* (1964), breaks new ground and is particularly good on post-Union administrative problems. To the making of books on Jacobitism there is no end; and that this has retarded the study of eighteenth-century Scotland is suggested in 'The Year '45', a judicious bibliographical article in *The Times Literary Supplement,* 3 November 1945. The best general accounts are: Sir C. Petrie, *The Jacobite Movement* (3rd edn., 1959); and G. H. Jones, *The Mainstream of Jacobitism* (1954), which is concerned mainly with plots and counter-plots. Of more specialised studies, the following can be recommended: C. H. Hartmann, *The Quest Forlorn* (1952), a somewhat blasé view, in marked contrast to D. Nicholas, *The Young Adventurer* (1949), which is clearly pro-Jacobite. That this was not the general attitude of eighteenth-century Scots is well brought out by Sir J. Fergusson, *Argyll and the Forty-Five* (1951). Kathleen Tomasson, *The Jacobite General* (1958), takes up the cudgels for Lord George Murray, pretty much as Winifred Duke had done in her *Lord George Murray and the '45* (1927). J. Prebble, *Culloden* (1961), is a shrill rendering of well-known matters.

While the Jacobites have engrossed so much attention the Namierite revolution has come and gone, leaving little mark on the study of politics in eighteenth-century Scotland. The approach, though an increasingly inadequate one, is still by way of biography. An obvious medium has been Henry Dundas, of whom there are three studies: by J. A. Lovat-Fraser (1916), H. Furber (1931), and C. Matheson (1933). Furber's work is regarded as standard, but, though well documented, it is not always *au fait* with the Scottish scene. A. Fergusson, *The Honourable Henry Erskine* (1882), is very diffuse but still of value, conveying as it does something of its subject's attractive personality. H. W. Meikle, *Scotland and the French Revolution* (1912), is really a political history from 1780 to 1830, and by no means as exhaustive as is generally supposed: it leans too heavily on H. Cockburn, especially the *Examination of the Trials for Sedition in Scotland* (2 vols., 1888), which is decidedly partisan. The working of the electoral system is described in E. and A. Porritt, *The Unreformed House of Commons* (2 vols., 1903), which gives a mass of ill-digested information. An indication of more recent trends of thought is to be found in the following articles: W. L. Burn, ' The General Election of 1761 at Ayr ', in *E.H.R.*, LII; J. Fergusson, ' " Making Interest " in Scottish County Elections ', in *S.H.R.*, XXVI; and W. Ferguson, ' Dingwall Burgh Politics and the Parliamentary Franchise in the Eighteenth Century ', in *S.H.R.*, XXXVIII.

(*b*) *Social and economic*

(i) *Primary sources.* Many sources illustrative of the rural scene have been published, notably: *Forfeited Estates Papers* (S.H.S.); *Monymusk Papers* (S.H.S.); *Life and Labour on an Aberdeenshire Estate, 1735–50* (Third Spalding Club); *Letters of Cockburn of Ormiston to his Gardener* (S.H.S.); *Household Book of Lady Grizell Baillie* (S.H.S.); *Scottish Population Statistics* (S.H.S.), which contains A. Webster's 'Analysis of the Population of Scotland, 1755'; *Survey of Lochtayside* (S.H.S.); *Survey of Assynt* (S.H.S.); *Argyll Estate Instructions* (S.H.S.); and V. Gaffney, *The Lordship of Strathavon* (Third Spalding Club).

In the later eighteenth century sources on agriculture became voluminous. A. Wight, *Present State of Husbandry in Scotland* (4 vols., 1778–84), is an excellent work; its findings can be compared with those given in the county agricultural surveys produced in the 1790s for the board of agriculture. A convenient list of these is given in an appendix to Handley, *Scottish Farming in the Eighteenth Century* (1953), and also in an appendix to Symon, *op. cit.* Background information on them is to be found in R. Mitchison, *Agricultural Sir John* (1962), an exuberant study of the fantastic Sir John Sinclair of Ulbster, who was instrumental in producing *The Statistical Account of Scotland* (21 vols., 1791–99), and who compiled *The Analysis of the Statistical Account* (2 vols., 1825–6). The *O.S.A.* covers the whole of Scotland, parish by parish. Contributions vary in quality, but generally ecclesiastical, agricultural, educational and social topics are given favoured treatment. Industry is not so well served, though some of the accounts take stock of coal-mining, textiles, and so on.

The printed sources so far have given poor coverage to trade and industry (cf. R. H. Campbell, ' The Industrial Revolution: A Revision Article ', in *S.H.R.*, XLVI). But it looks as if the balance may soon be redressed: Professor Campbell himself has made a beginning with his edition of *States of the Annual Progress of the Linen Manufacture, 1727–54* (1964), on the work of the Board of Manufactures. Much can also be gleaned from the periodical press, to which M. E. Craig, *Scottish Periodical Press, 1750–1789* (1931), is a good guide.

(ii) *Secondary works*. The main authority is H. Hamilton, *An Economic History of Scotland in the Eighteenth Century* (1963), which is erudite and compendious, with an excellent bibliography. The same author's *The Industrial Revolution in Scotland* (1932), is less detailed but covers the early nineteenth century as well and is still invaluable. On agriculture, J. Handley, *Scottish Farming in the Eighteenth Century* (1953), has been criticised as too gloomy and old-fashioned, but these strictures seem exaggerated. The same author's *Agricultural Revolution in Scotland* (1963), is a series of loosely connected essays, some of which are valuable. A. R. B. Haldane, *The Drove Roads of Scotland* (1952), brings out the importance of the cattle trade, especially to the Highlands. E. Burt, *Letters from the North of Scotland* (2 vols., 1st edn., 1754), purports to describe the Highlands in the early eighteenth century; but it is suspect and ought to be used very cautiously. Much more reliable insights are given by I. F. Grant, *Everyday Life on an Old Highland Farm* (1934). The best treatment of the Highlands from the economic standpoint is M. Gray, *The Highland Economy, 1750–1850* (1957). J. E. Donaldson, *Caithness in the Eighteenth Century* (1938), is also well-documented.

On trade and industry specialist studies are relatively meagre. A. Fell, *The Early Iron Industry of Furness and District* (1908), is bulky but only partly concerned with the activities of Furness ironmasters in Scotland. R. H. Campbell, *Carron Company* (1961), sheds much light on the growth of the iron industry from 1759 onwards. Two articles furnish some interesting details: G. Thomson, ' The Dalnotter Iron Company ', in *S.H.R.*, XXXV; and J. R. Hume and J. Butt, ' Muirkirk, 1786–1802: The creation of a Scottish industrial community ', in *S.H.R.*, XLV. Adam Smith, *Wealth of Nations* (2 vols., ed. Cannan, 1950), should not be overlooked, for it provides stimulating comments on many aspects of eighteenth-century Scotland. R. Bald, *A General View of the Coal Trade of Scotland* (1808), is a contemporary classic that ought to be reprinted. R. Page Arnot, *History of the Scottish Miners* (1955), is very sketchy on the eighteenth century. A. and N. Clow, *The Chemical Revolution* (1952), is a massive work which throws a flood of light on many facets of eighteenth-century Scottish life.

Transport is dealt with in the following: J. B. Salmond, *Wade in Scotland* (new edn. 1938), which describes the making of the military roads in the

Highlands from 1725 onwards; A. R. B. Haldane, *New Ways Through the Glens* (1962), carries the story forward to the work of Thomas Telford; and S. Smiles, *Lives of the Engineers* (5 vols., 1874) gives a good deal of attention to transport in his biographies of Telford, Watt, and others. E. A. Pratt, *Scottish Canals and Waterways* (1922), demonstrates the importance of canals in the first phase of the Industrial Revolution. L. Gardiner, *Stage-Coach to John-o'-Groats* (1961), is a good popular account of the rise of stage-coach services.

A thorough history of banking is much needed. A. W. Kerr, *History of Banking in Scotland* (4th edn., 1962), was an important pioneer study but now appears rather superficial. Much the same can be said of W. Graham, *The One Pound Note in the History of Banking in Great Britain* (1911). They can be eked out by specialist accounts, themselves of varying quality: C. A. Malcolm, *The Bank of Scotland, 1695–1945* (n.d.); N. Munro, *The History of the Royal Bank of Scotland, 1727–1927* (1928); R. S. Rait, *The History of the Union Bank of Scotland* (1930), which covers the numerous private banks which amalgamated to form the Union Bank; C. A. Malcolm, *The History of the British Linen Bank* (1950); and Anon., *Our Bank: the Story of the Commercial Bank of Scotland, 1810–1941* (1941).

Several papers in *Studies in Scottish Business History* (ed. P. L. Payne, 1967) deal with eighteenth-century themes.

The literature on social life is immense. There is much information in John Ramsay of Ochtertyre's observations, *Scotland and Scotsmen in the Eighteenth Century* (ed. A. Allardyce, 2 vols., 1888); and in *Letters of John Ramsay of Ochtertyre, 1799–1812* (S.H.S.). W. Alexander, *Sketches of Northern Rural Life in the Eighteenth Century* (1877), is excellent for the north-east Lowlands, as is E. Dunbar Dunbar, *Social Life in Former Days* (2 vols., 1865–6). J. Murray, *Social Life a Hundred Years Ago* (1905), summarises many topics dealt with in the O.S.A., to which it gives copious references. H. G. Graham, *The Social Life of Scotland in the Eighteenth Century* (var. edns.), remains a good introduction (and a splendid book), though a broad coverage on more analytical lines is now badly needed. M. Plant, *The Domestic Life of Scotland in the Eighteenth Century* (1952), confines itself too much to the upper classes and thus gives a distorted picture. M. Lochhead, *The Scots Household in the Eighteenth Century* (1948), is popular but disjointed.

On most aspects of urban life the publications of the Burgh Records Society should be consulted. H. Arnot, *History of Edinburgh* (1779), remains a prime source. J. Grant, *Old and New Edinburgh* (3 vols., 1883), is a good example of a nineteenth-century popular work. J. Kay, *A Series of Original Portraits and Caricature Etchings* (new edn., 1887), is a unique source, giving brief biographies as well as life-like caricatures of most of the notabilities of Edinburgh in the late eighteenth century. E. Topham, *Letters from Edinburgh in the years 1774 and 1775* (2 vols., 1780), is more sympathetic than English visitors were wont to be. For the capital, see *Edinburgh, 1767–1967: a Select List of Books* (1967).

Glasgow also has a considerable literature (for which see Mitchell and Cash). The most useful works are: J. Gibson, *History of Glasgow* (1777); and

G. Eyre Todd, *History of Glasgow* (3 vols., 1921–34), which is, however, rather pedestrian.

The Scots have never been denied the opportunity of seeing themselves 'as ithers see them'. Some visitors, mainly English, jotted down their impressions, and many have been printed: see A. Mitchell, *List of Travels and Tours in Scotland, 1296–1900* (1902). The main accounts are utilised in R. H. Coats, *Travellers' Tales of Scotland* (1913), and, less fully, in M. Lindsay, *The Discovery of Scotland* (1966)—both popular but engagingly readable works.

On emigration, see G. Donaldson, *The Scots Overseas* (1966), a succinct examination of a complex issue, with helpful bibliography. I. C. C. Graham, *Colonists from Scotland* (1956), deals with eighteenth-century emigration in more detail.

The literature of the period is an important source—notably, the works of Allan Ramsay senior for the earlier eighteenth century, of Robert Fergusson for the middle period, and of Robert Burns for the last quarter of the century. The best of Sir Walter Scott's novels also deal with late seventeenth- and eighteenth-century Scotland—*Old Mortality, Heart of Midlothian, Waverley, Redgauntlet* and *The Antiquary*. On this, consult J. Anderson, 'Sir Walter Scott as Historical Novelist', in *Studies in Scottish Literature*, IV. The novels of John Galt, particularly *The Annals of the Parish* and *The Provost*, are excellent illustrations of late eighteenth-century trends. In a wider prospect, D. Daiches, *The Paradox of Scottish Culture: the Eighteenth Century Experience* (1964), is a stimulating, if rather controversial, introduction. Chapters in the relevant volumes of the *Oxford History of English Literature*, by B. Dobree (1959), and more especially W. L. Renwick (1963) should be consulted.

(c) Ecclesiastical

(i) *Primary sources.* For the Church of Scotland, these are mainly to be found in *Acts of the General Assembly of the Church of Scotland, 1638–1842* (ed. T. Pitcairn *et al.*, 1843), and N. Morren, *Annals of the General Assembly of the Church of Scotland, 1752–66* (2 vols., 1840); A. Edgar, *Old Church Life in Scotland* (2 vols., 1885–6), gives many interesting references to church records. The records of many presbyteries have been printed—for which see M. B. Macgregor, *op. cit.*, pp. 180 ff. There are also many diaries and autobiographies (for a guide to them, see Fyfe, *op. cit*).

(ii) *Secondary works.* The best general work is J. Walker, *The Theology and Theologians of Scotland, chiefly of the Seventeenth and Eighteenth Centuries* (2nd edn., 1888). There are two good books on the Highlands: J. Mackay, *The Church in the Highlands* (1914), which is at its best for the eighteenth century; and J. Macinnes, *The Evangelical Movement in the Highlands of Scotland* (1951), a valuable work which is by no means restricted to church history. There are many biographies, most of which are either of poor quality or ancient vintage. The most useful are: W. Addison, *The Life and Writings of Thomas Boston of Ettrick* (1936); and A. R. Macewen, *The Erskines* (1900), a minor classic by a major historian. The older covenanted tradition is best savoured in J. Howie of Lochgoin, *The Scots Worthies* (1775, and numerous later edns.), a presbyterian martyrology which attained a great vogue.

(d) Cultural

(i) *Primary sources.* It is impossible to list here the works that might be considered under this head: reference can be made to *The Catalogue of an Exhibition of Eighteenth Century Scottish Books at the Signet Library Edinburgh* (1951), an interesting but not exhaustive compilation.

(ii) *Secondary works.* Older commentaries, though dated, often contain insights denied more recent authorities. Thus J. McCosh, *The Scottish Philosophy* (1875), and L. Stephen, *History of English Thought in the Eighteenth Century* (2 vols., 3rd edn., 1902), are well worth reading. H. Laurie, *Scottish Philosophy in its National Development* (1902), is an extremely lucid account which invites comparison with S. A. Grave, *The Scottish Philosophy of Common Sense* (1960). The so-called 'Enlightenment' commands increasing attention, mainly on sociological grounds. While interesting and revealing, such an approach does some violence to the subject, upgrading some rather secondary writers who fit the theory at the expense of more important thinkers who do not. Thus Hutcheson and Reid suffer excommunication: for them recourse has to be had to W. R. Scott, *Francis Hutcheson* (1900), and A. Campbell Fraser, *Thomas Reid* (1898). W. C. Lehmann, *Adam Ferguson* (1930), may claim to have initiated the sociological approach. The same author has produced a valuable study of *John Millar of Glasgow, 1735–1801* (1960). A good general treatment of this sort is G. Bryson, *Man and Society: The Scottish Inquiry of the Eighteenth Century* (1954), which has an extensive bibliography. E. C. Mossner has produced two major works on David Hume: *The Forgotten Hume* (1943), which treats of Hume as a man; and the massive, if prolix, *Life of David Hume* (1954). Editions, more or less critical, of eighteenth-century texts are now the fashion, such as Adam Smith's *Lectures on Rhetoric and Belles-Lettres* (ed. J. M. Lothian, 1963), and Adam Ferguson's *Essay on the History of Civil Society* (ed. D. Forbes, 1966).

For schools, as well as the more general texts already referred to, consult A. Law, *Education in Edinburgh in the Eighteenth Century* (1965); and D. J. Withrington, 'The S.P.C.K. and Highland Schools in Mid-Eighteenth Century', in *S.H.R.*, XLI.

On the arts the following studies are important: A. Smart, *The Life and Art of Allan Ramsay* (1952); A. T. Bolton, *The Architecture of Robert and James Adam* (2 vols., 1922); J. Lees-Milne, *The Age of Adam* (1947); and J. Fleming, *Robert Adam and his Circle* (1962). A. J. Youngson, *The Making of Classical Edinburgh* (1966), gives a brief but sumptuously illustrated account of the rise of the new town.

v. The Nineteenth Century

(a) Political

(i) *Primary sources.* Little archive material has been printed, but there is a great mass of printed Parliamentary Papers, covering many topics, for which reference should be made to the guides mentioned on p. 418.

For the early nineteenth century *The Letters of Sir Walter Scott* (ed. H. J. C. Grierson, 12 vols., 1932–7), are very informative on many subjects. H. Cockburn, *Memorials*, remains valuable (though it has constantly to be remembered that he had a strong Whig bias); the same author's *Letters on the Affairs of Scotland* (1874) illuminate Whig politics in the 1820s and the Reform Bill crises of 1830–32; and his *Journal* (2 vols., 1874) is a first-rate source up to 1848, particularly valuable for its treatment of the legal and political aspects of the Scottish church question.   A. B. Richmond, *Narrative of the Condition of the Manufacturing Population, and Proceedings of Government which led to the State Trials in Scotland* (1824), is a revealing piece of special pleading.   A. Somerville, *Autobiography of a Working Man* (1848), deals in part with social conditions in southern Scotland, a theme more fully developed in J. Younger, *Autobiography* (1881), which demonstrates the growth of working-class political consciousness.

R. M. W. Cowan, *The Newspaper in Scotland, a Study of its First Expansion, 1815–60* (1946) estimates the influence of the press on politics and society. Something of the quality of local newspapers can be savoured in J. Barron, *The Northern Highlands in the Nineteenth Century* (3 vols., 1903–13), which consists mainly of excerpts from the Inverness newspapers.   Early numbers of *The Edinburgh Review* (1803–) and of *Blackwood's Edinburgh Magazine* (1817–) deal at length with Scottish problems.

(ii) *Secondary works.*   The best effort at synthesis up to 1843 is W. L. Mathieson, *Church and Reform in Scotland, 1797–1843* (1916); but it is dated. H. Cockburn, *Life of Lord Jeffrey* (2 vols., 1852), is superficial.   A. Nicolson, *Memoirs of Adam Black* (1885), is largely taken up with the struggle between Whiggery and radicalism, which is also touched upon in G. O. Trevelyan, *Life and Letters of Lord Macaulay* (edn. 1889).   The Conservative viewpoint is presented in Sir A. Alison, *An Autobiography* (2 vols., 1883).   L. C. Wright, *Scottish Chartism* (1953), is the standard work; but reference should also be made to A. Wilson's chapter on ' Chartism in Glasgow ', in *Chartist Studies* (ed. A. Briggs, 1959).   Much has been written on Robert Owen: the best introduction is M. Cole, *Robert Owen of New Lanark* (1953).   A study of the activities of the Anti-Corn Law League in Scotland is very much needed. Some information is to be found in J. Morley, *Life of Richard Cobden* (2 vols., 1881); and in J. B. Mackie, *Life and Work of Duncan McLaren* (2 vols., 1888), which is virtually a history of mid-Victorian Scotland.   There is also much background material in the Marquess of Crewe, *Lord Rosebery* (2 vols., 1931), which is not entirely superseded by R. R. James, *Rosebery* (1963).   The early socialist movement is covered mainly by biographies.   H. F. West, *Cunninghame Graham* (1932), is supplemented by A. F. Tschiffely, *Don Roberto* (1937), another study of this exotic pioneer socialist.   His coadjutor, J. Keir Hardie, has been the subject of many biographies, of which the best are by W. Stewart (1921), H. Fyfe (1935), and E. Hughes (1956).   There is an excellent brief introduction to the labour movement by W. H. Marwick, *Labour in Scotland* (1948).   On this entire subject, see *An Interim Bibliography of the Scottish Working Class Movement* (ed I. McDougall, 1965).

For elections results, see T. Wilkie, *The Representation of Scotland: Parliamentary Elections since 1832* (1895).

On home rule and the rise of a nationalist movement, Sir R. Coupland, *Welsh and Scottish Nationalism* (1954), is suggestive but marred by factual errors. A better short account is W. H. Marwick, *Scottish Devolution* (1950).

Several articles elucidate specific themes: W. Ferguson, 'The Reform Act (Scotland) of 1832 ', in *S.H.R.*, XLV; H. J. Hanham, 'The Creation of the Scottish Office, 1881–87 ', in *Juridical Review*, N.S., X; D. W. Crowley, 'The " Crofters' Party ", 1885–92 ', in *S.H.R.*, XXXVIII; D. C. Savage, 'Scottish Politics, 1885–6 ', in *S.H.R.*, XL; J. G. Kellas, 'The Liberal Party and the Scottish Church Disestablishment Crisis ', in *E.H.R.*, LXXIXX; J. G. Kellas, 'The Liberal Party in Scotland, 1876–1895 ', in *S.H.R.*, XLIV; and D. W. Urwin, 'The Development of the Conservative Party Organisation in Scotland until 1912 ', in *S.H.R.*, XLIV.

(b) Social and economic

Parliamentary Papers are the main printed sources. *The New Statistical Account of Scotland* (15 vols., 1845), is on the same lines as *O.S.A.*, but fuller. J. H. Dawson, *Abridged Statistical History of Scotland* (1854), draws heavily on the *N.S.A.*, as do S. Lewis, *Topographical Dictionary of Scotland* (2 vols., 1846), and J. M. Wilson, ed., *Imperial Gazetteer of Scotland* (2 vols., n.d.). From 1801 onwards the decennial census returns are invaluable: *Scottish Population Statistics* (ed. J. G. Kyd, S.H.S.), conveniently summarises the main points, and so does D. F. Macdonald, *Scotland's Shifting Population, 1770–1850* (1937). J. Handley, *The Irish in Scotland, 1798–1845* (1943), and his *The Irish in Modern Scotland* (1947), are the standard works.

L. J. Saunders, *Scottish Democracy* (1950), describes the social structure of Scotland in the early nineteenth century; and W. H. Marwick, *Economic Developments in Victorian Scotland* (1936), also deals with social conditions. The poor-relief problem is covered by Sir G. Nicholls, *A History of the Scotch Poor Law* (1856), which is the best study, and more superficially by A. Cormack, *Poor Relief in Scotland* (1923). The social attitudes of the churches are discussed in S. Mechie, *The Church and Scottish Social Development, 1780–1870* (1960); and there is a slight but valuable monograph by J. H. Brotherston, *Observations on the Early Public Health Movement in Scotland* (1952).

For agriculture Symon, *op. cit.*, is particularly good. The social side of the industry is studied by G. Houston, 'Labour Relations in Scottish Agriculture before 1870 ', in *Agricultural History Review*, VI, which should be bracketed with G. Evans, 'Farm Servants' Unions in Aberdeenshire from 1870–1900 ', in *S.H.R.*, XXXI, and with E. H. Whetham, 'Prices and Production in Scottish Farming, 1850–70 ', in *Scottish Journal of Political Economy*, IX. A most revealing biography is C. Hope, *Memoir of George Hope of Fenton Barns* (1881), which illustrates the difficulties encountered by tenant farmers.

M. Gray, *op. cit.*, remains the best authority on economic developments in the Highlands. A large, but controversial and unscholarly, literature has sprung up on the ' Clearances '. J. Loch, *Account of the Improvements on the Estates of the Marquess of Stafford* (1820), remains the improvers' bible. D. Sage, *Memorabilia Domestica* (1889), was a contemporary Highland minister who failed to appreciate improvement. D. Macleod, *Gloomy Memories in the Highlands of Scotland* (n.d., edn. 1892), was even more denunciatory. A. Mackenzie, *The History of the Highland Clearances* (1883, 2nd edn. 1946), is a kind of sourcebook for denunciations of ' landlordism '. I. Grimble, *The Trial of Patrick Sellar* (1962), and J. Prebble, *The Highland Clearances* (1963), merely echo Mackenzie. R. Somers, *Letters from the Highlands* (1848), has a more authentic ring, and there is a mass of interesting material in the Napier Commission *Report on Crofting* (5 vols., 1884). But on this whole subject thorough research is long overdue.

The subject of local government is thoroughly covered in J. P. Day, *Public Administration in the Highlands and Islands* (1918).

For the development of industry D. Bremner, *The Industries of Scotland* (1869), is still useful but ripe for supersession. R. W. Dron, *The Coal-Fields of Scotland* (1902), is technical but contains much valuable information on the industry's problems in the nineteenth century. A. S. Cunningham deals with certain areas: *Mining in the Kingdom of Fife* (1913), and *Mining in Mid and East Lothian* (1926), both popular. R. Page Arnot, *op. cit.*, devotes most of his space to the nineteenth and twentieth centuries.

There is no adequate treatment of the iron industry. T. B. Mackenzie, *Life of J. B. Neilson* (1928), is a mere pamphlet, barely indicating the problems facing the industry in the early nineteenth century; and A. MacGeorge, *The Bairds of Gartsherrie* (1872), deals somewhat cursorily with a family of prominent ironmasters in the period of expansion in the mid-nineteenth century. The following articles by R. H. Campbell should be consulted: ' Investment in the Scottish Pig Iron Trade, 1830–48 ', in *Scottish Journal of Political Economy*, I, and ' Developments in the Scottish Pig Iron Trade, 1844–48 ', in *Journal of Economic History*, xv.

The rise of the Clyde shipbuilding industry is described in J. Shields, *Clyde Built* (1949), a popular work; and more cogently in C. R. Fay, *Round and About Industrial Britain*, ch. 7 (1952). There are the inevitable biographies, notably: J. Napier, *Robert Napier* (1904), and A. B. Bruce, *William Denny* (1888). But that the industry was not confined to the Clyde, see S. G. E. Lythe, ' Shipbuilding at Dundee down to 1914 ', in *Scottish Journal of Political Economy*, IX.

For the textile industries, A. J. Warden, *History of the Linen Trade* (1864), remains important. Cotton is dealt with by: W. H. Marwick, ' The Cotton Industry and the Industrial Revolution in Scotland ', in *S.H.R.*, xxi; G. M. Mitchell, ' The English and Scottish Cotton Industries ', in *S.H.R.*, xxiii; and W. O. Henderson, ' The Cotton Famine in Scotland, 1862–64 ', in *S.H.R.*,

XXX. M. Blair, *The Paisley Shawl* (1904), deals informatively with this specialised trade.

The following cover transport developments: G. Dott, *Early Scottish Colliery Wagonways* (1947), a pamphlet; W. M. Acworth, *The Railways of Scotland* (1890); and O. S. Nock, *Scottish Railways* (1950). There are many books on individual railway and shipping concerns.

(c) Ecclesiastical

The standard works already cited usually cover the early nineteenth century but tend to become sketchy thereafter. The Disruption produced a voluminous literature, of which the following are the most significant. T. Brown, *Annals of the Disruption* (var. edns.), has much interesting contemporary material. Three committed histories illustrate different loyalties: R. Buchanan, *The Ten Years' Conflict* (2 vols., new edn., 1852), strongly non-intrusionist; J. Bryce, *Ten Years of the Church of Scotland* (2 vols., 1850), as strongly reflects the Moderate standpoint; and A. Turner, *The Scottish Secession of 1843* (1859), in giving the Middle party version ' calls a plague o' both houses '. They make a fascinating and revealing trilogy, suggesting that ' history ' is largely a state of mind. W. Hanna, *Memoirs of Thomas Chalmers* (4 vols., 1852–53), is a prime source, and so also is T. Guthrie, *Autobiography and Memoir* (2 vols., 1874). They have been freely drawn upon by later writers. Of these the best are: H. Watt, *Thomas Chalmers and the Disruption* (1943); and G. D. Henderson, *Heritage: A Study of the Disruption* (1943), a brilliant little book. On a wider plane, J. R. Fleming, *History of the Church in Scotland, 1843–1929* (2 vols., 1927–32) is concerned mainly, though not exclusively, with the presbyterian churches. A valuable biography is P. C. Simpson, *Life of Principal Rainy* (2 vols., 1909), which is in effect a study of the Scottish presbyterian churches in the last half of the nineteenth century. J. Tulloch, *Movements of Religious Thought in Britain during the Nineteenth Century* (1885), pays special attention to Scotland.

(d) Cultural

In the later nineteenth century the cultural life of Scotland suffered a sharp decline, but the great tradition lasted until the 1830s. It is well illustrated in J. G. Lockhart, *Life of Sir Walter Scott* (best edn., 10 vols., 1902–03), a work of literature as well as a first-rate historical source. J. G. Lockhart, *Peter's Letters to his Kinsfolk* (var. edns.), powerfully evokes the Scottish scene, as does J. Wilson (' Christopher North '), *Noctes Ambrosianae* (var. edns.). J. A. Greig, *Francis Jeffrey of the Edinburgh Review* (1948), adds some significant touches, and much can be learned from D. Nichol Smith, ed., *Jeffrey's Literary Criticism* (1910). J. Clive, *Scotch Reviewers* (1957), demonstrates the importance of the *Edinburgh Review*. The earlier part of J. A. Froude's *Life of Thomas Carlyle* also contributes to understanding of the early nineteenth century. There is a pleasant, but not particularly deep, introduction by M. Joyce, *Edinburgh, the Golden Age* (1951); D. Young, *Edinburgh in the Age of Sir Walter Scott* (1965), is too discursive. Certain chapters of I. Jack, *English Literature, 1815–32* (1963), in the Oxford series, deal with aspects of Scottish literature.

G. E. Davie, *The Democratic Intellect: Scotland and her Universities in the Nineteenth Century* (1961), attributes the decline and fall to anglicising influences, but his views have not been generally accepted. The change may, in fact, merely have denoted a transition to a technological age, as is suggested by reading A. G. Clement and R. H. S. Robertson, *Scotland's Scientific Heritage* (1961). The old Scottish natural philosophy can be seen establishing new traditions in S. P. Thompson, *Life of Lord Kelvin* (2 vols., 1910), and in L. Campbell and W. Garnett, *Life of Clerk Maxwell* (1882). There are interesting recent assessments in C. Domb, ed., *Clerk Maxwell and Modern Science* (1963).

On the whole, the culture of Scotland in the later nineteenth century badly needs closer examination. D. Carswell, *Brother Scots* (1927), which consists of six splenetic biographical essays, is far too facile. G. Blake, *Barrie and the Kailyard School* (1951), suggests some likely explanations but is too brief to make them wholly convincing. The counterblast to the kailyairders is examined in J. Veitch, *George Douglas Brown* (1952).

VI. THE TWENTIETH CENTURY

So little in the way of primary material is in print that the distinction between primary and secondary material is at the moment scarcely worth maintaining. Statutes, white papers, and the press (particularly *The Scotsman*, *The Glasgow Herald*, *Daily Express*, *Bulletin*, and *Daily Record*) constitute the main available primary material.

(a) Political

There is no satisfactory text-book on the period. Party politics are covered, with varying degrees of success, in biographies and memoirs, notably: J. A. Spender, *Life of Campbell-Bannerman* (2 vols., 1923); R. Blake, *The Unknown Prime Minister* (1955), a study of A. Bonar Law; G. Elton, *Life of Ramsay MacDonald* (1939); and R. B. Haldane, *An Autobiography* (1929).

The rise of socialist political groups is touched upon in: W. Gallacher, *Revolt on the Clyde* (1936), and to a less instructive extent in its sequel, *Rolling of the Thunder* (1947), both engagingly idiosyncratic rather than accurate; D. Kirkwood, *My Life of Revolt* (1935), a simple record; T. Bell, *John Maclean: Fighter for Freedom* (1944), reflects Communist commitments, as does the same author's autobiography, *Pioneering Days* (1941); a more interesting and authentic picture is given by J. Paton, *Proletarian Pilgrimage* (1935), and its sequel *Left Turn!* (1936); and E. Shinwell, *Conflict without Malice* (1955), contributes a little both to the rise of socialist parties and to the parliamentary scene. Anon., *The Scottish Socialists: a Gallery of Contemporary Portraits* (1931), makes some shrewd assessments of leading figures.

Important works dealing with developments during and immediately following the first world war are: W. R. Scott and J. Cunnison, *Industries of the Clyde Valley during the War* (1924), and B. Pribićević, *The Shop-Stewards'*

Movement (1959), both of which cover the activities of the Clyde Workers' Committee; and R. K. Middlemas, *The Clydesiders* (1965), attempts to assess the influence of the group, but the handling of the Scottish scene is suspect.

For the inter-war period there are numerous *pièces d'occasion* that mix politics, economics and apocalyptic visions: most of them of left-wing provenance are listed in I. MacDougall, *op. cit.* Of the more extensive works the best are: G. McAllister, *James Maxton* (1935), which is preferable to J. McNair, *James Maxton* (1955); T. N. Graham, *Willie Graham* (n.d.); and T. Johnston, *Memories* (1952), an interesting but rather disappointing work which also deals with the second world war. Viscount Findhorn, *Within the Fringe* (1967), gives the recollections of another ex-secretary of state for Scotland, but also adds little. Sir D. Milne, *The Scottish Office and other Scottish Government Departments* (1958), outlines administration, and Sir W. E. Whyte, *Local Government in Scotland* (2nd revised edn. 1936) gives full references. A useful electoral study is S. B. Chrimes, ed., *The General Election in Glasgow, 1950* (1950); and a somewhat peculiar one is I. Budge and D. W. Urwin, *Scottish Political Behaviour* (1966).

J. M. MacCormick, *The Flag in the Wind* (1955), covers, from a rather personal standpoint, the rise of political nationalism, and A. M. Macewen, *The Thistle and the Rose* (1932), states the more moderate nationalist case. A. C. Turner, *Scottish Home Rule* (1951), is a brief attempt at an objective assessment. The Duchess of Atholl, *Working Partnership* (1958), adds vivid touches to many topics.

(b) Social and Economic

T. F. Henderson and F. Watt, *Scotland of Today* (1907), gives a chatty description of most aspects of Scottish life just before the first world war. The post-war depression produced a voluminous literature, most of it ephemeral. G. M. Thomson, *Scotland That Distressed Area* (1937), is a highly critical polemic which makes some shrewd points; R. M. Findlay, *Scotland at the Crossroads* (1937), condemns 'protection' and state intervention; C. A. Oakley, *Scottish Industry Today* (1937), is determinedly optimistic; and J. A. Bowie, *The Future of Scotland* (1939), makes the best analysis of the situation.

M. P. Fogarty, *Prospects of the Industrial Areas of Great Britain* (1945), does not neglect Scotland. Since 1947 basic information can be obtained from the annual official report on Industry and Employment (H.M.S.O.). J. Gollan, *Scottish Prospect* (1948), astringently examined post-war development plans and made some dolefully accurate predictions. A. Cairncross, ed., *The Scottish Economy* (1954), is a collection of essays on various industries and topics. G. McCrone, *Scotland's Economic Progress, 1951–60* (1965), is technical and not very conclusive. A. Moffat, *My Life with the Miners* (1965), is Marxist but good on developments after the second world war. M. Gaskin, *The Scottish Banks* (1965), is a comprehensive survey of their contemporary situation. C. A. Oakley, ed., *Scottish Industry* (1953), again provides a somewhat optimistic introduction to various manufactures.

On the Highlands the best works are: A. Collier, *The Crofting Problem* (1953), and F. Fraser Darling, *West Highland Survey* (1955).

On demographic studies, see *Scotland's Changing Population* (1946), seven papers on regional problems. *The Third Statistical Account of Scotland*, now in progress, should throw light on this and allied topics; but, unfortunately, the work is still incomplete and the published volumes (1952–) differ considerably in scope, accuracy, and even period.

(c) Ecclesiastical

J. R. Fleming, *op. cit.*, II is the best general treatment up to 1929; thereafter Burleigh, *op. cit.* R. Sjölinder, *Presbyterian Reunion in Scotland, 1907–1921* (1962), is scholarly and well-documented. C. A. Muir, *John White* (1958), is a detailed biography of one of the main architects of the union of 1929. J. Barr, *The Scottish Church Question* (1920), states the case for the opposition to union. J. Highet, *The Churches in Scotland Today* (1950), and the same author's *The Scottish Churches* (1960) are sociological studies replete with statistics. Two autobiographies that convey something of the situation of Church of Scotland ministers to day are: C. L. Warr, *The Glimmering Landscape* (1960), and H. C. Whitley, *Laughter in Heaven* (1962). I. Henderson, *Power Without Glory* (1967), is a strong anti-ecumenical tract, which finds little to laugh at below. The 'prescopalian' standpoint is well illustrated in J. K. S. Reid, *Presbyterians and Unity* (1962).

(d) Cultural

The main development has been the rise of a literary movement bent on emphasising its Scottish-ness. It is best studied in H. MacDiarmid, *Collected Poems* (1962), *Lucky Poet*, an autobiography (1943), *Contemporary Scottish Studies* (1926); E. Muir, *An Autobiography* (1954); and M. Lindsay, *The Scottish Renaissance* (1948), an incisive lecture.

Two of the most important figures are studied in: D. Glen, *Hugh MacDiarmid and the Scottish Renaissance* (1964), full and detailed with excellent bibliography; and I. S. Munro, *Leslie Mitchell: Lewis Grassic Gibbon* (1966), less detailed and not so penetrating.

Addenda

A. Chitnis, *The Scottish Enlightenment: a Social History* (1976); A. L. Drummond and J. B. Bulloch, *The Scottish Church, 1688–1843: the Age of the Moderates* (1973), and *The Church in Victorian Scotland, 1843–1874* (1975); W. Ferguson, *Scotland's Relations with England: a Survey to 1707* (1977); H. J. Hanham, *Scottish Nationalism* (1969); C. Harvie, *Scotland and Nationalism: Scottish Society and Politics, 1707–1977* (1977); J. R. Hunter, *The Making of the Crofting Community* (1976); J. Kellas, *Modern Scotland: the Nation since 1870* (1968), and *The Scottish Political System* (1973); D. N. MacCormick, ed., *The Scottish Debate: Essays on Scottish Nationalism* (1970); A. A. Maclaren, *Religion and Social Class: the Disruption Years in Aberdeen* (1974), and ed., *Social Class in Scotland: Past and Present* (1976); J. P. Mackintosh, *The Devolution of Power* (1968); R. Mitchison, *A History of Scotland* (1970); H. J. Paton, *The Claim of Scotland* (1968); T. C. Smout, *A History of the Scottish People 1560–1830* (1969).

Map of Scotland south of
Tay showing the main
locations of Industry.

600 feet and over.

Scale of Miles

0   10   20   30   40   50

INDEX